CURRENT,
STREAMLINED
COVERAGE

STUDENT-
FRIENDLY
APPROACH

INSTRUCTOR
SUPPORT

STUDENT
SUPPORT

6th
Canadian Edition

MARKETING

FREDERICK G. CRANE
QMA Consulting Group Limited

ROGER A. KERIN
Southern Methodist University

STEVEN W. HARTLEY
University of Denver

ERIC N. BERKOWITZ
University of Massachusetts

WILLIAM RUDELIUS
University of Minnesota

McGraw-Hill
Ryerson

Toronto Montréal Boston Burr Ridge, IL Dubuque, IA Madison, WI New York
San Francisco St. Louis Bangkok Bogotá Caracas Kuala Lumpur Lisbon London
Madrid Mexico City Milan New Delhi Santiago Seoul Singapore Sydney Taipei

McGraw-Hill
Ryerson

Marketing
Sixth Canadian Edition

ISBN: 0-07-093986-1

1 2 3 4 5 6 7 8 9 10 TCP 0 9 8 7 6

Printed and bound in Canada.

Senior Sponsoring Editor: Leanna MacLean
Marketing Manager: Charlotte Liu
Managing Editor, Development: Jennifer DiDomenico
Senior Production Coordinator: Jennifer Wilkie
Supervising Editor: Anne Nellis
Copy Editor: Rohini Herbert
Cover Design: Dianna Little
Cover Credit: © EuroStyle Graphics/Alamy
Interior Designer: Sharon Lucas
Photo Researcher: Karen Becker
Composition: Bookman Typesetting Company Inc.
Printer: Transcontinental Printing Group

Library and Archives Canada Cataloguing in Publication

Marketing / Frederick G. Crane ... [et al.]. — 6th Canadian ed.

Includes bibliographical references and index.
ISBN 0-07-093986-1

1. Marketing—Textbooks.   2. Marketing—Canada—Textbooks.
I. Crane, F. G.

HF5415.M293 2006   658.8   C2005-905011-X

∎∎∎
BRIEF CONTENTS

CONTENTS

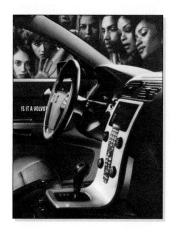

PART 3 TARGETING MARKETING OPPORTUNITIES 194

PART 4 SATISFYING MARKETING OPPORTUNITIES 252

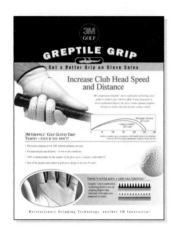

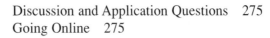

11   Managing Products and Brands   279

12   Managing Services   307

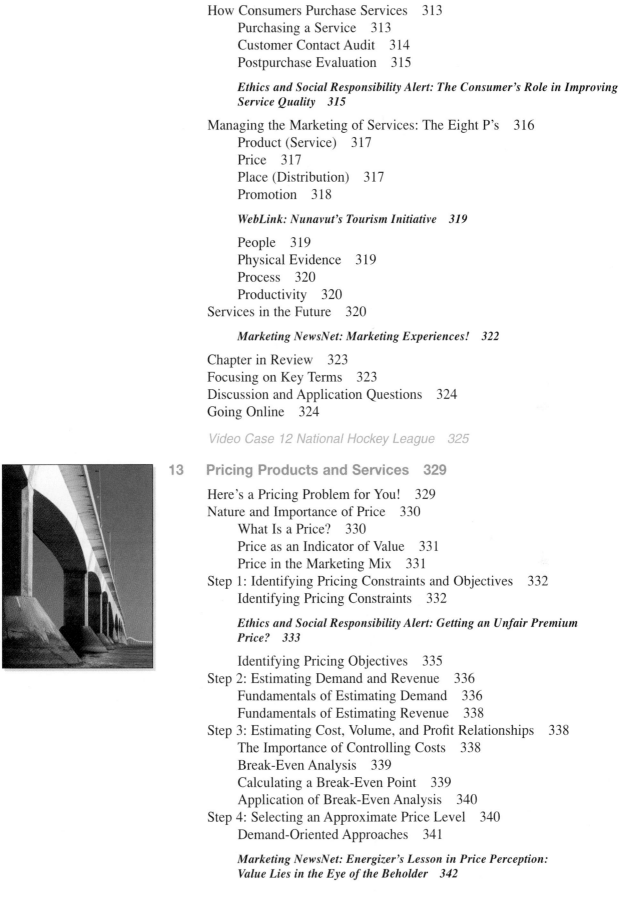

14   Managing Marketing Channels and Supply Chains   365

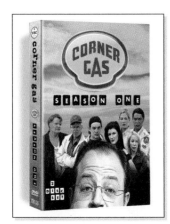

Changing Shopping Behaviour   415

***Ethics and Social Responsibility Alert: Biometric Payment Systems:
The Possible Dark Side   415***

Chapter in Review   416
Focusing on Key Terms   416
Discussion and Application Questions   417
Going Online   417

Video Case 15 Vaughan Mills Shopping Centre   418

**16   Integrated Marketing Communications and Direct
Marketing   421**

CTV Achieves Success with *Corner Gas* Using an Integrated
Marketing Communications Strategy   421
The Communication Process   422
Encoding and Decoding   423
Feedback   424
Noise   424
The Promotional Elements   424
Advertising   425
Personal Selling   426
Public Relations   426
Sales Promotion   427
Direct Marketing   427
Integrated Marketing Communications—Developing the
Promotional Mix   428
The Target Audience   428

***Marketing NewsNet: Gen Y Applies Multi-tasking to Media Consumption—
29 Hours per Day!   428***

The Product Life Cycle   429
Product Characteristics   430
Stages of the Buying Decision   431
Channel Strategies   432
Developing the Promotion Program   433
Identifying the Target Audience   434
Specifying Promotion Objectives   434
Setting the Promotion Budget   434
Selecting the Right Promotional Tools   436
Designing the Promotion   436
Scheduling the Promotion   436
Executing and Evaluating the Promotion Program   437

WebLink: A Look at One Agency's Approach to IMC   437

Direct Marketing   438
The Growth of Direct Marketing   438
The Value of Direct Marketing   439
Technological, Global, and Ethical Issues in Direct
Marketing   440

CURRENT, STREAMLINED COVERAGE

The Sixth Canadian Edition of *Marketing* is substantially revised, updated, and packed with new examples of marketing in Canada and around the world. You asked for new material, and we listened! In addition to new or expanded coverage of such topics as social marketing, Canada's e-marketplaces, buzz marketing, hybrid marketing channels, and new technologies (for example, VOIP, WI-FI, RFID, and biometrics), we have overhauled our examples and cases. Over 50 percent of all pedagogical features, including 10 new opening vignettes, 15 new Marketing NewsNet boxes, and 10 new video cases, are either new or updated in this edition. Please see the detailed list of changes below for some highlights.

Instructors also recommended a streamlined chapter structure that would allow them to cover all the important topics in their course, while making such topics as pricing easier for students to comprehend. The Sixth Canadian Edition addresses this concern with a 19-chapter structure that offers new streamlined and integrated Chapter 13 on Pricing Products and Services and Chapter 14 on Managing Marketing Channels and Supply Chains.

Finally, the Sixth Canadian Edition facilitates assessment with a stronger focus on learning objectives. Each chapter (1) begins with measurable learning objectives, and (2) ends with a new Chapter in Review feature, which is a summary of content related to each learning objective. The objectives are cross-referenced to specific Test Bank questions to allow construction of measurement instruments.

DETAILED LIST OF CHANGES

Chapter 1 – Marketing: Customer Value, Satisfaction, and Customer Relationships

- This chapter features a new opening vignette on Curves International, the fastest growing franchise chain in the world. It also highlights Curves' marketing program and provides a new chapter-ending video case on the company. There is new material on social marketing as well as customer value, customer satisfaction, customer relationship marketing (CRM), customer lifetime value, and eCRM. The experience of Canadian companies implementing CRM is also highlighted.

Chapter 2 – Developing Successful Marketing and Corporate Strategies

- The chapter opener has been revised to unveil the strategic changes at Bombardier. There is also new material on the concept of competition and expanded coverage of business portfolio analysis with an application of BCG using Kodak's shift from film to digital technology. New Appendix A—Creating an Effective Marketing Plan—features a new restaurant concept for Prince Rupert, British Columbia.

Chapter 3 – Scanning the Marketing Environment

- Chapter 3 provides a new look at Canada's marketing environment, including a discussion on the digital revolution as well as other new technologies, such as VOIP and WI-FI. The chapter also deals with global population trends and generational cohorts, including Gen Y, Gen X, and millennials. The latest demographic statistics on the Canadian marketplace, including population growth, ethnic diversity, and income, along with a new discussion of multicultural marketing are also discussed. The latest information on small business as a competitive trend in Canada is highlighted, as is new material on Canada's Privacy Act and the PIPEDA .

Chapter 4 – Ethics and Social Responsibility in Marketing

- Chapter 4 provides a new opening vignette on Canadian automakers and their approach to social responsibility. It also features Canadian research on business ethics, the inclusion of the Canadian Marketing Association's code of ethics, and a chapter ending video case on Starbucks Corporation.

Chapter 5 – Consumer Behaviour

- Chapter 5 provides coverage of new consumer behaviour regarding the impact and use of online technology and the consumer purchase process. It also discusses *buzz marketing* and provides new material on lifestyle or psychographic programs (including VALS, Social Values Tribes (Environics), the new Canadian PRIZM$_{CE}$ program) and the new Millward Brown Goldfarb Segments (including a Weblink so that students can determine which Goldfarb segment they belong to). There are also new boxes that deal with how you know you are Canadian. Finally, this chapter includes the latest material on French-Canadian buying behaviour.

Chapter 6 – Organizational Markets and Buyer Behaviour

- This chapter features a new opening vignette on Dofasco and better coverage of Canada's manufacturing sector. There is also new material on the forthcoming North American Product Classification system; eBay's expansion into online business-to-business trading—eBayBusiness.ca—and coverage of Canada's other new e-marketplaces.

Chapter 7 – Reaching Global Markets

- Chapter 7 provides updates on global trade, EU membership, the growing use of global brands, new considerations when customizing versus standardizing marketing practices in global markets, Canada's trade relationships with other nations, how Japanese consumers perceive Canadian products, and how small Canadian firms compete successfully in the global economy.

Chapter 8 – Marketing Research: From Information to Action

- Chapter 8 provides new material on e-mail, fax, Internet surveys, intercept interviews, and the use of mystery shoppers. It also includes coverage on information technology topics, such as the use of sales drivers and data mining. New perspectives on ethics in research are another updated feature of this chapter.

Chapter 9 – Identifying Market Segments and Targets

- Chapter 9 provides new and extended examples of segmentation strategies by Reebok, Wendy's, and Apple. It also introduces the concept of firmographics for segmenting business markets.

Chapter 10 – Developing New Products and Services

- Chapter 10 features a new chapter opener on 3M's new Greptile Grip golf glove. It also includes discussions of Volvo's YCC concept car and a new chapter-ending video case on 3M's Greptile Grip golf gloves.

Chapter 11 – Managing Products and Brands

- Chapter 11 provides an updated vignette on Clearly Canadian Beverages and its approach to brand management. New material is also offered on brand equity, brand licensing, fighting brands, and cohort brand management. The chapter contains an interesting feature on Molson's new beer—Molson Kick.

Chapter 12 – Managing Services

- Chapter 12 provides an update on the services sector in Canada, including an emphasis on services as experiences. There is new material on services marketing in the future, including new e-services, as well as continued coverage of the Eight P's of services marketing. The chapter concludes with an updated video case on the NHL.

Chapter 13 – Pricing Products and Services

- Based on the reviewers' recommendations to streamline and integrate the two pricing chapters into one, we replaced the two original chapters on pricing (Chapters 13 and 14) with the new integrated Chapter 13, which provides a more practical and easy-to-comprehend approach to pricing.

Chapter 14 – Managing Marketing Channels and Supply Chains

- Reviewers also suggested that we streamline and integrate the chapters on managing marketing channels and supply chains. Chapter 14 (originally Chapters 15 and 16) offers a comprehensive treatment of these topics, as well as new coverage on multichannel distribution, or hybrid marketing channels.

Chapter 15 – Retailing

- Chapter 15 provides a new updated opening on Tim Horton's strategy for growth, including its expansion into the United States. There is also new material on online retailing (etailing); technology in retailing, including RFID and biometrics; category management and multichannel retailing; online pharmacy retailing; and Zellers' repositioning in the Canadian retail marketplace. The chapter concludes with a video case featuring Canada's latest regional shopping centre—Vaughan Mills.

Chapter 16 – Integrated Marketing Communications and Direct Marketing

- Chapter 16 features how CTV successfully utilizes integrated marketing communications to promote its highly successful *Corner Gas* sitcom. The chapter also includes new topics, such as examples of SIMM and ezines, and features a new video case on UPS's IMC program.

Chapter 17 – Advertising, Sales Promotion, and Public Relations

- This chapter introduces one of Canada's most unique advertising and marketing communications firms—AdFarm. It also presents new Canadian content on the use of humour in advertising; updated statistics on ad spending by media type; new material on celebrity spokespersons; and new coverage of yellow pages advertising, satellite radio, Internet advertising, and sponsorship marketing. This chapter also introduces the concepts of recency and advergaming and provides new material on sales promotions in Canada, including sampling, and loyalty programs. A new video case on AdFarm rounds out the chapter.

Chapter 18 – Personal Selling and Sales Management

- An updated opening vignette, a new Marketing NewsNet on sales training for gender intelligence in Canada, and new material on sales quotas are the special features of this chapter.

Chapter 19 – Pulling It All Together: The Strategic Marketing Process

- Chapter 19 features a new opening vignette on WestJet and its marketing strategy. It also presents the latest research on business performance and what strategies really work; coverage on synergy, introducing the Molson-Coors merger and the TD and Banknorth merger; and new material on ROI marketing. It concludes with a new video case on WestJet.

STUDENT-FRIENDLY APPROACH

"I like the conversational, informal tone, and the layout is one that is visually appealing and nonthreatening for students. Essential topics are addressed, and there is very little clutter with other subtopics that may not be necessary to cover in a fundamentals course."

—Sherry Finney, Cape Breton University

"Overall, I would characterize it as a 'sure thing,' since it does a very good job presenting the scope of concepts relevant to marketing."

—Michael Mulvey, University of Ottawa

"It is comprehensive—giving us flexibility with our various programs. It is also reasonably easy to read for our students, who are coming in at a younger age from high school. There are many examples, photos, charts, etc. to add interest."

—Raymond Rodda, Cambrian College

"Students have been very positive about the text; they like the wealth of charts and visuals, good product and company examples, and are very pleased with the quizzes on the Web site."

—Peter Burgess, George Brown College

As evidenced by the quotations above, *Marketing* has developed an excellent reputation among Canadian instructors and students as a text that delivers key concepts in a student-friendly style without watering down the material. Our Sixth Canadian Edition continues to be characterized by:

- **A High-Engagement Style**. An easy-to-read, high-involvement, interactive writing style that engages students through active learning techniques, timely and interesting examples, and challenging applications.
- **Personalized Marketing**. A vivid and accurate description of businesses, marketing professionals, and entrepreneurs—through cases, exercises, and testimonials—that allow students to personalize marketing and identify possible career interests and role models.
- **Emphasis on Marketing Decision Making**. The use of extended examples, cases, and videos involving people making marketing decisions, which students can easily relate to text concepts.
- **A Strong Pedagogical Framework**. A rigorous pedagogical framework in the text, based on the use of learning objectives, concept checks, key terms, boxed applications, and Chapter in Review summaries, along with supportive student supplements, appeal to a wide range of learning styles.

Chapter Opening Vignettes introduce students to the chapter concepts ahead, using an exciting company example (10 vignettes are **new** to the Sixth Canadian Edition). For instance, in Chapter 1, the vignette zeroes in on the global success of Curves in Canada and around the world. The chapter-opening discussions are often integrated into narrative, exhibits, and boxed features throughout the chapter.

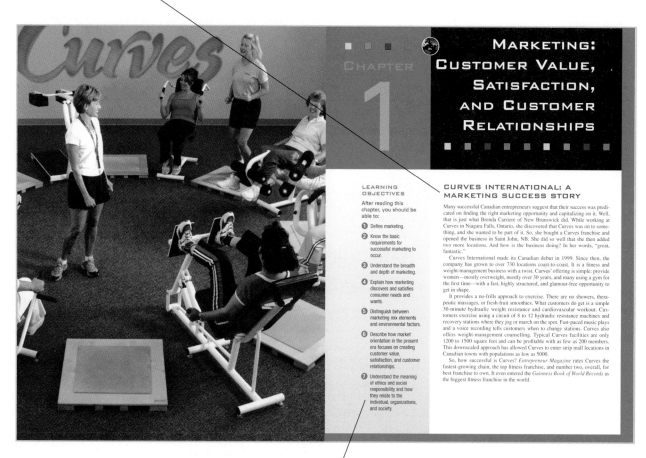

CHAPTER 1

MARKETING: CUSTOMER VALUE, SATISFACTION, AND CUSTOMER RELATIONSHIPS

LEARNING OBJECTIVES

After reading this chapter, you should be able to:

1. Define marketing.

2. Know the basic requirements for successful marketing to occur.

3. Understand the breadth and depth of marketing.

4. Explain how marketing discovers and satisfies consumer needs and wants.

5. Distinguish between marketing mix elements and environmental factors.

6. Describe how market orientation in the present era focuses on creating customer value, satisfaction, and customer relationships.

7. Understand the meaning of ethics and social responsibility and how they relate to the individual, organizations, and society.

CURVES INTERNATIONAL: A MARKETING SUCCESS STORY

Many successful Canadian entrepreneurs suggest that their success was predicated on finding the right marketing opportunity and capitalizing on it. Well, that is just what Brenda Carriere of New Brunswick did. While working at Curves in Niagara Falls, Ontario, she discovered that Curves was on to something, and she wanted to be part of it. So, she bought a Curves franchise and opened the business in Saint John, NB. She did so well that she then added two more locations. And how is the business doing? In her words, "great, fantastic."

Curves International made its Canadian debut in 1999. Since then, the company has grown to over 730 locations coast-to-coast. It is a fitness and weight-management business with a twist. Curves' offering is simple: provide women—mostly overweight, mostly over 30 years, and many using a gym for the first time—with a fast, highly structured, and glamour-free opportunity to get in shape.

It provides a no-frills approach to exercise. There are no showers, therapeutic massages, or fresh-fruit smoothies. What customers do get is a simple 30-minute hydraulic weight resistance and cardiovascular workout. Customers exercise using a circuit of 8 to 12 hydraulic resistance machines and recovery stations where they jog or march on the spot. Fast-paced music plays and a voice recording tells customers when to change stations. Curves also offers weight-management counselling. Typical Curves facilities are only 1200 to 1500 square feet and can be profitable with as few as 200 members. This downscaled approach has allowed Curves to enter strip mall locations in Canadian towns with populations as low as 5000.

So, how successful is Curves? *Entrepreneur Magazine* rates Curves the fastest-growing chain, the top fitness franchise, and number two, overall, for best franchise to own. It even entered the *Guinness Book of World Records* as the biggest fitness franchise in the world.

Learning Objectives open each chapter to help students preview chapter content and study effectively.

Concept Checks are checkpoints found at the end of each major chapter section, offering critical thinking and memory recall questions. These questions help students reflect on the text and test their comprehension of the material before moving on.

The organization must strike a difficult balance among the sometimes differing interests of these individuals and groups. For example, it is not possible to simultaneously provide the lowest-priced and highest-quality products to customers and pay the highest prices to suppliers, highest wages to employees, and maximum dividends to shareholders.

CONCEPT CHECK

1. What is marketing?
2. Marketing focuses on _____ and_____ prospective customers' needs and wants.
3. What four factors are needed for marketing to occur?

HOW MARKETING DISCOVERS AND SATISFIES CONSUMER NEEDS

The importance of discovering consumer needs is so critical to understanding marketing that we look at each of these two steps in detail next.

Marketing NewsNet boxes provide engaging, current examples of marketing applications in action. Fifteen Marketing NewsNets are **new** to the Sixth Canadian Edition, including boxes on the challenges of social marketing, protecting Canadian consumers' privacy, online pharmacies in Canada, buzz marketing and advergaming.

MARKETING NEWSNET — The Buzz on "Buzz"

Have you recently heard about a new product, movie, Web site, book, or restaurant from someone you know . . . or from a complete stranger? If so, you may have been buzzed.

Canadian research illustrates well the importance of word of mouth. For example, the Canadian Mood & Mindset online survey reveals that we do rely on each other for recommendations about products and services. The key to successful buzz, according to Lynn Fletcher of Arnold Worldwide Canada in Toronto, is to find the quarterbacks of buzz. Her company's research reveals that just 14 percent of the Canadian population comprised the quarter-backs of buzz. And they are influenced by geo...

agents to generate buzz about its product, service, or brand. When a client signs with BzzAgent, the company searches its databases for agents who match the profile of the client's target market. Agents sign up and receive sample products and some training on buzz creation. Each time an agent completes a buzz activity, he or she files an online report. Agents get to keep the products they promote and earn points redeemable for other products. It is not cheap, however; 1000 buzz agents for a 12-week buzz campaign can cost $85 000, exclusive of product samples. Finally, Proctor and Gamble has its own word-of-mouth or buzz-marketing arm, called Tremor. Not only do these Tremor members promote P&G's products, P...

Ethics and Social Responsibility Alert boxes increase awareness and assessment of current topics of ethical and social concern. **New** boxes in the Sixth Canadian Edition cover such topics as MRIA guidelines, biometric payment systems, and PETA's public relations campaigns.

ETHICS AND SOCIAL RESPONSIBILITY ALERT — Biometric Payment Systems: The Possible Dark Side

Makers of biometric payment systems assert that this technology has a big advantage over other payment systems: speed at the checkout counter. Here is how a biometric system works: (1) To enroll, a customer gives the retailer a blank cheque and valid ID to scan into a computer. (2) The customer then places each index finger on a tennis-ball-sized reader that captures fingerprints. (Other systems will use thumbprints or even scan your iris) (3) The customer selects a code to authorize debits from a checking account and to verify age. (4) Once enrolled, the customer makes purchases by placing a finger on the reader and entering a code (or PIN ID).

... scan biom... ... system ...

transaction in less than 15 seconds, compared with the 65 seconds it takes to process a cheque and the 50 seconds to process a credit card. And retailers will have the added benefit of saving the fees they normally pay to credit card companies.

However, many people are concerned about possible abuses and privacy concerns revolving around this technology. For some people, a fingerprint only means one thing: a police record. And this is making people wary of the technology. In fact, Dollar Rent a Car used fingerprinting in the past to combat theft of its cars but had to stop this practice after widespread complaints by customers. Moreover, many privacy experts suggest that the biometric syst... ... by ...

WebLink boxes encourage students to explore digital strategies that innovative companies and organizations are employing online. Eight are **new** to this edition, including WebLink boxes on Millward Brown Goldfarb segmentation, eBay, and the IAB of Canada and Internet Advertising.

Captivate TV Network offers "TV in Elevators."

played on screen before the movies are shown), even tons of bars, colleges, restaurants, and nightclubs! You have probably also seen advertising on video screens on gas pumps, ATMs, and in elevators! Another new form of advertising is called advergaming, as the accompanying Marketing NewsNet box discusses.

WEBLINK
HTTP://WWW.MCGRAWHILL.CA/COLLEGE/CRANE

IAB of Canada and Internet/Online Advertising

The Interactive Advertising Bureau (IAB) of Canada is a not-for-profit association with membership composed of publishers, advertisers, advertising agencies, and service associates in the Canadian online/interactive marketing industry. IAB Canada is dedicated to establishing and communicating interactive advertising best practices that optimize advertising investment, leading to increased stakeholder value. Go to its Web site (www.iabcanada.com). Select "Standards" on the main menu. Click on "Best Practices White Papers." Select "Online Ad Campaign Measuring" paper. Read about what has been learned so far about online ad measurement.

Chapter in Review sections are **new** summaries that group chapter content recaps by learning objective. Chapter in Review is followed by a list of **Key Terms** and **Discussion and Application Questions**.

CHAPTER IN REVIEW

1 *Define marketing.*

Marketing is an organizational function and a set of processes for creating, communicating, and delivering value to customers and for managing customer relationships in ways that benefit the organization and its stakeholders.

2 *Know the basic requirements for successful marketing to occur.*

For marketing to occur, it is necessary to have (a) two or more parties with unmet needs, (b) a desire and ability to satisfy them, (c) communication between the parties, and (4) something to exchange.

3 *Understand the breadth and depth of marketing.*

Marketing affects every person and organization. Both for-profit and nonprofit organizations perform marketing activities. They market products, services, and ideas that benefit consumers, organizations, and countries.

4 *Explain how marketing discovers and satisfies consumer needs and wants.*

The first objective in marketing is discovering the needs of prospective consumers. The second objective in marketing is satisfying the needs of targeted consumers. Because an organization cannot satisfy all consumer needs, it must concentrate its efforts on certain needs of a specific group of potential consumers or target market—one or more specific groups of potential consumers toward which an organization directs its marketing program. Having selected its target market, the organization then takes action to satisfy the customers' needs by developing a unique marketing program to appeal to that market.

5 *Distinguish between marketing mix elements and environmental factors.*

Four elements in a marketing program designed to satisfy customer needs are product, price, promotion, and place. These elements are called the marketing mix—the four Ps—or the controllable variables because they are under the general control of the marketing department within an organization. Environmental factors, also called uncontrollable variables, are largely beyond the organization's control. These include social, technological, economic, competitive, and regulatory forces.

focuses on creating customer value, satisfaction, and customer relationships.

Organizations with a market orientation focus their efforts on (1) continuously collecting information about customers' needs and competitors' capabilities, (2) sharing this information throughout the organization, and (3) using the information to create value, ensure customer satisfaction, and develop customer relationships. Organizations with a market orientation engage in customer relationship management (CRM)—the process of building and developing long-term relationships with customers by delivering customer value and satisfaction. Organizations engaging CRM understand the importance of the customer lifetime value (CLV)—the profits generated by the customer's purchase of an organization's product or service over the customer's lifetime. The concept of eCRM—a Web-centric, personalized approach to managing long-term customer relationships electronically, which includes interactive marketing, is changing the way buyers and sellers interact. Interactive marketing technology now allows for a level of customer interaction, individualization, and customer relationship management process to be carried out on a scale never before available. However, CRM, including eCRM, has not been easy to implement, and many experts are advocating new approaches to manage long-term customer relationships. One concept is concierge marketing (CM)—where an emphasis is placed on understanding why and how customers use a brand and building a process of customer benefits around that usage.

7 *Understand the meaning of ethics and social responsibility and how they relate to the individual, organizations, and society.*

Marketing managers must balance consumer, organizational, and societal interests. This involves issues of ethics and social responsibility. Ethics are the moral principles and values that govern the actions and decisions of an individual or group. Ethics serve as guidelines on how to act correctly and justly. Social responsibility means that individuals and organizations are part of a larger society and are accountable to that society for their actions. Some marketing experts stress the societal marketing concept, the view that an organization should discover and satisfy the needs of its consumers in a way that...

5 What are the four marketing elements might be used to reach the target market in question 4?

provides how an organization engaged with you? Explain.

Going Online is an exercise at the end of each chapter that asks students to go online and think critically about a specific company's use of the Internet, helping them apply knowledge of key chapter concepts, terms, and topics, as well as evaluate the success or failure of the company's efforts.

GOING ONLINE

Understanding Marketing Terms and Concepts

Marketing uses a number of terms and concepts that are often difficult to remember. But, the American Marketing Association (AMA), a professional body that represents thousands of marketers in Canada, the United States, and around the world, is a valuable source of information on marketing. In fact, on its Web site, the AMA actually has a comprehensive dictionary containing over 4000 marketing terms and concepts.

Go to www.marketingpower.com (the AMA's official Web site) and check out the marketing dictionary. Search for key terms and concepts that are of interest to you. This exercise should prove invaluable to you as you attempt to gain a better understanding of the marketing discipline. There are also numerous provincial chapters of the AMA in Canada. You may also wish to check out their Web sites for the latest marketing news in Canada.

STUDENT-FRIENDLY APPROACH

Each chapter concludes with a **Video Case** that provide an up-close look at a company example, reinforcing the chapter content and bringing the material to life. The video segments are available for viewing on the Online Learning Centre at www.mcgrawhill.ca/college/crane. Curves, Starbucks, Vaughan Mills, AdFarm, and WestJet are just a few of the exciting video cases available with the Sixth Canadian Edition.

---

visit us at www.mcgrawhill.ca/college/crane

VIDEO CASE 17 | AdFarm

INTRODUCTION

AdFarm is Canada's largest agricultural marketing communications firm and has been recognized as one of 50 Best Managed Companies in Canada. It focuses exclusively on providing marketing communications solutions for companies and organizations operating in the agriculture sector. AdFarm is a full service agency offering a complete range of marketing communications services, including advertising, public relations, issue management, media relations, direct marketing, and online marketing.

AdFarm is a collection of four successful regional agricultural marketing communications agencies that saw the opportunity to respond to the changing needs and expectations of industry leaders operating in a highly competitive, global market. These four firms believed that a combined organization operating with a single focus could compete successfully in serving the multi-billion dollar, global agricultural industry. AdFarm has offices in Calgary and Guelph as well as in Fargo, ND, and Kansas City, MO. AdFarm's past and current clients include some of the world's premiere agricultural leaders, such as Bayer CropScience, Dow Agro-Sciences, RBC Royal Bank (the largest bank serving agriculture in North America), Case New Holland, Mer-ial, No........... Animal He....... ...ain, Albe...

is communication technology made possible today as a result of the Internet, video conferencing, and collaborative tool technology.

ORGANIZATIONAL STRUCTURE

AdFarm is guided by a board of directors, a "round-table" advisory committee, and a management committee. The board includes six directors—three of whom are actively involved and three experienced businessmen who are *not* actively involved in the operations of the firm. The roundtable is composed of experienced agriculture and marketing communications professionals. This group has no legal or operating responsibilities but, rather, is a sounding board and a directional group to identify industry issues and trends and suggest directional paths that AdFarm should consider.

The AdFarm management committee, consisting of the CEO, the seven "function heads" who have responsibility for the key functions within the agency (account management, strategy, creative, public relations, consulting, finance & administration, and partnership services) plus three additional directors with specific agency responsibilities (AdFarm brand management, human resource management, and information technology man-......ment). T..... ....oup meet...... .... a mon....

A **new** sample marketing plan in Appendix A for a restaurant concept in Prince Rupert, BC serves as a valuable model for students in terms of form and content.

> Blue boxes explain significance of Marketing Plan elements

> Red boxes give writing style, format, and layout guidelines

> The Table of Contents provides quick access to the topics in the plan, usually organized by section and subsection headings.

> Seen by many experts as the single most important element in the plan, the Executive Summary "sells" the plan to readers through its clarity and brevity.

> The Company Description highlights the recent history of the organization.

FIVE-YEAR MARKETING PLAN
Frenz Steak and Seafood

Table of Contents

1. Executive Summary

The following plan outlines the marketing strategy and tactics for Frenz Steak and Seafood, a large casual-style restaurant opening during the summer of 2005 in Prince Rupert, British Columbia.

While the local restaurant sector is reasonably competitive, it is weighted toward small, independent restaurants. The absence of family restaurants, midrange franchise operations, and features common in larger markets (e.g., salad bars, child-friendly operations, high-calibre customer service) creates an opportunity for a new restaurant operator.

Frenz Steak and Seafood is positioned in the middle of the casual dining spectrum in pricing and cuisine quality, offering a wide selection of menu items. The restaurant has four distinguishing features—(1) a child-friendly environment, (2) a comfortable atmosphere created by skilled serving teams, (3) features lacking in local restaurants, and (4) the skilled use of publicity and promotional activities to establish a clear brand identity. As in franchise operations, Frenz segregates family dining from intimate dining and banquets, enabling the operator to target different market segments in one facility.

2. Company Description

Frenz Steak and Seafood is opening as a 100-seat restaurant in downtown Prince Rupert in July 2005. A casual-style restaurant, offering a selection of seafood, steaks, pastas, and pizzas, Frenz will also provide take-out and delivery services for cooked and ready-to-cook menu items.

Frenz is positioned at the middle of the casual dining spectrum in pricing and menu variety. Frenz will provide a comfortable, community atmosphere for people of all ages through a serving staff with a "can do" attitude, a child-friendly environment, and a décor reflecting the history of the community. The layout of the premises enables Frenz to target separate segments—family dining near the entrance, semiprivate booths farther back for intimate dining, and a separate banquet room for groups of up to 35 people.

The restau....... ....on atmosphe...... service, and marketin...... ....ll provide it with ..... fragm..... .... Ru.....

STUDENT SUPPORT

Student Online Learning Centre (OLC)

Visit the OLC at www.mcgrawhill.ca/college/crane for a complete set of learning and study tools that will help you improve your grades in Marketing. The OLC includes self-grading quizzes, marketing plan resources, streaming Video Cases, flashcards, *Globe and Mail* newsfeeds, and access to *Marketing Magazine*'s archives, Study to Go, the student Integrator, E-STAT, and premium content, such as learning objects and PowerWeb.

Study Guide

The Study Guide (ISBN 0-07-097336-9) has been completely revised for the Sixth Canadian edition to include more application- and scenario-based questions to help you apply your marketing knowledge. The Study Guide continues to provide a wide selection of questions and problems, along with answer keys, to help you to learn the material and succeed in the course!

Marketing Magazine

Students get free access to *Marketing Magazine*'s archives with purchase of the text. This real-world complement to the Sixth Canadian Edition is a great way to keep current in the marketing course.

E-STAT

E-STAT is an educational resource designed by Statistics Canada and made available to Canadian educational institutions. Using 450 000 current CANSIM (Canadian Socio-economic Information Management System) Time Series and the most recent—as well as historical—census data, E-STAT lets you bring data to life in colourful graphs and maps. Access to E-STAT is made available to purchasers of this book, via the Crane Online Learning Centre, by special agreement between McGraw-Hill Ryerson and Statistics Canada. The Online Learning Centre provides additional information.

Learning Objects

To assist students and instructors alike, McGraw-Hill Ryerson has developed a library of Marketing learning objects housed on the Online Learning Centre. Learning objects are designed to provide an interactive, audiovisual learning environment for topics that prove challenging to students. Contact your *i*Learning Sales Specialist to learn more about making this valuable resource available to your students.

PowerWeb

PowerWeb offers current articles related to marketing, weekly updates with assessment tools, informative and timely world news culled by a subject expert, Web links, and more. In addition, PowerWeb provides an array of helpful learning aids, including self-grading quizzes and interactive glossaries and exercises. Contact your *i*Learning Sales Specialist to learn more about making this valuable resource available to your students.

Student Integrator

Improve your grades! The Student Integrator is a tool that will help you find all the student support material that relates to a particular learning objective in *Marketing,* Sixth Canadian Edition. Access the student integrator at www.mcgrawhill.ca/college/crane.

Study to Go

Do you use a handheld Personal Digital Assistant (PDA)? McGraw-Hill Ryerson's Study To Go application gives you the opportunity to study any time, anywhere. And it is free for students using *Marketing,* Sixth Canadian Edition! To download quizzes, key terms, and flashcards, visit the Online Learning Centre at http://www.mcgrawhill.ca/college/crane.

Marketing, Sixth Canadian Edition, offers a complete, integrated supplements package for instructors to address all your needs.

SUPERIOR SERVICE

Service takes on a whole new meaning with McGraw-Hill Ryerson and *Marketing.* More than just bringing you the textbook, we have consistently raised the bar in terms of innovation and educational research—both in marketing and in education in general. These investments in learning and the education community have helped us understand the needs of students and educators across the country and allow us to foster the growth of truly innovative, integrated learning.

Integrated Learning Sales Specialist

Your Integrated Learning Sales Specialist is a McGraw-Hill Ryerson representative who has the experience, product knowledge, training, and support to help you assess and integrate all of the *Marketing* supplements, technology, and services into your course for optimum teaching and learning performance. Whether it is using our test bank software, helping your students improve their grades, or putting your entire course online, your *i*Learning Sales Specialist is there to help you do it. Contact your local *i*Learning Sales Specialist today to learn how to maximize all of McGraw-Hill Ryerson's resources!

*i*Learning Services Program

McGraw-Hill Ryerson offers a unique *i*Services package designed for Canadian faculty. Our mission is to equip providers of higher education with superior tools and resources required for excellence in teaching. For additional information visit http://www.mcgrawhill.ca/highereducation/iservices.

Teaching, Technology & Learning Conference Series

The educational environment has changed tremendously in recent years, and McGraw-Hill Ryerson continues to be committed to helping you acquire the skills you need to succeed in this new milieu. Our innovative Teaching, Technology & Learning Conference Series brings faculty together from across Canada with 3M Teaching Excellence award winners to share teaching and learning best practices in a collaborative and stimulating environment. Preconference workshops on general topics, such as teaching large classes and technology integration, are also offered. We will also work with you at your own institution to customize workshops that best suit the needs of your faculty at your institution.

INSTRUCTOR SUPPLEMENTS

Instructor's Online Learning Centre (OLC)

The OLC at www.mcgrawhill.ca/college/crane includes a password-protected Web site for instructors. The site offers downloadable supplements, including an Instructor's Manual, Microsoft® PowerPoint® slides, Alternate Cases, streaming Video Cases and Case Teaching Notes, as well as access to the integrator, *Marketing Magazine* and PageOut, the McGraw-Hill Ryerson Web site development centre.

Instructor's CD-ROM contains the Instructor's Manual, Test Bank in Rich Text Format, Computerized Test Bank, and Microsoft® PowerPoint® slides:

- **Instructor's Manual**
  The Instructor's Manual contains lecture notes, summaries of all boxed features, and answers to Concept Checks, Going Online, and Discussion Questions.
- **Test Bank in Rich Text Format**
  The Test Bank contains an extensive array of multiple choice and essay items categorized by level of learning (definition, conceptual, application) and by learning objective.
- **Computerized Test Bank**
  This flexible and easy-to-use electronic testing program allows instructors to create tests from book-specific items. It accommodates a wide range of question types, and instructors may add their own questions. Multiple versions of the test can be created and printed.
- **Microsoft® PowerPoint® Slides**
  These robust presentations offer high-quality visuals to bring key marketing concepts to life.

Enhanced PowerPoint® Presentations are available in a separate CD-ROM package, enriching the ICD version of the PowerPoints with video clips.

Video Case Studies

A unique series of 19 contemporary marketing cases are available on videotape (VHS) and DVD, as well as for download from the Online Learning Centre. Each video case corresponds with chapter-specific topics and the end-of-chapter case in the text. The Sixth Canadian Edition includes brand new videos, including Curves, Starbucks, Vaughan Mills, WestJet, AdFarm, and more! Several additional video cases are available exclusively on the Online Learning Centre.

Alternate Cases

An additional 22 alternate cases can be found in Appendix D on the Online Learning Centre, providing even more opportunities to bring the course content to life for students.

Video Case and Alternate Case Teaching Notes

This manual, available for download from the Online Learning Centre, includes helpful teaching suggestions for the video cases and alternate cases.

The Integrator

Keyed to the chapters and learning objectives of *Marketing,* Sixth Canadian Edition, the Integrator ties together all of the elements in your resource package, guiding you to where you will find corresponding coverage in each of the related support package components—be it the Instructor's Manual, Computerized Test Bank, PowerPoint® slides, Case Studies, or Online Learning Centre. Link to the Integrator via the Online Learning Centre at www.mcgrawhill.ca/college/crane.

Create a custom course Website with **PageOut**, free with every McGraw-Hill Ryerson textbook.

To learn more, contact your McGraw-Hill Ryerson publisher's representative or visit www.mhhe.com/solutions

Course Management

Visit www.mhhe.com/pageout to create a Web page for your course using our resources. PageOut is the McGraw-Hill Ryerson Web site development centre. This Web page-generation software is free to adopters and is designed to help faculty create an online course, complete with assignments, quizzes, links to relevant Web sites, and more—all in a matter of minutes.

In addition, content cartridges are available for the course management systems **WebCT** and **Blackboard**. These platforms provide instructors with user-friendly, flexible teaching tools. Please contact your local McGraw-Hill Ryerson *i*Learning Sales Specialist for details.

eInstruction's Classroom Performance System (CPS)

CPS is a student response system using wireless connectivity. It gives instructors and students immediate feedback from the entire class. The response pads are remotes that are easy to use and engage students.

- **CPS** helps you increase **student preparation, interactivity, and active learning** so that you can receive immediate feedback and know what students understand.
- **CPS** allows you to administer quizzes and tests and provide **immediate grading**.
- With **CPS**, you can create lecture questions that can be multiple-choice, true/false and subjective. You can even create questions on-the-fly as well as conduct group activities.
- **CPS** not only allows you to **evaluate classroom attendance, activity, and grading** for your course as a whole, but CPSOnline allows you to provide students with an immediate study guide. All results and scores can easily be imported into Excel and can be used with various classroom management systems.

CPS-ready content is available for use with *Marketing,* Sixth Canadian Edition. Please contact your *i*Learning Sales Specialist for more information on how you can integrate CPS into your marketing classroom.

Team Learning Assistant

The Team Learning Assistant (TLA) is a Web-based set of tools that promotes effective classroom teaming for faculty and students alike. TLA is organized into two toolboxes, one for students and one for faculty. The faculty toolbox contains teaching notes, helpful hints, and proven materials, designed for instructors who use teams in their courses. The professor determines how students will use the student tool box and then is able to track student performance data generated by the class. Located at http://www.mhhe-tla.com, the Team Learning Assistant features important advice on integrating teams into the syllabus and grading process, the importance of having a team contract and how to write one, details on peer and instructor evaluations, as well as meeting and conflict management.

These hands-on features bring the course to life

Instructor's Survival Kit (ISK): In-Class Activities and Product Props in a Box!

The ISK box contains an In-Class Activities Guide and product props for use in the classroom to illustrate marketing concepts and encourage student participation and collaboration. Today's students are more likely to learn and be motivated by active, participative experiences than by classic classroom lecture and discussion. The Instructor's Survival Kit contains these specific elements to enhance classroom interaction:

In-Class Activities: These in-class activities have received extremely positive feedback from our customers, both instructors and students. In-class activities may relate to a specific video case or example from the text.

Sample Products: *Marketing,* Sixth Canadian Edition utilizes examples of offerings from both large and small firms that will interest today's students. A number of new products are included in the Survival Kit, such as a 3M Post-it Flag Highlighter. Also, when appropriate, sample ads are included among our PowerPoint slides.

ACKNOWLEDGMENTS

DEVELOPMENT OF THE TEXT AND PACKAGE

To ensure continuous improvement of our product, we have utilized an extensive review and development process for each of our editions. Building on that history, the Sixth Canadian Edition's development process included several phases of evaluation by a broad panel of instructors.

Reviewers who were vital in helping us develop this edition include:

D. Wesley Balderson, University of Lethbridge

Debra Z. Basil, University of Lethbridge

E. Baumann, Humber College

Peter Burgess, George Brown College

John Cavaliere, Sault College of Applied Arts and Technology

Mary Ann Cipriano, Concordia University

Scott Colwell, University of Guelph

Kerry Dale Couet, Grant MacEwan College

Gary Dover, Georgian College

Webb Dussome, University of Alberta

Dwight Dyson, Centennial College

Janice Edwards, College of the Rockies

Sherry Finney, Cape Breton University

Ray Friedman, Lethbridge College

Bill Garbarino, Algonquin College

Elke Haggerty, Grant MacEwan College

Dwight R. Heinrichs, University of Regina

Valerie Hill, Algonquin College

Sandy Kalb, Ryerson University

Tammy Kiss, College of the Rockies

Melissa MacEachern, University of Prince Edward Island

Albert Mastromartino, Sir Sandford Fleming College

Miguel Morales, St. Mary's University

Michael S. Mulvey, University of Ottawa

Ewa Owczarczyk, Kwantlen University College

Beth Pett, Niagara College

Alan Richert, Confederation College

Lynne Ricker, Haskayne School of Business, University of Calgary

Raymond Rodda, Cambrian College

Steven G. Russell, Nova Scotia Agricultural College

Diana Serafini, Dawson College

Janice Seto, Nunavut Arctic College

John Shepherd, Northwest Community College

Harold J. Simpkins, John Molson School of Business, Concordia University

David J. Smith, Lakehead University

Rae Verity, Southern Alberta Institute of Technology

The preceding list demonstrates the amount of feedback and developmental input that went into the project, and we are deeply grateful to the numerous people who shared their ideas with us. Reviewing a book or supplement takes an incredible amount of energy and attention. We are glad that so many of our colleagues took the time to do it. Their comments inspired us to do our best in developing this new edition.

Thanks are due to faculty members who contributed to the text and supplements. They include:

Victor Bilodeau, Grant MacEwan College (Test Bank and PowerPoint Presentations)

Dwight Dyson, Centennial College (Instructor's Manual)

Sherry Finney, University of Cape Breton (Cybersurf video case)

David Nowell, Sheridan College (Online Learning Centre)

Ajax Persaud, University of Ottawa (Study Guide)

John Shepherd, Northwest Community College, with Trina O'Connor (new text Appendix A)

Many businesspeople and organizations also provided substantial assistance in making available information that appears in the text and supplements, much of it for the first time in university or college learning materials. Thanks are due to many individuals, including Susanne Boyce of CTV, Sean Durfy of WestJet, Kimberly Evans of West Edmonton Mall, Jason Finney of Cybersurf, Becky Frusher of Curves, Tom Hughes of Atlanta Spirit, Kim McConnell of AdFarm, Danielle Riposati of National Public Relations, and Steve Simic of Rogers Television.

Finally, we acknowledge the professional efforts of the McGraw-Hill Ryerson Higher Education Group staff. Completion of our book and its many supplements required the attention and commitment of many editorial, production, marketing, and research personnel. Thanks to Leanna MacLean, Senior Sponsoring Editor; Jennifer DiDomenico, Managing Editor, Development; Charlotte Liu, Marketing Manager; Anne Nellis, Supervising Editor, Jennifer Wilkie, Senior Production Coordinator, Rohini Herbert, Copy Editor, and Karen Becker, Freelance Photo Researcher.

I am responsible for the Canadianization of this text, and so any questions or concerns about the book should be directed to me. I would like to thank my co-authors for their input, encouragement, and continued support.

I am dedicating this edition of *Marketing* to my wife, Doreen, and daughters, Erinn, Jacquelyn, and Brenna. I am so blessed to have these loyal, beautiful, intelligent, socially conscious women in my life. I love each of you more than life itself. I am also dedicating this book to my best friend Ceilidh who loves me unconditionally; to my parents who have sacrificed to provide all their children a better life; and, most of all, to God, who, despite my failings, has continued to love me.

Frederick G. Crane

1

PART 1
Initiating the
Marketing
Process

PART 2
Understanding
Buyers and
Markets

PART 3
Targeting
Marketing
Opportunities

PART 4
Satisfying
Marketing
Opportunities

PART 5
Managing the
Marketing
Process

INITIATING THE MARKETING PROCESS

HOW PART 1 FITS INTO THE BOOK

Laying the foundation for the entire book, chapters in Part 1 explain what marketing and the strategic marketing process are and relate the importance of environmental, ethical, and social responsibility factors to a manager's marketing actions.

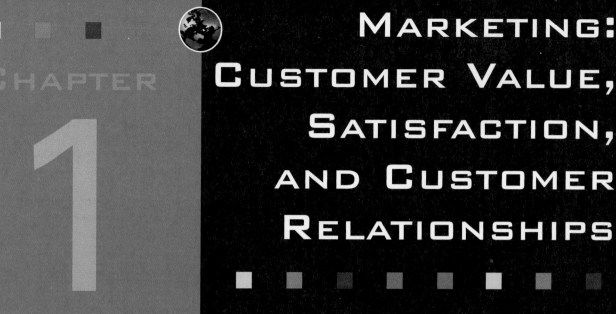

CHAPTER 1

MARKETING: CUSTOMER VALUE, SATISFACTION, AND CUSTOMER RELATIONSHIPS

LEARNING OBJECTIVES

After reading this chapter, you should be able to:

1 Define marketing.

2 Know the basic requirements for successful marketing to occur.

3 Understand the breadth and depth of marketing.

4 Explain how marketing discovers and satisfies consumer needs and wants.

5 Distinguish between marketing mix elements and environmental factors.

6 Describe how market orientation in the present era focuses on creating customer value, satisfaction, and customer relationships.

7 Understand the meaning of ethics and social responsibility and how they relate to the individual, organizations, and society.

CURVES INTERNATIONAL: A MARKETING SUCCESS STORY

Many successful Canadian entrepreneurs suggest that their success was predicated on finding the right marketing opportunity and capitalizing on it. Well, that is just what Brenda Carriere of New Brunswick did. While working at Curves in Niagara Falls, Ontario, she discovered that Curves was on to something, and she wanted to be part of it. So, she bought a Curves franchise and opened the business in Saint John, NB. She did so well that she then added two more locations. And how is the business doing? In her words, "great, fantastic."

Curves International made its Canadian debut in 1999. Since then, the company has grown to over 730 locations coast-to-coast. It is a fitness and weight-management business with a twist. Curves' offering is simple: provide women—mostly overweight, mostly over 30 years, and many using a gym for the first time—with a fast, highly structured, and glamour-free opportunity to get in shape.

It provides a no-frills approach to exercise. There are no showers, therapeutic massages, or fresh-fruit smoothies. What customers do get is a simple 30-minute hydraulic weight resistance and cardiovascular workout. Customers exercise using a circuit of 8 to 12 hydraulic resistance machines and recovery stations where they jog or march on the spot. Fast-paced music plays and a voice recording tells customers when to change stations. Curves also offers weight-management counselling. Typical Curves facilities are only 1200 to 1500 square feet and can be profitable with as few as 200 members. This downscaled approach has allowed Curves to enter strip mall locations in Canadian towns with populations as low as 5000.

So, how successful is Curves? *Entrepreneur Magazine* rates Curves the fastest-growing chain, the top fitness franchise, and number two, overall, for best franchise to own. It even entered the *Guinness Book of World Records* as the biggest fitness franchise in the world.

And why is Curves so successful? Well, its success lies in the subject of this book: marketing! Gary Heavin, the company founder, built the organization on a solid understanding of its customers' needs. He developed a unique value proposition to meet those needs. He focuses on ensuring customer satisfaction and on building long-term relationships with Curves' customers. This is the essence of modern marketing—customer value, satisfaction, and customer relationships—and Curves International illustrates how successful an organization can be if it truly embraces these marketing concepts. This business with over 9300 locations in more than 30 countries has encouraged more than four million women to exercise, most of them for the first time in their lives. And Curves is still growing, while its clients' waistlines are shrinking![1]

Interested in a Curves franchise? It will cost you about $40 000 plus monthly fees (5 percent of the membership dues collected, not to exceed $795). Those costs include equipment and marketing support. But the costs do not include leasing costs or staff. However, good luck finding a franchise, since most provinces have been completely sold out!

How will Curves International continue to grow in the future? By the time you reach the end of this chapter, you will know. In this chapter and in the rest of the book, we will introduce you to many of the people, organizations, ideas, activities, and jobs in marketing that have spawned the products and services that you find in the Canadian and global marketplaces.

Marketing affects all individuals, all organizations, all industries, and all countries. This text seeks not only to teach you marketing concepts but also to demonstrate marketing's many applications and how it affects our lives. This knowledge should make you a better consumer, enable you to be a more informed citizen, and even help you in your career.

In this chapter and those that follow, you will feel the excitement of marketing. You will be introduced to the dynamic changes that will affect all of us in the future and will also meet many men and women, such as Gary Heavin, whose marketing creativity sometimes achieved brilliant, extraordinary results. And who knows? Somewhere in these pages, like Brenda Carriere, you may find a career.

■ ■ ■
WHAT MARKETING IS AND WHAT IT IS NOT

Right now, we want you to take your very first marketing test. We know you are probably saying, "What a way to start off the book!" But do not get too stressed out. There is just one question, and it is the only time that we will ever ask you "not" to think before you answer. Quickly and honestly: what is the first word that comes to your mind when you hear the word "marketing"?

We are going to make an educated guess and predict that most of you will answer "advertising," "selling," or "common sense." In our classes, we have asked thousands of other students this same question and have found these to be the most typical answers. But *marketing is not advertising*. Although advertising is one of the most visible aspects of marketing, it is but one small element of marketing. *Marketing is not selling*. In fact, many marketing experts believe that effective marketing can reduce the need for selling.

Marketing is not merely common sense. While good marketers are sensible, perceptive, and intuitive, these traits alone are not sufficient for making successful marketing decisions. Effective marketing requires intimate knowledge and understanding of consumers and the marketplace, which goes beyond simple common sense.

We are very much aware of the misconceptions about marketing, including many negative ones. But marketing is not hucksterism; it is not about selling unwanted things and taking the customer's money. Nor is marketing about manipulating, fooling, or tricking the customer.[2] Therefore, in order to fully appreciate marketing, you need to understand what it is and what it is not.

Marketing: Defined

marketing
An organizational function and a set of processes for creating, communicating, and delivering value to customers and for managing customer relationships in ways that benefit the organization and its stakeholders.

The American Marketing Association, the professional body representing marketers in Canada, the United States, and other countries around the world, define **marketing** as an organizational function and a set of processes for creating, communicating, and delivering value to customers and for managing customer relationships in ways that benefit the organization and its stakeholders.[3] This definition stresses the importance of customer value and customer relationships, concepts that will be discussed in this chapter and throughout the text.

In order to create "value,"marketing seeks (1) to discover the needs and wants of prospective customers, and (2) to satisfy them. These prospective customers include both individuals buying for themselves or their households and organizations that buy for their own use (such as manufacturers) or for resale (such as wholesalers and retailers).

Requirements for Marketing to Occur

For marketing to occur, at least four factors are required: (1) two or more parties (individuals or organizations) with unsatisfied needs, (2) a desire and ability on their part to be satisfied, (3) a way for the parties to communicate, and (4) something to exchange.

Two or More Parties with Unsatisfied Needs   Suppose you have developed an unmet need—a desire for information about how computer and telecommunications are interacting to reshape the workplace—but you did not yet know that *Computer-World* magazine existed. Also unknown to you was that several copies of *Computer-World* were sitting on the magazine rack at your nearest bookstore, waiting to be purchased. This is an example of two parties with unmet needs: you, with a need for technology-related information, and your bookstore owner, needing someone to buy a copy of *ComputerWorld*.

Desire and Ability to Satisfy These Needs   Both you and the bookstore owner want to satisfy these unmet needs. Furthermore, you have the money to buy the item and the time to get to the bookstore. The store's owner has not only the desire to sell *ComputerWorld* but also the ability to do so, since it is stocked on the shelves.

A Way for the Parties to Communicate   The marketing transaction of buying a copy of *ComputerWorld* will never occur unless you know the product exists and its location. Similarly, the store owner will not stock the magazine unless there is a market of potential buyers nearby. When you receive a free sample in the mail or see the magazine on display in the bookstore, this communications barrier between you (the buyer) and your bookstore (the seller) is overcome.

Something to Exchange   Marketing occurs when the transaction takes place and both the buyer and seller exchange something of value. In this case, you exchange your money for the bookstore's magazine. Both you and the bookstore have gained something and also given up something, but you are both better off because you have each satisfied your unmet needs. You have the opportunity to read *ComputerWorld*, but you gave up some money; the store gave up the magazine but received money, which enables it to remain in business. This exchange process and, of course, the ethical and legal foundations of exchange are central to marketing.

The Breadth and Depth of Marketing

Marketing today affects every person and organization. To understand this, let us analyze (1) what a market is, (2) who markets, (3) what they market, (4) who buys and uses what is marketed, and (5) who benefits from these marketing activities.

market

People with the desire and ability to buy a specific product.

What Is a Market?   A **market** is people with the desire and ability to buy a specific product. All markets ultimately are people. Even when we say a firm bought a photocopier, we mean one or several people in the firm decided to buy it. People who are aware of their unmet needs may have the desire to buy the product, but that alone is not sufficient. People must also have the ability to buy, that is, have the authority, time, and money. People may even "buy" an idea that results in an action, such as having their blood pressure checked or turning down their thermostats to save energy.

Who Markets?   Every organization markets! It is obvious that business firms involved in manufacturing (McCain Foods, General Motors of Canada, Ericsson Canada), retailing (Canadian Tire, Modrobes, The Bay), and providing services (Canadian Broadcasting Corporation, Air Canada, Via Rail, Vancouver Canucks, E*trade.ca) market their offerings. Today, many other types of marketing are also popular. Nonprofit organizations (Winnipeg Ballet, Canadian Red Cross, Canadian Museum of Civilization, Toronto Metro Zoo) also engage in marketing.[4] Your college or university, for example, probably has a marketing program to attract students, faculty members, and donations. Places (cities, provinces, countries) often use marketing efforts to attract tourists, conventions, or businesses. The province of Ontario, for example, has a marketing campaign designed to persuade businesses to locate there. Organizations associated with special events or causes use marketing to inform and influence a target audience. These marketing activities range from government agencies encouraging AIDS (acquired immune deficiency syndrome) prevention to professional organizations, such as the Registered Nurses Association of Ontario using marketing to recruit and retain nurses in Ontario. Finally, individuals, such as politicians like Paul Martin, often use marketing to gain attention and voter preference.

What Is Marketed?   Goods, services, and ideas are marketed. *Goods* are physical objects, such as Crest toothpaste, Nikon cameras, or Apple computers, that satisfy consumer needs. *Services* are activities, deeds, or other basic intangibles, such as airline trips on WestJet airlines, financial advice from TD Waterhouse, or long-distance telephone calls offered by the Telus Group. *Ideas* are intangibles involving thoughts about actions or causes, such as donating to the Salvation Army or to the Trans Canada Trail project.

Marketing is used by nonprofit organizations, causes, and places.

social marketing
Marketing designed to influence the behaviour of individuals in which the benefits of the behaviour accrue to those individuals or to the society in general and not to the marketer.

The use of idea marketing has grown significantly over the past three decades, in particular, idea marketing that focuses on enhancing social ends is a prevalent part of today's marketplace. This is referred to as social marketing. **Social marketing** is designed to influence the behaviour of individuals by which benefits accrue to those individuals or to society in general and not to the marketer. For example, antismoking campaigns by Health Canada or the Canadian Cancer Society would be an example of social marketing. Social marketing can be conducted by for-profit and nonprofit organizations or by individuals. For instance, even your friend's attempt to influence you to eat a more healthy diet could be considered social marketing. A discussion of some of the issues involved in the use of social marketing can be found in the accompanying Marketing NewsNet box.[5]

ultimate consumers
People—whether 80 years or 8 months old—who use the goods and services purchased for a household.

organizational buyers
Those manufacturers, wholesalers, retailers, and government agencies that buy goods and services for their own use or for resale.

Who Buys and Uses What Is Marketed?   Both individuals and organizations buy and use goods and services that are marketed. **Ultimate consumers** are people—whether 80 years or 8 months old—who use the goods and services purchased for a household. In contrast, **organizational buyers** are units, such as manufacturers, retailers, or government agencies, that buy goods and services for their own use or for resale. Although the terms *consumers*, *buyers*, and *customers* are sometimes used for both ultimate consumers and organizations, there is no consistency on this. In this book, you will be able to tell from the example whether the buyers are ultimate consumers, organizations, or both.

Who Benefits?   In our free-enterprise society, there are three specific groups that benefit from effective marketing: consumers who buy, organizations that sell, and society as a whole. True competition among products and services in the marketplace ensures that we as Canadian consumers can find value from the best products, the

---

MARKETING NEWSNET   **The Challenges of Social Marketing**

Social marketing was developed more than three decades ago to combat such social problems as overpopulation, drug abuse, violence against women, use of tobacco products, and other behaviours that increase the chances of poor health. However, social marketing faces a set of challenges that may inhibit its full development. First, most people lack a clear understanding of what social marketing is and what role it should play it creating social change.

Second, the ends that social marketing promotes in resolving social problems may not be justified in the same way in which the ends of commercial marketing are justified. For example, instead of appealing to the fulfillment of needs and wants of the people it targets, social marketing must develop an objective notion of social welfare that justifies those ends. In seeking to change the behaviour of people with social problems, social marketers must be candid about the ends sought, the evidence that links those ends to the welfare of the people targeted, the means used to bring about those ends, and the sources of funding behind the social marketing effort.

Third, social marketers may not focus on the background and structural features that underlie the social problems they attack. In short, social marketing may only offer temporary solutions which may not significantly affect the underlying problems. For example, social marketers may tell students to stay in school but if those schools do not provide a safe and nurturing environment for the students to learn, then where is the benefit to the student to stay in school? Fourth, using marketing techniques may have the consequence of not giving those whose behaviour is to be changed a rights-based voice in the matter. For example, do social marketers have the right to tell a teen to use condoms?

In sum, social marketing is not a neutral, technical enterprise but a form of social activism. Both the social marketers and the targets of social marketing must be aware of this fact. And if social marketing is asking people to change their behaviour, the rationale for that change must be honestly and openly presented. These and other challenges must be addressed if social marketing is to reach its full development.

lowest prices, or exceptional service. Providing choices leads to consumer satisfaction and the quality of life that we have come to expect from our Canadian economic system.

Organizations that provide need-satisfying products combined with effective marketing programs—for example, McDonald's Restaurants of Canada, IBM Canada, and Microsoft Canada—have blossomed. But competition creates problems for ineffective competitors, and hundreds of Canadian businesses fail every year. Effective marketing actions result in rewards for organizations that serve customers and in thousands of marketing jobs for individuals all across the country.

Finally, effective marketing benefits society. It enhances competition, which, in turn, both improves the quality of products and services and lowers their prices. This makes countries more competitive in world markets and provides jobs and a higher standard of living for their citizens.

The Diverse Factors Influencing Marketing Activities

Although an organization's marketing activity focuses on assessing and satisfying consumer needs, countless other people, groups, and forces interact to shape the nature of its activities (Figure 1–1). Foremost is the organization itself, whose mission and objectives determine what business it is in and what goals it seeks. Within the organization, organizational leaders are responsible for establishing these goals. And the marketing department works closely with a network of other departments and employees to help provide the customer-satisfying products required for the organization to survive and prosper.

Figure 1–1 also shows the key people, groups, and forces outside the organization that influence marketing activities. The marketing department is responsible for facilitating relationships, partnerships, and alliances with the organization's customers, its shareholders (or often representatives of groups served by a nonprofit organization), its suppliers, and other organizations. Environmental forces, such as

■ **FIGURE 1–1** ■

An organization's marketing department relates to many people, groups, and forces

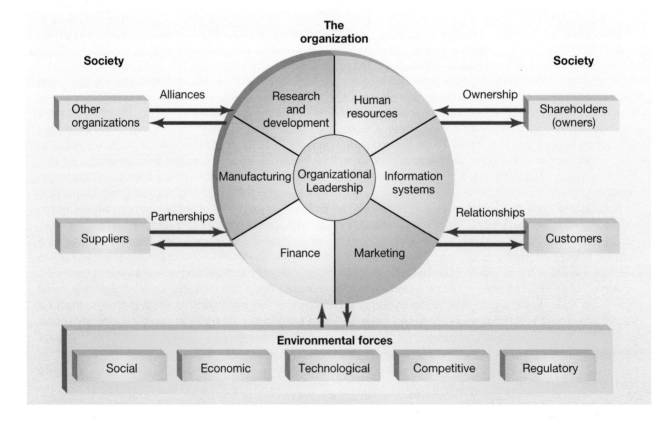

social, technological, economic, competitive, and regulatory factors, also shape an organization's marketing activities. Finally, an organization's marketing decisions are affected by and, in turn, often have an important impact on society as a whole.

The organization must strike a continual balance among the sometimes differing interests of these individuals and groups. For example, it is not possible to simultaneously provide the lowest-priced and highest-quality products to customers and pay the highest prices to suppliers, highest wages to employees, and maximum dividends to shareholders.

CONCEPT CHECK

1. What is marketing?

2. Marketing focuses on _____ and _____ prospective customers' needs and wants.

3. What four factors are needed for marketing to occur?

■ ■ ■
HOW MARKETING DISCOVERS AND SATISFIES CONSUMER NEEDS

The importance of discovering consumer needs is so critical to understanding marketing that we look at each of these two steps in detail next.

Discovering Consumer Needs

The first objective in marketing is discovering the needs of prospective customers. Sound simple? Well, it is not. In the abstract, discovering needs looks easy, but when you get down to the specifics of marketing, things can be difficult, and things can go wrong. For example, new product development experts estimate that 80 to 94 percent of the over 25 000 new consumable products (food, beverage, health, beauty, and other household and pet products) introduced in North America annually do not succeed in the long run. Robert M. McMath, who has studied over 40 000 of these new-product launches, has two key suggestions to marketers: (1) focus on what the customer benefit is, and (2) learn from the past.[6]

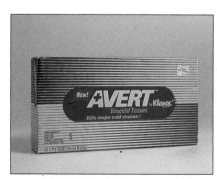

Why did Kimberly-Clark's Avert Virucidal tissues fail? See the section "Discovering Consumer Needs."

The solution to preventing new product failures does seem embarrassingly obvious. First, find out what consumers need and want. Second, produce what they need and want, and do not produce what they do not need or want. This is far more difficult than it sounds. For example, let us look at why Kimberly-Clark's Avert Virucidal tissues failed. First, the name confused consumers who could not quite understand what benefit a "virucidal" tissue provided. (It contained vitamin C derivatives that were supposed to keep germs from spreading when you blew into it.) Second, according to McMath, names that end in -cidal—such as homicidal or suicidal—do not put people in a buying mood. Ultimately, prospective customers were simply too confused and scared to risk putting their noses into Avert Virucidals.[7] So, today, firms spend billions of dollars annually on marketing and technical research that significantly reduces—but does not eliminate—new-product failure.

Consumer Needs and Consumer Wants   Should marketing try to satisfy consumer needs or consumer wants? The answer is both! Heated debates rage over this question, with regard to the definitions of needs and wants and the amount of freedom given to prospective customers to make their own buying decisions.

A *need* occurs when a person feels physiologically deprived of basic necessities, such as food, clothing, and shelter. A *want* is a felt need that is shaped by a person's knowledge, culture, and personality. So, if you feel hungry, you have developed a basic need and desire to eat something. Let us say you then want to eat an apple or a candy bar because based on your past experience and personality, you know these will satisfy your hunger need. Effective marketing, in the form of creating an awareness of good products at convenient locations, can clearly shape a person's wants.

At issue is whether marketing persuades prospective customers to buy the "wrong" things—say, a candy bar rather than an apple to satisfy hunger pangs. Certainly, marketing tries to influence what we buy. A question then arises: at what point do we want government and society to step in to protect consumers? Most consumers would say they want government to protect us from harmful drugs and unsafe cars, but what about candy bars, cereals, and soft drinks? Read the Ethics and Social Responsibility Alert box concerning the advertising of junk food directed at Canadian children.[8] What do you think about this issue? Sometimes, there are no clear-cut answers when it comes to the issue of what should be marketed and how. In fact, there is continuing debate over what constitutes human *need* and *want* and whether somebody has the right to determine for someone else what a need is and what a want is. Because even psychologists and economists still argue about the exact meanings of need and want, we shall avoid the semantic arguments and use the terms interchangeably in the rest of the book.

As shown in Figure 1–2, discovering needs involves looking carefully at prospective customers, whether they are children buying M&Ms, university students buying Rollerblade in-line skates, or firms buying photocopying machines. Principal activities of a firm's marketing department are to carefully scrutinize its consumers to understand what they need, to study industry trends, to examine competitors' products, and even to analyze the needs of a customer's customer.

Satisfying Consumer Needs

Marketing does not stop with the discovery of consumer needs. Because the organization obviously cannot satisfy all consumer needs, it must concentrate its efforts on certain needs of a specific group of potential consumers. This is the **target market** —one or more specific groups of potential consumers toward which an organization directs its marketing program.

target market
One or more specific groups of potential consumers toward which an organization directs its marketing program.

The Four P's: Controllable Marketing Mix Factors   Having selected the target market consumers, the firm must take steps to satisfy their needs. Someone in the organization's marketing department, often the marketing manager, must take action

■ FIGURE 1–2 ■
Marketing's first task: discovering consumer needs

Between their second and twelfth birthdays, Canadian children will see 200 000 television commercials. About 80 percent of food commercials aired during Saturday morning kids' TV shows are for products of low nutritional value, or what some refer to as junk food. Spots for high-sugar products—for example, candy and cereals—form the majority of such ads. In many cases, the ads contain what some experts label "weasel words," or words and phrases that are meant to mislead children—such as "part of a complete breakfast."

Many health experts are concerned about the diets of young Canadians, suggesting that they eat too many foods with poor nutritional value. Furthermore, poor eating habits, including the high rate of consumption of junk food, have led to a steady increase in childhood obesity over the past 30 years. This increase in childhood obesity has many health experts concerned because they believe it will contribute to many diseases in the decades to come, including higher rates of diabetes and cancer.

Nutritional experts suggest that because young children lack the decision-making ability to make wise food choices, something must be done to protect them from junk food advertising. But what? A complete ban on advertising junk food to children? Stricter regulations on what can be said and shown in such ads? Stronger parental involvement regarding food choices? There may not be a clear answer here. But this issue does reveal the possible ethical, social, or even legal aspects of marketing something as simple as a candy bar or a box of cereal.

and develop a complete marketing program that creates, communicates, and delivers value to a target market. This happens through the use of a combination of four tools, often called the four Ps—a useful shorthand reference to them first published by Professor E. Jerome McCarthy:[9]

- *Product.* A good, service, or idea to satisfy the consumer's needs.
- *Price.* What is exchanged for the product.
- *Promotion.* A means of communication between the seller and buyer.
- *Place.* A means of getting the product into the consumer's hands.

We will define each of the four P's more carefully later in the book, but for now, it is important to remember that they are the elements of the marketing mix, or simply the **marketing mix**. These are the marketing manager's controllable factors, the marketing actions of product, price, promotion, and place that he or she can take to create, communicate, and deliver value. The marketing mix elements are called controllable factors because they are under the control of the marketing department in an organization.

The Uncontrollable, Environmental Factors   There are a host of factors largely beyond the control of the marketing department and its organization. These factors can be placed into five groups (as shown in Figure 1–1): social, economic, technological, competitive, and regulatory forces. Examples are what consumers themselves want and need, changing technology, the state of the economy in terms of whether it is expanding or contracting, actions that competitors take, and government restrictions. These are the **environmental factors** in a marketing decision, the uncontrollable factors involving social, economic, technological, competitive, and regulatory forces. These five forces may serve as accelerators or brakes on marketing, sometimes expanding an organization's marketing opportunities and other times restricting them. These five environmental factors are covered in Chapter 3.

Traditionally, many marketing executives have treated these environmental factors as rigid, absolute constraints that are entirely outside their influence. Accordingly, some executives simply fail to anticipate and respond to these environmental factors. But recent studies have shown that forward-looking, action-oriented firms

marketing mix
The marketing manager's controllable factors; the marketing actions of product, price, promotion, and place that he or she can take to create, communicate, and deliver value.

environmental factors
The uncontrollable factors involving social, economic, technological, competitive, and regulatory forces.

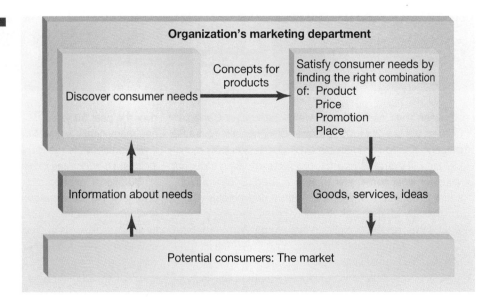

can take advantage of changes in the marketing environment by aligning their organizations to capitalize on such changes by introducing new technologies or competitive breakthroughs.

The Marketing Program

Effective relationship marketing strategies help marketing managers discover what prospective customers need. They must translate this information into some concepts for products the firm might develop (Figure 1–3). These concepts must then be converted into a tangible **marketing program**—a plan that integrates the marketing mix to provide a good, service, or idea to prospective buyers. These prospects then react to the offering favourably (by buying) or unfavourably (by not buying), and the process is repeated. As shown in Figure 1–3, in an effective organization this process is continuous: consumer needs trigger product concepts that are translated into actual products that stimulate further discovery of consumer needs.

marketing program
A plan that integrates the marketing mix to provide a good, service, or idea to prospective buyers.

A Marketing Program for Curves International

To see some specifics of an actual marketing program, let us return to the earlier example of Curves International, the women's fitness and weight-management business. Curves long-run strategy will focus on: (1) launching 200 new locations per month via the franchising route, (2) competing on a customer service dimension, and (3) expanding its product offerings.

Curves will focus on expanding in new markets in Canada, the United States, and other markets. The goal will be to not only be the largest fitness franchise in the world but also the largest weight-loss franchise. This will involve the development and marketing of books on dieting as well as vitamin products and protein shakes.

Curves believes this approach will be necessary for continued growth in the future. The company has already attracted numerous competitors that are trying to copy its business model. But such competitors as Slender Lady and Ladies' Workout Express do not concern Curves' CEO Gary Heavin. He argues the Curves will continue to dominate because of the focus on customer service and the relationships it builds with its clients.[10] Figure 1–4 shows the basic features of the Curves marketing

MIX ELEMENT	MARKETING PROGRAM FOR CURVES
Product	Simple 30-minute hydraulic weight resistance and ardiovascular fitness and weight-management program at a no-frills fitness centre/gym
	Curves vitamins, Curves protein shakes, diet books, Curves clothing, stretching mat, pedometer, wristwatch with heart rate monitor
Price	Initiation fee of $99 to $199
	Annual membership fee of $475 or monthly fee of $45 Curves vitamins $27–$35 for one month supply Curves protein shakes $30 for one month supply
Promotion	Word-of-mouth, print ads, broadcast ads
Place	Typically located in strip malls in cities and towns, offering convenience and accessibility

■ FIGURE 1–4 ■

Marketing Program for Curves

program. To get a better understanding of this company, go to the accompanying WebLink box to read the story of Curves International and its current and future marketing programs.

■ ■ ■

HOW MARKETING BECAME SO IMPORTANT

Marketing is a driving force in the modern global economy. To understand why this is so and some related ethical aspects, let us look at the (1) evolution of the market orientation, (2) ethics and social responsibility in marketing.

WEBLINK
HTTP://WWW.MCGRAWHILL.CA/
COLLEGE/CRANE

The Curves International Story

In this chapter, we introduced you to this wildly successful company: Curves International. To find out more about this company and its current and future marketing programs, visit www.curvesinternational.com. Be sure to read the founder's story and why he developed the company. Also, be sure to read how Curves intends to continue to grow in the future.

CONCEPT CHECK

1. An organization cannot satisfy the needs of all consumers, and so it must focus on one or more subgroups, which are its _____.

2. What are the four marketing mix elements that make up the organization's marketing program?

3. What are uncontrollable variables?

Evolution of the Market Orientation

Many market-oriented manufacturing organizations have experienced four distinct stages in the life of their firms. We can use Pillsbury, now part of General Mills, and General Electric as examples.

Production Era Goods were scarce in the early years in North America, and so buyers were willing to accept virtually any goods that were produced and make do with them as best they could. The central notion was that products would sell themselves, and so the major concern of business firms was production, not marketing. Robert Keith, a Pillsbury president, described his company at this stage: "We are professional flour millers. . . . Our basic function is to mill quality flour."[11] As shown in Figure 1–5, this production era generally continued through the 1920s.

Sales Era About that time, many firms discovered that they could produce more goods than their regular buyers could consume. Competition grew. The usual solution was to hire more salespeople to find new buyers. Pillsbury's philosophy at this stage was summed up simply by Keith: "We must hire salespersons to sell it [the flour] just as we hire accountants to keep our books." The role of the Pillsbury sales-force was simply to find consumers for the goods that the firm could produce best. This sales era continued into the 1950s for Pillsbury and into the 1960s for many other firms (see Figure 1–5).

Marketing Concept Era In the 1960s, marketing became the motivating force among many firms. Then the policy became: "we are in the business of satisfying needs and wants of consumers." This is really a brief statement of what has come to be known as the **marketing concept**; the idea is that an organization should (1) strive to satisfy the needs of consumers (2) while also trying to achieve the organization's goals.

    The statement of a firm's commitment to satisfying consumer wants and needs that probably launched the marketing concept appeared in a 1952 annual report of General Electric:[12] "The concept introduces . . . marketing . . . at the beginning rather than the end of the production cycle and integrates marketing into each phase of the business." This statement emphasizes that marketing ideas are fed into the production cycle from *after* an item is produced to *before* it is designed. Clearly, the marketing concept is a focus on the consumer. Unfortunately, many companies found that actually implementing the concept was very difficult.

Market Orientation Era An organization that has a **market orientation** focuses its efforts on (1) continuously collecting information about customers' needs and competitors' capabilities, (2) sharing this information throughout the

marketing concept
The idea that an organization should (1) strive to satisfy the needs of consumers (2) while also trying to achieve the organization's goals.

market orientation
Focusing efforts on (1) continuously collecting information about customers' needs and competitors' capabilities, (2) sharing this information throughout the organization, and (3) using the information to create value, ensure customer satisfaction, and develop customer relationships.

■ **FIGURE 1–5** ■■
Four different orientations in the history of North American business

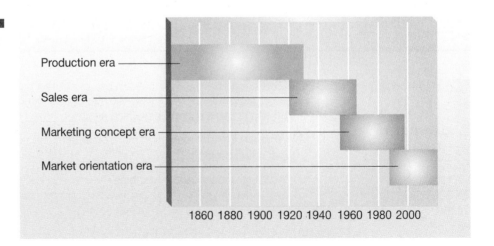

What type of value do these firms offer their customers? See the text.

customer value
The unique combination of benefits received by the customer that include quality, price, convenience, on-time delivery, and both before-sale and after-sale service.

organization, and (3) using the information to create value, ensure customer satisfaction, and develop customer relationships.

Customer value is defined as the unique combination of benefits received by the customer that include quality, price, convenience, on-time delivery, and both before-sale and after-sale service. As Chapter 5 will point out, Canadians are becoming increasingly "value conscious." And Canadian companies are attempting to provide unique value that they alone can deliver to their targeted markets. This unique customer value can come in the form of best price, best product, or best service.[13] For example, Wal-Mart attempts to offer its customers the best price. Starbucks claims to offer its customers the best product. And Canadian Tire delivers value through exceptional customer service.

customer satisfaction
The match between customer expectations of the product and the product's actual performance.

When customers believe they have received good value, they tend to be satisfied with their providers. **Customer satisfaction** is the match between customer expectations of the product and the product's actual performance. This is an important measure of the ability of a firm to successfully meet the needs of the customer. If the product fails to meet the customer's expectations, the customer will be dissatisfied. If the product performance matches expectations, the customer is satisfied. If the performance exceeds the customer's expectations, the customer is likely to be highly satisfied. Recent research involving successful Canadian and American entrepreneurs revealed that customer satisfaction is an important ingredient for the long-term success of businesses. Moreover, this same research found that customer value and satisfaction are critical for an organization in order to develop ongoing customer relationships.[14]

customer relationship management (CRM)
The process of building and developing long-term relationships with customers by delivering customer value and satisfaction.

Therefore, it is not surprising that organizations with a market orientation actually engage in **customer relationship management (CRM)**—the process of building and developing long-term relationships with customers by delivering customer value and satisfaction. CRM involves the use of relationship-centric strategies to optimize the long-term value of an organization's selected customers. Retaining customers over time, or managing the entire customer life cycle is a cost-effective way for firms to grow in competitive markets. Organizations engaging CRM understand the importance of the lifetime value of a customer, not just single transactions. **Customer lifetime value (CLV)** is the profit generated by the customer's purchase of an organization's product or service over the customer's lifetime. Kimberly-Clark, for example, reports that its retained customers buy about seven boxes of Kleenex per year and will spend over $1400 on facial tissue over a lifetime. Meanwhile, Lexus estimates that a retained and satisfied customer is worth over $600 000 in lifetime sales.[15]

customer lifetime value (CLV)
The profit generated by the customer's purchase of an organization's product or service over the customer's lifetime.

To be effective, CRM requires the involvement and commitment of managers and employees throughout the organization and the growing application of information technology. In fact, technology is a key CRM enabler. And with advances in information technology and changes in customer buying behaviour—specifically, online

eCRM

A Web-centric, personalized approach to managing long-term customer relationships electronically.

buying— the scope of CRM has been broadened to include **eCRM**—a Web-centric, personalized approach to managing long-term customer relationships electronically.[16] Expenditures on CRM initiatives in North America are expected to exceed $10 billion in 2006.[17]

An integral component of eCRM is interactive marketing. *Interactive marketing* involves two-way buyer–seller electronic communication in which the buyer can control the kind and amount of information received from the seller. For effective interactive marketing to occur, companies need to listen, understand, and respond to their customers' needs. Marketers must also treat customers as individuals and empower them to (1) influence the timing and extent of the buyer–seller interaction, and (2) have a say in the kind of products and services they buy, the information they receive, and, in some cases, even the prices they pay. Interactive marketing technology now allows for a level of customer interaction, individualization, and customer relationship management process to be carried out on a scale never before available.

However, many experts have suggested that CRM initiatives are suffering because the focus has been on getting CRM technology in place while neglecting to ask customers if they want a relationship and, if so, what type of relationship they want. Moreover, employees responsible for CRM implementation have also been neglected and not consulted about the rationale behind the CRM initiatives. In fact, some studies have shown that CRM successes are few and far between. And now, many companies believe that CRM has been overhyped, overpromised, and oversold and that it is not as easy to implement as once perceived and not as profitable as once believed.[18] Bank of Montreal, for example, has spent years trying to integrate CRM through the entire organization and is now just starting to see some of the rewards of CRM. The Royal Bank of Canada has had to totally restructure its departments to match the customer segments revealed through CRM initiatives in order to achieve CRM results. Outside of the Canadian financial services industry, a few other Canadian companies are achieving some success with CRM, including Telus, Bell, Sears, and Shoppers Drug Mart.[19] The Hudson's Bay Company has also invested heavily in CRM and is successfully leveraging its CRM technology and its customer database in order to build customer loyalty by providing good value and satisfaction.[20]

Still, these companies appear to be the exception and not the rule. Many experts see CRM as an evolutionary process that may take up to 20 years to embrace and implement successfully. Others believe that different models may be necessary if marketers are to truly build long-term successful and profitable relationships with customers. One emerging model is the concept of *concierge marketing* (CM)—

The Hudson's Bay Company engages in CRM activities to retain customers for life.

where the emphasis is placed on understanding why and how customers use a brand and on building a process of customer benefits around that usage. For example, Coldwell Bankers' CM program does not involve selling real estate per se. Instead, it offers banking services, moving companies, decorators, repair people—all reformulated in an one-stop-shop package. They have taken a marketing commodity, real estate, and turned it into concierge marketing. Their brand is at the centre of the home-buying process. Advocates of CM argue that the CRM programs often fail because many brands have become commoditized and marginalized; and if a brand lacks value in the minds of the customer, there is no brand loyalty. In that case, trying to sell more products to existing customers under the rubic of CRM will not work. With CM, on the other hand, the brand is at the centre of a customer-centric process. And, the brand is perceived as valuable to the customer because it is seen as a means to an end—improving the customer's quality of life.[21]

Ethics and Social Responsibility: Balancing the Interests of Different Groups

As organizations have changed their orientation, society's expectations of marketers have also changed. Today, the standards of marketing practice have shifted from an emphasis on producers' interests to consumers' interests. In addition, organizations are increasingly encouraged to consider the social and environmental consequences of their actions for all parties. Guidelines for ethical and socially responsible behaviour can help managers balance consumer, organizational, and societal interests.

ethics
The moral principles and values that govern the actions and decisions of an individual or group.

Ethics   Many marketing issues are not specifically addressed by existing laws and regulations. Should information about a firm's customers be sold to other organizations? Should advertising by professional service providers, such as accountants and lawyers, be restricted? Should consumers be on their own to assess the safety of a product? These questions may not involve strict legal issues but do raise some ethical questions. **Ethics** are the moral principles and values that govern the actions and decisions of an individual or group. Ethics serve as guidelines on how to act correctly and justly. In Chapter 4, we will discuss marketing ethics and how organizations must work to ensure that their employees not only live within the law but also practise ethical behaviour.

social responsibility
Individuals and organizations are part of a larger society and are accountable to that society for their actions.

societal marketing concept
The view that an organization should discover and satisfy the needs of its consumers in a way that also provides for society's well-being.

macromarketing
The aggregate flow of a nation's goods and services to benefit society.

micromarketing
How an individual organization directs its marketing activities and allocates its resources to benefit its customers.

Social Responsibility   While many ethical issues involve only the buyer and seller, others involve society as a whole. For example, suppose you change the oil in your old Chevy yourself and dump the used oil on a corner of your backyard. Is this just an transaction between you and the oil manufacturer? Not quite! The used oil may contaminate the soil, and so society will bear a portion of the cost of your behaviour. This example illustrates the issue of social responsibility. **Social responsibility** means that individuals and organizations are part of a larger society and are accountable to that society for their actions (see Chapter 4). In fact, some marketing experts stress the **societal marketing concept**, the view that an organization should discover and satisfy the needs of its consumers in a way that also provides for society's well-being.[22]

The societal marketing concept is directly related to **macromarketing**, which looks at the aggregate flow of a nation's goods and services to benefit society.[23] Macromarketing addresses such broad issues as whether marketing costs too much, whether advertising is wasteful, and what resource scarcities and pollution side-effects result from the marketing system. Macromarketing issues are addressed in this book, but the main focus is on how an individual organization directs its marketing activities and allocates its resources to benefit its customers,which is referred to as **micromarketing**. An overview of this approach appears in Chapter 2. Because of the importance of ethical and social responsibility issues in marketing today, Chapter 4 focuses on these topics, while they are also highlighted throughout the book.

1. Many firms have gone through four distinct orientations for their businesses: starting with the _____ era and ending with today's _____ era.

2. An organization that has a marketing orientation focuses its efforts on (1) _____ , (2) _____ and (3) _____ .

3. The process of building and developing long-term relationships with customers by delivering customer value and satisfaction is called _____ .

■ ■ ■
CHAPTER IN REVIEW

1 Define marketing.

Marketing is an organizational function and a set of processes for creating, communicating, and delivering value to customers and for managing customer relationships in ways that benefit the organization and its stakeholders.

2 Know the basic requirements for successful marketing to occur.

For marketing to occur, it is necessary to have (a) two or more parties with unmet needs, (b) a desire and ability to satisfy them, (c) communication between the parties, and (4) something to exchange.

3 Understand the breadth and depth of marketing.

Marketing affects every person and organization. Both for-profit and nonprofit organizations perform marketing activities. They market products, services, and ideas that benefit consumers, organizations, and countries.

4 Explain how marketing discovers and satisfies consumer needs and wants.

The first objective in marketing is discovering the needs of prospective consumers. The second objective in marketing is satisfying the needs of targeted consumers. Because an organization cannot satisfy all consumer needs, it must concentrate its efforts on certain needs of a specific group of potential consumers or target market—one or more specific groups of potential consumers toward which an organization directs its marketing program. Having selected its target market, the organization then takes action to satisfy the customers' needs by developing a unique marketing program to appeal to that market.

5 Distinguish between marketing mix elements and environmental factors.

Four elements in a marketing program designed to satisfy customer needs are product, price, promotion, and place. These elements are called the marketing mix—the four Ps—or the controllable variables because they are under the general control of the marketing department within an organization. Environmental factors, also called uncontrollable variables, are largely beyond the organization's control. These include social, technological, economic, competitive, and regulatory forces.

6 Describe how market orientation in the present era focuses on creating customer value, satisfaction, and customer relationships.

Organizations with a market orientation focus their efforts on (1) continuously collecting information about customers' needs and competitors' capabilities, (2) sharing this information throughout the organization, and (3) using the information to create value, ensure customer satisfaction, and develop customer relationships. Organizations with a market orientation engage in customer relationship management (CRM)—the process of building and developing long-term relationships with customers by delivering customer value and satisfaction. Organizations engaging CRM understand the importance of the customer lifetime value (CLV)—the profits generated by the customer's purchase of an organization's product or service over the customer's lifetime. The concept of eCRM—a Web-centric, personalized approach to managing long-term customer relationships electronically, which includes interactive marketing, is changing the way buyers and sellers interact. Interactive marketing technology now allows for a level of customer interaction, individualization, and customer relationship management process to be carried out on a scale never before available. However, CRM, including eCRM, has not been easy to implement, and many experts are advocating new approaches to manage long-term customer relationships. One concept is concierge marketing (CM)—where an emphasis is placed on understanding why and how customers use a brand and building a process of customer benefits around that usage.

7 Understand the meaning of ethics and social responsibility and how they relate to the individual, organizations, and society.

Marketing managers must balance consumer, organizational, and societal interests. This involves issues of ethics and social responsibility. Ethics are the moral principles and values that govern the actions and decisions of an individual or group. Ethics serve as guidelines on how to act correctly and justly. Social responsibility means that individuals and organizations are part of a larger society and are accountable to that society for their actions. Some marketing experts stress the societal marketing concept, the view that an organization should discover and satisfy the needs of its consumers in a way that also provides for society's well-being.

FOCUSING ON KEY TERMS

customer lifetime value (CLV) p. 17
customer relationship management (CRM) p. 17
customer satisfaction p. 17
customer value p. 17
eCRM p. 18
environmental factors p. 13
ethics p. 19
macromarketing p. 19
market p. 8
market orientation p. 16
marketing p. 7

marketing concept p. 16
marketing mix p. 13
marketing program p. 14
micromarketing p. 19
organizational buyers p. 9
social marketing p. 9
social responsibility p. 19
societal marketing concept p. 19
target market p. 12
ultimate consumers p. 9

DISCUSSION AND APPLICATION QUESTIONS

1 What value does the consumer receive by purchasing the following products or services? (a) Carnation Instant Breakfast, (b) Adidas running shoes, (c) Hertz Rent-A-Car, and (d) television home shopping programs.

2 Each of the four products, services, or programs in question 1 has substitutes. Respective examples are (a) a ham and egg breakfast, (b) regular tennis shoes, (c) taking a bus, and (d) a department store. What consumer value might these substitutes deliver instead of those mentioned in question 1?

3 What are the characteristics (e.g., age, income, education) of the target market customers for the following products or services? (a) *National Geographic* magazine, (b) *Wired* magazine, (c) Toronto Blue Jays baseball team, and (d) the Canadian Open tennis tournament.

4 A university in a metropolitan area wishes to increase its evening-school offerings of business-related courses, such as marketing, accounting, finance, and management. Who are the target market customers (students) for these courses?

5 What actions involving the four marketing mix elements might be used to reach the target market in question 4?

6 What environmental factors (uncontrollable variables) must the university in question 4 consider in designing its marketing program?

7 Curves International believes it can grow by taking the business globally. What are the advantages and disadvantages of trying to reach new global markets?

8 Provide a recent example of a shopping experience where you were very satisfied and one where you were very dissatisfied with your purchase. Explain why you were satisfied or dissatisfied. What impact will this experience have on your purchases from that organization?

9 Calculate the annual value of a specific purchase you make on a regular basis. For example, gasoline for your car. What would be the purchase value over a 10-year period? What does this tell you about the customer lifetime value concept?

10 Customer relationship management (CRM) is one of the hottest concepts in modern marketing. Do you have an example that illustrates how an organization has engaged in CRM with you? Explain.

| GOING ONLINE | Understanding Marketing Terms and Concepts |

Marketing uses a number of terms and concepts that are often difficult to remember. But, the American Marketing Association (AMA), a professional body that represents thousands of marketers in Canada, the United States, and around the world, is a valuable source of information on marketing. In fact, on its Web site, the AMA actually has a comprehensive dictionary containing over 4000 marketing terms and concepts.

Go to www.marketingpower.com (the AMA's official Web site) and check out the marketing dictionary. Search for key terms and concepts that are of interest to you. This exercise should prove invaluable to you as you attempt to gain a better understanding of the marketing discipline. There are also numerous provincial chapters of the AMA in Canada. You may also wish to check out their Web sites for the latest marketing news in Canada.

VIDEO CASE 1   Curves International

INTRODUCTION

In small towns and large cities all across Canada, groups of women are working out on fitness machines in a distinctively different type of fitness centre—Curves. Curves is the largest fitness franchise in the world with over 9300 locations worldwide. Curves clubs can be found in the United States, Canada, Europe, South America, The Caribbean, Mexico, Australia, and New Zealand. It is a fitness and weight-management facility dedicated to providing affordable, one-stop exercise and nutritional information for women.

Curves made its Canadian debut in 1999. Since then, the company has grown to over 730 locations coast-to-coast. It is a fitness and weight-management business with a twist. Curves' offering is simple: provide women—mostly overweight, mostly over 30 years of age, and many using a gym for the first time—with a fast, highly structured and glamour-free opportunity to get in shape. It is a no-frills approach to fitness. There are no showers, therapeutic massages, or fresh fruit smoothies. What customers do get is a simple 30-minute hydraulic weight resistance and cardio-vascular workout. Customers exercise using a circuit of eight to 12 hydraulic resistance machines and recovery stations where they jog or march on the spot. Fast-paced music plays and a voice recording tells customers when to change stations. It also offers a weight-management counselling program.

THE HISTORY OF CURVES

Over 27 years ago, Curves founder Gary Heavin dropped out of a pre-med program that he could no longer afford. He took over a failing health club and began to provide fitness services that would prevent illness. By age 30, Gary had built a fitness centre chain with 17 locations, and then... he lost it all. He decided to rebuild his business applying the many lessons he had learned from both his successes and his failures. He and his wife Diane opened their first Curves in 1992. This new concept of 30-minute fitness, strength training,

weight-loss guidance, and a comfortable environment designed for women was immediately successful. Diane had a passion for exercise and the perspective of an advertising executive. Together, Gary and Diane began to develop plans for franchising the concept, with the first franchise opening in 1995. By 1996, Curves had grown to 44 locations. By 1999, Curves had 860 locations and was chosen by *Entrepreneur* magazine as the number one best new franchise. It also opened its first location in Canada that year.

In 2000, Curves opened a location in Spain, and in 2001, Curves opened its doors in Mexico. In 2001, Curves had over 2200 locations. By 2002, the company expanded to 5000 clubs and opened its first club in the United Kingdom.

In 2005, after just 10 years in business, Curves had grown to over 9000 locations, with all Curves franchises being 100 percent independently owned and operated. Curves has been consistently ranked in *Entrepreneur* magazine as one of the best franchises in its annual surveys and was entered into the Guinness World Records as "The world's largest fitness centre franchise." Importantly, much of this phenomenal growth has been realized through the positive word-of-mouth from Curves members. With locations now in more than 30 countries, Curves has encouraged more than four million women to stay fit and manage their weight.

THE CURVES BUSINESS MODEL

Curves efficient business model allows the company to enter small Canadian markets, for example, in towns with populations as low as 5000. Typical Curves facilities are only 1200 to 1500 square feet compared with large clubs that run from 30 000–40 000 square feet. Moreover, Curves clubs can be profitable with as few as 200 members. Canadian franchisees pay about $40 000 for a franchise, plus $500 in monthly fees. Those costs include equipment and marketing support. But the costs do not include leasing costs or staff.

What is very interesting about Curves' business model is that it is not designed to take customers away from other fitness clubs. Instead, Curves creates its own markets and generates a new customer base—people who do not belong to other clubs and perhaps never even thought about joining a club. Company founder, Gary Heavin, saw an opportunity to cater to this particular target market, a market that competitors were overlooking or ignoring. He identified the basic needs of this target market and built the Curves organization around those needs. Importantly, he focuses the entire organization on ensuring customer satisfaction and on building long-term relationships with Curves' customers. And, as mentioned, this strategy is working, given that most new members to Curves join as a result of positive word-of-mouth from existing numbers.

FUTURE GROWTH

Curves International's future growth paths will include opening new franchise locations, domestically and internationally. But, it has also added new elements to its core business, including: a Curves line of clothing, Curves vitamins, Curves protein drink mix, and Curves workout and diet books. Other Curves-branded products are being marketed by Avon, including a stretching mat, a pedometer, and a wrist watch with a heart rate monitor. Curves also offers a corporate accounts program where companies can allow their female employees to join Curves at discounted rates.

While Curves has forever altered the fitness industry landscape and demonstrated tremendous growth over the past decade, it has also spurred on a wave of copycat fitness chains, such as Slender Lady and Ladies Workout Express, which may impact on its future growth. These companies are trying to copy the Curves business model and are attempting to compete in the same markets or markets similar to Curves's. But Curves intends to remain competitive in order to secure its future growth.

QUESTIONS

1 What trends in the environmental forces (social, economic, technological, competitive, and regulatory) identified in Figure 1–1 in the chapter (a) work for and (b) work against Curves International's potential growth in Canada?

2 How does Curves International illustrate the two critical aspects of marketing: identifying and satisfying customer needs?

3 Now that Curves is faced with copycat fitness chains, how should it respond?

4 In searching for new global markets to enter, (a) what are some criteria that Curves should use to select countries to enter, and (b) what three or four countries meet the criteria best and are the most likely candidates?

2

DEVELOPING SUCCESSFUL MARKETING AND CORPORATE STRATEGIES

LEARNING OBJECTIVES

After reading this chapter, you should be able to:

1. Describe the three organizational levels of strategy.

2. Describe why business, mission, culture, and goals are important in organizations.

3. Explain how organizations set strategic directions by assessing where they are now and seek to be in the future.

4. Describe the strategic marketing process and its three key phases: planning, implementation, and control.

5. Explain how the marketing mix elements are blended into a cohesive marketing program.

BOMBARDIER—A CANADIAN COMPANY MOVING PEOPLE ON A GLOBAL SCALE

In 1942, J. Armand Bombardier founded a company in Quebec named L'Auto-Neige Bombardier Limitee to manufacture tracked vehicles for transportation on snow-covered terrain. In 1967, the company became Bombardier Inc., and its growth has been impressive. Today, Quebec-based Bombardier is a world-leading manufacturer of innovative transportation solutions from regional aircraft and business jets to rail transportation equipment. It currently generates revenue of more than $15 billion. The company employees over 65 000 people, and 95 percent of its revenue comes from markets outside Canada.

The company's core businesses include aerospace, rail transportation, and Bombardier Capital. You are probably familiar with some of their aerospace products, including their CRJ regional aircraft used by airlines around the world, as well as their Learjet and Challenger business aircraft. You have probably also travelled on their rail vehicles or total transit systems.

But what makes Bombardier a Canadian success story? First, it has clearly defined the scope and nature of its businesses and the markets in which it competes (e.g., aerospace, rail transportation, financial services). Establishing core businesses provides needed focus to the company. Second, its clear, simple, and straight-forward mission "to be the world's leading manufacturer of planes and trains" creates a unity of purpose and inspiration for the entire organization. Third, Bombardier has outlined clear corporate goals and objectives as well as developed and articulated strategies to achieve those objectives.

The company also has a strong corporate culture that is focused on integrity, excellence, and innovation. Moreover, included in its written core values is the commitment to customers, including a customer orientation that emphasizes providing outstanding value and service to customers as well as a commitment to shareholders to create sustainable shareholder value through developing profitable products. The company also has a comprehensive code of ethics program, published in 12 languages, that makes a major commitment to social responsibility, including the establishment of a charitable foundation.

The company has made many strategic decisions throughout its corporate history in order to maintain its focus and profitability. Recently, it sold off its recreational products segment for $2.5 billion. This business, Bombardier Recreational Products, manufactures and markets snowmobiles (Ski-doo), watercraft, all-terrain vehicles (ATVs), and outdoor engines. The company believed this divestment was an appropriate strategic move in order for the company to exploit opportunities in the high-growth aerospace and rail transportation sectors. One opportunity the company seized in the aerospace sector is the on-demand charter or private aviation business. Bombardier Skyjet currently offers business travellers on-demand charter service for $1800 per hour.[1]

Chapter 2 describes how organizations define their business, set their mission and overall direction, and link these activities to marketing strategies. Because of today's intense competition and changing markets, firms must continuously revisit these tasks. In essence, this chapter describes how such organizations as Bombardier Inc. try to plan, implement, and control the strategic marketing process.

■ ■ ■
LEVELS OF STRATEGY IN ORGANIZATIONS

This chapter first distinguishes among different kinds of organizations and the various levels within them. It then compares strategies at three different levels in an organization, emphasizing the importance of activities at the functional level.

Today's Organizations: Kinds, Levels, and Teams

Large organizations today are extremely complex. All of us deal in some way with huge organizations every day, and so it is useful to understand (1) the two basic kinds of organizations, (2) the levels that exist in them and their link to marketing, and (3) the functional areas and cross-functional teams.

Kinds of Organizations   Today's organizations can be divided into business firms and nonprofit organizations. A *business firm* is a privately owned organization that serves its customers in order to earn a profit. Business firms must earn profits to survive. **Profit** is the reward to a business firm for the risk it undertakes in offering a product for sale: the money left over after a firm's total expenses are subtracted from its total revenues. In contrast to business firms, a *nonprofit organization* is a nongovernmental organization that serves its customers but does not have profit as an organizational goal. For simplicity, in the rest of the book, however, the terms *firm*, *company*, *corporation*, and *organization* are used to cover both business and nonprofit operations.

Levels in Organizations and How Marketing Links to Them   Whether explicit or implicit, organizations have a strategic direction. Marketing not only helps set this direction but also must help implement it. Figure 2–1 summarizes the focus of this direction at each of the three levels in an organization.

The **corporate level** is where top management directs overall strategy for the entire organization. Multimarket, multiproduct firms, such as Bombardier Inc. or Johnson & Johnson, really manage a portfolio of businesses, often termed strategic

profit
The reward to a business firm for the risk it undertakes in offering a product for sale; the money left over after a firm's total expenses are subtracted from its total revenues.

corporate level
Level at which top management directs overall strategy for the entire organization.

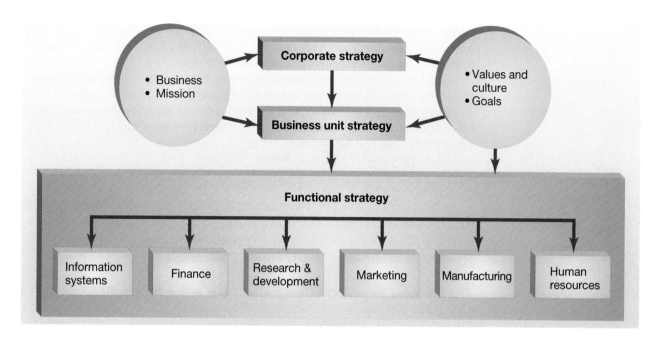

■ FIGURE 2–1 ■
The three levels of strategy
in organizations

business unit
An organization that markets a
set of related products to a
clearly defined group of
customers.

business unit level
Level at which business unit
managers set the direction for
their products and markets.

functional level
Level at which groups of
specialists actually create
value for the organization.

business units (SBUs), strategic business segments, or product-market units
(PMUs).[2] This level creates value for the shareholders of the firm, as measured by
share performance and profitability.

The term **business unit** refers to an organization that markets a set of related
products to a clearly defined group of customers. The **business unit level** is the
level at which business unit managers set the direction for their products and markets
to exploit value-creating opportunities. The strategic direction is more specific at the
business level of an organization. For less complex firms with a single business
focus, the corporate and business unit levels may merge.

Each business unit has marketing and other specialized activities (e.g., finance,
research and development, or human resource management) at the **functional
level**, which is where groups of specialists actually create value for the organization.
The term *department* generally refers to these specialized functions, such as the marketing department or information systems department. At the functional level, the
strategic direction becomes more specific and focused. So, just as there is a hierarchy
of levels within organizations, there is also a hierarchy of strategic directions set by
management at that level.

Because marketing's role is to look outward—to keep the organization focused on
creating customer value—its activities tie to each of the three levels in Figure 2–1. In
a large corporation with multiple business units, marketing may be called on to
assess consumer trends and analyze marketing opportunities to aid in corporate
strategic planning. At the business unit level, marketing may be asked to determine
how to compete in given market segments or to develop customer service programs
across all business units.

Where Things Happen: Functional Areas and Cross-Functional Teams   At
the lowest level in Figure 2–1, marketing serves as part of a team of functional specialists. It is at this level that strategy formulation at higher levels turns into strategy
implementation. In other words, marketing makes things happen! Customers are listened to, products are designed and produced, and customer needs are satisfied. The
marketing department does not work alone but works with all departments to deliver
customer value and satisfaction.

cross-functional teams
A small number of people from
different departments in an
organization who are mutually
accountable to a common set
of performance goals.

In practice, new-product development and other activities in many organizations
involve **cross-functional teams**, a small number of people from different
departments in an organization who are mutually accountable to a common set of

performance goals. Sometimes, very innovative firms develop cross-functional teams that consist of employees not only from different functional areas within the firm but also from its suppliers and customers.

Sometimes, cross-functional conflict can arise because other departments may see marketing's drive to implement the marketing concept and increase customer value as making their own jobs more difficult. The marketing department must make these other departments understand that without satisfied customers who buy the organization's product, there is no company and hence no jobs.

Strategy Issues in Organizations

Organizations need a *raison d'être*—a reason for their existence—and a direction. This is where their business, mission, organizational culture, and goals converge. As shown in Figure 2–1, business and mission apply to the corporate and business unit levels, while culture and goals relate to all three levels.

The Business Definition   Organizations, such as Bombardier, the Canadian Red Cross, and your college or university, exist for a purpose—to accomplish something for someone. At birth, most organizations have clear ideas about what "something" and "someone" mean. But as the organization grows over time, often its purpose grows fuzzy or unclear.

This is when the organization repeatedly asks some of its most difficult questions ever: What is our business? Who are our customers? What offerings should we provide to give these customers value? One guideline in defining the organization's business: try to understand the people served by the organization and the value they receive, which emphasizes the critical customer-driven focus that successful organizations possess.

Organizations must be careful not to define their businesses too narrowly or too broadly. If they do, they may lose sight of who their customers are and how to best serve them.[3] For example, with its focus on the customer, Disney does not view itself as being in the theme park or movie business but rather in the business of creating entertainment, fun, and fantasy for customers. Similarly, Medtronic, a world leader in heart pacemakers, is *not* in the medical device business but *is* in the business of alleviating pain, restoring health, and extending life. Ottawa-based Corel Corporation, maker of software products, including CorelDraw and WordPerfect, believes it is in business "to give customers boundless power to create. Anytime. Anywhere."

mission
A statement of the organization's scope.

The Mission   By properly defining its business, an organization can take steps to define its **mission**, a statement of the organization's scope that often identifies its customers, markets, products, technology, and values. Today, often used interchangeably with "vision," the "mission" statement frequently has an inspirational theme—something that can ignite the loyalty of employees and others with whom the organization comes in contact. Figure 2–2 provides the mission statement for a Holiday Inn in Burlington, Ontario. With this clearly defined mission, marketing activities at this Holiday Inn can be more focused and effective.

stakeholders
Individuals or groups, either within or outside an organization, that relate to it in what it does and how well it performs.

organizational culture
A set of values, ideas, and attitudes that is learned and shared among the members of an organization.

Organizational Culture   Organizations must connect not just with their employees but with all of their **stakeholders**, individuals or groups either within or outside an organization that relate to it in terms of what it does and how well it performs. Internal stakeholders include employees, officers, and board members. External stakeholders typically include customers, suppliers, distributors, governments, union, local communities, and the general public.

Whether at the corporate, business, or functional level, **organizational culture** exists in the unit, which is a set of values, ideas, and attitudes that is learned and shared among the members of an organization. As you read in the chapter opener,

■ **FIGURE 2–2** ■
Mission of the Holiday Inn Burlington

> The Holiday Inn Burlington is dedicated to providing quality hospitality product and service. Although we try to anticipate guest concerns before they arise, we understand that every customer is an individual who requires special attention. Therefore,
>
> If a customer has a need or want, we fill it.
>
> If a customer has a question, we find the answer.
>
> If a customer has a concern, we resolve it.
>
> If a customer is lost, we show them the way.

Bombardier has a strong culture that focuses on delivering quality products and good value to customers, respecting and appreciating employees, protecting the natural environment, and being a good corporate citizen of the communities within which it operates.

goals or **objectives**
Convert the mission into targeted levels of performance to be achieved.

Goals   **Goals** or **objectives** (the terms are used interchangeably in this textbook) convert the mission into targeted levels of performance to be achieved, often by a specific time. So, these goals measure just how well a mission is being accomplished. As shown in Figure 2–1, goals exist at the corporate, business, and functional levels. All lower-level goals must contribute to achieving the goals at the next, higher level. Firms can pursue several different types of goals:

- *Profit.* Classic economic theory assumes a firm seeks to maximize long-run profit, achieving as high a financial return on its investment as possible.
- *Sales revenue.* If profits are acceptable, a firm may elect to maintain or increase its sales level, even though profitability may not be maximized. Canadian Tire's goal over the next five years is to increase top-line growth (sales) as well as improve its profitability.
- *Market share.* A firm may choose to maintain or increase its market share, sometimes at the expense of greater profits if industry status or prestige is at stake. **Market share** is the ratio of sales revenue of the firm to the total sales revenue of all firms in the industry, including the firm itself.

market share
The ratio of sales revenue of the firm to the total sales revenue of all firms in the industry, including the firm itself.

- *Unit sales.* Sales revenue may be deceiving because of the effects of inflation, and so a firm may choose to maintain or increase the number of units it sells, such as cars, cases of breakfast cereal, or TV sets.
- *Quality.* A firm may target the highest quality products or services in its industry, as 3M does with its Six Sigma program; Loblaws' goal is to offer customers high-quality food products and a quality shopping experience.
- *Customer satisfaction.* Customers are the reasons the organization exists, and so their satisfaction is of vital importance. At Markham, Ontario–based IBM Canada, customer satisfaction is tracked just the same as financial revenue figures. At Maritime Life Assurance Company in Halifax, Nova Scotia, yearly bonuses paid to employees are based on customer satisfaction data.
- *Employee welfare.* A firm may recognize the critical importance of its employees by having an explicit goal stating its commitment to provide good employment opportunities and working conditions. Crystal Decisions Inc. owns a chalet at a Whistler resort that its employees can use; Pfizer Canada offers daycare facilities to its employees, and BC Biomedical offers flex-work opportunities.
- *Social responsibility.* A firm may seek to balance conflicting goals of consumers, employees, and shareholders to promote the overall welfare of all these groups, even at the expense of profits. Firms marketing on a global basis are often confronted with the notion of being "good global citizens." The Ethics and Social Responsibility Alert box deals with the concept of sustainable development, an issue relevant to global marketers.[4]

ETHICS AND SOCIAL RESPONSIBILITY ALERT

The Global Dilemma: How to Achieve Sustainable Development

Corporate executives and world leaders are increasingly asked to address the issue of "sustainable development." This term was formally defined in a 1987 United Nations report as meeting present needs "without compromising the ability of future generations to meet their own needs." What often happens is the achievement of profits for a firm and economic development for a country by adding jobs in highly polluting industries, thereby pushing cleanup actions into the future.

Eastern Europe and the nations of the former Soviet Union provide an example. Tragically, poisoned air and dead rivers are the legacies of seven decades of communist rule. With more than a third of the households of many of these nations below the poverty level, should the immediate goal be a cleaner environment or more food,

clothing, housing, and consumer goods? What should the heads of these governments do? What should Western firms trying to enter these new, growing markets do? What will be the impact on future generations?

3M developed an innovative program called Pollution Prevent Pays (3P) to reduce harmful environmental impacts, making a profit doing so. 3M estimates that the 3P program in the last quarter century has cut its pollution by 1.6 billion pounds while saving almost $900 million in raw materials and avoiding fines. The company's current environmental goal is: improve energy efficiency per pound of product by 20 percent while reducing waste per pound by 25 percent.

Should the environment or economic growth come first? What are the societal tradeoffs? Will profit-making firms adopt and implement a 3P kind of program?

Many Canadian private organizations that do not seek profits also exist. Examples include museums, such as the Montreal Museum for Fine Arts (www.mbam.qc.ca), symphony orchestras, such as the Edmonton Symphony Orchestra (www.edmonton symphony.com), hospitals, such as Saint Joseph's Hospital in Hamilton, Ontario (www.stjosham.on.ca), and research institutes, such as the Conference Board of Canada (www.conferenceboard.ca) and the Fraser Institute in Vancouver (www.fraserinstitute.ca). These organizations strive to serve consumers, members, or patrons with the greatest efficiency and the least cost.

Although technically not falling under the definition of "nonprofit organization," government agencies also perform marketing activities in trying to achieve their goal of serving the public good. For example, Industry Canada (www.ic.gc.ca) is a federal government department responsible for fostering a competitive, knowledge-based Canadian economy. The department works with Canadians in all parts of the country and throughout the economy to improve conditions for investment, improve Canada's innovation performance, increase Canada's share of global trade, and build a fair, efficient, and competitive marketplace. Some of their marketing initatives include promoting investment and trade, promoting tourism, and facilitating small business development.

CONCEPT CHECK

1. What are the three levels in today's large organizations?

2. What is the difference between an organization's mission and its culture?

3. Give an example of a goal for a business and a goal for a nonprofit organization.

SETTING STRATEGIC DIRECTIONS

Setting strategic directions involves answering two other difficult questions: (1) Where are we now? (2) Where do we want to go?

A Look Around: Where Are We Now?

Asking an organization where it is at the present time involves identifying its customers, competencies, and competitors. More detailed approaches of assessing "where are we now?" include both SWOT analysis (see Figure 2–7) and environmental scanning (Chapter 3), which may be done at each of the three levels in the organization.

Customers   A sound strategic direction is set by knowing in complete detail who an organization's customers and prospective customers are and the type of products and services (value) they are seeking. Moreover, where, how, and in what form they want this value delivered must also be known. Without such intimate knowledge, an organization's strategic direction may be misaligned and finite corporate resources wasted. In order to stay close to their customers and to understand their needs, every employee at R.C. Purdy's Chocolates of Vancouver (www.purdys.com) actually serves customers.

Competencies   "What do we do best?" asks about the organization's capabilities or competencies. **Competencies** are an organization's special capabilities, including the skills, technologies, and resources that distinguish it from other organizations.

Exploiting these competencies can lead to organizational success.[5] Competencies should be distinctive enough to provide a **competitive advantage**, a unique strength relative to competitors that is often based on quality, time, cost, innovation, or customer intimacy.[6]

For example, if 3M has a goal of generating a specific portion of its sales from new products, it must have a supporting competency in research and development and new-product marketing. Canadian Tire believes one of its competitive advantages is its ability to stay close to the customer (customer intimacy). It is able to do so, in part, because of its strategic retail locations. In fact, 92 percent of the Canadian

competencies

An organization's special capabilities, including skills, technologies, and resources, that distinguish it from other organizations.

competitive advantage

A unique strength relative to competitors, often based on quality, time, cost, innovation, or customer intimacy.

Kodak today must make a series of difficult marketing decisions. From what you know about cameras and photos, assess Kodak's sales opportunities for the four products shown here. For some possible answers and a way to show these opportunities graphically, see the text and Figure 2–3.

Eastman Kodak Company

www.kodak.com

Kodak digital cameras

Kodak film sold in the U.S., Canada, and Western Europe

Kodak self-service kiosks in retail outlets

Kodak printers (to print digital photos at home)

population lives within 15 minutes of a Canadian Tire store, and more than 40 percent of Canadian adults shop there every week. Once the customer is in the store, Canadian Tire associates attempt to provide outstanding customer service.

Another strategy is to develop a competency in producing high-quality products. **Quality** here means those features and characteristics of a product that influence its ability to satisfy customer needs. Firms often try to improve quality through **benchmarking**—discovering how others do something better than your own firm so that you can imitate or leapfrog the competition. Benchmarking can also involve studying operations in completely different businesses and applying this new knowledge to your own business.

Competitors   In today's fiercely competitive and globalized economy, the lines among competitive sectors are increasingly blurred. Many companies face a complex array of competitors. So, successful firms continuously assess both who the competitors are and how they are changing in order to respond with their own competitive strategies. For example, Shoppers Drug Mart competes directly with other pharmacies, such as Rexall, Pharma Plus, Medicine Shoppe, and IDA/Guardian. At the same time, it also competes against supermarkets and mass merchandisers, such as Loblaws, Safeway, and Wal-Mart, who are also in the pharmacy business. Given the competitive landscape, Shoppers has initiated new merchandising programs, lower prices, new outlets, and better promotion of its private-label Life brand products. In another competitive arena, we have Blockbuster Video, which competes directly against other video rental retailers, but at the same time, it competes with Wal-Mart, which can actually sell videos for as cheaply as renting them from Blockbuster. This has changed Blockbuster's approach to video rentals which now includes allowing consumers to keep the videos longer and pushing the sales of videos instead of rentals. You will read more about direct and "intertype competition" in Chapter 15 when we discuss retailing in Canada.

Growth Strategies: Where Do We Want to Go?

Knowing where the organization is at the present time enables managers to set a direction for the firm and start to allocate resources to move toward that direction. Two techniques to aid in these decisions are (1) business portfolio, and (2) market-product analyses.

Business Portfolio Analysis   The Boston Consulting Group's (BCG) *business portfolio analysis* uses quantified performance measures and growth targets to analyze a firm's business units (called strategic business units, or SBUs, in the BCG analysis) as though they were a collection of separate investments.[7] While used at the strategic business unit level here, this BCG analysis has also been applied at the product line or individual product or brand level. More than 75 percent of the largest firms in North America have used it in some form. BCG, an internationally known management consulting firm, advises its clients to locate the position of each of its SBUs on a growth-share matrix (Figure 2–3).

The vertical axis is the *market growth rate,* which is the annual rate of growth of the specific market or industry in which a given SBU is competing. The horizontal axis is the *relative market share,* defined as the sales of the SBU divided by the sales of the largest firm in the industry. A relative market share of 10× (at the left end of the scale) means that the SBU has 10 times the *share* of its largest competitor, whereas a share of 0.1× (at the right end of the scale) means it has only 10 percent of the *sales* of its largest competitor.

BCG has given specific names and descriptions to the four resulting quadrants in its business portfolio analysis matrix based on the amount of cash they generate for or require from the firm:

quality
Those features and characteristics of a product that influence its ability to satisfy customer needs.

benchmarking
Discovering how others do something better than your own firm so you can imitate or leapfrog competition.

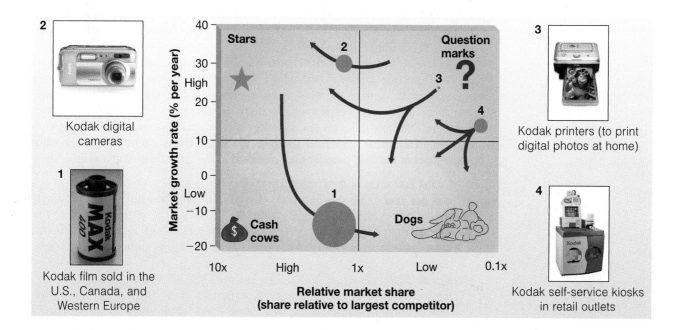

2

Kodak digital cameras

1

Kodak film sold in the U.S., Canada, and Western Europe

3

Kodak printers (to print digital photos at home)

4

Kodak self-service kiosks in retail outlets

■ **FIGURE 2–3** ■

Boston Consulting Group portfolio analysis for Kodak, as it might appear in 2005.

- *Cash cows* are SBUs that typically generate large amounts of cash, far more than they can invest profitably in their own product line. They have a dominant share of a slow-growth market and provide cash to pay large amounts of company overhead and to invest in other SBUs.
- *Stars* are SBUs with a high share of high-growth markets that may need extra cash to finance their own rapid future growth. When their growth slows, they are likely to become cash cows.
- *Question marks* or *problem children* are SBUs with a low share of high-growth markets. They require large injections of cash just to maintain their market share, much less increase it. Their name implies management's dilemma concerning these SBUs: choosing the right ones to invest in and phasing out the rest.
- *Dogs* are SBUs with a low share of low-growth markets. Although they may generate enough cash to sustain themselves, they do not hold the promise of ever becoming real winners for the firm. Dropping SBUs that are dogs may be required, except when relationships with other SBUs, competitive considerations, or potential strategic alliances exist.[8]

A firm's SBUs often start as question marks and go counterclockwise around Figure 2–3 to become stars, then cash cows, and finally dogs. Because most firms have limited influence on the market growth rate, their main alternative in a business portfolio analysis framework is to try to change the relative market share. To accomplish this, management makes conscious decisions on what role each SBU should have in the future and either injects or removes cash from it.

Four Kodak SBUs are shown as they appeared in 2005 and can serve as an example of BCG analysis. The area of each circle in Figure 2–3 is roughly proportional to the corresponding SBU's 2005 sales revenue. In a more complete analysis, its other SBUs would be included. This Kodak example also shows the agonizing strategic decisions that must be made by executives in firms in an industry facing revolutionary change—the situation Kodak faces in the camera and film business with the arrival of digital technology.

More than a century ago, Kodak virtually invented the photography industry. Nicknamed "Big Yellow" for its film packages, until about 2000, Kodak relied not on its cameras for the bulk of its revenues and profits but on its film for the billions of photographs taken every year. Two factors changed that: (1) more competition from film manufacturers like Fuji, and (2) the popularization of digital cameras that need no conventional film.

So, in late 2003, Kodak's CEO Daniel Karp announced a shift in Kodak's strategic priorities from film to digital technology. Experts, both supporters and critics, have weighed in with their opinions of the new priorities. One thing, however, is eminently clear. The success of Kodak's strategy and its product lines shown in Figure 2–3 depends on how millions of consumers like you take pictures and convert your pictures into useful images over the next decade. Here is a snapshot of the sales opportunities of the four product lines reflected in the comments of analysts:

1. *Kodak film sales in the United States, Canada, and Western Europe.* An $8 billion per year "cash cow" in 2003, Kodak film sales are still its biggest single source of revenue. In its "death throes," Kodak film sales are expected to decline 10 to 12 percent per year through 2006.[9] Sales will not be helped by the 2004 announcement that Kodak will soon stop selling film cameras in these countries.[10]

2. *Kodak digital cameras.* A $1 billion business in 2003, Kodak's "filmless imaging market" is expected to grow from 30 percent of its 2003 revenues to 60 percent in 2006.[11] Sales of its popular line of EasyShare digital cameras grew 87 percent in 2003 over sales in 2002.[12] Kodak clearly expects its digital cameras to be a "star" soon. The challenge: it is no. 2 in market share behind Sony in North America with new rivals emerging, such as Nokia's cell phones with digital cameras.

3. *Kodak printers (to print digital photos at home).* With 82 percent of digital prints made this way in 2003, this might look like a clear BCG star with Kodak's expected new line of home printers. But industry analysts expect this in-home segment to decline substantially because of the hassle.[13] And with Kodak competing with established printer manufacturers, such as Hewlett-Packard and Canon, this "question mark" could also become a "dog."

4. *Kodak self-service kiosks in retail outlets.* With only about 1 percent of the market in printed pictures in 2003, these self-service machines used to take up to four minutes to make an 8 × 10 photo. But in early 2004, Kodak announced a self-service kiosk that can convert a roll of 35-mm film into prints in only seven minutes. As shown in Figure 2–3, an innovative technology (the kiosks) for a slowly dying product (the film) faces big unknowns, also because Japanese copiers are well entrenched in these outlets.[14]

Are these BCG projections valid? Your use of digital cameras and how you make their prints hold the answer. Kodak strategies on selling film in developing markets are discussed later in the chapter.

The primary strength of business portfolio analysis lies in forcing a firm to place each of its SBUs in the growth-share matrix, which, in turn, suggests which SBUs will be cash producers and cash users in the future. Weaknesses are that it is often difficult (1) to get the needed information, and (2) to incorporate competitive information into business portfolio analysis.[15]

Market-Product Analysis   Firms can also view growth opportunities in terms of markets and products. Let us think of it this way: for any product, there is both a current market (consisting of existing customers) and a new market (consisting of potential customers). And for any market, there is a current product (what they are now using) and a new product (something they might use if it were developed). These four market-product strategies are shown in Figure 2–4.[16]

As Unilever attempts to increase sales revenues of its Ben & Jerry's business, it must consider all four of the alternative market-product strategies shown in Figure 2–4. For example, it can try to use *market penetration*—a marketing strategy of

■ **FIGURE 2–4** ■
Four market-product
strategies: alternative ways
to expand sales revenues for
Ben & Jerry's

Markets	PRODUCTS	
	Current	**New**
Current	**Market penetration** Selling more Ben & Jerry's super premium ice cream to existing customers	**Product development** Selling a new product, such as children's clothing, under the Ben & Jerry's brand in current markets
New	**Market development** Selling more Ben & Jerry's super premium ice cream in South American markets for the first time	**Diversification** Selling a new product, such as children's clothing, in South American markets for the first time

increasing sales of present products in existing markets, in this case by increasing sales of Ben & Jerry's present ice cream products to existing consumers. There is no change in either the basic product line or the market served, but increased sales are possible—either by selling more ice cream (through better promotion or distribution) *or* by selling the same amount of ice cream at a higher price to its existing customers.

Market development, a marketing strategy of selling existing products to new markets, is a reasonable alternative for Ben & Jerry's. South America, for example, is a good possible new market. There is good news and bad news for this marketing strategy: as the income of South American households increases, consumers may be able to buy more ice cream, but the Ben & Jerry's brand is relatively unknown there.

Product development is a marketing strategy of selling new products to existing markets. Figure 2–4 shows that the firm could try leveraging the Ben & Jerry's brand by selling its own Ben & Jerry's brand of children's clothing in current markets. This, of course, has dangers because customers may not be able to see a clear connection between the company's expertise in ice cream and, say, children's clothing.

Diversification is a marketing strategy of developing new products and selling them in new markets. This is a potentially high-risk strategy for Ben & Jerry's, as for most firms, because the company has neither previous production experience nor marketing experience on which to draw. For example, in trying to sell a Ben & Jerry's brand of children's clothing in South America, the company has expertise neither in producing children's clothing nor in marketing to South American consumers.

Which strategies will Ben and Jerry's follow? Keep your eyes, ears, and taste buds working to discover the marketing answers.

**CONCEPT
CHECK**

1. What are competencies, and why are they important?

2. What is business portfolio analysis?

3. What are the four market-product strategies?

■ ■ ■
THE STRATEGIC MARKETING PROCESS

After the organization assesses where it is at and where it wants to go, other questions emerge:

1. How do we allocate our resources to get where we want to go?

2. How do we convert our plan to actions?

3. How do our results compare with our plans, and do deviations require new plans?

How can Ben & Jerry's identify new ice cream flavours and social responsibility programs that contribute to its mission? The text describes how the strategic marketing process and its SWOT analysis can help.

strategic marketing process
Process whereby an organization allocates its marketing mix resources to reach its target markets.

marketing plan
A road map for the marketing activities of an organization for a specified future period of time, such as one year or five years.

This same approach is used in the **strategic marketing process**, whereby an organization allocates its marketing mix resources to reach its target markets. This process is divided into three phases: planning, implementation, and control (Figure 2–5).

The strategic marketing process is so central to the activities of most organizations that they formalize it as a **marketing plan**, which is a road map for the marketing activities of an organization for a specified future period of time, such as one year or five years. Appendix A at the end of this chapter provides guidelines for writing a marketing plan and also presents a sample marketing plan for a new restaurant called Frenz located in Prince Rupert, B.C. The sequence of activities that follow parallels the elements of the marketing plan that appear in Appendix A.

Strategic Marketing Process: The Planning Phase

As shown in Figure 2–5, the planning phase of the strategic marketing process consists of the three steps shown at the top of the figure: (1) situation analysis, (2) market-product focus and goal setting, and (3) the marketing program. Let us use the recent marketing planning experiences of several companies to look at each of these steps.

Figure 2–5 also shows how the strategic marketing process integrates the chapters in this book. Chapters 2 through 8 provide the information for the situation (SWOT) analysis, step 1 of the planning phase. Step 2, developing a market-product focus and goals for the product, is covered in Chapters 9 and 10. The elements of the marketing program in step 3—the 4Ps—are discussed in Chapters 10 through 18. The book concludes with Chapter 19, which ties together the planning, implementation, and control phases of the strategic marketing process.

situation analysis
Taking stock of where the firm or product has been recently, where it is now, and where it is headed in terms of the organization's plans and the external factors and trends affecting it.

Step 1: Situation (SWOT) Analysis   The essence of **situation analysis** is taking stock of where the firm or product has been recently, where it is now, and where it is headed in terms of the organization's plans and the external factors and trends affecting it. The situation analysis box in Figure 2–5 is the first of the three steps in the planning phase.

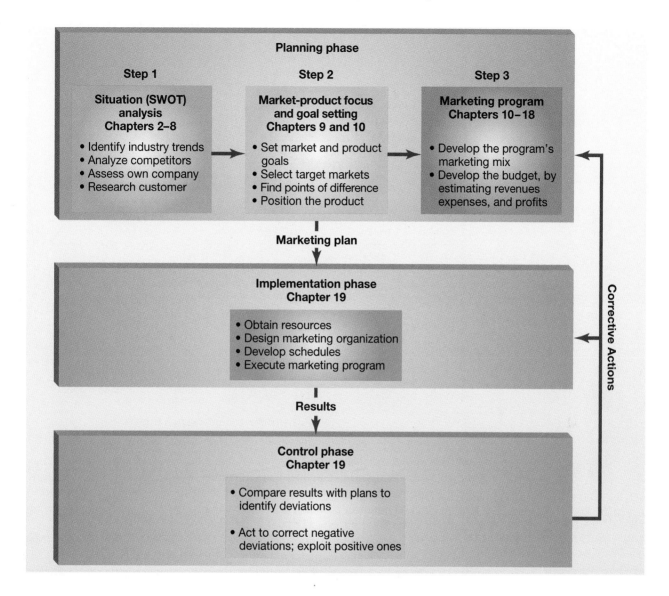

■ FIGURE 2–5 ■
The strategic marketing process

SWOT analysis
An acronym describing an organization's appraisal of its internal **S**trengths and **W**eaknesses and its external **O**pportunities and **T**hreats.

An effective shorthand summary of the situation analysis is a **SWOT analysis**, an acronym describing an organization's appraisal of its internal Strengths and **W**eaknesses and its external **O**pportunities and **T**hreats. Both the situation and SWOT analyses can be done at the level of the entire organization, the business unit, the product line, or the specific product. As an analysis moves from the level of the entire organization to the specific product, it, of course, gets far more detailed. For small firms or those with basically a single product line, an analysis at the firm or product level is really the same thing.

The SWOT analysis is based on an exhaustive study of the four areas shown in step 1 of the planning phase of the strategic marketing process (see Figure 2–5). Knowledge of these areas forms the foundation on which the firm builds its marketing program:

- Identifying trends in the firm's industry.
- Analyzing the firm's competitors.
- Assessing the firm itself.
- Researching the firm's present and prospective customers.

Let us assume you are the Unilever vice-president responsible for integrating Ben & Jerry's into Unilever's business. You might do the SWOT analysis shown in Figure 2–6 on the next page. Note that your SWOT table has four cells formed by the

■ **FIGURE 2–6** ■

Ben & Jerry's: a SWOT
analysis to get it growing
again

Location of Factor	TYPE OF FACTOR	
	Favorable	Unfavorable
Internal	**Strengths** • Prestigious, well-known brand name • major share of the super premium ice cream market • Can complement Unilever's existing ice cream brands • Widely recognized for its social responsibility actions	**Weaknesses** • Danger that B&J's social responsibility actions may add costs, reduce focus on core business • Need for experienced managers to help growth • Flat sales and profits in recent years
External	**Opportunities** • Growing demand for quality ice cream in overseas markets • Increasing demand for frozen yogurt and other low-fat desserts • Success of many firms in extending successful brand in one product category to others	**Threats** • Consumer concern about fatty desserts; B&J customers are the type who read new government-ordered nutritional labels • Competes with giant Pillsbury and its Haagen-Dazs brand • International downturns increase the risks for B&J in European and Asian markets

combination of internal versus external factors (the rows) and favourable versus unfavourable factors (the columns) that summarize Ben & Jerry's strengths, weaknesses, opportunities, and threats. This SWOT analysis can identify Ben & Jerry's flavours that do not meet customer tastes and wind up in its "Flavour Graveyard," as described in the WebLink box.

A SWOT analysis helps a firm identify the strategy-related factors in these four cells that can have a major effect on the firm. The goal is not simply to develop the SWOT analysis but to translate the results of the analysis into specific actions to help the firm grow and succeed. The ultimate goal is to identify the *critical* factors affecting the firm and then build on vital strengths, correct glaring weaknesses, exploit significant opportunities, and avoid disaster-laden threats. That is a big order.

WEBLINK

HTTP://WWW.MCGRAWHILL.CA/
COLLEGE/CRANE

Ben & Jerry's Flavours: From Chocolate Fudge Brownie Ice Cream and One Sweet Whirled Novelty Bars to . . . the Flavour Graveyard

Ben & Jerry's markets its flavours of ice cream, frozen yogurt, sorbet, and novelty bars in response to both consumer . . . ahem! . . . tastes and important causes it supports, a practice continued even after being sold to Unilever in 2000. For more than a decade, the brownies for Ben & Jerry's popular Chocolate Fudge Brownie ice cream have been supplied by Greyston Bakery, a nonprofit organization that trains, employs, and houses low-income people in the area. Recently, Ben & Jerry's teamed up with the award-winning Dave Matthews Band and SaveOurEnvironment.org to fight global warming by creating the One Sweet Whirled ice cream flavour in pints and novelty bars. But not all flavours last. The ones that don't survive wind up in Ben & Jerry's "Flavour Graveyard." To see Ben & Jerry's current flavours as well as those "dearly departed flavours" in the Flavour Graveyard, visit "Our Products" at www.benjerry.com. Have any of your favourite flavours been "laid to rest"?

The Ben and Jerry's SWOT analysis in Figure 2–6 can be the basis for these kinds of specific actions. An action in each of the four cells might be:

- *Build on a strength.* Find specific efficiencies in distribution with Unilever's existing ice cream brands.
- *Correct a weakness.* Recruit experienced managers from other consumer product firms to help stimulate growth.
- *Exploit an opportunity.* Develop a new line of low-fat frozen yogurts to respond to consumer health concerns.
- *Avoid a disaster-laden threat.* Focus on less risky international markets, such as Mexico.

Step 2: Market-Product Focus and Goal Setting   Determining which products will be directed toward which customers (step 2 of the planning phase in Figure 2–5) is essential for developing an effective marketing program (step 3). This decision is often based on **market segmentation**, which involves aggregating prospective buyers into groups, or segments, that (1) have common needs and (2) will respond similarly to a marketing action. Ideally, a firm can use market segmentation to identify the segments on which it will focus its efforts—its target market segments—and develop one or more marketing programs to reach them.

market segmentation
Aggregating prospective buyers into groups, or segments, that (1) have common needs and (2) will respond similarly to a marketing action.

As always, understanding the customer is essential. In the case of Medtronic, executives researched a potential new market in Asia by talking extensively with doctors in India and China. They learned that these doctors saw some of the current state-of-the-art features of heart pacemakers as unnecessary and too expensive. Instead, they wanted an affordable pacemaker that was reliable and easy to implant. This information led Medtronic to develop and market a new product, the Champion heart pacemaker, directed at the needs of this Asian market segment.

Goal setting involves setting measurable marketing objectives to be achieved. Such objectives would be different depending on the level of marketing involved. For a specific market, the goal may be to introduce a new product, such as Medtronic's Champion pacemaker in Asia or Toyota's launch of its hybrid car, the Prius. For a specific brand or product, the goal may be to create a promotional campaign or pricing strategy that will get more consumers to purchase. For an entire marketing program, the objective is often a series of actions to be implemented over several years.

Using the strategic marketing process shown in Figure 2–5, let us examine Medtronic's five-year plan to reach the "affordable and reliable" segment of the pacemaker market:[17]

- *Set marketing and product goals.* The chances of new-product success are increased by specifying both market and product goals. Based on their market research showing the need for a reliable yet affordable pacemaker, Medtronic executives set the following as their goal: design and market such a pacemaker in the next three years that could be manufactured in China for the Asian market.
- *Select target markets.* The Champion pacemaker will be targeted at cardiologists and medical clinics performing heart surgery in India, China, and other Asian countries.

points of difference
Characteristics of a product that make it superior to competitive substitutes.

- *Find points of difference.* **Points of difference** are those characteristics of a product that make it superior to competitive substitutes. Just as a competitive advantage is a unique strength of an entire organization compared with its competitors, points of difference are the unique characteristics of one of its products that make it superior to the competitive products it faces in the marketplace. For the Champion pacemaker, the key points of difference are *not* the state-of-the-art features that drive up production costs and are important to only a minority of patients. Instead, they are high quality, long life, reliability, ease of use, and low cost.

The Champion: Medtronic's high-quality, long-life, low-cost heart pacemaker for an Asian market segment.

- *Position the product.* The pacemaker will be "positioned" in cardiologists' and patients' minds as a medical device that is high quality and reliable with a long, nine-year life. The name Champion is selected after testing acceptable names among doctors in India, China, Pakistan, Singapore, and Malaysia.

Details in these four elements of step 2 provide a solid foundation to use in developing the marketing program, the next step in the planning phase of the strategic marketing process.

Step 3: Marketing Program   Activities in step 2 tell the marketing manager which customers to target and which customer needs the firm's product offerings can satisfy—the *who* and *what* aspects of the strategic marketing process. The *how* aspect—step 3 in the planning phase—involves developing the program's marketing mix and its budget.

Figure 2–7 shows components of each marketing mix element that are combined to provide a cohesive marketing program. For the five-year marketing plan of Medtronic, these marketing mix activities include the following:

- *Product strategy.* Offer a Champion brand heart pacemaker with features needed by Asian patients at an affordable price.
- *Price strategy.* Manufacture Champion to control costs so that it can be priced below $1000 (in U.S. dollars)—a fraction of the price of the state-of-the-art pacemakers offered in Western markets.
- *Promotion strategy.* Feature demonstrations at cardiologist and medical conventions across Asia to introduce the Champion and highlight the device's features and application.
- *Place (distribution) strategy.* Search out, utilize, and train reputable medical distributors across Asia to call on cardiologists and medical clinics.

■ FIGURE 2–7 ■

Elements of the marketing mix that comprise a cohesive marketing program

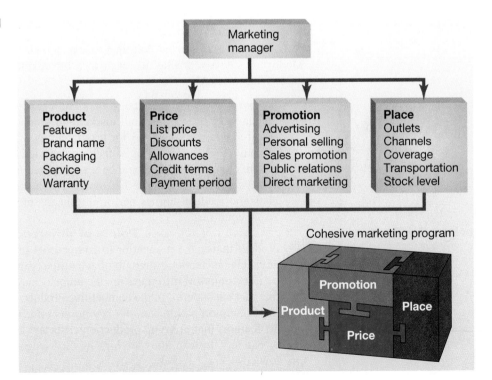

Putting this marketing program into effect requires that the firm commit time and money to it in the form of a sales forecast and budget that must be approved by top management.

1. What is the difference between a strength and an opportunity in a SWOT analysis?

2. What is market segmentation?

3. What are points of difference, and why are they important?

Strategic Marketing Process: The Implementation Phase

As shown in Figure 2–5, the result of the tens or hundreds of hours spent in the planning phase of the strategic marketing process is the firm's marketing plan. Implementation, the second phase of the strategic marketing process, involves carrying out the marketing plan that emerges from the planning phase. If the firm cannot put the marketing plan into effect—in the implementation phase—the planning phase was a waste of time. Figure 2–5 also shows the four components of the implementation phase: (1) obtaining resources, (2) designing the marketing organization, (3) developing schedules, and (4) actually executing the marketing program designed in the planning phase. Eastman Kodak provides a case example.

Obtaining Resources   In late 2003, Kodak CEO Daniel Karp announced his bold plan (discussed earlier) to re-energize the filmmaker for the new age of digital cameras and prints. Karp needed money to implement the plan, and so he cut shareholder dividends by 72 percent to invest the $3 billion saved in Kodak's digital technologies.[18] And in early 2004, Karp announced a painful cut of up to 15 000 jobs over the next three years to provide additional money to invest in Kodak's digital future.[19]

Designing the Marketing Organization   A marketing program needs a marketing organization to implement it. Figure 2–8 shows the organization chart of a typical

Kodak is pursuing opportunities for sales of film cameras and film in China.

manufacturing firm, giving some details of the marketing department's structure. Four managers of marketing activities are shown to report to the vice-president of marketing. Several regional sales managers and an international sales manager may report to the manager of sales. This marketing organization, as a part of the corporate team, is responsible for converting marketing plans to reality.

In the 1990s, a number of large consumer products firms changed the title of the head of the marketing department from "vice-president of marketing" to "chief marketing officer" (CMO), but the responsibilities have stayed largely the same.[20]

Developing Schedules   Effective implementation requires goals, deadlines, and schedules. To implement his plan to focus on Kodak's digital business opportunities, Karp set some key goals:[21]

- Boost sales from $13 billion in 2003 to $16 billion in 2006 and $20 billion in 2010.
- Increase the share of Kodak's revenues from its digital businesses from 30 percent in 2003 to 60 percent in 2006.

To achieve these goals, Karp worked with key Kodak executives to schedule the acquisition of and partnering with firms having digital expertise, the phase-out of its film cameras, and the launch of new lines of digital cameras.

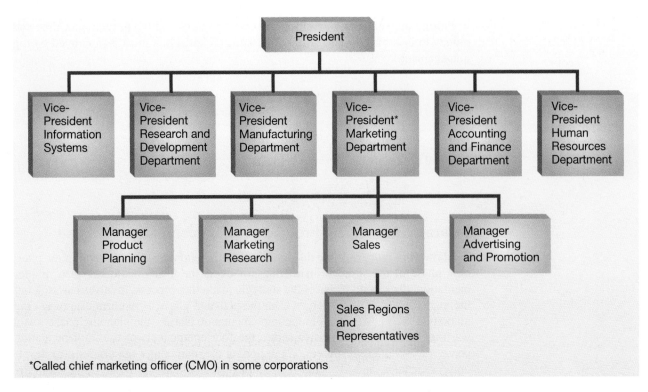

*Called chief marketing officer (CMO) in some corporations

■ **FIGURE 2-8** ▪▪

Organization of a typical manufacturing firm, showing a breakdown of the marketing department

marketing strategy
The means by which a marketing goal is to be achieved, usually characterized by a specified target market and a marketing program to reach it.

marketing tactics
Detailed day-to-day operational decisions essential to the overall success of marketing strategies.

Executing the Marketing Program   Marketing plans are meaningless pieces of paper without effective execution of those plans. This effective execution requires attention to detail for both marketing strategies and marketing tactics. A **marketing strategy** is the means by which a marketing goal is to be achieved, usually characterized by a specified target market and a marketing program to reach it. Although the term *marketing strategy* is often used loosely, it implies both the end sought (target market) and the means to achieve it (marketing program). At this marketing strategy level, Kodak will seek to increase sales of film cameras and film in emerging markets, such as India, China, and Eastern Europe, where low prices, simplicity, and convenience are important.[22]

To implement a marketing program successfully, hundreds of detailed decisions are often required. These decisions, called **marketing tactics**, are detailed day-to-day operational decisions essential to the overall success of marketing strategies. At Kodak, writing ads and setting prices for its new lines of digital cameras are examples of marketing tactics.

Marketing strategies and marketing tactics shade into each other. Effective marketing program implementation requires excruciating concern for both.

Strategic Marketing Process: The Control Phase

The control phase of the strategic marketing process seeks to keep the marketing program moving in the direction set for it (see Figure 2–5). Accomplishing this requires the marketing manager (1) to compare the results of the marketing program with the goals in the written plans to identify deviations, and (2) to act on these deviations—correcting negative deviations and exploiting positive ones.

Comparing Results with Plans to Identify Deviations   In late 2003, as Daniel Karp looked at the company's sales revenues from 1998 through 2003, he did not like what he saw: the very flat trend, or AB in Figure 2–9. Extending the 1998–2003

FIGURE 2–9

Evaluation and control of Kodak's marketing program

trend to 2010 along BC shows declining sales revenues, a totally unacceptable, no-growth strategy.

Karp set a growth target of 5 to 6 percent annually, line BD in Figure 2–9, that will give sales revenues of $16 billion in 2006 and $20 billion in 2010. This reveals a wedge-shaped shaded gap in the figure. Planners call this the *planning gap,* the difference between the projection of the path to reach a new goal (line BD) and the projection of the path of the results of a plan already in place (line BC).

The ultimate purpose of the firm's marketing program is to "fill in" this planning gap—in Kodak's case, to move its future sales revenue line from the no-growth line BC up to the challenging target of line BD. But poor performance can result in actual sales revenues being far less than the targeted levels. This is the essence of evaluation: comparing actual results with planned objectives.

Acting on Deviations   When evaluation shows that actual performance fails to meet expectations, managers need to take corrective actions. And when actual results are far better than the plan called for, creative managers find ways to exploit the situation. Two possible Kodak midcourse corrections for both positive and negative deviations from targets illustrate these management actions:

- *Exploiting a positive deviation.* If Kodak's film strategy in India and China shows promise, it might partner with more local companies to produce cameras and film and to process film.
- *Correcting a negative deviation.* However, if Indian and Chinese consumers choose to skip film cameras and jump directly to digital ones, Kodak will likely need to partner with different business firms in these countries.

The strategic marketing process is discussed in greater detail again in Chapter 19.

CONCEPT CHECK

1. What is the control phase of the strategic marketing process?

2. How do the objectives set for a marketing program in the planning phase relate to the control phase of the strategic marketing process?

■ ■ ■

CHAPTER IN REVIEW

1 *Describe the three organizational levels of strategy.*
Most large business firms and nonprofit organizations are divided into three levels of strategy: (*a*) the corporate level, where top management directs overall strategy for the entire organization; (*b*) the business unit level, where business unit managers set the direction for their products and markets to exploit value-creating opportunities; and (*c*) the functional level, where groups of specialists actually create value for the organization.

2 *Describe why business, mission, culture, and goals are important in organizations.*
Organizations exist to accomplish something for someone. To give organizations direction and focus, they continuously assess their business, mission, culture, and goals. First, an organization defines what its business is—the set of customer needs, such as transportation, it wants to satisfy. Next, an organization defines its mission, which is a statement that describes its customers, markets, and products and inspires loyalty from its stakeholders. An organization's culture serves to connect it with its stakeholders based on a set of shared values, ideas, and attitudes. Finally, the organization's goals measure how well it accomplishes its mission at each organizational level by providing specific targeted levels of performance to be achieved, such as sales and profits, by a specific time period.

3 *Explain how organizations set strategic directions by assessing where they are now and seek to be in the future.*
Managers of an organization ask two key questions to set a strategic direction. The first question—Where are we now?—requires an organization to (*a*) assess its customers to determine whether its direction must be modified based on changes in consumer trends; (*b*) re-evaluate its competencies to ensure that its special capabilities still provide a competitive advantage; and (*c*) analyze its current and potential competitors from a global perspective to determine

whether any business definition modifications are needed. The second question—Where do we want to go?—requires an organization to actually set a direction and allocate resources to move it in that direction. Business portfolio and market-product analyses are two useful techniques to do this.

4 *Describe the strategic marketing process and its three key phases: planning, implementation, and control.*
An organization uses the strategic marketing process to allocate its marketing mix resources to reach its target markets. This process consists of three phases, which are usually formalized in a marketing plan. The planning phase consists of (*a*) a situation (SWOT) analysis of the organization's strengths, weaknesses, opportunities, and threats; (*b*) a market-product focus through market segmentation, points of difference analysis, and goal setting; and (*c*) a marketing program that specifies the budget and activities (marketing strategies and tactics) for each marketing mix element. The implementation phase carries out the marketing plan that emerges from the planning phase. It has four key elements: obtaining resources, designing the marketing organization, developing schedules, and executing the marketing program. The control phase compares the results from the implemented marketing program with the marketing plan's goals to identify the "planning gaps" and take actions to exploit positive deviations or correct negative ones.

5 *Explain how the marketing mix elements are blended into a cohesive marketing program.*
A marketing manager uses information obtained during the SWOT analysis, market-product focus, and goal-setting steps in the planning process to develop marketing strategies and marketing tactics for each marketing mix element for a given product, which are then implemented, as specified in the marketing plan, as a marketing program.

■ ■ ■

FOCUSING ON KEY TERMS

benchmarking p. 32
business unit p. 27
business unit level p. 27
competencies p. 31
competitive advantage p. 31
corporate level p. 26
cross-functional teams p. 27
functional level p. 27
goals p. 29
market segmentation p. 39
market share p. 29
marketing plan p. 36

marketing strategy p. 42
marketing tactics p. 42
mission p. 28
objectives p. 29
organizational culture p. 28
points of difference p. 39
profit p. 26
quality p. 32
situation analysis p. 36
stakeholders p. 28
strategic marketing process p. 36
SWOT analysis p. 37

DISCUSSION AND APPLICATION QUESTIONS

1 (*a*) Explain what a mission statement is. (*b*) Using Holiday Inn as an example from the chapter, explain how it gives a strategic direction to its organization. (*c*) Create a mission statement for your own career.

2 How might top management try to change the "culture" of its organization?

3 What competencies best describe (*a*) your college or university, (*b*) your favourite restaurant, and (*c*) the company that manufactures the computer you own or use most often?

4 Why does a product often start as a question mark and then move counterclockwise around BCG's growth-share matrix shown in Figure 2–3?

5 Many Canadian universities have traditionally offered an undergraduate degree in liberal arts (the product) to full-time 18- to 22-year-old students (the market). How might such an institution use the four market-product expansion strategies shown in Figure 2–4 to compete in the twenty-first century?

6 What is the main result of each of the three phases of the strategic marketing process? (*a*) planning, (*b*) implementation, and (*c*) control.

7 Select one strength, one weakness, one opportunity, and one threat from the SWOT analysis for Ben & Jerry's shown in Figure 2–6, and suggest a specific possible action that Unilever might take to exploit or address each one.

8 The goal-setting step in the planning phase of the strategic marketing process sets quantified objectives for use in the control phase. What actions are suggested for a marketing manager if measured results are below objectives? Above objectives?

GOING ONLINE		How Mission Statements Compare

In April 2000, Unilever N.V., a multinational consumer products firm, bought Ben & Jerry's, adding to its portfolio of other famous North American ice cream brands, such as Breyers All Natural, Good-Humor, Klondike, and Popsicle. As a condition of the buyout, Unilever must continue to donate 7.5 percent of all pretax profits to the Ben & Jerry's Foundation to fund organizations that engage in socially responsive activities, a critical aspect of Ben & Jerry's mission. In early 2004, Unilever revised its mission in response to its Path to Growth strategy that was launched in February 2000. Go to Ben & Jerry's Web site (www.benjerry.com) and Unilever's Web site (www.unilever.com) to compare the mission statement of both firms.

1 How are the mission statements of these organizations similar? How are they different?

2 Which mission statement do you believe will lead to "sustainable, profitable growth for our businesses and long-term value creation for our shareholders and employees" (from the "Introducing Unilever" promotional brochure)?

Do you want to get better grades and stay up to date with current issues in marketing? Visit the Online Learning Centre at www.mcgrawhill.ca/college/crane for practice tests, video cases, resources for building a marketing plan, *Globe and Mail* headlines, access to *Marketing Magazine*, and other learning and study tools.

VIDEO CASE 2   Specialized Bicycle Components, Inc.: Ride the Red "S"

The speaker leans forward with both intensity and pride in his voice. "We're in the business of creating a bike that delivers the customer their best possible ride," he explains. "When the customer sees our red 'S,' they say this is the company that understands the cyclist. It's a company of riders. The products they make are the rider's products." The speaker is Chris Murphy, director of marketing for Specialized Bicycle Components, Inc.—or just "Specialized" to serious riders.

THE COMPANY

Specialized was founded in 1974 by Mike Sinyard, a cycling enthusiast who sold his VW van for the $1500 startup capital. Mike started out importing hard-to-find "specialized" bike components, but the company began to produce its own bike parts by 1976. Specialized introduced the first major production mountain bike in the world in 1980, revolutionizing the bike industry, and since then has maintained a reputation as the technological leader in the bike and bike accessory market. In fact, since the company's founding, its formal mission statement has remained unchanged: "To give everyone the best ride of their life!"

The company continues to innovate. In addition to hiring bicycling enthusiasts, Specialized created the first professional mountain bike racing team, a dedicated BMX program, and an elite road racing program. Racers often serve as design consultants and "test pilots" for new technologies. The company banks on the perception, and reality, that this race-proven technology trickles down to the entire line of Specialized bikes and products.

Today, Specialized produces a full range of high-end and entry-level road bikes, mountain bikes, commuter/city bikes, children's bikes, and BMX bikes. The company also offers an extensive line of bike accessories, including helmets, water bottles, jerseys, tires, and shoes. As Chris says, "The customer is buying the ride from us, not just the bike."

THE ENVIRONMENT

The bike market is driven by innovation and technology, and with the market becoming more crowded and competitive. Specialized divides the bike market into two categories: (1) the retailer, and (2) the end-user consumer. While its focus in designing the product is on the end-user consumer, it only sells directly to the retailer and realizes a strong relationship with the dealers is a key factor for success. Steve Meineke, president of Specialized USA (the domestic unit of

Specialized), refers to the on-floor salesperson as "our most important partner."

The end-user consumer is broken down into two target age groups: the 18- to 25-year-old college students and the 30- to 40-year-old professional "techies." To differentiate itself from the rest of the market, Specialized positioned itself as the innovator in bike design—its models are what the rest of the industry imitates.

Cycling is the seventh most popular recreational activity in the United States behind walking, swimming, camping, fishing, exercising with equipment, and bowling. About 11 million adults in the United States ride a bicycle regularly and spend approximately $5 billion each year on new bicycles, parts, and accessories. Bicycle sales have declined slightly in recent years, however, as the 1990s surge in mountain bike sales has slowed. One explanation is that mountain bikes—which account for one-third of all bicycle sales—are so durable that consumers have not needed to replace them. Does Chris believe this trend will hurt Specialized? "We believe we will see growth in the next six or seven years as the entry level participants trade up—trade their lower-end bikes for higher-end bikes," he explains.

Other factors suggest that the industry will grow in the future. The popularity of Lance Armstrong, the seven-times Tour de France champion, has increased the interest in road bikes, which currently represent 5 percent of the market. In addition, new full-suspension technology and improved ergonomic frame designs have attracted many new customers to the "comfort" bike category. Finally, recent research shows

that while 94 percent of people who ride bicycles do so for recreation or fitness, a growing number are using bicycles as a form of transportation.

The bicycle industry consists of four channels of distribution—independent bicycle retailers, mass merchants, sporting goods stores, and other outdoor retailers and mail order merchants. Specialized now has an extensive global distribution network of 5000 retailers in 35 countries in Asia, North America, South America, and Australia.

THE ISSUES

How can Specialized stay at the forefront of an industry that now includes more than 20 manufacturers? Strategic placement in the marketplace is one way. Specialized recently designed its own server, the World Ride Web, on the Internet (www.specialized.com). The Web site offers international mountain bike trail and road bike trail directories, e-mail access to Specialized engineers, a trail preservation network, and a dealer directory that connects users directly to dealer home pages. Specialized believes guest appearances on TV talk shows and displays in retail shops help keep the Specialized name in front of the end-user consumer.

Targeting its other market segment, the dealers, Specialized launched a "Best Ride Tour." It loaded up trailers full of the new models and visited 30 cities nationwide, enabling retailers and shop employees to test ride the bikes they will be ordering for the coming year—"Ride Before You Buy."

Specialized is also eager to become involved in joint ventures to keep its technological edge, including one with Du Pont that led to a more aerodynamic wheel. Specialized also entered into a distribution relationship with GripShift, allowing the high-end gear manufacturer access to its extensive dealer network.

Specialized sponsors races, provides racer support teams, initiates mountain biking safety programs, and is involved in trail-access advocacy groups all over the world. Specialized supplies bicycles and equipment to many of the top racing teams in the world, such as Domina Vacanze that raced in the 2004 Tour de France.

But, as it was in Specialized's early years, Mike sees a commitment to top quality and design as the most important factor for future success: "Even though we've been around for 20 years, this company still feels like it has something to prove. I expect it will always be that way."

QUESTIONS

1   Do a SWOT analysis for Specialized. Use Figure 2–6 as a guide. In assessing internal factors (strengths and weaknesses), use the material provided in the case. In assessing external factors (opportunities and threats), augment the case material with what you see happening in the bicycle industry.

2   As part of step 2 of the planning phase and using your SWOT analysis, select target markets on which you might focus for present and potential bikers.

3   As part of step 3 of the planning phase and using your answers in questions 1 and 2 above, outline Specialized's marketing programs for the target market segments you chose.

"New ideas are a dime a dozen," observes Arthur R. Kydd, "and so are new products and new technologies." Kydd should know. As chief executive officer of St. Croix Venture Partners, he and his firm have provided the seed money and venture capital to launch more than 60 startup firms in the last 25 years. Today, those firms have more than 5000 employees. Kydd elaborates:

> I get 200 to 300 marketing and business plans a year to look at, and St. Croix provides startup financing for only two or three. What sets a potentially successful idea, product, or technology apart from all the rest is markets and marketing. If you have a real product with a distinctive point of difference that satisfies the needs of customers, you may have a winner. And you get a real feel for this in a well-written marketing or business plan.[1]

This appendix (1) describes what marketing and business plans are, including the purposes and guidelines in writing effective plans; and (2) provides a sample marketing plan.

MARKETING PLANS AND BUSINESS PLANS

After explaining the meanings, purposes, and audiences of marketing plans and business plans, this section describes some writing guidelines for them and what external funders often look for in successful plans.

Meanings, Purposes, and Audiences A *marketing plan* is a road map for the marketing activities of an organization for a specified future period of time, such as one year or five years.[2] It is important to note that no single "generic" marketing plan applies to all organizations and all situations. Rather, the specific format for a marketing plan for an organization depends on the following:

- *The target audience and purpose.* Elements included in a particular marketing plan depend heavily on (1) who the audience is, and (2) what its purpose is. A marketing plan for an internal audience seeks to point the direction for future marketing activities and is sent to all individuals in the organization who must implement the plan or who will be affected by it. If the plan is directed to an external audience, such as friends, banks, venture capitalists, or potential investors, for the purpose of raising capital, it has the additional function of being an important sales document. In this case, it contains elements such as the strategic plan/focus, organization, structure, and biographies of key personnel that would rarely appear in an internal marketing plan. Also, the financial information is far more detailed when the plan is used to raise outside capital. The elements of a marketing plan for each of these two audiences are compared in Figure A–1 on the next page.
- *The kind and complexity of the organization.* A small neighbourhood restaurant has a somewhat different marketing plan from that of Nestlé, which serves international markets. The restaurant's plan would be relatively simple and directed at serving customers in a local market. In Nestlé's case, because there is a hierarchy of marketing plans, various levels of detail would be used—such as the entire organization, the business unit, or the product/ product line.
- *The industry.* Both the restaurant that serves a local market and Medtronic that sells heart pacemakers globally analyze competition. Not only are their geographic thrusts far different, but the complexities of their offerings and hence the time periods likely to be covered by their plans also differ. A one-year marketing plan may be adequate for the restaurant, but Medtronic may need a five-year planning horizon because product-development cycles for complex, new medical devices may be three or four years.

In contrast to a marketing plan, a *business plan* is a road map for the entire organization for a specified future period of time, such as one year or five years.[3] A key difference between a marketing plan and a business plan is that the business plan contains details on the research and development (R&D)/operations/manufacturing activities of the organization. Even for a manufacturing business, the marketing plan is probably 60 or 70 percent of the entire business plan. For such businesses as a small restaurant or an auto repair shop, their marketing and business plans are virtually identical. The elements of a business plan typically targeted at internal and external audiences appear in the two right-hand columns in Figure A–1.

The Most-Asked Questions by Outside Audiences   Lenders and prospective investors reading a business or marketing plan that is used to seek new capital are probably the toughest audiences to satisfy. Their most-asked questions include the following:

1. Is the business or marketing idea valid?
2. Is there something unique or distinctive about the product or service that separates it from substitutes and competitors?
3. Is there a clear market for the product or service?
4. Are the financial projections realistic and healthy?
5. Are the key management and technical personnel capable, and do they have a track record in the industry in which they must compete?
6. Does the plan clearly describe how those providing capital will get their money back and make a profit?

Rhonda M. Abrahms, author of *The Successful Business Plan*, observes that "within the first five minutes of reading your . . . plan, readers must perceive that the answers to these questions are favourable."[4] While her comments apply to plans seeking to raise capital, the first five questions just listed apply equally well to plans for internal audiences.

Writing and Style Suggestions   There are no magic one-size-fits-all guidelines for writing successful marketing and business plans. Still, the following writing and style guidelines generally apply:[5]

■ **FIGURE A–1** ■■

Elements in typical marketing and business plans targeted at different audiences

Element of the plan	Marketing plan		Business plan	
	For internal audience (to direct the firm)	For external audience (to raise capital)	For internal audience (to direct the firm)	For external audience (to raise capital)
1. Executive summary	✓	✓	✓	✓
2. Description of company		✓		✓
3. Strategic plan/focus		✓		✓
4. Situation analysis	✓	✓	✓	✓
5. Market-product focus	✓	✓	✓	✓
6. Marketing program strategy and tactics	✓	✓	✓	✓
7. R&D and operations program			✓	✓
8. Financial projections	✓	✓	✓	✓
9. Organization structure		✓		✓
10. Implementation plan	✓	✓	✓	✓
11. Evaluation and control	✓		✓	
Appendix A: Biographies of key personnel		✓		✓
Appendix B, etc.: Details on other topics	✓	✓	✓	✓

- Use a direct, professional writing style. Use appropriate business terms without jargon. Present and future tenses with active voice ("I will write an effective marketing plan.") are generally better than past tense and passive voice ("An effective marketing plan was written by me.").
- Be positive and specific to convey potential success. At the same time, avoid superlatives ("terrific," "wonderful"). Specifics are better than glittering generalities. Use numbers for impact, justifying projections with reasonable quantitative assumptions, where possible.
- Use bullet points for succinctness and emphasis. As with the list you are reading, bullets enable key points to be highlighted effectively.
- Use A-level (the first level) and B-level (the second level) headings under the numbered section headings to help readers make easy transitions from one topic to another. This also forces the writer to organize the plan more carefully. Use these headings liberally, at least one every 200 to 300 words.
- Use visuals, where appropriate. Photos, illustrations, graphs, and charts enable massive amounts of information to be presented succinctly.
- Aim for a plan 15 to 35 pages in length, not including financial projections and appendixes. An uncomplicated small business may require only 15 pages, while a high-technology startup may require more than 35 pages.
- Use care in layout, design, and presentation. Laser printers give a more professional look than do ink-jet printers. Use 11- or 12-point type (you are now reading 10.5-point type) in the text. Use a serif type (with "feet," like that you are reading now) in the text because it is easier to read, and sans serif (without "feet") in graphs and charts, as in Figure A–1. A bound report with an attractive cover and clear title page adds professionalism.

These guidelines are used, where possible, in the sample marketing plan that follows.

■ ■ ■

SAMPLE FIVE-YEAR MARKETING PLAN FOR FRENZ STEAK AND SEAFOOD

To help interpret the marketing plan for Frenz Steak and Seafood that follows, we suggest some guidelines.

Interpreting the Marketing Plan

The sample marketing plan for Frenz Steak and Seafood, a fictitious restaurant, was written by Professor John Shepherd of the College of New Caledonia. Trina O'Connor, who has extensive restaurant experience in Prince Rupert, British Columbia, provided invaluable assistance during the preparation of the sample marketing plan. Notes in the margins next to the plan fall into two categories:

1. *Substantive notes* are shaded blue and elaborate on the significance of an element in the marketing plan and are keyed to chapter references in this text.
2. *Writing style, format, and layout notes* are shaded in red and explain the editorial or visual rationale for the element.

A closing word of encouragement! Writing an effective marketing plan is hard—but challenging and satisfying—work. However, dozens of the authors' students have used effective marketing plans they wrote for class in their interviewing portfolio to show prospective employers what they could do and to help them get their first job.

Blue boxes explain significance of Marketing Plan elements

Red boxes give writing style, format, and layout guidelines

The Table of Contents provides quick access to the topics in the plan, usually organized by section and subsection headings.

Seen by many experts as the single most important element in the plan, the Executive Summary "sells" the plan to readers through its clarity and brevity.

The Company Description highlights the recent history of the organization.

FIVE-YEAR MARKETING PLAN
Frenz Steak and Seafood

Table of Contents

1. Executive Summary

The following plan outlines the marketing strategy and tactics for Frenz Steak and Seafood, a large casual-style restaurant opening during the summer of 2005 in Prince Rupert, British Columbia.

While the local restaurant sector is reasonably competitive, it is weighted toward small, independent restaurants. The absence of family restaurants, midrange franchise operations, and features common in larger markets (e.g., salad bars, child-friendly operations, high-calibre customer service) creates an opportunity for a new restaurant operator.

Frenz Steak and Seafood is positioned in the middle of the casual dining spectrum in pricing and cuisine quality, offering a wide selection of menu items. The restaurant has four distinguishing features—(1) a child-friendly environment, (2) a comfortable atmosphere created by skilled serving teams, (3) features lacking in local restaurants, and (4) the skilled use of publicity and promotional activities to establish a clear brand identity. As in franchise operations, Frenz segregates family dining from intimate dining and banquets, enabling the operator to target different market segments in one facility.

2. Company Description

Frenz Steak and Seafood is opening as a 100-seat restaurant in downtown Prince Rupert in July 2005. A casual-style restaurant, offering a selection of seafood, steaks, pastas, and pizzas, Frenz will also provide take-out and delivery services for cooked and ready-to-cook menu items.

Frenz is positioned at the middle of the casual dining spectrum in pricing and menu variety. Frenz will provide a comfortable, community atmosphere for people of all ages through a serving staff with a "can do" attitude, a child-friendly environment, and a décor reflecting the history of the community. The layout of the premises enables Frenz to target separate segments—family dining near the entrance, semiprivate booths farther back for intimate dining, and a separate banquet room for groups of up to 35 people.

The restaurant's focus on atmosphere, service, and marketing will provide it with a competitive advantage in the fragmented Prince Rupert market. This plan describes how Frenz can establish a leading position in the Prince Rupert marketplace, prior to its expansion to other Northern B.C. communities.

To improve readability, each numbered section usually starts on a new page. (This is not always done in this plan to save space.)

The Strategic Focus and Plan sets the strategic direction for the entire organization, a direction with which proposed actions of the marketing plan must be consistent. This section is not included in all marketing plans. See Chapter 2.

The qualitative Mission/Vision statement focuses the activities of Frenz Steak and Seafood for the stakeholder groups to be served. See Chapter 2.

The Goals section sets both the nonfinancial and financial targets—where possible in quantitative terms—against which the company's performance will be measured. See Chapter 2.

Lists use parallel construction to improve readability—in this case a series of infinitives starting with "To . . ."

The Situation Analysis is a snapshot to answer the question, "Where are we now?" See Chapter 2.

3. Strategic Focus and Plan

The corporate strategy of Frenz Steak and Seafood and its (1) mission/vision, (2) goals, and (3) core competences and sustainable competitive advantage are described below.

<u>Mission/Vision</u>

Frenz is a restaurant where patrons can leave their worries at the door and enjoy a fun atmosphere where they feel valued and part of a community. It is a meeting place where people of all ages and all backgrounds can enjoy a good meal.

<u>Goals</u>

- Nonfinancial goals
  1. To become known as the leading restaurant and an employer of choice throughout the Northwest.
  2. To establish similar restaurants in Terrace and Smithers by year 2010.
- Financial goals
  1. To achieve breakeven point for each restaurant by the end of its first year of operation.
  2. To achieve a before-tax profit of $50 000 for each Frenz Steak and Seafood in its second year of operations.

<u>Core Competency and Sustainable Competitive Advantage</u>

The core competency of a Frenz restaurant is its customer-centred atmosphere, where people can eat good food in a friendly, casual, and child-friendly environment.

Frenz will achieve a sustainable competitive advantage through careful selection of serving staff, a focus on training, leadership by example, and a supportive environment where employees are valued. Frenz will implement design elements commonly found in franchise restaurants.

4. Situation Analysis

The situation analysis begins with a SWOT analysis (strengths, weaknesses, opportunities, and threats), followed by analyses of the Canadian food services industry, existing Prince Rupert restaurants, and the Prince Rupert market.

The SWOT Analysis identifies strengths, weaknesses, opportunities, and threats to provide a solid foundation as a springboard to identify subsequent actions in the marketing plan. See Chapter 2.

Each long table, graph, or photo is given a figure number and title. It then appears as soon as possible after the first reference in the text, accommodating necessary page breaks. This also avoids breaking long tables like this one in the middle. Short tables or graphs that are less than 3 cm are often inserted in the text without figure numbers because they do not cause serious problems with page breaks.

Effective tables seek to summarize a large amount of information in a short amount of space.

The text discussion of Figure 1 (the SWOT Analysis table) elaborates on its more important elements. This "walks" the reader through the information from the vantage of the plan's writer. In terse plans this accompanying discussion is sometimes omitted, but is generally desirable to give the reader an understanding of what the company sees as the critical SWOT elements.

SWOT Analysis

The SWOT analysis for Frenz is summarized in Figure 1, showing the internal and external factors that could affect the restaurant's competitive success.

FIGURE 1. SWOT Analysis for the Frenz Restaurant Concept

Internal Factors	Strengths	Weaknesses
Management	Experienced and entrepreneurial management.	Limited supply of qualified and experienced personnel in Northwest British Columbia.
Offering	Casual dining, service-oriented concept targeting multiple market segments.	A wide range of restaurants serving the Prince Rupert market.
Marketing	A detailed marketing plan which focuses on low cost publicity and promotional activities.	Limited funds available during the startup could restrict marketing activities.
Personnel	Human resource and management practices should attract high-quality employees.	Limited regional labour force of trained cooks and quality serving personnel.
Finance	Adequate startup and working capital financing.	Limited access to external financing until a track record is established.
Manufacturing	Partnership with Northwest Community College's Culinary Arts Program.	Limited access to experienced and talented chefs in the region.
Product Development	Partnership with College Culinary Arts Program.	Limited in-house capacity for the development of new cuisine.
External Factors	**Opportunities**	**Threats**
Consumer/Social	Local residents are accustomed to eating at restaurants and to take-out.	Price sensitivity would impact a premium pricing strategy.
Competitive	Fragmented industry populated by small, owner-operated restaurants	Entry of a professionally managed midrange restaurant franchise.
Technological	No fundamental technological changes anticipated.	Increased automation would benefit franchise and chain restaurants.
Economic	Several port-related projects could stimulate economic recovery in the region.	Protracted recession in primary industries has resulted in local job losses and lower household incomes.
Legal/Regulatory	Health regulations benefit well-managed operations.	Few barriers to entry for entrants into the industry.

In the company's favour are such internal factors as the strength of the concept, detailed planning, and a management team with restaurant experience. Favourable external factors include the fragmented nature of the local restaurant sector and gaps in the local market.

Frenz faces adverse factors, both internally and externally. Business startups are a risky proposition, especially in the restaurant sector. Statistics Canada figures indicate that new food service operations have a 22-percent chance of surviving eight years. Staffing the restaurant with qualified, cheerful serving and cooking staff will be a challenge. Finally, a declining population base, job losses in the resource sector, reduced household incomes, and the discretionary nature of restaurant sales reduce the attractiveness of the Prince Rupert market.

The Industry Analysis section provides the backdrop for the subsequent, more detailed analysis of competition, the company, and the company's customers. Without an in-depth understanding of the industry, the remaining analysis may be misdirected. See Chapter 2.

Industry Analysis

The food services sector is a $47 billion industry in Canada. The industry grew rapidly during the 1970s and 1980s due to changing consumer demographics. The increasing numbers of double-income and single-parent households eroded the time available to cook at home. One result has been the growing popularity of take-out and delivery services, with 60 percent of meals and snacks in 2003 eaten away from home.

After two decades of rapid expansion, the percentage of household food dollars spent at restaurants and bars plateaued in 1997 and has changed little over the past seven years. Attributing factors include competition from ready-to-heat meals sold at grocery stores and increased value consciousness among consumers. Fierce competition for market share among national chains and constant innovation are now the norm.

The food services industry suffered during the early 2000s due to a recession and external events, such as the September 11 terrorist attacks in the United States, the Iraqi conflict, and outbreaks of SARS and mad cow disease in Canada. According to the Canadian Restaurant and Food Services Association, the profit margins of Canadian food services operators fell to 4.6 percent in 2002. Restaurants and bars lost market share in 2003 to grocery and liquor stores, with households spending only 23 percent of their food and drink dollars at restaurants and bars.

Restaurant sales are strongly correlated with household disposable incomes. For example, household spending in restaurants in 2003 ranged from $1878 in B.C. to $1022 in Newfoundland. Restaurant sales recovered in 2004 with B.C. recording a 7.8-percent growth rate, a reflection of an improved economy.

Even though relatively brief, this in-depth treatment of the food services industry demonstrates to the plan's readers the company's understanding of the industry in which it competes. It gives both external and internal readers confidence that the company thoroughly understands its own industry.

Statistics Canada classifies foodservices operations as full-service restaurants (39 percent market share), limited-services restaurants (28 percent), accommodations food services (10 percent), social and contract caterers (6 percent), and bars (5 percent). There are four categories of restaurants in Canada's foodservices industry: quick service, family-style, casual, and fine dining.

Quick-service restaurants, including fast-food outlets, sandwich bars, and delivery pizzerias, capture the largest share of consumer's dollars and are visited most often. Family-style restaurants are table-service or self-service restaurants with inexpensive to moderately priced menus. These restaurants specialize in one type of food, often feature a children's menu, and sometimes offer a take-out option. Family restaurant revenues have remained fairly constant throughout the year.

Casual dining restaurants offer full table service, a bar, an atmosphere-type concept, or a food speciality. Menu entrées are priced in the moderate to expensive range, and revenues are highest during the summer months. Fine dining restaurants are the priciest, focusing on service and high-quality cuisine.

<u>Overview of the Prince Rupert Restaurant Market</u>
Prince Rupert is a small port community on British Columbia's North Coast, 700 kilometres west of Prince George. The city has nearly 35 restaurants, mainly situated along Second and Third Avenues in the downtown core and Cow Bay, one kilometre north along the waterfront.

The local trade is unusual in its limited number of fast-food outlets and low penetration by major national chains and franchises. The lack of franchise operations, such as Pizza Hut, White Spot, and ABC Restaurants, is puzzling, as communities of similar size have a much larger franchise presence. Past failures of such franchises as Pizza Hut, Boston Pizza, KFC, and Dairy Queen are hard to explain.

Local dining is heavily weighted toward small, independent casual-style restaurants offering a wide selection of menu items and take-out services. There are a few speciality restaurants offering menus restricted to one ethnic cuisine (e.g., Panago Pizza), a few fast-food franchises, and many ethnic restaurants. The sector is relatively competitive due to the number of establishments and offers reasonable prices.

The B.C. North Coast has experienced years of economic decline. Several port-related projects are in the planning stage, creating hope but no economic benefit to date. Despite a significant population decline, however, very few restaurants have closed up until now.

<u>Competitive Analysis</u>
Frenz will face competition from casual dinning and hotel restaurants. The most direct competitor is Rodhos Pizza and Steakhouse, a full-service, sit-down restaurant offering a selection of Greek, Italian, and western cuisine. Rodhos offers good food for moderate prices, a good atmosphere, and decent service. However, it has cramped seating, a drab façade, and limited parking.

Several casual dining restaurants in Prince Rupert are located along Third Avenue, including Cu's Steak House and Seafood, Galaxy Gardens, West End, and Stardust. Galaxy Gardens is probably the most notable, offering a selection of Cantonese, seafood, and western cuisines at a midrange price. Galaxy Gardens is a well-maintained 100-seat restaurant, offering home delivery and catering services.

The Howard Johnson Highliner Inn, the Coast Prince Rupert Hotel, and the Crest Motor Hotel are the three largest and best-maintained hotels. The Crest Motor Hotel is a four-star hotel, with a popular lounge and restaurant and an excellent view of the harbour. A combination of desirable ambience, high-quality customer service, and ongoing marketing activities has secured it the top spot in the local market. The Prince Rupert Hotel has a restaurant offering excellent meals at a reasonable price and is quite successful at attracting local residents.

As with the Industry Analysis, the Competitive Analysis demonstrates that the company has a realistic understanding of who its major competitors are and what their marketing strategies are. Again, a realistic assessment gives confidence to both internal and external readers that subsequent marketing actions in the plan rest on a solid foundation. See Chapters 2, 3, 8, and 9.

This page uses a "block" style and does *not* indent each paragraph, although an extra space separates each paragraph. Compare this page with page 54, which has indented paragraphs. Most readers find indented paragraphs in marketing plans and long reports are easier to follow.

The Company Analysis provides details of the company's strengths and marketing strategies that will enable it to achieve the mission, vision, and goals identified earlier. See Chapters 2, 8, and 19.

The higher-level "A heading" of Customer Analysis has a more dominant typeface and position than the lower-level "B heading" of B.C. Industry Survey. These headings introduce the reader to the sequence and level of topics covered. The organization of this textbook uses this kind of structure and headings.

Satisfying customers and providing genuine value to them is why organizations exist in a market economy. This section addresses the question of "Who are the customers for Frenz Steak and Seafood" citing relevant survey data? See Chapters 5, 6, 7, 8, and 9.

One kilometre north in Cow Bay, Smile's Seafood Cafe, Breakers Pub, and the Cow Bay Cafe are popular restaurants. Breakers is a well-liked local pub with a reasonable menu selection, an outside patio, and the usual pub activities. Smile's Seafood Cafe is a well-known seafood restaurant, which, however, has only limited space.

Frenz Steak and Seafood will benefit from weak spots in local restaurants and underserved market segments. In particular, there are no family restaurants or midrange, franchise operations in Prince Rupert; there is a lack of salad bars; and only McDonalds focuses on the children's market. Advertising, with the exception of that for the Crest, is limited to Yellow Pages and the door-to-door delivery of brochures to households.

Company Analysis

The operations manager has 10 years of local restaurant experience, with several years in a management capacity. The company president, a Certified General Accountant, will handle the financial, accounting, and marketing aspects of the venture.

Recruitment and retention of motivated, qualified serving staff and cooks are crucial to achieving a sustainable competitive advantage. The management team will work closely with Northwest Community College's Culinary Arts Program to access a reliable supply of chefs for a growing operation.

Customer Analysis

B.C Industry Survey. The BC Restaurant and Food Services Association conducted an online survey in March 2004 (see Figure 2). The survey concluded that 60 percent of B.C. residents dine out about 2 to 10 times per month and 44 percent spend from $100 to $600 per month at restaurants. The heaviest users are those in the 18- to 34-year age group, two-thirds of whom dine out six or more times a month.

Singles dine out more often than do families with children, and the dining habit declines with age. Dining out for lunch (48 percent) and supper (46 percent) is equally popular. However, eat-out lunches are preferred over dinners among people in the 45- to 54-year age group. There is a trend toward healthier eating, with 33 percent of B.C. residents reducing their consumption of red meats, carbohydrates, and heavier sauces, and asking more questions about food preparation. As summarized by Figure 2, B.C. residents are not adventuresome in their culinary experiences, with only 14 percent interested in trying out new cuisine.

FIGURE 2. Favourite Cuisine among B.C. Residents, 2004 Ipsos-Reid Poll

Favourite Type of Cuisine	Percentage of Poll Respondents
North American/Canadian	36%
Chinese	16%
Japanese	15%
Italian	13%
East Indian	7%

This section demonstrates the company's insights into major trends that have a potentially large impact.

Consumer Trends. One customer trend is toward healthier eating. A 1994 report of the National Institute of Nutrition concluded that 87 percent of Canadians are concerned about nutrition. However, the report concluded that it is taste, not nutrition, that governs what Canadians eat. People want healthier food but are unwilling to compromise on taste. In a backlash, some consumers have rejected healthy foods in favour of higher-fat foods but feel some guilt as a result.

Consumers give themselves small rewards to feel good, even if this feeling only lasts a few moments. People who cannot afford to buy big-ticket items buy small ones as self-indulgence. A lack of wage growth has led to greater value consciousness among customers. According to Charles Suddaby, a hospitality consultant, "people want good food at a reasonable price with perceived value in terms of quality, freshness, presentation, and service."

In addition, families are having to deal with increasing time pressures. Faced with long working hours in a tough employment market, expensive day-care, and reduced support systems, time has become the most precious commodity in many households. Home cooking has therefore been assigned a low priority.

Local Population. According to the 2001 Census, Prince Rupert had a population of 15 302, with another 6256 people living in the isolated North Coast and Queen Charlotte Islands/Haida Qwaii communities. Being a port community, Prince Rupert has a diverse ethic mix, including 30 percent people of First Nations descent and 10 percent of Asian descent, mainly Vietnamese, Chinese, Filipino, and South Asian. Over half of the people living elsewhere in the Queen Charlotte Regional District are of First Nations descent.

Current local demographics resemble those of the 1970s. A large proportion of the population consists of young families with children. Over 30 percent of the Prince Rupert's population is under 20 years of age and fairly few over the age of 54. The numbers of households with single individuals, common-law couples, or single parents with children are higher than provincial norms. Median household income is slightly higher than the provincial average, but past censuses reported a flat distribution, with a many households earning more than $70 000 and less than $20 000.

Prince Rupert is a blue-collar community with relatively few knowledge-industry workers and professionals. Traditionally, a large percentage of the workforce was employed in commercial fishing fleet, fish processing plants, logging operations, and pulp mills and at the Port of Prince Rupert. A significant drop in local population since 2001, related to the closure of the pulp mill, a downturn in port shipments, and downsizing of the fishing industry, is having an undetermined effect on demographics. The population of Prince Rupert and the Queen Charlotte Regional District declined by 12 percent between 1996 and 2001.

Prince Rupert residents seem to dine out a lot, probably for reasons different from those of other Canadians. Families face fewer time pressures due to a slower pace, the absence of long commutes to work, and the proximity of facilities that are within easy walking distances. Restaurants serve as social meeting places, where people converse and exchange news. Frequent rains discourage outdoor activities, and the range of leisure activities is limited.

Market Potential. On the basis of the B.C. figure of $1878 per household and the 2001 Canada Census data, it can be said that Prince Rupert residents probably spend $10 to $11 million a year at restaurants. An unknown percentage of these dollars is spent during shopping trips to Vancouver, Terrace, and Prince George.

Residents of North Coast communities regularly visit Prince Rupert for shopping, sports, and entertainment. As dining options in small communities are really limited, they might spend $2 to $3 million at Prince Rupert restaurants per year. Finally, people travelling through Prince Rupert constitute another secondary market, perhaps spending a total of $1 million spent a year. In total, the market potential for restaurant food and alcohol sales is probably in the range of $12 million.

5. Market-Product Focus

This section outlines the marketing objectives for Frenz Steak and Seafood, identifying target markets, points of difference, and restaurant positioning.

Marketing and Product Objectives – Marketing objectives are divided into two categories, short-term and long-term.

One-Year Marketing Objectives

- To create local awareness of the Frenz concept.
- To stimulate trial and repeat purchases by consumers in target market segments.
- To achieve a 6-percent market share and $600 000 in sales, by the end of the first year.
- To achieve recognition that Frenz is the place to go for a good time.
- To become known as a "good corporate citizen" in Prince Rupert.

Five-Year Marketing Objectives

- To become known as a leading restaurant and restaurant employer of choice in Northwest British Columbia.
- To establish restaurants in two other Northern communities, achieving breakeven points for all restaurants established.

Side annotations:

Size of headings should give a professional look to the report and not overwhelm the reader. These two headings are too large.

As noted in Chapter 10, the chances of success for a new product are significantly increased if objectives are set for the product itself and if target market segments are identified for it. This section makes these explicit for Frenz Steak and Seafood. The objectives also serve as the planned targets against which marketing activities are measured in program implementation and control.

A heading should be spaced closer to the text that follows (and that it describes) than the preceding section to avoid confusion for the reader. This rule is not followed for the Target Markets heading, which now unfortunately appears to "float" between the preceding and following paragraphs.

Target markets

Frenz targets several market segments within Prince Rupert as its primary market. People in North Coast communities and travellers constitute secondary markets.

This section identifies the specific niches or target markets toward which the company's products are directed. When appropriate and when space permits, this section often includes a market-product grid. See Chapter 9.

Given the considerable size of the population of children, it is surprising that only McDonalds targets children, offering kid's meals and activities. A market also exists for intimate dinners for singles, families without children, and couples who would appreciate an evening away from the kids. A combination of good food, friendly service, and a degree of privacy should appeal to this market.

Frenz is located in the downtown core, within blocks of bank branches, government offices, and business offices. The former Epicurean restaurant had steady lunch traffic in spite of its limited staff. Larger groups, such as office Christmas parties, can be handled in the banquet room.

First Nations people comprise 30 percent of the population, and there is a higher percentage of offshore communities. Targeting of this segment presents problems due to its decentralized and fragmented nature. In the past, Epicurean prepared ready-to-cook meals for delivery to isolated First Nations communities. According to Tourism Prince Rupert, 125 000 people travel through the community each year; 100 000 Alaska cruise ship passengers visited Prince Rupert during the summer of 2005.

Points of Difference
Frenz Steak and Seafood has four distinguishing characteristics:

An organization cannot grow by offering only "me-too products or services." The greatest single factor in a new product's or services failure is the lack of significant "points of difference" that sets it apart from competitors' substitutes. This section makes these points of difference explicit. See Chapter 10.

- A child-friendly environment, including trained servers, kids menus, colouring placemats, parties, kid promotions, and so on.
- A comfortable, community atmosphere created by serving teams with a "can do" attitude and a décor that reflects "Prince Rupert."
- The introduction of features lacking in local restaurants—salad bars, flame grill entrées, vegetarian dishes, and healthy menus.
- The use of advertising, promotions and publicity to establish a brand identity, create a sense of excitement, and target specific market segments.

Positioning
Frenz Steak and Seafood is positioned in the middle of the casual dining spectrum in pricing and cuisine quality. The restaurant differentiation is its atmosphere, its use of features common in franchise restaurants, and its targeting of distinct market segments.

A positioning strategy helps communicate the company's unique points of difference of its products to prospective customers in a simple, clear way. This section describes this positioning. See Chapters 9 and 10.

Everything that has gone before in the marketing plan sets the stage for the marketing mix actions—the 4 Ps—covered in the marketing program. See Chapters 10 through 19.

The section describes in detail key elements of the company's product strategy. See Chapters 10, 11, and 12.

6. Marketing Program

The four elements of the marketing program for Frenz are described below.

<u>Product Strategy</u>

Frenz will have daily specials, lunch, dinner, children's menus, and take-out menus. The lunch menu consists of a salad bar, hot sandwiches, chicken fingers, pizzas, pizza submarines, burgers, milk shakes, and the usual side dishes.

The dinner menu includes appetizers and a selection of western cuisine: a salad bar, pizza, seafood, pasta, flame-grilled steak, chicken, ribs, side dishes, deserts, and vegetarian and healthy-choice entrées. Paper inserts will draw attention to daily specials and specialty entrées for the "Round the World" promotion, where T-shirts are given to patrons who eat meals from a certain number of countries. A selection of specialty coffees, wines, domestic and imported beers, and cocktails are listed on the beverage menu.

The children's menu offers the usual children's dishes (e.g., burger, chicken nuggets, hot dogs, French fries) and scaled-down portions of popular adult meals. The take-out menu includes cooked and ready-to-heat dishes, along with larger quantities of items, such as pasta trays. Apparently, the old Epicurean restaurant flew ready-to-heat meals on a regular basis to isolated North Coast communities, where no restaurants exist.

Recognizing that the meal itself is only one part of the overall culinary experience, Frenz will create a fun, community atmosphere through signage, a cheerful serving staff, and furnishings that reflect Prince Rupert's industrious past (e.g., older tables, black-and-white photographs from the past, and so on). The possibility of opening up the front of the kitchen—so that patrons can see food being prepared—will be explored.

The Price Strategy section makes the company's price point very clear, along with its price position relative to potential substitutes. When appropriate and when space permits, this section might contain a break-even analysis. See Chapter 13.

Price Strategy

The strategy of Frenz is to match the prices of popular casual dining restaurants, in particular, Rodhos Pizza–Steak & Seafood House, Galaxy Gardens, and Stardust Restaurant (see Figure 3). For the restaurant's take-out and delivery services, 2-for-1 pizzas and family specials are available with a 10-percent discount for pickups. The goal is to avert a price war by matching the competition's prices.

FIGURE 3. Price Ranges for Key Prince Rupert Restaurants

Restaurant	Appetizers	Lunches	Dinners
Boulets' Seafood House	$4.95 – $15.95	–	$15.95 – $37.00
Coast Prince Rupert Hotel	–	$6.95 – $9.95	$9.70 – $13.65
Crest Hotel	$7.95 – $16.95	$6.95 – $16.95	$8.95 – $39.95
Galaxy Gardens Restaurant	–	$5.50 – $13.75	$8.50 – $34.95
Cu's Steakhouse & Seafood	$2.95 – $8.95	$4.95 – $13.95	$11.95 – $24.95
Rodhos Pizza – Steak	$2.95 – $6.95	–	$7.50 – $29.95
Stardust Restaurant	$2.75 – $6.95	$5.20 – $10.00	$8.65 – $27.00

The Place Strategy is described here. See Chapters 14, and 15.

Place (Distribution) Strategy

The planned location for Frenz Steak and Seafood is the old Epicurean restaurant building, among a cluster of restaurants on Second Avenue, including Rodhos, Rain, and Zorba's Pizza. Second Avenue is the second busiest street in town, passing through the downtown core en route to the Via Rail station and B.C.–Alaska Ferry terminals.

The building provides ample space for a 100-seat restaurant and flexibility for its interior layout. Since the premises were previously occupied by a restaurant, leasehold improvements and overall startup costs are reduced. Frenz might operate a food cart in Mariner's Park to serve the 3000 passengers and crew arriving in town on cruise ships. Large vessels are scheduled to visit Prince Rupert three days a week during the summer of 2005.

Advertising, Publicity, and Promotional Activities

Print Material. The plan is designed to create local awareness and a sense of excitement among local residents. Print material, menus, and signage will have the same style of lettering, logo (two people with an arm on each other's shoulder), and a common theme—*"Where good friends gather."* Standard templates for menus, print advertisements, and brochures will be prepared.

In smaller cities, such as Prince Rupert, the opening of a restaurant in a prominent location generates a lot of local interest. Details concerning the venture will be kept under wraps, with the local rumour mill kept primed with conflicting stories.

Elements of the Promotion Strategy are highlighted in terms of the key promotional activities the company is emphasizing. For space reasons the company's online strategies are not shown in the plan. See Chapters 16, 17, and 18.

Publicity. Prior to opening, interviews are planned with local newspapers, television stations, and radio talk shows. These interviews will focus on human-interest stories, the company's vision and mission, and a belief in Prince Rupert's future. Subsequently, Frenz will regularly update local reporters and offer to contribute to a regular newspaper column on such topics as healthy eating, wine selection, and so on.

Lunches. Frenz will open with a lunch menu and a take-out service, expanding into dinner offerings after employees gain experience. The lunch menus, with $1-off coupons attached, will be liberally distributed to downtown offices. Frenz will have a loyalty program to encourage regular visits and a discount program for college and high school students. Lunch deliveries to offices will help distinguish Frenz, as in the case of the old Epicurean restaurant, from competitors who typically open at 4 p.m.

Take-Out Service. A take-out and delivery brochure, containing coupons for entrées and side dishes, will be delivered twice a year as a newspaper insert to North Coast households. A menu and a coupon for a side dish will be attached to each meal delivered or picked up. Distinctive signage will be attached to each delivery vehicle.

Customer Database. Serving staff and delivery personnel will ask patrons' permission to enter personal information into a database, with their names entered into a draw. If they so desire, patrons will be reminded by phone of upcoming anniversaries, birthdays, or special events in their lives.

Grand Opening. A grand opening party will celebrate the start of evening dining at Frenz. The restaurant could partner with a suitable charity, such as the SPCA, to use the grand opening as a fundraising event. A radio station, such as CHTK, could co-sponsor the fundraiser and provide an announcer to talk between songs and a live-on-location broadcast at a reduced price. Daytime activities could include a draw for a Vancouver weekend getaway, gourmet cooking classes, free samples, and fun activities for children. The evening dinner will be a black-tie fundraising event with suitable live entertainment, advertised by press releases, posters, and community event announcements. Tickets will be sold in advance at the usual locations.

Advertising. Frenz Steak and Seafood will sponsor the noon news of CHTK Radio for six months and place a one-third page advertisement in the Yellow Pages.

Children's Events. Serving staff will be selected for a distinctive personality and trained on catering to kids. Children will have separate menus, crayon placemats, birthday parties (e.g., a free ice cream treat and "happy birthday" sung by serving staff), and a wall for birthday photographs and artwork provided by kids.

Sponsorships. A small budget will be available to sponsor sports teams, youth activities, community events, and not-for-profit organizations. Donations will be in the form of gift certificates and food donations.

Fantasy Getaways. Three fantasy getaway promotions are planned for the first year during the dreary winter months: Hawaiian Luau, Amazon Adventure, and Valentines Day. Invitations will be mailed to regular customers and staff actively involved in organizing these fun events.

Visitor Promotions. Frenz will place advertisements in Tourism Prince Rupert promotional materials and drop off copies of its brochures at points of entry. A cross-promotion will be arranged with local motels, and regular visits to the Park Avenue Campground will help promote Frenz among overnight visitors.

7. Five-Year Financial Projections

The five-year financial forecast for Frenz Steak and Seafood is presented below:

	Projections ($ thousands)				
	Year 1	Year 2	Year 3	Year 4	Year 5
Restaurants	1	1	2	2	3
Revenue	$600	$800	$1400	$1600	$2200
Cost of Sales	222	296	518	592	814
Labour Costs	186	248	434	496	682
Other Costs	144	192	336	384	528
Operating Profit	$48	$64	$112	$128	$176

The financial forecasts are prepared on the basis of conservative assumptions. Given the sophistication of the marketing plan and the restaurant concept, the forecasted sales figures are probably too low.

All the marketing mix decisions covered in the just-described marketing program have both revenue and expense effects. These are summarized in this section of the marketing plan. See Appendix B.

Because this table is very short, it is woven into the text, rather than given a figure number and title.

The five-year financial projections are often based on judgment forecasts. Gross revenue and then operating profit—critical to the restaurant's survival—are also projected. Often times, multiple forecasts using different forecast scenarios are included in the appendix to the plan.

The Organization of Frenz Steak and Seafood appears here. It reflects the bare-bones organizational structure of successful small businesses. Often a more elaborate marketing plan will show the new positions expected to be added as the firm grows. See Chapter 19.

The Implementation Plan shows how the company will turn plans into results. Action-item lists are often used to set deadlines and assign responsibilities for the many tactical marketing decisions needed to enter a new market. See Chapter 19.

8. Organization

The organizational structure for the fifth year of operation is summarized in Figure 4. Initially, the management structure will simple, consisting of a President/CEO and a Restaurant Manager. Later, as the operation expands, the restaurant manager will assume the role of Vice-President of Operations, overseeing the operation of all restaurants.

FIGURE 4. Organization Chart, Year 5

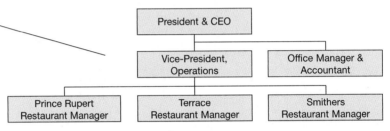

9. Implementation Plan

The task of opening a new restaurant, particularly one that targets several market segments, is a complex one. As any restaurant has only one chance to make a first impression, each Frenz restaurant will be opened in two stages over a period of two to three months.

Lunch menus and pickup and take-out services will be first offered. These services are straightforward in terms of staffing and the range of menu items. Once these operations begin to run smoothly, the grand opening for evening dining is planned for each location. The expected schedule of restaurant openings is summarized in Figure 5.

FIGURE 5. Schedule of Restaurant Openings

Community	Year
Prince Rupert	2005
Terrace	2007
Smithers	2009

The essence of Evaluation and Control is comparing actual sales with the targeted values set in the plan and taking appropriate actions. See Chapter 19.

10. Evaluation and Control

Annual budgets will be prepared for each restaurant and the overall operation. Actual sales and expenses will be compared with these targets and variances investigated. Weekly sales by product category will be tracked and the results of each promotional activity evaluated.

Management will work with each restaurant to modify tactical marketing campaigns as required, adapting the marketing mix to the unique nature of each community. The speed of the chain's expansion will depend on the sales and financial performance in each community served.

Appendix A: Biographical Sketches of Key Personnel

Appendix B: Detailed Financial Projections

Various appendices may appear at the end of the plan, depending on the purpose and audience for them. For example, resumes of key personnel or detailed financial spreadsheets often appear in appendices. For space reasons, these are not shown here.

iPod

10,000 songs* in your pocket. Works with Mac® or PC. The new iPod.™

CHAPTER 3

SCANNING THE MARKETING ENVIRONMENT

LEARNING OBJECTIVES

After reading this chapter, you should be able to:

1 Explain how environmental scanning provides information about social, economic, technological, competitive, and regulatory forces.

2 Describe how social forces, such as demographics, and culture and economic forces, such as macroeconomic conditions and consumer income, affect marketing.

3 Describe how technological changes can affect marketing.

4 Discuss the forms of competition that exist in a market, key components of competition, and the impact of competition on corporate structures.

5 Explain the major legislation that ensures competition and protects consumers in Canada.

IT'S SHOW TIME!

Don't blink, because the world of entertainment is changing faster than anyone imagined possible. Online music, high-definition televisions, digital photography, computer-based media centres, and software for making movies are just some of the many products new to the entertainment industry. The revolution began with the combination of Apple's iPod music player, which can store 10 000 songs in a device smaller than a deck of cards, and its iTunes Music Store, which sells more than 10 000 000 songs each month for just $0.99 each. Other new forms of digital entertainment products include digital video recorders (DVRs), which record TV shows on hard drives instead of tape, and home entertainment "hubs," which utilize wireless networks to link digital devices from around the home. And now there is even an iPod for movies.

Suddenly, the music, television, photography, movie, and computer industries are converging. Musicians, recording companies, television networks, camera companies, movie studios, computer companies, retail stores, and consumers like you are part of a completely different entertainment marketplace. How did this happen? The marketing environment changed!

First, consumers changed. They gradually made it clear that they preferred more convenient and customer-friendly approaches to purchasing music, television programming, movies, and photographs. Second, technology changed. High-speed Internet became available to millions of users, computers with improved storage capabilities and CD burners were introduced, high-resolution displays became smaller and less expensive, and file-transfer software was developed. Third, the regulatory environment changed. You may remember the first file-sharing service, Napster, was sued by the recording industry and ordered to stop helping users exchange copyrighted material. The ruling led to new agreements between music labels and such services as iTunes and sparked a worldwide debate about copyright protection. Finally, competitive forces have changed. Such companies as Disney, Pixar, Apple, Hewlett-Packard, Sony, Napster, A&M Records, and many others are now in an environment where they might be competitors or partners. Apple, for example, has created a partnership that allows Hewlett-Packard to resell its music player under the HP brand, but it is competing with Microsoft, Sony, and RealNetworks to become the industry standard in the music-downloading business. All of these changes, and the trends they suggest, led one expert to predict that "how we watch movies, look at photos, listen to music, even read a book promises to change profoundly in the next decade."[1]

Many businesses operate in environments where important forces change. Anticipating and responding to changes, such as those experienced by the entertainment industry, often means the difference between marketing success and failure. This chapter describes how the marketing environment has changed in the past and how it is likely to change in the future.

■ ■ ■
ENVIRONMENTAL SCANNING IN THE NEW MILLENNIUM

environmental scanning
The process of continually acquiring information on events occurring outside the organization to identify and interpret potential trends.

Changes in the marketing environment are a source of opportunities and threats to be managed. The process of continually acquiring information on events occurring outside the organization to identify and interpret potential trends is called **environmental scanning**.

Tracking Environmental Trends

Environmental trends typically arise from five sources: social, economic, technological, competitive, and regulatory forces. As shown in Figure 3–1 and described later in this chapter, these forces affect the marketing activities of a firm in numerous ways. To illustrate how environmental scanning is used, consider the following trend:

> Coffee industry marketers have observed that the percentage of adults who drink coffee has declined from 75 percent in 1962 to 51 percent in 2003. Age-specific analysis, however, indicates that the percentage of 18- to 24-year-olds who drink coffee has risen from 19 percent in 1998 to 29 percent today.[2]

What types of businesses are likely to be influenced by this trend? What future would you predict for coffee?

■ FIGURE 3–1 ■
Environmental forces affecting the organization as well as its suppliers and customers

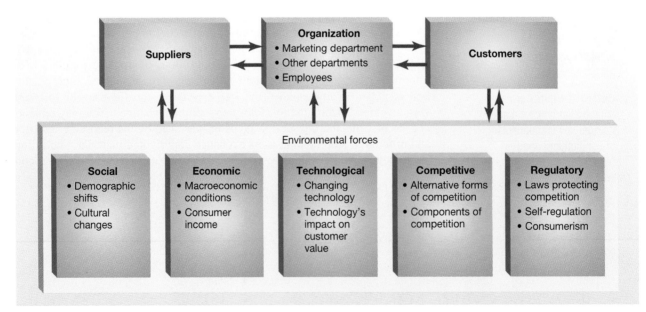

You may have concluded that this trend is likely to influence coffee manufacturers, coffee shops, and supermarkets. If so, you are absolutely correct—manufacturers have responded by offering new flavours and seasonal blends, coffee shops are automating to prepare drinks faster, and supermarkets have added coffee boutiques and gourmet brands to try to reverse the trend. Predicting the future of coffee requires assumptions about the number of years the trends will continue and the rate of increase or decline in various age groups. Did you consider these issues in your analysis? Because experts make different assumptions, their forecasts range from a 30-percent decline to a 7-percent increase by 2008, a range that probably includes your forecast.

Environmental scanning also involves explaining trends. Why has coffee consumption been declining? One explanation is that consumers are switching from coffee to other beverages, such as soft drinks, juices, or water. This idea is supported by the fact that soft drink consumption has increased from 87 litres per person in 1970 to 204 litres in 2003. Another explanation is that preferences have shifted to more expensive types of coffee, and consumers have reduced their use to maintain the same level of expenditure. Identifying and interpreting trends, such as the decline in coffee consumption, and developing explanations, such as those offered in this paragraph, are essential to successful environmental scanning.[3]

An Environmental Scan of Canada

What other trends might affect marketing in the future? A firm conducting an environmental scan of the marketplace might uncover key trends, such as those listed in Figure 3–2 for each of the five environmental factors.[4] Although the list of trends is far from complete, it reveals the breadth of an environmental scan—from the growing diversity of the Canadian population, the shift to the service-sector economy, to the increasing use of wireless technology. These trends affect consumers and the businesses and organizations that serve them. Such trends are covered as the five environmental forces are described in the following pages.

■ **FIGURE 3–2** ■

An environmental scan of
Canada's marketplace

ENVIRONMENTAL FORCE	TREND IDENTIFIED BY AN ENVIRONMENTAL SCAN
Social	• Declining differences in gender roles and buying patterns • Growing diversity of the Canadian population • Aging • Obesity
Economic	• Shift to service-sector economy • Growth in electronic commerce • Increase in savings and money management as many workers approach retirement
Technological	• Increasing use of wireless broadband technology • The dramatic growth of the open source (free) software movement, started by Linux • Advances in biotechnology, cosmetic surgery, and cancer drugs
Competitive	• The growing influence of China as the world leader in technology manufacturing • Mergers and acquisitions to create scale and improve competitiveness • Increased focus on empowering workers to improve performance
Regulatory	• New legislation related to digital copyright, intellectual property protection, and consumer privacy • Increased emphasis on free trade • Deregulation of industries to encourage competition

■ ■ ■
SOCIAL FORCES

social forces
Forces of the environment that include the demographic characteristics of the population and its values.

demographics
The study of the characteristics of a human population. These characteristics include population size, growth rate, gender, marital status, ethnicity, income, and so forth.

The **social forces** of the environment include the demographic characteristics of the population and its values. Changes in these forces can have a dramatic impact on marketing strategy.

Demographics

Demographics is the study of the characteristics of a human population. These characteristics include population size, growth rate, gender, marital status, ethnicity, income, and so forth. Several organizations, such as the United Nations, monitor the world population profile, while other organizations, such as Statistics Canada, provide information on the Canadian population.

The World Population at a Glance   The most recent estimates indicate that there are 6.3 billion people in the world today and that the population is likely to grow to 9 billion by 2050. While this growth has led to the term *population explosion,* the increases have not occurred worldwide—they are primarily in the developing countries of Africa, Asia, and Latin America. In fact, India is predicted to have the world's largest population in 2050 with 1.6 billion people, and China will be a close second with 1.3 billion people. Figure 3–3 shows the declining proportion of the world's population in North America, Europe, Australia, and Japan.[5]

Another important global trend is the shifting age structure of the world population. It is expected that the number of people older than 65 will more than double in the coming decades, while the number of youth will grow at a much lower rate. Again, the magnitude of this trend varies by region, and the developed countries such as Canada are expected to face a high growth rate of the elderly age group. Global income levels and living standards have also been increasing, although the averages across countries are very different. Per capita income, for example, ranges from $43 000 in Luxembourg, to $24 000 in Canada, to $800 in Afghanistan.

For marketers, such global trends have many implications. Obviously, the relative size of such countries as India and China will mean they represent huge markets for many product categories. Elderly populations in the developed countries are likely to save less and begin spending their funds on health care, travel, and other retirement-related products and services. Economic progress in the developing countries will lead to growth in entrepreneurship, new markets for infrastructure related to manufacturing, communication, and distribution, and the growth of exports.[6]

■ **FIGURE 3–3** ■■

The changing distribution of the world population

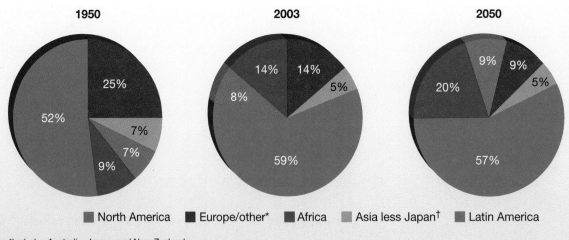

*Includes Australia, Japan, and New Zealand.
†Includes Oceania except for Australia and New Zealand.

The Canadian Population   Studies of the demographic characteristics of the Canadian population suggest several important trends. Generally, the population of Canada is becoming older and more diverse. In 2006, the Canadian population has been estimated at slightly over 32 million. The population of Canada is expected to be over 33 million by 2011.[7] With Canada's declining birth rate, the principal source of growth in the Canadian population will be from immigration, which will add even more diversity to the Canadian population.

If current trends in the life expectancy, birth rates, and immigration continue, niche markets based on age, life stage, family structure, geographic location, and ethnicity will become increasingly important. The global trend toward an older population is particularly true in Canada. For example, by 2011, almost 15 percent of the Canadian population will be over the age of 65, while only 10 percent of the population will be between 0 and 9 years of age.[8]

baby boomers

The generation of those born between 1946 and 1964.

Generational Cohorts   A major reason for the greying of Canada is that the **baby boomers**—the generation of those born between 1946 and 1964—are growing older. As the baby boomers have aged, their participation in the workforce and their earnings have increased, making them an important consumer market. This group accounts for the majority of the purchases in most consumer product and service categories. In the future, baby boomers' interests will reflect concern for their children and grandchildren, their own health and retirement, and companies will need to position products to respond to these interests. Generally, baby boomers are receptive to anything that makes them look and feel younger. Olay's Total Effects product line, for example, includes anti-aging moisturizers, cleansing cloths, and restoration treatments designed for this age group. This aging baby boomer group is also starting to experience health problems related to aging, such as incontinence and erectile dysfunction (ED). In fact, there is a heated ED marketing war in Canada as drug companies vie for share in a $150 million ED drug market.

Generation X

The population of those born between 1965 and 1976.

The baby boom cohort is followed by **Generation X**, which includes the population of those born between 1965 and 1976. This group represents about 15 percent of the Canadian population. This period is also known as the "baby bust" because the number of children born each year was declining during that period. This is a generation of consumers who are self-reliant, entrepreneurial, supportive of ethnic diversity, and better educated than any previous generation. They are not prone to extravagance and are likely to pursue lifestyles that are a blend of caution, pragmatism, and traditionalism. For example, Generation X is saving, planning for

Which generational cohorts are these advertisers trying to reach?

Generation Y
Those born between 1977 and 1994.

retirement, and taking advantage of retirement plans much earlier than did the boomer generation. As the baby boomers move into grandparenthood, Generation X is becoming the new parent market. In response, some brands that Generation X helped popularize are expanding their offerings. Tommy Hilfiger and DKNY, for example, have launched children's lines for the babies of Generation X parents.

The generational cohort labelled **Generation Y** includes those born between 1977 and 1994. This was a period of increasing births, which resulted from baby boomers having children, and is often referred to as the "echo-boom" or "baby boomlet." Generation Y exerts influence on music, sports, computers, videogames, and especially wireless phones. Generation Y views wireless communication as a lifeline to friends and family and has been the first to use text messaging, wireless phone games, and built-in cameras. This is also the group that includes recent and future 21-year-olds—the beginning of adult responsibilities and many new consumer activities. The accompanying Marketing NewsNet box describes some of the important changes that many "Gen Ys" face.[9] The term *millennials* is also used, with inconsistent definitions, to refer to younger members of Generation Y and sometimes to those born since 1994.

Because the members of each generation are distinctive in their attitudes and consumer behaviour, marketers have been studying the many groups or cohorts that make up the marketplace and have developed *generational marketing* programs for them. For example, Toyota Canada recently developed a spin-off company to develop and market a new brand of vehicles called Scion to appeal to the Generation Y group while still marketing their traditional brands, such as the Toyota Camry to the baby boomers. In addition, global marketers have discovered that many of the Canadian generational differences also exist outside of Canada.[10]

The Canadian Family   The types of families in Canada are changing in both size and structure. The average family size in Canada is about three persons. In 1971, one in three Canadian families consisted of the once-typical scenario of a husband working outside the home, with a wife inside the home with their children. Today, only one in seven families fall into this category. The dual-income family is the norm in Canada, representing almost 65 percent of all husband–wife families.

blended family
Family formed by the merging into a single family of two previously separated units.

About 50 percent of all first marriages in Canada end in divorce. Thus, the single-parent family is also becoming more typical and is more socially acceptable. But the majority of divorced people eventually remarry, giving rise to the **blended family**,

MARKETING NEWSNET   **IDEAS AHEAD**   Generation Y is Turning 21

There are several million members of the Generational Y cohort. About 20 percent of them have already reached the age of 21, and the rest are not far behind. Why is this important? Because much more than legal privileges begin when someone turns 21. The transition to adulthood signals a period when many people graduate from university or college, look for their first full-time job, start forming their own households, purchase their first new car and home, and select savings and retirement funds. They also begin developing brand loyalties that could last a lifetime. As a result, 21-year-olds are just beginning a path of extraordinary influence on the marketplace.

Generation Y is known as a savvy, demanding, and sometimes marketing-skeptical group, and so marketers are eager to better understand them. By the time these individuals reach 21 years of age, they have received millions of advertisements; spent thousands of dollars; and probably have taken out a credit card in their names. Of course, marketers know there is a lot more to know about these 21-year-olds. But if they watch them closely, they may see some opportunities to design and deliver unique product and service offerings to cater to this group, and, of course, produce some more ads designed exclusively with them in mind!

one formed by the merging into a single family of two previously separated units. Today, many Canadians are finding themselves as a step-parent, step-child, step-sibling, or some other member of a blended family. In fact, Hallmark Cards specially designs cards and verses for such blended families. But many people do not remarry, and single-parent families now represent almost 20 percent of all family units in Canada.

Population Shifts   Since the mid-1970s there had been a major shift in the Canadian population from rural to urban areas. In fact, more than 80 percent of Canadians are urban dwellers. Most Canadians live in **census metropolitan areas** (CMAs), geographic labour markets having a population of 100 000 persons or more. About 65 percent of the Canadian population is located in the top 27 CMAs in the country, which include such cities as Toronto, Montreal, Vancouver, Ottawa, and Edmonton. Moreover, four major urban regions are emerging in Canada, representing over 50 percent of the Canadian population. These important regions are the Golden Horseshoe in Ontario (Oshawa, Toronto, Hamilton, and St. Catherines–Niagara, Kitchener, Guelph, and Barrie); Montreal and adjacent regions (Salaberry-de-Valleyfield, Saint-Jean-sur-Richelieu, Saint-Hyacinthe, Sorel, Joliette, and Lachute); British Columbia's Lower Mainland and southern Vancouver Island; and the Calgary–Edmonton corridor. With the concentration of the population in or near the CMAs and key urban regions, marketers can reach large segments of the Canadian population efficiently and effectively.

census metropolitan areas
Geographic labour markets having a population of 100 000 persons or more.

Ethnic Diversity   While we often think of Canada as consisting of French and English Canadians, close to 3 out of 10 Canadians are of neither French nor British descent. While the majority of the non-British, non-French populations are of European descent, there has been a major growth in other ethnic groups and visible minorities in Canada. In fact, 80 different ethnic groups are represented in Canada. And, close to 70 percent of all immigrants to Canada are now classified as visible minorities, primarily people from China, Southeast Asia, Africa, and India. Visible minorities are projected to represent between 21 and 25 percent of the Canadian population by 2017. The largest groups will be South Asians, Chinese, and Blacks.[11]

Much of the ethnic population in Canada can be found in major metropolitan cities, such as Toronto, Vancouver, Montreal, Calgary, and Edmonton. Close to 20 percent of the populations in those cities register their native language as something other than English or French. Marketers have recognized the growing ethnic diversity in Canada and have developed **multicultural marketing** programs, which are combinations of the marketing mix that reflect the unique attitudes, ancestry, communication preferences, and lifestyles of ethnic Canadians. For example, HSBC Bank, the Royal Bank, and Bell Canada, all engage in multicultural marketing. CIBC actually has an Aboriginal banking unit that develops multicultural marketing programs to cater to Aboriginal clients. Even Canadian retailers, such as Sears Canada, IKEA, and The Brick, have responded to the growing ethnic population in Canada by developing and executing new multicultural marketing programs.[12]

multicultural marketing
Combinations of the marketing mix that reflect the unique attitudes, ancestry, communication preferences, and lifestyles of ethnic Canadians.

culture
The set of values, ideas, and attitudes that are learned and shared among the members of a group.

Ford and CIBC are companies that engage in multicultural marketing in Canada.

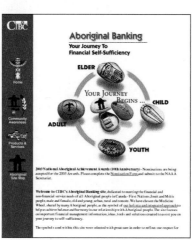

Culture

A second social force, **culture**, incorporates the set of values, ideas, and attitudes that are learned and shared among the members of a group. Because many of the elements of culture influence consumer buying patterns, monitoring national and global cultural trends in important in marketing. Cross-cultural analysis needed for global marketing is discussed in Chapter 7. Some noteworthy cultural trends in Canada are discussed here.

Changing Attitudes and Values In recent years, Canadians have experienced notable cultural changes that have affected consumer attitudes and values. For example, attitudes toward work, lifestyles, and consumption are evolving. For example, more than 65 percent of Canadian women work outside the home. In fact, women now make up over 46 percent of the Canadian labour force. But with more working women, the number of tasks to do is expanding, while the time available to do them is shrinking. This has led to the phenomenon of *time poverty*. Therefore, many Canadian consumers, particularly working women, are living harried lives and want to do business with companies that can offer them greater convenience. Many businesses are responding by offering express lanes of checkouts, longer store hours, drive-through windows, delivery services, and electronic shopping. Sobey's Inc., a major supermarket, offers its time-pressed shoppers the convenience of one-stop shopping, including groceries, in-store pharmacies, wellness centres, and banking services. The Hudson's Bay Company offers its customers the option of shopping in its retail stores or on the Internet via its online store HBC.com. The Bay and Imperial Oil have teamed up to allow customers to use The Bay and Zellers credit cards at Esso stations across Canada. Esso even allows customers to pay for their purchases with its electronic "Speedpass" payment system.

Companies are also creating new products to meet the convenience imperative demanded by consumers. From soup to desserts, products now come in hands-free versions for easier consumption. The concept of "dashboard dining" is now a major trend in the food industry with car-friendly products and packaging popping up everywhere. The Campbell Soup Company, for example, now offers "Soup at Hand" for the busy commuter.[13]

Many Canadians are changing their attitudes toward health. Fitness activity and sports participation are on the rise. Many Canadians are also changing their eating habits. Sales of low-fat, no-fat, low-carb, and organic foods are growing. Quiznos, for example, now offers 20 new low-carb subs. Many Canadians are drinking healthier beverages including bottled water and juices, instead of traditional soft drinks. Health-conscious Canadians are also buying more health supplements and medical self-diagnostic kits. For example, sales of multivitamins and calcium supplements are soaring, and such brands as Centrum, Shoppers Drug Mart's Life brand, and Roots Canada's vitamin lines are enjoying growth. Lifescan Canada is doing well with its self-testing kits that can monitor cholesterol or test for colorectal cancer.

Responding to consumer demand for value, Sobeys offers a value-based line of products that come with a low-price guarantee.

However, while some Canadians are trying to be more healthy, the medical community suggests that obesity is becoming a major public health threat. In fact, obesity in Canada is reaching epidemic proportions and is even showing up in young children. Some firms are responding to this trend by marketing plus-sized clothing. In fact, Canadian retailers report clothing sales to larger women are growing three times the overall rate.[14]

value consciousness
The concern for obtaining the best quality, features, and performance of a product or service for a given price.

Another change in the attitudes of Canadians is the trend toward **value consciousness**—or the concern for obtaining the best quality, features, and performance of a product or service for a given price. Innovative marketers have responded to this new orientation in numerous ways. Holiday Inn Worldwide offers customers Holiday Express Hotels, which feature comfortable accommodations with room rates lower the traditional Holiday Inns. Sobey's Inc., one of Canada's top food retailers, offers customers its Smart Choice brand of products, which is a private-label, value-based line that comes with a low-price guarantee. Canada's major banks offer lower-interest credit cards, some with value-added enhancements, such as frequent flyer programs and cash-back offers. Even Canada's sports and entertainment industries are appealing to the value-conscious customer. For example, the Toronto Blue Jays are now promoting the value and affordability of attending the SkyDome (now Rogers Centre) to watch professional baseball.[15]

CONCEPT CHECK

1. Describe three generational cohorts.

2. Why are many companies developing multicultural marketing programs?

3. What is a census metropolitan area?

■ ■ ■
ECONOMIC FORCES

economy
Pertains to the income, expenditures, and resources that affect the cost of running a business and household.

The second component of the environmental scan, the **economy**, pertains to the income, expenditures, and resources that affect the cost of running a business and household. We will consider two aspects of these economic forces: a macroeconomic view of the marketplace and a microeconomic perspective of consumer income.

Macroeconomic Conditions

Of particular concern at the macroeconomic level is the inflationary or recessionary state of the economy, whether actual or perceived by consumers or businesses. In an inflationary economy, the cost to produce and buy products and services escalates as prices increase. From a marketing standpoint, if prices rise faster than consumer incomes do, the number of items consumers can buy decreases.

Whereas inflation is a period of price increases, recession is a time of slow economic activity. Businesses decrease production, unemployment rises, and many consumers have less money to spend. The Canadian economy experienced recessions in the early 1970s, early 1980s, and early 1990s. The Canadian economy was relatively healthy in the late 1990s, but with the dot-com collapse in 2000, the "new economy" evaporated, triggering an economic slowdown beginning in 2001. The Canadian economy is now showing signs of recovery but is still considered a slow-growth economy. The Conference Board of Canada is forecasting low rates of inflation, lower employment, and lower growth in the gross domestic product (GDP) for 2006–2008.

Assessing consumer expectations of an inflationary and recessionary economy is an important element of environmental scanning. Consumer spending, which accounts for two-thirds of Canadian economic activity, is affected by expectations of the future. Surveys of consumer expectations are tracked over time by researchers, who ask such questions as "Do you expect to be better off or worse off financially a year from now?" Surveyors record the share of positive and negative responses to this question and related ones to develop an index, sometimes called a consumer confidence or consumer sentiment index. The higher the index, the more favourable are consumer expectations. Many firms evaluate such indexes in order to plan production levels. DaimlerChrysler, for example, uses such indexes to plan its automobile production levels in order to avoid overproducing cars during a recessionary economy.

Consumer Income

The microeconomic trends in terms of consumer income are also important issues for marketers. Having a product that meets the needs of consumers may be of little value if they are unable to purchase it. A consumer's ability to buy is related to income, which consists of gross, disposable, and discretionary components.

gross income
The total amount of money made in one year by a person, household, or family unit.

Gross Income   The total amount of money made in one year by a person, household, or family unit is referred to as **gross income**. Average gross family income in Canada is slightly over 72 000. But family income in Canada varies by province as well as by the education level and profession of the head(s) of the family. For example, the majority of families earning $75 000 or more are headed by university graduates. It also varies by province and territory. Read the WebLink box to learn about the median family income in your province or territory.

disposable income
The money a consumer has left after paying taxes to use for such necessities as food, shelter, clothing, and transportation.

Disposable Income   The second income component, **disposable income**, is the money a consumer has left after paying taxes to use for such necessities as food, shelter, clothing, and transportation. Thus, if taxes rise at a faster rate than does disposable income, consumers must economize. The average Canadian household saw about 20 percent of their expenditures go to personal income tax, while food, shelter, clothing, and transportation accounted for over 47 percent of total household expenditures. The cost of transportation has now outstripped the cost of food, with transportation accounting for over 13 percent of total household expenditures, while food accounted for only 11 percent. The cost of automobiles and their maintenance, as well as rising fuel costs, explain the spike in transportation costs.[16]

discretionary income
The money that remains after paying for taxes and necessities.

Discretionary Income   The third component of income is **discretionary income**, the money that remains after paying for taxes and necessities. Discretionary income is used for luxury items, such as vacations at a Four Seasons resort. An obvious problem in defining discretionary versus disposable income is determining whether something is a luxury or a necessity. Observation can be a way to make this determination—if a family has Royal Doulton china, Rolex watches, and Lexus

WEBLINK
HTTP://WWW.MCGRAWHILL.CA/
COLLEGE/CRANE

Family Income in Canada by Province and Territory

Obviously, marketers collect and use environmental information to better understand consumers. One key aspect of an environmental scan is to collect and compare economic data about particular markets or market segments. In general, marketers will want to look at what is "typical" or "average" about the entire population. However, they also want to look at any differences that might exist. As

the text stated earlier the average or median family income in Canada varies by province and territory. Go to the Statistics Canada Web site (www12.statcan.ca/english/census01/products/highlights/income) to find out what the median family income is for your home province and territory. What are the implications to marketers if your province or territory is above or below the median?

As consumers' discretionary income increases, so does the enjoyment of pleasure travel.
Four Seasons Hotels
www.fourseasons.com

automobiles, one could assume that they have, or had, discretionary income. Still, it is important to note that a product defined as a necessity by one individual may be viewed as a luxury by another. For example, some Canadians view a microwave oven as a necessity, while others see it as a luxury item.

■ ■ ■
TECHNOLOGICAL FORCES

technology
Inventions or innovations from applied science or engineering research.

Our society is in a period of dramatic technological change. **Technology**, the third environmental force, refers to inventions or innovations from applied science or engineering research. Each new wave of technological innovation can replace existing products and companies. Do you recognize the items pictured on the next page and what they may replace?

Technology of Tomorrow

Technological change is the result of research, and so it is difficult to predict. Some of the most dramatic technological changes occurring now, however, include the following:

Technological change leads to new products. What products might be replaced by these innovations?

1. Advances in nanotechnology, the science of unimaginably small electronics, will lead to smaller microprocessors, efficient fuel cells, and cancer-detection sensors.
2. High-definition televisions and programming will become the industry standard.
3. In the next five years, as much as 50 percent of all telephone calls could be made over the Internet.
4. Companies will begin building software databases so that lines of code can be "reused."

These trends in technology are already seen in today's marketplace. Cablevision recently launched a high-definition-only service called Voom, which carries 25 high-definition (HD) channels. Voice over Internet protocol (VoIP) companies, such as Vonage, offer very low-cost, over-the-Internet telephone services, and Xerox has already saved $30 million in two years by "reusing" software. Other such technologies as flash memory, music downloading services, and plasma screen televisions are likely to replace or substitute for existing products and services, such as floppy disks or compact disc recorders (CDRs), music stores and CDs, and televisions with cathode ray tubes (CRTs) or projection screens.[17]

Technology's Impact on Customer Value

Advances in technology are having important effects on marketing. First, the cost of technology is plummeting, causing the customer value assessment of technology-based products to focus on other such dimensions as quality, service, and relationships. When Plaxo introduced its address book software, it gave the product away at no charge, reasoning that satisfied customers would later buy upgrades and related products. A similar approach is now used by many cellular telephone vendors, who charge little for the telephone if the purchase leads to a telephone service contract.[18]

Technology also provides value through the development of new products. Many automobile manufacturers now offer customers a navigation system that uses satellite signals to help the driver reach any destination. Under development are radarlike collision avoidance systems that disengage cruise control, reduce the engine speed, and even apply the brakes.[19] Other new products likely to be available soon include a "smart ski" with an embedded microprocessor that will adjust the flexibility of the ski to snow conditions; injectable health monitors that will send glucose level,

Examples of recycling by rePlanet and precycling by Lever.

oxygen level, and other clinical information to a wristwatch-like monitor; and electronic books that will allow you to download any volume and view it on pages coated with electronic "ink" and embedded electrodes.[20]

Technology can also change existing products and the ways they are produced. Many companies are using technological developments to allow *recycling* products through the manufacturing cycle several times. The *Canadian Plastics Association* reports that grocery and trash plastic bags, for example, are being recycled to produce other plastic bags and even recycled into plastic lumber.[21] In Squamish, B.C., Moore Enviro Systems Inc. now produces shingles made of used tires called Moo Roof.[22] The roof comes with a 50-year warranty. Another approach is *precycling*—efforts by manufacturers to reduce waste by decreasing the amount of packaging they use. The development of new packaging materials, for example, has allowed DuPont to produce a collapsible pouch as an alternative to milk cartons in school lunch programs.[23]

Electronic Business Technologies

marketspace

An information- and communication-based electronic exchange environment mostly occupied by sophisticated computer and telecommunication technologies and digitized offerings.

The transformative power of technology may be best illustrated by the rapid growth of the **marketspace,** an information- and communication-based electronic exchange environment mostly occupied by sophisticated computer and telecommunication technologies and digitized offerings. Any activity that uses some form of electronic communication in the inventory, exchange, advertisement, distribution, and payment of goods and services is often called **electronic commerce.** Network technologies are now used for everything from filing expense reports, to monitoring daily sales, to sharing information with employees, to communicating instantly with suppliers.

electronic commerce

Any activity that uses some form of electronic communication in the inventory, exchange, advertisement, distribution, and payment of goods and services.

intranet

An Internet/Web-based network used within the boundaries of an organization.

Many companies have adapted Internet-based technology internally to support their electronic business strategies. An **intranet,** for example, is an Internet/Web-based network used within the boundaries of an organization. It is a private Internet that may or may not be connected to the public Internet. **Extranets,** which use Internet-based technologies, permit communication between a company and its supplier, distributors, and other partners (such as advertising agencies). The Marketing NewsNet box on the next page describes how the latest Internet development—the Wi-Fi revolution—is transforming the way companies do business.[24]

extranet

Uses Internet-based technologies, permit communication between a company and its supplier, distributors, and other partners.

COMPETITIVE FORCES

competition
Alternative firms that could provide a product to satisfy a specific market's needs.

The fourth component of the environmental scan, **competition,** refers to the alternative firms that could provide a product to satisfy a specific market's needs. There are various forms of competition, and each company must consider its present and potential competitors in designing its marketing strategy.

Alternative Forms of Competition

There are four basic forms of competition that form a continuum from pure competition to monopolistic competition to oligopoly to pure monopoly. Chapter 13 contains further discussions on pricing practices under these four forms of competition.

At one end of the continuum is *pure competition,* in which every company has a similar product. Companies that deal in commodities common to agribusiness (for example, wheat, rice, and grain) often are in a pure competition position, in which distribution (in the sense of shipping products) is important but other elements of marketing have little impact.

In the second point on the continuum, *monopolistic competition,* the many sellers compete with their products on a substitutable basis. For example, if the price of coffee rises too much, consumers may switch to tea. Coupons or sales are frequently used marketing tactics.

Oligopoly, a common industry structure, occurs when a few companies control the majority of industry sales. Because there are few sellers in an oligopolistic situation, price competition among firms is not desirable because it would lead to reduced revenue for all producers. Instead, nonprice competition is common, which means competing on other dimensions of the marketing mix, such as product quality, distribution, and/or promotion. Canada is sometimes referred to by some economists as the "land of oligopoly" because it has several major industries that can be considered oligopolistic, including the airline industry and the banking industry.

The final point on the continuum, *monopoly*, occurs when only one firm sells the product or service. It has been common for producers of goods and services considered essential to a community: water, electricity, or telephone service. Typically, marketing plays a small role in a monopolistic setting because it is regulated by a provincial or the federal government. Government control usually seeks to ensure price protection for the buyer.

Components of Competition

In developing a marketing program, companies must consider the factors that drive competition: entry, bargaining power of buyers and suppliers, existing rivalries, and substitution possibilities.[25] Scanning the environment requires a look at all of them. These factors relate to a firm's marketing mix decisions and may be used to create a barrier to entry, increase brand awareness, or intensify a fight for market share.

Entry   In considering the competition, a firm must assess the likelihood of new entrants. Additional producers increase industry capacity and tend to lower prices. A company scanning its environment must consider the possible **barriers to entry** for other firms, which are business practices or conditions that make it difficult for new firms to enter the market. Barriers to entry can be in the form of capital requirements, advertising expenditures, product identity, distribution access, or switching costs. The higher the expense of the barrier, the more likely it will deter new entrants.

barriers to entry
Business practices or conditions that make it difficult for new firms to enter the market.

Power of Buyers and Suppliers   A competitive analysis must consider the power of buyers and suppliers. Powerful buyers exist when they are few in number, there are low switching costs, or the product represents a significant share of the buyer's total costs. This last factor leads the buyer to exert significant pressure for price competition. A supplier gains power when the product is critical to the buyer and when it has built up the switching costs.

Existing Competitors and Substitutes   Competitive pressures among existing firms depend on the rate of industry growth. In slow-growth settings, competition is more heated for any possible gains in market share. High fixed costs also create competitive pressures for firms to fill production capacity. For example, airlines offer discounts for making early reservations and charge penalties for changes or cancellations in an effort to fill seats, which represent a high fixed cost.

Small Businesses as Competitors

While large companies provide familiar examples of the forms and components of competition, small businesses make up the majority of the competitive landscape for most businesses. In fact, in Canada there are over 2.7 million small- and medium-sized enterprises (SMEs), and they generate half of the country's total gross domestic product (GDP), employ 6 out of 10 Canadians, and create the bulk of all new jobs.[26] Economic growth in Canada is largely tied to the activities of SMEs, and entrepreneurs who start new businesses provide new competition for existing large companies.

CONCEPT CHECK

1. What is the difference between a consumer's disposable income and discretionary income?

2. How does technology impact customer value?

3. In pure competition, there are a _____ number of sellers.

■ ■ ■
REGULATORY FORCES

regulation
Restrictions the provincial and federal laws place on business with regard to the conduct of its activities.

For any organization, the marketing and broader business decisions are constrained, directed, and influenced by regulatory forces. **Regulation** consists of restrictions the provincial and federal laws place on business with respect to the conduct of its activities. Regulation exists to protect companies as well as consumers. Much of the regulation from the federal and provincial levels has been passed to ensure competition and fair business practices. For consumers, the focus of legislation is to protect them from unfair trade practices and ensure their safety.

Protecting Competition and Consumers

Legislation and regulations exist in Canada at all three levels of government—federal, provincial, and municipal—to protect and encourage a competitive environment, which is deemed desirable because it permits the consumer to determine which competitor will succeed and which will fail.

Competition Act
The key legislation designed to protect competition and consumers in Canada.

The Competition Act The key legislation designed to protect competition and consumers in Canada is the **Competition Act**, which replaced the Combines Investigation Act. The Combines legislation, in effect since 1923, has been found to be rather ineffectual. The Competition Act was introduced in two stages, in 1975 and 1986. The purpose of the Competition Act is:

> to maintain and encourage competition in Canada in order to promote the efficiency and adaptability of the Canadian economy, in order to expand opportunities for Canadian participation in world markets while at the same time recognizing the role of foreign competition in Canada, in order to ensure that small- and medium-sized enterprises have an equitable opportunity to participate in the Canadian economy and in order to provide consumers with competitive prices and product choices.[27]

In essence, the Act is designed to protect and to balance the interests of competitors and consumers. The Bureau of Competition Policy, which is part of Industry Canada, is responsible for administering and enforcing the provisions of the Act. The Act contains both criminal and noncriminal provisions.

Criminal offences under Part VI of the Act include conspiracy (e.g., price fixing), bid rigging, discriminatory and predatory pricing, price maintenance, and misleading or deceptive marketing practices, such as double ticketing or bait-and-switch selling.

Noncriminal reviewable matters under Part VIII of the Act include mergers, abuse of dominant position, refusal to deal, consignment selling, exclusive dealing, tied selling, market restriction, and delivered pricing. The Director of the Bureau of Competition Policy refers these matters to the Competition Tribunal under noncriminal law standards. The tribunal was established when the Act took effect and is governed by the Competition Tribunal Act. The tribunal adjudicates all reviewable matters under the Act.

Industry Canada is responsible for most of the legislation affecting business practices in Canada. Figure 3–4 lists the more significant federal legislation that protects competition and consumers in Canada. Marketers must also be cognizant of the fact that in addition to federal laws and regulations, there are many more at the provincial level. Many provinces have their own departments of consumer affairs in order to administer any such legislation and regulations enacted on the provincial government level.

Unfortunately, the laws and regulations at the provincial level vary from province to province. A marketer may find it necessary to adapt some aspect of the marketing mix or some broader business practice, depending on the province. For example, in Quebec, there are specific laws dealing with store signage, packaging, and labelling. Additionally, advertising directed toward children is prohibited in Quebec. Many

■ FIGURE 3–4 ■

Major federal legislation designed to protect competition and consumers

Bank Cost Borrowing Act	Hazardous Products Act
Bankruptcy Act	Income Tax Act
Bills of Exchange Act	Industrial Design Act
Board of Trade Act	Maple Products Industry Act
Broadcasting Act	Motor Vehicle Safety Act
Canada Agricultural Products	Offical Languages Act
Standards Act	Patent Act
Canada Cooperative Association Act	Personal Information and Electronic
Canada Corporations Act	Documents Act
Canada Dairy Products Act	Precious Metals Marketing Act
Canadian Human Rights Act	Privacy Act
Competition Act	Small Loans Act
Consumer Packaging and Labelling Act	Standards Council of Canada Act
Copyright Act	Textile Labelling Act
Criminal Code	The Interest Act
Department of Consumer and	Timber Marketing Act
Corporate Affairs Act	Trade-Marks Act
Electricity Inspection Act and Gas	True Labelling Act
Inspection Act	Weights and Measures Act
Fish Inspection Act	Winding-up Act
Food and Drugs Act	

provinces, including Quebec, also have consumer protection acts and/or business or trade practices acts.

Self-Regulation

self-regulation

An alternative to government control where an industry attempts to police itself.

The government has provided much legislation to create a competitive business climate and protect the consumer. An alternative to government control is **self-regulation**, where an industry attempts to police itself. The Canadian Broadcasting Association, whose members include major television networks and radio stations across the country, has a code of ethics that helps govern the conduct of its members in terms of protecting the consumer against deceptive trade practices, such as misleading advertising. Similarly, the Advertising Standards Council, the self-regulatory arm of the Canadian Advertising Foundation, has established the Canadian Code of Advertising Standards for its members to follow. The members of this organization consist of major advertising agencies that are responsible for allocating the bulk of advertising dollars in Canada. The Canadian Radio-television and Telecommunications Commission (CRTC), the federal agency responsible for licensing and regulating broadcasting in Canada, is in favour of greater industry self-regulation.

The Canadian Marketing Association, whose members represent 80 percent of direct-marketing sales in Canada, has mandated that its members comply with the consumer's right to privacy and honour consumers who request not to be contacted by telephone or mail for selling purposes. Critics argue that telemarketers in Canada demonstrate what is wrong with self-regulation efforts: noncompliance by members and enforcement.

Another well-known self-regulatory group is the Better Business Bureau (BBB). This organization is a voluntary alliance of companies whose goal is to help maintain fair business practices. Although the BBB has no legal power, it does try to use "moral suasion" to get members to comply with its regulations.

consumerism

A grassroots movement started in the 1960s to increase the influence, power, and rights of consumers in dealing with institutions.

Consumerism

Regulation by government and self-regulation by industry help in protecting the consumer in the marketplace. But the consumer can also play a direct and active role. **Consumerism** is a movement to increase the influence, power, and rights of consumers in dealing with institutions. Modern consumerism in Canada and the United States really began in the 1960s. U.S. President John F. Kennedy, in a speech entitled "Consumer Bill of Rights," outlined four basic consumer rights: (1) the right to safety, (2) the right to be informed, (3) the right to choose, and (4) the right to be heard. Although not passed as laws, these proclaimed rights serve as the basis for modern consumerism. Shortly after President Kennedy's Consumer Bill of Rights was unveiled in the United States, the Canadian government formed the Department of Consumer and Corporate Affairs, making it the agency responsible for protecting consumers and regulating corporate activities.

Canada also has many independent consumer organizations that advance the cause of consumerism. The Consumers Association of Canada (CAC) is the largest consumer group working on behalf of the Canadian consumer. The CAC serves as a channel for supplying consumers' views to government and industry, providing consumer information, and studying consumer problems and presenting recommended solutions to those problems. In addition to ensuring that the four original consumer rights are protected, the consumer movement also includes consumer demands for environmentally safe products and ethical and socially responsible business practices, including the right to privacy.

The Privacy Act (PA) and Personal Information Protection and Electronic Documents Act (PIPEDA) were enacted by the federal government to protect Canadian citizens' privacy and to ensure that information on individuals is collected, used and disclosed legally and ethically. However, recent research shows that 80 percent of Canadians are unaware of this legislation.[28] Yet, Canadian consumers are concerned

ETHICS AND SOCIAL RESPONSIBILITY ALERT

Protecting Canadian Consumers' Privacy

While new legislation is in place to protect consumer privacy in Canada, some argue that companies should go beyond the legal letter of the law to ensure consumer rights with regard to privacy. Amanda Maltby, an authority on privacy, and vice-president of Public Affairs and Communications at the Canadian Marketing Association, has some advice for marketers in terms of the ethical and responsible use of consumer information. She suggests that every organization should designate a privacy officer who will be responsible for ensuring that the organization complies with privacy laws. She also suggests that companies should clearly identify how they intend to use customer data, now and in the future, and receive consent from the customer for the collection, use, and disclosure of personal information. If marketing lists are to be made available to third parties, companies must obtain consent from customers. The collection of personal information should also be limited to that which is necessary for the purposes identified by the organization, such as maintaining service records.

Marketers are also obligated to keep personal information on customers as accurate, complete, and up-to-date as possible. Safeguards should be in place for protecting customer information to ensure against unauthorized access, alteration, or use. Organizations should be prepared to publicize their information-handling practices through all customer touch points in their business. All staff should also be trained regarding the privacy policies of the organization. Consumers should be made aware that they have a right to know if the marketers holds personal information about them, and such information needs to be made available to the customer on request. The consumer also has a right to correct erroneous information. Finally, an organization must establish formal inquiry and complaint-handling mechanisms and make sure that these procedures are known to the consumers who inquire or complain.

Maltby suggests that all organizations need to adhere to these principles in order to comply with the law. Moreover, they should go beyond the minimal requirements set by law in order to ensure consumer rights to privacy as well as give consumers confidence in the organization's ability to safeguard personal information. What are your thoughts regarding consumer privacy rights in Canada? Do Maltby's principles go far enough? What other obligations do firms have regarding the protection of customer privacy?

about their privacy. Canadian companies that have collected or are collecting customer information should be proactive and responsible to ensure customer privacy. In fact, some experts suggest this should be top priority for organizations. See the Ethics and Social Responsibility Alert box for a discussion of this topic.[29]

CONCEPT CHECK

1. The _____ Act is the most important legislation designed to protect competition and consumers in Canada.

2. An alternative to legislation protecting competition and consumers is self-_____ .

3. What is consumerism?

■ ■ ■

CHAPTER IN REVIEW

1 *Explain how environmental scanning provides information about social, economic, technological, competitive, and regulatory forces.*

Many businesses operate in environments where important forces change. Environmental scanning is the process of acquiring information about these changes to allow marketers to identify and interpret trends. There are five environmental forces businesses must monitor: social, economic, technological, competitive, and regulatory. By identifying trends related to each of these forces, businesses can develop and maintain successful marketing programs. Several trends that most businesses are monitoring include the growing diversity of the Canadian population, the increasing use of wireless technology, and new legislation related to consumer privacy.

2 *Describe how social forces, such as demographics, and culture and economic forces, such as macroeconomic conditions and consumer income, affect marketing.*

Demographic information helps describe the world population, the Canadian population, generational cohorts, such as baby boomers, Generation X, and Generation Y, the structure of the Canadian family, and ethnic diversity. Ethnic diversity, for example, has led to multicultural marketing programs in Canada. Cultural trends in Canada indicate that many individuals are suffering from time poverty and are more interested in health and fitness. Still, obesity persists and is a public health problem. Economic forces include the strong relationship between consumers' expectations about the economy and their spending.

3 *Describe how technological changes can affect marketing.*

Technological innovations can replace existing products and services. Digital cameras, for example, have reduced the need for film, and music-downloading services are changing how consumers buy music. Changes in technology can also have an impact on consumer value by reducing the cost of products, improving the quality of products, and providing new products that were not previously feasible. Electronic commerce, including the Wi-Fi revolution, is transforming the way companies do business.

4 *Discuss the forms of competition that exist in the market, key components of competition, and the impact of small businesses as competitors.*

There are four forms of competition: pure competition, monopolistic competition, oligopoly, and monopoly. The key components of component include the likelihood of new competitors, the power of buyers and suppliers, and the presence of competitors and possible substitutes. While large companies are often used as examples of marketplace competitors, there are over two million small- and medium-sized enterprises in Canada that have a significant impact on the economy and the competitive landscape.

5 *Explain the major legislation that ensures competition and protects consumers in Canada.*

Regulation exists to protect competition and consumers. The key legislation in Canada that ensures a competitive marketplace and consumer protection is the Competition Act. Self-regulation through such organizations as the Canadian Marketing Association and the Better Business Bureau provides an alternative to federal and provincial regulations.

■ ■ ■
FOCUSING ON KEY TERMS

baby boomers p. 71
barriers to entry p. 81
blended family p. 72
census metropolitan areas p. 73
competition p. 80
Competition Act p. 82
consumerism p. 83
culture p. 73
demographics p. 70
discretionary income p. 76
disposable income p. 76
economy p. 75
electronic commerce p. 79

environmental scanning p. 68
extranet p. 79
generation X p. 71
generation Y p. 72
gross income p. 76
intranet p. 79
marketspace p. 79
multicultural marketing p. 73
regulation p. 82
self-regulation p. 83
social forces p. 70
technology p. 77
value consciousness p. 75

■ ■ ■
DISCUSSION AND APPLICATION QUESTIONS

1 For many years, Gerber has manufactured baby food in small, single-serving containers. In conducting an environmental scan, identify three trends or factors that might significantly affect this company's future business; then propose how Gerber might respond to these changes.

2 Describe the new features you would add to an automobile designed for an aging baby boomer. In what magazines would you advertise to appeal to this target market?

3 New technologies are continuously improving and replacing existing products. Although technological change is often difficult to predict, suggest how the following companies and products might be affected by the Internet and digital technologies: (a) Kodak cameras and film, (b) Air Canada, and (c) the Museum of Art.

4 Historically, a couple of large firms dominated the Canadian brewing industry (Labatt and Molson). But now, they

face competition from many regional brands and microbreweries. In terms of the continuum of competition, how would you explain this change?

5 What role does marketing play now in the deregulated Canadian airline industry? What elements of the marketing mix or more of less important now?

6 The Johnson Company manufacturers buttons and pins with slogan and designs. These pins are inexpensive to produce and are sold in retail outlets, such as discount stores, hobby shops, and bookstores. Little equipment is needed for a new competitor to enter the market. What strategies should Johnson consider to create effective barriers to entry?

7 Today's consumer is more value-conscious. How could a retail home improvement centre sell the same products but still offer the consumer greater perceived value? What specific things could the retailer do?

GOING ONLINE	Using the Web to Scan the Canadian Marketing Environment

Many sources of information might be useful in conducting an environmental scan. One particularly useful Web site is Statistics Canada's site (www.statcan.ca). Statistics Canada is the source for Canadian statistics on Canadian population trends, consumer expenditures, the economy, and so on. Use this site to answer the following questions:

1 What is the current population of Canada? What is the projected population of Canada in 2017?

2 How many people are aged 90 and over in Canada? (That's right, 90.)

3 How many single-parent families are there in Canada?

Do you want to get better grades and stay up to date with current issues in marketing? Visit the Online Learning Centre at www.mcgrawhill.ca/college/crane for practice tests, video cases, resources for building a marketing plan, *Globe and Mail* headlines, access to *Marketing Magazine*, and other learning and study tools.

*Learning*Centre

Marketing

"Terry was looking for a keyboard player to be in the band he was just starting," remembers Jimmy Jam of Flyte Tyme Productions, Inc. "I had sort of rebelled because I had first thought of myself as a drummer," says Jam. But after he listened and heard how good the drummer was, he told Terry, "I'll be the keyboard player."

The conversation took place a few weeks after Terry Lewis and Jimmy Jam met at a summer math program for gifted junior high school students, sponsored by a local university. The two came to prominence in the early 1980s as members of the funk band "The Time" that appeared as the opener on many of Prince's early tours. The pair still credit Prince for much of their tenacious work ethic and eclectic musical tastes. After leaving the band, Terry and Jimmy started a music production company—Flyte Tyme—creating the new name by adapting the old one. Now in their early forties, the two have worked together for 20 years, most of it in Flyte Tyme Productions (www.flytetyme.com), where their clients include Mary J. Blige, Boyz II Men, Mariah Carey, Aretha Franklin, Janet Jackson, Patti LaBelle, Usher, TLC, and many others.

THE MUSIC

Sunglasses, fedoras, and sharp suits are Jam and Lewis's signature image, but—curiously—they have no signature sound. Instead, their approach is to tailor tunes for each artist. Janet Jackson's steamy ballads do not sound anything like Patti LaBelle's big Diane Warren ballads. They also work in a wide variety of music genres—from gospel (Yolanda Adams) and country (Rissi Palmer) to jazz (Herb Alpert) and pop (Mariah Carey).

Flyte Tyme's successes are impressive. They produced Usher's no. 1 pop hit "U Remind Me," which held the top spot on the charts for four weeks. They also produced an album for Japanese pop star, Hikaru Utada, which climbed to the top of Japan's pop charts, selling four million copies in two weeks. And then there are such projects as creating music for the NBA All-Star game!

These and other hits put Flyte Tyme in extraordinary company. Having produced 16 no. 1 singles on *Billboard*'s pop chart, they are second only to the producer for the Beatles (with 23) and tied with the producer for Elvis Presley. Flyte Tyme has also produced more than 40 Top-10 hits and more than 100 albums that have reached gold, platinum, and multi-platinum status. They are three-time Grammy winners for Producer of the

Year, Best R&B Song, and Best Dance Recording. Most recently, they were nominated for the fourth consecutive year for Producer of the Year. In an industry where consumers' preferences, technology, competition, and the regulatory environment change at an extraordinary pace, Flyte Tyme has managed to stay on top for more than 20 years!

THE TEAM AND ITS FORMULA FOR SUCCESS

How have Jam and Lewis stayed at the top of the music game so long? Janet Jackson's answer: "There are no egos involved." Terry Lewis echoes this and says about his relationship with Jam: "He's the best partner a person could have. We've never had a contract—we've never had one argument in twenty-something years, not saying we don't disagree about things but our attitudes are the *best* idea wins. Not the right, not the wrong, but the *best*!"

"What we try to do is get everybody relaxed—check the egos at the door, that kind of thing. We find that we do it a lot more with new artists than with the older, more established artists," explains Jam. "Psychology is a big part of producing. Some artists like to work right away, others like to play pool, have lunch, talk on the phone, then they mosey in and record," he says. "If you think of Janet Jackson or Mariah Carey—the people who you would think of as superstars, you would think that they would bring a superstar ego with them. But it's almost the opposite," says Jam. "New artists often come to Flyte Tyme with a feeling they have to prove something. And what happens is, you don't really get a natural performance," says Jam.

Another of Flyte Tyme's special strengths: adapting the music and lyrics to an artist's unique talents, not

visit us at www.mcgrawhill.ca/college/crane

the other way around. Their interest in many types of music and their experience with many artists allow them to add new ideas to the creative process. Still, Flyte Tyme may work on several different versions based on its perceptions of what radio stations or MTV will play.

Jam and Lewis work on both the music and lyrics for many of their songs, but Jam leans slightly more toward the melodies and Lewis toward the vocals and lyrics. In fact, Lewis keeps "The Book of Titles," and any time someone says something clever or in an interesting way, it goes into the book. "Music is the soundtrack of life," says Lewis. "The inspiration for words I just take from watching people, and life has a lot of verses in it," he adds.

MARKETING, DISTRIBUTION, COMPETITION

Selecting the best music ideas requires an instinct to find the right blend of art and business. The elements of the art include a huge respect for and understanding of the artists, an interest in a broad palette of musical sounds, and a good ear for melodies and vocals. The business components of their formula include understanding many of the factors—such as consumers, technology, and competition—that influence their business.

Music artists walking in the door of Flyte Tyme receive an array of services: a studio facility with Jam, Lewis, and an experienced staff providing ideas, direction, and focus—"trying to get things out of them they didn't know they had in them," says Lewis. Flyte Tyme Records, the marketing arm, develops the artist's image,

the marketing plan, advertising, and distribution—everything to get the record or CD on the rack to be sold. "If you have $100 000 to spend on promotion, you can do a nice music video and then you can spend a lot of time trying to get it played on MTV or BET or VH1 or any of the appropriate video channels," says Jam. Or sometimes, the music calls for a different strategy, Flyte Tyme's "groundhog approach." For example, in the early 1990s with one of its bands, Flyte Tyme piled the band in a Winnebago and hit college campuses.

Today, Flyte Tyme creates a lot of that same groundhog buzz with its Web site, where the music audience can learn about Flyte Tyme's artists and activities. Jam and Lewis note that the new fee-based online music services are a great tool for providing the public access to music. In addition, while the delivery system—buying a CD at a retail store, downloading music from the Internet, or burning a CD—does not affect the process of Flyte Tyme's making the music in the studio, adapting to the environmental changes is important. "Change doesn't frighten us," says Lewis, "and we change with time."

QUESTIONS

1   Based on the case information and what you know about today's music industry, conduct an environmental scan for Flyte Tyme to identify key trends. For each of the five environmental forces (social, economic, technological, competitive, and regulatory), identify trends likely to influence it in the near future.

2   About 80 percent of startup businesses fail within five years. What reasons explain Flyte Tyme's continuing success?

3   What marketing factors and actions must Jimmy Jam and Terry Lewis consider in developing music (*a*) for a new, unknown artist, and (*b*) an established artist, such as Janet Jackson?

4   What promotional and distribution strategies should Flyte Tyme use to get its music in front of prospective buyers?

CHAPTER 4

ETHICS AND SOCIAL RESPONSIBILITY IN MARKETING

LEARNING OBJECTIVES

After reading this chapter, you should be able to:

1. Explain the differences between legal and ethical behaviour in marketing.

2. Identify factors that influence ethical and unethical behaviour in marketing.

3. Describe the different concepts of social responsibility.

4. Recognize unethical and socially irresponsible consumer behaviour.

CANADIAN AUTOMAKERS MAKE A COMMITMENT TO CANADA

Canadian automobile manufacturers have a longstanding tradition of social responsibility and dedication to the country. They are involved in multifaceted efforts to support the communities in which they operate and to protect the natural environment of Canada. They have a history of supporting countless charities and other worthy causes and have even established specific foundations to support these charities and causes.

For example, General Motors of Canada is committed to being a good corporate citizen, and its philanthropic contributions are evidence of that citizenship. Some of the organizations that GM supports are the YMCA, Junior Achievement, the United Way, Scouts Canada and Girl Guides Canada, and the Stratford Festival. GM Volunteer PLUS International is a corporate citizenship program, created and funded by the GM Corporation to encourage and support GM employees' volunteer efforts within GM communities. General Motors of Canada Limited also provides postsecondary education scholarships and bursaries for students across Canada. The Partnership for the Advancement of Collaborative Engineering Education (PACE), a corporate alliance between General Motors, EDS, and Sun Microsystems, also provides funding to prepare mechanical designers, engineers, and analysts with the skills to compete in the future. For example, the University of British Columbia received an in-kind contribution with a commercial value of approximately $240 million.

Improved global environmental quality is a goal at General Motors of Canada. Accordingly, it has established a corporate philosophy and policy—*The General Motors Environmental Principles.* As a responsible corporate citizen, General Motors is dedicated to protecting human health, natural resources, and the global environment. This dedication reaches farther than compliance with the law to encompass the integration of sound environmental practices into its business decisions. General Motors of Canada Limited also supports a variety of environmental organizations whose objectives, goals, and activities are aligned with the General Motors Environmental Principles.

Ford Motor Company of Canada has also made a commitment to Canadian environment. Its facilities are ISO14001-certified, and the company has made a major commitment to the 3Rs (reduce, reuse, recycle). It is committed to reduce emissions, energy use, and waste; reuse (almost all parts/components delivered to Ford plants are in returnable pallets/containers); and recycle (95 percent of all solid nonhazardous waste at its facilities is recycled; and all Canadian-built Ford vehicles exceed the industry average of 75 percent recyclability).

Nissan Canada developed the Nissan Canada Foundation as a signal of its commitment to the Canadian community. This foundation was established to help Canadian senior citizens, who represent a substantial portion of the population. The foundation has three main goals; (1) to raise funds, (2) to distribute those funds to nonprofit organizations that serve senior citizens (e.g., Meals on Wheels), and (3) to raise awareness about the needs and concerns of seniors.

Toyota Canada is a sponsor of the Special Olympics. It is also an ISO14001-certified company that has made a major commitment to the Canadian environment. For example, its manufacturing activities focus around the vehicle life cycle. It seeks to increase the fuel economy of its vehicles, decrease the environmental impact of manufacturing, curtail packaging waste, energy use, and water pollution, as well as improve end-of-life vehicle recycling. Toyota works with environmental partners, including Evergreen Canada and Earth Day Canada, to ensure a healthy environment for all Canadians.[1]

This chapter focuses on ethics and social responsibility in marketing. You will see that some Canadian companies recognize that while ethically and socially responsible behaviour often comes with a price tag, the price for unethical and socially irresponsible behaviour is often much higher. In essence, in this marketplace, companies *can* "do well by doing good."

■ ■ ■
NATURE AND SIGNIFICANCE OF MARKETING ETHICS

ethics
The moral principles and values that govern the actions and decisions of an individual or group.

As defined in Chapter 1, **ethics** are the moral principles and values that govern the actions and decisions of an individual or group.[2] Simply put, ethics serve as guidelines on how to act correctly and justly when faced with moral dilemmas. For marketing managers, ethics concern the application of moral principles and values to marketing decision making.

Ethical/Legal Framework in Marketing

A good starting point for understanding the nature and significance of ethics is the distinction between legality and ethicality of marketing decisions. Figure 4–1 helps you visualize the relationship between laws and ethics.[3] While ethics deal with personal and moral principles and values, **laws** are society's values and standards that are enforceable in the courts.[4]

laws
Society's values and standards that are enforceable in the courts.

In general, what is illegal is also unethical. For example, deceptive advertising is illegal. It is also unethical because it conflicts with the moral principles of honesty and fairness. But not all unethical conduct is illegal. For instance, price gouging is usually not illegal but is often viewed as unethical. Marketing managers often find

■ FIGURE 4–1 ■

Classifying marketing
decisions according to
ethical and legal
relationships

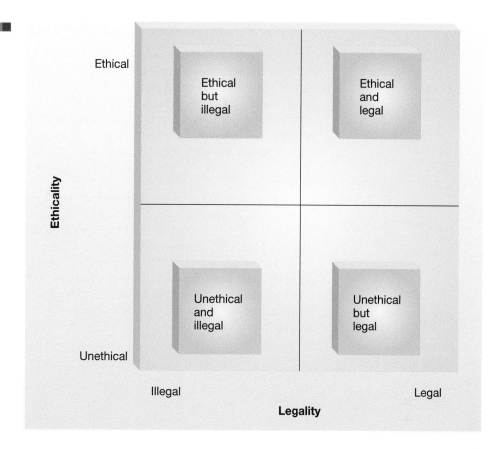

themselves in many situations where they must make judgments in defining ethical
and legal boundaries. For some, the distinction between ethics and laws can sometimes lead to the rationalization that if a behaviour is within legal limits, then it is not
really unethical. For example, a group of Canadian business students surveyed were
asked: "Is it okay to charge a higher price than normal when you know the customer
really needs the product and will pay the higher price?" Almost 35 percent of the
business students who took part in the survey responded yes.[5] How would you have
answered this question?

Now consider the following situations. After reading each, assign it to the cell in
Figure 4–1 that you think best fits the situation along the ethical–legal continuum.

1. Several companies meet and agree to bid rigging for sealed tendered government contract work. Bid rigging is illegal under the Competition Act because it
   eliminates free and open competition.
2. A company uses a technique called "slugging," or selling under the guise of
   research. Once prospective customers agree to take part in the research, the
   salespeople switch to their sales pitch.
3. A real estate agent sells a high-rise condo unit to a customer, primarily because
   the customer loves the city view from the condo windows. The agent knows that
   in one year another high-rise will be built, effectively blocking the view so
   important to the customer. The agent decides not to tell that to the customer.
4. A company interviews a very qualified female for an industrial sales position.
   She is more qualified than any males who have been interviewed. However, the
   company knows that some male purchasing agents prefer to deal with a male
   salesperson, and so they hire a less qualified male applicant.

Do these situations fit neatly into Figure 4–1 as clearly defined ethical and legal or
unethical and illegal? Some probably do not. As you read further in this chapter, you
will be asked to consider other ethical dilemmas.

Current Perceptions of Ethical Behaviour

There has been much discussion about the possible deterioration of personal morality and ethical standards on a global scale. The news media offer well-publicized examples of personal dishonesty, hypocrisy, cheating, and greed. There also has been a public outcry about the ethical practices of businesspeople. In particular, there is widespread concern over unethical marketing practices, such as price fixing, bribery, deceptive advertising, and unsafe products. Recent Canadian research shows that most business students surveyed feel that the ethical standards of business have declined over the years and believe the situation is not likely to improve in the future.[6]

There are at least four possible reasons why the state of perceived ethical business conduct is at its present level. First, there is increased pressure on businesspeople to make decisions in a society characterized by diverse value systems.[7] Second, there is a growing tendency for business decisions to be judged publicly by groups with different values and interests. Third, the public's expectations regarding ethical business behaviour have increased. Finally, and most disturbing, ethical business conduct may have declined. EthicScan Canada, an organization that monitors the ethical performance of hundreds of Canadian companies, seems to have confirmed this decline.[8]

CONCEPT CHECK

1. What are ethics?

2. What are laws?

UNDERSTANDING ETHICAL MARKETING BEHAVIOUR

Researchers have identified numerous factors that influence ethical marketing behaviour.[9] Figure 4–2 presents a framework that shows these factors and their relationships.

Societal Culture and Norms

As described in Chapter 3, *culture* incorporates the set of values, ideas, and attitudes that are learned and shared among members of a group. Culture also serves as a socializing force that dictates what is morally right and just. This means that moral standards are relative to particular societies. These standards often reflect the laws and regulations that affect social and economic behaviour, which can create moral

■ FIGURE 4–2 ■

A framework for understanding ethical behaviour

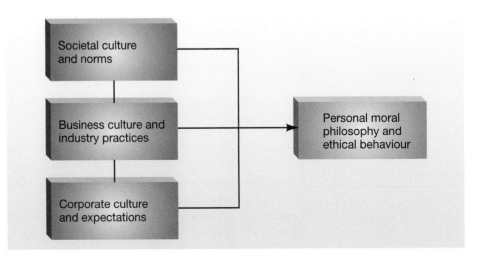

MARKETING NEWSNET   Global Business Software Piracy

By 2005, the Internet will link an estimated 1.17 billion Internet users worldwide. The many benefits of the Internet often overshadow its dark side: business software piracy. The explosive growth of the Internet is making piracy easy because pirated copies of software can be distributed and downloaded quickly and globally with the click of a mouse. The Software & Information Industry Association (SIIA) and the Business Software Alliance (BSA) estimate that one in every three business software applications in use in the world is pirated. Piracy means lost jobs, wages, tax revenues, and a potential barrier to success for startup software companies around the globe.

It is estimated that the unauthorized copying of business software costs North American producers more than $12 billion in worldwide sales annually. Software piracy has become pandemic in many countries. According to SIIA/BSA estimates, 70 percent of the software in Eastern Europe is pirated, followed by rates of 60 percent and 59 percent in the Middle East and Africa and Latin America, respectively. Countries with the highest piracy rates are Vietnam (98%), China (91%), Russia (89%), and Lebanon and Oman (88% each). For comparison, the piracy rate is 25 percent in the United States and 41 percent in Canada.

dilemmas. For example, Levi Strauss decided to end much of its business dealings in China because of what the company called "pervasive human rights abuses." According to its vice-president for corporate marketing: "There are wonderful commercial opportunities in China. But when ethical issues collide with commercial appeal, we try to ensure ethics as the trump card. For us, ethical issues precede all others."[10]

Actions that restrain trade, fix prices, deceive buyers, and result in unsafe products are considered morally wrong in Canada and other countries. However, different cultures view marketing practices differently. Consider the use of another's ideas, copyright, trademark, or patent. These are viewed as intellectual property, and unauthorized use is illegal and unethical in Canada.

Outside Canada, however, is another story.[11] Unauthorized use of copyrights, trademarks, and patents is routine in some countries, such as China, Mexico, and Korea, and costs the authorized owners billions of dollars annually. In Korea, for instance, copying is partly rooted in its society's culture. According to international trade officials, many Koreans have the idea that the thoughts of one person should benefit all, and the Korean government rarely prosecutes infringements. Copyright infringement in the global business software industry is particularly widespread with the explosive growth of the Internet. Copies of software can be distributed and downloaded quickly and globally, with a click of the mouse. Read the accompanying Marketing NewsNet box to find out where the unauthorized use of business software is most prevalent.[12]

Business Culture and Industry Practices

Societal culture provides a foundation for understanding moral and ethical behaviour in business activities. *Business cultures* "comprise the effective rules of the game, the boundaries between competitive and unethical behaviour, [and] the codes of conduct in business dealings."[13] Consumers have witnessed numerous instances where business cultures in the brokerage (insider trading), insurance (deceptive sales practices), and defence (bribery) industries went awry. Business culture affects ethical conduct both in the exchange relationship between sellers and buyers and in the competitive behaviour among sellers.

Ethics of Exchange   The exchange process is central to the marketing concept. Ethical exchanges between sellers and buyers should result in both parties being better off after a transaction.[14]

caveat emptor
The legal concept of "let the buyer beware" that was pervasive in Canadian business culture before the 1960s.

Prior to the 1960s, the legal concept of **caveat emptor**—let the buyer beware—was pervasive in Canadian business culture. The growth and strength of the consumer movement resulted in this concept becoming an unacceptable marketplace philosophy. A codification of ethics between buyers and sellers was established, with consumers recognizing their rights to safety, to be informed, to choose, and to be heard.

The right to safety manifests itself in industry and federal safety standards for most products sold in Canada. However, even the most vigilant efforts to ensure safe products cannot foresee every possibility. Mattel's experience with its Cabbage Patch Snacktime Kids doll is a case in point.[15] The doll was designed to "eat" plastic french fries, celery, and other tidbits by drawing them into its motorized mouth. Despite exhaustive laboratory and in-home testing, Mattel executives did not consider that a child's hair might become caught in the doll's mouth and cause harm. Unfortunately, this happened. Mattel immediately pulled the dolls from store shelves, refunded buyers, and discontinued the product.

The right to be informed means that marketers have an obligation to give consumers complete and accurate information about products and services. This right also applies to the solicitation of personal information over the Internet and its subsequent use by marketers.[16] For example, a recent survey of Web sites indicated that 92 percent collect personal information, such as consumer e-mail addresses, telephone numbers, shopping habits, and financial data. Yet, only two-thirds of Web sites inform consumers what is done with this information once obtained. Because consumers often assume that personal information is confidential, it was therefore understandable that subscribers to America Online (AOL) balked when AOL proposed giving member information to partners who could then telemarket to them. AOL backed down.

Relating to the right to choose, many supermarket chains now demand "slotting allowances" from manufacturers, in the form of cash rebates or free goods, to stock new products. This practice could limit the number of new products available to consumers and interfere with their right to choose. One critic of this practice remarked: "If we had had slotting allowances a few years ago, we might not have had granola, herbal tea, or yogurt."[17]

Finally, the right to be heard means that consumers should have access to company- and/or public-policy makers regarding comments or complaints about products and services. Many Canadian companies have set up consumer service departments to deal with customer comments and complaints. In fact, it was consumer complaints about late-night and repeated calls by telemarketers that led to greater limitations on telemarketing practices.

Ethics of Competition   Business culture also affects ethical behaviour in competition. Two kinds of unethical behaviour are most common: (1) economic espionage, and (2) bribery.

economic espionage
The clandestine collection of trade secrets or proprietary information about a company's competitors.

Economic espionage is the clandestine collection of trade secrets or proprietary information about a company's competitors. This practice is illegal and unethical and includes such activities as trespassing, theft, fraud, wire tapping, and searching a competitor's trash. Many Canadian and American firms have uncovered espionage in some form, costing them billions of dollars a year.[18] This practice is most prevalent in high-technology industries, such as electronics, specialty chemicals, industrial equipment, aerospace, and pharmaceuticals, where technical know-how and secrets separate industry leaders from followers.

But espionage can occur anywhere—the toy industry and even the cookie industry! Procter & Gamble charged that competitors photographed its plants and production lines, stole a sample of its cookie dough, and infiltrated a confidential sales presentation to learn about its technology, recipe, and marketing plan. The competitors paid Procter & Gamble $120 million in damages after a lengthy dispute.[19]

The second form of unethical competitive behaviour is giving and receiving bribes and kickbacks. Bribes and kickbacks are often disguised as gifts, consultant

WEBLINK
HTTP://WWW.MCGRAWHILL.CA/
COLLEGE/CRANE

The Corruption Perceptions Index

The use of bribery as a means to win and retain business varies widely by country. Transparency International, based in Germany, periodically polls employees of multinational firms and institutions as well as political analysts and ranks countries on the basis of their perceived level of bribery to win or retain business. To obtain the most recent ranking, visit the Transparency International Web site at www.transparency.org/cpi/index.html.

Scroll through the Corruption Perceptions Index to see where Canada stands in the worldwide rankings. How about our neighbours, the United States and Mexico? Any surprises? Which country listed in the most recent ranking has the highest ranking, and which has the lowest ranking?

fees, and favours. This practice is more common in business-to-business and government marketing than in consumer marketing.

In general, bribery is most evident in industries experiencing intense competition and in countries in earlier stages of economic development. According to a recent United Nations' study, 15 percent of all companies in industrialized countries have to pay bribes to win or retain business. In Asia, this figure is 40 percent. In Eastern Europe, 60 percent of all companies must pay bribes to do business. A recent poll of senior executives engaged in global marketing revealed that Bangladesh and Nigeria were the most likely countries to evidence bribery to win or retain business. Iceland and Finland were the least likely.[20] Bribery on a worldwide scale is monitored by Transparency International. Visit its Web site described in the accompanying WebLink box, and view the most recent country rankings on this practice.

Corporate Culture and Expectations

A third influence on ethical practices is corporate culture. *Corporate culture* is a set of values, ideas, and attitudes that is learned and shared among the members of an organization. The culture of a company demonstrates itself in the dress ("We don't wear ties"), sayings ("The IBM Way"), and manner of work (team efforts) of employees. Culture is also apparent in the expectations for ethical behaviour present in formal codes of ethics and the ethical actions of top management and co-workers.

code of ethics
A formal statement of ethical principles and rules of conduct.

Codes of Ethics   A **code of ethics** is a formal statement of ethical principles and rules of conduct. Research shows that 85 percent of Canadian companies surveyed had some sort of ethics code.[21] Ethics codes typically address such issues as contributions to government officials and political parties; relations with customers, competitors, and suppliers; conflicts of interest; and accurate recordkeeping. Nortel Networks provides ethical guidance to its employees through its *Living the Commitments* code, which all employees must follow when conducting business on a worldwide basis. However, an ethics code is rarely enough to ensure ethical behaviour. One of the reasons for this is the lack of specificity of ethics codes. Ultimately, it is the employee who often judges whether a specific behaviour is really unethical. The Canadian Marketing Association, the largest marketing organization in Canada, whose members include Microsoft Canada, Bank of Montreal, The Shopping Channel, and Bell Canada has a code of ethics that is compulsory for all members to follow. Portions of this code are shown in Figure 4–3. For a copy of the complete code of ethics, visit www.the-cma.org.

■ FIGURE 4-3 ■■

Excerpt from the Canadian Marketing Association Code of Ethics and Standards of Practice (abridged). The full document is available at www.the-cma.org.

CANADIAN MARKETING ASSOCIATION

A1 Purpose of Code of Ethics and Standards of Practice

Preamble: Marketers acknowledge that the establishment and maintenance of high standards of practice are a fundamental responsibility to the public, essential to winning and holding public confidence, and the foundation of a successful and independent information-based marketing industry in Canada. Canadian Marketing Association members include Canada's major financial institutions, insurance companies, publishers, cataloguers and charitable organizations, relationship marketers, and those engaged in electronic commerce and multimedia marketing.

A2 Application and Governing Legislation

A2.2 Members of the Canadian Marketing Association recognize an obligation—to the public, to the integrity of the discipline in which they operate, and to each other—to practice to the highest standards of honesty, truth, accuracy, and fairness.

B Accuracy of Representation

B1 Accuracy: Offers must be clear and truthful and shall not misrepresent a product, service, solicitation, or program and shall not mislead by statement, or technique of demonstration or comparison.

C Constituent Elements and Characteristics of the Offer

C1 Disclosure: The offer shall contain clear and conspicuous disclosure of the following terms: the exact nature of what is offered; the price; the terms of payment, including any additional charges, such as shipping and handling; and, the consumer's commitment and any ongoing obligation in placing an order.

D Fulfilment Practices

D1 Shipment: Goods offered shall be shipped within 30 days of the receipt of a properly completed order, or within the time limit stated in the original offer.

E Media-Specific Standards of Practice

E1 Broadcast

E1.2 Misrepresentation: Marketers shall not employ presentations likely to mislead reasonable consumers that the presentation is news, information, public service, or entertainment programming.

E2 Printed Media

E2.2 Description: All printed materials shall accurately and fairly describe the product or service offered. Type size, colour, contrast, style, placement, or other treatment shall not be used to reduce the legibility or clarity of the offer, exceptions to the offer, or terms and conditions.

E3 Telephone

E3.3 Privacy: No marketer shall knowingly call any person who has an unlisted or unpublished telephone number, except where the telephone number was furnished by the customer to that marketer.

E4 Internet and Other Electronic Media

E4.1.2 e-Mail Purpose: Organizations must identify the purpose for which an individual's e-mail address is being requested prior to or at the time the e-mail address is collected.

F Product Safety

F1 Products offered by marketers shall be safe in normal use and, where applicable, shall conform to product safety regulations established by Health and Welfare Canada and by the Canadian Standards Association, and/or other recognized Canadian authorities.

G Special Considerations in Marketing to Children

G2 Responsibility: Marketing to children (someone who has not reached his or her 13th birthday) imposes a special responsibility on marketers. Marketers shall recognize that children are not adults and that not all marketing techniques are appropriate for children.

H Special Considerations in Marketing to Teenagers

Continued

■ FIGURE 4–3 ■
Continued

H2 Responsibility: Marketing to teenagers (someone who has reached his or her 13th birthday but has not yet reached the age of majority in his or her province or territory of residence) imposes special responsibilities on marketers. Marketers will use discretion and sensitivity in marketing to teenagers, to address the age, knowledge, sophistication, and maturity of teenagers. Marketers should exercise caution that they do not take advantage of or exploit teenagers.

I Protection of the Environment

I1 Environmental Responsibility: Marketers recognize and acknowledge a continuing responsibility to manage their businesses to minimize environmental impact. This responsibility shall include use of targeted marketing techniques to improve mail efficiency; use of recycled papers and environmentally benign inks and other materials; use of materials recycling programs; and, the active encouragement of environmental responsibility among members of the business community. In addition, marketers shall use the CMA's Do Not Mail program to reduce unwanted mailings and thereby reduce wasted materials.

I2 Three Rs: Marketers shall incorporate the "Three Rs" (reduce, reuse, and recycle) of environmental responsibility in the operation of their businesses.

J Protection of Personal Privacy

Privacy: All marketers shall recognize and abide by the seven principles of personal privacy adopted by the Canadian Marketing Association (e.g., Principle #1: Giving consumers control of how information about them is used).

K Enforcement Procedures for the Standards of Practice

With permission from the Canadian Marketing Association, 2004.

2004 © Canadian Marketing Association.

Ethical Behaviour of Management and Co-workers A second reason for violating ethics codes rests in the perceived behaviour of top management and co-workers.[22] Observing peers and top management and gauging responses to unethical behaviour play an important role in individual actions. For example, what message do employees receive when they see personnel being rewarded for engaging in unethical behaviour and see others punished for refusing to engage in unethical behaviour? Clearly, ethical dilemmas often bring personal and professional conflict. In many cases, **whistle-blowers**, employees who report unethical or illegal actions of their employers, often face recrimination. Some firms, such as General Dynamics and Dun & Bradstreet, have appointed ethics officers who are responsible for safeguarding such individuals.[23]

Personal Moral Philosophy and Ethical Behaviour

Ultimately, ethical choices are based on the personal moral philosophy of the decision maker. Moral philosophy is learned through the process of socialization with friends and family and by formal education. It is also influenced by the societal, business, and corporate cultures in which a person finds himself or herself. Moral philosophies are of two types: (1) moral idealism, and (2) utilitarianism.[24]

Moral Idealism **Moral idealism** is a personal philosophy that considers certain individual rights or duties as universal (e.g., right to freedom) regardless of the outcome. This philosophy is favoured by moral philosophers and consumer interest groups. This philosophy also applies to ethical duties, such as informing the consumer about the safety hazards of a particular product or even conducting a large-scale recall of a defective product, regardless of cost, in order to uphold that consumer right to safety.

Utilitarianism An alternative perspective on moral philosophy is **utilitarianism**, which is a personal moral philosophy that focuses on "the greatest good for the greatest

---

whistle-blowers
Employees who report unethical or illegal actions of their employers.

moral idealism
A personal moral philosophy that considers certain individual rights or duties as universal, regardless of the outcome.

utilitarianism
A personal moral philosophy that focuses on the "greatest good for the greatest number" by assessing the costs and benefits of the consequences of ethical behaviour.

number" by assessing the costs and benefits of the consequences of ethical behaviour. If the benefits exceed the costs, then the behaviour is ethical. If not, then the behaviour is unethical. This philosophy underlies the economic tenets of capitalism and, not surprisingly, is embraced by many business executives and students.[25]

Utilitarian reasoning was apparent in Nestlé Canada's original decision to add peanut product additives to some of the company's chocolate snacks. However, some consumers, albeit only a small percentage of Canadians, are severely allergic to peanuts. Still, Nestlé was intent on pursuing this strategy until many Canadians protested the move. In the end, Nestlé decided to cancel the proposed practice and took out advertising in major newspapers to announce its decision. While the vast majority of Canadians may have enjoyed the newly formulated snacks, and certainly would not have been harmed by them, protestors believed that some consumers may have been harmed by this proposed practice. The views of the protestors prevailed in this case, even though Nestlé could have used the "greatest good for the greatest number" argument.[26]

An appreciation for the nature of ethics, coupled with a basic understanding of why unethical behaviour arises, alerts a person to when and how ethical issues exist in marketing decisions. Ultimately, ethical behaviour rests with the individual, but the consequences affect many.

CONCEPT CHECK

1. What is caveat emptor?

2. What is a code of ethics?

3. What is meant by moral idealism?

UNDERSTANDING SOCIAL RESPONSIBILITY IN MARKETING

social responsibility
The idea that organizations are part of a larger society and are accountable to that society for their actions.

As we saw in Chapter 1, the societal marketing concept stresses marketing's social responsibility by not only satisfying the needs of consumers but also providing for society's welfare. **Social responsibility** means that organizations are part of a larger society and are accountable to that society for their actions. Like ethics, agreement on the nature and scope of social responsibility is often difficult to come by, given the diversity of values present in different societal, business, and corporate cultures.[27]

Concepts of Social Responsibility

Figure 4–4 shows three concepts of social responsibility: (1) profit responsibility, (2) stakeholder responsibility, and (3) societal responsibility.

Profit Responsibility *Profit responsibility* holds that companies have a simple duty—to maximize profits for their owners or shareholders. This view is expressed by Nobel Laureate Milton Friedman, who said, "There is one and only one social responsibility of business—to use its resources and engage in activities designed to increase its profits so long as it stays within the rules of the game, which is to say, engages in open and free competition without deception or fraud."[28] Genzyme—the maker of Ceredase, a drug that treats a genetic illness called Gaucher's disease that affects 20 000 people worldwide—has been criticized for apparently adopting this view in its pricing practices. A Genzyme spokesperson responded by saying that Ceredase profits are below industry standards and that the company freely gives the drug to patients without insurance.[29]

■ FIGURE 4-4   ■
Three concepts of social responsibility

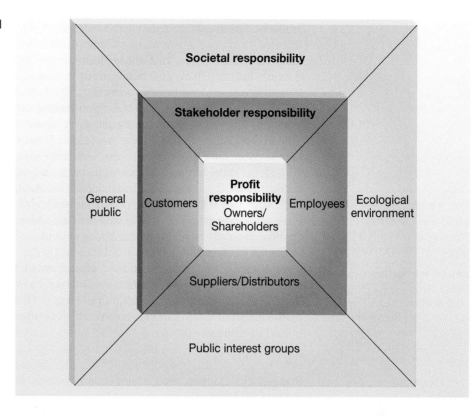

Stakeholder Responsibility   Frequent criticism of the profit view has led to a broader concept of social responsibility. *Stakeholder responsibility* focuses on the obligations an organization has to those who can effect achievement of its objectives. These constituencies include customers, employees, suppliers, and distributors. Source Perrier S.A., the supplier of Perrier bottled water, exercised this responsibil-

Which of the three concepts of social responsibility do you think Perrier applied when it learned of quality problems with its popular water? Read the text to learn how the company responded to this problem and its reasoning.

ity when it recalled 160 million bottles of water in 120 countries after traces of a toxic chemical were found in 13 bottles. The recall cost the company $35 million, and $40 million more was lost in sales. Even though the chemical level was not harmful to humans, Source Perrier's president believed he acted in the best interests of the firm's consumers, distributors, and employees by removing "the least doubt, as minimal as it might be, to weigh on the image of the quality and purity of our product".[30]

Societal Responsibility   An even broader concept of social responsibility has emerged in recent years. *Societal responsibility* refers to obligations that organizations have to the (1) preservation of the ecological environment, and (2) general public. Concerns about the environment and public welfare are represented by interest and advocacy groups, such as Greenpeace, an international environmental organization.

green marketing
Marketing efforts to produce, promote, and reclaim environmentally sensitive products.

Chapter 3 detailed the growing importance of ecological issues in marketing. Companies have responded to this concern through what is termed **green marketing** —marketing efforts to produce, promote, and reclaim environmentally sensitive products. Green marketing takes many forms.[31] The Canadian aluminum industry recycles nearly two-thirds of all aluminum cans for reuse. The Food and Consumer Products Manufacturers of Canada (formerly GPMC) has a program known as the Grocery Industry Packaging Stewardship Initiative, which is designed to promote responsible waste and product recycling. Black Photo of Ontario has factored the environment into everything it does, from product conception to manufacturing, distribution, and sales. Mercedes-Benz has designed its S-class sedans and 500/600 SEC luxury coupes to be entirely recyclable. These voluntary responses to environmental issues have been implemented with little or no additional cost to consumers.

A global undertaking to further green marketing efforts is the ISO 14001 initiative developed by the International Standards Organization (ISO) in Geneva, Switzerland. **ISO 14001** consists of worldwide standards for environmental quality and green marketing practices. These standards are embraced by 118 countries, including Canada, members of the European Union, and most Pacific Rim countries.[32]

Socially responsible efforts on behalf of the general public are also becoming more common. A formal practice is **cause marketing**, which occurs when the charitable contributions of a firm are tied directly to the customer revenues produced through the promotion of one of its products.[33] This definition distinguishes cause marketing from a firm's standard charitable contributions, which are outright donations. For example, Procter & Gamble raises funds for the Special Olympics when consumers purchase selected company products, and MasterCard International linked usage of its card with fundraising for institutions that combat cancer, heart disease, child abuse, drug abuse, and muscular dystrophy. Avon Products, Inc. focuses on different issues in different countries: breast cancer in the United States, Canada, Philippines, Mexico, Venezuela, Malaysia, and Spain; programs for women who care for senior citizens in Japan; emotional and financial support for mothers in Germany; and AIDS in Thailand. Cause marketing programs incorporate all three

ISO 14001
Worldwide standards for environmental quality and green marketing practices.

cause marketing
Occurs when the charitable contributions of a firm are tied directly to the customer revenues produced through the promotion of one of its products.

Marketing and social responsibility programs are often integrated, as is the case with McDonald's. Its concern for ill children is apparent in the opening of another Ronald McDonald House for children and their families.

McDonald's
www.mcdonalds.com

concepts of social responsibility by addressing public concerns, satisfying customer needs, and enhancing corporate sales and profits.[34]

The Social Audit

social audit
A systematic assessment of a firm's objectives, strategies, and performance in the domain of social responsibility.

Converting socially responsible ideas into actions involves careful planning and monitoring of programs. Many companies develop, implement, and evaluate their social responsibility efforts by means of a **social audit**, which is a systematic assessment of a firm's objectives, strategies, and performance in the domain of social responsibility. Frequently, marketing and social responsibility programs are integrated, as is the case with McDonald's. The company's concern for the needs of families with children who are chronically or terminally ill was converted into Ronald McDonald Houses around the world. These facilities, located near treatment centres, enable family members to stay together during a child's care. In this case, McDonald's is contributing to the welfare of a portion of its target market.

A social audit consists of five steps:[35]

1. Recognition of a firm's social expectations and the rationale for engaging in social responsibility endeavours.
2. Identification of social responsibility causes or programs consistent with the company's mission.
3. Determination of organizational objectives and priorities for programs and activities it will undertake.
4. Specification of the type and amount of resources necessary to achieve social responsibility objectives.
5. Evaluation of social responsibility programs and activities undertaken and assessment of future involvement.

sustainable development
Conducting business in a way that protects the natural environment while making economic progress.

Corporate attention to social audits will increase as companies seek to achieve sustainable development and improve the quality of life in a global economy.[36] **Sustainable development** involves conducting business in a way that protects the natural environment while also making economic progress. Ecologically responsible initiatives, such as green marketing, represent one such initiative. Research initiatives related to working conditions at offshore manufacturing sites that produce goods for North American companies focus on quality-of-life issues. Public opinion surveys show that consumers are concerned about working conditions under which products are made in Asia and Latin America. Some companies, such as Reebok, Nike, Liz Claiborne, Levi Strauss, and Mattel, have responded by imposing codes of conduct to reduce harsh or abusive working conditions at offshore manufacturing facilities.[37] Reebok, for example, now monitors the production of its sporting apparel and equipment to ensure that no child labour is used in making its products.

Companies that evidence societal responsibility have been rewarded for their efforts. Research has shown that these companies (1) benefit from favourable word-of-mouth among consumers, and (2) typically outperform less responsible companies on financial performance.[38]

Turning the Table: Consumer Ethics and Social Responsibility

Consumers also have an obligation to act ethically and responsibly in the exchange process and in the use and disposition of products. Unfortunately, consumer behaviour is spotty on both counts.

Unethical practices of consumers are a serious concern to marketers.[39] These practices include filing warranty claims after the claim period, misredeeming coupons, making fraudulent returns of merchandise, providing inaccurate information on credit applications, tampering with utility meters, tapping cable TV lines, illegally downloading music, movies, and software from the Internet, and submitting phony insurance claims. The cost to marketers in lost sales revenue and prevention expenses is huge. For example, consumers who redeem coupons for unpurchased products or use coupons destined for other products cost manufacturers millions of dollars each year. Unauthorized downloading of music, movies, and software from the Internet cost companies billions of dollars per year in lost sales. Electrical utilities lose 1 to 3 percent of yearly revenues due to meter tampering. Retailers lose billions of dollars yearly from shoplifting.

Consumer purchase, use, and disposition of environmentally sensitive products relates to consumer social responsibility. Research indicates that consumers are generally sensitive to ecological issues.[40] However, research also shows that consumers (1) may be unwilling to sacrifice convenience and pay potentially higher prices to protect the environment, and (2) lack the knowledge to make informed decisions dealing with the purchase, use, and disposition of products.[41]

For example, a Cap Gemini Ernst & Young/Maritz Automotive study showed that Canadians are, indeed, increasingly concerned about the environment. More than 80 percent of Canadians polled claimed that when purchasing a new car, environmental concerns are a factor. The research even indicates that Canadian consumers might be willing to pay more for a "greener" car. However, they would do so only as long as the greater environmental friendliness does not come at the expense of performance and styling. Not surprisingly, sales of "greener" vehicles in Canada have been dismal. Canadians appear to be saying, "give us an alternative-fuel vehicle (a "greener" car) that is stylish and outperforms our current vehicles, otherwise forget it."[42]

Many marketers suggest that consumers must become aware of and increase their demand for environmentally sensitive products. For example, producers of environmentally certified lumber say the market for "green wood" is very small in Canada. Certified lumber comes from forest companies that use sustainable harvesting practices and produce wood products with the least environmental impact. J. D. Irving Co., a Canadian timber and energy conglomerate, has been pursuing certification of its forest lands. The company suggests that consumers should look for and demand wood products from certified forests. In doing so, consumers could end widespread clear-cutting, chemical spraying, and other destructive forestry practices. "Green wood" products can be easily identified by a trademark product label: a green cross superimposed on a globe.

Ultimately, marketers and consumers are accountable for ethical and socially responsible behaviour. The twenty-first century will prove to be a testing period for both.

CONCEPT CHECK

1. What is meant by social responsibility?

2. Marketing efforts to produce, promote, and reclaim environmentally sensitive products are called _____.

3. What is a social audit?

■ ■ ■
CHAPTER IN REVIEW

1 *Explain the differences between legal and ethical behaviour in marketing.*

A good starting point for understanding the nature and significance of ethics is the distinction between legality and ethicality of marketing decisions. Whereas ethics deal with personal moral principles and values, laws are society's values and standards that are enforceable in the courts. This distinction can lead to the rationalization that if a behaviour is within reasonable ethical and legal limits, then it is not really illegal or unethical. Judgment plays a large role in defining ethical and legal boundaries in marketing. Ethical dilemmas arise when acts or situations are not clearly ethical and legal or unethical and illegal.

2 *Identify factors that influence ethical and unethical marketing decisions.*

Four factors influence ethical marketing behaviour. First, societal culture and norms serve as socializing forces that dictate what is morally right and just. Second, business culture and industry practices affect ethical conduct both in the exchange relationships between buyers and sellers and the competitive behaviour among sellers. Third, corporate culture and expectations are often defined by corporate ethics codes and the ethical behaviour of top management and co-workers. Finally, an individual's personal moral philosophy, such as moral idealism or utilitarianism, will dictate ethical choices. Ultimately, ethical behaviour rests with the individual, but the consequences affect many.

3 *Describe the different concepts of social responsibility.*

Social responsibility means that organizations are part of a larger society and are accountable to that society for their actions. There are three concepts of social responsibility. First, profit responsibility holds that companies have a simple duty: to maximize profits for their owners or shareholders. Second, stakeholder responsibility focuses on the obligations an organization has to those who can effect the achievement of its objectives. Those constituencies include consumers, employees, suppliers, and distributors. Finally, societal responsibility focuses on obligations that organizations have to the preservation of the ecological environment and the general public. Companies are placing greater emphasis on societal responsibility today and are reaping the rewards of positive word of mouth from their consumers and favourable financial performance.

4 *Recognize unethical and socially irresponsible consumer behaviour.*

Consumers, like marketers, have an obligation to act ethically and responsibly in the exchange process and in the use and disposition of products. Unfortunately, consumer behaviour is spotty on both counts. Unethical consumer behaviour include filing warranty claims after the claim period, misredeeming coupons, pirating music, movies, and software from the Internet, and submitting phony insurance claims, among other behaviours. Consumer purchase, use, and disposition of environmentally sensitive products relate to consumer social responsibility. Even though consumers are sensitive to ecological issues they (*a*) may be unwilling to sacrifice convictions and pay potentially higher prices to protect the environment, and (*b*) lack the knowledge to make informed decisions dealing with the purchase, use, and disposition of products.

■ ■ ■
FOCUSING ON KEY TERMS

cause marketing p. 102
caveat emptor p. 96
code of ethics p. 97
economic espionage p. 96
ethics p. 92
green marketing p. 101
ISO 14001 p. 102

laws p. 92
moral idealism p. 99
social audit p. 103
social responsibility p. 100
sustainable development p. 103
utilitarianism p. 99
whistleblowers p. 99

■ ■ ■
DISCUSSION AND APPLICATION QUESTIONS

1 What concepts of moral philosophy and social responsibility are applicable to the practices of the Canadian automakers described in the introduction to this chapter? Why?

2 Where would the following situations fit in Figure 4–1? (*a*) exaggerating the performance of a product to get a sale, and (*b*) selling a used automobile knowing it had a major mechanical problem and not telling the buyer.

3 A recent survey of Canadian business students asked, "Is calling your office pretending to be sick in order to take the day off ethical or unethical behaviour?" How would you respond to this question?

4 Compare and contrast moral idealism and utilitarianism as alternative personal moral philosophies.

5 How would you evaluate Milton Friedman's view of the social responsibility of a firm?

6 The text lists several unethical practices of consumers. Can you name others? Why do you think consumers engage in unethical conduct?

7 Cause marketing programs have become popular. Describe two such programs that you are familiar with.

The Canadian Centre for Ethics & Corporate Policy is a charitable, registered, independent ethics centre. It works with its own contributors and with other organizations involved in business ethics. The Centre is a volunteer-driven organization comprising corporations and individuals dedicated to developing and maintaining an ethical organizational culture. Visit its Web site at www.ethicscentre.com, and click on the newsletter icon. *Management Ethics* is the Centre's bimonthly publication. Choose some topics from Chapter 4 pertaining to ethics or social responsibility that interest you, such as codes of ethics, ethical behaviour of management, sustainable development, and so on. Read some of the current and back issues of the newsletter. Update at least one example in the text related to your chosen topics.

Do you want to get better grades and stay up to date with current issues in marketing? Visit the Online Learning Centre at www.mcgrawhill.ca/college/crane for practice tests, video cases, resources for building a marketing plan, *Globe and Mail* headlines, access to *Marketing Magazine*, and other learning and study tools.

VIDEO CASE 4   Starbucks Corporation: Serving More Than Coffee

Wake up and smell the coffee—Starbucks is everywhere! As the world's number one specialty coffee retailer, Starbucks serves more than 25 million customers in its stores every week. The concept of Starbucks goes far beyond being a coffeehouse or coffee brand. It represents the dream of its founder, Howard Schultz, who wanted to take the experience of an Italian—specifically, Milan–espresso bar to every corner of every city block in the world. So, what is the *Starbucks experience*? According to the company,

> You get more than the finest coffee when you visit Starbucks. You get great people, first-rate music, a comfortable and upbeat meeting place, and sound advice on brewing excellent coffee at home. At home you're part of a family. At work you're part of a company. And somewhere in between there's a place where you can sit back and be yourself. That's what a Starbucks store is to many of its customers–a kind of "third place" where they can escape, reflect, read, chat, or listen.

But there is more. Starbucks has embraced corporate social responsibility like few other companies. A recent Starbucks Corporate Social Responsibility Annual Report described the company's views on social responsibility:

> Starbucks defines corporate social responsibility as conducting our business in ways that produce social, environmental, and economic benefits to the communities in which we operate. In the end, it means being responsible to our stakeholders.
>
> There is a growing recognition of the need for corporate accountability. Consumers are demanding more than "product" from their favourite brands. Employees are choosing to work for companies with strong values. Shareholders are more inclined to invest in business with outstanding corporate reputations. Quite simply, being socially responsible is not only the right thing to do; it can distinguish a company from its industry peers.

Starbucks not only recognizes the central role that social responsibility plays in its business. It also takes constructive action to be socially responsible.

THE COMPANY

Starbucks is the leading retailer, roaster, and brand of specialty coffee in the world, with more than 7500 retail locations in North America, Latin America, Europe, the Middle East, and the Pacific Rim. Beginning in 1971 with a single retail location in Seattle, Washington, Starbucks became a Fortune 500 company in 2003 with annual sales exceeding $4 billion. In addition, Starbucks is ranked as one of the "Ten Most Admired Companies in America" and one of the "100 Best Companies to Work For" by *Fortune* magazine. It has been recognized as one of the "Most Trusted Brands" by *Ad Week* magazine. *Business Ethics* magazine placed Starbucks twenty-first in its list of the "100 Best Citizens" in 2003. Starbucks' performance can be attributed to a passionate pursuit of its mission and adherence to six guiding principles. Both appear in Figure 1.

COMMITMENT TO CORPORATE SOCIAL RESPONSIBILITY

Starbucks continually emphasizes its commitment to corporate social responsibility. Speaking at the annual shareholders meeting in March 2004, Howard Schultz said,

> From the beginning, Starbucks has built a company that balances profitability with a social conscience. Starbucks business practices are even more relevant today

■ FIGURE 1   ■■
Starbucks Mission Statement and Guiding Principles

Establish Starbucks as the premier purveyor of the finest coffee in the world while maintaining our uncompromising principles as we grow.

The following six principles will help us measure the appropriateness of our decisions:

1. Provide a great work environment and treat each other with respect and dignity.
2. Embrace diversity as an essential component in the way we do business.
3. Apply the highest standards of excellence to the purchasing, roasting, and fresh delivery of our coffee.
4. Develop enthusiastically satisfied customers all the time.
5. Contribute positively to our communities and our environment.
6. Recognize that profitability is essential to our future success.

as consumers take a cultural audit of the goods and services they use. Starbucks is known not only for serving the highest quality coffee, but for enriching the daily lives of its people, customers, and coffee farmers. This is the key to Starbucks ongoing success and we are pleased to report our positive results to shareholders and partners (employees).

Each year, Starbucks makes public a comprehensive report on its corporate social responsibility initiatives. A central feature of this annual report is the alignment of the company's social responsibility decisions and actions with the Starbucks Mission Statement and Guiding Principles. The Starbucks 2003 Corporate Social Responsibility Report, titled "Living Our Values," focused on six topical areas: (*a*) partners, (*b*) diversity, (*c*) coffee, (*d*) customers, (*e*) community and environment, and (*g*) profitability.

Partners

Starbucks employs some 74 000 people around the world. The company considers its employees as partners following the creation of Starbucks stock option plan in 1991, called "Bean Stock." The company believes that giving eligible full- and part-time employees an ownership in the company and sharing the rewards of Starbucks' financial success has made the sense of partnership real. In addition, the company has one of the most competitive employee benefits and compensation packages in the retail industry. Ongoing training, career advancement opportunities, partner recognition programs, and diligent efforts to ensure a healthy and safe work environment have all contributed to the fact that Starbucks has one of the lowest employee turnover rates within the restaurant and fast food industry.

Diversity

Starbucks strives to mirror the customers and communities it serves. On a quarterly basis, the company monitors the demographics of its workforce to determine whether they reflect the communities in which Starbucks operates. In 2003, Starbucks' U.S. workforce comprised 63 percent women and 24 percent visible minorities. The company also is engaged in a joint venture called Urban Coffee Opportunities (UCO) created to bring Starbucks stores to diverse neighbourhoods. There were 52 UCO locations employing almost 1000 Starbucks partners at the end of 2003.

Supplier diversity is also emphasized. To do business with Starbucks as a diverse supplier, that company must be 51 percent owned, operated, and managed by women, minorities, or socially disadvantaged individuals and meet Starbucks requirements of quality, service, value, stability, and sound business practice. The

company spent $80 million with diverse suppliers in 2003, $95 million with diverse suppliers in 2004.

Coffee

Starbucks' attention to quality coffee extends to its coffee growers located in more than 20 countries. Sustainable development is emphasized. This means that Starbucks pays coffee farmers a fair price for the beans; that the coffee is grown in an ecologically sound manner; and that Starbucks invests in the farming communities where its coffees are produced.

One longstanding initiative is Starbucks' partnership with Conservation International, a nonprofit organization dedicated to protecting soil, water, energy, and biological diversity worldwide. Starbucks is particularly focused on environmental protection and helping local farmers earn more for their crops. In 2003, Starbucks invested more than $1 million in social programs, notably health and education projects, that benefited farming communities in nine countries, from Columbia to Indonesia.

Customers

Starbucks served customers in 32 countries in 2003. The company and its partners are committed to providing each customer the optimal Starbucks experience every time they visit a store. For very loyal Starbucks customers, that translates into 18 visits per month on average.

Making a connection with customers at each store and building the relationship a customer has with Starbucks *baristas,* or coffee brewers, is important in creating the Starbucks experience. Each barista receives 24 hours of training in customer service and basic retail skills, as well as "Coffee Knowledge" and "Brewing the Perfect Cup" classes. Baristas are taught to anticipate the customers' needs and to make eye contact while carefully explaining the various coffee flavours and blends. Starbucks also enhances the customer relationship by soliciting feedback and responding to patrons' experiences and concerns. Starbucks Customer Relations reviews and responds to every inquiry or comment, often within 24 hours in the case of telephone calls and e-mails.

Community and Environment

Efforts to contribute positively to the communities it serves and the environments in which it operates are emphasized in Starbucks' guiding principles. "We aren't in the coffee business, serving people. We are in the people business, serving coffee," says Howard Schultz. Starbucks and its partners have been recognized for volunteer support and financial contributions to a wide variety of local, national, and international social, economic, and environmental initiatives. For example, the "Make Your Mark" program rewards partners' gifts of time for volunteer work with charitable donations from Starbucks. In addition, Starbucks is a supporter of CARE International, a nonprofit organization dedicated to fighting global poverty.

Starbucks is also committed to environmental responsibility. Starbucks has been a long-time involvement with Earth Day activities. It has instituted companywide energy and water conservation programs and waste reduction, recycling, and reuse initiatives proposed by partner *Green Teams*.

Profitability

At Starbucks, profitability is viewed as essential to its future success. When the Starbucks' guiding principles were conceived, profitability was included but intentionally placed last on the list. This was done not because profitability was the least important. Instead, it was believed that adherence to the five other principles would ultimately lead to good financial performance. In fact, it has.

QUESTIONS

1   How does Starbucks' approach to social responsibility relate to the three concepts of social responsibility described in the text?

2   What role does sustainable development play in Starbucks' approach to social responsibility?

PART 1
Initiating the
Marketing
Process

PART 2
Understanding
Buyers and
Markets

PART 3
Targeting
Marketing
Opportunities

PART 4
Satisfying
Marketing
Opportunities

PART 5
Managing the
Marketing
Process

UNDERSTANDING BUYERS AND MARKETS

HOW PART 2 FITS INTO THE BOOK

Chapters in Part 2 stress how marketing seeks to serve the needs and wants of potential buyers, whether they are individuals and household consumers, organizations, or global customers.

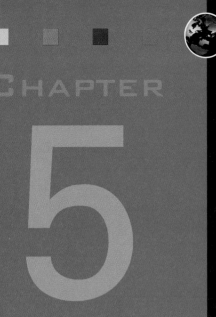

CHAPTER 5

CONSUMER
BEHAVIOUR

LEARNING OBJECTIVES

After reading this chapter, you should be able to:

1 Describe the stages in the consumer purchase decision process.

2 Distinguish among three variations of the consumer purchase decision process: routine, limited, and extended problem solving.

3 Identify major psychological influences on consumer behaviour.

4 Identify the major sociocultural influences on consumer behaviour.

GETTING TO KNOW THE AUTOMOBILE CUSTOM(H)ER AND INFLUENC(H)ER

Who buys more than 60 percent of new cars and light trucks? Who spends billions on new and used cars and trucks and automotive accessories? Who influences 85 percent of all vehicle-buying decisions? Women. Yes, women.

Women are a driving force in the North American automotive industry. Enlightened automakers, such as Volvo, have hired women designers, engineers, and marketing executives to better understand and serve this valuable automobile consum(h)er and influenc(h)er of purchase decisions. What have they learned? First, women cast the deciding vote in the family-car purchase and, of course, make the final decision in all of their own purchase decisions. Second, sleek exteriors and interior designs that fit a driver's proportions as well as easy vehicular entry and exit, minimal maintenance, good visibility, storage space, and effortless parking are important to women . . . and men. "We have found that by meeting women's expectations, we exceeded those of most men," says Hans-Olov Olsson, president and CEO of Volvo Cars, a unit of Ford Motor Company. Not surprisingly, 54 percent of Volvo buyers in North America are women.

Third, women approach car buying in a deliberate manner. They frequently visit auto-buying Web sites and scan car advertisements to gather information, but recommendations of friends and relatives matter most. Women shop an average of three dealerships before making a purchase decision—one more than men. While only a third of women say that price is the most influential factor when they shop for a car, 73 percent say price determines their final decision. Finally, automakers have learned that the great majority of women dislike the car-buying process.

Recognition of women as purchasers and influencers in car and truck buying has also altered the behaviour of dealers. Many dealers now use a one-price policy and have stopped negotiating a vehicle's price. Industry research indicates that 68 percent of new-car buyers dread the price negotiation process involved in buying a car, and women often refuse to do it at all![1]

consumer behaviour

The actions a person takes in purchasing and using products and services, including the mental and social processes that precede and follow these actions.

This chapter examines **consumer behaviour**, the actions a person takes in purchasing and using products and services, including the mental and social processes that precede and follow these actions. This chapter shows how the behavioural sciences help answer such questions as why people choose one product or brand over another, how they make these choices, and how companies use this knowledge to provide value to consumers.

■ ■ ■

CONSUMER PURCHASE DECISION PROCESS

purchase decision process

The stages a buyer passes through in making choices about which products and services to buy.

Behind the visible act of making a purchase lies an important decision process that must be investigated. The stages a buyer passes through in making choices about which products and services to buy is the **purchase decision process**. This process has the five stages shown in Figure 5–1: (1) problem recognition, (2) information search, (3) alternatives evaluation, (4) purchase decision, and (5) postpurchase behaviour.

Problem Recognition: Perceiving a Need

Problem recognition, the initial step in the purchase decision, is perceiving a difference between a person's ideal and actual situations that is big enough to trigger a decision.[2] This can be as simple as finding an empty milk carton in the refrigerator; noting, as a first-year university student, that your high school clothes are not in the style that other students are wearing; or realizing that your laptop computer may not be working properly.

In marketing, advertisements or salespeople can activate a consumer's decision process by showing the shortcomings of competing (or currently owned) products. For instance, an advertisement for an MP3 player could stimulate problem recognition because it emphasizes "maximum music from one device."

Information Search: Seeking Value

■ **FIGURE 5–1** ■■
Purchase decision process

After recognizing a problem, a consumer begins to search for information, the next stage in the purchase decision process. First, you may scan your memory for previous experiences with products or brands.[3] This action is called *internal search*. For

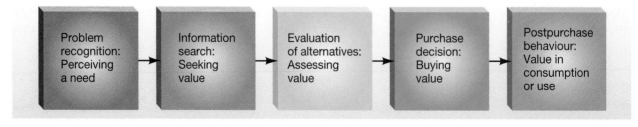

frequently purchased products, such as shampoo and conditioner, this may be enough. Or a consumer may undertake an *external search* for information.[4] This is especially needed when past experience or knowledge is insufficient, the risk of making a wrong purchase decision is high, and the cost of gathering information is low. The primary sources of external information are (1) *personal sources*, such as relatives and friends whom the consumer trusts; (2) *public sources*, including various product-rating organizations, such as *Consumer Reports*, government agencies, and TV "consumer programs"; and (3) *marketer-dominated sources*, such as information from sellers that includes advertising, company Web sites, salespeople, and point-of-purchase displays in stores.

Suppose you are considering buying a portable MP3 player. You will probably tap several information sources: friends and relatives, MP3 advertisements, brand and company Web sites, and stores carrying MP3 players (for demonstrations). You might also study comparable evaluation of various MP3 players as found in *Consumer Reports*, published in either hard copy or found online. In fact, online information search has become very popular with 75 percent of Canadians claiming to have searched for product information online last year.[5] Also, many Canadians are turning to Web logs, or blogs, for information. A **blog** is a Web site that contains an online personal journal that contains reflections, comments, and often hyperlinks provided by the writer. Consumers can find a wide variety of information on these blogs, including people's personal experiences with products and companies.

Alternative Evaluations: Assessing Value

The information search stage clarifies the problem for the consumer by (1) yielding brand names, (2) suggesting criteria to use to judge the various brands, and (3) developing consumer value perceptions. The brands that you become aware of during your search become part of your *awareness set*. The criteria you consider when evaluating MP3 players are called **evaluative criteria**—factors that represent both the objective attributes of a brand (such as locate speed) and the subjective ones (such as brand prestige) you use to compare different products and brands.[6] Only the brands that meet your criteria become part of your evoked set, or **consideration set**—the group of brands that a consumer would consider acceptable from among all the brands which he or she is aware of.[7]

Consumers often have several criteria for evaluating brands. Knowing this, companies seek to identify the most important evaluative criteria that consumers use when judging brands and often display these criteria in advertisements. The goal is to create in the consumer's mind the best brand or best value for the money sought by him or her and other consumers. For example, if you were buying a new MP3 player, your selection criteria might consist of price, sound quality, ease of use, or some other combination of these and other criteria. Companies developing MP3 players would have to demonstrate to you that their brands met your criteria and do so better than did the competitors'.

Purchase Decision: Buying Value

Having examined the alternatives in the consideration set, you are almost ready to make a purchase decision. Two choices remain: (1) from whom to buy, and (2) when to buy. For a product like an MP3 player, the information search process probably involved visiting retail stores, seeing different brands in catalogues, and viewing an MP3 player on a seller's Web site. The choice of which seller to buy from will depend on such considerations as the terms of sale, past experience buying from the seller, and the return policy. Often, a purchase decision involves a simultaneous evaluation of both product attributes and seller characteristics. For example, you might choose the second

blog
A Web site that contains an online personal journal that contains reflections, comments, and often hyperlinks provided by the writer.

evaluative criteria
Factors that represent both the objective attributes of a brand (such as locate speed) and the subjective ones (such as brand prestige) you use to compare different products and brands.

consideration set
The group of brands that a consumer would consider acceptable from among all the brands which he or she is aware of.

A satisfactory or unsatisfactory consumption or use experience is an important factor in postpurchase behaviour. Marketer attention to this stage can pay huge dividends as described in the text.

most preferred brand of MP3 player at a store with a liberal refund and return policy versus the most preferred brand at a store with more conservative policies.

Deciding when to buy is frequently determined by a number of factors. For instance, you might buy sooner if one of your preferred brands is on sale or its manufacturer offers a rebate. Other such factors as the store atmosphere, pleasantness of the shopping experience, salesperson persuasiveness, time pressure, and financial circumstances could also affect whether a purchase decision is made or postponed.[8]

Postpurchase Behaviour: Value in Consumption or Use

After buying a product, the consumer compares it with his or her expectations and is either satisfied or dissatisfied. If the consumer is dissatisfied, marketers must decide whether the product was deficient or consumer expectations were too high. Product deficiency may require a design change; if expectations are too high, perhaps the company's advertising or the salesperson oversold the product's features.

Sensitivity to a customer's consumption or use experience is extremely important in a consumer's value perception. For example, research on long-distance telephone services provided by Sprint and AT&T indicates that satisfaction or dissatisfaction affects consumer value perceptions.[9] Studies show that satisfaction or dissatisfaction affects consumer communications and repeat-purchase behaviour. Satisfied buyers tell three other people about their experiences. Dissatisfied buyers complain to nine people.[10] Satisfied buyers also tend to buy from the same seller each time a purchase occasion arises. The financial impact of repeat-purchase behaviour is significant.[11] Accordingly, such firms as General Electric (GE), Johnson & Johnson, Coca-Cola, and British Airways focus attention on postpurchase behaviour to maximize customer satisfaction and retention. These firms, among many others, now provide toll-free telephone numbers, offer liberalized return and refund policies, and engage in staff training to handle complaints, answer questions, and record suggestions. For example, GE operates a database that stores 750 000 answers about 8500 of its models in 120 product lines to handle three million calls annually. Such efforts produce positive postpurchase communications among consumers and contribute to relationship building between sellers and buyers.

Often, a consumer is faced with two or more highly attractive alternatives, such as a Panasonic or Sony MP3 player. If you choose the Panasonic, you may think, "Should I have purchased the Sony?" This feeling of postpurchase psychological tension or anxiety is called **cognitive dissonance**. To alleviate it, consumers often attempt to applaud themselves for making the right choice. So, after your purchase, you may seek information to confirm your choice by asking friends such questions as, "Don't you like my new MP3 player?" or by reading ads of the brand you chose. You might even look for negative features about the brand you did not buy and decide that that brand was not right for you. Firms often use ads or follow-up calls from salespeople in this postpurchase stage to comfort buyers that they made the right decision. For many years, Buick ran an advertising campaign with the message, "Aren't you really glad you bought a Buick?"

Involvement and Problem-Solving Variations

Sometimes, consumers do not engage in the five-stage purchase decision process. Instead, they skip or minimize one or more stages, depending on the level of **involvement,** the personal, social, and economic significance of the purchase to the consumer.[12] High-involvement purchase occasions typically have at least one of three characteristics: The item to be purchased (1) is expensive, (2) can have serious personal consequences, or (3) could reflect on one's social image. For these occasions, consumers engage in extensive information search, consider many product

cognitive dissonance
Feeling of postpurchase psychological tension or anxiety.

involvement
The personal, social, and economic significance of the purchase to the consumer.

attributes and brands, form attitudes, and participate in word-of-mouth communication. Low-involvement purchases, such as toothpaste and soap, and barely involving to most of us, but audio and video systems and automobiles are very involving. There are three general variations in the consumer purchase decision process based on consumer involvement and product knowledge. Figure 5–2 shows some of the important differences between the three problem-solving variations.[13]

Extended Problem Solving   In extended problem solving, each of the five stages of the consumer purchase decision process is used in the purchase, including considerable time and effort on external information search and in identifying and evaluating alternatives. Several brands are in the consideration set, and these are evaluated on many attributes. Extended problem solving exists in high-involvement purchase situations for such items as automobiles and elaborate audio systems.

Limited Problem Solving   In limited problem solving, consumers typically seek some information or rely on a friend to help them evaluate alternatives. In general, several brands might be evaluated using a moderate number of different criteria. You might use limited problem solving in choosing a toaster, a restaurant for lunch, and other purchase situations in which you have little time or effort to spend.

Routine Problem Solving   For such products as table salt and milk, consumers recognize a problem, make a decision, and spend little effort seeking external information and evaluating alternatives. The purchase process for such items is virtually a habit and typifies low-involvement decision making. Routine problem solving is typically the case for low-priced, frequently purchased products.

Involvement and Marketing Strategy   Low and high consumer involvement has important implications for marketing strategy. If a company markets a low-involvement product and its brand is a market leader, attention is placed on (1) maintaining product quality, (2) avoiding stockout situations so that buyers do not substitute a competing brand, and (3) advertising messages that reinforce a consumer's

■ **FIGURE 5–2** ■
Comparison of problem-solving variations

CHARACTERISTICS OF THE CONSUMER PURCHASE DECISION PROCESS	HIGH ◀ CONSUMER INVOLVEMENT ▶ LOW		
	EXTENDED PROBLEM SOLVING	LIMITED PROBLEM SOLVING	ROUTINE PROBLEM SOLVING
Number of brands examined	Many	Several	One
Number of sellers considered	Many	Several	Few
Number of product attributes evaluated	Many	Moderate	One
Number of external information sources used	Many	Few	None
Time spent searching	Considerable	Little	Minimal

Help keep your heart running strong: New Tropicana® Healthy Heart™

knowledge or assures buyers they made the right choice. Market challengers have a different task. They must break buying habits and use free samples, coupons, and rebates to encourage trial of their brand. Advertising messages will focus on getting their brand into a consumer's consideration set. For example, Campbell's V8 vegetable juice advertising message—"I could have had a V8!"—was targeted at consumers who routinely purchased fruit juices and soft drinks. Challengers can also link their brand attributes with high-involvement issues. Tropicana does this by linking the natural attributes of orange juice with adult health concerns.

Marketers of high-involvement products recognize that their consumers constantly seek and process information about objective and subjective brand attributes, form evaluative criteria, rate product criteria for various brands, and combine these ratings for an overall brand evaluation—like that described in the MP3 player purchase decision. Market leaders freely supply consumers with product information through advertising and personal selling and create chat rooms on their company or brand Web sites. Market challengers capitalize on this behaviour through comparative advertising that focuses on existing product attributes and often introduce novel evaluative criteria for judging competing brands. Increasingly, challengers benefit from Internet search engines, such as MSN Search and Google, that assist buyers of high-involvement products.

Situational Influences

situational influences

Have an impact on your purchase decision process: (1) the purchase task, (2) social surroundings, (3) physical surroundings, (4) temporal effects, and (5) antecedent states.

Often the purchase situation will affect the purchase decision process. Five **situational influences** have an impact on your purchase decision process: (1) the purchase task, (2) social surroundings, (3) physical surroundings, (4) temporal effects, and (5) antecedent states.[14] The purchase task is the reason for engaging in the decision in the first place. Information searching and evaluating alternatives may differ, depending on whether the purchase is a gift, which often involves social visibility, or for the buyer's own use. Social surroundings, including the other people present when a purchase decision is made, may also affect what is purchased. Physical surroundings, such as decor, music, and crowding in retail stores, may alter how purchase decisions are made. Temporal effects, such as time of day or the amount of time available, will influence where consumers have breakfast and lunch and what is ordered. Finally, antecedent states, which include the consumer's mood or the amount of cash on hand, can influence purchase behaviour and choice.

Figure 5–3 on the next page shows the many influences that affect the consumer purchase decision process. The decision to buy a product also involves important psychological and sociocultural influences, the two important topics discussed in the remainder of this chapter. Marketing mix influences are described in Chapters 10 through 18.

CONCEPT CHECK

1. What is the first stage in the consumer purchase decision process?

2. The brands a consumer considers buying out of the set of brands in a product class which the consumer is aware of is called the _____.

3. What is the term for postpurchase anxiety?

■ FIGURE 5–3 ■

Influences on the consumer purchase decision process

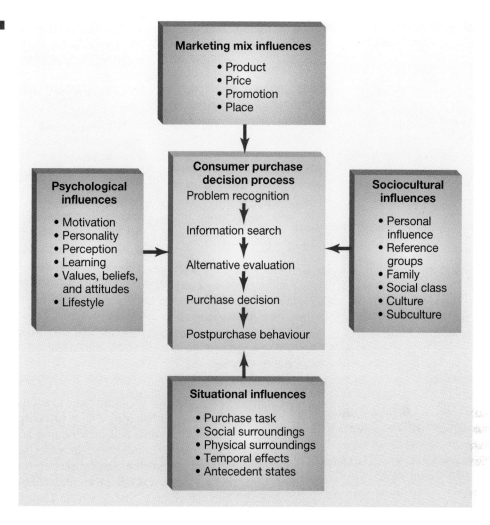

PSYCHOLOGICAL INFLUENCES ON CONSUMER BEHAVIOUR

Psychology helps marketers understand why and how consumers behave as they do. In particular, such concepts as motivation and personality; perception; learning; values, beliefs, and attitudes; and lifestyle are useful for interpreting buying processes and directing marketing efforts.

Motivation and Personality

Motivation and personality are two familiar psychological concepts that have specific meanings and marketing implications. They are both used frequently to describe why people do some things and not others.

motivation

The energizing force that causes behaviour that satisfies a need.

Motivation   Motivation is the energizing force that causes behaviour that satisfies a need. Because consumer needs are the focus of the marketing concept, marketers try to arouse these needs.

An individual's needs are boundless. People possess physiological needs for such basics as water, sex, and food. They also have learned needs, including esteem, achievement, and affection. Psychologists point out that these needs are hierarchical; that is, once physiological needs are met, people seek to satisfy their learned needs. Figure 5–4 shows one need hierarchy and classification scheme that contains five

■ **FIGURE 5–4** ■

Hierarchy of needs

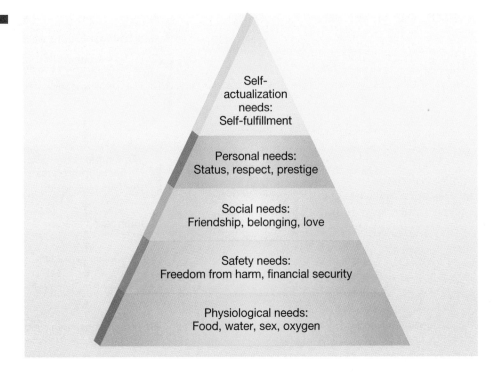

need classes.[15] *Physiological needs* are basic to survival and must be satisfied first. A Burger King advertisement featuring a juicy hamburger attempts to activate the need for food. *Safety needs* involve self-preservation and physical well-being. Smoke detector and burglar alarm manufacturers focus on these needs. *Social needs* are concerned with love and friendship. Dating services and fragrance companies try to arouse these needs. *Personal needs* are represented by the need for achievement, status, prestige, and self-respect. The American Express Gold Card and Harry Rosen men's wear appeal to these needs. Sometimes, firms try to arouse multiple needs to stimulate problem recognition. For example, Michelin combines security with parental love to promote tire replacement. *Self-actualization* needs involve personal fulfillment, such as completing your degree.

Personality   **Personality** refers to a person's consistent behaviours or responses to recurring situations. Although numerous personality theories exist, most identify key traits—enduring characteristics within a person or in his or her relationships with others. Such traits include assertiveness, extroversion, compliance, dominance, and aggression, among others. Research suggests that compliant people prefer known brand names and use more mouthwash and toilet soaps. In contrast, aggressive types use razors, not electric shavers, apply more cologne and after-shave lotions, and purchase signature goods, such as the Birks blue box, Yves St. Laurent, and Donna Karan as an indicator of status.[16] Cross-cultural analysis also suggests that residents of different countries have a **national character**, or a distinct set of personality characteristics common among people of a country or society.[17] For example, Canadians are more deliberate and cautious about purchasing anything without examining it.

These personality characteristics are often revealed in a person's **self-concept**, which is the way people see themselves and the way they believe others see them. Marketers recognize that people have an actual self-concept and an ideal self-concept. The *actual self* refers to how people actually see themselves. The *ideal self* describes how people would like to see themselves. These two self "images" are reflected in the products and brands a person buys, including automobiles, home appliances and furnishings, magazines, clothing, grooming and leisure products, and,

---

personality

A person's consistent behaviours or responses to recurring situations.

national character

A distinct set of personality characteristics common among people of a country or society.

self-concept

The way people see themselves and the way they believe others see them.

ETHICS AND SOCIAL RESPONSIBILITY ALERT

The Ethics of Subliminal Messages

For almost 50 years, the topic of subliminal perception and the presence of subliminal messages embedded in commercial communications has sparked debate. To some, the concept of subliminal messages is a hoax. To others, the possibility of a person being influenced without their knowledge is either an exciting or a frightening concept. Many experts suggest that the use of subliminal messages by marketers, effective or not, is deceptive and unethical.

But there are marketers who occasionally pursue opportunities to create these messages. For example, a recent book by August Bullock, *The Secret Sales Pitch: An Overview of Subliminal Advertising*, is devoted to this topic. Bullock identifies images and advertisements that he claims contain subliminal messages and describes techniques that can be used for conveying these messages.

Do you believe that attempts to implant subliminal messages in electronic and print media are a deceptive practice and unethical, regardless of their intent?

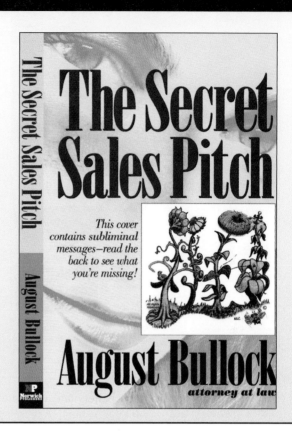

frequently, the stores a person shops. The importance of self-concept is summed up by a senior executive at Barnes & Noble: "People buy books for what the purchase says about them—their taste, their cultivation, their trendiness."[18]

Perception

perception
The process by which an individual selects, organizes, and interprets information to create a meaningful picture of the world.

One person sees a Cadillac as a mark of achievement; another sees it as ostentatious. This is the result of **perception**—the process by which an individual selects, organizes, and interprets information to create a meaningful picture of the world.

Selective Perception   Because the average consumer operates in a complex environment, the human brain attempts to organize and interpret information through a filtering process called *selective perception*. The four stages of selective perception are selective exposure, selective attention, selective comprehension, and selective retention. First, consumers are not exposed to all information or messages in the marketplace. In other words, there is *selective exposure*. For example, you may watch CTV, but not CBC television. In doing so, you do not expose yourself to any information broadcast on the CBC network. Because of selective exposure, marketers must work to determine where consumers are most likely to be exposed to information.

But even if a consumer is exposed to a message, either by accident or design, the consumer may not attend to that message. In general, with *selective attention*, the consumer will pay attention only to messages that are consistent with their attitudes

Why does the Good Housekeeping seal for Clorox's new Fresh Step Crystals cat litter appear in the ad, and why does Mary Kay, Inc. offer a free sample of its new Velocity brand fragrance through its Web site? The answers appear in the text.

Clorox Fresh Step
www.freshstep.com

Mary Kay Velocity
www.mkvelocity.com

subliminal perception
Means that you see or hear messages without being aware of them.

perceived risk
The anxieties felt because the consumer cannot anticipate the outcomes of a purchase but believes that there may be negative consequences.

and beliefs and will ignore those that are inconsistent. Consumers are also more likely to attend to messages when they are relevant or of interest to them. For example, a consumer is likely to pay attention to an ad about a product they just bought or to an ad for a product they are interested in buying.

Selective comprehension involves interpreting information so that it is consistent with one's attitudes and beliefs. A marketer's failure to understand this can have disastrous results. For example, Toro introduced a small, lightweight snowblower called the Snow Pup. Even though the product worked, sales failed to meet expectations. Why? Toro later found out that consumers perceived the name to mean that Snow Pup was a toy or too light to do any serious snow removal. When the product was renamed "Snow Master," sales increased sharply.[19]

Selective retention means that consumers do not remember all the information they see, read, or hear, even minutes after exposure to it. This affects the internal and external information search stage of the purchase decision process. This is why furniture and automobile retailers often give consumers product brochures to take home after they leave the showroom.

Because perception plays such an important role in consumer behaviour, it is not surprising that the topic of subliminal perception is a popular item for discussion. **Subliminal perception** means that you see or hear messages without being aware of them. The presence and effect of subliminal perception on behaviour is a hotly debated issue, with more popular appeal than scientific support. Indeed, evidence suggests that such messages have limited effects on behaviour.[20] If these messages did influence behaviour, would their use be an ethical practice? (See the accompanying Ethics and Social Responsibility Alert box.[21])

Perceived Risk   Perception plays a major role in the perceived risk in purchasing a product or service. **Perceived risk** represents the anxieties felt because the consumer cannot anticipate the outcomes of a purchase but believes that there may be negative consequences. Examples of possible negative consequences are the size of the financial outlay required to buy the product (Can I afford $200 for those skis?), the risk of physical harm (Is bungee jumping safe?), and the performance of the product (Will the hair colouring work?). A more abstract form is psychosocial (What will my friends say if I wear that sweater?). Perceived risk affects information search because the greater the perceived risk, the more extensive the external search phase is likely to be.

Recognizing the importance of perceived risk, companies develop strategies to reduce the consumer's risk and encourage purchases. These strategies and examples of firms using them include the following:

- Obtaining seals of approval: Canadian Standards Association (CSA) seal or the Good Housekeeping seal for Fresh Step Crystals cat litter.
- Securing endorsements from influential people: Athletes promoting milk consumption.
- Providing free trials of the product: sample packages of General Mills Cheerios Snack Mix or Mary Kay's Velocity fragrance.
- Giving extensive usage instructions: Clairol haircolouring.
- Providing warranties and guarantees: Cadillac's four-year, 80 000-kilometre, Gold Key bumper-to-bumper warranty.

Learning

Much consumer behaviour is learned. Consumers learn which sources to use for information about products and services, which evaluative criteria to use when assessing alternatives, and, more generally, how to make purchase decisions. **Learning** refers to those behaviours that result from (1) repeated experience, and (2) thinking.

learning
Those behaviours that result from (1) repeated experience, and (2) thinking.

Behavioural Learning   *Behavioural learning* is the process of developing automatic responses to a situation built up through repeated exposure to it. Four variables are central to how consumers learn from repeated experience: drive, cue, response, and reinforcement. A *drive* is a need that moves an individual to action. Drives, such as hunger, might be represented by motives. A *cue* is a stimulus or symbol perceived by consumers. A *response* is the action taken by a consumer to satisfy the drive, and a *reinforcement* is the reward. Being hungry (drive), a consumer sees a cue (a billboard), takes action (buys a hamburger), and receives a reward (it tastes great!).

Marketers use two concepts from behavioural learning theory. *Stimulus generalization* occurs when a response elicited by one stimulus (cue) is generalized to another stimulus. Using the same brand name for different products is an application of this concept, such as Tylenol Cold & Flu and Tylenol P.M. *Stimulus discrimination* refers to a person's ability to perceive differences in stimuli. Consumers' tendency to perceive all light beers as being alike led to Budweiser Light commercials that distinguished among many types of "lights" and Bud Light.

Cognitive Learning   Consumers also learn through thinking, reasoning, and mental problem solving without direct experience. This type of learning, called *cognitive learning*, involves making connections between two or more ideas or simply observing the outcomes of others' behaviours and adjusting your own accordingly. Firms also influence this type of learning. Through repetition in advertising, such messages as "Advil is a headache remedy" attempt to link a brand (Advil) and an idea (headache remedy) by showing someone using the brand and finding relief.

brand loyalty
A favourable attitude toward and consistent purchase of a single brand over time.

Brand Loyalty   Learning is also important because it relates to habit formation—the basis of routine problem solving. Furthermore, there is a close link between habits and **brand loyalty**, which is a favourable attitude toward and consistent purchase of a single brand over time. Brand loyalty results from the positive reinforcement

Bad news. Your toothpaste won't make it past the soup.*

Unless you use Colgate Total. Most toothpastes can't fight plaque after you eat or drink, when teeth become more vulnerable to bacteria. But Colgate Total is different. Its unique formula has an antibacterial ingredient that attaches to teeth to protect for 12 hours. Even after eating and drinking.

Colgate Total

12 Hour Protection

EXTRA POWER. EXTRA GENTLE.

Extra Strength BAYER Plus.
Extra strong for your pain, plus extra gentle for your stomach.

Nothing's stronger for tough body pain, aching joints and minor arthritis than Extra Strength BAYER Plus. Just two caplets release 1000 milligrams of BAYER Aspirin. Plus an ingredient that helps protect against the occasional upset stomach some aspirin users may experience.

THE POWER OF **BAYER**

Attitudes toward Colgate toothpaste and Extra Strength Bayer Aspirin were successfully changed by these ads. How? Read the text to find out how marketers can change consumer attitudes toward products and brands.

Colgate-Palmolive
www.colgate.com

Bayer Corporation
www.bayer.ca

values
Personally or socially preferable modes of conduct or states of existence that are enduring.

beliefs
A consumer's subjective perception of how well a product or brand performs on different attributes.

attitude
A learned predisposition to respond to an object or class of objects in a consistently favourable or unfavourable way.

of previous actions. So, a consumer reduces risk and saves time by consistently purchasing the same brand of shampoo and has favourable results—healthy, shining hair. There is evidence of brand loyalty in many commonly purchased products in Canada and the global marketplace. However, the incidence of brand loyalty appears to be declining in North America, Mexico, European Union nations, and Japan.[22]

Values, Beliefs, and Attitudes

Values, beliefs, and attitudes play a central role in consumer decision making all related marketing actions.

Values　**Values** are personally or socially preferable modes of conduct or states of existence that are enduring. In essence, values are ideas people hold to be important or believe to be good. Values vary by level of specificity. We speak of Canadian core values, including material well-being and humanitarianism. We also have personal values, such as thriftiness and ambition. Marketers are concerned with both but focus mostly on personal values.

Beliefs　**Beliefs** are a consumer's subjective perception of how well a product or brand performs on different attributes. Beliefs are based on personal experience, advertising, and discussions with other people.

Attitudes　An **attitude** is a "learned predisposition to respond to an object or class of objects in a consistently favourable or unfavourable way."[23]

Attitudes are shaped by our values and beliefs. For example, personal values affect attitudes by influencing the importance assigned to specific product attributes. Suppose thriftiness is one of your personal values. When you evaluate cars, fuel economy (a product attribute) becomes important. If you believe (a belief) that a specific car has this attribute, you are likely to have a favourable attitude toward it.

Attitude Change   Marketers use three approaches to try to change consumer attitudes toward products and brands, as shown in the following examples.[24]

1. *Changing beliefs about the extent to which a brand has certain attributes.* To allay consumer concern that Aspirin use causes an upset stomach, Bayer Corporation successfully promoted the gentleness of its Extra Strength Bayer Plus Aspirin.
2. *Changing the perceived importance of attributes.* Pepsi-Cola made freshness an important product attribute when it stamped freshness dates on its cans. Prior to doing so, few consumers considered cola freshness an issue. After Pepsi spent about $25 million on advertising and promotion, a consumer survey found that 61 percent of cola drinkers believed freshness dating was an important attribute.
3. *Adding new attributes to the product.* Colgate-Palmolive included a new antibacterial ingredient tricloson, in its Colgate Total toothpaste and spent $100 million marketing the brand. The result? Colgate replaced Crest as the market leader for the first time in 25 years.

Lifestyle

lifestyle

A mode of living that is identified by how people spend their time and resources, what they consider important in their environment, and what they think of themselves and the world around them.

Lifestyle is a mode of living that is identified by how people spend their time and resources, what they consider important in their environment, and what they think of themselves and the world around them. The analysis of consumer lifestyles, called psychographics, has produced many insights into consumer behaviour. For example, lifestyle analysis has proven useful in segmenting and targeting consumers for new and existing products and services (Chapter 9).

Psychographics, in essence, the practice of combining psychology and demographics, is often used to uncover consumer motivations for buying and using products and services. There are several well-known psychographic systems developed by various researchers, including: (1) the VALS system developed by SRI Consulting Business Intelligence (SRIC-BI), (2) Monitor MindBase developed by Yankelovich Partners, and (3) PRIZM developed by Claritas. Until recently, these psychographic systems have been American-based. But, VALS is now available for the Japanese and British markets, and PRIZM has now been adapted for the Canadian market.

Two home-grown psychographics systems developed for the Canadian market are: (1) The Goldfarb Segments developed by Millward Brown Goldfarb Consultants of Toronto, and (2) The Social Values Tribes developed by the Canadian firm Environics.

The Goldfarb Segments are based on activities, interests, and opinions research involving a large sample of Canadian adults. Nine lifestyle or psychographic segments have been identified and labelled as seen in Figure 5–5. Visit the Millward Brown Goldfarb Web site as shown in the accompanying WebLink box, and fill out the survey to see which psychographic segment you belong to.[25]

The Social Values Tribes system is based on values and attitudes tracked using a sociocultural map which harmonizes Canadian demographics with such values as

WEBLINK
HTTP://WWW.MCGRAWHILL.CA/
COLLEGE/CRANE

Identify Which Goldfarb Segment You Belong To

Millward Brown Goldfarb has a Canadian psychographic system that consists of nine segments. Go to the Web site www.mbgoldfarb.com, and click on the Psychographic Analysis icon. There you will be asked to take the psychographic test (Click on Take the Test). Answer the questions, and you will receive your results, including not only the segment you belong to but the characteristics of the segment.

■ **FIGURE 5-5** ■

Millward Brown Goldfarb
Segment

Source: Reprinted with permission of
Millward Brown

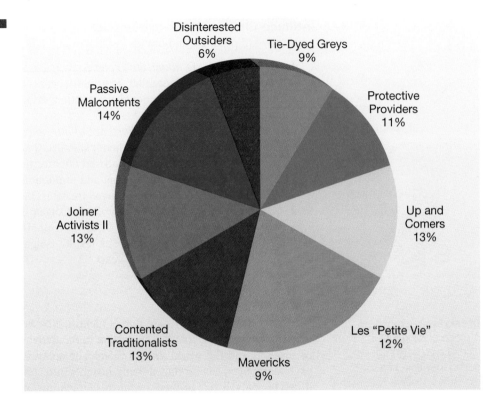

rejection of authority, destiny control, and pursuit of happiness. The tribes are grouped using pre-boomer, boomer, and post-boomer cohorting. In partnership with Claritas, Environics has combined its Social Values Tribes system with the U.S.-based PRIZM system to create $PRIZM_{CE}$, a new Canadian geodemographics and psychographics system that consists of 66 lifestyle types. Only 16 of the Canadian segments or clusters correspond to the 66 original segments or clusters found in the American version of PRIZM, while 50 are unique to Canada, including such groups as Les Chics and Lunch @ Tim's.

Given our globalized economy, one firm set out to determine if discernable lifestyle segments cut across cultures, regardless of differences in geographics, languages or other factors. Global Scan developed by BSBW is a psychographics system based on surveys of 15 000 consumers in 14 countries (Australia, Canada, Columbia, Finland, France, Germany, Hong Kong, Indonesia, Japan, Mexico, Spain, the United Kingdom, the United States, and Venezula). It measures more than 250 values and attitudes, in addition to demographics, media usage, and buying preferences. BSBW discovered that five global lifestyle segments emerged: strivers, achievers, pressured, adapters, and traditionals. These segments exist in all 14 countries, but the percentage of the population in each group varies by country. Still, this psychographic system allows global marketers insight into how to segment and target consumers in these different countries.

■ ■ ■
SOCIOCULTURAL INFLUENCES ON CONSUMER BEHAVIOUR

Sociocultural influences, which evolve from a consumer's formal and informal relationships with other people, also exert a significant impact on consumer behaviour. These involve personal influence, reference groups, family, social class, culture, and subculture.

Personal Influence

A consumer's purchases are often influenced by the views, opinions, or behaviours of others. Two aspects of personal influence are important to marketing: opinion leadership and word-of-mouth activity.

opinion leaders
Those knowledgeable about or users of particular products and services, and so their opinions influence others' choices.

Opinion Leadership   Individuals who exert direct or indirect social influence over others are called **opinion leaders**. Opinion leaders are considered to be knowledgeable about or users of particular products and services, and so their opinions influence others' choices. Opinion leadership is widespread in the purchase of cars and trucks, clothing and accessories, club membership, consumer electronics, vacation locations, and financial investments. A study by *Popular Mechanics* magazine identified 18 million opinion leaders who influence the purchases of some 85 million consumers for do-it-yourself products.

About 10 percent of adults are opinion leaders.[26] Identifying, reaching, and influencing opinion leaders is a major challenge for companies. Some firms use sports figures or celebrities as spokespersons to represent their products, for example, actor Pierce Brosnan and tennis player Anna Kournikova for Omega watches, in the hope that they are opinion leaders. Others promote their products in those media believed to reach opinion leaders. Still others use more direct approaches. For example, DaimlerChrysler Corporation invited influential community leaders and business executives to test-drive its new models. Some 6000 accepted the offer, and 98 percent said they would recommend their tested car. The company estimated that the number of favourable recommendations totalled 32 000.

word of mouth
The influencing of people during conversations.

Word of Mouth   The influencing of people during conversations is called **word of mouth**. Word of mouth is the most powerful and authentic information source for consumers because it typically involves friends viewed as trustworthy. According to a recent study, 67 percent of consumer product sales are directly based on word-of-mouth activity among friends, family, and colleagues. For services, word of mouth plays an even stronger role, with 70 percent of Canadians saying they used word of mouth when selecting a bank and 95 percent when choosing a physician.[27]

Firms use actors or athletes as spokespersons to represent their products, for example, Pierce Brosnan and Anna Kournikova for Omega watches, in the hope that they are opinion leaders.

Omega
www.omega.com

MARKETING NEWSNET   The Buzz on "Buzz"

Have you recently heard about a new product, movie, Web site, book, or restaurant from someone you know . . . or from a complete stranger? If so, you may have been buzzed.

Canadian research illustrates well the importance of word of mouth. For example, the Canadian Mood & Mindset online survey reveals that we do rely on each other for recommendations about products and services. The key to successful buzz, according to Lynn Fletcher of Arnold Worldwide Canada in Toronto, is to find the quarterbacks of buzz. Her company's research reveals that just 14 percent of the Canadian population comprised the quarterbacks of buzz. And they are not defined by gender, age, regions, education, or income. What sets them apart is attitude. Inspirationals are the ones with the knowledge, the ones that have the idea. They are about 4 percent of this population. Connectors, the remaining 10 percent, are defined by their sociability. Put them together, and you can create buzz about your brand, your company, or your idea. CTV's successful series, *Corner Gas*, used buzz that helped make the series one of the more successful homegrown TV programs in recent history. To kick-start the buzz, preview screeners were sent to members of the media and to a list of inspirationals and connectors. A well-focused public relations campaign, on-air promotion, an integrated Web site promotion, a cross-country standup tour, branded premiums, and free gas giveaways rounded out the promotional campaign to support the series and to generate even more buzz. According to CTV, the buzz about the series continues at dinner conversations across the country.

On the other hand, if organizations have difficulty locating and engaging inspirationals and connectors, they can simply hire outside firms to generate buzz. BzzAgent, for example, can provide an organization with an army of buzz agents to generate buzz about its product, service, or brand. When a client signs with BzzAgent, the company searches its databases for agents who match the profile of the client's target market. Agents sign up and receive sample products and some training on buzz creation. Each time an agent completes a buzz activity, he or she files an online report. Agents get to keep the products they promote and earn points redeemable for other products. It is not cheap, however; 1000 buzz agents for a 12-week buzz campaign can cost $85 000, exclusive of product samples. Finally, Proctor and Gamble has its own word-of-mouth or buzz-marketing arm, called Tremor. Not only do these Tremor members promote P&G's products, P&G also farms them out to other companies, such as Kraft, and Coca-Cola. Tremor members work for free, except the coupons and product samples they receive. There continues to be a lot of buzz about buzz, and more and more Canadian organizations are interested in finding out how to generate it.

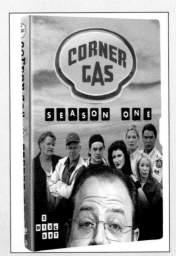

The power of personal influence has prompted firms to promote positive word of mouth and retard negative word of mouth. For instance, "teaser" advertising campaigns are run in advance of new-product introductions to stimulate conversations. Other techniques, such as advertising slogans, music, and humour, also heighten positive word of mouth. Many commercials shown during the Super Bowl, for instance, are created expressly to initiate conversations about the advertisements and featured product or service the next day. Increasingly, companies recruit and deploy people to produce *buzz*—popularity created by consumer word of mouth. Read the accompanying Marketing NewsNet box to learn more about buzz.[28]

On the other hand, rumours about Kmart (snake eggs in clothing), McDonald's (worms in hamburgers), Corona Extra beer (contaminated beer), and Snickers candy bars in Russia (a cause of diabetes) have resulted in negative word of mouth, none of which was based on fact. Overcoming or neutralizing negative word of mouth is difficult and costly. Marketers have found that supplying factual information, providing toll-free numbers for consumers to call the company, and giving appropriate product demonstrations have proven helpful.

The power of word of mouth has been magnified by the Internet through online forums, chat rooms, bulletin boards, and Web sites. In fact, Ford uses special software to monitor online messages and find out what consumers are saying about its vehicles.

Reference Groups

reference groups
People to whom an individual looks as a basis for self-appraisal or as a source of personal standards.

Reference groups are people to whom an individual looks as a basis for self-appraisal or as a source of personal standards. Reference groups affect consumer purchases because they influence the information, attitudes, and aspiration levels that help set a consumer's standards. For example, one of the first questions one asks others when planning to attend a social occasion is, "What are you going to wear?" Reference groups have an important influence on the purchase of luxury products but not of necessities—reference groups exert a strong influence on the brand chosen when its use or consumption is highly visible to others.

Consumers have many reference groups, but three groups have clear marketing implications. A *membership group* is one to which a person actually belongs, including fraternities and sororities, social clubs, and the family. Such groups are easily identifiable and are targeted by firms selling insurance, insignia products, and charter vacations. An *aspiration group* is one that a person wishes to be a member of or wishes to be identified with, such as a professional society. Firms frequently rely on spokespeople or settings associated with their target market's aspiration group in their advertising. A *dissociative group* is one that a person wishes to maintain a distance from because of differences in values or behaviours.

Family Influence

Family influences on consumer behaviour result from three sources: consumer socialization, passage through the family life cycle, and decision making within the family or household.

consumer socialization
The process by which people acquire the skills, knowledge, and attitudes necessary to function as consumers.

Consumer Socialization   The process by which people acquire the skills, knowledge, and attitudes necessary to function as consumers is **consumer socialization**.[29] Children learn how to purchase (1) by interacting with adults in purchase situations, and (2) through their own purchasing and product usage experiences. Research shows that children evidence brand preferences at age two, and these preferences often last a lifetime.[30] This knowledge prompted Sony to introduce "My First Sony," a line of portable audio equipment for children; Time, Inc., to launch *Sports Illustrated for Kids;* Polaroid to develop the Cool Cam camcorder for children between ages 9 and 14; and Yahoo! and America Online to offer special areas where young audiences can view their children's menu—Yahooligans! and Kids Only, respectively.

family life cycle
The distinct phases that a family progresses through from formation to retirement, each phase bringing with it identifiable purchasing behaviours.

Family Life Cycle   Consumers act and purchase differently as they go through life. The **family life cycle** concept describes the distinct phases that a family progresses through from formation to retirement, each phase bringing with it identifiable purchasing behaviours.[31] Figure 5–6 illustrates the traditional progression as well as contemporary variations of the family life cycle. Today, the traditional family—

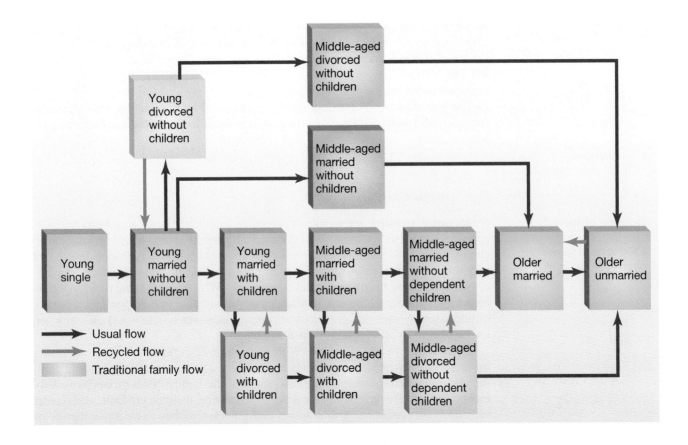

Young
divorced
without
children

Middle-aged
divorced
without
children

Middle-aged
married
without
children

Young
single

Young
married
without
children

Young
married
with
children

Middle-aged
married
with
children

Middle-aged
married
without
dependent
children

Older
married

Older
unmarried

Usual flow
Recycled flow
Traditional family flow

Young
divorced
with
children

Middle-aged
divorced
with
children

Middle-aged
divorced
without
dependent
children

■ FIGURE 5–6 ■

Modern family life cycle

married couples with children younger than 18 years—constitute less than one-third of all households. The remaining households include single parents; unmarried couples; divorced, never-married, or widowed individuals; and older married couples whose children no longer live at home.

Young singles' buying preferences are for nondurable items, including prepared foods, clothing, personal care products, and entertainment. They represent a target market for recreational travel, automobile, and consumer electronics firms. Young married couples without children are typically more affluent than young singles because usually both spouses are employed. These couples exhibit preferences for furniture, housewares, and gift items for each other. Young marrieds with children are driven by the needs of their children. They make up a sizable market for life insurance, various children's products, and home furnishings. Single parents with children are the least financially secure of households with children. Their buying preferences are affected by a limited economic status and tend toward convenience foods, child care services, and personal care items.

Middle-aged married couples with children are typically better off financially than their younger counterparts. They are a significant market for leisure products and home improvement items. Middle-aged couples without children typically have a large amount of discretionary income. These couples buy better home furnishings, status automobiles, and financial services. Persons in the last two phases—older married and older unmarried—make up a sizable market for prescription drugs, medical services, vacation trips, and gifts for younger relatives.

Family Decision Making A third influence in the decision-making process occurs within the family. Two decision-making styles exist: spouse-dominant and joint decision making. With a joint decision-making style, most decisions are made by both husband and wife. Spouse-dominant decisions are those for which either the husband or the wife is responsible. Research indicates that wives tend to have the most say

The Haggar Clothing Co. recognizes the important role women play in the choice of men's clothing. The company directs a large portion of its advertising toward women because they influence and purchase men's clothing.

Haggar Clothing Co.

www.haggar.com

In the **female** the ability to match colors comes at an early age.

In the **male** it comes when he marries a female.

The City Canada three-button, crepe jacket, 100% cotton, French-yarn shirt, Bedford cord pants, and a touch of color.

HAGGAR
Stuff you can work with.

when purchasing groceries, children's toys, clothing, and medicines. Husbands tend to be more influential in home and car maintenance purchases. Joint decision making is common for cars, vacations, houses, home appliances and electronics, and medical care. As a rule, joint decision making increases with the education of the spouses.[32]

Roles of individual family members in the purchase process are another element of family decision making. Five roles exist: (1) information gatherer, (2) influencer, (3) decision maker, (4) purchaser, and (5) user. Family members assume different roles for different products and services. This knowledge is important to firms.[33] For example, 89 percent of wives either influence or make outright purchases of men's clothing. Knowing this, Haggar Clothing, a menswear marketer, now advertises in women's magazines, such as *Vanity Fair* and *Redbook*. Even though women are often the grocery decision maker, they are not necessarily the purchaser. More than 40 percent of all food-shopping dollars are spent by male customers. Increasingly, preteens and teenagers are the information gatherers, influencers, decision makers, and purchasers of products and services for the family, given the prevalence of working parents and single-parent households.[34] Children under 12 directly influence billions of dollars in annual family purchases. Teenagers also influence billions of dollars in annual family purchases and spend millions of their own money annually. These figures help explain why, for example, Nabisco, Johnson & Johnson, Apple Computer, Kellogg, P&G, Sony, and Oscar Mayer, among countless other companies, spend more than close to $40 billion annually in media that reach preteens and teens.

Social Class

social class

The relatively permanent, homogeneous divisions in a society into which people sharing similar values, lifestyles, interests, and behaviour can be grouped.

A more subtle influence on consumer behaviour than direct contact with others is the social class to which people belong. **Social class** may be defined as the relatively permanent, homogeneous divisions in a society into which people sharing similar values, interests, and behaviour can be grouped. A person's occupation, source of income (not level of income), and education determine his or her social class. Generally speaking, three major social class categories exist—upper, middle, and lower—with subcategories within each. This structure has been observed in Canada, the United States, the United Kingdom, Western Europe, and Latin America.[35]

To some degree, persons within social classes exhibit common attitudes, lifestyles, and buying behaviours. Compared with the middle classes, people in the lower classes have a more short-term time orientation, are more emotional than rational in their reasoning, think in concrete rather than abstract terms, and see fewer personal opportunities. Members of the upper classes focus on achievements and the future and think in abstract or symbolic terms.

Companies use social class as a basis for identifying and reaching particularly good prospects for their products and services. In general, people in the upper classes are targeted by companies for such items as financial investments, expensive cars, and evening wear. The middle classes represent a target market for home improvement centres, automobile parts stores, and personal hygiene products. Firms also recognize differences in media preferences among classes: lower and working classes prefer sports and scandal magazines, middle classes read fashion, romance, and celebrity (*People*) magazines, and upper classes tend to read literary, travel, and news magazines, such as *Maclean's*.

Culture and Subculture

As described in Chapter 3, culture incorporates the set of values, ideas, and attitudes that are learned and shared among members of a group. This we often refer to as, say, Canadian culture, American culture, British culture, or Japanese culture. (Cultural underpinnings of Canadian buying patterns are described in Chapter 3, while Chapter 7 explores the role of culture in global marketing.) Read the accompanying Marketing NewsNet box to discover "how you know you are Canadian."[36]

subcultures

Subgroups within the larger, or national, culture with unique values, ideas, and attitudes.

Subgroups within the larger, or national, culture with unique values, ideas, and attitudes are referred to as **subcultures**. Subcultures can be identified by age (e.g., baby boomers versus Generation X), geography (e.g., Western Canadian versus Atlantic Canadian), and ethnicity. Here, we focus on ethnic subcultures.

An *ethnic subculture* is a segment of a larger society whose members are thought, by themselves and/or by others, to have a common origin and to participate in shared activities believed to be culturally significant. Common traits, such as customs, language, religion, and values, hold ethnic subcultures together.

Canada has traditionally thought of itself as a cultural mosaic, a pluralist society, rather than a melting pot. In this case, ethnic groups did not necessarily join the mainstream culture. This was referred to as the *salad bowl phenomenon*, where a potpourri of people mix but do not blend. However, new Canadian research indicates that Canada's ethnic population is becoming integrated into the cultural mainstream in a single generation. This has implications for marketers wanting to appeal to ethnic Canadians and for ethnic media attempting to reach ethnic groups. Assimilation means a loss of ethnic markets.[37]

French-Canadian Subculture   There are over seven million French-speaking Canadians, about 25 percent of the total Canadian population. The overwhelming majority of French Canadians live in Quebec. Research shows that French-speaking Quebecers do differ from other Canadians on a variety of dimensions, including consumption behaviour.[38] PRIZM$_{CE}$, the geodemographic and psychographic system mentioned earlier in the chapter has found that the French Quebecers are very different from other Canadians. In fact, 15 of the 66 segments or clusters in the PRIZM$_{CE}$ system are distinctly Quebecois, including Les Chics, MiniVan & Vin Rouge, and Quebec Rustics. Other research has also confirmed that French Canadians are different from other Canadians in many ways.

For example, asked what is most important to them, Quebecers are more likely than other Canadians to say "enjoying life" and "seeking happiness." In fact, Quebecers enjoy living in the moment and are prone to seeking instant gratification. They are also more tolerant and open-minded than English Canadians on a variety of

MARKETING NEWSNET   How You Know You Are Canadian

IDEAS AHEAD

While we share an undefended border and similar demographics with the United States, Canada is *not* the United States. In fact, according to Michael Adams, Canadian author of the book, *Sex in the Snow*, we are, socially and culturally, very different from Americans. He suggests that while Americans are individualistic, self-reliant, and religious and espouse personal freedom, Canadians, on the other hand, are pragmatic, socialistic, and espouse group rights.

But, besides what academics and other researchers purport to say about Canadians, what are some everyday tell-tale signs that you are Canadian? According to *The New Canadian Magazine,* there are plenty of ways to tell you are Canadian. They developed a list of the "Top 10 Things About Being Canadian": (10) health care; (9) the world's largest hockey stick—Duncan, BC; (8) being the only country to successfully invade the United States and burn its capital to the ground; (7) "if my grandmother had wheels, I would have been a bus"—Jean Chretien; (6)

Hockey Night in Canada and Don Cherry; (5) colourful money; (4) The Friendly Giant and Mr. Dressup; (3) toboggans and toques; (2) beer; and (1) we are *not* American.

The magazine offers even more proof that you are Canadian: (1) your local newspaper covers the national news on two pages but requires six pages for hockey; (2) you know that the last letter of the English alphabet is always pronounced "zed" not "zee"; (3) "eh?" is a very important part of your vocabulary and is more polite than, "huh?"; (4) you understand the request "Could you pass me a serviette, I dropped my poutine on the chesterfield"; and (5) you know that Casey and Finnegan were not part of a Celtic musical group.

And what is the result of this unique Canadian identity? The Pew Research Center recently released a study that showed Canadians are among the happiest people on earth, with over 90 percent of Canadians surveyed reporting they are satisfied with their lives!

issues. For instance, French Canadians are more likely to believe that everybody should be free to do their own thing, compared with English Canadians. For example, 89 percent of Quebecers agree that homosexuals are the same as everyone else, while only 73 percent of Ontarians think so. Quebecers are also more likely to support euthanasia than are other Canadians. They are also more open-minded and least likely to say that extramarital affairs are immoral. While the birth rate might be among the lowest in the world, Quebecers nevertheless love kids; 78 percent of Quebecers say having a child is an experience every woman should have compared with 58 percent of English Canadians.

More Quebecers also say they feel the need to be closer to nature, 77 percent compared with only 58 percent in the rest of Canada. In fact, Quebec has the highest percentage of hunters and fishermen in the world. "Cottage Country" might be big in Ontario, but ask Canadians if they prefer country life to city life, and 67 percent of Quebecers say yes, compared with 46 percent of Ontarians.

Quebecers also like to be comfortable at home. Over 70 percent of Quebecers describe their homes as "always having that lived in look" compared with only 45 percent of English Canadians. It is also true about the backyard; 16 percent of homes in Quebec have a swimming pool compared with 6 percent in the rest of Canada. Yet, Quebecers do not appear too keen to fix things around the house; just 22 percent say that they only do DIY projects if they absolutely have to. They are also less likely than English Canadians to own power tools.

Quebecers are very loyal to their province. In fact, 41 percent of Quebecers claim they identify first and foremost with their province, while 32 percent do so with Canada. Quebecers are also loyal to their heritage; 66 percent of Quebecers feel the need to demonstrate and sustain their traditions and symbols, compared with 47 percent of English Canadians. They are also keen to understand their roots. Give Quebecers access to the Internet, and they become genealogists.

More so than other Canadians, French Canadians also feel a need to be with people whose outlook on life and sense of values are similar to their own. French

Canadians say they feel closer to people who have the same religious, national, or ethnic background as their own. However, interestingly enough, Quebecers feel closer to Americans than to the rest of Canada; 34 percent of Quebecers support the idea of annexing to the United States versus 15 percent of Ontarians; 30 percent would live and work in the United States if given the opportunity, compared with 24 percent of Ontarians. Furthermore, French Quebecers have seemingly moved away from their Catholic roots with almost one-quarter (22 percent), significantly more than any other region of the country, saying their belief in God has declined over the years. But Quebecers are more likely to say they believe in an "afterlife but not necessarily a heaven or a hell." They are also most likely to believe in the ability to "channel or communicate with the dead."

Quebecers like to talk. They call radio stations and they chat online. In fact, Yahoo! Canada's French-language portal is very busy in Quebec. Quebecers are also obsessed with the lives of their stars, big and small. The most watched TV program in Quebec is called *Tout le monde en parle*—a talk show appropriately called "everybody is talking about it."

Quebecers tend to have eccentric tastes. For example, the immensely popular TV show *La Petite Vie* was a celebration of kitsch taste. And you still see plenty of planters made of old tires painted white when you cruise around the province.

For Quebecers, shopping is not a chore but a source of pleasure; 56 percent of Quebecers describe shopping as an experience that is relaxing and enjoyable, while only 45 percent feel this way in English Canada. They are also more brand loyal than are other Canadians and more likely to say that they have traditional tastes. Also, two-thirds of Quebecers feel the need to add their own touch to the things they buy, compared with 48 percent of English Canadians. Quebecers are more likely to say they follow their instincts than listen to experts. Yet, Quebecers like advertising more than do other Canadians. But they are no more likely to believe its claim than are English Canadians, and they are more likely than other Canadians to say that they have been offended by an ad.

Quebecers prefer to plan their shopping, and more Quebecers shop with a grocery list compared with other Canadians. Quebecers use coupons more than do English Canadians, but they do not appear to think of themselves as either bargain hunters (34 percent in French Canada versus 43 percent in English Canada) or smart shoppers (29 percent in French Canada versus 35 percent in English Canada). They do, however, feel a greater need to evaluate the quality and value of the products they buy (75 percent in French Canada versus 57 percent in English Canada). Metro-Richelieu, a Quebec grocery chain, has found that Quebecers do consult the chain's weekly circulars. The firm has also found that Metro's EconoMetro plan, a program that offers discount coupons and weekly money-saving tips has also been a hit with Quebecer shoppers.

Quebecers like to buy things that pleasure the senses. For example, they like fine restaurants and fine wines. Moreover, 38 percent of Quebecers have used bath additives in the past six months, compared with only 21 percent of Canadians in the rest of Canada; 30 percent of Quebec women say they do not feel complete without perfume, compared with 23 percent of women in the rest of Canada. Quebecois women are very fashion-conscious, and upscale brands, such as Prada, Coach, and Seven Jeans, sell well in Quebec. In fact, Quebecers compare with New Yorkers in terms of their fashion sense. They also enjoy looking good and young; 58 percent of Quebecers say they will do whatever they can to look as young as possible, compared with 31 percent of English Canadians. Beauty products sell well in Quebec, including upscale brands, such as Lancome.

The financial services industry is different in Quebec. More than 60 percent of the province's financial services market remains in the hands of two players that are almost nonexistent in English Canada: the Mouvement Desjardins (the federation of Quebec credit unions) and the National Bank. Both players deploy integrated and

Quebec-specific communications that resonate in this market. However, the personal saving rate is lower in Quebec than in the rest of Canada, and there is a greater proportion of the population in Quebec with less than $50 000 in their RRSPs than anywhere else in Canada. This may be explained by their desire to live life in the here and now.

To be successful in marketing to French Canadians living in Quebec, marketers must be sensitive to the wants and needs of the Quebecois consumers and appreciate the inherent differences between them and other Canadians. In addition to cultural and lifestyle differences, there are also other issues that marketers must address. Commercial advertising to children is prohibited, and there are greater restrictions on alcohol advertisements. Provincial regulations require that labels and packages be in both French and English, while storefront signage be only in French.

Acadian Subculture   Many Canadians assume that French Canadians are basically the same. Even though the majority of French-speaking Canadians reside in Quebec, another special group of French-speaking Canadians live outside of Quebec. These people are the Acadians, most of whom live in New Brunswick and are proud of their distinctive heritage. The Acadians are often referred to as the "forgotten French market."

Acadians are different from French Quebecers in many ways. In terms of consumption, Acadians are very fashion-oriented and tend to dine out more often than their French counterparts in Quebec. Acadians are very price-conscious. They also prefer companies that speak to them in their language, which is slightly different from French Québécois.

Chinese-Canadian Subculture   The Chinese-Canadian market currently represents over 3 percent of Canada's population, but it is one of the fastest-growing subcultures in Canada. This ethnic group is composed predominantly of immigrants from Hong Kong and Taiwan and is concentrated largely in Toronto and Vancouver.

Chinese Canadians have unique values. While most Canadians value straight-line thinking (logic), the Chinese value circular thinking (what goes around comes around). They value work, family, and education. They have different purchasing patterns and often perceive products differently from other Canadians. This group also appreciates companies that speak to them in their language. For example, many firms produce ads in Mandarin or Cantonese and run them in specialty publications, such as the *Sing Tao*, a Toronto newspaper for Chinese readers.

The average Chinese Canadian has a higher income, is better educated, is less likely to be unemployed, and is significantly younger than the general Canadian population. Because of these characteristics, many firms see Chinese Canadians as a viable target market for a variety of products. For example, the Royal Bank sees them as good prospects for RRSPs and mutual fund products, while RogersCantel markets its cellular phones to this group.

Other Ethnic Subcultures   Many other ethnic Canadians can be found in large metropolitan centres or clustered in certain geographic areas. Kitchener-Waterloo has a large German Canadian population, Winnipeg is home to many Ukrainian Canadians, and Toronto has a large number of Italian Canadians. The emerging trend in Canada today is that 70 percent of all immigrants to this country are visible minorities. In addition to Asia, many new Canadians are coming from Africa, India, and Latin America.[39] Marketers must appreciate the fact that these new ethnic Canadians may carry with them distinctive social and cultural behaviours that will affect their buying patterns. Subcultural research and sensitivity can aid organizations in developing effective marketing strategies designed to appeal to these groups.[40] For example, a common misconception is that ethnic Canadians have less spending power than Canadian-born people. However, studies show that arriving immigrants are bringing in large amounts of capital. This is particularly true of immigrants from Hong Kong, who have migrated and continue to migrate here due to mainland China's takeover of Hong Kong. Moreover, it has been found that foreign-born Canadians earn more money, comparatively, than do native-born Canadians.

CONCEPT CHECK	**1.** What are the two primary forms of personal influence? **2.** Which types of reference groups are marketers concerned with? **3.** What is an ethnic subculture?

■ ■ ■

CHAPTER IN REVIEW

1 *Describe the stages in the consumer purchase decision process.*

The consumer purchase decision process consists of five stages. They are problem recognition, information search, alternative evaluation, purchase decision, and postpurchase behaviour. Problem recognition is perceiving a difference between a person's ideal and actual situation big enough to trigger a decision. Information search involves remembering previous purchase experiences (internal search) and external search behaviour, such as seeking information from other sources. Alternative evaluation clarifies the problem for the consumer by (*a*) yielding brand names that might meet the criteria, (*b*) suggesting the evaluative criteria to use for the purchase, and (*c*) developing consumer value perceptions. The purchase decision involves the choice of an alternative, including from whom to buy and when to buy. Postpurchase behaviour involves the comparison of the chosen alternative with a consumer's expectations, which leads to satisfaction or dissatisfaction and subsequent purchase behaviour.

2 *Distinguish among three variations of the consumer purchase decision process: routine, limited, and extended problem solving.*

Consumers do not always engage in the five-stage purchase decision process. Instead, they skip or minimize one or more stages depending on the level of involvement—the personal, social, and economic significance of the purchase. For low-involvement purchase occasions, consumers engage in routine problem solving. They recognize a problem, make a decision, and spend little effort seeking external information and evaluating alternatives. For high-involvement purchase occasions, each of the five stages of the consumer purchase decision process is used, including considerable time and effort on external information search and in identifying and evaluating alternatives. With limited problem solving, consumers typically seek some information or rely on a friend to help them evaluate alternatives.

3 *Identify major psychological influences on consumer behaviour.*

Psychology helps marketers understand why and how consumers behave as they do. In particular, psychological concepts, such as motivation and personality; perception; learning; values, beliefs, and attitudes; and lifestyle are useful for interpreting buying processes. Motivation is the energizing force that stimulates behaviour to satisfy a need. Personality refers to a person's consistent behaviours or responses to recurring situations. Perception is the process by which an individual selects, organizes, and interprets information to create a meaningful picture of the world. Consumers filter information through selective attention, selective exposure, comprehension, and retention.

Much consumer behaviour is learned. Learning refers to those behaviours that result from (*a*) repeated experience, and (*b*) reasoning. Brand loyalty results from learning. Values, beliefs, and attitudes are also learned and influence how consumers evaluate products, services, and brands. A more general concept is lifestyle. Lifestyle, also called psychographics, combines psychology and demographics and focuses on how people spend their time and resources, what they consider important in their environment, and what they think of themselves and the world around them.

4 *Identify major sociocultural influences on consumer behaviour.*

Sociocultural influences, which evolve from a consumer's formal and informal relationships with other people, also affect consumer behaviour. These involve personal influence, reference groups, the family, social class, culture, and subculture. Opinion leadership and word-of-mouth behaviour are two major sources of personal influence on consumer behaviour. Reference groups are people whom an individual looks to as a basis for self-approval or as source of personal standards. Family influences on consumer behaviour result from three sources: consumer socialization; passage through the family life cycle; and decision making within the family or household. A more subtle influence on consumer behaviour than direct contact with others is the social class to which people belong. Persons within social classes tend to exhibit common values, attitudes, beliefs, lifestyles, and buying behaviours. Finally, a person's culture and subculture have been shown to influence product preferences and buying patterns.

■ ■ ■

FOCUSING ON KEY TERMS

attitude p. 124
beliefs p. 124
blog p. 115
brand loyalty p. 123
cognitive dissonance p. 116
consideration set p. 115
consumer behaviour p. 114
consumer socialization p. 129
evaluative criteria p. 115
family life cycle p. 129
involvement p. 116
learning p. 123
lifestyle p. 125
motivation p. 119

national character p. 120
opinion leaders p. 127
perceived risk p. 122
perception p. 121
personality p. 120
purchase decision process p. 114
reference groups p. 129
self-concept p. 120
situational influences p. 118
social class p. 131
subcultures p. 132
subliminal perception p. 122
values p. 124
word of mouth p. 127

■ ■ ■

DISCUSSION AND APPLICATION QUESTIONS

1 Outline the consumer purchase decision process you used to select your college or university. Discuss your perceived problem; information sources used; awareness set, evaluative criteria, consideration set; and how happy you are with your decision.

2 Suppose research at Panasonic reveals that prospective buyers are anxious about buying high-definition television sets. What strategies might you recommend to the company to reduce consumer anxiety?

3 A Porsche salesperson was taking orders on new cars because he was unable to satisfy the demand with the limited number of cars in the showroom and lot. Several persons had backed out of the contract within two weeks of signing the order. What explanation can you give for this behaviour, and what remedies would you recommend?

4 Which social class would you associate with each of the following items or actions: (*a*) tennis club membership, (*b*)

an arrangement of plastic flowers in the kitchen, (*c*) *True Romance* magazine, (*d*) *Maclean's* magazine, (*e*) formally dressing for dinner frequently, and (*f*) being a member of a bowling team.

5 Assign one or more levels of the hierarchy of needs and the motives described in Figure 5–5 to the following products: (*a*) life insurance, (*b*) cosmetics, (*c*) *The Financial Post,* and (*d*) hamburgers.

6 With which stage in the family life cycle would the purchase of the following products and services be most closely identified: (*a*) bedroom furniture, (*b*) life insurance, (*c*) a Caribbean cruise, (*d*) a house mortgage, and (*e*) children's toys?

7 "The greater the perceived risk in a purchase situation, the more likely that cognitive dissonance will result." Does this statement have any basis given the discussion in the text? Why?

GOING ONLINE	The Impact of Online Reviews of Your Perception of Products

Go to www.amazon.ca. Click on Music—Bestsellers. Pick a CD you do not own and have not heard but might be interested in buying. Click on customer Reviews. What do you think about the reviews? Are you more likely or less

likely to buy the CD now? Now, click on a CD you own or have heard. Click on customer reviews. What do you think about the reviews? What are your thoughts about your purchase now after reading the reviews?

Do you want to get better grades and stay up to date with current issues in marketing? Visit the Online Learning Centre at www.mcgrawhill.ca/college/crane for practice tests, video cases, resources for building a marketing plan, *Globe and Mail* headlines, access to *Marketing Magazine*, and other learning and study tools.

VIDEO CASE 5　　The Consumer on the Couch

To retailers, there is no question more important than "why do consumers buy?" Understanding the influences that affect purchasing behaviour can spell the difference between commercial success and failure.

Paco Underhill is a New York City–based "retail anthropologist" who has been retained by dozens of top-flight companies, including the Canadian Imperial Bank of Commerce, Burger King, and Calvin Klein, to determine what attracts customers to their locations, what makes them linger, and what makes them spend. His empirical findings, many of which are documented in his *Why We Buy: The Science of Shopping,* are based mainly on analysis of tens of thousands of hours of clandestine videotaping of shoppers in action. Underhill's studies have significantly expanded our understanding of the purchase decision process while raising important questions about the privacy rights of consumers.

SHAPE UP OR SHIP OUT

At last count, the retail sector recorded sales of $277 billion and provided 12 percent of all jobs (about 1.75 million positions) in Canada. But while the sector has 100 percent more stores than it did 15 years ago, it has only 15 percent more customers. As participants in a key economic sector that is subject to tremendous domestic competition, Canadian retailers must do everything they can to understand consumer needs and motivations.

Their need for greater insight into consumer behaviour became critical in the mid-1990s, when international retailers began to vie for market share in Canada. Global competitors with deep pockets, such as Wal-Mart, Pottery Barn, and Payless ShoeSource, threatened the viability of many domestic firms. According to Underhill, Canada can expect even more competition from foreign retailers in the years ahead. Part of the problem, as he sees it, is that most Canadian outlets are "frumpy." By this, he means more than unattractive; he means that most are not designed with shoppers in mind. As he says in the *Venture* video, "If the 20th century was about marketers being leaders, the 21st century is about marketers being followers." Satisfying consumer expectations is the key to success at the cash register.

At the same time, Underhill is a stalwart fan of such firms as Canadian Tire, which completely redesigned its hardware stores to curb the market penetration of big-box competitors, such as Home Depot and Wal-Mart. Such examples show clearly that domestic firms can compete successfully for the attention of increasingly fickle shoppers. And Underhill believes they must. "In the Canadian marketplace," he says, "retailers must shape up or go out of business."

READING THE RETAIL LANDSCAPE

Traditional market research on consumer behaviour has been done through analysis of barcodes scanned at the cash register and from direct surveys of shoppers conducted via telephone, one-on-one interviews, or focus groups. While the resulting data are valuable, rarely do they shed light on the discrepancy between what customers say about the process of making purchasing choices and what they actually do at the store. Consequently, Underhill and like-minded students of shopping are less concerned with what people buy than why they so often fail to buy.

To gain more understanding of shoppers, some retailers have turned to in-store customer surveillance. Using hidden cameras that videotape consumers as they approach, enter, and exit a store, and supplementing that evidence with surreptitious observations by in-store "trackers" who add a more qualitative dimension, retail anthropologists provide micro-level documentation of consumer behaviour. Nothing escapes their scrutiny. The result, when time-series data are compiled, is a telling view of a single store's failings as a shopping environment from the perspective of the customer. Retailers who have implemented changes based on such evidence attest that catering directly to the needs of their existing customer base has significantly improved their bottom line.

FOUR KEY OBSERVATIONS

A Sharp Turn to the Right

Eighty percent of buying decisions are made on the shop floor, and so the layout of the shop floor and the manner in which customers are lured onto it are crucial to raising sales volumes and profit levels. The fact that people will not read more than three or four words in a shop window, for example, implies that window displays must be primarily visual in content. And contrary to popular belief, the entry to a store is not the ideal location for a retailer's most desirable goods; rather, it is a commercially dead zone where customers orient themselves but almost never buy. Reserving the entry for a display that appeals to the senses and pulls uncommitted shoppers into the bowels of the store where they will spend is the best tactic.

But the real key to effective layout, says Underhill, is the tendency of almost all customers to enter a store and turn, immediately, to the right. That is the prime spot for snagging a customer's attention. In fact, Underhill has determined that sales can be increased as much as 15 percent merely by shifting the cash register from the right side of a store to the left. Once they have made that initial right turn, customers navigate the store in a counterclockwise orbit. Articles placed strategically along that path are much more likely to be purchased.

Appealing to the Senses

Underhill has found a strong, direct correlation between sensory stimulation and sales volume. The idea is akin to creating a bazaar-like atmosphere within the store: fill the air with a seductive scent, let customers sample some delicious food, place clothing so that it can be touched, and watch sales increase. Have a salesperson talk to the customer while they taste or touch the merchandise, and the odds of them buying increase by half again. Let them try on an article of clothing, and the odds get even better. In short, involving them directly with the product pays big dividends.

Women Are a Retailer's Best Friends

Seventy percent of shoppers are women, and women are believed to influence as much as 85 percent of all retail purchasing decisions. And if two women shop together, they will spend almost twice as much time in the store as a male–female couple. All of which is important in view of the strong relationship between the time spent shopping and the amount spent.

After observing shoppers for some 20 years, Underhill is adamant that women care much more than men do about the shopping experience. Enhance a store's atmosphere according to the interests and concerns of the female shopper, and the typical customer will stay longer and spend more. Generous, well-lit display spaces rank high on the list of vital enhancements, but pristine washrooms and garbage cans in fitting rooms matter, too. Provide amenities for male companions and children, and the sales volume climbs even further. The Chapters-Indigo book chain, with its wide aisles, consistent lighting, clear signs, comfortable chairs, and aromatic coffee-house corner has been a particularly apt pupil when it comes to designing what Underhill defines as "female-friendly" retail space.

Butt-Brushing

Culturally and socially, Western women are averse to anything that touches their posteriors. Video after video in the Underhill archives shows that females who inadvertently back into awkwardly placed display racks or narrowly spaced rows of shelving will leave a store immediately. And with them goes the potential sale. This is what he calls the "butt-brush factor," and it exemplifies the respect for unspoken customer sensitivities that every retailer must possess if they wish to succeed in business.

MEETING FUTURE CONSUMER NEEDS

Underhill says that change is good but that constant change is better. He is referring not only to modifying today's retailing methods but also to the importance of anticipating and addressing the needs of traditionally neglected customers and emerging markets. The first kind of change deals with tactical options, while the second is about choosing a long-term, strategic marketing direction. To assist companies in this, he has identified a number of key opportunities that lie ahead:

- the high-income seniors' market
- marketing to ethnic and minority groups
- addressing the needs of women who are buying nontraditional products (e.g., technology, automobiles, hardware)
- addressing the needs of men who are doing the family shopping and buying clothing

If retailers have what Underhill calls the "good manners" to identify and satisfy the different needs and expectations of these diverse groups, he is convinced they will profit.

QUESTIONS

1 Identify specific examples of Canadian retailers whose sales have been affected by international competitors. What behavioural factors can you cite to account for their success or failure?

2 If a single store offers a range of merchandise that appeals to various demographic groups, how can it hope to satisfy all their needs?

3 Corporate collection of customer data without permission has been controversial in the online retail world. How does that situation differ, if at all, from the methods typically employed by retail anthropologists like Paco Underhill?

4 What are the principal behavioural factors that need to be considered in addressing the rapidly growing seniors market? Discuss how a retailer selling goods or services via the Internet might use this information.

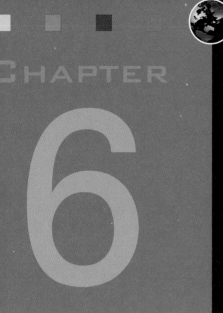

ORGANIZATIONAL MARKETS AND BUYER BEHAVIOUR

LEARNING OBJECTIVES

After reading this chapter, you should be able to:

1. Distinguish among industrial, reseller, and government organizational markets.

2. Describe the key characteristics of organizational buying that make it different from consumer buying.

3. Explain how buying centres and buying situations influence organizational purchasing.

4. Recognize the importance and nature of online buying in industrial, reseller, and government organizational markets.

DOFASCO INC. : ACHIEVING SUCCESS IN THE BUSINESS-TO-BUSINESS (B2B) MARKETPLACE

Established in 1912, Hamilton (Ontario)–based Dofasco is Canada's largest steel producer and one of North America's most progressive and profitable steelmakers. It is a market leader in an industry that is an important component of the Canadian economy and employs almost 7500 Canadians. Dafasco produces a wide range of steel products, such as high-quality flat, rolled, and tubular steels and laser-welded blanks. It is also Canada's only producer of tinplate.

Dofasco markets its products to a variety of business customers. The automotive industry is its single largest market. In fact, its success in that market can be attributed to its creative initiative called the "body-in-white." The stripped-down shell of a major automotive customer's best-selling vehicle was purchased by Dafasco for the purpose of showing car manufacturers how new steel technology could reduce weight, cuts costs, and strengthen overall design. This program resulted in improved strength, a 25-percent reduction in weight, and a 3-percent lower production cost. Dofasco's body-in-white program began a new trend that has since become an industry standard. You might not have known this, but you are probably driving around in a vehicle constructed, at least in part, from Dofasco steel. Dofasco also serves other major customers, including the construction, energy, manufacturing, pipe and tube, appliance, container, and distribution industries. It is a leader in steel products for residential framing, and a premier supplier of cold rolled steel for appliances.

Dofasco considers its customer-focused *Solutions in Steel*™ strategy a major competitive advantage when competing in the B2B marketplace. This strategy has helped transform Dafasco from a simple manufacturer of steel to the producer of innovative, value-added steel products designed to solve the immediate and future needs of its customers.

In short, Dofasco exemplifies what it takes to be successful in the B2B marketplace. The company understands the customers' needs; it partners with them to create unique solutions to their needs; it builds a partnership relationship with customers based on trust; and it delivers customer value and ensures customer satisfaction. In fact, Dofasco ranked second overall among 27 North American steel suppliers in an industry-recognized customer satisfaction survey. This has translated into outstanding results: five million tonnes of steel to its customers and over $4 billion in sales.[1]

This chapter examines the types of organizational buyers; key characteristics of organizational buying, including online buying; some typical buying decisions in organizational or business markets; and how firms like Dofasco can be successful in marketing to business customers.

▪ ▪ ▪
THE NATURE AND SIZE OF ORGANIZATIONAL MARKETS

business marketing
The marketing of goods and services to companies, governments, or not-for-profit organizations for use in the creation of goods and services that they can produce and market to others.

Business marketing is the marketing of goods and services to companies, governments, or not-for-profit oganizations for use in the creation of goods and services that they can produce and market to others. This is also sometimes referred to as business-to-business, or B2B, marketing. Because many Canadian business school graduates take jobs in firms that engage in business marketing, it is important to understand the fundamental characteristics of organizational buyers and their buying behaviour.

organizational buyers
Those manufacturers, wholesalers, retailers, and government agencies that buy goods and services for their own use or for resale.

Organizational buyers are those manufacturers, retailers, and government agencies that buy goods and services for their own use or for resale. For example, all these organizations buy computers and telephone services for their own use. However, manufacturers buy raw materials and parts that they reprocess into the finished goods they sell, whereas retailers resell goods they buy without reprocessing them. Organizational buyers include all the buyers in a nation, except the ultimate consumers. These organizational buyers purchase and lease tremendous volumes of capital equipment, raw materials, manufactured parts, supplies, and business services. In fact, because they often buy raw materials and parts, process them, and sell the upgraded product several times before it is purchased by the final organizational buyer or ultimate consumer, the aggregate purchases of organizational buyers in a year are far greater than those of ultimate consumers.

Organizational buyers are divided into three markets: (1) industrial, (2) reseller, and (3) government markets.

Industrial Markets

industrial firm
An organizational buyer that, in some way, reprocesses a good or service it buys before selling it again to the next buyer.

There are thousands of firms in the industrial, or business, market in Canada. **Industrial firms**, in some way, reprocess a good or service they buy before selling it again to the next buyer. This is certainly true of a steel mill that converts iron ore into steel. It is also true (if you stretch your imagination) of a firm selling services, such as a bank that takes money from its depositors, reprocesses it, and "sells" it as loans to its commercial borrowers.

There has been a marked shift in the scope and nature of the industrial marketplace. Service industries are growing and currently make the greatest contribution to Canada's gross domestic product (GDP). Because of the importance of service firms, service marketing is discussed in detail in Chapter 12. Industrial firms and primary industries currently account for about 22 percent of Canada's GDP. Nevertheless, primary industries (e.g., farming, mining, fishing, and forestry) and the manufacturing sector are important components of Canada's economy. There are about 40 000 manufacturers in Canada whose estimated value of shipments are over $545 billion.[2]

For an understanding of the role of manufacturing in the Canadian exonomy, read the accompanying Marketing NewsNet box.

Reseller Markets

reseller
A wholesaler or retailer that buys physical products and sells them again without any processing.

Wholesalers and retailers who buy physical products and sell them again without any reprocessing are **resellers**. Over 200 000 retailers and over 65 000 wholesalers are currently operating in Canada. Some of the largest retailers in Canada include The Hudson's Bay Co., Sears Canada, and Costco. Some major wholesalers are Cargill, MedisHealth, and Federated Co-Operatives. These companies participate in B2B marketing. In later chapters, we see how manufacturers use wholesalers and retailers in their distribution ("place") strategies as channels through which their products reach ultimate consumers. In this chapter, we look at resellers mainly as organizational buyers in terms of (1) how they make their own buying decisions, and (2) which products they choose to carry.

Government Markets

government units
The federal, provincial, and local agencies that buy goods and services for the constituents they serve.

Government units are the federal, provincial, and local agencies that buy goods and services for the constituents they serve. Their annual purchases vary in size from the billions of dollars for a federal department, such as the Department of Defence, to millions or thousands of dollars for a local university or school. The bulk of the buying at the federal government level is done by the Department of Supply and

---

MARKETING NEWSNET   **The Importance of Canada's Manufacturing Sector**

While Canada has been transitioning into a services-based economy, the manufacturing sector still plays an important role in the national economy. According to the Canadian Manufacturers & Exporters Association (CME), manufacturing employs 2.2 million Canadians directly, and another 2.5 million depend on the sector for their livelihood. Directly, manufacturing accounts for 22 percent of Canada's economic activity. But when spinoffs are included, such as the purchases of goods and services in Canada, manufacturers drive 55 percent of the economy. Every $1 of manufacturing in Canada generates $3 in total economic activity. Pay in the manufacturing sector averages $45 000 or 15 percent more than the national average of $35 000. And, more manufacturers (83 percent) have employee-training programs than any other sector of the economy.

Nearly 70 percent of all goods manufactured in Canada are exported and manufactured products account for 90 percent of Canada's merchandise exports. Manufacturers perform 75 percent of private sector R&D in Canada and 30 percent of business investment in nonresidential construction, machinery, and equipment.

Because of the importance of the manufacturing sector in Canada, SourceCAN was developed. SourceCAN is a free e-marketplace and a collaborative partnership arrangement among Industry Canada, the Canadian Commercial Corporation, and HyperNet Inc. SourceCan matches Canadian products and services with thousands of business opportunities posted by domestic and foreign corporations and governments. Through an international tender feeding system, small- and medium-sized Canadian companies can source bids, post opportunities, and pursue strategic partnerships, all within a secure online trading environment. SourceCAN also offers foreign firms a comprehensive and up-to-date Canadian capabilities database, exposing Canadian businesses to the global marketplace. You can visit the site at www.sourcecan. com.

Services Canada. Most provincial governments have a government services department that does the buying on the provincial level. Hundreds of government departments, including agencies and Crown corporations, such as CBC, VIA Rail, and the Royal Canadian Mint, must purchase goods and services to operate. The federal government is a large organizational consumer making total purchases of goods and services in excess of $240 billion annually.[3]

Global Organizational Markets

Industrial, reseller, and government markets also exist on a global scale. In fact, many of Canada's top exporters, including Bombardier, Canadian Pacific, DuPont Canada, Maple Leaf Foods, and Pratt & Whitney, focus on organizational customers, not ultimate consumers.

Most world trade involves manufacturers, resellers, and government agencies buying goods and services for their own use or for resale to others. The exchange relationships often involve numerous transactions spanning the globe. For example, Honeywell, Micro Switch Division sells its fibre-optic technology and products to manufacturers of data communication systems worldwide, through electronic component resellers in more than 20 countries, and directly to national governments in Europe and elsewhere. Europe's Airbus Industrie, the world's largest aircraft manufacturer, sells its passenger airplanes to Air Canada, which flies Canadian businesspeople to Asia. Ontario-based Inco, one of the world's largest nickel producers, is a global business participant marketing its products to customers around the world. In fact, it exports 90 percent of its products to global organizational markets.

■ ■ ■
MEASURING DOMESTIC AND GLOBAL INDUSTRIAL, RESELLER, AND GOVERNMENT MARKETS

North American Industry Classification System (NAICS)

Provides common industry definitions for Canada, Mexico, and the United States, which facilitate the measurement of economic activity in the three member countries of NAFTA.

The measurement of industrial, reseller, and government markets is an important first step for a firm interested in gauging the size of one, two, or all three of these markets in Canada and around the world. This task has been made easier with the **North American Industry Classification System (NAICS)**.[4] NAICS provides common industry definitions for Canada, Mexico, and the United States, which facilitate the measurement of economic activity in the three member countries of the North American Free Trade Agreement (NAFTA). NAICS replaced the Standard Industrial Classification (SIC) system, a version of which has been in place for more than 50 years in the three NAFTA member countries. The SIC neither permitted comparability across countries nor accurately measured new or emerging industries. Furthermore, NAICS is consistent with the International Standard Industrial Classification of All Economic Activities, published by the United Nations, to facilitate measurement of global economic activity.

The NAICS groups economic activity to permit studies of market share, demand for goods and services, import competition in domestic markets, and similar studies. NAICS designates industries with a numerical code in a defined structure. A six-digit coding system is used. The first two digits designate a sector of the economy, the third

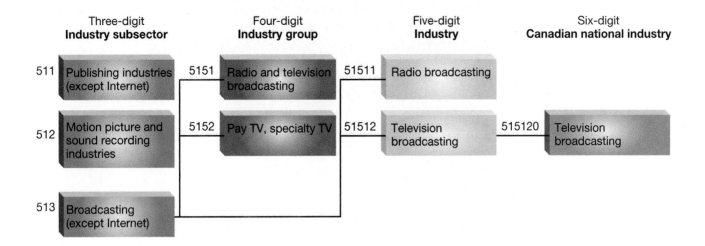

Three-digit **Industry subsector**	Four-digit **Industry group**	Five-digit **Industry**	Six-digit **Canadian national industry**
511 Publishing industries (except Internet)	5151 Radio and television broadcasting	51511 Radio broadcasting	
512 Motion picture and sound recording industries	5152 Pay TV, specialty TV	51512 Television broadcasting	515120 Television broadcasting
513 Broadcasting (except Internet)			

■ **FIGURE 6–1** ■
NAICS breakdown for information and cultural industries sector: NAICS code 51 (abbreviated)

digit designates a subsector, and the fourth digit represents an industry group. The fifth digit designates a specific industry and is the most detailed level at which comparable data are available for Canada, Mexico, and the United States. The sixth digit designates individual country-level national industries. Figure 6–1 presents an abbreviated breakdown within the Information Industries Sector (code 51) to illustrate the classification scheme.

The NAICS permits a firm to find the NAICS codes of its present customers and then obtain NAICS-coded lists for similar firms. Also, it is possible to monitor NAICS categories to determine the growth in various sectors and industries to identify promising marketing opportunities. However, NAICS codes, like the earlier SIC codes, have important limitations. The NAICS assigns one code to each organization based on its major economic activity, and so large firms that engage in many different activities are still given only one NAICS code. A second limitation is that five-digit national industry codes are not available for all three countries because the respective governments will not reveal data when too few organizations exist in a category.

A further refinement in the measurement or organizational markets is expected in 2007 with the publication of the *North American Product Classification System* (NAPCS). The NAPCS will provide a classification system for products and services that is consistent across Canada, Mexico, and the United States and international classification systems, such as the Central Product Classification System of the United Nations. The NAICS and NAPCS represent the continued effort toward economic integration in North America and the world.

CONCEPT CHECK

1. What are the three main types of organizational buyers?

2. What is the North American Industry Classification System (NAICS)?

■ ■ ■
CHARACTERISTICS OF ORGANIZATIONAL BUYING

Organizations are different from individuals, and so buying for an organization is different from buying for yourself or your family.[5] True, in both cases, the objective in making the purchase is to solve the buyer's problem—to satisfy a need or

CHARACTERISTICS   **DIMENSIONS**

Market characteristics	• Demand for business products and services is derived. • Few customers typically exist, and their purchase orders are large.
Product or service characteristics	• Products or services are technical in nature and purchased on the basis of specifications. • There is a predominance of raw and semifinished goods purchased. • Heavy emphasis is placed on delivery time, technical assistance, postsale service, and financing assistance.
Buying process characteristics	• Technically qualified and professional buyers exist and follow established purchasing policies and procedures. • Buying objectives and criteria are typically spelled out, as are procedures for evaluating sellers and products (services). • Multiple buying influences exist, and multiple parties participate in purchase decisions. • Reciprocal arrangements exist, and negotiation between buyers and sellers is commonplace. • Online buying over the Internet is widespread.
Marketing mix characteristics	• Direct selling to organizational buyers is the rule, and physical distribution is very important. • Advertising and other forms of promotion are technical in nature. • Price is often negotiated, evaluated as part of broader seller and product (service) qualities, typically inelastic owing to derived demand, and frequently affected by trade and quantity discounts.

■ **FIGURE 6–2** ■

Key characteristics of organizational buying behaviour

organizational buying behaviour

The decision-making process that organizations use to establish the need for products and services and identify, evaluate, and choose among alternative brands and suppliers.

derived demand

Demand for industrial products and services driven by, or derived from, demand for consumer products and services.

want. But unique objectives and policies of an organization put special constraints on how it makes buying decisions. Understanding the characteristics of organizational buying is essential in designing effective marketing programs to reach these buyers.

Organizational buying behaviour is the decision-making process that organizations use to establish the need for products and services and identify, evaluate, and choose among alternative brands and suppliers. Key characteristics of organizational buying behaviour are listed in Figure 6–2 and discussed next.[6]

Demand Characteristics

Consumer demand for products and services is affected by their price and availability and by consumers' personal tastes and discretionary income. By comparison, demand for business products and services is derived. **Derived demand** means that the demand for business products and services is driven by, or derived from, demand for consumer products and services. For example, the demand for MacMillan Bloedel's pulp and paper products is based on consumer demand for newspapers, Domino's "keep warm" pizza-to-go boxes, Federal Express packages, and disposable diapers. Derived demand is often based on expectations of future consumer demand. For instance, Whirlpool purchases parts for its washers and dryers in anticipation of consumer demand, which is affected by the replacement cycle for these products and by consumer income.

Ultimately, most demand is derived from consumer demand, the exception being demand derived from government purchases. Therefore, because of the importance of the concept of derived demand, business marketers are always paying close attention to consumer demand forecasts and reports.[7]

Size of the Order or Purchase

The size of the purchase involved in organizational buying is typically much larger than that in consumer buying. The value of a single purchase made by an organization often runs into the thousands or millions of dollars. For example, Motorola was awarded an $88-million contract to install a cellular phone system in Brazil.[8] With so much money at stake, most organizations place constraints on their buyers in the form of purchasing policies or procedures. Buyers must often get competitive bids from at least three prospective suppliers when the order is above a specific amount, such as $5000. When the order is above an even higher amount, such as $50 000, it may require the review and approval of a vice-president or even the president of the company. Knowing how the size of the order affects buying practices is important in determining who participates in the purchase decision and makes the final decision and also the length of time required to arrive at a purchase agreement.

Number of Potential Buyers

Firms selling consumer products or services often try to reach thousands or millions of individuals or households. For example, your local supermarket or bank probably serves thousands of people, and Kelloggs Canada tries to reach more than 10 million Canadian households with its breakfast cereals and probably succeeds in selling to a third or half of these in any given year. In contrast, firms selling to organizations are often restricted to far fewer buyers. Bombardier can sell its business jets to a few thousand organizations throughout the world, and B. F. Goodrich sells its original equipment tires to fewer than 10 car manufacturers.

Organizational Buying Objectives

Organizations buy products and services for one main reason: to help them achieve their objectives. For business firms, the buying objective is usually to increase profits through reducing costs or increasing revenues. 7-Eleven buys automated inventory systems to increase the number of products that can be sold through its convenience stores and to keep them fresh. Nissan Motor Company switched its advertising agency because it expects the new agency to devise a more effective ad campaign to help it sell more cars and increase revenues. To improve executive decision making, many firms buy advanced computer systems to process data. The objectives of non-profit firms and government agencies are usually to meet the needs of the groups they serve. Thus, a hospital buys a high-technology diagnostic device to serve its patients better. Understanding buying objectives is a necessary first step in marketing to organizations. Recognizing the high costs of energy, Sylvania promotes to prospective buyers cost savings and increased profits made possible by its fluorescent and halogen lights. Many companies today have broadened their buying objectives to include environmental considerations. For example, The Home Depot no longer purchases lumber from companies that harvest timber from the world's endangered forests.[9] Successful business marketers recognize that understanding buying objectives is a necessary first step in marketing to organizations.

Organizational Buying Criteria

organizational buying criteria
The objective attributes of the supplier's products and services and the capabilities of the supplier itself.

In making a purchase, the buying organization must weigh key buying criteria that apply to the potential supplier and what it wants to sell. **Organizational buying criteria** are the objective attributes of the supplier's products and services and the capabilities of the supplier itself. These criteria serve the same purpose as the evaluative criteria used by consumers and described in Chapter 5. Seven of the most commonly used criteria are (1) price, (2) ability to meet the quality specifications required for the item, (3) ability to meet required delivery schedules, (4) technical capability, (5) warranties and claim policies in the event of poor performance, (6) past performance on previous contracts, and (7) production facilities and capacity.[10] Suppliers that meet or exceed these criteria create customer value.

Organizational buyers who purchase products and services in a global marketplace often supplement their buying criteria with supplier ISO 9000 certification. **ISO 9000 standards**, developed by the International Standards Organization (ISO) in Geneva, Switzerland, refer to standards for registration and certification of a manufacturer's quality management and assurance system based on an on-site audit of practices and procedures. ISO certification is administered in Canada by SCC (Standards Council of Canada: www.scc.ca). Many Canadian companies that market globally have achieved this certification.[11]

Many organizational buyers today are transforming their buying criteria into specific requirements that are communicated to prospective suppliers. This practice, called **reverse marketing**, involves the deliberate effort by organizational buyers to build relationships that shape suppliers' products, services, and capabilities to fit a buyer's needs and those of its customers.[12] For example, consider Deere & Company, the maker of John Deere farm, construction, and lawn-care equipment. Deere employs 94 supplier-development engineers who work full-time with the company's suppliers to improve their efficiency and quality and reduce their costs. According to a Deere senior executive, "Their quality, delivery, and costs are, after all, our quality, delivery, and costs."[13] Harley-Davidson also emphasizes supplier collaboration in its product design.[14]

With many Canadian manufacturers using a "just-in-time" (JIT) inventory system that reduces the inventory of production parts to those to be used within hours or days, on-time delivery is becoming an even more important buying criterion and, in some instances, a requirement. Caterpillar trains its key suppliers at its Quality Institute in JIT inventory systems and conducts supplier seminars on how to diagnose, correct, and implement continuous quality improvement programs. The just-in-time inventory system is discussed further in Chapter 14.

ISO 9000 standards
Registration and certification of a manufacturer's quality management and quality assurance system.

reverse marketing
The deliberate effort by organizational buyers to build relationships that shape suppliers' products, services, and capabilities to fit a buyer's needs and those of its customers.

ETHICS AND SOCIAL RESPONSIBILITY ALERT

Scratching Each Other's Back: The Ethics of Reciprocity in Organizational Buying

Reciprocity, the buying practice in which two organizations agree to purchase each other's products and services, is frowned upon by Industry Canada because it restricts the normal operation of the free market. Reciprocal buying practices do exist, however, in a variety of forms, including certain types of countertrade arrangements in international marketing. Furthermore, the extent to which reciprocity is viewed as an ethical issue varies across cultures. In many Asian countries, for instance, reciprocity is often a positive and widespread practice.

Reciprocity is occasionally addressed in the ethics codes of companies or their purchasing policies. For instance, IBM describes its reciprocity policy in the company's Global Procurement Principles and Practices Statement:

> IBM's goal is to buy goods and services which have the best prices, quality, delivery, and technology. IBM has a policy against reciprocal buying arrangements because those arrangements can interfere with this goal.

Do you think reciprocal buying is unethical?

Buyer–Seller Relationships and Supply Partnerships

Another distinction between organizational and consumer buying behaviour lies in the nature of the relationship between organizational buyers and suppliers. Specifically, organizational buying is more likely to involve complex negotiations concerning delivery schedules, price, technical specifications, warranties, and claim policies. These negotiations also can last for an extended period of time. This was the case when the Lawrence Livermore National Laboratory recently acquired two IBM supercomputers—each with capacity to perform 360 trillion mathematical operations per second—at a cost of $290 million.[15]

reciprocity
An industrial buying practice in which two organizations agree to purchase each other's products and services.

Reciprocal arrangements also exist in organizational buying. **Reciprocity** is an industrial buying practice in which two organizations agree to purchase each other's products and services. Industry Canada frowns on reciprocal buying because it restricts the normal operation of the free market. However, the practice exists and can limit the flexibility of organizational buyers in choosing alternative suppliers. Regardless of the legality of reciprocal buying, do you believe this practice is ethical? (See the accompanying Ethics and Social Responsibility Alert box.)[16]

Long-term relationships are also prevalent.[17] As an example, International Truck and Engine Corporation (formerly Navistar) has a long-term relationship with Cummins, which sells engine technology to International for its heavy-duty trucks.[18]

supply partnership
A relationship that exists when a buyer and its supplier adopt mutually beneficial objectives, policies and procedures for the purpose of lowering the cost and/or increasing the value of products and services delivered to the ultimate consumers.

In some cases, buyer–seller relationships develop into supply partnerships.[19] A **supply partnership** exists when a buyer and its supplier adopt mutually beneficial objectives, policies, and procedures for the purpose of lowering the cost and/or increasing the value of products and services delivered to the ultimate consumer. Intel, the world's largest manufacturer of microprocessors and the "computer inside" most personal computers, is a case in point. Intel supports its suppliers by offering them quality management programs and by investing in supplier equipment that produces fewer product defects and boosts supplier productivity. Suppliers, in turn, provide Intel with consistent high-quality products at a lower cost for its customers, the makers of personal computers, and finally you, the ultimate customer. Retailers, too, are forging partnerships with their suppliers. Wal-Mart and Zellers have such a relationship with Procter & Gamble for ordering and replenishing P&G's products in their stores. By using computerized cash register scanning equipment and direct electronic linkages to P&G, these retailers can tell P&G what merchandise is needed, along with how much, when, and to which store to deliver it on a daily basis. Because supply partnerships also involve the physical distribution of goods, they are again discussed in Chapter 14 in the context of supply chains.

The Buying Centre: A Cross-Functional Group

For routine purchases with a small dollar value, a single buyer or purchasing manager often makes the purchase decision alone. In many instances, however, several people in the organization participate in the buying process. The individuals in this group, called a **buying centre**, share common goals, risks, and knowledge important to a purchase decision. For most large multistore chain resellers, such as Sears, 7-Eleven convenience stores, or Zellers, the buying centre is highly formalized and is called a *buying committee*. However, most industrial firms or government units use informal groups of people or call meetings to arrive at buying decisions.

buying centre
The group of people in an organization who participate in the buying process and share common goals, risks, and knowledge important to a purchase decision.

The importance of the buying centre requires that a firm marketing to many industrial firms and government units understand the structure, technical and business functions represented, and behaviour of these groups. One researcher has suggested four questions to provide guidance in understanding the buying centre in these organizations:[20] Which individuals are in the buying centre for the product or service? What is the relative influence of each member of the group? What are the buying

criteria of each member? How does each member of the group perceive our firm, our products and services, and our salespeople?

Answers to these questions are difficult to come by, particularly when dealing with industrial firms, resellers, and governments outside Canada.[21] For example, Canadian firms are often frustrated by the fact that Japanese buyers "ask a thousand questions" but give few answers, sometimes rely on third-party individuals to convey views on proposals, are prone to not "talk business," and often say yes to be courteous when they mean no. Firms in the global chemical industry recognize that production engineering personnel have a great deal of influence in Hungarian buying groups, while purchasing agents in the Canadian chemical industry have relatively more influence in buying decisions.

People in the Buying Centre   The composition of the buying centre in a given organization depends on the specific item being bought. Although a buyer or purchasing manager is almost always a member of the buying centre, individuals from other functional areas are included, depending on what is to be purchased. In buying a million-dollar machine tool, the president (because of the size of the purchase) and the production vice-president or manager would probably be members. For key components to be incorporated in a final manufactured product, a cross-functional group of individuals from research and development (R&D), engineering, and quality control are likely to be added. For new word-processing equipment, experienced secretaries who will use the equipment would be members. Still, a major question in penetrating the buying centre is finding and reaching the people who will initiate, influence, and actually make the buying decision.

Roles in the Buying Centre   Researchers have identified five specific roles that an individual in a buying centre can play.[22] In some purchases, the same person may perform two or more of these roles.

- *Users* are the people in the organization who actually use the product or service, such as a secretary who will use a new word processor.
- *Influencers* affect the buying decision, usually by helping define the specifications for what is bought. The information systems manager would be a key influencer in the purchase of a new mainframe computer.
- *Buyers* have formal authority and responsibility to select the supplier and negotiate the terms of the contract. The purchasing manager probably would perform this role in the purchase of a mainframe computer.
- *Deciders* have the formal or informal power to select or approve the supplier that receives the contract. Whereas in routine orders the decider is usually the buyer or purchasing manager, in important technical purchases, it is more likely to be someone from R&D, engineering, or quality control. The decider for a key component being incorporated in a final manufactured product might be any of these three people.
- *Gatekeepers* control the flow of information in the buying centre. Purchasing personnel, technical experts, and secretaries can all keep salespeople or information from reaching people performing the other four roles.

buy classes
Three types of organizational buying situations: new buy, straight rebuy, and modified rebuy.

Buying Situations and the Buying Centre   The number of people in the buying centre largely depends on the specific buying situation. Researchers who have studied organizational buying identify three types of buying situations, called **buy classes**. These buy classes vary from the routine reorder, or *straight rebuy*, to the completely new purchase, termed *new buy*. In between these extremes is the *modified rebuy*. Some examples will clarify the differences.[23]

BUYING CENTRE DIMENSION	BUY-CLASS SITUATION	
	NEW BUY	**STRAIGHT/MODIFIED REBUY**
People involved	Many	Few
Decision time	Long	Short
Problem definition	Uncertain	Well-defined
Buying objective	Good solution	Low-price supplier
Suppliers considered	New/present	Present
Buying influence	Technical/operating personnel	Purchasing agent

■ **FIGURE 6–3** ■■

How the buying situation affects buying centre behaviour

- *Straight rebuy.* Here, the buyer or purchasing manager reorders an existing product or service from the list of acceptable suppliers, probably without even checking with users or influencers from the engineering, production, or quality control departments. Office supplies and maintenance services are usually obtained as straight rebuys.
- *Modified rebuy.* In this buying situation, the users, influencers, or deciders in the buying centre want to change the product specifications, price, delivery schedule, or supplier. Although the item purchased is largely the same as with the straight rebuy, the changes usually necessitate enlarging the buying centre to include people outside the purchasing department.
- *New buy.* Here, the organization is a first-time buyer of the product or service. This involves greater potential risks in the purchase, and so the buying centre is enlarged to include all those who have a stake in the new buy. Procter & Gamble's purchase of a multi-million dollar fibre-optic network to link its corporate offices from Corning, Inc. represented a new buy.[24]

Figure 6–3 summarizes how buy classes affect buying centre tendencies in different ways.[25]

The marketing strategies of sellers facing each of these three buying situations can vary greatly because the importance of personnel from functional areas, such as purchasing, engineering, production, and R&D, often varies with (1) the type of buying situation, and (2) the stage of the purchasing process.[26] If it is a new buy for the manufacturer, you should be prepared to act as a consultant to the buyer, work with technical personnel, and expect a long time for a buying decision to be reached. However, if the manufacturer has bought the component part from you before (a straight or modified rebuy), you might emphasize a competitive price and a reliable supply in meetings with the purchasing agent.

CONCEPT CHECK

1. What one department is almost always represented by a person in the buying centre?

2. What are the three types of buying situations or buy classes?

■ ■ ■

CHARTING THE ORGANIZATIONAL BUYING PROCESS

Organizational buyers, like consumers, engage in a decision process when selecting products and services. As defined earlier in this chapter, organizational buying behaviour is the decision-making process that organizations use to establish the need for products and services and identify, evaluate, and choose among alternative brands and suppliers. There are important similarities and differences between the two decision-making processes. To better understand the nature of organizational

STAGE IN THE BUYING DECISION PROCESS	CONSUMER PURCHASE: MP3 PLAYER FOR A STUDENT	ORGANIZATIONAL PURCHASE: EARPHONES FOR AN MP3 PLAYER
Problem recognition	Student does not like the features of the portable CD player now owned and desires a new MP3 player.	Marketing research and sales departments observe that competitors are improving the earphones on their MP3 models. The firm decides to improve the earphones on its own new models, which will be purchased from an outside supplier.
Information search	Student uses own and friends' past experience, ads, the Internet, and *Consumer Reports* to collect information and uncover alternatives.	Design and production engineers draft specifications for earphones. The purchasing department identifies suppliers of MP3 player earphones.
Alternative evaluation	Alternative MP3 players are evaluated on the basis of important attributes desired in a MP3 player, and several stores are visited.	Purchasing and engineering personnel visit with suppliers and assess (1) facilities, (2) capacity, (3) quality control, and (4) financial status. They drop any suppliers not satisfactory on these factors.
Purchase decision	A specific brand of MP3 player is selected, the price is paid, and the student leaves the store.	They use (1) quality, (2) price, (3) delivery, and (4) technical capability as key buying criteria to select a supplier. Then they negotiate terms and award a contract.
Postpurchase behaviour	Student re-evaluates the purchase decision, may return the MP3 player to the store if it is unsatisfactory, and looks for supportive information to justify the purchase.	They evaluate suppliers using a formal vendor rating system and notify the supplier if earphones do not meet their quality standard. If the problem is not corrected, they drop the firm as a future supplier.

■ FIGURE 6–4 ■■

Comparing the stages in consumer and organizational purchases

buying behaviour, we first compare it with consumer buying behaviour and then describe an actual organizational purchase in detail.

Stages in the Organizational Buying Process

As shown in Figure 6–4 (and covered in Chapter 5), the five stages a student might use in buying an MP3 player also apply to organizational purchases. However, comparing the two right-hand columns in Figure 6–4 reveals some key differences. For example, when a MP3 player manufacturer buys earphones for its units from a supplier more individuals are involved, supplier capability becomes more important, and the postpurchase evaluation behaviour is more formalized.

The earphone-buying decision process is typical of the steps made by organizational buyers. Let us now examine in detail the decision-making process for a more complex product—machine vision systems.

Buying a Machine Vision System

Machine vision is widely regarded as one of the keys to the factory of the future. The chief elements of a machine vision system are its optics, light source, camera, video processor, and computer software. Vision systems are mainly used for product inspection. They are also becoming important as one of the chief elements in the information feedback loop of systems that control manufacturing processes. Vision systems, selling for around $25 000, are mostly sold to original equipment manufacturers (OEMs) who incorporate them in still larger industrial automation systems that sell for $200 000 to $300 000.

Finding productive applications for machine vision involves the constant search for technology and designs that satisfy user needs. The buying process for machine vision components and assemblies is frequently a new buy because many machine vision systems contain elements that require some custom design. Let us track five purchasing stages that a company, such as the Industrial Automation Division of Siemens, a large German industrial firm, would follow when purchasing components and assemblies for the machine vision systems it produces and installs.

Problem Recognition Sales engineers constantly canvass industrial automation equipment users, such as Ford Motor Company, Grumman Aircraft, and many Asian and European firms, for leads on upcoming industrial automation projects. They also keep these firms current on Siemens' technology, products, and services. When a firm needing a machine vision capability identifies a project that would benefit from Siemens' expertise, company engineers typically work with the firm to determine the kind of system required to meet the customer's need.

make-buy decision
An evaluation of whether components and assemblies will be purchased from outside suppliers or built by the company itself.

After a contract is won, project personnel must often make a **make-buy decision**—an evaluation of whether components and assemblies will be purchased from outside suppliers or built by the company itself. (Siemens produces many components and assemblies.) When these items are to be purchased from outside suppliers, the company engages in a thorough supplier search and evaluation process.

Information Search Such companies as Siemens (www.siemens.com) employ a sophisticated process for identifying outside suppliers of components and assemblies. For standard items, such as connectors, printed circuit boards, and components, for example, resistors and capacitors, the purchasing agent consults the company's purchasing databank, which contains information on hundreds of suppliers and thousands of products. All products in the databank have been prenegotiated as to price, quality, and delivery time, and many have been assessed using **value analysis**—a systematic appraisal of the design, quality, and performance of a product to reduce purchasing costs.

value analysis
A systematic appraisal of the design, quality, and performance of a product to reduce purchasing costs.

For one-of-a-kind components or assemblies, such as new optics, cameras, and light sources, the company relies on its engineers to keep current on new developments in product technology. This information is often found in technical journals and industry magazines or at international trade shows where suppliers display their most recent innovations. In some instances, supplier representatives might be asked to make presentations to the buying centre at Siemens. Such a group often consists of a project engineer; several design, system, and manufacturing engineers; and a purchasing agent.

Alternative Evaluation Three main buying criteria are used to select suppliers: price, performance, and delivery. Other important criteria include assurance that a supplier will not go out of business during the contractual period, assurance that the supplier will meet product quality and performance specifications, and service during the contractual period. Typically, two or three suppliers for each standard component and assembly are identified from a **bidders' list**—a list of firms believed to be qualified to supply a given item. This list is generated from the company's purchasing databank as well as from engineering inputs. Specific items that are unique or one-of-a-kind may be obtained from a single supplier after careful evaluation by the buying centre.

bidders' list
A list of firms believed to be qualified to supply a given item.

Firms selected from the bidders' list are sent a quotation request from the purchasing agent, describing the desired quantity, delivery date(s), and specifications of the components or assemblies. Suppliers are expected to respond within 30 days.

The purchase of machine vision systems involves a lengthy organizational buying process.

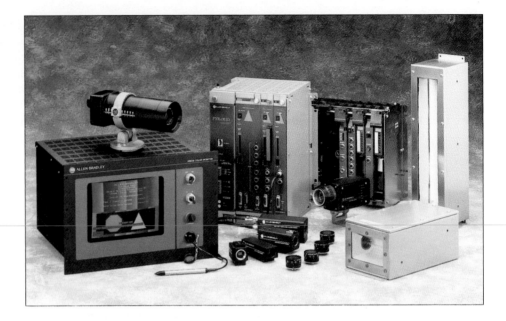

Purchase Decision   Unlike the short purchase stage in a consumer purchase, the period from supplier selection to order placement to product delivery can take several weeks or even months. Even after bids for components and assemblies are submitted, further negotiation concerning price, performance, and delivery terms is likely. Sometimes, conditions related to warranties, indemnities, and payment schedules have to be agreed on. The purchase decision is further complicated by the fact that two or more suppliers of the same item might be awarded contracts. This practice can occur when large orders are requested. Furthermore, suppliers who are not chosen are informed why their bids were not selected.

Postpurchase Behaviour   As in the consumer purchase decision process, postpurchase evaluation occurs in the industrial purchase decision process, but it is formalized and often more sophisticated. All items purchased are examined in a formal product-acceptance process. The performance of the supplier is also monitored and recorded. Performance on past contracts determines a supplier's chances of being asked to bid on future purchases, and poor performance may result in a supplier's name being dropped from the bidders' list.

The preceding example of an organizational purchase suggests four lessons for marketers to increase their chances of selling products and services to organizations. Firms selling to organizations must (1) understand the organization's needs, (2) get on the right bidders' list, (3) find the right people in the buying centre, and (4) provide value to the organizational buyer.

CONCEPT CHECK

1. What is a make-buy decision?

2. What is a bidders' list?

ONLINE BUYING IN ORGANIZATIONAL MARKETS

Organizational buying behaviour and business marketing continues to evolve with the application of Internet/Web technology. Organizations dwarf consumers in terms of both online transactions made and purchase volume.[27] In fact, organizational

eBay, Inc., is a true Internet phenomenon. By any measure, it is the predominant person-to-person trading community in the world.

eBay recently introduced a trading platform for the millions of small businesses in Canada, the United States, and around the world. When you go to the eBayBusiness Web site (www.ebaybusiness.com) of the Canadian site (http://business.ebay.ca), you will find a homepage structured for the small business marketplace. The site is easy for small business buyers and sellers to navigate and features many industry marketplaces and a dozen cross-industry products, such as office equipment, metalworking, and professional photography. Transactions on eBayBusiness exceed sales of $2 billion annually.

eBay is always updating its industry marketplaces. Go to the industry listing on the homepage. What types of industries are most prominent? Are products for all three kinds of organizational markets—industrial, reseller, and government—available?

"I save so much on eBay, I recommend it to my clients.

www.ebaybusiness.com

eBaY Business

buyers account for about 80 percent of the total worldwide dollar value of all online transactions. It is projected that online organizational buyers around the world will purchase between $6 trillion and $7.5 trillion worth of products and services by 2007. Organizational buyers in North America will account for about 60 percent of these purchases.

Prominence of Online Buying in Organizational Markets

Online buying in organizational markets is prominent for three major reasons.[28] First, organizational buyers depend heavily on timely supplier information that describes product availability, technical specifications, application uses, price, and delivery schedules. This information can be conveyed quickly via Internet/Web technology. Second, this technology has been shown to substantially reduce buyer order processing costs. At General Electric, online buying has cut the cost of a transaction from $50 to $100 per purchase to about $5. Third, business marketers have found that Internet/Web technology can reduce marketing costs, particularly sales and advertising expense, and broaden their potential customer base for many types of products and services. For these reasons, online buying is popular in all three kinds of organizational markets. For example, airlines order more than $400 million in spare parts from the Boeing Web site each year. Customers of Provigo, a large Canadian food wholesaler, can buy online, while provincial and municipal governments across Canada also engage in online purchasing.

Online buying can assume many forms. Organizational buyers can purchase directly from suppliers. For instance, a buyer might acquire a dozen desktop photocopiers from Xerox.com. This same buyer might purchase office furniture and supplies through a reseller, such as Office Depot at officedepot.com. Increasingly, organizational buyers and business marketers are using e-marketplaces and online auctions to purchase and sell products and services.

E-Marketplaces: Virtual Organizational Markets

e-marketplaces

Online trading communities, called e-marketplaces, that bring together buyers and supplier organizations.

A significant development in organizational buying has been the creation of online trading communities, called **e-marketplaces**, that bring together buyers and supplier organizations. These online communities go by a variety of names, including B2B exchanges and e-hubs, and make possible the real-time exchange of information, money, products, and services.

E-marketplaces can be independent trading communities or private exchanges.[29] Independent e-marketplaces act as a neutral third-party and provide an Internet technology trading platform and a centralized market that enable exchanges between buyers and sellers. They charge a fee for their service and exist in settings that have one or more of the following features: (1) thousands of geographically dispersed buyers and sellers, (2) volatile prices caused by demand and supply fluctuations, (3) time sensitivity due to perishable offerings and changing technologies, and (4) easily comparable offerings between a variety of suppliers. Well-known independent e-marketplaces include PlasticsNet (plastics), FreeMarkets (industrial parts, raw material, and commodities), Empori.com and XSAg.com (agricultural products). Small business buyers and sellers, in particular, benefit from independent e-marketplaces. These e-marketplaces offer them an economical way to expand their customer base and reduce the cost of products and services. eBay recently launched eBayBusiness to serve the small businesses market in Canada and the United States. You can learn about how B2B exchanges work and eBayBusiness in the accompanying WebLink box.[30]

Large companies tend to favour private exchanges that link them with their network of qualified suppliers and customers. Private exchanges focus on streamlining a company's purchase transactions with its suppliers and customers. Like independent e-marketplaces, they provide a technology trading platform and central market for buyer–seller interactions. They are not a neutral third party, however, but represent the interests of their owners. For example, Worldwide Retail Exchange performs the buying function for its 62 retail members, including Best Buy, The Gap, Radio Shack, Safeway, Target, and Walgreen. Procuron, developed by Canadian telecommunications and Banking institutions, such as Bell Canada and CIBC, offer a one-stop source of 6000 business goods and services and the Global Healthcare Exchange and its Canadian counterpart GHX Canada, engages in the buying and selling of health care products for 1400 hospitals and more than 100 health care suppliers, such as Abbott Laboratories, Johnson & Johnson, and U.S. Surgical. Each of these private exchanges has saved their members $1 billion due to efficiencies in purchase transactions.

Online Auctions in Organizational Markets

Online auctions have grown in popularity among organizational buyers and business marketers. Many e-marketplaces offer this service. Two general types of auctions are common: (1) a traditional auction, and (2) a reverse auction.[31] Figure 6–5 shows how buyer and seller participants and price behaviour differ by type of auction. Let us look at each auction type more closely to understand the implications of each for buyers and sellers.

traditional auction

A seller puts an item up for sale, and would-be buyers are invited to bid in competition with each other.

In a **traditional auction** a seller puts an item up for sales and would-be buyers are invited to bid in competition with each other. As more would-be buyers become involved, there is an upward pressure on bid prices. Why? Bidding is sequential. Prospective buyers observe the bids of others and decide whether or not to increase the bid price. The auction ends when a single bidder remains and "wins" the item with its highest price. For example, eBayBusiness uses a traditional auction. Traditional auctions are also used to dispose of excess merchandise. For example, Dell Inc. sells surplus, refurbished, or closeout computer merchandise at its dellauction.com Web site.

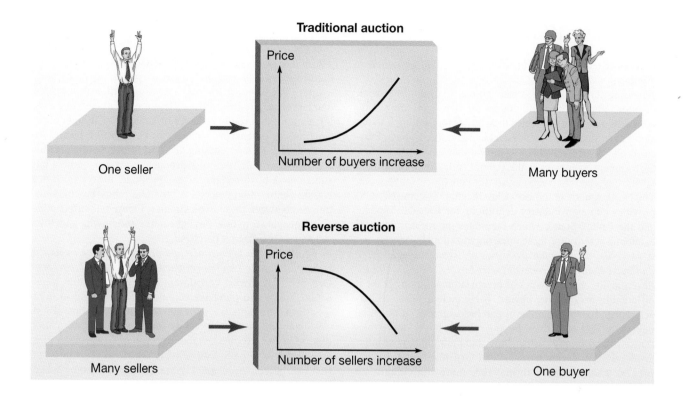

■ FIGURE 6–5 ■
How buyer and seller participants and price behaviour differ by type of online auction

reverse auction
A buyer communicates a need for a product or service, and would-be suppliers are invited to bid in competition with each other.

A reverse auction works in the opposite direction from a traditional auction. In a **reverse auction**, a buyer communicates a need for a product or service and would-be suppliers are invited to bid in competition with each other. As more would-be suppliers become involved, there is a downward pressure on bid prices for the buyer's business. Why? Like traditional auctions, bidding is sequential and prospective suppliers observe the bids of others and decide whether or not to decrease the bid price. The auction ends when a single bidder remains and "wins" the business with its lowest price. Reverse auctions benefit organizational buyers by reducing the cost of their purchases. As an example, Global eXchange Services, which runs online reverse auctions, claims it saved General Electric $780 million on the purchase of $6 billion worth of products and services.

Clearly, buyers welcome the lower prices generated by reverse auctions. Some suppliers also favour reverse auctions because they give them a chance to capture business that they might not have otherwise had because of a longstanding purchase relationship between the buyer and another supplier. On the other hand, suppliers say that reverse auctions put too much emphasis on prices, discourage consideration of other important buying criteria, and threaten supply partnership opportunities.[32]

CONCEPT CHECK

1. What are e-marketplaces?

2. In general, which type of online auction creates upward pressure on bid prices, and which type creates downward pressure on bid prices?

CHAPTER IN REVIEW

1 *Distinguish among industrial, reseller, and government organizational markets.*
There are three different organizational markets: industrial, reseller, and government. Industrial firms, in some way, reprocess a product or service they buy before selling it to the next buyer. Resellers—wholesalers and retailers—buy physical products and sell them again without any reprocessing. Government agencies, at the federal, provincial, and local levels, buy goods and services for the constituents they serve. The North American Industry Classification System (NAICS) provides common industry definitions for Canada, Mexico, and the United States, which facilitates the measurement of economic activity for these three organizational markets.

2 *Describe the key characteristics of organizational buying that make it different from consumer buying.*
Seven major characteristics of organizational buying make it different from consumer buying. These include demand characteristics, size of the order or purchase, number of potential buyers, buying objectives, buying criteria, buyer–seller relationships and supply partnerships, and multiple buying influences within organizations. The organizational buying process itself is more formalized, more individuals are involved, supplier capability is more important, and the post-purchase evaluation behaviour often includes performance of the supplier and the item purchased. Figure 6–4 details how the purchase of an MP3 player differs between a consumer purchase and an organizational purchase. The case study describing the purchase of machine vision systems by an industrial firm illustrates this process in greater depth.

3 *Explain how buying centres and buying situations influence organizational purchasing.*
Buying centres and buying situations have an important influence on organizational purchasing. A buying centre consists of a group of individuals who share common goals, risks, and knowledge important to a purchase decision. A buyer or purchasing manager is almost always a member of a buying centre. However, other individuals may affect organizational purchasing due to their unique roles in a purchase

decision. Five specific roles that a person may play in a buying centre include user, influencer, buyer, decider, and gatekeeper. The specific buying situation will influence the number of people in and the different roles played in a buying centre. For a routine reorder of an item—a straight rebuy situation—a purchasing manager or buyer will typically act alone in making a purchasing decision. When an organization is a first-time purchaser of a product or service—a new buy situation—a buying centre is enlarged and all five roles in a buying centre often emerge. A modified rebuy buying situation lies between these two extremes. Figure 6–3 offers additional insights into how buying centres and buying situations influence organization purchasing.

4 *Recognize the importance and nature of online buying in industrial, reseller, and government organizational markets.*
Organizations dwarf consumers in terms of online transactions made and purchase volume. Online buying in organizational markets is popular for three reasons. First, organizational buyers depend on timely supplier information that describes product availability, technical specifications, application uses, price, and delivery schedules. This information can be conveyed quickly via Internet technology. Second, this technology substantially reduces buyer order processing costs. Third, business marketers have found that Internet technology can reduce marketing costs, particularly sales and advertising expense, and broaden their customer base. Two developments in online buying have been the creation of e-marketplaces and online auctions. E-marketplaces provide a technology trading platform and a centralized market for buyer–seller transactions and make possible the real-time exchange of information, money, products, and services. These e-marketplaces can be independent trading communities, such as freemarkets, or private exchanges, such as the worldwide retail exchange. Online traditional and reverse auctions represent a second major development. With traditional auctions, the highest-priced bidder "wins." conversely, the lowest-priced bidder "wins" with reverse auctions.

FOCUSING ON KEY TERMS

bidders' list p. 153
business marketing p. 142
buy classes p. 150
buying centre p. 149
derived demand p. 146
e-marketplaces p. 156
government units p. 143
industrial firm p. 142
ISO 9000 standards p. 148
make-buy decision p. 153
North American Industry Classification System (NAICS) p. 144

organizational buyers p. 142
organizational buying behaviour p. 146
organizational buying criteria p. 147
reciprocity p. 149
reseller p. 143
reverse auction p. 157
reverse marketing p. 148
supply partnership p. 149
traditional auction p. 156
value analysis p. 153

■ ■ ■
DISCUSSION AND APPLICATION QUESTIONS

1 Describe the major differences among industrial firms, resellers, and government units in Canada.

2 Explain how the North American Industry Classification System (NAICS) might be helpful in understanding industrial, reseller, and government markets, and discuss the limitations inherent in this system.

3 List and discuss the key characteristics of organizational buying that make it different from consumer buying.

4 What is a buying centre? Describe the roles assumed by people in a buying centre and what useful questions should be raised to guide any analysis of the structure and behaviour of a buying centre.

5 Effective marketing is of increasing importance in today's competitive environment. How can firms more effectively market to organizations?

6 A firm that is marketing multi-million dollar wastewater treatment systems to cities has been unable to sell a new type of system. To date, the firm's marketing efforts have been directed to city purchasing departments to be included on approved bidders' lists. Talks with city-employed personnel have indicated that the new system is very different from current systems and therefore city sanitary and sewer department engineers, directors of these two departments, and city council members are unfamiliar with the workings of the system. Consulting engineers, hired by cities to work on the engineering and design features of these systems and paid on a percentage of system cost, are also reluctant to favour the new system. (*a*) What roles do the various individuals play in the purchase process for a wastewater treatment system? (*b*) How could the firm improve the marketing effort behind the new system?

■
GOING ONLINE   Navigating the NAICS

The North American Industrial Classification System (NAICS) structures industrial sectors into their component industries. The NAICS can be accessed at http://www.statcan.ca/english/Subjects/Standard/naics/2002/naics02-menu.htm. A person only has to click NAICS codes to obtain industry breakdowns.

You have been hired by a large industrial firm as a market analyst. Your first assignment is to identify the kinds of companies and services that fall into the Utilities Sector (code 22) and make a presentation to senior management. Your immediate supervisor advises you that senior management would be interested in the following information:

1 How many three-, four-, five-, and six-digit industries exist in the Utilities Sector?

2 How is the sector structured? That is, how would you display this subsector using the framework shown in Figure 6–1?

Do you want to get better grades and stay up to date with current issues in marketing? Visit the Online Learning Centre at www.mcgrawhill.ca/college/crane for practice tests, video cases, resources for building a marketing plan, *Globe and Mail* headlines, access to *Marketing Magazine*, and other learning and study tools.

VIDEO CASE 6   Lands' End: Where Buyers Rule

Organizational buying is a part of the marketing effort that influences every aspect of business at Lands' End. As senior vice-president of operations Phil Schaecher explains, "When we talk about purchasing at Lands' End, most people think of the purchase of merchandise for resale, but we buy many other things aside from merchandise, everything from the simplest office supply to the most sophisticated piece of material-handling equipment." As a result, Lands' End has developed a sophisticated approach to organizational buying, which is one of the keys to its incredible success.

THE COMPANY

The company started by selling sailboat equipment, duffle bags, rainsuits, and sweaters from a basement location in Chicago's old tannery district. In its first catalogue, the company name was printed with a typing error—the apostrophe in the wrong place—but the fledgling company could not afford to correct and reprint it. So, ever since, the company name has been Lands' End—with the misplaced apostrophe.

When the company outgrew its Chicago location, founder Gary Comer relocated it to Dodgeville, Wisconsin, because he had fallen in love with its rolling hills and changing seasons. The original business ideas were simple: "Sell only things we believe in, ship every order the day it arrives, and unconditionally guarantee everything." Over time, the company developed eight principles of doing business:

1. Never reduce the quality of a product to make it cheaper.
2. Price products fairly and honestly.
3. Accept any return for any reason.
4. Ship items in stock the day after the order is received.
5. What is best for the customer is best for Lands' End.
6. Place contracts with manufacturers who are cost-conscious and efficient.
7. Operate efficiently.
8. Keep overheads low.

These principles became the guidelines for the company's dedicated local employees and helped create extraordinary expectations from Lands' End customers.

Today, Lands' End is one of the world's largest direct merchants, with annual sales of traditionally styled clothing, luggage, and home products exceeding $1.4 billion. The products are offered through catalogues, the Internet, and retail stores. Last year, Lands' End distributed more than 260 million catalogues designed for specific segments, including *The Lands' End Catalog, Lands' End Men, Lands' End Women, Lands' End Kids, Lands' End for School, Lands' End Home,* and *Lands' End Corporate.* In a typical day, catalogue shoppers place more than 40 000 telephone calls to the company. The Lands' End Web site (www.lands end.com) also offers every Lands' End product and a wide variety of Internet shopping innovations, such as a 3-D model customized to each customer (called My Virtual Model™); a "personal shopper," to suggest products that match the consumer's preferences; and a feature that allows customers to "chat" online directly with a customer service representative. Lands' End operates stores in the United States, the United Kingdom, and Japan. Selected Lands' End merchandise is also sold at Sears following the purchase of Lands' End by Sears in 2002.

The company's goal is to please customers with the highest levels of quality and service in the industry. Lands' End maintains the high quality of its products through several important activities. For example, the company works directly with mills and manufacturers to retain control of quality and design. "The biggest difference between Lands' End and some other retailers or catalogue businesses is that we actually design all the product here and we do all the specifications. Therefore, the manufacturer is building that product directly to our specs, we are not buying off of somebody else's line," explains Joan Mudget, vice-president of quality assurance. In addition, Lands' End tests its products for comfort and fit by paying real people (local residents and children) to "wear-test" and "fit-test" all types of garments.

Service has also become an important part of the Lands' End reputation. Customers expect prompt, professional service at every step—initiating the order, making selections, shipping, and follow-up (if necessary). Some of the ways Lands' End meets these expectations include offering the simplest guarantee in the industry ("Guaranteed. Period.") toll-free telephone lines open 24 hours-a-day 364 days a year, continuous product training for telephone representatives, and two-day shipping. Lands' End operators even send personal responses to all e-mail messages, approximately 230 000 per year.

ORGANIZATIONAL BUYING AT LANDS' END

The sixth Lands' End business principle (described above) is accomplished through the company's organizational buying process. First, its buyers specify fabric

quality, construction, and sizing standards, which typically exceed industry standards, for current and potential Lands' End products. Then, the buyers literally search around the world for the best possible source of fabrics and products. Once a potential supplier is identified, one of the company's 150 quality assurance personnel makes an information-gathering visit. The purpose of the visit is to understand the supplier's values, to assess four criteria (economic, quality, service, and vendor), and to determine if the Lands' End standards can be achieved.

Lands' End evaluations of potential suppliers lead to the selection of what the company hopes will become long-term partners. As Mudget explains, "When we're looking for new manufacturers, we are looking for the long term. I think one of the most interesting things is we're not out there looking for new vendors every year to fill the same products." In fact, Lands' End believes that the term *supplier* does not adequately describe the importance the company places on the relationships. Lands' End suppliers are viewed as allies, supporters, associates, colleagues, and stakeholders in the future of the company. Once an alliance is formed, the product specifications and the performance on those specifications are regularly evaluated.

Lands' End buyers face a variety of buying situations. Straight rebuys involve reordering an existing product—such as shipping boxes—without evaluating or changing specifications. Modified rebuys involve changing some aspect of a previously ordered product—such as the collar of a knit shirt—based on input from consumers, retailers, or other people involved in the purchase decision. Finally, new buys involve first-time purchases—such as Lands' End addition of men's suits to its product line. The complexity of the process can vary with the type of purchase. Schaecher explains,

"As you get more complicated in the purchase there are more things you look at to decide on a vendor."

FUTURE CHALLENGES FOR LANDS' END

Lands' End faces several challenges as it pursues improvements in its organizational buying process. First, new technologies offer opportunities for fast, efficient, and accurate communication with suppliers. Ed Smidebush, general inventory manager, describes a new system at Lands' End: "Our quick response system is a computerized system where we transmit electronically to our vendors each Sunday night, forecast information as well as stock positions and purchase order information so that on Monday morning this information will be incorporated directly into their manufacturing reports so that they can prioritize their production." Occasionally, Lands' End must work with its suppliers to improve their technology and information system capabilities.

Another challenge for Lands' End is to anticipate changes in consumer interests. While it has many years of experience with retail consumers, preferences for colours, fabrics, and styles change frequently, requiring buyers to constantly monitor the marketplace. In addition, Lands' End's more recent offerings to corporate customers require constant attention "because business customers' wants and incentives, and the environment in which they're shopping, are very different from consumers at home," explains marketing manager Hilary Kleese.

Finally, Lands' End must anticipate the quantities of each of its products that consumers are likely to order. To do this, historical information is used to develop forecasts. One of the best tests of their forecast accuracy is the holiday season, when Lands' End receives more than 100 000 calls each day. Having the right products available is important because, as every employee knows from Principle 4, every order must be shipped the day after it is received.

QUESTIONS

1 Who is likely to comprise the buying centre in the decision to select a new supplier for Lands' End? Which of the buying centre members are likely to play the roles of users, influencers, buyers, deciders, and gatekeepers?

2 Which stages of the organizational buying decision process does Lands' End follow when it selects a new supplier? What selection criteria does the company utilize in the process?

3 Describe purchases Lands' End buyers typically face in each of the three buying situations: straight rebuy, modified rebuy, new buy.

CHAPTER 7

REACHING GLOBAL MARKETS

LEARNING OBJECTIVES

After reading this chapter, you should be able to:

1 Describe the nature and scope of world trade from a global perspective and its implications for Canada.

2 Identify the major trends that have influenced the landscape of global marketing in the past decade.

3 Identify the environmental factors that shape global marketing efforts.

4 Name and describe the alternative approaches companies use to enter global markets.

5 Explain the distinction between standardization and customization when companies craft worldwide marketing programs.

MATTEL'S GLOBAL MARKETING IS MORE THAN CHILD'S PLAY

Mattel is rewriting the rules for toy marketing on a global scale. As the world-wide leader in the design, manufacture, and marketing of toys and family products, Mattel successfully markets its best-selling Barbie®, Hot Wheels®, and Fisher-Price® brands in more than 150 countries.

Mattel's global marketing success can be linked to its new-product development effort. Toy developers are encouraged to think globally from the moment a new toy is conceived, with an eye to developing products that are likely to have universal appeal. Why? Mattel's research with children in dozens of countries has yielded a novel insight: children are more alike than they are different in their product preferences. Today, Mattel markets as much as 80 percent of its product offerings to a global audience, with just 20 percent geared to individual country markets. Mattel's product introductions are also global in scope. For example, Mattel recently launched Rapunzel Barbie on the same day in 59 countries supported by a televised advertising campaign broadcast in 35 languages. The widening international reach of retailing giants, such as Wal-Mart, Target, and French-based Carrefour SA (the world's second-largest retailer), also permits Mattel to coordinate its store merchandising campaigns on a global scale.

Mattel's global marketing orientation has paid huge dividends. More than 40 percent of the company's sales come from outside North America. One Barbie is sold every three seconds somewhere in the world.[1]

This chapter describes the global marketing environment at the dawn of the twenty-first century. It also highlights the many ways successful companies like Mattel engage in global marketing.

■ ■ ■
DYNAMICS OF WORLD TRADE

The dollar value of world trade has more than doubled in the past decade and will exceed $11.5 trillion in 2008. Manufactured goods and commodities account for 75 percent of world trade. Service industries, including telecommunications, transportation, insurance, education, banking, and tourism, represent the other 25 percent of world trade.

World Trade Flows

All nations and regions of the world do not participate equally in world trade. World trade flows reflect interdependencies among industries, countries, and regions and manifest themselves in country, company, industry, and regional exports and imports.

countertrade
The practice of using barter rather than money for making global sales.

■ FIGURE 7–1 ■
Illustrative world trade flows for manufactured goods and commodities (billions of dollars)

Global Perspective   Figure 7–1 shows the estimated dollar value of exports and imports among North American countries, Europe, Asian/Pacific Rim countries, and the rest of the world, including intraregional trade flows.[2] The United States, Europe, Canada, China, and Japan together account for more than two-thirds of world trade.

Not all trade involves the exchange of money for goods or services. In a world where 70 percent of all countries do not have convertible currencies or where government-owned enterprises lack sufficient cash or credit for imports, other means of payment are used. An estimated 15 to 20 percent of world trade involves **countertrade**, the practice of using barter rather than money for making global sales.[3]

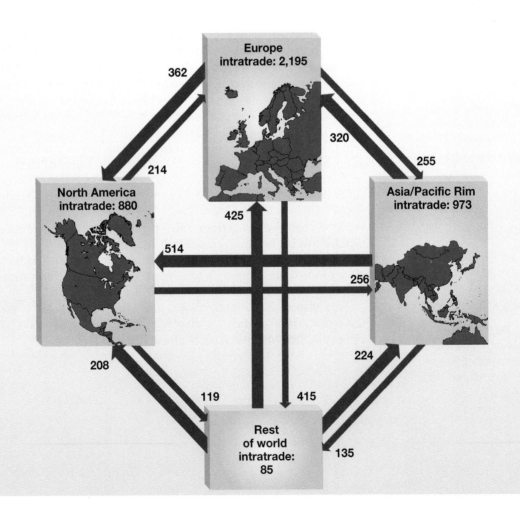

Countertrade is popular with many Eastern European nations, Russia, and Asian countries. For example, the Malaysian government recently exchanged 20 000 tonnes of rice for an equivalent amount of Philippine corn. Volvo of North America delivered automobiles to the Siberian police force when Siberia had no cash to pay for them. It accepted payment in oil, which it then sold for cash to pay for media advertising.[4]

A global perspective on world trade views exports and imports as complementary economic flows: a country's imports affect its exports and exports affect its imports. Every nation's imports arise from the exports of other nations. As the exports of one country increase, its national output and income rise, which, in turn, leads to an increase in the demand for imports. This nation's greater demand for imports stimulates the exports of other countries. Increased demand for exports of other nations energizes their economic activity, resulting in higher national income, which stimulates their demand for imports. This phenomenon is called the **trade feedback effect** and is one argument for free trade among nations.

trade feedback effect
A country's imports affect its exports and exports affect its imports.

gross domestic product
The monetary value of all goods and services produced in a country during one year.

balance of trade
The difference between the monetary value of a nation's exports and imports.

Canadian Perspective   Canada's **gross domestic product** (GDP), the monetary value of all goods and services produced in a country during one year, is valued at over $1 trillion. Canada exports a significant percentage of the goods and services it produces. In fact, it exports almost 45 percent of GDP, making it an important trading nation.

The difference between the monetary value of a nation's exports and imports is called the **balance of trade.** When a country's exports exceed its imports, it incurs a surplus in its balance of trade. When imports exceed exports, a deficit has occurred. Canada maintains an overall surplus in its balance of trade at this time.

Almost every Canadian is affected by Canada's trading activity. The effects vary from the products we buy (Samsung computers from Korea, Waterford crystal from Ireland, Lindemans wine from Australia) to those we sell (Moosehead beer to Sweden, Inniskillin ice wines to the EU, and Bombardier aircraft to Norway) and the additional jobs and improved standard of living that can result from world trade.

World trade flows to and from Canada reflect demand and supply interdependencies for goods and services among nations and industries. While Canada trades with dozens of other countries, the three largest importers of Canadian goods and services are the United States (about 80 percent), Japan, and the European Union (EU). These countries are also the top three exporters to Canada. The EU and Japan enjoy trade surpluses with our country, while the United States incurs a trade deficit.[5]

Trade is so important to Canada that it is one of the federal government's key priorities. It is so critical to the growth of the Canadian economy that the government established what it calls Team Canada Inc. (TCI), a network of more than 20 federal departments and agencies that work to help Canadian firms find new global markets and assist them in competing in those markets.

Competitive Advantage of Nations

As companies in many industries find themselves competing against foreign competitors at home and abroad, government policy makers around the world are increasingly asking why some companies and industries in a country succeed globally while others lose ground or fail. Michael Porter suggests a "diamond" to explain a nation's competitive advantage and why some industries and firms become world leaders.[6] He identified four key elements, which appear in Figure 7–2:

1. *Factor conditions.* These reflect a nation's ability to turn its natural resources, education, and infrastructure into a competitive advantage. Consider Holland, which exports 59 percent of the world's cut flowers. The Dutch lead the world in the cut-flower industry because of their research in flower cultivation, packaging, and shipping—not because of their weather.

Porter's "diamond" of
national competitive
advantage

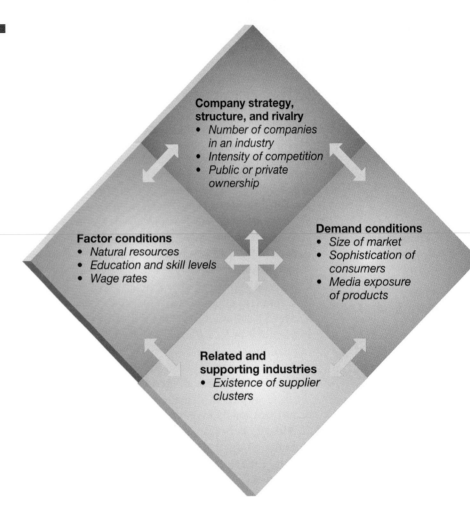

2. *Demand conditions.* These include both the number and sophistication of domestic customers for an industry's product. Japan's sophisticated consumers demand quality in their TVs and radios, thereby making Japan's producers, such as Sony, Sanyo, Matsushita, and Hitachi, some of the world leaders in the electronics industry.

3. *Related and supporting industries.* Firms and industries seeking leadership in global markets need clusters of world-class suppliers that accelerate innovation. The German leadership in scientific and industrial instrumentation relates directly to the cluster of supporting German precision engineering suppliers.

4. *Company strategy, structure, and rivalry.* These factors include the conditions governing the way a nation's businesses are organized and managed, along with the intensity of domestic competition. The Italian shoe industry has become a world leader because of intense domestic competition among such firms as MAB, Bruno Magli, and Rossimoda, which has made shoes for Christian Dior and Anne Klein Couture.

In Porter's study, case histories of firms in more than 100 industries were analyzed. While the strategies employed by the most successful global competitors were different in many respects, a common theme emerged—a firm that succeeds in global markets has first succeeded in intense domestic competition. Hence, competitive advantage for global firms grows out of relentless, continuing improvement, innovation, and change.

It is important to note, however, that it is not essential to be a giant company to compete successfully in global markets. Numerous small Canadian firms succeed in

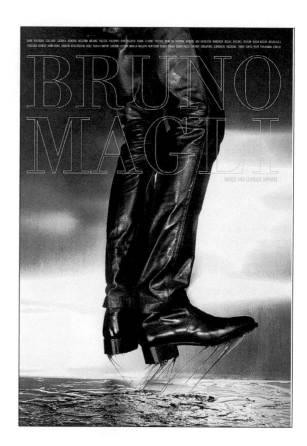

Sharp and Bruno Magli have succeeded in the global marketplace as well as in their domestic markets.

foreign markets because they find niche markets, sell innovative products, successfully leverage technology or licensing arrangements, or establish unique market positioning. In fact, Porter's study for the Canadian government on Canada's global competitiveness recommended, among other things, that Canadian firms should utilize such strategies as opposed to attempting to sell price-oriented commodities in global markets. He believes that by investing in R&D, and enhancing domestic competition, Canadian firms can improve their global competitiveness.[7] The Marketing NewsNet box on the next page provides some examples of some smaller Canadian firms that have found success in global markets.

CONCEPT CHECK

1. What is the trade feedback effect?

2. What variables influence why some companies and industries in a country succeed globally, while others lose ground or fail?

MARKETING IN A BORDERLESS ECONOMIC WORLD

Global marketing has and continues to be affected by a growing borderless economic world. Four trends in the past decade have significantly influenced the landscape of global marketing:

Trend 1: Gradual decline of economic protectionism by individual countries.

Trend 2: Formal economic integration and free trade among nations.

Trend 3: Global competition among global companies for global customers.

Trend 4: Development of networked global marketspace.

As you read in this chapter, Canada is a trading nation. Many Canadian firms are global leaders in their product categories, and yet, many are not huge corporations or mega-brand firms. Many smaller Canadian companies are successful globally by finding niche markets, selling innovative products, successfully leveraging technology or licensing arrangements, or establishing unique market positioning.

For example, one of Canada's independent breweries, Moosehead, in Saint John, New Brunswick, has achieved major success in global markets with its premium quality beer. Its international sales department is very busy supplying such markets as Australia, Chile, Ireland, Japan, Switzerland, and New Zealand. Another small Canadian company, W.F. Buckley has been successful in global markets due to the unique positioning of its Buckley's Mixture cough remedy product. Buckley's "It tastes awful. And it works" slogan has allowed it to achieve 10-percent market share of the Canadian cough and cold category

and to capture a significant share in global markets, such as the United States, the Caribbean, Australia, and New Zealand.

Toronto-based Spinmaster Toys is also a Canadian success story. Started in 1994 by three college students, the company has grown to be one of the top 10 global toy manufacturers in just 10 years. Spinmaster focuses on developing innovative products and utilizing strong licensing arrangements with some of the world's leading brands, including Disney, McDonald's, Marvel, and Hershey. Finally, Inniskillin Wines of Ontario has achieved global success with its niche icewine product. Its VAQ Icewine is a unique dessert beverage sold to upscale wine consumers at a $50 price tag for a 375-mL bottle. In an extremely competitive wine market, against players many times its size, Inniskillin has found success with this special niche product. These companies are just a few examples of Canadian firms that demonstrate that size is not a key factor in competing in global markets.

Decline of Economic Protectionism

protectionism

The practice of shielding one or more industries within a country's economy from foreign competition through the use of tariffs or quotas.

Protectionism is the practice of shielding one or more industries within a country's economy from foreign competition through the use of tariffs or quotas. The economic argument for protectionism is that it limits the outsourcing of jobs, protects a nation's political security, discourages economic dependency on other countries, and encourages the development of domestic industries. Read the accompanying Ethics and Social Responsibility Alert box and ask yourself if protectionism has an ethical and social responsibility dimension.[8]

tariffs

A government tax on goods or services entering a country, primarily serve to raise prices on imports.

Tariffs and quotas discourage world trade as depicted in Figure 7–3. **Tariffs,** which are a government tax on goods or services entering a country, primarily serve to raise prices on imports. The average tariff on manufactured goods in industrialized countries is 4 percent. However, wide differences exist across nations. For example, European Union countries have a 10-percent tariff on cars imported from Japan, which is about four times higher than the tariff imposed by the United States on Japanese cars.

The effect of tariffs on world trade and consumer prices is substantial. Consider rice exports to Japan. Experts claim that if the Japanese rice market were opened to imports by lowering tariffs, lower prices would save Japanese consumers over $8 billion annually. Similarly, tariffs imposed on bananas by European Union countries cost consumers $4 billion a year. Ecuador (the world's largest banana exporter), Mexico, Guatemala, and Honduras have negotiated a reduction in this levy before 2007.

quota

A restriction placed on the amount of a product allowed to enter or leave a country.

A **quota** is a restriction placed on the amount of a product allowed to enter or leave a country. Quotas can be mandated or voluntary and may be legislated or negotiated by governments. Import quotas seek to guarantee domestic industries access to a certain percentage of their domestic market. For example, there is a limit on

■ **FIGURE 7–3** ■

How protectionism affects
world trade

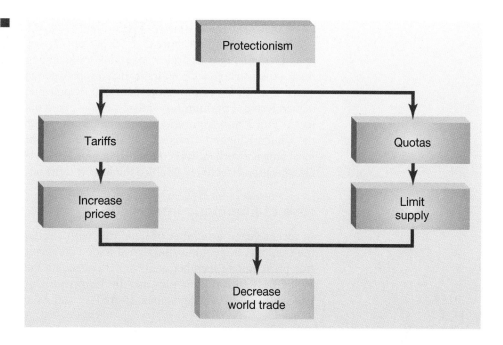

imported television sets to the United Kingdom and Italian quotas on Japanese motorcycles. Canada also imposes quotas which ultimately result in Canadian consumers usually paying higher prices for various goods.

Every country engages in some form of protectionism. However, protectionism has declined over the past 50 years due, in large part, to the *General Agreement on Tariffs and Trade (GATT)*. This international treaty was intended to limit trade barriers and promote world trade through the reduction of tariffs, which it did. However, GATT did not explicitly address nontariff trade barriers, such as quotas, and world trade in services, which often sparked heated trade disputes between nations.

As a consequence, the major industrialized nations of the world formed the **World Trade Organization** (WTO www.wto.org) in 1995 to address a broad

World Trade Organization
Organization formed in 1995 to address a broad array of world trade issues.

ETHICS AND SOCIAL
RESPONSIBILITY
ALERT

Global Ethics and Global Economics—
The Case of Protectionism

World trade benefits from free and fair trade among nations. Nevertheless, governments of many countries continue to use tariffs and quotas to protect their various domestic industries. Why? Protectionism earns profits for domestic producers and tariff revenue for government. There is a cost, however. Protectionist policies cost Japanese consumers between $75 billion and $110 billion annually. Canadian consumers pay billions each year in higher prices because of tariffs and other protective restrictions.

Sugar and textile import quotas in the United States, automobile and banana import tariffs in many European countries, beer import tariffs in Canada, and rice import tariffs in Japan protect domestic industries but also interfere with world trade for these products. Regional trade agreements, such as those found in the provisions of the European Union and the North American Free Trade Agreement, may also pose a situation whereby member nations can obtain preferential treatment in quotas and tariffs but nonmember nations cannot.

Protectionism, in its many forms, raises an interesting global ethical question. Is protectionism, no matter how applied, an ethical practice?

array of world trade issues.[9] There are 147 WTO member countries, including Canada, accounting for more than 90 percent of world trade. The WTO is a permanent institution that sets rules governing trade among its members through panels of trade experts who decide on trade disputes between members and issue-binding decisions. The WTO reviews more than 200 disputes annually. For instance, the WTO denied Kodak's multimillion-dollar damage claim that the Japanese government protected Fuji Photo from import competition. In another decision, the WTO allowed the United Kingdom, Ireland, and the European Union to reclassify U.S.-produced local area network (LAN) computer equipment as telecommunications gear. The new classification effectively doubled the import tariff on these American goods.

Rise of Economic Integration

In recent years, a number of countries with similar economic goals have formed transnational trade groups or signed trade agreements for the purpose of promoting free trade among member nations and enhancing their individual economies. Three of the best-known examples are the European Union (or simply EU), the North American Free Trade Agreement (NAFTA), and Asian Free Trade Areas.

European Union   The European Union consists of 25-member countries that have eliminated most barriers to the free flow of goods, services, capital, and labour across their borders (Figure 7–4).[10] This single market houses more than 380 million consumers. In addition, 12 countries have adopted a common currency called the *euro*. Adoption of the euro has been a boon to electronic commerce in the EU by eliminating the need to continually monitor currency exchange rates.

The EU creates abundant marketing opportunities because firms no longer find it necessary to market their products and services on a nation-by-nation basis. Rather, pan-European marketing strategies are possible due to greater uniformity in product and packaging standards; fewer regulatory restriction on transportation, advertising, and promotion imposed by countries; and removal of most tariffs that affect pricing practices. For example, Colgate-Palmolive Company now markets its Colgate toothpaste with one formula and package across EU countries at one price. Similarly, Black & Decker—the maker of electrical hand tools, appliances, and other consumer products— now produces 8, not 20, motor sizes for the European market, resulting in production and marketing cost savings. These practices were previously impossible because of different government and trade regulations. Europe-wide distribution from fewer locations is also feasible, given open borders. French tire maker Michelin has closed 180 of its European distribution centres and now uses just 20 to serve all EU countries.

North American Free Trade Agreement   The North American Free Trade Agreement lifted many trade barriers among Canada, Mexico, and the United States and created a marketplace with more than 400 million consumers.[11] Negotiations are under way to expand NAFTA to create a 34-country Free Trade Area of the Americas. This agreement would include the United States, Canada, Mexico, Latin America, and the Caribbean countries.

NAFTA has stimulated trade flows among member nations as well as cross-border retailing, manufacturing, and investment. For example, NAFTA paved the way for Wal-Mart to move to Mexico and Mexican supermarket giant, Gigante, to move into the United States. Whirlpool Corporation's Canadian subsidiary stopped making washing machines in Canada and moved that operation to Ohio. Whirlpool then shifted the production of kitchen ranges and compact dryers to Canada. Ford invested $60 million in its Mexico City manufacturing plant to produce smaller cars and light trucks for global sales.

■ **FIGURE 7-4** ■

The countries of the European Union in 2005

European Union
www.europa.eu.int

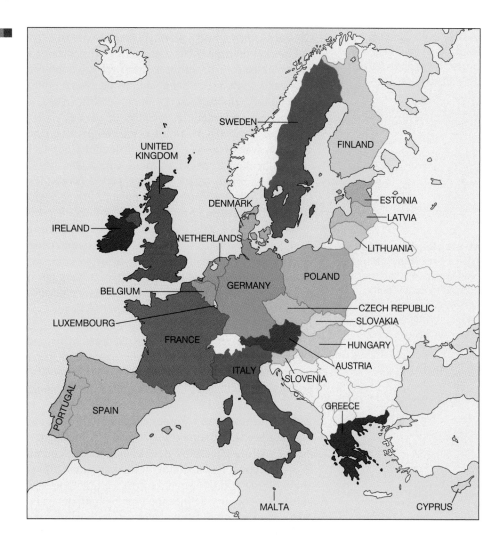

Other Free Trade Agreements   Other significant trade agreements include the Asia-Pacific Economic Cooperation (APEC) forum, which was established to promote economic integration around the Pacific Rim and to sustain economic growth. APEC currently has 21 members, including Australia, Canada, China, Japan, Peru, Russia, and the United States. APEC is a powerful trading group and accounts for a significant component of total world exports and imports. Another trade agreement is the ASEAN Free Trade Area (AFTA), established by the member nations of the Association of Southeast Asian Nations, which include Indonesia, Malaysia, Philippines, Singapore, Thailand, Brunei, Vietnam, Laos, Myanmar, and Cambodia.

Canada has also entered into various bilateral, or two-way, trade agreements with numerous countries. For example, the Canada–Israel Free Trade Agreement improves market access for agri-food products of export interest to both Canada and Israel and eliminates tariffs on virtually all manufactured goods.

A New Reality: Global Competition among Global Companies for Global Consumers

The emergence of a largely borderless economic world has created a new reality for marketers of all shapes and sizes. Today, world trade is driven by global competition among global companies for global consumers.

global competition
Exists when firms originate, produce, and market their products and services worldwide.

strategic alliances
Agreements among two or more independent firms to cooperate for the purpose of achieving common goals, such as a competitive advantage or customer value creation.

Global Competition　　**Global competition** exists when firms originate, produce, and market their products and services worldwide. The automobile, pharmaceutical, apparel, electronics, aerospace, and telecommunication fields represent well-known industries with sellers and buyers on every continent. Other industries that are increasingly global in scope include soft drinks, cosmetics, ready-to-eat cereals, snack chips, and retailing.

Global competition broadens the competitive landscape for marketers. The familiar "cola war" waged by Pepsi-Cola and Coca-Cola in Canada has been repeated around the world, including India, China, and Argentina. Procter & Gamble's Pampers and Kimberly-Clark's Huggies have taken their disposable diaper rivalry from Canada to Western Europe. Boeing and Europe's Airbus vie for lucrative commercial aircraft contracts on virtually every continent.

Collaborative relationships also are becoming a common way to meet the demands of global competition. Global **strategic alliances** are agreements among two or more independent firms to cooperate for the purpose of achieving common goals, such as a competitive advantage or customer value creation. For instance, several of the world's largest telecommunication equipment makers, including Ericsson (Sweden), Nortel (Canada), Siemens (Germany), and 3Com (USA), formed Juniper Networks, Inc., an alliance created to build devices to speed global Internet communications. General Mills and Nestlé of Switzerland created Cereal Partners Worldwide for the purpose of fine-tuning Nestlé's European cereal marketing and distributing of General Mills cereals worldwide. This global alliance produces more than $1 billion in sales in 130 countries.[12]

Global Companies　　Three types of companies populate and compete in the global marketplace: (1) international firms, (2) multinational firms, and (3) transnational firms.[13] All three employ people in different countries, and many have administrative, marketing, and manufacturing operations (often called *divisions* or *subsidiaries*) around the world. However, a firm's orientation toward and strategy for global markets and marketing defines the type of company it is or attempts to be.

An *international firm* engages in trade and marketing in different countries as an extension of the marketing strategy in its home country. Generally speaking, these firms market their existing products and services in other countries the same way they do in their home country. Avon, for example, successfully distributes its product

Pepsi-Cola, now available in more than 190 countries and territories, accounts for a quarter of all soft drinks sold internationally. This Brazilian ad—"How to make jeans last 10 years"—features the popular Diet Pepsi brand targeted at weight-conscious consumers.

PepsiCo, Inc.
www.pepsico.com

MARKETING NEWSNET

IDEAS AHEAD

The Global Teenager—A Market of 500 Million Consumers with $100 Billion to Spend

The "global teenager" market consists of 500 million 13- to 19-year-olds in Europe, North and South America, and the industrialized nations of Asia and the Pacific Rim, who have experienced intense exposure to television (MTV broadcasts in 166 countries), movies, travel, the Internet, and global advertising by such companies as Benetton, Sony, Nike, and Coca-Cola. The similarities among teens across these countries are greater than their differences. For example, a global study of middle-class teenagers' rooms in 25 industrialized countries indicated it was difficult, if not impossible, to tell whether the rooms were in Vancouver, Mexico City, Tokyo, Rio de Janeiro, Sidney, or Paris. Why? Teens spend $100 billion annually for a common gallery of products: Sony video

games, Tommy Hilfiger apparel, Levi's blue jeans, Nike athletic shoes, Swatch watches, and Procter & Gamble Clearasil acne medicine.

Teenagers around the world appreciate fashion and music, and desire novelty and trendier designs and images. They also acknowledge an Americanization of fashion and culture based on another study of 6500 teens in 26 countries. When asked what country had the most influence on their attitudes and purchase behaviour, 87 percent of those from Latin America, 80 percent of the Europeans, and 80 percent of those from Asia named the United States. This phenomenon has not gone unnoticed by parents. As one parent in India said, "Now the youngsters dress, talk, and eat like Americans."

---

multidomestic marketing strategy

Use of as many different product variations, brand names, and advertising programs as countries in which they do business.

global marketing strategy

The practice of standardizing marketing activities when there are cultural similarities and adapting them when cultures differ.

line through direct selling in Asia, Europe, and South America, employing virtually the same marketing strategy used in North America.

A *multinational firm* views the world as consisting of unique parts and markets to each part differently. Multinationals use a **multidomestic marketing strategy**, which means that they have as many different product variations, brand names, and advertising programs as countries in which they do business. For example, Lever Europe, a division of Unilever, markets its fabric softener known as Snuggle in Canada in 10 different European countries under seven brand names, including Kuschelweich in Germany, Coccolino in Italy, and Mimosin in France. These products have different packages, different advertising programs, and occasionally different formulas. Procter & Gamble markets Mr. Clean, its multipurpose cleaner, in North America and Asia. But you will not find Mr. Clean in other parts of the world. In Latin America, Mr. Clean is Mastro Limpio. Mr. Clean is Mr. Proper in Europe, Africa, and the Middle East.

A *transnational firm* views the world as one market and emphasizes cultural similarities across countries or universal consumer needs and wants more than differences. Transnational marketers employ a **global marketing strategy**—the practice of standardizing marketing activities when there are cultural similarities and adapting them when cultures differ. This approach benefits marketers by allowing them to realize economies of scale from their production and marketing activities.

Global marketing strategies are popular among many business-to-business marketers, such as Caterpillar and Komatsu (heavy construction equipment) and Texas Instruments, Intel, Hitachi, and Motorola (semiconductors). Consumer goods marketers, such as Timex, Seiko, and Swatch (watches), Coca-Cola and Pepsi-Cola (cola soft drinks), Mattel and LEGO (children's toys), Gillette (personal care products), L'Oréal and Shiseido (cosmetics), and McDonald's (quick-service restaurants),

global brand

A brand marketed under the same name in multiple countries with similar and centrally coordinated marketing programs.

successfully execute this strategy. Each of these companies markets a **global brand**—a brand marketed under the same name in multiple countries with similar and centrally coordinated marketing programs.[14] Global brands have the same product formulation or service concept, deliver the same benefits to consumers, and use consistent advertising across multiple countries and cultures. This is not to say that global brands are not sometimes tailored to specific cultures or countries. However, adaptation is only used when necessary to better connect the brand to consumers in different markets. Consider McDonald's.[15] This global marketer has adapted its proven formula of "food, fun, and families" across 119 countries. Although the Golden Arches and Ronald McDonald appear worldwide, McDonald's tailors other aspects of its marketing program. It serves beer in Germany, wine in France, and coconut, mango, and tropical mint shakes in Hong Kong. Hamburgers are made with different meat and spices in Japan, Thailand, India, and the Philippines. But McDonald's world-famous French fry is standardized. Its French fry in Beijing, China, tastes like that in Paris, France, which tastes like that in your neighbourhood.

global consumers

Consumer groups living in many countries or regions of the world who have similar needs or seek similar features and benefits from products or services.

Global Consumers   Global competition among global companies often focuses on the identification and pursuit of global consumers as described in the accompanying Marketing NewsNet box.[16] **Global consumers** consist of consumer groups living in many countries or regions of the world who have similar needs or seek similar features and benefits from products or services.[17] Evidence suggests the emergence of a global middle-income class, a youth market, and an elite segment, each consuming or using a common assortment of products and services, regardless of geographic location. A variety of companies have capitalized on the global consumer. Whirlpool, Sony, and IKEA have benefited from the growing global middle-income class desire for kitchen appliances, consumer electronics, and home furnishings, respectively. Levi's, Nike, Coca-Cola, and Benetton have tapped the global youth market. DeBeers, Chanel, Gucci, Rolls Royce, and Sotheby's and Christie's, the world's largest fine art and antique auction houses, cater to the elite segment for luxury goods worldwide.

Nestlé features multiple country and language Web sites that customize content and communicate with consumers in their native tongue. The Web site for Peru shown here is an example. Read the text to learn how many Web sites and languages Nestlé uses.

Nestlé S. A.

www.nestle.com

Emergence of a Networked Global Marketspace

The use of Internet technology as a tool for exchanging goods, services, and information on a global scale is the fourth trend affecting world trade.[18] Some one billion

businesses, educational institutions, government agencies, and households world-wide are expected to have Internet access by 2007. The broad reach of this technology suggests that its potential for promoting world trade is huge. In fact, sales arising from electronic commerce are projected to represent 10 percent of world trade in 2007, up from about 1 percent in 2001.

The promise of a networked global marketspace is that it enables the exchange of goods, services, and information from companies *anywhere* to customers *anywhere* at *any time* and at a lower cost. This promise has become a reality for buyers and sellers in industrialized countries that possess the telecommunications infrastructure necessary to support Internet technology. In particular, companies engaged in business-to-business marketing have spurred the growth of global electronic commerce. Ninety percent of global electronic commerce revenue arises from business-to-business transactions among a dozen countries in North America, Western Europe, and the Asia/Pacific Rim region. Industries that have benefited from this technology include industrial chemicals and controls, maintenance, repair, and operating supplies, computer and electronic equipment and components, aerospace parts, and agricultural and energy products. The United States, Canada, the United Kingdom, Germany, Sweden, Japan, China, and Taiwan are among the most active participants in worldwide business-to-business electronic commerce.

Marketers recognize that the networked global marketspace offers unprecedented access to prospective buyers on every continent. Companies that have successfully capitalized on this access manage multiple country and language Web sites that customize content and communicate with consumers in their native tongues. Nestlé, the world's largest packaged food manufacturer, coffee roaster, and chocolate maker is a case in point. The company operates 53 individual country Web sites in 20 languages that span five continents.

CONCEPT CHECK

1. What is protectionism?

2. Among which countries was the North American Free Trade Agreement was designed to promote free trade?

3. What is the difference between a multidomestic marketing strategy and a global marketing strategy?

■ ■ ■
A GLOBAL ENVIRONMENTAL SCAN

Global companies conduct continuing environmental scans of the five sets of environmental factors described earlier in Figure 3–1 (social, economic, technological, competitive, and regulatory forces). This section focuses on three kinds of uncontrollable environmental variables—cultural, economic, and political-regulatory—that affect global marketing practices in strikingly different ways from those in domestic markets.

Cultural Diversity

cross-cultural analysis
Involves the study of similarities and differences among consumers in two or more nations or societies.

Marketers must be sensitive to the cultural underpinnings of different societies if they are to initiate and consummate mutually beneficial exchange relationships with global consumers. A necessary step in this process is **cross-cultural analysis,** which involves the study of similarities and differences among consumers in two or more nations or societies.[19] A thorough cross-cultural analysis involves an understanding of and an appreciation for the values, customs, symbols, and language of other societies.

Values   As defined in Chapter 5, values are personally or socially preferable modes of conduct or states of existence that are enduring. Understanding and working with these aspects of a society's values are important factors in global marketing. For example,

- McDonald's does not sell beef hamburgers in its restaurants in India because the cow is considered sacred by almost 85 percent of the population. Instead, McDonald's sells the McMaharajah: two all-mutton patties, special sauce, lettuce, cheese, pickles, and onions on a sesame-seed bun.
- Germans have not been overly receptive to the use of credit cards, such as Visa or MasterCard, and installment debt to purchase goods and services. Indeed, the German word *Schuld* is the same for debt as well as for guilt.

These examples illustrate how cultural values can influence behaviour in different societies. Cultural values become apparent in the personal values of individuals that affect their attitudes and beliefs and the importance assigned to specific behaviours and attributes of goods and services. These personal values affect consumption-specific values, such as the use of installment debt by Germans, and product-specific values, such as the importance assigned to credit card interest rates.

customs

Norms and expectations about the way people do things in a specific country.

Customs   **Customs** are the norms and expectations about the way people do things in a specific country. Clearly, customs can vary significantly from country to country. For example, 3M Company executives were perplexed when the company's Scotch-Brite floor-cleaning product initially produced lukewarm sales in the Philippines. When a Filipino employee explained that consumers there customarily clean floors by pushing coconut shells around with their feet, 3M changed the shape of the pad to a foot, and sales soared! Some other customs are unusual to Canadians. Consider, for example, that in France, men use more than twice the number of cosmetics than women do and that Japanese women give Japanese men chocolates on Valentine's Day.

Customs also relate to the nonverbal behaviour of individuals in different cultural settings. For example, in many European countries, it is considered impolite not to have both hands on the table in business meetings. A simple gesture in a commercial such as pointing a finger, is perfectly acceptable in Western culture but is perceived as an insult in Middle and Far Eastern countries. Direct eye contact is viewed positively in North and Latin America but negatively in Japan. Casual touching is also inappropriate in Japan, while men hold hands in Middle Eastern countries as a sign of friendship. Business executives in Japan like to hold their opinions, listen longer, and pause before responding in meetings. Sometimes, the silence is misread by North American executives as lack of response.[20]

cultural symbols

Things that represent ideas and concepts.

semiotics

The field of study that examines the correspondence between symbols and their role in the assignment of meaning for people.

Cultural Symbols   **Cultural symbols** are things that represent ideas and concepts. Symbols or symbolism play an important role in cross-cultural analysis because different cultures ascribe different meanings to things. So important is the role of symbols that a field of study, called **semiotics**, has emerged that examines the correspondence between symbols and their role in the assignment of meaning for people. By adroitly using cultural symbols, global marketers can tie positive symbolism to their products and services to enhance their attractiveness to consumers. However, improper use of symbols can spell disaster. A culturally sensitive global marketer will know that[21]

- North Americans are superstitious about the number 13, and Japanese feel the same way about the number 4. *Shi,* the Japanese word for four, is also the word for death. Knowing this, Tiffany & Company sells its fine glassware and china in sets of five, not four, in Japan.
- "Thumbs-up" is a positive sign in Canada. However, in Russia and Poland, this gesture has an offensive meaning when the palm of the hand is shown, as AT&T learned. The company reversed the gesture depicted in ads, showing the back of the hand, not the palm.

What cultural lesson did Coca-Cola executives learn when they used the Parthenon in a global advertising campaign?

Cultural symbols evoke deep feelings. Consider how executives at Coca-Cola Company's Italian office learned this lesson. In a series of advertisements directed at Italian vacationers, the Eiffel Tower, the Empire State Building, and the Tower of Pisa were turned into the familiar Coca-Cola bottle. However, when the white marble columns in the Parthenon that crowns Athens' Acropolis were turned into Coca-Cola bottles, the Greeks were outraged. Greeks refer to the Acropolis as the "holy rock," and a government official said the Parthenon is an "international symbol of excellence" and that "whoever insults the Parthenon insults international culture." Coca-Cola apologized for the ad.[22]

Global markets are also sensitive to the fact that the "country of origin or manufacture" of products and services can symbolize superior or poor quality in some countries. For example, Russian consumers believe products made in Japan and Germany are superior in quality to products from North America and the United Kingdom. Japanese consumers believe Japanese products are superior to those made in Europe and North America. However, recently, Canadian firms marketing in Japan have discovered that Japanese like the "Canadian-ness" of products, and so brands and labels that say "Canada" add cachet for Japanese consumers.[23]

Language Global marketers should know not only the native tongues of countries in which they market their products and services but also the nuances and idioms of a language. Even though about 100 official languages exist in the world, anthropologists estimate that at least 3000 different languages are spoken. There are 11 official languages spoken in the European Union, and Canada has two official languages (English and French). Seventeen major languages are spoken in India alone.

English, French, and Spanish are the principal languages used in global diplomacy and commerce. However, the best language to communicate with consumers is their own, as any seasoned global marketer will attest to. Unintended meanings of brand names and messages have ranged from the absurd to the obscene:

- When the advertising agency responsible for launching Procter & Gamble's successful Pert shampoo in Canada realized that the name means "lost" in French, it substituted the brand name Pret, which means "ready."
- In Italy, Cadbury Schweppes, the world's third-largest soft drink manufacturer, realized that its Schweppes Tonic Water brand had to be renamed Schweppes Tonica because "il water" turned out to be the idiom for bathroom.
- The Vicks brand name common in North America is German slang for sexual intimacy; therefore, Vicks is called Wicks in Germany.

back translation

Retranslating a word or phrase into the original language by a different interpreter to catch errors.

Experienced global marketers use **back translation**, where a translated word or phrase is retranslated into the original language by a different interpreter to catch errors. For example, IBM's first Japanese translation of its "Solutions for a small planet" advertising message yielded "Answers that make people smaller." The error was caught and corrected. Nevertheless, unintended meanings still occur in the most unlikely situations. Just ask the logo designers for a line of Nike athletic shoes. The designers intended to portray "Air" with stylized flames on the shoe heel.

In Canada, all packages and labels must be printed in both English and French, and most major companies also run their ads in both languages. Here are both the English and French versions of a service ad for Hewlett-Packard. The company's Web site is multilingual, too.

Hewlett-Packard

www.hp.com

Unfortunately, the logo inadvertently resembled the Arabic script for the word "Allah," the Arabic word for God. After receiving complaints from Muslim leaders, Nike apologized and withdrew the offending shoes from the market.

The use of language in global marketing is assuming greater importance in an increasingly networked and borderless economic world. For example, Oracle Corporation, a leading worldwide supplier of software, now markets its products by language groups instead of through 145 country-specific efforts. The French group markets to France, Belgium, Switzerland, and Canada. A Spanish-language group oversees Spain and Latin America. Eight other language groups—English, Japanese, Korean, Chinese, Portuguese, Italian, Dutch, and German—cover Oracle's top revenue-producing countries.[24]

Cultural Ethnocentricity   The tendency for people to view their own values, customs, symbols, and language favourably is well known. However, the belief that aspects of one's culture are superior to another's is called *cultural ethnocentricity* and is a sure impediment to successful global marketing.

An outgrowth of cultural ethnocentricity exists in the purchase and use of goods and services produced outside of a country. Global marketers are acutely aware that certain groups within countries disfavour imported products, not on the basis of price, features, or performance, but purely because of their foreign origin. **Consumer ethnocentrism** is the tendency to believe that it is inappropriate, indeed immoral, to purchase foreign-made products.[25] Ethnocentric consumers believe that buying imported products is wrong because such purchases are unpatriotic, harm domestic industries, and cause domestic unemployment.[26]

consumer ethnocentrism
The tendency to believe that it is inappropriate, indeed immoral, to purchase foreign-made products.

Economic Considerations

Global marketing is also affected by economic considerations. Therefore, a scan of the global marketplace should include (1) a comparative analysis of the economic development in different countries, (2) an assessment of the economic infrastructure in these countries, (3) measurement of consumer income in different countries, and (4) recognition of a country's currency exchange rates.

Stage of Economic Development   There are about 260 countries in the world today, each of which is at a slightly different point in terms of its stage of economic development. However, they can be classified into two major groupings that will help the global marketer better understand their needs:

- *Developed* countries have somewhat mixed economies. Private enterprise dominates, although they have substantial public sectors as well. Canada, the United States, Japan, and most of Western Europe can be considered developed.
- *Developing* countries are in the process of moving from an agricultural to an industrial economy. There are two subgroups within the developing category: (1) those that have already made the move, and (2) those that remain locked in a preindustrial economy. Such countries as Poland, Hungary, Israel, Venezuela, Singapore, and South Africa fall into the first group. In the second group are Afghanistan, Sri Lanka, Tanzania, and Chad, where living standards are low and improvement will be slow.

A country's stage of economic development affects and is affected by other economic factors, as described next.

Economic Infrastructure   The *economic infrastructure*—a country's communications, transportation, financial, and distribution systems—is a critical consideration in determining whether to try to market to a country's consumers and organizations. Parts of the infrastructure that North Americans or Western Europeans take for granted can be huge problems elsewhere—not only in the developing nations but even in countries of the former Soviet Union, Eastern Europe, the Indian subcontinent, and China, where such an infrastructure is assumed to be in place. Consider, for instance, the transportation and distribution systems in these countries. Two-lane roads that limit average speeds to 55 or 65 kilometres per hour are commonplace—and a nightmare for firms requiring prompt truck delivery. In China, the bicycle is the preferred mode of transportation. This is understandable because China has few navigable roads outside its major cities, where 80 percent of the population lives. In India, Coca-Cola uses large tricycles to distribute cases of Coke along narrow streets in many cities. Wholesale and retail institutions tend to be small and are operated by new owner-managers still learning the ways of a free market system.

The communication infrastructures in these countries also differ. This infrastructure includes telecommunications systems and networks in use, such as telephones, cable television, broadcast radio and television, computers, satellites, and wireless telephones. In general, the communication infrastructure in many developing countries is limited or antiquated compared with that of the developed countries. But

The Coca-Cola Company has made a huge financial investment in bottling and distribution facilities in Russia.

The Coca-Cola Company
www.thecoca-cola
company.com

notable exceptions exist. China, for example, will have the largest number of Internet users in the world by 2008.[27]

Even the financial and legal systems can cause problems. Formal operating procedures among financial institutions and private properties did not exist under communism and are still limited. As a consequence, it is estimated that two-thirds of the commercial transactions in Russia involve nonmonetary forms of payment. The legal red tape involved in obtaining title to buildings and land for manufacturing, wholesaling, and retailing operations also has been a huge problem. Nevertheless, the Coca-Cola Company invested $750 million from 1991 through 1998 to build bottling and distribution facilities in Russia, Allied Lyons spent $30 million to build a plant to make Baskin-Robbins ice cream, and Mars opened a $200-million candy factory outside Moscow.[28]

Consumer Income and Purchasing Power   A global marketer selling consumer goods must also consider what the average per-capita or household income is among a country's consumers and how the income is distributed to determine a nation's purchasing power. Per-capita income varies greatly between nations. Average yearly per-capita income in EU countries is more than $20 000 and is less than $300 in some developing countries, such as Vietnam. A country's income distribution is important because it gives a more reliable picture of a country's purchasing power. Generally speaking, as the proportion of middle-income-class households in a country increases, the greater a nation's purchasing power tends to be. Figure 7–5 shows the worldwide disparity in the percentage distribution of households by level of purchasing power. In established market economies, such as those in North America and

■ **FIGURE 7–5** ■

How purchasing power differs around the world

Source: Reprinted with the permission of PRIMEDIA Business Magazines & Media, Inc. Copyright © 2002. All rights reserved.

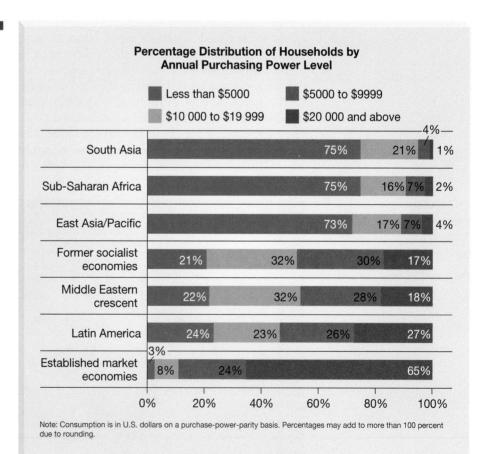

Percentage Distribution of Households by Annual Purchasing Power Level

■ Less than $5000   ■ $5000 to $9999
  $10 000 to $19 999   ■ $20 000 and above

Region	Less than $5000	$5000 to $9999	$10 000 to $19 999	$20 000 and above
South Asia	75%	21%	4%	1%
Sub-Saharan Africa	75%	16%	7%	2%
East Asia/Pacific	73%	17%	7%	4%
Former socialist economies	21%	32%	30%	17%
Middle Eastern crescent	22%	32%	28%	18%
Latin America	24%	23%	26%	27%
Established market economies	3% / 8%	24%		65%

Note: Consumption is in U.S. dollars on a purchase-power-parity basis. Percentages may add to more than 100 percent due to rounding.

Western Europe, 65 percent of households have an annual purchasing capability of $20 000 or more. In comparison, 75 percent of households in the developing countries of South Asia have an annual purchasing power of less than $5000.[29]

Seasoned global marketers recognize that people in the developing countries often have government subsidies for food, housing, and health care that supplement their income. Accordingly, people with seemingly low incomes are actually promising customers for a variety of products. For example, a consumer in South Asia earning the equivalent of $250 per year can afford Gillette razors. When that consumer's income rises to $1000, a Sony television becomes affordable, and a new Volkswagen or Nissan can be bought with an annual income of $10 000. In the developing countries of Eastern Europe, a $1000 annual income makes a refrigerator affordable, and $2000 brings an automatic washer within reach.

Income growth in the developing countries of Asia, Latin America, and Eastern Europe is expected to stimulate world trade well into the twenty-first century. The number of consumers in these countries earning the equivalent of $10 000 per year is expected to surpass the number of consumers in North America, Japan, and Western Europe combined by 2007.

Currency Exchange Rates   Fluctuations in exchange rates among the world's currencies are of critical importance in global marketing. Such fluctuations affect everyone—from international tourists to global companies.

currency exchange rate
The price of one country's currency expressed in terms of another country's currency.

A **currency exchange rate** is the price of one country's currency expressed in terms of another country's currency, such as the Canadian dollar expressed in Japanese yen or Swiss francs. Failure to consider exchange rates when pricing products for global markets can have dire consequences.[30]

Exchange-rate fluctuations have a direct impact on the sales and profits made by global companies. When foreign currencies can buy more Canadian dollars, for example, Canadian products are less expensive for foreign customers. Short-term fluctuations, however, can have a significant effect on the profits of global companies. Hewlett-Packard gained nearly a half million dollars of additional profit through exchange rate fluctuation in one year. On the other hand, Honda lost over $400 million on its European operations due to currency swings in the Japanese yen compared with the euro and the British pound.

Political-Regulatory Climate

The political and regulatory climate for marketing in a country or region of the world lies not only in identifying the current climate but also in determining how long a favourable or unfavourable climate will last. An assessment of a country or regional political-regulatory climate includes an analysis of its political stability and trade regulations.

Political Stability   Trade among nations or regions depends on political stability. Billions of dollars have been lost in the Middle East and Africa as a result of internal political strife and war. Such losses encourage careful selection of politically stable countries and regions of the world for trade.

Political stability in a country is affected by numerous factors, including a government's orientation toward foreign companies and trade with other countries. These factors combine to create a political climate that is favourable or unfavourable for marketing and financial investment in a country or region of the world. Marketing managers monitor political stability using a variety of measures and often track country risk ratings supplied by such agencies as the PRS Group. Visit the PRS Group Web site shown in the accompanying WebLink box to see the most recent political risk ratings for countries.

Trade Regulations Countries have a variety of rules that govern business practices within their borders. These rules often serve as trade barriers.[31] For example, Japan has some 11 000 trade regulations. Japanese car safety rules effectively require all automobile replacement parts to be Japanese and not North American or European; public health rules make it illegal to sell Aspirin or cold medicine without a pharmacist present. The Malaysian government has advertising regulations stating that "advertisements must not project or promote an excessively aspirational lifestyle," Greece bans toy advertising, and Sweden outlaws all advertisements to children. And, until recently, the EU banned Canadian icewine from its markets because the icewine's alcohol content was beyond accepted levels.

Trade regulations also appear in free trade agreements among countries. European Union nations abide by some 10 000 rules that specify how goods are to be made and marketed. For instance, the rules for a washing machine's electrical system are detailed on more than 100 typed pages. There are also regulations related to contacting consumers via telephone, fax, and e-mail without their prior consent. The European Union's ISO 9000 quality standards, though not a trade regulation, have the same effect on business practice. These standards, described in Chapter 6, involve registration and certification of a manufacturer's quality management and quality assurance system. Many European companies require suppliers to be ISO 9000 certified as a condition of doing business with them. Certified companies have undergone an on-site audit that includes an inspection of its facilities to ensure that documented quality control procedures are in place and that all employees understand and follow them.

**CONCEPT
CHECK**

1. Semiotics involves the study of _____ .

2. When foreign currencies can buy more U.S. dollars, are American products more or less expensive for a foreign consumer?

■ ■ ■
GLOBAL MARKET-ENTRY STRATEGIES

Once a company has decided to enter the global marketplace, it must select a means of market entry. Four general options exist: (1) exporting, (2) licensing, (3) joint venture, and (4) direct investment.[32] As Figure 7–6 demonstrates, the amount of financial commitment, risk, marketing control, and profit potential increases as the firm moves from exporting to direct investment.

Exporting

exporting
Producing goods in one country and selling them in another country.

Exporting is producing goods in one country and selling them in another country. This entry option allows a company to make the least number of changes in terms of its product, its organization, and even its corporate goals. Host countries usually do not like this practice because it provides less local employment than under alternative means of entry.

Indirect exporting is when a firm sells its domestically produced goods in a foreign country through an intermediary. It involves the least amount of commitment and risk but will probably return the least profit. This kind of exporting is ideal for the company that has no overseas contacts but wants to market abroad. The intermediary is often a broker or agent that has the marketing know-how and the resources necessary for the effort to succeed.

Direct exporting occurs when a firm sells its domestically produced goods in a foreign country without intermediaries. Most companies become involved in direct exporting when they believe their volume of sales will be sufficiently large and easy to obtain that they do not require intermediaries. For example, the exporter may be approached by foreign buyers that are willing to contract for a large volume of purchases. Direct exporting involves more risk than indirect exporting for the company but also opens the door to increased profits.

W. K. Buckley Ltd. uses an indirect exporting strategy to market its cough remedy product (Buckley's Mixture) in the Australian market and a direct exporting

■ **FIGURE 7–6** ■ ■
Alternative global market-entry strategies

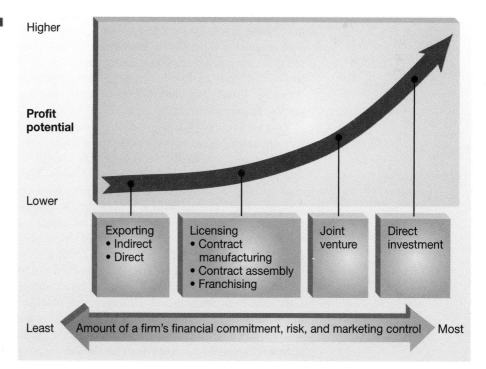

McDonald's uses franchising as a market-entry strategy, and more than 60 percent of the company's sales came from foreign operations.

McDonald's
www.mcdonalds.com

strategy for the United States market. Reif Estate Winery in Niagara-on-the-Lake and Andrés Wines of Grimsby, Ontario, both engage in exporting their Canadian wines to the European Union as well as other foreign markets, where sales have grown significantly.

Licensing

Under licensing, a company offers the right to a trademark, patent, trade secret, or other similarly valued items of intellectual property in return for a royalty or a fee. In international marketing, the advantages to the company granting the licence are low risk and a capital-free entry into a foreign country. The licensee gains information that allows it to start with a competitive advantage, and the foreign country gains employment by having the product manufactured locally. W. K. Buckley Ltd. used licensing for entering Holland.

There are some serious drawbacks to this mode of entry, however. The licensor forgoes control of its product and reduces the potential profits gained from it. In addition, while the relationship lasts, the licensor may be creating its own competition. Some licensees are able to modify the product somehow and enter the market with product and marketing knowledge gained at the expense of the company that got them started. To offset this disadvantage, many companies strive to stay innovative so that the licensee remains dependent on them for improvements and successful operation. Finally, should the licensee prove to be a poor choice, the name or reputation of the company may be harmed.

Two variations of licensing, *contract manufacturing* and *contract assembly,* represent alternative ways to produce a product within the foreign country. With contract manufacturing, a Canadian company may contract with a foreign firm to manufacture products according to stated specifications. The product is then sold in the foreign country or exported back to Canada. With contract assembly, the Canadian company may contract with a foreign firm to assemble (not manufacture) parts and components that have been shipped to that country. In both cases, the advantage to the foreign country is the employment of its people, and the Canadian firm benefits from the lower wage rates in the foreign country. Contract manufacturing and assembly in the developing countries had sparked controversy in the toy, textile, and apparel industries, where poor working conditions, low pay, and child labour practices have been documented. However, this practice has been an economic boon to many developing countries. For example, Taiwan makes more than half of the world's notebook computers, contracting for Dell and IBM, and this has generated personal income and employment for the Taiwanese people.

A third variation of licensing is franchising. Franchising is one of the fastest-growing market-entry strategies. Franchises include soft-drink, motel, retailing, fast-food, and car rental operation and a variety of business services. McDonald's is a premier global franchiser: more than 70 percent of the company's stores are franchised, and over 60 percent of the company's sales come from foreign operations.[33]

Joint Venture

joint venture

An arrangement in which a foreign company and a local firm invest together to create a local business, sharing ownership, control, and profits of the new company.

When a foreign country and a local firm invest together to create a local business, it is called a **joint venture**. These two companies share ownership, control, and profits of the new company. Investment may be made by having either of the companies buy shares in the other or by creating a third and separate entity. This was done by Caterpillar, Inc., the world's largest manufacturer of earth-moving and construction equipment. When it created NEVAMASH with its joint-venture partner, Kirovsky Zvod, a large Russian manufacturer of heavy equipment.

The advantages of this option are twofold. First, one company may not have the necessary financial, physical, or managerial resources to enter a foreign market alone. Ford and Volkswagen formed a joint venture to make four-wheel-drive vehicles in Portugal. Second, a government may require or strongly encourage a joint venture before it allows a foreign company to enter its market. This is the case in China. Today, more than 75 000 Chinese–foreign joint ventures operate in China, including W. K. Buckley Ltd. and its joint-venture partner.[34]

The disadvantages arise when the two companies disagree about policies or courses of action for their joint venture or when governmental bureaucracy bogs down the effort. For example, Canadian firms often prefer to reinvest earnings gained, whereas some foreign companies may want to spend those earnings. Or a Canadian firm may want to return profits earned to Canada, while the local firm or its government may oppose this—the problem now faced by many potential joint ventures in Eastern Europe, Russia, Latin America, and South Asia.

Direct Investment

direct investment

A domestic firm actually investing in and owning a foreign subsidiary or division.

The biggest commitment a company can make when entering the global market is **direct investment**, which entails a domestic firm actually investing in and owning a foreign subsidiary or division. Examples of direct investment are Toyota's automobile plant in Ontario and Hyundai's plant in Quebec. Many Canadian-based companies are also switching to this mode of entry. Alcan Aluminium built a recycling plant in Worrington, England, and Ganong Brothers owns a plant that manufactures chocolates in Thailand. And New Brunswick–based McCain Foods, a global leader in the frozen-food industry has 55 production facilities on six continents. It is the world's largest processor of frozen french fries, producing, in fact, one-third of all frozen French fries in the world.

For many firms, direct investment often follows one of the other three market-entry strategies. For example, Ernst & Young, an international accounting and management consulting firm, entered Hungary first by establishing a joint venture with a local company. Ernst & Young later acquired the company, making it a subsidiary with headquarters in Budapest. Following the success of its European and Asian exporting strategy, Harley-Davidson now operates wholly owned subsidiaries in Germany, Italy, and Japan.

The advantages to direct investment include cost savings, better understanding of local market conditions, and fewer local restrictions. Firms entering foreign markets using direct investment believe that these advantages outweigh the financial commitments and risks involved.

CONCEPT CHECK

1. What mode of entry could a company follow if it has no previous experience in global marketing?
2. How does licensing differ from a joint venture?

CRAFTING A WORLDWIDE MARKETING PROGRAM

The choice of a market-entry strategy is a necessary first step for a marketer when joining the community of global companies. The next step involves the challenging task of designing, implementing, and controlling marketing programs worldwide.

Successful global marketers standardize global marketing programs whenever possible and customize them wherever necessary. The extent of standardization and customization is often rooted in a careful global environment scan supplemented with judgment based on experience and marketing research.

Product and Promotion Strategies

Global companies have five strategies for matching products and their promotion efforts to global markets. As Figure 7–7 shows, the strategies focus on whether a company extends or adapts its product and promotion message for consumers in different countries and cultures.

A product may be sold globally in one of three ways: (1) in the same form as in its home market, (2) with some adaptations, or (3) as a totally new product:[35]

1. *Product extension.* Selling virtually the same product in other countries is a product extension strategy. It works well for such products as Coca-Cola, McCain frozen French fries, Gillette razors, Wrigley's gum, Levi's jeans, Sony consumer electronics, Harley-Davidson motorcycles, and Nokia cell phones. As a general rule, product extension seems to work best when the consumer market target for the product is alike across countries and cultures—that is, consumers share the same desires, needs and uses for the product.

2. *Product adaptation.* Changing a product in some way to make it more appropriate for a country's climate or consumer preferences is a product adaptation strategy. Gerber baby food comes in different varieties in different countries. Vegetable and Rabbit Meat is a favourite in Poland. Freeze-Dried Sardines and Rice is popular in Japan. Maybelline's makeup is formulaically adapted in labs

■ FIGURE 7–7 ■

Five product and promotion strategies for global marketing

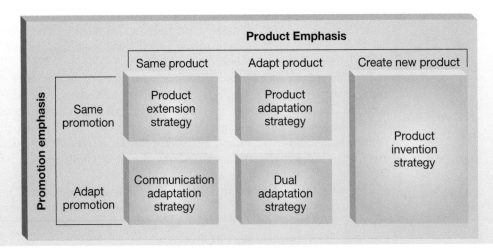

to suit local skin types and weather across the globe, including an Asia-specific mascara that does not run during the rainy season.

3. *Product invention.* Alternatively, companies can invent totally new products designed to satisfy common needs across countries. Black & Decker did this with its Snake Light Flexible Flashlight. Created to address a global need for portable lighting, the product became a best seller in North America, Europe, Latin America, and Australia and is the most successful new product developed by Black & Decker. Similarly, Whirlpool developed a compact, automatic clothes washer specifically for households in the developing countries with annual household incomes of $2000. Called Ideale, the washer features bright colours because washers are often placed in a home's living areas, not hid in laundry rooms (which do not exist in many homes in the developing countries). Demand for this product exceeded forecasts when it was introduced in Brazil, China, and India.

An identical promotion message is used for the product extension and product adaptation strategies around the world. Gillette uses the same global message for its men's toiletries: "Gillette, the Best a Man Can Get."

Global companies may also adapt their promotion message. For instance, the same product may be sold in many countries but advertised differently. As an example, L'Oréal, a French health and beauty products marketer, introduced its Golden Beauty brand of sun-care products through its Helena Rubenstein subsidiary in Western Europe with a communication adaptation strategy. Recognizing the cultural and buying motive differences related to skin care and tanning, Golden Beauty advertising features dark tanning for northern Europeans, skin protection to avoid wrinkles among Latin Europeans, and beautiful skin for Europeans living along the Mediterranean Sea, even though the products are the same.

Other companies use a dual adaptation strategy by modifying both their products and promotion messages. Nestlé does this with Nescafé coffee. Nescafé is marketed using different coffee blends and promotional campaigns to match consumer preferences in different countries. For example, Nescafé, the world's largest brand of coffee, generally emphasizes the taste, aroma, and warmth of shared moments in its advertising around the world. However, Nescafé is advertised in Thailand as a way to relax from the pressures of daily life.

These examples illustrate the simple rule applied by global companies: Standardize product and promotion strategies whenever possible and customize them wherever necessary. This is the art of global marketing.[36]

Distribution Strategy

Distribution is of critical importance in global marketing. The availability and quality of retailers and wholesalers, as well as transportation, communication, and warehousing facilities, are often determined by a country's stage of economic development. Figure 7–8 outlines the channel through which a product manufactured in one country must travel to reach its destination in another country. The first step involves the seller; its headquarters is the starting point and is responsible for the successful distribution to the ultimate consumer.

The next step is the channel between two nations, moving the product from one country to another. Intermediaries that can handle this responsibility include resident buyers in a foreign country, independent merchant wholesalers who buy and sell the product, or agents who bring buyers and sellers together.

Once the product is in the foreign nation, that country's distribution channels take over.[37] These channels can be very long or surprisingly short depending on the product line. In Japan, fresh fish go through three intermediaries before getting to a retail outlet. Conversely, shoes go through only one intermediary. In other cases, the

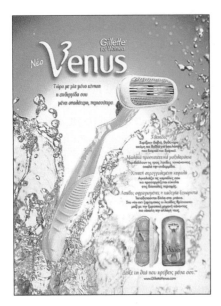
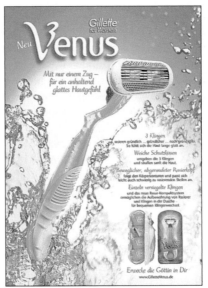
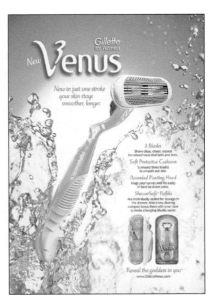

Gillette delivers the same global message whenever possible, as shown in the Gillette for Women Venus ads from Greece, Germany, and Canada.

The Gillette Company

www.gillette.com

channel does not even involve the host country. Procter & Gamble sells its soap door to door in the Philippines because there are no other alternatives in many parts of that country. The sophistication of a country's distribution channels increase as its economic infrastructure develops. Supermarkets facilitate selling products in many nations, but they are not popular or available in many others where culture and lack of refrigeration dictate shopping on a daily rather than a weekly basis. For example, when Coke and Pepsi entered China, both had to create direct-distribution channels, investing in refrigerator units for small retailers.

Pricing Strategy

Global companies also face many challenges in determining a pricing strategy as part of their worldwide marketing effort. Individual countries, even those with free trade agreements, may impose considerable competitive, political, and legal constraints on the pricing latitude of global companies. For example, Wal-Mart was told by German antitrust authorities that the prices in its stores were too low, relative to competitors, and faced a fine for violating the country's trade if the prices were not raised.[38] Of course, economic factors, such as the costs of production, selling, and tariffs, plus transportation and storage costs, also affect global pricing decisions.

Pricing too low or too high can have dire consequences. When prices appear too low in one country, companies can be charged with dumping, a practice subject to severe penalties and fines. **Dumping** is when a firm sells a product in a foreign country below its domestic price or below its actual cost. This is often done to build a company's share of the market by pricing at a competitive level. Another reason is that the products being sold may be surplus or cannot be sold domestically and, therefore, are already a burden to the company. The firm may be glad to sell them at almost any price.

dumping

Occurs when a firm sells a product in a foreign country below its domestic price or below its actual cost

■ **FIGURE 7–8** ■

Channels of distribution in global marketing

grey market

A situation where products are sold through unauthorized channels of distribution.

When companies price their products very high in some countries but competitively in others, they face a grey market problem. A **grey market,** also called *parallel importing,* is a situation where products are sold through unauthorized channels of distribution. A grey market comes about when individuals buy products in a lower-priced country from a manufacturer's authorized retailer, ship them to higher-priced countries, and then sell them below the manufacturer's suggested retail price through unauthorized retailers. Many well-known products have been sold through grey markets, including Olympus cameras, Seiko watches, IBM personal computers, and Mercedes-Benz cars.

CONCEPT CHECK

1. Products may be sold globally in three ways. What are they?

2. What is dumping?

CHAPTER IN REVIEW

1 *Describe the nature and scope of world trade from a global perspective and its implications for Canada.*

A global perspective on world trade views exports and imports as complementary economic flows: a country's imports affect its exports, and exports affects its imports. World trade flowing to and from Canada reflects demand and supply interdependencies for goods among nations and industries. Canada is a trading nation and currently maintains a surplus in it balance of trade. The largest importers of Canadian goods and services are the United States, Japan, and the EU.

2 *Identify the major trends that have influenced the landscape of global marketing in the past decade.*

Four major trends have influenced the landscape of global marketing in the past decade. First, there has been a gradual decline of economic protectionism by individual countries, leading to a reduction in tariffs and quotas. Second, there is growing economic integration and free trade among nations, reflected in the creation of the European Union and the North American Free Trade Agreement. Third, there is increased global competition among global companies for global consumers, resulting in firms adopting global marketing strategies and promoting global brands. And finally, a networked global marketspace has emerged using Internet technology as a tool for exchanging goods, services, and information on a global scale.

3 *Identify the environmental factors that shape global marketing efforts.*

Three major environmental factors shape global marketing efforts. First, there are cultural factors, including values, customs, cultural symbols, and language. Economic factors also shape global marketing efforts. These include a country's stage of economic development and economic infrastructure, consumer income and purchasing power, and currency exchange rates. Finally, political-regulatory factors in a country or region of the world create a favourable or unfavourable climate for global marketing efforts.

4 *Name and describe the alternative approaches companies use to enter global markets.*

Companies have four alternative approaches for entering global markets. These are exporting, licensing, joint venture, and direct investment. Exporting involves producing goods in one country and selling them in another country. Under licensing, a company offers the right to a trademark, patent, trade secret, or similarly valued items of intellectual property in return for a royalty or fee. In a joint venture, a foreign company and a local firm invest together to create a local business. Direct investment entails a domestic firm actually investing in and owning a foreign subsidiary or division.

5 *Explain the distinction between standardization and customization when companies craft worldwide marketing programs.*

Companies distinguish between standardization and customization when crafting worldwide marketing programs. Standardization means that all elements of the marketing program are the same across countries and cultures. Customization means that one or more elements of the marketing program are adapted to meet the needs or preferences of consumers in a particular country or culture. Global marketers apply a simple rule when crafting worldwide marketing programs: standardize marketing programs whenever possible and customize them wherever necessary.

■ ■ ■
FOCUSING ON KEY TERMS

■ ■ ■
DISCUSSION AND APPLICATION QUESTIONS

1   What is meant by this statement: "Quotas are a hidden tax on consumers, whereas tariffs are a more obvious one"?

2   Is the trade feedback effect described in the text a long-run or short-run view on world trade flows? Explain your answer.

3   Since English is the official language in Australia, some Canadian global companies might select it as an easy market to enter. Others believe that this similarity in language could make it harder to successfully enter that market. Who is right? Why?

4   How successful would a television commercial in Japan be if it featured a husband surprising his wife in her dressing area on Valentine's Day with a small box of chocolates containing four candies? Why?

5   As a novice in global marketing, which alternative for global market-entry strategy would you be likely to start with? Why? What other alternatives do you have for a global market entry?

6   Coca-Cola is sold worldwide. In some countries, Coca-Cola owns the bottling facilities; in others, it has signed contracts with licensees or relies on joint ventures. When selecting a licensee in each country, what factors should Coca-Cola consider?

| GOING ONLINE | | Getting to Know the WTO |

The World Trade Organization is the only international organization dealing with the global rules of trade among nations. Its intended function is to ensure that trade flows as smoothly, predictably, and freely as possible. Understanding how the WTO operates is a necessary prerequisite for global marketing.

Visit the WTO Web site at www.wto.org to learn more about how this organization functions and the issues it faces. A useful starting point for familiarizing yourself with the WTO is to find answers to the following questions:

1   Countries are constantly seeking WTO membership. How many countries are now members of this organization? Which country is the newest member?

2   What are the 10 most common misunderstandings about the WTO identified by this organization?

VIDEO CASE 7 — CNS Breathe Right® Strips: Going Global

"It's naive to treat 'international' as one big market—particularly within OTC," explains Marti Morfitt, president and CEO of CNS, the company that manufactures Breathe Right® nasal strips. "There are many discrete, unique markets, and local expertise is needed to understand the dynamics within each and address them effectively."

"OTC" refers to over-the-counter medical products, such as aspirin or cough syrup, that customers can buy without a doctor's prescription. Breathe Right nasal strips qualify as an OTC product. But, that does not mean there is not a lot of technology and medical science behind it.

Breathe Right nasal strips are innovative adhesive strips with patented dual flex bars inside. When attached to the nose, they gently lift and hold open nasal passages, making it easier to breathe. Breathe Right strips are used for a variety of reasons, all to help breathe better through the nose: athletes hoping to play their best (particularly when wearing mouth guards); snorers (and their spouses hoping for a quiet night's sleep); and allergy, sinusitis, and cold sufferers looking for drug-free relief from nasal congestion.

HOW IT ALL BEGAN

Breathe Right strips were invented by Bruce Johnson, a chronic nasal congestion sufferer. At times, Johnson put straws or paper clips in his nose at night to keep his nasal passages open. He eventually came up with a prototype for Breathe Right strips. He brought his invention to CNS, Inc., which recognized its market potential. CNS took the strips to the U.S. Food and Drug Administration for approval of claims for relief of snoring and nasal congestion.

CNS, a small company, had a limited marketing budget. However, it got a big public relations break when Jerry Rice, the wide receiver for the San Francisco 49ers, wore a Breathe Right strip on national TV and scored two touchdowns during the 49ers' 1995 Super Bowl victory. Demand for the strips soared.

"What really helped sales of Breathe Right strips was that CNS had done a very effective job of getting press kits in the hands of news and sports media," says Morfitt. "When people on television asked, 'What is that funny looking thing on his nose?' the reporters could talk about how the strip was an effective consumer product for everyone. And a $1.4 million business turned into a $45 million business in just one year," she explains.

THE DECISION TO GO GLOBAL

As awareness and trial were building domestically, CNS began to get inquiries from people in other countries asking where they could buy these strips. In 1995, CNS decided to take advantage of the global interest and introduce Breathe Right strips internationally.

What countries did CNS choose to enter with its Breathe Right strips? "Countries we focus on are those with a large OTC market, high per-capita spending in the OTC market, and future prospects for growth," says Kevin McKenna, vice-president for international at CNS. All these factors relate to market size. "But the real key to success in a market is a local partner that is entrepreneurial and has an ability to execute in terms of achieving distribution and sales."

IMPORTANCE OF LOCAL PARTNERS

Dynamic world market changes in the last 30 years have influenced opportunities for global sales of Breathe Right strips. Key trends include increased availability of OTC products formerly available only by prescription and a global push toward self-care, spurred by the increasing cost of health and medical care. Additionally, OTC products have extended beyond the traditional boundary of the pharmacy and into grocery and other channels; and the role of the pharmacist has expanded from that of medical professional to one that includes selling and marketing OTC products to consumers.

At the same time, changes were taking place within CNS. When Morfitt joined CNS in 1998, she began pulling together a new management group with extensive experience in marketing consumer packaged goods, including globally. CNS began seeking "hungry" international partners who would bring greater localized market expertise and direct-selling capabilities than past partners. Morfitt also wanted partners with demonstrated entrepreneurial spirit to match that of the new management team.

The company's partner in Italy, BluFarm Group, uses its local knowledge and direct selling skills to partner with pharmacists to teach them how to increase sales of Breathe Right strips in their stores. In Italy, as throughout much of Europe, OTC products, such as antacids, aspirin, and nasal strips, are typically placed behind pharmacy counters and therefore not visible to customers. The only way to sell a product is for a

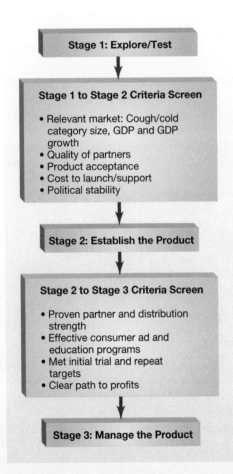

MANAGING GLOBAL GROWTH

Today, Breathe Right strips are sold in over 25 countries, and global sales make up a growing percentage of CNS business each year. To ensure the Breathe Right brand continues to meet growth expectations, CNS now uses a three-stage approach to penetrate and develop new markets:

- Stage 1: Explore/test the concept
  - Use screening criteria to identify high-potential markets
  - Identify potential partners
  - Validate concept with research
  - Develop strategy and launch test market
- Stage 2: Establish the product
  - Penetrate the marketplace
  - Refine messages for local market
  - Evaluate partnership and marketing strategies
- Stage 3: Manage the product
  - Achieve sustainability/profitability
  - Exploit new product and new use opportunities

Overall, this approach starts with what works domestically and extends it into new markets, paying close attention to local needs and customs. Throughout the three stages, CNS conducts market research and makes financial projections.

As shown in the figure, at each stage of the market development process, performance must be met for the product to enter the next stage. Once success with Breathe Right nasal strips is established in a country, the groundwork is laid and international partners have the ability to introduce other Breathe Right products, such as Snore Relief™ Throat Spray, and Vapor Shot™ personal vaporizer.

LOOKING FORWARD

"We believe the Breathe Right brand has great potential, both domestically and around the world," says Morfitt. "Growth will come both from further expansion of Breathe Right nasal strips and from other drug-free, better-breathing line extensions," says Morfitt.

QUESTIONS

1 What are the advantages and disadvantages for CNS taking Breathe Right strips into international markets?

2 What are the advantages to CNS of (*a*) using its three-stage process to enter new global markets, and (*b*) having specific criteria to move through the stages?

3 Using the CNS criteria, with what you know, which countries should have highest priority for CNS?

4 Which single segment of potential Breathe Right strip users would you target to enter new markets?

5 Which marketing mix variables should CNS emphasize the most to succeed in a global arena? Why?

customer to ask for it by name. BluFarm Group recognized the importance of in-store advertising and sales execution to build awareness and created point-of-sale materials, such as window and counter displays (see photo) to let customers know that Breathe Right strips were available in the store. "BluFarm's ability to capture consumers' awareness of Breathe Right strips as they walk in the retailer's door has beneficial results for CNS, BluFarm, pharmacists, and consumers," says McKenna.

"Working with an experienced local partner helps overcome surprises in global markets," says Nick Naumann, senior marketing communications manager at CNS. One surprise: Universal Product Codes (UPC) on packaging are not "universal"—they are used only in the United States and Canada. "Different forms of those codes in other countries can take a few weeks to six months or more of government review to obtain," he says.

Even the same packaging colours do not work around the globe. Research with domestic consumers revealed that they wanted darker packaging to suggest the strips' use at night by snorers and those with stuffed noses. "'Too grim and negative' Asian and European consumers told us," says Naumann. Breathe Right strips in those countries have a lighter, airier look than the domestic packages, to convey the open feeling one gets from the nasal strips.

PART

3

PART 1	PART 2	PART 3	PART 4	PART 5
Initiating the Marketing Process	Understanding Buyers and Markets	Targeting Marketing Opportunities	Satisfying Marketing Opportunities	Managing the Marketing Process

TARGETING
MARKETING
OPPORTUNITIES

HOW PART 3 FITS INTO THE BOOK

The two chapters in Part 3 discuss key marketing methods—techniques to help discover the potential buyers for a product or services and determine their needs and wants; then focusing marketing efforts on those key segments most likely to buy the product or service.

CHAPTER 8

MARKETING RESEARCH: FROM INFORMATION TO ACTION

TEST SCREENINGS: LISTENING TO CONSUMERS TO REDUCE MOVIE RISKS!

Blockbuster movies are essential for today's fiercely competitive world of film making, examples being *Spider-Man*, *Tough Love*, *Shoeless Joe*, and *3000*.

What's in a Movie Name?   Can't remember those last three movies, even after scratching your head? Well, test screenings by the studios—a form of marketing research—found that moviegoers had problems with those titles. Here is what happened:

- *Tough Love* became *Gigli* when audiences did not like the name of the mob comedy starring Jennifer Lopez and Ben Affleck. Unfortunately, even the name change did not help this movie, which bombed at the box-office.
- *Shoeless Joe* became *Field of Dreams* because audiences thought Kevin Costner might be playing a homeless person.
- *3000* became *Pretty Woman* when audiences did not have a clue what the number meant. *Hint*: It was the amount of dollars to spend an evening with Julia Roberts.[1]

Film makers want movie titles that are concise, attention-getting, capture the essence of the film, and have no legal restrictions—basically, the same factors that make a good brand name.

The Risks in Today's Blockbuster Movies   Bad weather, poor scripts, temperamental stars who stomp off the set, and too-costly special effects are just some of the nightmares faced by movie producers. Today's films average more than $100 million to produce and market.[2] So, some studios try to reduce their new-movie gamble by planning a multi-episode film series—*Harry Porter*, *Matrix*, *Lord of the Rings*, and *Spider-Man* being examples. But there are hidden dangers. As Harry Potter and Hermoine Granger age, will their characters be credible, and will young moviegoers, the target audience, still *buy tickets*? Shooting all the movies in a sequence at one time, like it was done for the *Lord of the Rings* triology, also poses huge marketing and marketing research issues. Most of the $320 million invested in the three movies would have been lost had the first in the sequence, *The Fellowship of the Ring*, been a disaster. The third film in the *Matrix* triology, *The Matrix Revolutions*, highlights the multi-film problem: ticket sales did not reach the production costs, to say nothing of the tens of millions of dollars spent on marketing the film.[3]

Spider-Man 2 was a pleasant shock among multi-episode film series by outselling the original movie. Its $500 million gross sales the first three weeks in theatres around the world easily covered its $200 million production budget and $50 million marketing costs. The producers are hoping for the same results when *Spider-Man 3* is released.[4]

Using Market Research to Reduce Movie Risk   Is research on movie titles expensive? Very! But the greater expense is selecting a bad title that can kill a movie and cost the studio millions of dollars—not to mention the careers of producers and directors! So, movie studios use marketing research to reduce their risks.

For test screenings, 300 to 400 prospective movie-goers are recruited to attend a "sneak preview" of a film before its release. After viewing the movie, the audience fills out an exhaustive survey to critique the title, plot, characters, music, and ending—as well as the marketing program (posters, trailers)—to identify improvements to make in the final edit of the movie.[5]

Without reading ahead, think about answers to these questions:

- Whom would you recruit for these test screenings?
- What questions would you ask audience members to help you in editing or modifying the title or parts of the film?

Virtually every major movie produced today uses test screenings to obtain the key reactions of consumers likely to be in the target market. Figure 8–1 summarizes some of the key questions that are used in these test screenings, both to select the people for the screenings and to obtain key reactions of those sitting in the screenings. Note how specific the studios action is for each question asked, such as "Change the title ending." This is an example of effective, action-oriented marketing research.

Here are some examples of changes to movies that have resulted from this kind of marketing research:

- *Making the plot move faster*. Disney cut a duet by Pocahontas and John Smith in *Pocahontas* because it got in the way of the action and confused test audiences.
- *Reaching a market segment more effectively*. More action footage was added for Kevin Costner when preview screening showed young males were less enthusiastic about *The Bodyguard* than were young females.[6]
- *Changing an ending*. *Fatal Attraction* had probably the most commercially successful "ending-switch" of all time. In its sneak previews, audiences liked everything but the ending, which had Alex (Glenn Close) committing suicide and managing to frame Dan (Michael Douglas) as her murderer by leaving his fingerprints on the knife she used. The studio shot $1.3 million of new scenes for the ending that regular audiences eventually saw.[7]

POINT WHEN ASKED	KEY QUESTIONS	USE OF QUESTIONS
Before the test screening	• How old are you?	• Find people who fit the profile of target audience for movie.
	• How frequently do you pay to see movies?	• Find people who frequently attend movies.
After the test screening	• What do you think of the title?	• Change movie title.
	• What title would you suggest?	
	• Were any characters too distasteful? Who? How?	• Change aspects of some characters.
	• How did you like the ending? If you did not like it, how would you change it?	• Change or clarify ending.
	• Would you recommend the movie to a friend?	• Overall indicator of liking of and/or satisfaction with movie.

■ **FIGURE 8–1** ■■

Marketing research questions asked in test screenings of movies, and how they are used

The switch in endings for *Fatal Attraction* that resulted from audience reactions to test screenings reduced the studio's risk and undoubtedly contributed to the movie's box-office success. But even good marketing research cannot guarantee success. Test screenings caused the studio to shoot a new ending for JLo and Ben Affleck in *Gigli*. Audiences hated that Ben Affleck's character died in the original ending, which they felt was too dark and inconsistent with the rest of the movie. The reshoot was not enough. Besides being a disaster at the box office, *Gigli* was nominated for "worst picture" and eight other "Razzies," the highest-profile bad-movie anti-Oscars given by voters of the Golden Raspberry Awards.[8]

Movie studios also use tracking studies, in which prospective movie-goers in the target audience are asked three key questions about an upcoming film release:[9]

- Are you aware of a particular film?
- Are you interested in seeing it?
- Would it be your first choice on a certain weekend?

Studios then use the data collected to forecast the movie's opening-weekend box office sales or run last-minute ads to increase awareness and interest: the "buzz" or word-of-mouth for the film. In some cases, a studio may postpone or advance a film's release depending on the results for other movies scheduled for release at that time.

These examples show how marketing research is the link between marketing strategy and decisive decisions, the main topic of this chapter. Also, marketing research is often used to help a firm develop sales forecasts, the final topic in the chapter.

■ ■ ■

WHAT IS MARKETING RESEARCH?

marketing research
The process of defining a marketing problem and opportunity, systematically collecting and analyzing information, and recommending actions to improve an organization's marketing activities.

Marketing research is the process of defining a marketing problem or opportunity, systematically collecting and analyzing information, and recommending actions to improve an organization's marketing activities.[10] Broadly speaking, assessing the needs and wants of consumers and providing information to help design an organization's marketing program to satisfy them is the principal role that marketing research performs. This means that marketing research attempts to identify and define both marketing problems and opportunities and to generate and evaluate marketing actions. Although marketing research can provide few answers with complete assurance, it can reduce risk and uncertainty to increase the likelihood of the success of marketing decisions. It is a great help to the marketing managers who must make final decisions. Conducted properly, marketing research can solve most marketing-related problems that an executive might have. However, marketing research should not be designed to simply replace an executive's good sense, experience, or intuition but rather should be used in conjunction with those skills and as a way of taking out some of the guesswork in the marketing decision-making process.

■ ■ ■ TYPES OF MARKETING RESEARCH

To understand the variety of research activity, it is helpful to categorize different types of marketing research. Marketing research is often classified on the basis of either technique or function. Surveys, experiments, and observation are a few research techniques with which you may be familiar. However, categorizing research by its purpose or function shows how the nature of the marketing problem influences the choice of research techniques. The nature of the problem will determine whether the research is (1) exploratory, (2) descriptive, or (3) causal.

Exploratory Research

Exploratory research is preliminary research conducted to clarify the scope and nature of the marketing problem. It is generally carried out to provide the researcher with a better understanding of the dimensions of the problem. Exploratory research is often conducted with the expectation that subsequent and more conclusive research will follow. For example, the Dairy Farmers of Canada, an association representing dairy producers in the country, wanted to discover why milk consumption was declining in Canada.

They conducted a search of existing literature on milk consumption, talked to experts in the field, and even conducted preliminary interviews with consumers to get ideas about why consumers were drinking less milk. This exploratory research helped the association to crystallize the problem and identify issues for more detailed follow-up research. We examine exploratory research as an integral component of the basic marketing research process later in the chapter.

The Dairy Farmers of Canada conducted three types of marketing research in an effort to solve the problem of decline in milk consumption. For details, read the text.

Dairy Farmers of Canada
www.dairyfarmers.org

Fact: Milk is recommended for its many vital nutrients.

Descriptive Research

Descriptive research is research designed to describe the basic characteristics of a given population or to profile particular marketing situations. Unlike exploratory research, with descriptive research, the researcher has a general understanding of the marketing problem and is seeking conclusive data that answer the questions necessary to determine a particular course of action. Examples of descriptive research would include profiling product purchasers (e.g., the Canadian shopper at the health food store), describing the size and characteristics of markets (e.g., the Canadian pizza restaurant market), detailing product usage patterns (e.g., ATM usage by Canadian bank customers), or outlining consumer attitudes toward particular brands (e.g., Canadian attitudes toward national, private, and generic brands).

Magazines, radio stations, and television stations almost always do descriptive research to identify the characteristics of their audiences in order to present them to prospective advertisers. As a follow-up to its exploratory research, the Dairy Farmers of Canada conducted descriptive research to determine the demographic characteristics of milk consumers, current usage patterns, and consumer attitudes toward milk consumption.

Causal Research

Causal research is research designed to identify cause-and-effect relationships among variables. In general, exploratory and descriptive research normally precede causal research. With causal research, there is typically an expectation about the relationship to be explained, such as predicting the influence of a price change on product demand. In general, researchers attempt to establish that one event (e.g., a price change) will produce another event (e.g., a change in demand). Typical causal research studies examine the effect of advertising on sales; the relationship between price and perceived quality of a product; and the impact of a new package on product sales. When the Dairy Farmers of Canada conducted its descriptive research on milk consumers, it discovered that many believed milk was too fattening and too high in cholesterol. The association felt that these beliefs might be related to the overall decline in milk consumption in Canada. To test this assumption, the association ran a television advertising campaign to demonstrate that milk was a healthful product and essential to a person's diet. In its tracking studies, it found that the ad campaign did change consumer attitudes toward milk, which, in turn, was causally related to a subsequent increase in milk consumption. We refer to causal research later in this chapter when we deal with experiments as a basic research technique.

CONCEPT CHECK	**1.** What is marketing research? **2.** What is the difference among exploratory, descriptive, and causal research?

THE MARKETING RESEARCH PROCESS

Marketing research should always be conducted on the basis of the *scientific method*, a process of systematically collecting, organizing, and analyzing data in an unbiased, objective manner. Marketing research must meet two basic principles of the scientific method—reliability and validity. *Reliability* refers to the ability to replicate research results under identical environmental conditions. In other words, if a research project were to be conducted for the second, third, or fourth time, the results should be the same. Marketers need to have reliable information to make effective decisions. If the results of a study are not reliable, the research can do more harm than no research at all. *Validity* involves the notion of whether the research measured what was intended to be measured. In other words, does the research tell marketers what they need to know? You should keep the concepts of reliability and validity in mind as we discuss the marketing research process.

Figure 8–2 outlines the basic marketing research process. The figure is perhaps an oversimplification of the process, since marketing research does not always follow such a neat and ordered sequence of activities. However, all marketing research consists of four basic stages: (1) defining the problem, (2) determining the research design, (3) collecting and analyzing data, and (4) drawing conclusions and preparing a report.

In reviewing Figure 8–2, you can see that the researcher has a number of decisions and choices to make during the stages of the process. For example, the red boxes in Figure 8–2 indicate stages in the process where a choice of one or more techniques or methods must be made. The dotted line indicates the researcher's choice to bypass the exploratory research stage of the process.

■ **FIGURE 8–2** ■■

The basic marketing research process

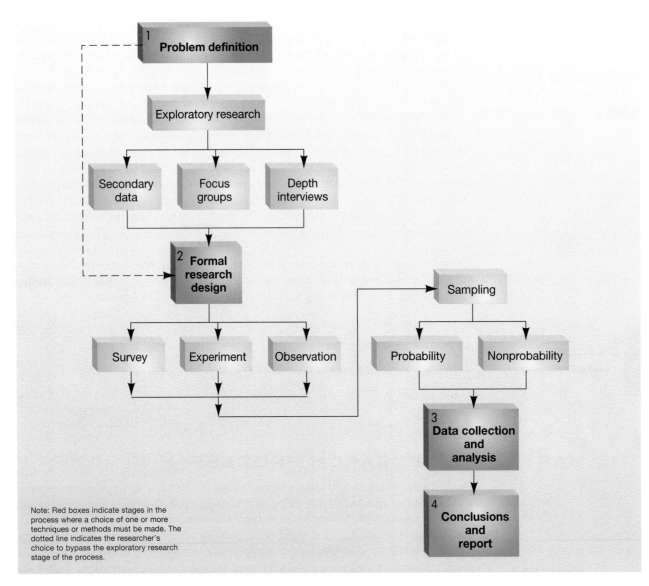

Note: Red boxes indicate stages in the process where a choice of one or more techniques or methods must be made. The dotted line indicates the researcher's choice to bypass the exploratory research stage of the process.

■ ■ ■
PROBLEM DEFINITION

The first step in the marketing research process is to properly define the scope and nature of the marketing problem to be investigated. In general, the term *problem* suggests that something has gone wrong. In reality, to the marketing researcher, the word *problem* may also mean something to explore or an opportunity to define, or a current marketing situation to monitor or evaluate. Sometimes, the problem is obvious, but in other cases, the problem may be more difficult to identify and define. In either case, the marketing researcher must fully understand and properly identify the problem at hand.

The marketing research process is often initiated by the marketing manager, who will approach the marketing researcher with a problem that requires information for decision making. For example, suppose you were the marketing manager for cranberry juice at Ocean Spray. You want to know if Asian consumers who have never heard of cranberries would buy cranberry juice. You also have other problems. The word "cranberry" is not part of any foreign language, and so you would have to find a name for it and its juice. Also, if you are going to take the product to Asia, you have to find a way to encourage consumers there to try the new product.[11] The marketing researcher has to fully understand these problems. The researcher must also remember that the best place to begin a research project is at the end. In other words, the researcher must know what is to be accomplished through the research process. In this case, as the marketing manager, what you really want to know is: Is there a market opportunity in Asia for cranberry juice? If so, how can it be exploited?

Proper problem definition is critical, since research based on incorrect problem definition will be a waste of resources. Good marketing researchers adhere to the old adage "a problem well defined is a problem half-solved." If the research problem is clear, the chances of collecting the necessary information to solve the problem are increased.

<table>
<tr><td>CONCEPT
CHECK</td><td>

1. What are reliability and validity?

2. What are the four basic stages in the marketing research process?
</td></tr>
</table>

Exploratory Research

Your colleague, the marketing researcher at Ocean Spray, has to make a decision early on in the marketing research process. Should exploratory research be conducted in an attempt to help answer the question: is there a market opportunity in Asia for cranberry juice? As we saw earlier in the chapter, exploratory research is preliminary research conducted to clarify the scope and nature of the marketing problem. In general, it is designed to provide the researcher with a better understanding of the dimensions of the problem and is often conducted with the expectation that subsequent and more conclusive research may follow.

Most researchers will usually conduct some basic exploratory research during the early stage of the research process. The extent of the exploratory research will depend on the magnitude of the problem as well as its complexity. If the researcher decides to conduct exploratory research, he or she has three basic techniques to choose from: (1) secondary data analysis, (2) focus groups, and (3) depth interviews.

secondary data
Facts and figures that have been recorded before the project at hand.

Secondary Data Exploratory research almost always involves the use of **secondary data** (or historical data)—data previously collected and assembled for

Should Ocean Spray introduce cranberry juice in Asia when consumers there have never heard of cranberries? See the text.

Ocean Spray

www.oceanspray.com

primary data

Facts and figures that are newly collected for the project.

some project other than the one at hand. **Primary data**, on the other hand, are data gathered and assembled specifically for the project at hand. As a rule, researchers gather secondary data before collecting primary data. In general, secondary data can be obtained more quickly and at a lower cost compared with primary data. However, there can be problems with secondary data. The required information may not exist, and if it does, it may not be current or particularly pertinent to the problem at hand. Still, most researchers agree that investigating secondary data sources can save researchers from "reinventing the wheel."

Researchers examine secondary data both inside and outside the organization. Internal secondary data include financial statements, research reports, customer letters, and customer lists. What did your colleague in marketing research at Ocean Spray discover during the secondary data search efforts? She was able to discover that Ocean Spray did attempt to introduce a bland cranberry juice in Japan—named "Cranby"—and the attempt fizzled, and the product was pulled off the market. As a marketing manager, this information does provide some background, but you still have more questions than answers about the possible marketing opportunity in Asia.

Sources of external secondary data can be wide and varied. One key source, for example, is the federal government, which makes data available through Statistics Canada or local libraries. Statistics Canada completes the *Census of Canada* once every decade and updates certain census data every few years. The census provides detailed information on Canadian households. Statistics Canada also prepares annual or biannual reports, including the *Family Expenditure Guide*, which gives a detailed breakdown of how families spend their money. These basic sources of information are used by manufacturers and retailers to identify the characteristics and trends of ultimate consumers.

Statistics Canada produces many other census reports that are vital to business firms selling goods and services to organizations. Such reports include the *Census of Manufacturers*, which lists the number and size of manufacturing firms by industry group, as well as other information, including values of shipments and wages paid.

A marketing researcher can obtain from Statistics Canada its annual *Marketing Research Handbook* or the *Canada Year Book*, which includes a summary of key information often necessary to aid marketing decision making. Statistics Canada also has a database system known as CANSIM (Canadian Socio-Economic Information Management System), which marketers can access directly to examine aggregate data.

In addition to government-supplied data, trade associations, universities, and business periodicals provide detailed data of value. For example, one business periodical, *Sales and Marketing Management* (S&MM), publishes special issues each year that provide useful data for firms selling both consumer and industrial products. The most famous publication by *S&MM* is its *Annual Survey of Buying Power*. *The Financial Post* produces a publication called *Canadian Markets*, which provides demographic information and data on consumer spending power in provinces, cities, and towns across the country.

Such companies as MapInfo and ACNielsen offer both standard and customized information services to other firms on a subscription, or for-fee, basis. MapInfo can provide information on any geographic area of any size in Canada that highlights population, income, and retail expenditure trends in that area. Figure 8–3 shows some of the secondary data sources available to marketers in Canada. There are also hundreds of useful online databanks and specialized data services, such as Dow Jones, Dialog, and Infoglobe. The WebLink box provides examples.

New marketing data services have also emerged that offer *single-source data*, which is information provided by a single firm on household demographics and lifestyles, product purchases, media habits, and responses to sales promotions, such as coupons and free samples. The principal advantage of single-source data is the ability of one service to collect, analyze, interrelate, and present all this information. For consumer product firms, such as Procter & Gamble, sales data from various channels are critical when allocating marketing resources among such channels. As a result, P&G uses single-source data providers, such as Information Resources' InfoScan and ACNielsen's ScanTrack, to collect product sales and coupon/free sample redemptions that have been scanned at the checkout counter from supermarket, drug, convenience, and mass merchandise retailers. Campbell Soup, maker of Swanson frozen dinners, used the information from a single-source data provider to shift

■ **FIGURE 8–3** ■

Sources of secondary data

SELECTED GUIDES, INDEXES, AND DIRECTORIES

Business Periodical Index
Canadian Almanac and Directory
Canadian Business Index
Canadian News Index
Canadian Periodical Index
Canadian Statistics Index
Canadian Trade Index
Directory of Associations in Canada
Fraser's Canadian Trade Directory
Predicasts Index
Scott's Directories
Standards Periodical Directory
Ulrich's International Periodicals Directory

SELECTED PERIODICALS AND NEWSPAPERS

Advertising Age
Adweek
American Demographics
Business Horizons
Canadian Business
Canadian Consumer
Forbes
Fortune
Harvard Business Review
Journal of Advertising
Journal of Advertising Research
Journal of Consumer Research
Journal of Marketing
Journal of Marketing Management
Journal of Marketing Research
Journal of Personal Selling and Sales Management
Journal of Retailing
Journal of Small Business
Marketing Magazine

Marketing & Media Decisions
Marketing News
Progressive Grocer
Sales and Marketing Management
The Globe and Mail
The Financial Post
The Financial Post Magazine
The Wall Street Journal

SELECTED STATISTICS CANADA PUBLICATIONS

Annual Retail Trade
Canadian Economic Observer
Canada Yearbook
Family Expenditure Guide
Market Research Handbook
Statistics Canada Catalogue

SELECTED TRADE SOURCES

ACNielsen
Conference Board of Canada
Dun & Bradstreet Canada
Financial Post Publishing
Find/SVP
Gale Research
MacLean Hunter Research Bureau
MapInfo Canada
Predicasts International
R. L. Polk

SELECTED DATABASES

CANSIM (Statistics Canada)
Dialog
Dow Jones
Infoglobe
Infomart
The Source

WEBLINK
HTTP://WWW.MCGRAWHILL.CA/COLLEGE/CRANE

Online Databases Useful in Marketing

Information in online databases available through the Internet divide into two categories: (1) indexes to articles in publications, which are accessed through keyword searches; and (2) statistical and directory data on households, products, and companies.

Online databases of indexes, abstracts, and full-text information from journals and periodicals include:

- LexisNexis' Academic Universe, which gives full-text information from more than 5000 periodicals and publications. (www.lexis-nexis.com)
- ProQuest databases, which contain academic articles from more than 8000 management, marketing, and business periodicals and journals. (www.proquest.com)

Statistical and directory information about households, products, and companies through online databases include:

- FIS online, which gives data on more than 28 000 companies that are traded on the NYSE, AMEX, and NASDAQ stock exchanges. (www.fisonline.com)
- Statistics Canada, which provides census data and detailed information on Canadian households, as well as industrial and retail trade information. (www.statcan.ca)
- Portals and search engines, such as Google (www.google.com or www.google.ca), a portal to the entire Internet. Users click on links to browse by topic or enter key words for specific searches.

Some of these sites are accessible only if a subscription fee has been paid by an organization. To check out these sites, access your college or university Web site, click on the icon for your library, and then click on these or other useful databases to which your institution subscribes.

its TV ad campaign from a serious to a light theme, which increased the sales of Swanson dinners.

Getting back to our marketing researcher at Ocean Spray and the cranberry juice in Asia question, she discovers some external secondary data, specifically a study on Taiwan consumers that shows increased consumption of juice beverages. Still, the study is not specific to cranberry juice and is about four years old. As marketing manager, you realize you still have a high degree of uncertainty about the possible marketing opportunity in Asia. So, you ask your colleague in marketing research to continue the exploratory stage of the marketing process.

focus groups
An informal session of 6 to 10 past, present, or prospective customers, in which a discussion leader, or moderator, asks their opinions about the firm's and its competitors' products.

Focus Groups A very popular exploratory research technique designed to obtain primary data is the use of focus groups. **Focus groups** are informal interview sessions in which 6 to 10 persons, relevant to the research project, are brought together in a room with a moderator to discuss topics surrounding the marketing research problem. The moderator poses questions and encourages the individuals to answer in their own words and to discuss the issues with each other. Often, the focus-group sessions are watched by observers through one-way mirrors, and/or the sessions are videotaped. Of course, participants should be informed they are being observed and/or taped. Focus-group sessions often provide the marketer with valuable information for decision making or can uncover other issues that should be researched in a more quantitative fashion.[12]

Britain's Lewis Woolf Griptight, a manufacturer of infant and toddler products, conducted focus group sessions about possible brand names for their products before bringing a new product line to market. British consumers turned their thumbs down on using "Griptight" as a brand name for kids' products because they thought it sounded like "a carpet glue, a denture fixative, a kind of tire." So, the firm called its product line Kiddiwinks™—a British word for children.

depth interviews
A detailed, individual interview with a person relevant to the research project.

Depth Interviews Another exploratory research technique used to obtain primary data involves the use of depth interviews. **Depth interviews** are detailed individual interviews with people relevant to the research project. The researcher questions

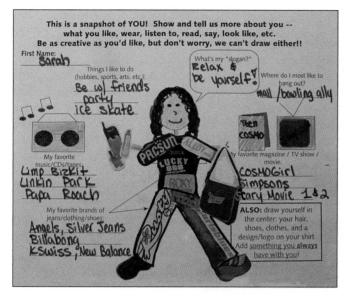

the individual at length in a free-flowing conversational style to obtain information that may help solve the marketing problem being investigated. Sometimes these interviews can take a few hours, and they are often recorded on audio- or videotape.

Hamburger Helper did not fare too well with consumers when General Mills first introduced it. Initial instructions called for cooking separately a half pound of hamburger, which was later mixed with the noodles. Depth interviews revealed that consumers did not think the recipe called for enough meat and that they did not want the hassle of cooking in two different pots. So, the Hamburger Helper product manager changed the recipe to call for a full pound of meat and to allow users to prepare the meal in one dish; this converted a potential failure into a success.

Researchers have also become creative in devising other exploratory research techniques. For example, finding "the next big thing" for consumers has become the obsession in many industries. In order to unearth the next big thing, marketing researchers have developed some unusual techniques sometimes referred to as "fuzzy front-end" methods. These techniques are designed to identify elusive consumer tastes or trends far before typical consumers have themselves recognized them. For example, having consumers take a photo of themselves every time they snack resulted in General Mills' Homestyle "Pop Secret" popcorn, which delivers the real butter and bursts of salt in microwave popcorn that consumers thought they could only get from the stovetop variety.[13]

Other unusual techniques are also being used to try to spot trends early. For example, Teenage Research Unlimited had teenagers complete a drawing to help discover what teenagers like, wear, listen to, and read.[14] Other companies hire "cool hunters," people with tastes far ahead of the curve, to identify the "next big things" likely to sweep popular culture. Wet Seal and Skechers use this method to anticipate teenage girls' fashion picks and footwear trends.[15]

CONCEPT CHECK

1. What are secondary data?

2. What are focus groups?

■ ■ ■
FORMAL RESEARCH DESIGN

After identifying and clarifying the marketing problem, with or without exploratory research, the researcher must determine the basic framework for finding a solution to the problem. At the formal research design stage, the researcher produces a plan that outlines the method and procedures for collecting and analyzing the required information. The plan includes the objectives of the research; the sources of information to be used; the research methods (e.g., survey, experiment); the sampling plan; and the schedule and cost of the research.

In selecting basic research methods, the researcher must make decisions. In general, the objectives of the research, the available data sources, the nature of the information required, and timing and cost considerations will determine which research method will be chosen. The basic methods the researcher can choose for descriptive and causal research include: (1) survey, (2) experiment, and (3) observation.

Survey

survey

A research technique used to generate data by asking people questions and recording their responses on a questionnaire.

The most common research method of generating new or primary data is the use of surveys. A **survey** is a research technique used to generate data by asking people questions and recording their responses on a questionnaire. Surveys can be conducted by personal interview, mail, telephone, e-mail, fax, or Internet. In choosing these alternatives, the marketing researcher must balance cost against the expected quality of information obtained. Personal interview surveys have the major advantage of enabling the interviewer to be flexible in asking probing questions or getting reactions to visual materials but are very costly to conduct. Mail surveys are usually biased because those likely to respond have had especially positive or negative experiences with a given product, service, or brand. While telephone surveys allow flexibility, they are increasingly difficult to complete because respondents may hang up on the interviewer. Also, with many unlisted telephone numbers, it is becoming increasingly more difficult to obtain representative samples. E-mail, fax, and Internet surveys are restrictive in that they are limited to respondents having the technology.[16]

The high cost of reaching respondants in their homes through personal interview surveys has led to a dramatic increase in the use of *mall intercept interviews*, which are personal interviews of consumers at shopping centres. These face-to-face interviews reduce the cost of personal visits to consumers in their homes while providing flexibility to show respondents visual cues, such as ads or actual product samples. However, a critical disadvantage of mall intercept interviews is that the people selected for the interviews may not be representative of the consumers targeted for the interviews, causing possible bias in results.

Sometimes, marketers will survey over time the same sample of people, commonly known as a survey *panel*. A panel can consist of a sample of consumers, stores, or experts, from which researchers can take a series of measurements. For example, a consumer's switch from one brand of breakfast cereal to another can be measured with panel data. The use of panels is becoming more popular with marketers as they attempt to obtain ongoing information about their constituents. Panel data are often incorporated into information systems, which are discussed later in the chapter.

When marketers decide to use surveys to ask questions, they assume that (1) the right questions are being asked, (2) people will understand the questions being asked, (3) people know the answers to the questions, (4) people will answer the questions truthfully, and (5) the researchers themselves will understand the answers provided. Marketers must concern themselves not only with asking the right questions but also with how to properly word those questions. Proper phrasing of a question is vital to uncovering useful marketing information.

Figure 8–4 shows typical problems to guard against in wording questions to obtain meaningful answers from respondents. For example, in the question about whether you eat at fast-food restaurants regularly, the word "regularly" is ambiguous. Two people might answer "yes" to the question, but one might mean "once a day" while the other means "once or twice a year." Both answers appear as "yes" to the researcher who tabulates them, but they suggest that dramatically different marketing actions be directed to each of these two prospective consumers. Therefore, it is essential that marketing research questions be worded precisely so that all respondents interpret the same question similarly. Marketing researchers must also take great care not to use "leading" questions (wording questions in a way to ensure a particular response), which can lead to a very distorted picture of the respondents' actual feelings or opinions.

In Figure 8–5, we can see the number of different formats that questions can take in a survey instrument. The questions presented are taken from a Wendy's survey that assessed fast-food preferences among present and prospective consumers. Question 1 is an example of an *open-end question*, which the respondent can answer in his or her own words. In contrast, questions in which the respondent simply checks an answer are *closed-end* or *fixed alternative questions*. Question 2 is an example of the

■ FIGURE 8-4 ■

Typical problems in wording questions

PROBLEM	SAMPLE QUESTION	EXPLANATION
Leading question	Why do you like Wendy's fresh meat hamburgers better than those of competitors?	Consumer is led to make statements favouring Wendy's hamburgers
Ambiguous question	Do you eat at fast-food restaurants regularly? ☐ Yes ☐ No	What is meant by word *regularly*—once a day, once a month, or what?
Unanswerable question	What was the occasion for your eating your first hamburger?	Who can remember the answer? Does it matter?
Two questions in one	Do you eat Wendy's hamburgers and chili? ☐ Yes ☐ No	How do you answer if you eat Wendy's hamburgers but not chili?
Nonexhaustive question	Where do you live? ☐ At home ☐ In dormitory	What do you check if you live in an apartment?
Non–mutually exclusive answers	What is your age? ☐ Under 20 ☐ 20–40 ☐ 40 and over	What answer does a 40-year-old check?

■ FIGURE 8-5 ■

Sample questions from Wendy's survey

1 What things are most important to you when you decide to eat out and go to a restaurant?

_____

_____

_____

_____

_____

_____

2 Have you eaten fast-food restaurant food in the past month?
☐ Yes ☐ No

3 If you answered "yes" to Question 2, how often do you eat fast food?
☐ Once a week or more ☐ Two or three times a month ☐ Once a month or less

4 How important is it to you that a fast-food restaurant satisfy you on the following characteristics? Check the box that describes your feelings.

CHARAC-TERISTIC	VERY IMPOR-TANT	SOME-WHAT IMPOR-TANT	IMPOR-TANT	UN-IMPOR-TANT	SOME-WHAT UNIM-PORTANT	VERY UNIM-PORTANT
Taste of food	☐	☐	☐	☐	☐	☐
Cleanliness	☐	☐	☐	☐	☐	☐
Price	☐	☐	☐	☐	☐	☐
Variety on menu	☐	☐	☐	☐	☐	☐

5 Check the space on the scale below that describes how you feel about Wendy's on the characteristics shown.

CHARACTERISTIC	CHECK THE SPACE DESCRIBING HOW WENDY'S IS		
Taste of food	Tasty	_ _ _ _ _ _ _ _ _ _	Not tasty
Cleanliness	Clean	_ _ _ _ _ _ _ _ _ _	Not clean
Price	Inexpensive	_ _ _ _ _ _ _ _ _ _	Expensive
Variety on menu	Broad	_ _ _ _ _ _ _ _ _ _	Narrow

Continued

■ FIGURE 8-5 ■
(Concluded)

6 Check the box that describes your agreement or disagreement with the following statements.

STATEMENT	STRONGLY AGREE	AGREE	DON'T KNOW	DISAGREE	STRONGLY DISAGREE
Adults like to take their families to fast-food restaurants.	☐	☐	☐	☐	☐
Our children have a say in where the family eats.	☐	☐	☐	☐	☐

7 How important are each of the following information sources when you select a fast-food restaurant?

SOURCE OF INFORMATION	VERY IMPORTANT SOURCE	SOMEWHAT IMPORTANT SOURCE	NOT AN IMPORTANT SOURCE
Television	☐	☐	☐
Newspapers	☐	☐	☐
Radio	☐	☐	☐
Billboards	☐	☐	☐
Flyers	☐	☐	☐

8 In the past month, how often have you eaten at each of these three fast-food restaurants?

RESTAURANT	ONCE A WEEK OR MORE	TWO OR THREE TIMES A MONTH	ONCE A MONTH OR LESS
Burger King	☐	☐	☐
McDonald's	☐	☐	☐
Wendy's	☐	☐	☐

9 Please answer the following questions about you and your household.
  a Are you   ☐ Male   ☐ Female
  b Are you   ☐ Single   ☐ Married   ☐ Other (widowed, divorced)
  c How many children under age 18 live in your home?
     ☐ 0   ☐ 1   ☐ 2   ☐ 3 or more
  d What is your age?
     ☐ under 25   ☐ 25–44   ☐ 45 or over
  e What is your approximate total annual household income?
     ☐ Less than $15 000   ☐ $15 000–$49 999   ☐ $50 000 or more

simplest fixed alternative question, a *dichotomous question* that allows only a "yes" or "no" answer. A fixed alternative question with three or more choices uses a scale. Question 5 is an example of a question that uses a *semantic differential scale*, a nine-point scale in which the opposite ends have one- or two-word adjectives that have opposite meanings. For example, depending on how clean the respondent believes that Wendy's is, he or she would check the left-hand space on the scale, the right-hand space, or one of the seven intervening points. Question 6 uses a *Likert scale*, in which the respondent is asked to indicate the extent to which he or she agrees or disagrees with a statement.

The questionnaire in Figure 8–5 is an excerpt of a precisely worded survey that provides valuable information to the marketing researcher at Wendy's. Questions 1 to 8 inform him or her about the likes and dislikes in eating out, frequency of eating out at fast-food restaurants generally and at Wendy's specifically, and sources of information used in making decisions about fast-food restaurants. Question 9 gives details about the personal or household characteristics which can be used in trying to segment the fast-food market, a topic discussed in Chapter 9.

Surveys of distributors—retailers and wholesalers in the marketing channel—are also very important for manufacturers. A reason given for the success of many Japanese consumer products in Canada, such as Sony Walkmans and Toyota automobiles, is the emphasis that Japanese marketers place on obtaining accurate information from their distributors.

Electronic technology has revolutionized the traditional concept of surveys. Today, respondents can walk up to a kiosk in a shopping centre, read questions off a screen, and key their answers into a computer on a touch screen. For example, Labatt Breweries Ltd. has used an interactive kiosk in the shape of a beer can and rewards customers with coupons as a thank-you for completing an electronic survey. Even fully automated systems exist for conducting surveys by telephone. An automated voice questions respondents over the telephone, who key in their replies on a touch-tone telephone.

Experiment

experiment
Obtaining data by manipulating factors under tightly controlled conditions to test cause and effect.

Another method that can be used by marketing researchers to generate primary data is the experiment. Marketing experiments offer the potential for establishing cause-and-effect relationships (causal research). An **experiment** involves the manipulation of an independent variable (cause) and the measurement of its effect on the dependent variable (effect) under controlled conditions.

In marketing experiments, the independent variables are often one or more of the marketing mix variables—sometimes called the marketing *drivers*—such as product features, price, or promotion used. An ideal dependent variable usually is a change in purchases by an individual, household, or entire organization. If actual purchases cannot be used as a dependent variable, factors that are believed to be highly related to purchases, such as preferences in a taste test or intentions to buy, are used.

Wendy's changes continuously in response to changing customer wants while keeping its "Fresh, hot'n juicy®" image.

Wendy's Restaurant
www.wendys.com

Test marketing led to Grocery Gateway's entry into the Internet-based retail grocery business.

Grocery Gateway

www.grocerygateway.com

A potential difficulty with experiments is that an extraneous (or outside) variable can distort the results of an experiment and affect the dependent variable.

Experiments can be conducted in the field or in a laboratory. In *field experiments*, the research is conducted in the real world, such as in a store or bank, or on the street, wherever the behaviour being studied occurs naturally. Field experiments can be expensive but are a good way to determine people's reactions to changes in the elements of the marketing mix. Test marketing is probably the most common form of field experiments. Kraft Canada used test marketing before introducing its microwavable, prebaked cookie to the Canadian marketplace. And Toronto-based Grocery Gateway, Canada's first fully integrated Internet grocery retailer, used test marketing before entering the online grocery business. Remember your problem regarding cranberry juice at Ocean Spray? You wanted to know if Asian consumers would buy cranberry juice when they had never tasted cranberries? Perhaps your marketing research colleague might recommend taste tests in Asia to gauge consumers' responses to the product.

Because marketers cannot control all the conditions in the field, they sometimes turn to a laboratory setting. Laboratories are not the real world but do offer highly controlled environments. Unlike in the field, the marketer has control over all the factors that may impact the behaviour under investigation.

For example, in a field experiment, the marketer may wish to examine the impact of a price reduction on the sales of a particular product. The competition, however, may see the price reduction and offer their own price deal, thus interfering with the possible results of the field experiment. This does not occur in a laboratory setting. Many companies are using laboratory settings where they can control conditions but can do so in a real-world fashion, such as simulated supermarkets or test stores. Here, they can experiment with changes in aisle displays, packaging changes, or other variables that may affect buyer behaviour without the fear of other extraneous factors influencing the results.

Observation

observation
Watching, either mechanically or in person, how people behave.

Another basic research method used to obtain primary data is observation. In general, **observation** involves watching, either mechanically or in person, how people behave. In some circumstances, the speed of events or the number of events being observed make mechanical or electronic observation more appropriate than personal observation. Retailers, for example, can use electronic cameras to count the number of customers entering or leaving a store.

A classic form of mechanical observation is Nielsen Media Researcher's "people meter," which is a box attached to television sets, VCRs, cable boxes, and satellite dishes in selected households in Canada and the United States in order to determine the size of audiences watching television programs delivered by the networks. When a household member watches TV, he or she is supposed to push a button on a remote and push it again when viewing stops. The information is transmitted and analyzed by Nielsen in order to measure who in the household is watching what program on every TV set owned.

This information is used to calculate ratings for each TV program, which, in turn, is used to set advertising rates for such programs. But people meters have limitations—as with all observations collected mechanically. Critics do not believe the devices accurately measure who is watching a given TV program or what is actually watched. Moreover, people meters cannot measure large segments of the population that watch TV programs at parties, hotels, or sports bars. A new "passive, portable people meter" is now being tested by Nielsen and Arbitron, a service firm that also measures cable TV viewership as well as radio listenership. This device, which is the size of a pager, is carried by consumers and automatically detects inaudible codes in the programming of TV, cable, and radio broadcasters, at both in-home and outside venues. Each night, participants place the meter into a base station, which then transmits the data to Nielsen/Arbitron for analysis.[17]

Nielsen also uses an electronic meter to record Internet user behaviour. These data are collected by tracking the actual mouse clicks made by users as they surf the Internet via a meter installed on their home or work computers. Nielsen has been able to identify the Web sites that have the largest audiences, the top advertising banners viewed, the top Internet advertisers, and global Internet usage for selected countries.

Watching consumers in person or by videotaping them are other observational approaches used to collect primary data. For example, Aurora Foods observes how consumers bake cakes in its Duncan Hines test kitchens to see if baking instructions on the cake box are understood and followed correctly. In order to develop better products Fisher-Price uses its licensed nursery schools to observe how children use or abuse toys. Gillette marketing researchers actually videotaped consumers brushing their teeth in their own bathrooms to find out how they really brush—not just how they say they brush. The result: Gillette's new Oral-B CrossAction toothbrush that is supposed to do a better job![18]

ethnographic research
Observational approach to discover subtle emotional reactions as consumers encounter products in their "natural use environment."

A specialized observational approach is **ethnographic research**, in which anthropologists and other trained observers seek to discover subtle emotional reactions as consumers encounter products in their "natural use environments," such as in homes, cars, or hotels. For example, Best Western, a hotel chain, paid couples to videotape themselves as they spent three to seven days on a cross-country car trip. From this, Best Western found that women usually decided when to pull off the road and where to stay—the reverse of what was found during focus group research. The result: Best Western targets women more often with its promotional messages.[19] Read the accompanying Marketing NewsNet box to see just how a new shower head came to market as a result of ethnographic research.[20]

Another novel approach to obtaining observational data is the hiring of *mystery shoppers*. Companies hire people to pose as real customers and have them go through an exchange process and record their observations in detailed reports. For example, a mystery shopper might be paid to travel to a vacation resort, eat at restaurants, play golf, open up bank accounts, test-drive new cars at auto dealers, or shop

How do you do marketing research on such things as toothbrushes and fashion products for teenagers? For some creative answers, see the text.

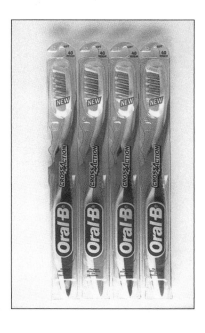

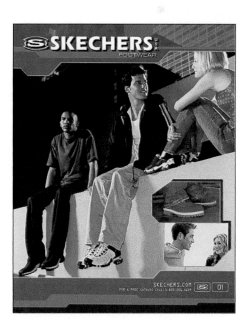

for groceries or clothes. The information they provide based on their observations often gives marketers unique insight that cannot be obtained any other way. There are Canadian mystery shopping companies, just in case you want a job like this!

Personal observation is both useful and flexible, but it can be costly and unreliable, especially when different observers report different conclusions in watching the same activities. Also, although observation can reveal what people do, it cannot determine why they do it, such as why they are buying or not buying a product. To determine why consumers behave as they do, marketing researchers must talk with consumers and record their responses. This is usually accomplished through the use of surveys.

Is There an Optimal Research Design?

In short, there is no optimal research design. A researcher may choose among a variety of alternative methods for solving a particular marketing problem. A good marketing researcher understands that there is likely to be more than one way to tackle a problem. The ability to select the most appropriate research design develops with experience. Inexperienced researchers often embrace the survey method as the best design because they are most familiar with this method. More experienced researchers, on the other hand, recognize the value of other methods and can often put together creative research designs that can solve marketing problems more quickly and less expensively. Experienced researchers often note that the proper definition of marketing plays a central role in determining the most appropriate research design.

MARKETING NEWSNET

The Naked Truth: Marketing Researchers Search for the Perfect Shower Head

As this chapter points out, a specialized observational research method is called *ethnographic research*. In short, researchers observe consumers interacting with products in their natural use environment. Before Moen Inc. put its new massaging shower head, the Revolution, on the market, it wanted to see what consumers thought about the new product design. But Moen did not want to just give consumers the shower head and later ask them if they liked it or not. The company wanted to see the consumers actually using the product . . . in the shower. So, it hired QualiData Research Inc. to do some observational research. Moen believed that people would not be able or willing to articulate what they really wanted in a shower head or why they liked or did not like the new shower head that Moen had developed. QualiData believed the only way to get real answers would be to watch people use the product in the shower. Obviously, not everyone would be willing to allow a stranger to observe or videotape them showering in the buff. So, Moen and QualiData decided to enlist nudists as their volunteers. They wanted at least 20 people, males and females of various ethnicities, who varied in age and body type. For $250 each, the volunteers allowed the researchers to come into their homes. They answered the researchers' questions about their lifestyles, while other team members installed a tiny video camera in the shower of each volunteer.

What truths did the videos reveal? Well, they showed that most people have only one hand free while they shower and that most people close their eyes sporadically while showering. The videos also showed that often bathroom lighting did not penetrate the shower curtain. Because of these constraints, people showering had a hard time fumbling around with massage settings. As a result of the research, the new Revolution massaging shower head has a peanut-shaped control dial below the water stream that allows consumers to constantly adjust the force and pulse of the water while providing coverage. The centre of the shower head spins and wobbles so that each stream of water twists and twirls, hence the name Revolution.

The Revolution appears to be a hit, selling out in many stores. Moen executives are not surprised, given the research effort to unearth consumer preferences. Oh—the cost of the shower head is about $60. Moen believes consumers will pay that price, given that it engineered the product exactly to consumer specifications!

Sampling

sampling
The process of selecting subsets from a population.

Although sampling is an inherent component of the research design stage, it is a distinctive aspect of the research process. The researcher's sampling plan indicates who is to be sampled, how large a sample is needed, and how the sampling units will be selected. Rarely does a research project involve a complete census of every person in the research population. This is because of the time and cost involved in conducting a census. Thus, sampling is used. **Sampling** is the process of gathering data from a subset of the total population rather than from all members (census) of that particular population. A *sample*, then, is a subset from a larger population.

If proper statistical procedures are followed, a researcher does not need to select every member in a population because a properly selected sample should be representative of the population as a whole. However, errors can and do occur in sampling, and the reliability of the data obtained through sampling can sometimes become an issue. Thus, the first and most critical sampling question for researchers to ask is: who is to be sampled?

Another key question concerns the sample size: how big should the sample be? As mentioned, it is usually unrealistic to expect a census of the research population be conducted. In general, larger samples are more precise than smaller ones, but proper sampling can allow a smaller subset of the total population to provide a reliable measure of the whole.

The final question in the sampling plan concerns how to select the sampling units. There are two basic sampling techniques: probability and nonprobability sampling. **Probability sampling** involves precise rules to select the sample such that each element of the population has a specific known chance of being selected. For example, if your university wants to know how last year's 1000 graduates are doing, it can put their names in a bowl and randomly select 100 names of graduates to contact. The chance of being selected—100/1000 or 0.10—is known in advance, and all graduates have an equal chance of being contacted. This procedure helps select a sample (100 graduates) that should be representative of the entire population (the 1000 graduates) and allows conclusions to be drawn about the entire population.

probability sampling
Using precise rules to select the sample such that each element of the population has a specific known chance of being selected.

nonprobability sampling
Using arbitrary judgments to select the sample so that the chance of selecting a particular element may be unknown or zero.

Nonprobability sampling involves the use of arbitrary judgment by the marketing researcher to select the sample so that the chance of selecting a particular element of the population is either unknown or zero. If your university decided to talk to 100 of last year's graduates but only those who lived closest to the university, many class members would be arbitrarily eliminated. This has introduced a bias, or possible lack of representativeness, which may make it dangerous to draw conclusions about the entire population of the graduating class. Nonprobability samples are often used when time and budgets are limited and are most often used for exploratory research purposes. In general, marketing researchers use data from such samples with caution.

CONCEPT CHECK

1. What is a survey?

2. Which research method offers the potential for establishing cause-and-effect relationship?

3. What is sampling?

■ ■ ■

DATA COLLECTION AND ANALYSIS

Once the research design has been formalized, the process of gathering or collecting data begins. Sometimes referred to as *fieldwork*, data collection at this stage of the research process includes all the activities that the researcher (and staff) undertakes to obtain data from the identified sources or respondents. Since there are several research methods that could be used by the researcher, this means there may be multiple ways to collect the data. For example, with the survey method, data may be collected by telephone, mail, or personal interview.

However the data are collected, it is important to minimize errors in the process. Most research experts agree that the data collection stage of the research process is one of the major sources of error in marketing research. Some of the errors that occur are a result of a variety of problems ranging from failure to select the right respondents to incorrect recording of observations. Competent and well-trained researchers inside the organization or those employed by outside research companies can go a long way in ensuring proper data collection.

The next step for the marketing researcher is data analysis. Mark Twain once observed, "Collecting data is like collecting garbage. You've got to know what you're going to do with the stuff before you collect it." In essence, the marketing researcher must know *why* the data are being collected and *how* to analyze them effectively in order for the data to have any value in decision making.

The level of analysis conducted on the data depends on the nature of the research and the information needed to provide a solution to the marketing problem. For survey data, frequency analysis is completed—calculating the responses question by question. The researcher may then wish to identify patterns in the data or examine how data pertaining to some questions may relate to data obtained from asking other questions. Probably the most widely used technique for organizing and analyzing marketing data is cross-tabulation. This method is particularly useful for market segmentation analysis.

■ ■ ■
CONCLUSIONS AND REPORT

At this stage of the process, the marketing researcher, often in conjunction with marketing management, must review the analysis and ask: what does this information tell us? A critical aspect of the marketing researcher's job is to interpret the information and make conclusions with regard to managerial decision making. The researcher must prepare a report to communicate the research findings. Included in this report should be suggestions for actions that might be taken by the organization to solve the marketing problem.

The researcher must be careful not to overwhelm management with technical terminology. Rather, the report should highlight the important results and conclusions in a clear and concise manner. Ultimately, the marketing researcher and management must work closely together to ensure proper interpretation of the research results. In addition, management must make a commitment to act—to make decisions based on the research and their good judgment and knowledge of the situation. In other words, someone must "make something happen" to see that a solution to the marketing problem gets implemented. Failure to act on the research findings creates an appearance that the marketing research effort is of little value. Finally, once implemented, the proposed solution should be monitored to ensure that intended results do occur.

■ ■ ■
ETHICAL ISSUES IN THE MARKETING RESEARCH PROCESS

According to the Marketing Research and Intelligence Association (MRIA), Canada's national association for professional marketing researchers, 9 in 10 Canadians support marketing and survey research and believe it serves a valuable societal purpose. However, unethical practices by some individual organizations are threatening the goodwill that Canadians have toward research.[21] Ethical issues can arise in the marketing researchers' relationships with all parties involved in the research

ETHICS AND SOCIAL RESPONSIBILITY ALERT

Standards for Public Release of Marketing Research Results in Canada

Marketing Research and Intelligence Association (MRIA) (www.camro.org), Canada's national association for professional marketing researchers, has developed a set of guidelines and recommendations for all its members to follow when releasing marketing research results to the public. The guidelines are as follows:

1. Include the following key facts in the report: sample size and population surveyed; sponsor of study; survey method (e.g., telephone, online, intercept); timing (when the project was done); and a statement of sample error/margin of error (i.e., ±2.5%/19 times out of 20).

2. Make the following facts available to the public upon request (if not included in the report): name of practitioner (who did the research); sampling method (e.g., random, custom list); weighting procedures, if used; and exact wording and order of questions.

3. Always differentiate between scientific and nonscientific studies.

4. Where appropriate, use the caveat that research is not necessarily predictive of future outcomes but rather captures opinion at one point in time.

MRIA has also issued additional standards regarding the reporting of qualitative research (e.g., focus groups, depth interviews). These guidelines include: clearly defining the recruiting specifications (e.g., product usage, party affiliation, specific demographic specification); inclusion of a statement of nonprojectability—results of qualitative research are not statistically projectable to the population at large; and in qualitative reporting, noninclusion of percentages or precise proportions. Such expressions as *some*, *most*, or *a few* may be used.

What do you think about MRIA's guidelines? Do they address all the possible ethical and socially responsible aspects of reporting research to the public?

process, including the respondents, the general public, their organizations, and/or clients. Professional marketing researchers must make ethical decisions regarding the collecting, using, and reporting of research data. Examples of unethical behaviour include failure to report problems with research results because of incomplete data, reporting only favourable results, using deception to collect information, and breaching the confidentiality of respondents.[22] Many companies are also collecting clickstream data when consumers go online, and sometimes these data are used for marketing purposes without the knowledge and consent of the consumer. The MRIA has developed formal ethical standards, guidelines, and policies for all its members to adhere to with regard to all aspects of marketing research. An example of a formal set of guidelines pertaining to the release of marketing research results is seen in the Ethics and Social Responsibility Alert box.[23]

USING INFORMATION TECHNOLOGY TO TRIGGER MARKETING ACTIONS

Today's marketing managers can be drowned in such an ocean of data that they need to adopt strategies for dealing with complex, changing views of the competition, the market, and the consumer. The Internet and the PC power of today provide a gateway to exhaustive data sources that vary from well organized and correct to disorganized and incorrect.

The Marketing Manager's View of Sales "Drivers"

Figure 8–6 shows a marketing manager's view of the product or brand "drivers," the factors that influence buying decisions of a household or organization and, hence,

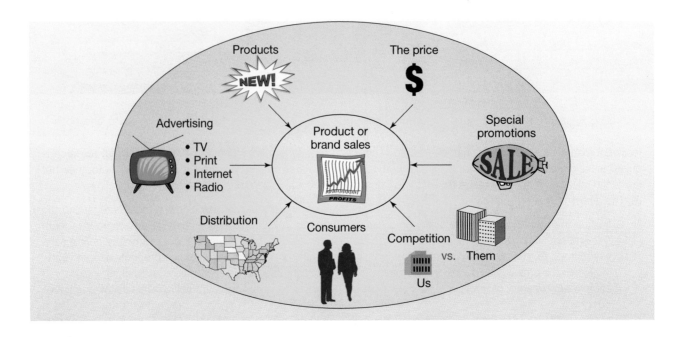

■ FIGURE 8–6 ■

Product and brand drivers: factors that influence sales

SOURCE: Used by permission of Ford Consulting Group, Inc.

sales. These drivers include both the controllable marketing mix factors, such as product and distribution, as well as uncontrollable factors, such as competition and the changing tastes of households or organizational buyers.

Understanding these drivers involves managing this ocean of data. Sometimes, hundreds of thousands of bits of data are created each week. Sources feeding this database ocean range from internal data about sales and customers to external data from syndication services and TV ratings. The marketer's task is to convert this data ocean into useful information on which to base informed decisions. In practice, some market researchers distinguish *data*—the facts and figures—from *information*—the distilled facts and figures whose interpretation leads to marketing actions.

Current information about products, competitors, and customers is almost always accessed and analyzed by computer. So, today, these activities fall under the broader term of **information technology**, which involves a computer and communication system to satisfy an organization's needs for data storage, processing, and access.

information technology

A computer and communication system to satisfy an organization's needs for data storage, processing, and access.

Key Elements of an Information System

Figure 8–7 shows how marketing researchers and managers use information technology to frame questions that provide answers leading to marketing actions. At the bottom of Figure 8–7, the marketer queries the databases in the information system with marketing questions that need answers. These questions go through statistical models that analyze the relationships existing among the data. The databases form the core, or *data warehouse,* where the ocean of data is collected and stored. After the search of this data warehouse, the models select and link the pertinent data, often presenting them in tables and graphics for easy interpretation. Marketers can also use *sensitivity analysis* to query the database with "what if" questions to determine how a hypothetical change in a driver, such as advertising, can affect sales.

Data Mining: A New Approach to Searching the Data Ocean

Traditional marketing research typically involves identifying possible drivers and then collecting data: Increasing couponing (the driver) during spring will increase trial by first-time buyers (the result). Marketing researchers then try to collect information to attempt to verify the truth of the relationship.

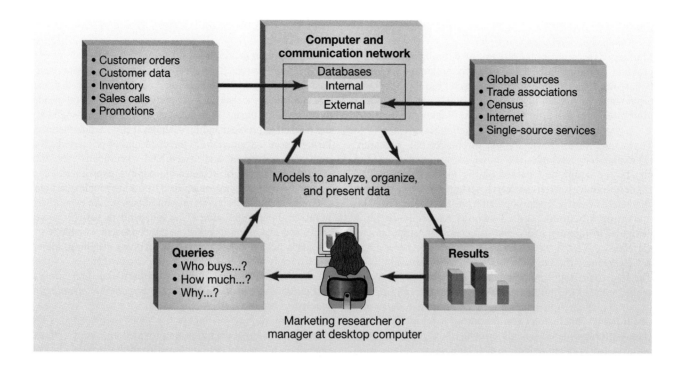

■ FIGURE 8-7 ■■

How marketing researchers and managers use information technology to turn information into action

data mining

The extraction of hidden predictive information from large databases

In contrast, **data mining** is the extraction of hidden predictive information from large databases. Catalogue companies, such as Sears Canada and Lands' End, use data mining to find statistical links that suggest particular marketing actions. Data mining, in fact, often plays a critical role in a company's customer relationship management (CRM) efforts. Through data mining, a company can monitor customer behaviour and determine appropriate strategies based on that behaviour. For example, one catalogue company studies about 3500 variables over the lifetime of a customer's relations with the company and its catalogue. It found that customers who change residences are three times more likely to buy new tables and decorative products than other customers who do not change residences. So, the company actually created a catalogue geared to customers who have recently moved.

Some purchase patterns are common sense. Peanut butter and grape jelly purchases link and might suggest a joint promotion between Kraft peanut butter and Welch's grape jelly. Other patterns link seemingly unrelated purchases. Supermarkets mined checkout data scanners and discovered that men buying diapers in the evening sometimes buy a six-pack of beer as well. So, the supermarkets placed diapers and beer near each other. Placing potato chips between them increased sales on all three.

Still, the success in data mining ultimately depends on humans—the marketing managers and researchers—and their judgments in how to select, analyze, and interpret the information.

CONCEPT CHECK

1. What does a marketing manager mean when she talks about a sales "driver"?

2. How does data mining differ from traditional marketing research?

■ ■ ■

CHAPTER IN REVIEW

1 *Know what marketing research is.*

Marketing research is the process of defining a marketing problem or opportunity, systematically collecting and analyzing information, and recommending actions to improve an organization's marketing activities. Marketing research is used by executives to aid in the decision-making process.

2 *Explain the different types of marketing research.*

There are three basic types of marketing research: (1) exploratory research—preliminary research conducted to clarify the scope and nature of the marketing problem, (2) descriptive research—research designed to describe basic characteristics of a given population or to profile particular marketing situations, and (3) causal research—research designed to identify cause-and-effect relationships among variables.

3 *Understand the stages in the marketing research process.*

The four basic stages in the marketing research process generally are: (1) defining the problem, (2) determining the research design, (3) collecting and analyzing data, and (4) drawing conclusions and preparing a report. The first stage—problem definition—is critical, since research based on incorrect problem definition will be a waste of resources. At the research design stage, the researcher produces a plan that outlines the methods and procedures for collecting and analyzing the required information. The plan includes the objectives of the research, the sources of information to be used, the research methods, the sampling plan, and the schedule and cost of the research.

4 *Explain the use of secondary data, surveys, experiments, and observation in marketing research.*

The marketing research can utilize secondary data—data previously collected and assembled for some other project than the one at hand. These data consist of information from both inside and outside the organization that may provide some insight into the marketing problem and its solution. If it does not, the marketing researcher may turn to the collecting of primary data—new data gathered and assembled specifically for the project—which can be obtained via surveys, experiments, and observation. A survey generates data by asking people questions and recording their responses on a questionnaire. An experiment involves the manipulation of an independent variable (e.g., price) and measuring its effect on the dependent variable (e.g., purchase behaviour). Observation involves watching, either mechanically or in person, how people actually behave.

5 *Explain how information technology and data mining link massive amounts of marketing information to meaningful marketing actions.*

Today's marketing managers are often overloaded with data—from internal data to those provided on, say, TV viewing habits or on grocery purchases from the scanner data at checkout counters. This can involve millions of bits of new information in a week or a month. So, information technology enables massive amounts of marketing data to be stored, processed, and accessed. Using this information technology, databases are queried using data mining to find statistical relationships to aid in marketing decisions and actions.

■ ■ ■

FOCUSING ON KEY TERMS

data mining p. 219
depth interviews p. 206
ethnographic research p. 213
experiment p. 211
focus groups p. 206
information technology p. 218
marketing research p. 199

nonprobability sampling p. 215
observation p. 212
primary data p. 204
probability sampling p. 215
sampling p. 215
secondary data p. 203
survey p. 208

■ ■ ■
DISCUSSION AND APPLICATION QUESTIONS

1 Is it possible to make effective marketing decisions without marketing research?

2 Why is the problem definition stage of the marketing research process probably the most important stage?

3 You plan to open an ice cream shop in your town. What type of exploratory research would you conduct to help determine its feasibility? You find the exploratory research does not answer all your questions. You decide to do a survey to determine whether you should open the shop. What kind of questions will you ask? Whom do you ask?

4 Suppose you are trying to determine the top three favourite department stores in your area. You show customers at a shopping mall a list of department stores and ask them to rank their three favourite stores from 1 to 3 (with 1 being the favourite). What problems can occur with the survey?

5 Your university bookstore wants to find out students' opinions about the store's merchandise, prices, and customer service. What type of marketing research would you recommend to the store?

6 You are a marketing researcher observing what people do when selecting bread in a supermarket. You are behind a one-way mirror, and the customers do not know they are being observed. During the course of the day, you observe several people shoplifting a smaller snack product near the bread section. You know personally two of the shoplifters you see. What are the ethical problems you face in this situation?

7 You plan to open a new rent-a-car business. You have drafted a survey you want to distribute to airline passengers. The survey will be left at the airports, and respondents will mail the surveys back in a prepaid envelope. Some of the questions you plan to use are shown below. Use Figure 8–4 to (*a*) identify the problem with each question, and (*b*) correct it. (**Note**: Some questions may have more than one problem.)

a. Do you own your own car or usually rent one?
_____ Yes _____ No

b. What is your age? _____ 21–30 _____ 30–40 _____ 41–50 _____ 50+

c. How much did you spend on rental cars last year?
_____ $100 or less _____ $101–$400 _____ $401–$800 _____ $800–$1000 _____ $1000 or more

d. What is a good daily rental car rate? _____

| | | What's New in Marketing Research? |

WorldOpinion calls its Web site "The World's Market Research Web Site." To check out the latest marketing research news, job opportunities, and directories of more than 8500 research locations in 99 countries, go to www.worldopinion.com, and do the following:

1. Click on the "News" link on WorldOpinion's home page to read about the current news and issues facing the market research industry.
2. Click on "The Frame" link, a set of online articles published by Survey Sampling, International.

Do you want to get better grades and stay up to date with current issues in marketing? Visit the Online Learning Centre at www.mcgrawhill.ca/college/crane for practice tests, video cases, resources for building a marketing plan, *Globe and Mail* headlines, access to *Marketing Magazine*, and other learning and study tools.

VIDEO CASE 8 — Ford Consulting Group, Inc.: from Data to Actions

"The fast pace of working as a marketing professional isn't getting any easier," agrees David Ford, as he talks with Mark Rehborg, Tony's Pizza brand manager. "The speed of communication, the availability of real-time market information, and the responsibility for a brand's profit make marketing one of the most challenging professional jobs today."

Mark responds, "Ten years ago, we could reach 80 percent of our target market with 3 television spots—but today, to reach the same 80 percent, we would have to buy 97 spots. We haven't the luxury to be complacent—our core consumer, the 6- to 12-year-old 'big kid,' is part of a savvy, wired culture that is changing rapidly."

THE COMPANY AND ITS CLIENTS

David Ford, president of Ford Consulting Group (FCG), assists clients such as Tony's in translating the market and sales information into marketing actions. Mark executes ideas that will draw consumers to Tony's and manages sales and profit performance. He distributes budgeted funds to promote the product. Feedback from the sales force requesting promotion funds is a common occurrence.

The information that FCG consultants and Tony's use most often for this analysis comes from places like AC Nielsen's ScanTrack and Information Resources' InfoScan (IRI) that summarize sales data from grocery stores and other outlets that scan purchases at the checkout.

FCG's typical consulting project involves helping clients make sense of their existing information, *not* in helping clients collect more information. Most often the client has a critical time deadline for FCG's data analysis and action recommendations: The client "wants" the answer a week ago, about four days *before* it hires FCG!

The project that follows is typical of the work Ford Consulting Group (www.fordconsultinggroup.com) undertakes for a client. The data are hypothetical, but the situation is a very typical one in the grocery products industry. Here's a snapshot of some of the terms in the case:

- "You" have just come on the job, as the new marketing person.
- "NE" is the Northeastern sales region of Tony's.
- "SE, NW, SW" are the other sales regions.

PART 1: A TYPICAL QUESTION, ON A TYPICAL DAY

Let's dive into the background of a typical question you might face, on a typical day. On the opposite page are some memos you are given (one from Mark to you) as background.

You dig into Lauretta's data files and develop Table 1 that shows how Tony's is doing in the company's four sales regions and the entire United States on key marketing dimensions. Without reading further, take a deep breath and try to answer question 1 below.

PART 2: UNCOVERING THE TRUTH

Let's assume your analysis (question 1) shows NE is a problem, so we need to understand what's going on in the NE. You dig into the data and develop Table 2. It shows the situation for the four largest supermarket chains in the Northeast sales region that carry Tony's. Now answer question 2.

QUESTIONS

1 Study Table 1. (*a*) How does the situation in the Northeast compare with the other regions in the United States? (*b*) What appears to be the reason(s) that sales are soft? (*c*) Write a 150-word e-mail with attachments to Mark Rehborg, your boss, giving your answers to *b*.

2 Study Table 2. (*a*) What do you conclude from this information? (*b*) Summarize your conclusions in a 150-word e-mail with attachments to Mark, who needs them for a meeting tomorrow with Margaret, the Northeast sales region manager. (*c*) What marketing actions might your memo suggest?

TO: Mark Rehborg, Tony's Brand Manager
FROM: Steve Quam, Tony's Field Sales
CC: Margaret Loiaza, NE Sales Region Manager

RE: Feedback on Sales Call at Food-Fast

Hi Mark—

Our sales call at Food-Fast wasn't so great. They don't see how our Tony's is going to sell well enough to justify the additional shelf-space. I also talked to Margaret and she said that second quarter may be weaker than planned across all the NE, and I should give you a heads-up. (She's on vacation this week, Aruba!) She's planning to schedule some time with you to talk about additional promotion money to do catch-up in the third quarter. She'll be there next week.

Steve

TO: You, the New Marketing Person
FROM: Mark Rehborg, Tony's Brand Manager (Your Boss)

RE: Small Project due Friday

Hi You,

Can you help out here? I've got a meeting with Margaret on Friday afternoon, and she's concerned that Food-Fast and the whole NE is going to need some additional promotion dollars.

Lauretta started the analysis and was hurt in a kick-boxing accident yesterday and won't be back to work for a week. Her files are attached. Can you look through her files and summarize what's going on in the NE and the rest of the U.S.? Does Margaret need more promotion money?

Let's discuss Friday AM.

Mark

TABLE 1. COMPARISON OF TONY'S PERFORMANCE, BY REGION

REGION	QUARTERLY CHANGE IN VOLUME (%)	DISTRIBUTION[a] (%)	PRICE ($)	PRICE GAP[b] ($)	PROMOTION	
					SUPPORT[c] (%)	VOLUME[d] (%)
NE	3%	93%	$1.29	18	7%	14%
SE	5	95	1.11	21	9	16
NW	8	98	1.19	11	8	15
SW	6	96	1.25	0	8	15
U.S.	6	97	1.19	0	8	15

[a] % of outlets carrying Tony's.
[b] Price gap 5 (Our price) 2 (Competitor's price).
[c] Promotion support 5 % of the time brand was promoted.
[d] Promotion volume 5 % of the volume sold on promotion.

TABLE 2. COMPARISON OF MAJOR SUPERMARKET CHAINS IN THE NORTHEAST

SUPER-MARKET CHAIN	QUARTERLY CHANGE IN VOLUME (%)	DISTRIBUTION[a] (%)	PRICE ($)	PRICE GAP[b] ($)	PROMOTION	
					SUPPORT[c] (%)	VOLUME[d] (%)
Save-a-lot	5%	95%	$1.39	110	10%	19%
Food-Fast	0	90	1.28	21	3	4
Get-Fresh	0	90	1.30	11	3	4
Dollars-Off	7	97	1.34	15	7	14

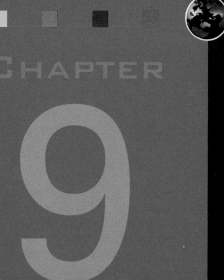

IDENTIFYING MARKET SEGMENTS AND TARGETS

SNEAKERS MARKETING WARS: HIP-HOP, YAO MING, AND THREE BILLION TRILLION CHOICES

In today's sneakers war among Reebok, Nike, Adidas, and others, a new shoe introduction can have the effect of a toy pop gun—or a salvo across a battleship's bow. That's how serious the competition is. And Reebok recently launched a marketing strategy that challenges conventional wisdom.

New Segments and Strategies   Reebok is reaching a new market segment and getting publicity for its entire sneaker line by signing endorsements with popular rappers and hip-hop music stars. Example: S. Carter Collection by Rbk. Don't recognize the S. Carter name? The street-inspired S. Carter Collection is named for hip-hop star Jay-Z, who was originally known as Shawn Carter. With their flat soles and soft leather, the S. Carter low tops (opposite page) are a long way from the look of Reebok's traditional "performance" athletic shoes.[1]

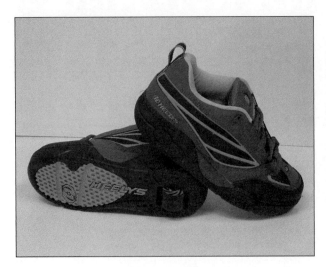

The look is not all that is unusual about Jay-Z's endorsement agreement with Reebok. Basketball star Yao Ming and tennis star Venus Williams have endorsement agreements with Reebok not only for their own footwear lines but also to promote its entire line and not to wear products from competitors. Yao Ming's $70 million contract with Reebok also will help it market its sports lines in his native China. But Jay-Z agrees to promote only his line of Reebok shoes, which means he is allowed to wear competing brands in public. Can you imagine Tiger Woods wearing a Reebok hat in the Canadian Open golf tournament—and his Nike sponsor being happy about it? Reebok says the "standard, more restrictive deal would have risked tagging its rapper allies as walking billboards for the corporation, hurting their countercultural appeal."[2]

What do you need in the sneaker business to stand out from the pack when consumers are faced with hundreds of athletic shoe choices, often on sneaker "walls" in sporting goods stores? The answer: all sneaker manufacturers are searching for new market segments of consumers and ways to differentiate their products from their global competitors. This challenge applies to the giants, such as Reebok and Nike, which are aggressively marketing new lines of superfast sneakers for track athletes, sleek soccer shoes, and sporty street apparel.[3] Competitive sneaker upstarts frequently target narrow market niches. For example, Heelys sneakers come with an imbedded, detachable wheel in the shoe's heel. In 2001, its first year of operation, Heelys sneakers were so hot that retailers sold one million pairs.

And what about the "three billion trillion choices" mentioned in the heading of this section? This was the number of different athletic shoe designs that Customatix claimed was possible if you ordered from its design-your-own-customized-shoes Web site. Customatix's strategy targeted a niche segment of athletic shoe buyers who wanted shoes designed to their unique wants and needs. And where are Customatix and its three billion trillion choices today? Gone—a silent victim in early 2004 to the sneaker marketing wars that proved too competitive.

Competitive Trends

Reebok also has recently signed deals with the NBA ($175 million) and the NFL ($250 million) to be their exclusive team uniform providers while offering branded apparel to consumers. And beginning in 2005, Reebok will be the provider of footwear to Major League Baseball players not under contract with other manufacturers. As a result of intense competition in the sneaker market, Nike acquired Converse, maker of basketball shoes worn by legends Magic Johnson and Larry Bird. The Sporting Goods Manufacturers Association (SGMA) and the NPD Group identified the following trends to consider in planning for the sneaker wars for 2005 and beyond:[4]

- *Age segments.* Teenagers/college-aged consumers comprise more than 32 percent of total sales; they are the largest segment, and spend more for sneakers than older consumers.
- *Gender segments.* Both men and women are important segments—women because their sales growth is higher than men, and men because they still buy more in total (double) at higher average prices.
- *Price segments.* More than 62 percent of sneakers purchased today cost less than $50 per pair.
- *Sport segments.* Running shoes are number one (29 percent market share); basketball shoes are number two (21 percent); and cross-training shoes are number three (13 percent). Basketball sales are up, but cross-training is down slightly.

- *Lifestyle segments.* Most recent sales growth in sneakers is due to casual styles that have a strong fashion component, where the retro look is prominent. Almost three-fourths of all sneakers are purchased for casual rather than for sports or fitness purposes. However, sales of higher-priced performance shoes rose dramatically in 2003 and 2004.

The strategies sneaker manufacturers use to satisfy the needs of different customers illustrate successful market segmentation, the main topic of this chapter. After discussing why markets need to be segmented, this chapter covers the steps a firm uses in segmenting and targeting a market, positioning its offering to the marketplace, and forecasting sales.

■ ■ ■
WHY SEGMENT MARKETS?

A business firm segments its markets so that it can respond more effectively to the wants of groups of potential buyers and thus increase its sales and profits. Not-for-profit organizations also segment the clients they serve to satisfy client needs more effectively while achieving the organization's goals. Let us use the situation of sneaker buyers finding their ideal Reebok shoes to describe (1) what market segmentation is, and (2) when it is necessary to segment markets.

What Market Segmentation Means

People have different needs and wants, even though it would be easier for marketers if they did not. Market segmentation involves aggregating prospective buyers into groups that (1) have common needs, and (2) will respond similarly to a marketing action. **Market segments** are the relatively homogeneous groups of prospective buyers that result from the market segmentation process. Each market segment consists of people who are relatively similar to each other in terms of their consumption behaviour.

The existence of different market segments has caused firms to use a marketing strategy of **product differentiation**. This strategy involves a firm's using different marketing mix activities, such as product features and advertising, to help consumers perceive the product as being different from and better than competing products. The perceived differences may involve physical features or nonphysical ones, such as image or price. The Reebok example discussed below shows how the company is using market segmentation, product differentiation, and market-product grids to develop effective marketing strategies.

market segments
The relatively homogeneous groups of prospective buyers that result from the market segmentation process.

product differentiation
Strategy involves a firm's using different marketing mix activities, such as product features and advertising, to help consumers perceive the product as being different from and better than competing products.

Segmentation: Linking Needs to Actions   The process of segmenting a market and selecting specific segments as targets is the link between the various buyers' needs and the organization's marketing program (Figure 9–1). Market segmentation is only a means to an end: to lead to tangible marketing actions that can increase sales and profitability.

Market segmentation first stresses the importance of grouping people or organizations in a market according to the similarity of their needs and the benefits they are

■ **FIGURE 9–1** ■
Market segmentation—linking market needs to an organization's marketing program

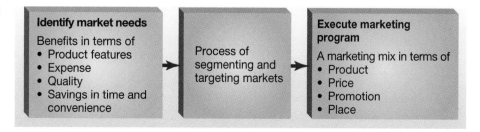

Identify market needs	Process of segmenting and targeting markets	Execute marketing program
Benefits in terms of • Product features • Expense • Quality • Savings in time and convenience		A marketing mix in terms of • Product • Price • Promotion • Place

looking for in making a purchase. Second, such needs and benefits must be related to specific marketing actions the organization can take. These actions may involve separate products or other aspects of the marketing mix, such as price, advertising, or distribution strategies.

How Reebok's Segmentation Strategy Developed   In 1979, Paul Fireman, who had dropped out of college to run his family's business, wandered through an international trade fair and saw Reebok's custom track shoes. He bought the North American licence from the British manufacturer and started selling running shoes in 1981.

In a brilliant marketing decision, Fireman introduced soft-leather aerobic dance shoes in flamboyant colours—the Reebok Freestyle—in 1982. Figure 9–2 shows that Reebok has introduced a variety of shoes since 1982—from tennis and basketball shoes in 1984 to cross-training shoes in 1988 and golf shoes in 1997. For simplicity, Figure 9–2 covers only shoes and does not show nonshoe lines, like fitness water (2001) and NBA/NFL apparel (2002).

Reebok's $3-billion-a-year sneaker business has a huge need to generate sales from new opportunities. As a result, Reebok has expanded both the markets it targets and the products it develops to satisfy this need, as detailed in Figure 9–2.

Using Market-Product Grids   A **market-product grid** is a framework to relate the market segments of potential buyers to products offered or potential marketing actions by the firm. The market-product grid in Figure 9–2 shows different market segments of sneaker users as rows in the grid, and the columns show the different shoe product lines chosen by Reebok. In a complete market-product grid analysis, each cell in the grid can show the estimated market size of a given product sold to a specific market segment.

The cells with red boxes in Figure 9–2, labelled P, represent Reebok's primary target market segment when it introduced each type of shoe. The blue boxes, labelled S,

---

market-product grid

A framework to relate the market segments of potential buyers to products offered or potential marketing actions by the firm.

■ FIGURE 9–2 ■

Market-product grid showing how different Reebok shoes reach segments of customers with different needs

---

MARKET SEGMENT		PRODUCT								
GENERAL	GROUP WITH NEED	RUNNING SHOES	AEROBIC SHOES	TENNIS SHOES	BASKETBALL SHOES	KIDS SHOES	WALKING SHOES	CROSS-TRAINING SHOES	GOLF SHOES	S. CARTER SHOES
		(1981)	(1982)	(1984)	(1984)	(1984)	(1986)	(1988)	(1997)	(2003)
Performance-oriented 30%	Runners	P						P		
	Aerobic/fitness exercisers		P					P		
	Tennis players			P				P		
	Basketball players				P			P		
	Golfers								P	
	Adventure seekers							P		
Nonathletic-oriented 70%	Walkers	S	S	S	S		P	P		
	Children					P				
	Comfort/style-conscious	S	S	S	S		S	S		
	Street fashion									P

Key: ▨ P = Primary market   ▨ S = Secondary market

MARKETING NEWSNET — Sneaker Strategies—Who's Doing What

Cross beams, shock absorbers, and cushions. Off-the-shelf versus design-your-own-shoe with numerous design combinations. These are some of the innovative technologies and strategies used by sneaker manufacturers to attract new consumers and differentiate their products from those offered by competitors.

Reebok

Reebok's Premier Series of shoes targets the specific needs of runners and features the new DMX Shear and Foam cushioning and Play Dry™ moisture management technologies. Because one style does not fit all, Reebok designed the Premier Control ($100) for runners whose feet tend to turn outward and the Premier Road ($85) with extra cushioning for pavement runners, two of several in the Premier line. From its new NFL® Collection, the Reebok NFL Game Day DMX cross-training shoe ($80) displays the official NFL logo and features an "X-Beam," similar to a cross beam used in buildings, to hold the foot in place and a "tongue pull ring" to tighten the laces of the shoe.

Nike

The "Michael-inspired" Air Jordan basketball shoe was originally launched in 1985. Today's Air Jordan XIX ($165) basketball shoe incorporates the latest Zoom Air cushioning technology. The Air Jordan XIX also features the radically new "Tech-Flex" lace cover for instep support, a carbon fibre midfoot shank plate for lateral support, and an adjustable strap for a more snug fit. Nike also lets you design your own running or basketball shoes at www.nikeid.com. Nike's MJ replacement? Basketball phenom LeBron James, with a reported $90 million basketball shoe and jersey contract.

Vans

Vans has targeted the rising wave of skateboard, snowboard, biking, and outdoor enthusiasts. To reach its skateboard shoe market, Vans relies on its endorsing athletes to design and market its signature lines and promote its skateboard events. Vans had a breakthrough when Foot Locker carried its shoes in more than 2700 retail outlets.

represent the secondary target market segments that also bought these products. In some cases, Reebok discovered that large numbers of people in a segment not originally targeted for a particular shoe style bought it anyway. Today, Reebok products are purchased by two types of segments: performance-oriented consumers (30 percent), who buy sneakers and apparel for athletic purposes; and nonathletic-oriented consumers (70 percent), who buy sneakers and apparel for comfort, style, price, or other nonathletic reasons. But as Figure 9–2 depicts, two segments of consumers in the nonathletic-oriented category, comfort/style conscious and walker, bought running, aerobic, and cross-trainer shoes not initially targeted at their respective segments. When this trend became apparent to Reebok in 1986, it introduced its walking shoe line directly at the walker segment.

Reebok tries to upgrade its products continuously; the years shown in Figure 9–2 are the first year that Reebok entered that segment. For example, in 2003, it upgraded many of its kid and adult shoes using microprocessor technologies. Figure 9–2 shows its 2003 introduction of the S. Carter Collection by Rbk, designed for a street-fashion target market.

What segmentation strategy will Reebok use to take it further into the twenty-first century? Only Reebok knows, but it will certainly involve trying to differentiate its products more clearly from its global competitors and perhaps target new or retarget existing global consumers. The Marketing NewsNet box[5] describes how Reebok, Nike, and Vans have succeeded in using market segmentation and product differentiation strategies to reach special groups of customers.

When to Segment Markets

A business firm goes to the trouble and expense of segmenting its markets when it expects that this will increase its sales, profit, and return on investment. When expenses are greater than the potentially increased sales from segmentation, a firm should not attempt to segment its market. However, three specific situations that illustrate effective use of market segmentation are the cases of: (1) one product and multiple market segments, (2) multiple products and multiple market segments, and (3) "segments of one," or mass customization.

One Product and Multiple Market Segments   When a firm produces only a single product or service and attempts to sell it to two or more market segments, it avoids the extra costs of developing and producing additional versions of the product, which often entail extremely high research, engineering, and manufacturing expenses. In this case, the incremental costs of taking the product into new market segments are typically those of a separate promotional campaign or a new channel of distribution. Although these expenses can be high, they are rarely as large as those for developing an entirely new product.

Does Harry Potter appeal only to the kids' segment? See the text for the answer to this amazing publishing success.

Movies, magazines, and books are single products frequently directed to two or more distinct market segments. Movie companies often run different TV commercials or magazine ads featuring different aspects of a newly released film (love, or drama, or spectacular scenery) that are targeted to different market segments. *Time* magazine now publishes more than 300 editions usually targeting unique geographic and demographic segments using a special mix of advertisements.

Harry Potter's phenomenal five-book success is based both on author J. K. Rowling's fiction-writing wizardry and on her publisher's creativity in marketing to pre-teen, teen, and adult segments of readers. By the end of 2003, almost one billion Harry Potter books had been sold globally, and the books were often at the top of fiction best-seller lists—for *adults. Harry Potter and the Order of the Phoenix,* the fifth book in the series, had a record-shattering initial press run of 8.5 million copies.[6] Although multiple TV commercials for movies and separate covers or advertisements for magazines or books are expensive, they are minor compared with the costs of producing an entirely new movie, magazine, or book for another market segment.

Multiple Products and Multiple Market Segments   Reebok's different styles of shoes, each targeted at a different type of user, are an example of multiple products aimed at multiple markets. Manufacturing these different styles of shoes is clearly more expensive than producing only a single style but seems worthwhile if it serves customers' needs better, does not reduce quality or increase price, and adds to the sales revenues and profits.

Marketing experts increasingly emphasize the two-tier marketing strategies—what some call "Tiffany/Wal-Mart strategies." Many firms are now offering different variations of the same basic product or service to high-end and low-end segments. Gap's Banana Republic chain sells blue jeans for $58, whereas its Old Navy stores sell a slightly different version for $22. The Walt Disney Company carefully markets two distinct Winnie-the-Poohs—such as the original line-drawn figures on fine china sold at Nordstrom and a cartoonlike Pooh on polyester bedsheets sold at Wal-Mart. The lines between customer segments often blur, however, as shown by the Cadillacs and Mercedes in Wal-Mart parking lots.[7]

Segments of One: Mass Customization   Canadian marketers are rediscovering today what their ancestors running the corner general store knew a century ago: every customer is unique, has unique wants and needs, and desires special tender loving care from the seller—the essence of customer relationship management (CRM). Economies of scale in manufacturing and marketing during the past century made mass-produced goods so affordable that most customers were willing to compromise their individual tastes and settle for standardized products. Today's Internet ordering and flexible manufacturing and marketing processes have made *mass*

WEBLINK

HTTP://WWW.MCGRAWHILL.CA/
COLLEGE/CRANE

GLOBAL ACCESS

Customizing Your Own Designer Shoes

Don't like the looks of those things on your feet right now? If you think your style instincts could design you a better running or basketball shoe, go to www.nikeid.com. There you can design your own shoe, customizing up to 11 elements for one of four shoe models. All possible combinations of these 11 design elements should create enough design variations for shoes to fit your unique style and feet.

customization possible, tailoring goods or services to the tastes of individual customers on a high-volume scale. The WebLink box shows how mass customization lets you design your own personalized running shoe.

Mass customization is the next step beyond *build-to-order* (BTO), manufacturing a product only when there is an order from a customer. Dell Computer uses BTO systems that trim work-in-progress inventories and shorten delivery times to customers. Dell's three-day deliveries are made possible by restricting its computer line to only a few basic modules and stocking a variety of each. This gives customers a good choice with quick delivery—Dell PCs can be assembled in four minutes. Most Dell customization comes from spending 90 minutes loading the unique software each customer selects. But even this system falls a bit short of total mass customization with virtually unlimited specification of features by customers.[8]

The key to successful product differentiation and market segmentation strategies is finding the ideal balance between satisfying a customer's individual wants and achieving organizational **synergy**, the increased customer value achieved through performing organizational functions more efficiently. The "increased customer value" can take many forms: more products, improved quality on existing products, lower prices, easier access to product through improved distribution, and so on. So, the ultimate criterion for an organization's marketing success is that customers should be better off as a result of the increased synergies.

synergy
The increased customer value achieved through performing organizational functions more efficiently.

CONCEPT CHECK

1. Market segmentation involves aggregating prospective buyers into groups that have two key characteristics. What are they?

2. When should a firm segment its markets?

STEPS IN SEGMENTING AND TARGETING MARKETS

The process of segmenting a market and then selecting and reaching the target segments is divided into the five steps discussed in this section, as shown in Figure 9–3. Segmenting a market is not an exact science—it requires large doses of common sense and managerial judgment.

Let us have you put on your entrepreneur's hat to use the market segmentation process to choose target markets and take useful marketing actions. Suppose you own a Wendy's fast-food restaurant next to a large urban university that offers both day and evening classes. Your restaurant specializes in the Wendy's basics: hamburgers, french fries, Frosty desserts, and chili. Even though you are part of a chain and have some restrictions on menu and decor, you are free to set your hours of business and to undertake local advertising. How can market segmentation help?

■ FIGURE 9-3 ■

The five key steps in
segmenting and targeting
markets link market needs of
customers to the
organization's marketing
program

■ FIGURE 9-3 ■

The five key steps in segmenting and targeting markets link market needs of customers to the organization's marketing program

Step 1: Group Potential Buyers into Segments

It is not always a good idea to segment a market. Grouping potential buyers into meaningful segments involves meeting some specific criteria that answer the questions: would segmentation be worth doing, and is it possible? If so, the next step is to find specific variables that can be used to create the various segments.

Criteria to Use in Forming the Segments   A marketing manager should develop market segments that meet five main criteria:

- *Potential for increased profit.* The best segmentation approach is the one that maximizes the opportunity for future profit and return on investment (ROI). If this potential is maximized without segmentation, do not segment. For not-for-profit organizations, the criterion is the potential for serving client users more effectively.
- *Similarity of needs of potential buyers within a segment.* Potential buyers within a segment should be similar in terms of a marketing action, such as product features sought or advertising media used.
- *Difference of needs of buyers among segments.* If the needs of the various segments are not very different, combine them into fewer segments. A different segment usually requires a different marketing action which, in turn, means greater costs. If increased sales do not offset extra costs, combine segments and reduce the number of marketing actions.
- *Potential of a marketing action to reach a segment.* Reaching a segment requires a simple but effective marketing action. If no such action exists, do not segment.
- *Simplicity and cost of assigning potential buyers to segments.* A marketing manager must be able to put a market segmentation plan into effect. This means being able to recognize the characteristics of potential buyers and then assigning them to a segment without encountering excessive costs.

Ways to Segment Consumer Markets   Figure 9–4 shows the main dimensions used to segment Canadian consumer markets. These include geographic, demographic, psychographic, and behavioural segmentation. By examining Figure 9–4, you can also see that a number of variables can be used within each dimension for segmentation purposes. What you should remember is that segmenting markets is not a pure science—it requires large doses of common sense and managerial judgment. A marketer may have to use several dimensions and multiple variables within each dimension to form proper market segments. Let us take a look at how some marketers might segment consumer markets using the information in Figure 9–4.

- *Geographic segmentation.* Using geographic segmentation, a marketer segments based on where consumers live. Geographic variables, such as countries, regions, provinces, counties, cities, or even neighbourhoods, could be used.

MAIN DIMENSIONS	VARIABLES	TYPICAL BREAKDOWNS
Geographic segmentation	Region	Atlantic, Quebec, Ontario, Prairies, British Columbia
	City or census metropolitan area (CMA) size	Under 5000; 5000–19 999; 20 000–49 000; 50 000–99 999; 100 000–249 000; 250 000–499 999; 500 000–999 000; 1 000 000–3 999 999; 4 000 000+
	Density	Urban; suburban; rural
	Climate	East; West
Demographic segmentation	Age	Infant; under 6; 6–11; 12–17; 18–24; 25–34; 35–49; 50–64; 65+
	Gender	Male; female
	Family size	1–2; 3–4; 5+
	Life stage	Infant; preschool; child; youth; collegiate; adult; senior
	Birth era	baby boomer (1946–1964); Generation X (1965–1976); baby Boomlet/Generation Y (1977–1994)
	Marital status	Never married; married; separated; divorced; widowed
	Income	Under $10 000; $10 000–19 999; $20 000–29 999; $30 000–39 999; $40 000–54 999; $55 000–74 999; $75 000+
	Occupation	Professional; managerial; clerical; sales; labourers; students; retired; housewives; unemployed
	Education	Grade school or less; some high school; high school graduate; some college; college graduate
	Race	White; Black; Asian; Native; other
	Home ownership	Own home; rent home
Psychographic segmentation	Personality/Lifestyle	Gregarious; compulsive; extroverted; introverted
	Lifestyle (Millward BrownGoldfarb)	Structured; discontented; fearful; assured; resentful; caring Protective providers; Up & Comers; Les "Petite Vie"; Mavericks; etc.
Behavioural segmentation	Benefits sought	Quality; service; low price
	Usage rate	Light user; medium user; heavy user
	User status	Nonuser; ex-user; prospect; first-time user; regular user
	Loyalty status	None, medium, strong

■ FIGURE 9-4 ■

Segmentation variables and breakdowns for Canadian consumer markets

Marketers often find that Canadians differ in terms of needs or preferences based on the region in which they live. This is a form of geographic segmentation. For example, Colgate-Palmolive markets Arctic Power, its cold-water detergent, on an energy-cost-saving dimension in Quebec, but as a clothes saver (cold-water washing is easier on clothes) in Western Canada.

- *Demographic segmentation.* One of the most common ways to segment consumer markets is to use demographic segmentation, or segmenting a market based on population characteristics. This approach segments consumers according to such variables as age, gender, income, education, occupation, and so forth. Cyanamid Canada Inc. uses age as a segmentation variable, producing and marketing its vitamins to various age groups, including children, young adults, and older Canadians. Centrum Select, for instance, is specifically designed for adults over 50. Trimark Investments of Ontario segments the financial services market by gender, targeting males and females with different products and different advertising campaigns. General Electric uses family size as a segmentation variable, targeting smaller families with compact microwaves and larger families with extra-large refrigerators. You should note, however, that a single demographic variable may not be sufficient in understanding and segmenting a given market.[9] Thus, many marketers combine a number of demographic variables that might clearly distinguish one segment from another. For example, cosmetics companies, such as Clinique, combine gender, income, and occupation in order to examine market segments for different lines of cosmetic products.

- *Psychographic segmentation.* Marketers use psychographic segmentation when they segment markets according to personality or lifestyle. It has been found that people who share the same demographic characteristics can have very different psychographic profiles. As we saw in Chapter 5, personality traits have been linked to product preferences and brand choice. In addition, a person's lifestyle (his or her activities, interests, and opinions) also affects the types of products, the brands of products, and how they may be purchased. Remember the Millward Brown Goldfarb Segments from Chapter 5? Well, for example, Canadians classified as protective providers are very price conscious but enjoy outdoor activities, such as gardening, golfing, and fishing. On the other hand, the Up & Comers want instant gratification, and the Tie-Dyed Greys are eco-conscious consumers.[10]

- *Behavioural segmentation.* When marketers use consumers' behaviour with or toward a product to segment the market, they are using behavioural segmentation. A powerful form of behavioural segmentation is to divide the market according to the benefits consumers seek from a product category. Using *benefits sought*, the marketer examines the major benefits consumers look for in the product category, the kinds of consumers who look for each benefit, and the major brands that deliver each benefit. For example, Telus Mobility and Bell Mobility both market their wireless communications products and services to young adults under 24 years of age who want text messaging "rather than talk" in order to ensure privacy. On the other hand, Rogers AT&T targets CEOs of large businesses who want to improve employee productivity through the use of wireless technology.

usage rate

Quantity consumed or patronage—store visits—during a specific period; varies significantly among different customer groups.

80/20 rule

A concept that suggests 80 percent of a firm's sales are obtained from 20 percent of its customers.

Wireless communications providers target young adults seeking specific benefits from wireless technology.

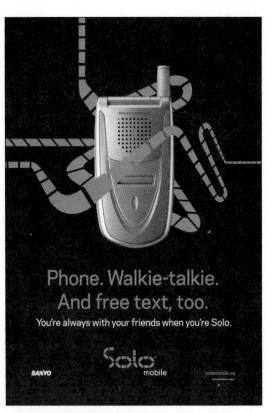

Phone. Walkie-talkie. And free text, too.
You're always with your friends when you're Solo.

Solo mobile
SANYO   solomobile.ca

Another behavioural segmentation variable often used by marketers is **usage rate**—quantity consumed or patronage during a specific period, which varies significantly among different customer groups. Air Canada, for example, focuses on usage rate for its frequent-flyer program, which is designed to encourage passengers to use its airline repeatedly. Usage rate is sometimes referred to in terms of the **80/20 rule**, a concept that suggests that 80 percent of a firm's sales are obtained from 20 percent of its customers. The percentages in the 80/20 rule are not really fixed; rather, the rule suggests that a small fraction of customers provide a large fraction of sales. For example, Air Canada pays special attention to the business travel segment that comprises only 20 percent of the airline seats but 40 percent of overall revenues.

Research shows that the fast-food market can also be segmented into light, medium, or heavy users. For every $1 spent by a light user in a fast-food restaurant, each heavy user spends about $5.[11] This is the reason for the emphasis in almost all marketing strategies on effective ways to reach heavy users of products and services. Thus, as a Wendy's restaurant owner you want to keep the heavy-user segment constantly in mind. With advances in information technology, marketers are now able to conduct detailed segmentation studies. Some Canadian telecommunications companies, for example, can now segment on the basis of more than 100 criteria, from calling patterns to promotional response.

Variables to Use in Forming Segments for Wendy's   Now, in determining one or two variables to segment the market for your Wendy's restaurant, very broadly, we find two main markets: students and nonstudents. To segment the students, we could try a variety of demographic variables, such as age, gender, year in school, or university major, or psychographic variables, such as personality or lifestyle. But none of these variables really meets the five criteria listed previously—particularly the fourth criterion: leading to a feasible marketing action to reach the various segments. Four student segments that *do* meet these criteria include the following:

- Students living in dormitories (residence halls, fraternity houses).
- Students living near the university in apartments.
- Day commuter students living outside the area.
- Night commuter students living outside the area.

These segmentation variables are really a combination of where the student lives and the time he or she is on campus (and near your restaurant). For nonstudents who might be customers, similar variables might be used:

- Faculty and staff members at the university.
- People who live in the area but are not connected with the university.
- People who work in the area but are not connected with the university.

Ways to Segment Organizational Markets   Variables for segmenting organizational markets are shown in Figure 9–5. A product manager at Xerox responsible for its new network colour printer might use a number of these segmentation variables, as follows:

- *Geographic segmentation.* The product manager might segment on the basis of region or actual location of the potential customer. Firms located in a census metropolitan area (CMA) might receive a personal sales call, whereas those outside the CMA might be contacted by phone.

■ **FIGURE 9–5** ■
Dimensions used to segment Canadian organizational markets

MAIN DIMENSIONS	VARIABLES	TYPICAL BREAKDOWNS
Geographic segmentation	Region	Atlantic, Quebec, Ontario, Prairies, British Columbia
	Location	In CMA; not in CMA
Demographic segmentation	NAICS code	2-digit: section; 3-digit: subsection; 4-digit: Industry Group
	Number of employees	1–19; 20–99; 100–249; 250+
	Annual sales volume	Less than $1 million; $1–10 million; $10–100 million; over $100 million
Behavioural segmentation	Benefits sought	Quality; customer service; low price
	Usage rate	Light user; medium user; heavy user
	User status	Nonuser; ex-user; prospect; first-time user; regular user
	Loyalty status	None, medium, strong
	Purchase method	Centralized; decentralized; Individual; group
	Type of buy	New buy; modified rebuy; straight rebuy

What variables might Xerox use to segment the organizational markets for its answer to colour copying problems? For the possible answer and related marketing actions, see the text.

Xerox Corporation

It's hot and cool at the same time. The Xerox Phaser® 8400 is the fastest color printer in the world for under $1000. There's a new way to look at it.

- *Demographic segmentation.* Firms might be categorized by the North American Industry Classification System (NAICS). Manufacturers, for example, with global customers might have different printing needs than do retailers or lawyers serving local customers.
- *Behavioural segmentation.* The market might also be segmented on the basis of benefits sought. Xerox may decide to focus on firms looking for quality product and good customer service as opposed to those looking for simply low prices. The product manager might also segment the market on the basis of usage rate, recognizing that larger, more globally oriented firms are more likely to be heavy users.

Some experts have combined geographic, demographic, and behavioural segmentation variables used in segmenting organizational markets to produce a segmentation concept known as firmographics. *Firmographics* involves both organizational characteristics, such as location, size of firm, industry category, corporate activities, business objectives, and buying objectives, and characteristics of the composition of the organization, such as the income distribution of employees, age, gender, and education of the workforce. Organizations with distinguishing firmographics are then grouped into market segments.[12]

Step 2: Group Products to Be Sold into Categories

As important as grouping customers into segments is finding a means of grouping the products you are selling into meaningful categories. If the firm has only one product or service, this is not a problem, but when it has dozens or hundreds, these must be grouped in some way so that buyers can relate to them. This is why department stores and supermarkets are organized into product groups, with the departments or aisles containing related merchandise. Likewise, manufacturers have product lines that are the groupings they use in the catalogues sent to customers.

What are the groupings for your Wendy's restaurant? It could be the item purchased, such as a Frosty, chili, hamburgers, and french fries, but this is where judgment—the qualitative aspect of marketing—comes in. Students really buy an

eating experience, or a meal that satisfies a need at a particular time of day, and so the product grouping can be defined by meal or time of day as breakfast, lunch, between-meal snack, dinner, and after-dinner snack. These groupings are more closely related to the way purchases are actually made and permit you to market the entire meal, not just your french fries or Frosties.

Step 3: Develop a Market-Product Grid and Estimate Size of Markets

Developing a market-product grid means labelling the markets (or horizontal rows) and products (or vertical columns), as shown in Figure 9–6. In addition, the size of the market in each cell, or the market-product combination, must be estimated. For your restaurant, this involves estimating the number of, or sales revenue obtained from, each kind of meal that can reasonably be expected to be sold to each market segment. This is a form of the usage rate analysis discussed earlier in the chapter.

The market sizes in Figure 9–6 may be simple "guesstimates" if you do not have time for formal marketing research (as discussed in Chapter 8). But even such crude estimates of the size of specific markets using a market-product grid are far better than the usual estimates of the entire market.

■ **FIGURE 9–6** ■

Selecting a target market for your fast-food restaurant next to an urban university (target market is shaded)

	PRODUCTS: MEALS				
MARKETS	**BREAK-FAST**	**LUNCH**	**BETWEEN-MEAL SNACK**	**DINNER**	**AFTER-DINNER SNACK**
STUDENT					
Dormitory	0	1	3	0	3
Apartment	1	3	3	1	1
Day commuter	0	3	2	1	0
Night commuter	0	0	1	3	2
NONSTUDENT					
Faculty or staff	0	3	1	1	0
Live in area	0	1	2	2	1
Work in area	1	3	0	1	0

Key: 3 = Large market; 2 = Medium market; 1 = Small market; 0 = No market.

Step 4: Select Target Markets

A firm must take care to choose its target market segments carefully. If it chooses too narrow a group of segments, it may fail to reach the volume of sales and profits it needs. If it selects too broad a group of segments, it may spread its marketing efforts so thin that the extra expenses more than offset the increased sales and profits.

Criteria to Use in Choosing the Target Segments　　Two different kinds of criteria are present in the market segmentation process: (1) those to use in dividing the market into segments (discussed earlier), and (2) those to use in actually choosing the target segments. Even experienced marketing executives often confuse these two different sets of criteria. The five criteria to use in actually selecting the target segments apply to your Wendy's restaurant in this way:

- *Market size.* The estimated size of the market in the segment is an important factor in deciding whether it is worth going after. There is really no market for breakfasts among campus students (see Figure 9–6); so why devote any marketing effort toward reaching a small or non-existent market?
- *Expected growth.* Although the size of the market in a segment may be small now, perhaps it is growing significantly or is expected to grow in the future. For example, the segment using drive-through ordering is growing three times faster than the eat-inside segment. So, having a fast-service drive-through facility may be critical for your restaurant's success.
- *Competitive position.* Is there a lot of competition in the segment now or is there likely to be in the future? The less the competition, the more attractive the segment is. For example, if the university cafeterias announce a new policy of "no meals on weekends," this segment is suddenly more promising for your restaurant.

ETHICS AND SOCIAL RESPONSIBILITY ALERT

De-selection of Customers or Customer Segments

Obviously, every organization has a right to determine the customer segments it wants to serve. And no one will dispute that organizations can do so as long as they are not discriminating against customers on the basis of race, ethnicity, or gender. However, as you have learned in this chapter, not all customers have the same value to an organization. In fact, in a world of high-technology and sophisticated segmentation analysis, many organizations are now able to discern the true costs and bottom-line value of individual consumers and/or given customer segments.

In most cases, good segmentation analysis reveals these hard numbers to show the real costs and contribution margins of certain customers. When this information is presented to executives, they may have to make some tough decisions. In some cases, it might mean to de-market or de-select certain customers. In other words, a firm might "fire" or quit the customer or invoke such practices as charging additional fees or restricting access to certain customer service levels, which might force some customers to find another alternative to do business with.

One bank, for example, determined through detailed segmentation analysis that certain customers were clearly less profitable, or even unprofitable, to serve compared with others. They started to charge a fee to those high-cost, low-profit customers if they used a teller at a branch or if they phoned a call centre for customer assistance. Many of these customers, upon finding charges of $2 per contact, decided to leave the bank, which is exactly what the bank intended. Others simply complained about unfair treatment and sought to have those fees removed from their statements. Another financial services company, finding that only their business-to-business (B2B) segment was highly profitable, simply stopped serving the business-to-consumer (B2C) market segment and informed those customers that they were exiting the B2C segment of the market, thus forcing this segment to find a new provider.

What do you think about the de-selection of customers or customer segments? Does a company have the right to de-select customers after segmentation analysis reveals that these customers are more costly to serve and/or contribute less to the profitability of the organization compared with other customers? If so, who will serve these customers?

- *Cost of reaching the segment.* A segment that is inaccessible to a firm's marketing actions should not be pursued. For example, the few nonstudents who live in the area may not be economically reachable with ads in newspapers or other media. As a result, do not waste money trying to advertise to them.
- *Compatibility with the organization's objectives and resources.* If your restaurant does not have the cooking equipment to make breakfasts and has a policy against spending more money on restaurant equipment, then do not try to reach the breakfast segment.

As is often the case in marketing decisions, a particular segment may appear attractive according to some criteria and very unattractive according to others.

Choose the Segments   Ultimately, a marketing executive has to use these criteria to choose the segments for special marketing efforts. As shown in Figure 9–6, let us assume you have written off the breakfast market for two reasons: too small market size and incompatibility with your objectives and resources. In terms of competitive position and cost of reaching the segment, you choose to focus on the four student segments and not the three nonstudent segments (although you are certainly not going to turn away business from the nonstudent segments). This combination of market-product segments—your target market—is shaded in Figure 9–6. In some cases, after selecting target markets, a firm may discover some segments may be too costly or unprofitable to serve. This may lead to de-selection of certain customers or segments, as the Ethics and Social Responsibility Alert box points out.

Step 5: Take Marketing Actions to Reach Target Markets

The purpose of developing a market-product grid is to trigger marketing actions to increase revenues and profits. This means that someone must develop and execute an action plan.

How can Wendy's target different market segments, such as drive-through customers, with different advertising programs? For the answer, see the text and Figure 9–7.

Your Wendy's Segmentation Strategy   With your Wendy's restaurant, you have already reached one significant decision: there is a limited market for breakfast, and so you will not open for business until 10:30 a.m. In fact, Wendy's first attempt at a breakfast menu was a disaster and was discontinued in 1986. Wendy's evaluates possible new menu items continuously, to compete not only with McDonald's and Burger King but also with a complex array of supermarkets, convenience stores, and gas stations that sell reheatable packaged foods as well as new "easy-lunch" products.

Another essential decision is where and what meals to advertise to reach specific market segments. An ad in the student newspaper could reach all the student segments, but you might consider this "shotgun approach" too expensive and want a more focused "rifle approach" to reach smaller segments. If you choose three segments for special actions (Figure 9–7), advertising actions to reach them might include:

- *Day commuters* (an entire market segment). Run ads inside commuter buses and put flyers under the windshield wipers of cars in parking lots used by day commuters. These ads and flyers promote all the meals at your restaurant to a single segment of students—a horizontal cut through the market-product grid.
- *Between-meals snacks* (directed to all four student markets). To promote eating during this downtime for your restaurant, offer "Ten percent off all purchases between 2:00 and 4:30 p.m. during the winter term." This ad promotes a single meal to all four student segments—a vertical cut through the market-product grid.

■ FIGURE 9-7 ■■
Advertising actions to reach
specific student segments

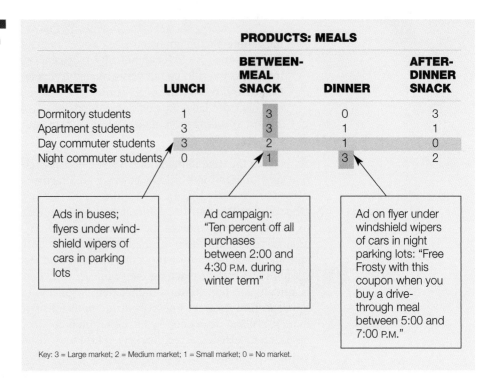

PRODUCTS: MEALS

MARKETS	LUNCH	BETWEEN-MEAL SNACK	DINNER	AFTER-DINNER SNACK
Dormitory students	1	3	0	3
Apartment students	3	3	1	1
Day commuter students	3	2	1	0
Night commuter students	0	1	3	2

Ads in buses; flyers under windshield wipers of cars in parking lots

Ad campaign: "Ten percent off all purchases between 2:00 and 4:30 P.M. during winter term"

Ad on flyer under windshield wipers of cars in night parking lots: "Free Frosty with this coupon when you buy a drive-through meal between 5:00 and 7:00 P.M."

Key: 3 = Large market; 2 = Medium market; 1 = Small market; 0 = No market.

- *Dinners to night commuters.* The most focused of all three campaigns, this ad promotes a single meal to a single student segment. The campaign might consist of a windshield flyer offering a free Frosty with the coupon when the customer buys a drive-through meal between 5:00 and 7:00 p.m.

Apple's Ever-Changing Segmentation Strategy   Steve Jobs and Steve Wozniak did not realize that they were developing today's multibillion-dollar PC industry when they invented the Apple I computer in a garage on April Fool's Day, 1976. Hobbyists, who were the initial target market, were not interested in the product. However, when the Apple II computer was displayed at a computer trade show in 1977, consumers loved it and Apple Computer was born. Typical of young companies, Apple focused on its products and had little concern for its markets. When IBM—"Big Blue"—entered the PC market in 1981, Apple was forced to become a "real company," much to the disappointment of its creative young engineers who were likened to "Boy Scouts without adult supervision."[13]

Fast-forward to the twenty-first century. Jobs believes that the personal computer entered the Age of the Digital Lifestyle in 2001. In a keynote address, Jobs said that "the proliferation of digital devices—CD players, MP3 players, cell phones, handheld organizers, digital cameras, digital camcorders, and more—will never have enough processing power and memory to stand alone." Jobs enthusiastically proclaimed, "the Mac can become the digital hub of this new digital lifestyle." By repositioning Apple as the "digital hub" with "killer apps," such as iTunes, iMovie, iDVD, iPhoto, and GarageBand—now bundled as iLife—Jobs believes consumers can take full advantage of the new digital lifestyle era.[14]

In most segmentation situations, a single product does not fit into an exclusive market niche. Rather, there is overlap among products in the product line and also among the markets to which they are directed. But a market segmentation strategy enables Apple to offer different products to meet the needs of different market segments, as shown in the accompanying Marketing NewsNet box. Stay tuned to see if Steve Jobs and these market-product strategies for his vision of the digital lifestyle era are on target. He is betting the company on it![15]

Original Apple II

What market segments for Apple's computers are represented by these products? The Marketing NewsNet and text discussion provide insights into Apple's market segmentation strategy.

Apple Computer

www.apple.com

Market–Product Synergies: A Balancing Act

Recognizing opportunities for key synergies—that is, efficiencies—is vital to success in selecting target market segments and making marketing decisions. Market–product grids illustrate where such synergies can be found. How? Let us consider Apple's market–product grid in the accompanying Marketing NewsNet box and examine the difference between marketing synergies and product synergies shown there.

- *Marketing synergies.* Running horizontally across the grid, each row represents an opportunity for efficiency in terms of a market segment. Were Apple to focus on just one group of consumers, such as the medium/large business segment, its marketing efforts could be streamlined. Time would not have to be spent learning about the buying habits of students or college faculty. So, it could probably do a single ad piece to reach the medium/large business target segment (the yellow row), highlighting the only products they would need to worry about developing: Power Mac G5, the PowerBook G4, and the iMac G5. Although clearly this is not Apple's strategy today, focusing on a single customer segment is a common marketing strategy for new companies.
- *Product synergies.* Running vertically down the market-product grid, each column represents an opportunity for efficiency in research and development (R&D) and production. If Apple wanted to simplify its product line, reduce R&D and production expenses, and manufacture only one computer, which might it choose? According to the market–product grid, Apple might do well to focus on the iMac G5 (the brown column), since the iMac G5 is purchased by most consumer segments—in this case, every segment.

Apple's Segmentation Strategy—Camp Runamok No Longer

Camp Runamok was the nickname given to Apple Computer in the early 1980s because the innovative company had no coherent series of product lines directed at identifiable market segments.

Today, Apple has targeted its various lines of Macintosh computers at specific market segments, as shown in the market–product grid below. Because the market–product grid shifts as a firm's strategy changes, the one below is based on Apple's product lines in late 2004. This market–product grid is a simplification because each product grouping consists of a line of Apple hardware products. Nevertheless, the grid suggests the market segmentation strategy Steve Jobs is using to compete in what he sees as the Age of the Digital Lifestyle, as described in the text.

MARKETS		HARDWARE PRODUCTS					
SECTOR	**SEGMENT**	Power Macintosh G5	PowerBook G4	iMac G5	iBook	eMac	iPod
CONSUMER	Individuals	✓	✓	✓	✓	✓	✓
CONSUMER	Small/home office	✓	✓	✓	✓	✓	
CONSUMER	Students			✓	✓	✓	✓
CONSUMER	Teachers	✓	✓	✓		✓	
PROFESSIONAL	Medium/large business	✓	✓	✓			
PROFESSIONAL	Creative	✓	✓	✓			✓
PROFESSIONAL	College faculty	✓	✓	✓			✓
PROFESSIONAL	College staff			✓	✓	✓	

A choice to take advantage of marketing synergies can often come at the expense of production ones because a single customer segment will likely require a variety of products, each of which will have to be designed and manufactured. The company saves money on marketing but spends more in production. Conversely, if product synergies are emphasized, marketing will have to address the concerns of a wide variety of consumers, which costs more time and money. Marketing managers responsible for developing a company's product line must balance both product and marketing synergies as they try to increase the company's profits.

CONCEPT CHECK

1. What are some criteria used to decide which segments to choose for targets?

2. In a market–product grid, what factor is estimated or measured for each of the cells?

3. What is the difference between marketing synergies and product synergies in a market–product grid?

■ ■ ■
POSITIONING THE PRODUCT

product positioning
The place an offering occupies in consumers' minds on important attributes relative to competitive products

product repositioning
Changing the place an offering occupies in a consumer's mind relative to competitive products.

When a company introduces a new product, a decision critical to its long-term success is how prospective buyers view it in relation to those products offered by its competitors. **Product positioning** refers to the place an offering occupies in consumers' minds on important attributes relative to competitive products. In contrast, **product repositioning** involves *changing* the place an offering occupies in a consumer's mind relative to competitive products.

Two Approaches to Product Positioning

There are two main approaches to positioning a new product in the market. *Head-to-head positioning* involves competing directly with competitors on similar product attributes in the same target market. Using this strategy, Dollar competes directly with Avis and Hertz.

Differentiation positioning involves seeking a less competitive, smaller market niche in which to locate a brand. McDonald's initially tried to appeal to the health-conscious segment and introduced its low-fat McLean Deluxe hamburger to avoid direct competition with Wendy's and Burger King. Companies also follow a differentiation positioning strategy among brands within their own product line to try to minimize cannibalization of a brand's sales or shares.

perceptual map
A means of displaying or graphing in two dimensions the location of products or brands in the minds of consumers to enable a manager to see how consumers perceive competing products or brands relative to its own and then take marketing actions.

Product Positioning Using Perceptual Maps

A key to positioning a product effectively is the perceptions of consumers. In determining a brand's position and the preferences of consumers, companies obtain three types of data from consumers:

1. Identification of the important attributes for a product class.
2. Judgments of existing brands with respect to these important attributes.
3. Ratings of an "ideal" brand's attributes.

From these data, it is possible to develop a **perceptual map**, a means of displaying or graphing in two dimensions the location of products or brands in the minds of consumers to enable a manager to see how consumers perceive competing products or brands relative to its own and then take marketing actions.

Figure 9–8 shows how a perceptual map can be used to develop positioning strategies for (1) milk drinks for children, and (2) chocolate milk for adults. The perceptual map in Figure 9–8 shows the positions that consumer beverages might occupy in the minds of consumers. Note that even these positions vary from one consumer to another. But for simplicity, assume these are the positions on the beverage perceptual map of typical North Americans.

Positioning Milk Drinks for Children   Assume that you work for a dairy or soft-drink company trying to develop for school children milk drinks that have more nutrition than soft drinks but more appeal than regular or chocolate milk. You can start by looking for holes or gaps in the perceptual map in Figure 9–8 that suggest a possible position for a milk drink that would have more nutritional value than soft drinks. Here is what companies did:

How can dairies put more zip into chocolate milk sales? To discover their successful positioning strategy, see the text.

- *Finding a position for milk drinks.* Marketing managers looked at this kind of perceptual map and picked a position about at point C in Figure 9–8. This is in a relatively big gap between regular milk and fruit-flavoured drinks and shows the increased nutritional value of the milk drinks.
- *Developing the product and flavours.* In mid-2003, Coca-Cola and Cadbury Schweppes PLC both developed "dairy drinks" positioned at point C, with just

Good nutrition is an increasing concern. It gets highlighted in comparing recent annual capita consumption of soft drinks versus milk: 52 gallons (197 l) of soft drinks versus 25 gallons (95 l) of milk, even with all milk's benefits of calcium and vitamins.[16] Here are two product positioning actions featuring milk products to address these nutrition concerns.

MILK DRINKS FOR KIDS: POSITIONING A NEW PRODUCT   Nutrition is a special concern for North American school children, where childhood obesity is growing. Soft-drink companies, criticized heavily for pushing soda sales in schools, are seeking both to "buff their image and build sales."[17] Study the perceptual map at the right and identify (a) in which lettered location a beverage company might position new milk drinks, and (b) what the product and some flavours might be to appeal to schoolchildren.

CHOCOLATE MILK FOR ADULTS: REPOSITIONING AN EXISTING PRODUCT   Several years ago, dairies got the idea to target chocolate milk sales at a new market—adults. Note on the perceptual map where adults positioned chocolate milk then, and suggest (a) in which lettered location dairies might reposition chocolate milk targeted at adults, and (b) what kind of packaging might appeal to them.

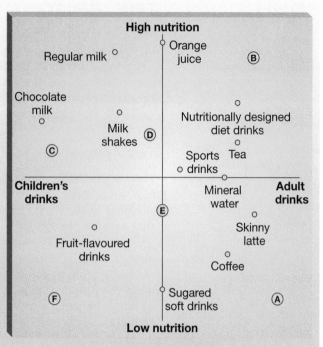

■ **FIGURE 9–8** ■

Using positioning and perceptual maps to increase milk sales to children and adults

over half being regular milk and the rest being water, sugar, and flavourings. Although calories and sugar are concerns, these drinks have nutritional value that is missing in soft drinks. Sample flavours? Cadbury's Raging Cow started with five flavours, including Chocolate Insanity, Piña Colada Chaos, and Jamocha Frenzy.[18]

Not to be left behind, some dairies have responded with new 100 percent milk drinks with extra sugar and flavours like Pleasin' Punch and Root Beer Float. The position of these milk drinks, sample flavours, and their packaging appear in Figure 9–9.

Repositioning Chocolate Milk for Adults   A few years ago, dairies, struggling to increase milk sales, hit on a wild idea: Try to reposition chocolate milk to make it appeal to adults. The term *adults* in this sense probably means 18 years old and older. The dairies' arguments are nutritionally powerful. For example, chocolate milk provides calcium and vitamins, critically important in adult diets. And dieters get a more filling, nutritious beverage than with a soft drink for about the same calories.[19] Here is what some dairies have done:

- *Finding a new position for chocolate milk in the minds of adults.* In Figure 9–8, dairies sought to do two things: (1) move chocolate milk to the right to make it a more respectable "adult drink," and (2) move it up on the nutrition scale. The result is a repositioning at about point B in Figure 9–8, a dramatic move as shown in Figure 9–9.
- *Packaging "adult" chocolate milk.* Sample packages, some designed to fit in car beverage holders, are shown in Figure 9–9. The result has been a significant increase in chocolate milk consumption among adults. Have you seen chocolate milk in containers like these in your college cafeteria?

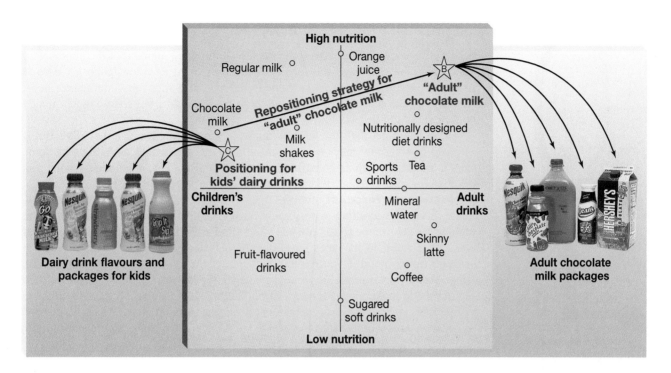

■ FIGURE 9–9 ■

Strategies for positioning dairy drinks for kids and repositioning chocolate milk to reach adults

With the success of these drinks, dairies are now offering other new, nonchocolate grown-up milks, such as a caramel Dulce de Leche milk and a coffee-flavoured milk with decaffeinated Brazilian roast coffee that tastes like coffee ice cream. And Krispy Kreme in its doughnut shops sells hot and cold milk in such flavours as vanilla, cinnamon, and raspberry, plus its signature "original Kreme."[20]

And for the superadventurous, there are *carbonated* flavoured milk beverages.[21] Question 6 in the end-of-chapter Discussion and Application Questions asks you to identify the target market and positioning strategies for these beverages.

■ ■ ■
SALES FORECASTING TECHNIQUES

Forecasting or estimating potential sales is critical when segmenting and selecting target markets. Good sales forecasts are also important for a firm as it schedules production.[22]

market (industry) potential

The maximum total sales of a product by all firms to a segment during a specified time period under specified environmental conditions and marketing efforts of the firms.

sales (company) forecast

The total sales of a product that a firm expects to sell during a specified time period under specified environmental conditions and its own marketing efforts.

The term **market potential**, or **industry potential**, refers to the maximum total sales of a product by all firms to a segment during a specified time period under specified environmental conditions and marketing efforts of the firms. For example, the market potential for cake mix sales to Canadian consumers in 2008 might be 1.2 million cases—what Pillsbury, Betty Crocker, Aurora Foods, and other cake mix producers would sell to Canadian consumers under the assumptions that (1) past patterns of dessert consumption continue, and (2) the same level of promotional effort continues relative to other desserts. The term **sales forecast**, or **company forecast**, refers to the total sales of a product that a firm expects to sell during a specified time period under specified environmental conditions and its own marketing efforts. For example, Betty Crocker might develop a sales forecast of 400 000 cases of cake mix for consumers in 2008, assuming consumers' dessert preferences remain constant and competitors do not change prices.

Three main sales forecasting techniques are often used: (1) judgments of the decision maker, (2) surveys of knowledgeable groups, and (3) statistical methods.

How might a marketing manager for Wilson tennis rackets forecast sales through 2007? Use a lost-horse forecast, as described in the text.

direct forecast
Estimating the value to be forecast without any intervening steps.

lost-horse forecast
Making a forecast using the last known value and modifying it according to positive or negative factors expected in the future.

survey of buyers' intentions forecast
Asking prospective customers if they are likely to buy the product during some future time period.

salesforce survey forecast
Asking the firm's salespeople to estimate sales during a coming period.

trend extrapolation
Extending a pattern observed in past data into the future.

linear trend extrapolation
The pattern is described with a straight line.

Judgments of the Decision Maker

Probably 99 percent of all sales forecasts are simply the judgment of the person who must act on the results of the forecast—the individual decision maker. A **direct forecast** involves estimating the value to be forecast without any intervening steps. Examples appear daily: How many quarts of milk should I buy? How much money should I get out of the ATM?

You probably get the same cash withdrawal most times you use the ATM. But if you need to withdraw more than the usual amount, you would probably take some intervening steps (such as counting the cash in your pocket or estimating what you will need for special events this week) to obtain your direct forecast.

A **lost-horse forecast** involves making a forecast using the last known value and modifying it according to positive or negative factors expected in the future. The technique gets its name from how you would find a lost horse: go to where it was last seen, put yourself in its shoes, consider those factors that could affect where you might go (to the pond if you are thirsty, the hayfield if you are hungry, and so on), and go there. For example, a product manager for Wilson's tennis rackets in 2006 who needed to make a sales forecast through 2009 would start with the known value of 2006 sales and list the positive factors (more tennis courts, more TV publicity) and the negative ones (competition from other sports, high prices of graphite and ceramic rackets) to arrive at the final series of annual sales forecasts.

Surveys of Knowledgeable Groups

If you wonder what your firm's sales will be next year, ask people who are likely to know something about future sales. Two common groups that are surveyed to develop sales forecasts are prospective buyers and the firm's salesforce.

A **survey of buyers' intentions forecast** involves asking prospective customers if they are likely to buy the product during some future time period. For industrial products with few prospective buyers, this can be effective. There are only a few hundred customers in the entire world for Boeing's largest airplanes, and so Boeing surveys them to develop its sales forecasts and production schedules.

A **salesforce survey forecast** involves asking the firm's salespeople to estimate sales during a coming period. Because these people are in contact with customers and are likely to know what customers like and dislike, there is logic to this approach. However, salespeople can be unreliable forecasters—painting too rosy a picture if they are enthusiastic about a new product and too grim a forecast if their sales quota and future compensation are based on it.

Statistical Methods

The best-known statistical method of forecasting is **trend extrapolation**, which involves extending a pattern observed in past data into the future. When the pattern is described with a straight line, it is **linear trend extrapolation**. Suppose that in early 2000 you were a sales forecaster for the Xerox Corporation and had actual sales running from 1988 to 1999 (Figure 9–10). Using linear trend extrapolation, you draw a line to fit the past data and project it into the future to give the forecast values shown for 2000 to 2006.[23]

If in 2004 you want to compare your forecasts with actual results, you are in for a surprise—illustrating the strength and weakness of trend extrapolation. Trend extrapolation assumes that the underlying relationships in the past will continue into the future, which is the basis of the method's key strength: simplicity. If this assumption proves correct, you have an accurate forecast. However, if this proves wrong, the forecast is likely to be wrong. In this case, your forecasts from 2001 through 2003 were too high, as shown in Figure 9–10, largely because of fierce competition in the photocopying industry.

■ **FIGURE 9–10** ■

Linear trend extrapolation of
sales revenues of Xerox,
made at the start of 2000

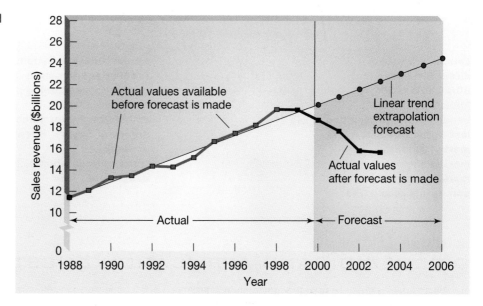

CONCEPT CHECK	**1.** Why do marketers use perceptual maps in product positioning decisions?
	2. What are the three kinds of sales forecasting techniques?
	3. How do you make a lost-horse forecast?

■ ■ ■
CHAPTER IN REVIEW

1 *Explain what market segmentation is and when to use it.*
Market segmentation involves aggregating prospective buyers into groups that (*a*) have common needs, and (*b*) will respond similarly to a marketing action. Organizations go to the trouble and expense of segmenting their markets when it increases their sales, profits, and ability to serve customers better.

2 *Identify the five steps involved in segmenting and targeting markets.*
Step 1 is to group potential buyers into segments. Buyers within a segment should have similar characteristics to each other and respond similarly to marketing actions, such as a new product or a lower price. Step 2 involves putting related products to be sold into groups. In step 3, organizations develop a market-product grid with estimated size of markets in each of the market-product cells of the resulting table. Step 4 involves selecting the target market segments on which the organization should focus. Step 5 involves taking marketing mix actions—often in the form of a marketing program—to reach the target market segments.

3 *Recognize the different factors used to segment consumer and organizational markets.*
Factors used to segment consumer markets include customer characteristics (geographic, demographic, psychographic, and behavioural variables). Organizational markets use related variables, often combining them to create what is called firmographics.

4 *Know how to develop a market–product grid to identify a target market and recommend resulting actions.*
Organizations use five key criteria to segment markets, whose groupings appear in the rows of the market–product grid. Groups of related products appear in the columns. After estimating the size of market in each cell in the grid, they select the target market segments on which to focus. They then identify marketing mix actions—often in a marketing program—to reach the target market most efficiently.

5 *Explain how marketing managers position products in the marketplace.*
Marketing managers often locate competing products on two-dimensional perceptual maps to visualize the products in the minds of consumers. They then try to position new products or reposition existing products in this space to attain the maximum sales and profits.

6 *Describe three approaches to developing a sales forecast for a company.*
One approach uses subjective judgments of the decision maker, such as direct or lost-horse forecasts. Surveys of knowledgeable groups is a second method. It involves obtaining such information as the intentions of potential buyers or estimates of the salesforce. Statistical methods involving extending a pattern observed in past data into the future is a third example. The best-known example is linear trend extrapolation.

■ ■ ■

FOCUSING ON KEY TERMS

company forecast p. 245
direct forecast p. 246
80/20 rule p. 234
industry potential p. 245
linear trend extrapolation p. 246
lost-horse forecast p. 246
market potential p. 245
market segments p. 227
market–product grid p. 228
perceptual map p. 243

product differentiation p. 227
product positioning p. 243
product repositioning p. 243
sales forecast p. 245
salesforce survey forecast p. 246
survey of buyers' intentions forecast p. 246
synergy p. 231
trend extrapolation p. 246
usage rate p. 234

■ ■ ■

DISCUSSION AND APPLICATION QUESTIONS

1 What variables might be used to segment these consumer markets? (*a*) lawnmowers, (*b*) frozen dinners, (*c*) dry breakfast cereals, and (*d*) soft drinks.

2 What variables might be used to segment these industrial markets? (*a*) industrial sweepers, (*b*) photocopiers, (*c*) computerized production control systems, and (*d*) car rental agencies.

3 In Figure 9–6, the dormitory market segment includes students living in college-owned residence halls, sororities, and fraternities. What market needs are common to these students that justify combining them into a single segment in studying the market for your Wendy's restaurant?

4 You may disagree with the estimates of market size given for the rows in the market–product grid in Figure 9–6. Estimate the market size, and give a brief justification for these market segments: (*a*) dormitory students, (*b*) day commuters, and (*c*) people who work in the area.

5 Suppose you want to increase revenues for your fast-food restaurant even further. Referring to Figure 9–7, what advertising actions might you take to increase revenues from (*a*) dormitory students, (*b*) dinners, and (*c*) after-dinner snacks from night commuters?

6 In 1999, entrepreneurs Mary Ann and George Clark founded MacFarms, Inc., to introduce milk beverages with enough appeal to wean children from soft drinks and athlete-oriented drinks. Their patented invention: carbonated milk beverages in various flavours. Look again at Figure 9–8 and (*a*) select one of the lettered positions on the perceptual map, and (*b*) suggest packaging for these drinks.

7 For which of the following variables would linear trend extrapolation be more accurate? (*a*) Annual population of Canada, or (*b*) annual sales of cars produced in Canada by General Motors. Why?

GOING ONLINE   **Apple's Latest Market-Product Strategies**

In its 25-year history, Apple Computer has initiated a series of creative market segmentation strategies, with new product lines targeted at specific market segments. For the latest updates of Apple's market-product strategies, go to www.apple-history.com, and click on the "Intro" and "History" menu options. As you read the narrative, identify the new and remaining markets

Apple has targeted with new and existing products compared with those described in the text and the Marketing NewsNet box. Do you think Apple will succeed in its quest to lead us into the digital lifestyle age? Can Apple survive as a niche PC marketer like BMW has with autos? Why, or why not?

Do you want to get better grades and stay up to date with current issues in marketing? Visit the Online Learning Centre at www.mcgrawhill.ca/college/crane for practice tests, video cases, resources for building a marketing plan, *Globe and Mail* headlines, access to *Marketing Magazine*, and other learning and study tools.

VIDEO CASE 9 · Cybersurf Corporation

On May 18, 2004, Jason Finney, vice-president Product Development of Cybersurf Corp. ("Cybersurf") (TSX Venture: CY), one of Canada's leading Internet services and technology companies, sat in his downtown Calgary office and read over the company's latest press release:

"Cybersurf announced today that it has begun selling high-speed Cable Internet over Shaw's Network in Shaw's Calgary area serving the market as of May 17, 2004.

For the time being, Cybersurf will be operating with the benefit of a resale arrangement pursuant to the terms of a decision rendered by the Canadian Radio Television and Telecommunications Commission (CRTC).... Pursuant to that decision, Shaw must open additional markets (serving areas) to Cybersurf for resale in two-week intervals upon request sequentially after the first market is opened .... Cybersurf has already requested from Shaw the Vancouver area market as its next market.

Cybersurf has had ... agreements with Shaw since November 2002 that entitle it to direct intersection with the Shaw Network in each Shaw serving area west of Thunder Bay, Ontario, to Victoria, British Columbia .... Cybersurf hopes for fulfillment of those agreements with Shaw for direct access in most major western markets in the near future but will in the interim operate under a resale arrangement regime with Shaw in its various markets.

Combined with current and planned intersections with Rogers Cable in Ontario, ... and (other) agreements in Ontario and Quebec with Bell, Cybersurf will be the first Internet Service Provider to possess national high-speed access on its own Network, and will also be the first Independent to access Shaw's Network.

Calgarians can visit http://www.get3web.com to sign up for Cybersurf's Cable High Speed service immediately. Cybersurf plans to roll out 3webXS for Broadband in Vancouver on June 2, 2004."[24]

Jason was elated about this development. After over a year and a half of negotiations with Shaw, and the necessity of repeated intervention by the CRTC, Cybersurf was finally in a position to provide Canadians in the west with a competitive alternative to traditional Internet Service Providers (ISPs), such as Telus, MTS, and Shaw. Basically, the details of the agreement between Cybersurf and Shaw are such that Shaw will make its high-speed Internet service available to Cybersurf for resale as its own branded ISP service. This service will be sold at a 25-percent discount from Shaw's lowest retail rate, including promotions and discounts, until such time that Shaw complies with Third Party Internet (Access) Agreement ("TPIA") as mandated by

the CRTC. In 2003, Cybersurf had signed a similar TPIA with Rogers Cable Inc. as well as a wholesale DSL agreement with Bell to allow the provision of an unlimited 3web High Speed service to customers throughout Ontario and Quebec.

As a result of this most recent agreement with Shaw, Cybersurf would be able to provide western Canadians high-speed Internet access close to the price that the competitors were charging for dial-up service. The company had already captured a significant portion of the dial-up market and Finney hoped that this would be the breakthrough that Cybersurf needed to allow them to gain a foothold in the high-speed market in Canada.

CYBERSURF—THE COMPANY

Cybersurf is a Canadian technology company dedicated to the development and deployment of innovative software solutions for Internet service, Internet portal, and new media applications. Products include direct user targeting and guaranteed ad message delivery software; a comprehensive, turnkey portal that any ISP can adopt as its own; and animation technology that delivers television quality to a user's desktop.

Cybersurf's product applications are designed to maximize available resources, reduce operating costs and create new revenue opportunities. Cybersurf's technology solutions provide a cost-effective structure to companies that use them. The company's mission since 1995 has been to provide the highest quality products and services to its Canadian customers at the lowest possible prices.

3WEB'S MISSION STATEMENT

3web Corp., a wholly owned subsidiary of Cybersurf Corp., is one of Canada's largest independent ISPs. Through its 3webXS service, 3web provides its subscribers with premium, unlimited Internet access across the country, at a fraction of the cost of competing services. 3web Corp. has served hundreds of thousands of Canadians from coast to coast with dial-up service since 1998, providing Internet access in 30 major centres.

According to the 3web Web site (www.get3web.com), what customers get with 3web is "value-priced communication products and services for significantly less than the competition, but at a quality level equal to or better than the others." It offers a total communications solution, providing high-speed Internet access, dial-up Internet access, and long distance plans that suit individual needs.

3WEBXS FOR BROADBAND HIGH SPEED

Management of Cybersurf has known that their customers have wanted cost-conscious high-speed Internet access for a long time. Several months of careful planning, involving infrastructure provision agreements, has finally come to fruition. Finney knew that while dial-up remained a strong growth market for Cybersurf, they also needed to cater to the portion of their customers who were beginning to search for a high-speed Internet product. By offering a competitively priced high-speed option, Finney was confident that Cybersurf would be able to meet the evolving needs of their current customer base while attracting new customers in the market for a low-cost cable Internet alternative.

Once the affiliation with Shaw was secured, 3web immediately began to promote itself as "Canada's best deal in both Cable and DSL high-speed Internet access!" 3web states that it offers its customers the same quality, same speed broadband service as Bell™, Rogers, Shaw, and Telus but for less, a lot less. In a product/feature comparison chart shown on the 3web Web site, 3web's price for unlimited high-speed service (regular not lite) ranges from 29.95/month to 24.95/month (discounted price for those customers who also sign up for long distance service). Monthly rates for five other major ISP competitors are also shown, and these range from $29.95 (lite service only) to $54.95/month. In addition, connection speeds promoted by 3web are just as fast as or faster than all other competitors. 3web also offers free unlimited dial-up access with a subscription to either a cable or DSL high-speed account. For travelling customers, this can be a significant added bonus and is unique to a 3web subscription, given that all other competing ISPs have limitations for the number of dial-up hours allowed.

DIAL-UP AND HIGH-SPEED INTERNET MARKET IN CANADA

If Cybersurf is to remain a major player in the Internet market in Canada, management knows that movement toward the provision of high-speed access is imperative. According to research conducted by Industry Canada, "The use of Internet has grown considerably in recent years. In 1999, 29 percent of households (3.3 million connected households) had either dial-up or high-speed Internet access at home. As of December

2002, there were approximately 7.4 million subscribers of dial-up, DSL, or cable Internet access in Canada, of which over 46 percent had a high-speed connection."[25] In terms of who is actually using the Internet, rates of Internet use vary across family types; however, singe-family households with unmarried children under the age of 18 had the highest rate of Internet use from any location in 2001, about 80 percent. This proportion was double the level of 38 percent in 1997. As well, research has revealed that all households of all income levels experienced increases in Internet adoption. In 2001, 87 percent of the households in the highest income bracket used the Internet, up from 58 percent in 1997. In contrast, while only 32 percent of the households with the lowest income level regularly used the Internet in 2001, this was still almost triple the rate of 12 percent in 1997.[26]

The rapid growth of the Internet and its expanding applications has transformed it from a specialty service with a limited market to a mass-market service targeting a wide audience.

FUTURE OUTLOOK

Finney believes many Canadians want "the freedom of choice" that comes with having an independent provider as an alternative to Canada's dominant ISPs. This new offering would allow users to connect to the Internet with an independent provider that focuses on the needs of today's average user by providing quality service at the best possible price. As he sat back and reflected again on the news release, Finney could not help but feel confident about the positioning and acceptance of this new product offering in the marketplace.

QUESTIONS

1 Define positioning strategy, and select a statement from the case that best depicts 3web's positioning approach.

2 Explain the relationship between market segmentation and product positioning.

3 Identify and describe the two major markets for ISPs in Canada.

4 Visit 3web's Web site (www.get3web.com), and provide examples of how 3web's product positioning is demonstrated in their Internet advertising.

5 Research the Web sites of some of the ISP competitors mentioned in this case. What are the primary elements of their positioning strategies?

PART

4

SATISFYING MARKETING OPPORTUNITIES

HOW PART 4 FITS INTO THE BOOK

The chapters in Part 4 cover the marketing mix—the four P's—that are the key product, price, place, and promotion actions marketing managers use to implement their marketing program.

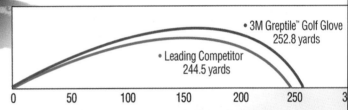
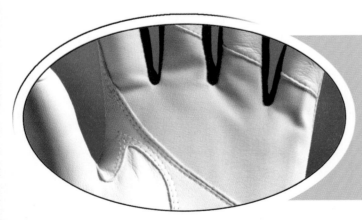

DEVELOPING NEW PRODUCTS AND SERVICES

LEARNING OBJECTIVES

After reading this chapter, you should be able to:

1 Recognize the various terms that pertain to products and services.

2 Identify the ways in which consumer and business goods and services can be classified.

3 Explain the implications of alternative ways of viewing "newness" in new products and services.

4 Describe the factors contributing to a product's or service's failure.

5 Explain the purposes of each step of the new-product process.

3M'S NEW GREPTILE GRIP GOLF GLOVE: HOW TO GET TO THE TOP OF THE LEADER BOARD

"We look around the company for under-utilized technologies that can result in exciting new products for niche markets," says Dr. George Dierberger, marketing and international manager for Sports and Leisure Products at 3M™. Turning 3M's micro-replication technology into a golf glove is a prime example.

To ensure that retailers will carry the innovative 3M Greptile™ Grip golf glove and that prospective golfers will buy and use it, Dierberger helps them discover its benefits and learn about the technology behind it. The benefits: to help golfers wearing the glove to hit longer drives and more accurate shots, thus getting lower scores through improved control of the golf club swing under both wet and dry conditions. Here is a quick take on the marketing issues Dierberger faced when introducing this new product:[1]

- *The product*? A golf glove that integrates 3M's revolutionary Greptile urethane gripping material, a technology that consists of thousands of "microscopic fingers," into a golf glove. The material is sewn in the "gripping channel" of the lower fingers and upper palm on the underside of the glove to reduce the slip of a golfer's grip when swinging the club.
- *The target market*? Golfers who want to improve their scores—only, say, 100 percent of the market. But then the market segments get more specific: golfers playing in hot or humid conditions, or those needing a stronger grip due to their skill level, age, or arthritis.
- *The special marketing task*? Leverage 3M's strong brand reputation for using its world-class technologies to introduce innovative, high-quality products in the adhesives, office supply, health care, and other markets as a means of entering the intensely competitive golf equipment market.

Dierberger and his marketing and engineering staff created the ad for distributors and retailers (shown on page 254). 3M has developed a two-stage marketing program for the golf glove: initially, a moderately priced 3M Greptile Grip golf glove will be sold in mass merchandise retailers, such as Wal-Mart. Then, 3M will introduce a premium version of the golf glove in golf course pro shops, golf superstores, sporting goods superstores, and sporting goods retailers. The team's continuing challenge is to communicate the product's benefits in its packaging and promotions to its targeted retailers and customers to overcome the lack of 3M brand recognition in a market dominated by FootJoy, Titleist, Nike, and other golf glove marketers.

A brief look at some 3M products shows how its new-product research has enabled the company to become a global leader in adhesive technology. This has led to dozens of 3M adhesive products. Some examples, varying by the degree of adhesive stickiness, include:

- *Permanent adhesive bonding.* VHB™ (for "very high bond") tape made with high-strength acrylic, pressure-sensitive adhesives that can make a continuous bond stronger than spot welds or rivets for such applications as for cargo trailers and highway signs.
- *One-time adhesion.* Nexcare™ Tattoo™ Waterproof Bandages for kids that combine superior, waterproof wound protection, with fun designs.
- *Multiple-time adhesion.* Post-it® Notes that enable you to stick and unstick that note to your friend over and over again.
- *No adhesion, but better gripping.* The Greptile Grip golf glove with its urethane gripping material that was discussed above.

The essence of marketing is in developing such products as a new, technologically advanced adhesive to meet buyer needs. A **product** is a good, service, or idea consisting of a bundle of tangible and intangible attributes that satisfies consumers and is received in exchange for money or some other unit of value. Tangible attributes include physical characteristics, such as colour or sweetness, and intangible attributes include better health or more wealth. Hence, a product includes the breakfast cereal you eat, the accountant who fills out your tax return, or your local art museum.

The life of a company often depends on how it conceives, produces, and markets new products. This is the exact reason that 3M spends $1.1 billion on research annually and has over 5000 engineers and scientists around the globe looking for what *BusinessWeek* calls the Next Big Thing for 3M.[2] Later, we describe how 3M strives to "delight its customers" using cross-functional teams and "Six Sigma" initiatives.

This chapter covers decisions involved in developing and marketing new products and services. Chapters 11 and 12 discuss the process of managing existing products and services, respectively.

product
A good, service, or idea consisting of a bundle of tangible and intangible attributes that satisfies consumers and is received in exchange for money or some other unit of value.

■ ■ ■
THE VARIATIONS OF PRODUCTS

A product varies in terms of whether it is a consumer or business good. For most organizations, the product decision is not made in isolation because companies often offer a range of products. To better appreciate the product decision, let us first define some terms pertaining to products.

Product Line and Product Mix

A **product line** is a group of products that are closely related because they satisfy a class of needs, are used together, are sold to the same customer group, are distributed through the same type of outlets, or fall within a given price range. Polaroid Canada has two major product lines consisting of cameras and film; Nike's product lines are shoes and clothing; the Toronto Hospital for Sick Children's product lines consist of

product line
A group of products that are closely related because they satisfy a class of needs, are used together, are sold to the same customer group, are distributed through the same outlets, or fall within a given price range.

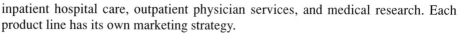

inpatient hospital care, outpatient physician services, and medical research. Each product line has its own marketing strategy.

Within each product line is the *product item*, a specific product as noted by a unique brand, size, or price. For example, Downy softener for clothes comes in 360-mL and 700-mL sizes; each size is considered a separate item and assigned a distinct ordering code, or *stock-keeping unit* (*SKU*).

product mix
The number of product lines offered by a company.

The third way to look at products is by the **product mix**, or the number of product lines offered by a company. Cray Research has a single product line consisting of supercomputers, which are sold mostly to governments and large businesses. Pillsbury Canada, however, has many product lines, including Green Giant canned and frozen vegetables, Pillsbury refrigerated baked goods, Prima Pasta, Old El Paso Mexican foods, and Underwood meat spreads.

Classifying Products

consumer goods
Products purchased by the ultimate consumer.

business goods
Products that assist directly or indirectly in providing products for resale (also known as *B2B goods, industrial goods, or organizational goods*).

Both the federal government and companies classify products, but for different purposes. The government's classification method helps it collect information on industrial activity. Companies classify products to help develop similar marketing strategies for the wide range of products offered. Two major ways to classify products are by type of user and degree of product tangibility.

Type of User   A major type of product classification is based on the type of user. **Consumer goods** are products purchased by the ultimate consumer, whereas **business goods** (also called B2B goods, industrial goods, or organizational goods) are products that assist directly or indirectly in providing products for resale. In many instances, the differences are distinct: Oil of Olay face moisturizer and Bass shoes are clearly consumer products, whereas Cray computers and high-tension steel springs are business goods used in producing other products or services.

Specialty goods, such as Raymond Weil watches, require distinct marketing programs to reach narrow target markets.

There are difficulties, however, with this classification because some products can be considered both consumer and business items. An HP computer can be sold to consumers as a final product or to business firms for office use. Each classification results in different marketing actions. Viewed as a consumer product, the HP would be sold through computer stores or direct from its Web site. As a business product, the HP might be sold by a salesperson offering discounts for multiple purchases. Classifying by the type of user focuses on the market and the user's purchase behaviour, which determine the marketing mix strategy.

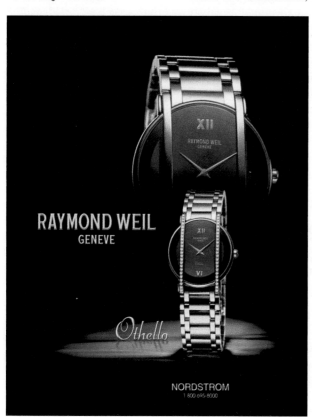

Degree of Tangibility   Classification by degree of tangibility divides products into one of three categories. First is a *nondurable good*, an item consumed in one or a few uses, such as food products and fuel. A *durable good* is one that usually lasts over an extended number of uses, such as appliances, automobiles, and stereo equipment. *Services* are defined as activities, deeds, or other basic tangibles offered for sale to consumers in exchange for money or something else of value. According to this classification, government data indicate that Canada has a service economy, the reason for a separate chapter (Chapter 12) on the topic.

This classification method also provides direction for marketing actions. Nondurable products, such as

Wrigley's gum, are purchased frequently and at relatively low cost. Advertising is important to remind consumers of the item's existence, and wide distribution in retail outlets is essential. A consumer wanting Wrigley's Spearmint Gum would most likely purchase another brand of spearmint gum if Wrigley's were not available. Durable products, however, generally cost more than nondurable goods and last longer, and so consumers usually deliberate longer before purchasing them. Therefore, personal selling is an important component in durable-product marketing because it assists in answering consumer questions and concerns.

Services and New-Product Development   Developing new services, like a new airline service or a new television show, is often difficult to observe step by step. Nevertheless, service innovations do occur and can have a major impact on our lives. For example, online banking and online brokerage firms have revolutionized the financial services industry, while online travel agencies have changed the way we make travel reservations.

■ ■ ■
CLASSIFYING CONSUMER AND BUSINESS GOODS

Because the buyer is the key to marketing, consumer and business product classifications are discussed in greater detail.

Classification of Consumer Goods

convenience goods
Items that the consumer purchases frequently and with a minimum of shopping effort.

shopping goods
Items for which the consumer compares several alternatives on such criteria as price, quality, or style.

specialty goods
Items that a consumer makes a special effort to search out and buy.

unsought goods
Items that the consumer either does not know about or knows about but does not initially want.

Convenience, shopping, specialty, and unsought products are the four types of consumer goods. They differ in terms of (1) effort the consumer expends on the decision, (2) attributes used in purchase, and (3) frequency of purchase.

Convenience goods are items that the consumer purchases frequently, conveniently, and with a minimum of shopping effort. **Shopping goods** are items for which the consumer compares several alternatives on criteria, such as price, quality, or style. **Specialty goods** are items, such as Tiffany sterling silver, that a consumer makes a special effort to search out and buy. **Unsought goods** are items that the consumer either does not know about or knows about but does not initially want. Figure 10–1 shows how the classification of a consumer product into one of these four types results in different aspects of the marketing mix being stressed. Different degrees of brand loyalty and amounts of shopping effort are displayed by the consumer for a product in each of the four classes.

The manner in which a consumer good is classified depends on the individual. One person may view a camera as a shopping good and visit several stores before deciding on a brand, whereas a friend may view cameras as a specialty good and will only buy a Nikon.

Classification of Business Goods

A major characteristic of business goods is that their sales are often the result of *derived demand*; that is, sales of business goods frequently result (or are derived) from the sale of consumer goods. For example, if consumer demand for Ford cars (a consumer product) increases, the company may increase its demand for paint-spraying equipment (a business good). Business goods may be classified as production or support goods.

production goods
Items used in the manufacturing process that become part of the final product.

Production Goods   Items used in the manufacturing process that become part of the final product are **production goods.** These include raw materials, such as grain or lumber, as well as component parts. For example, a company that

TYPE OF CONSUMER GOOD

BASIS OF COMPARISON	CONVENIENCE	SHOPPING	SPECIALTY	UNSOUGHT
Product	Toothpaste, cake mix, hand soap, laundry detergent	Cameras, TVs, briefcases, clothing	Rolls Royce cars, Rolex watches	Burial insurance, thesaurus
Price	Relatively inexpensive	Fairly expensive	Usually very expensive	Varies
Place (distribution)	Widespread; many outlets	Large number of selective outlets	Very limited	Often limited
Promotion	Price, availability, and awareness stressed	Differentiation from competitors stressed	Uniqueness of brand and status stressed	Awareness is essential
Brand loyalty of consumers	Aware of brand, but will accept substitutes	Prefer specific brands, but will accept substitutes	Very brand loyal; will not accept substitutes	Will accept substitutes
Purchase behaviour of consumers	Frequent purchases; little time and effort spent shopping	Infrequent purchases; needs much comparison shopping time	Infrequent purchases; needs extensive search and decision time	Very infrequent purchases; some comparison shopping

■ **FIGURE 10–1** ■
Classification of consumer goods

support goods
Items used to assist in producing other goods and services.

manufactures door hinges used by GM in its car doors is producing a component part. As noted in Chapter 6, the marketing of production goods is based on such factors as price, quality, delivery, and service. Marketers of these products tend to sell directly to business users.

Support Goods   The second class of business goods is **support goods**, which are items used to assist in producing other goods and services. Support goods include installations, accessory equipment, supplies, and services.

- *Installations* consist of buildings and fixed equipment. Because a significant amount of capital is required to purchase installations, the business buyer deals directly with construction companies and manufacturers through sales representatives. The pricing of installations is often by competitive bidding.
- *Accessory equipment* includes tools and office equipment and is usually purchased in small-order sizes by buyers. As a result, instead of dealing directly with buyers, sellers of business accessories use distributors to contact a large number of buyers.
- *Supplies* are similar to consumer convenience goods and consist of such products as stationery, paper clips, and brooms. These are purchased with little effort, using the straight rebuy decision sequence discussed in Chapter 6. Price and delivery are key factors considered by the buyers of supplies.
- *Services* are intangible activities to assist the business buyer. This category can include maintenance and repair services and advisory services, such as tax or legal counsel, where the seller's reputation is critical.

CONCEPT CHECK

1. Explain the difference between product mix and product line.

2. What are the four main types of consumer goods?

3. To which type of good (business or consumer) does the term *derived demand* generally apply?

■ ■ ■

NEW PRODUCTS AND WHY THEY SUCCEED OR FAIL

New products are the lifeblood of a company and keep it growing, but the associated financial risks are large. Before discussing how new products reach the stage of commercialization when they are in the market, we will begin by looking at *what* a new product is.

What Is a New Product?

The term *new* is difficult to define. Is Sony's PlayStation Portable (PSP) *new* when there was a PlayStation 2? Is Microsoft's Xbox *new* when Microsoft has not been a big player in video games before? What does *new* mean for new-product marketing? Newness from several points of view and some marketing implications of this newness are discussed below.

As you read the discussion about what "new" means in new-product development, think how it affects the marketing strategies of Sony and Microsoft in their new videogame launches.

Sony Corporation
www.sony.com

Microsoft Corporation
www.microsoft.com

Newness Compared with Existing Products   If a product is functionally different from existing products, it can be defined as new. Sometimes, this newness is revolutionary and creates a whole new industry, as in the case of the Apple II computer. At other times, additional features are added to an existing product to try to make it appeal to more customers. An example appearing in the accompanying Marketing NewsNet box describes the convergence of cell phones, PDAs, digital cameras, and portable music players in a single device.[3] So, digital device manufacturers are suddenly facing competitors from completely different industries than they faced a decade ago. But another result is that today's consumers face difficult decisions about which of almost countless features they want in buying their new digital devices.

MARKETING NEWSNET

**Blindsided in the Twenty-First Century—
The Convergence of Digital Devices**

Mobile phones that provide wireless voice communications virtually anywhere. Personal digital assistants, or PDAs, that give handheld computerized organization of appointments, addresses, telephone numbers, and so on. Digital cameras that can electronically capture and distribute digitized images. Portable music players such as the Apple iPod store and play back hundreds of tunes. In the late 1990s, companies selling these digital products had it relatively easy: just deliver the *single* core benefit that defined their respective product classes.

But that was the twentieth century—when electronic devices "stayed at home" in their own industry. But in today's twenty-first century, whole industries—industries that used to be completely separate—are colliding and their products often overlap.

What has happened is that improvements in key technologies have transformed the landscape of the digital consumer electronics marketplace. Consumers, who in the past had purchased these devices separately, now want features from each to be incorporated into a unified product. This collision of these industries has birthed what some call the "convergent digital device."

Blindsided by the revolutionary changes in technology and consumer tastes, digital device marketers now face competition from unexpected places. Motorola, Nokia, and Samsung now market mobile phones that integrate a digital camera, voice recorder, phonebook organizer, and Internet and e-mail access. PalmOne now offers a PDA with a mobile phone and Internet and e-mail access.

Apple iPods have the capability to store and play video in addition to voice and music, and Nokia and other wireless phone companies offer phones that play CD-quality music including downloadable tunes.

Some experts believe that television, handheld gaming, integrated hands-free mobile phone, and satellite radio will be the next set of convergent digital devices to appear on the horizon and integrate voice, data, and video communication technologies to meet the future needs of consumers.

Newness in Legal Terms   Industry Canada, the federal government's department that regulates business practices, has determined that a product can be called "new" for only up to 12 months.

Newness from the Company's Perspective   Successful companies are starting to view newness and innovation in their products at three levels. At the lowest level, which usually involves the least risk, is a product line extension. This is an incremental improvement of an existing product for the company, such as Frosted Cheerios or Diet Cherry Coke or Gillette Venus for Women—extensions of the basic Cheerios or Diet Coke or men's Gillette Mach3 product lines, respectively. At the next level is a significant jump in innovation or technology, such as Sony's leap from the micro tape recorder to the Walkman. The third level is true innovation, a truly revolutionary new product, like the first Apple computer in 1976. Effective new product programs in large firms deal at all three levels.

Newness from the Consumer's Perspective   A fourth way to define new products is in terms of their effects on consumption. This approach classifies new products according to the degree of learning required by the consumer, as shown in Figure 10–2.

	LOW	Degree of New Consumer Learning Needed	HIGH
BASIS OF COMPARISON	**CONTINUOUS INNOVATION**	**DYNAMICALLY CONTINUOUS INNOVATION**	**DISCONTINUOUS INNOVATION**
Definition	Requires no new learning by consumers	Disrupts consumer's normal routine but does not require totally new learning	Establishes new consumption patterns among consumers
Examples	Sensor and New Improved Tide	Electric toothbrush, compact disc player, and automatic flash unit for cameras	VCR, home computer, speech recognition software
Marketing emphasis	Generate awareness among consumers and obtain widespread distribution	Advertise benefits to consumers, stressing point of differentiation and consumer advantage	Educate consumers through product trial and personal selling

■ FIGURE 10–2 ■
Consumption effects define newness

With *continuous innovation,* no new behaviours must be learned. Gateway's introduction of the first plasma flat-panel TV started a revolution among TV buyers.[4] Gateway's new TV does not require buyers to learn new TV-watching behaviours and therefore is a continuous innovation. Under these conditions, the beauty of this innovation is that effective marketing simply depends on generating awareness and having strong distribution in appropriate outlets, not completely re-educating customers.

With *dynamically continuous innovation*, only minor changes in behaviour are required for use. An example is built-in, fold-down child seats, such as those available in DaimlerChrysler minivans. Built-in car seats for children require only minor bits of education and changes in behaviour, and so the marketing strategy is to *educate* prospective buyers on their benefits, advantages, and proper use.

A *discontinuous innovation* involves making the consumer learn entirely new consumption patterns in order to use the product. After decades of research, IBM introduced its ViaVoice speech recognition software. If you are using ViaVoice you are able to speak to your computer and watch your own words appear on your computer screen, and you can also open Windows programs with your voice. The risk that IBM faced in introducing this discontinuous innovation was that people had to learn new behaviours in producing word-processed memos and reports. Hence, marketing efforts for discontinuous innovations involve educating consumers on both the benefits and proper use of the innovative product—activities that can cost millions of dollars.

Why Products Succeed or Fail

We all know of giant product or service success stories, such as Microsoft Windows and CNN. Yet, thousands of product failures that occur every year cost Canadian businesses millions of dollars. Recent research suggests that it takes about 3000 raw unwritten ideas to produce a single commercially successful new product.[5] To learn marketing lessons and convert potential failures to successes, we can analyze why new products fail and then study several failures in detail. As we go through the new-product process later in the chapter, we can identify ways such failures might have been avoided—admitting, of course, that hindsight is clearer than foresight.

Marketing Reasons for New-Product Failures   Both marketing and nonmarketing factors contribute to new-product failures, as shown in the accompanying Marketing NewsNet box. Using the research results from several studies[6] on new-product success and failure and also those described in the Marketing NewsNet, we can identify critical marketing factors—sometimes overlapping—that often separate new-product winners and losers:

1. *Insignificant "point of difference."* Shown as the most important factor in the Marketing NewsNet, a distinctive "point of difference" is essential for a new product to defeat competitive ones—through having superior characteristics that deliver unique benefits to the user. In the mid-1990s, General Mills introduced "Fingos," a sweetened cereal flake about the size of a corn chip. Consumers were supposed to snack on them dry, but they did not.[7] The point of difference was not important enough to get consumers to give up eating competing snacks, such as popcorn, potato chips, or Cheerios, from the box late at night.

2. *Incomplete market and product definition before product development starts.* Ideally, a new product needs a precise **protocol**, a statement that, before product development begins, identifies (1) a well-defined target market; (2) specific customers' needs, wants, and preferences; and (3) what the product will be and do. Without this precision, loads of money disappear as research and development (R&D) tries to design a vague product for a phantom market. Apple Computer's hand-sized Newton computer, which intended to help keep the user organized, fizzled badly because no clear protocol existed.

3. *Too little market attractiveness.* Market attractiveness refers to the ideal situation every new-product manager looks for: a large target market with high growth and real buyer need. But often, when looking for ideal market niches, the target market is too small and competitive to warrant the R&D, production, and marketing expenses necessary to reach it. In the early 1990s, Kodak discontinued its Ultralife lithium battery. With its 10-year shelf life, the battery was

protocol

A statement that, before product development begins, identifies (1) a well-defined target market; (2) specific customers' needs, wants, and preferences; and (3) what the product will be and do.

New-product success or failure? For the special problems these products face, see the text.

MARKETING NEWSNET

IDEAS AHEAD

What Separates New-Product Winners and Losers

What makes some products winners and others losers? Knowing this answer is a key to a new-product strategy. R. G. Cooper and E. J. Kleinschmidt studied 203 new products to find the answers shown below.

The researchers defined the "product success rate" of new products as the percentage of products that reached the company's own profitability criteria. Product "winners" are the best 20 percent of performers, and "losers" are the worst 20 percent. For example, for the first factor in the table below, 98 percent of the winners had a major point of difference compared with only 18 percent of the losers.

Note that the table below includes both marketing and nonmarketing factors. Most of the marketing factors tie directly to the reasons cited in the text for new-product failures that are taken from a number of research studies.

FACTOR AFFECTING PRODUCT SUCCESS RATE	PRODUCT "WINNERS" (BEST 20%)	PRODUCT "LOSERS" (WORST 20%)	% DIFFERENCE (WINNERS–LOSERS)
1. Point of difference, or uniquely superior product	98%	18%	80%
2. Well-defined product before actual development starts	85	26	59
3. Synergy, or fit, with firm's R&D and manufacturing capabilities	80	29	51
4. Quality of execution of technological activities	76	30	46
5. Quality of execution of activities before actual development starts	75	31	44
6. Synergy, or fit, with marketing mix activities	71	31	40
7. Quality of execution of marketing mix activities	71	32	39
8. Market attractiveness, ones with large markets and high growth	74	43	31

touted as lasting twice as long as an alkaline battery. Yet, the product was available only in the 9-volt size, which accounts for less than 10 percent of the batteries sold in North America.

4. *Poor execution of the marketing mix*: name, package, price, promotion, distribution. Coca-Cola thought its Minute Maid Squeeze-Fresh frozen orange juice concentrate in a squeeze bottle was a hit. The idea was that consumers could make one glass of juice at a time, and the concentrate stayed fresh in the refrigerator for more than a month. After two test markets, the product was finished. Consumers loved the idea, but the product was messy to use, and the advertising and packaging did not educate them effectively on how much concentrate to mix.

5. *Poor product quality on critical factors*. Overlapping somewhat with point 1, this factor stresses that problems on one or two critical factors can kill the product, even though the general quality is high. For example, the Japanese, like the British, drive on the left side of the road. Until 1996, North American car makers sent Japan few right-drive cars—unlike German car makers, who exported right-drive models in a number of their brands.[8]

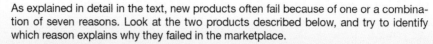

Why did these new products fail?

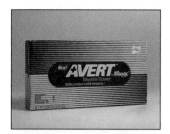

As explained in detail in the text, new products often fail because of one or a combination of seven reasons. Look at the two products described below, and try to identify which reason explains why they failed in the marketplace.

- Kimberly-Clark's "Avert Virucidal" tissues that contained vitamin C derivatives scientifically designed to kill cold and flu germs when users sneezed, coughed, or blew their nose into them.

- OUT! International's Hey! There's A Monster In My Room spray that was designed to rid scary creatures from kids' rooms and had a bubble-gum fragrance.

Compare your insights with those in the text.

6. *Bad timing.* The product is introduced too soon, too late, or at a time when consumer tastes are shifting dramatically. Bad timing gives new-product managers nightmares. IBM, for example, killed several laptop computer prototypes because competitors introduced better, more advanced machines to the marketplace before IBM could get there.

7. *No economical access to buyers.* Grocery products provide an example. Today's mega-supermarkets carry 30 000 different SKUs. With new food products introduced each day, the fight for shelf space is tremendous in terms of costs for advertising, distribution, and shelf space.[9] Because shelf space is determined in terms of sales per square foot, Thirsty Dog! (a zesty beef-flavoured, vitamin-enriched, mineral-loaded, lightly carbonated bottled water for your dog) must displace an existing product on the supermarket shelves, a difficult task with the precise measures of revenues per square foot these stores use.

A Look at Some Failures   Before reading further, study the product failures described in Figure 10-3, and try to identify which of the reasons is the most likely explanation for their failure. The two examples are discussed in greater detail below.

Kimberly-Clark's Avert Virucidal tissues lasted 10 months in a test market before being pulled from the shelves. People did not believe the claims and were frightened by the name. So, the tissue probably failed because of not having a clear point of difference, a bad name, and, hence, bad marketing mix execution—probably reasons #1 and #4 on the list in the text.

Out! International's "Hey! There's A Monster In My Room" spray was creative and cute when introduced in 1993. But the name probably kept the kids awake at night more than their fear of the monsters because it suggested the monster was still hiding in the room. Question: Wouldn't calling it the "Monster-Buster Spray" have licked the name problem? It looks like the spray was never really defined well in a protocol (reason #2) and definitely had poor name execution (reason #4).

Simple marketing research on consumers should have revealed the problems. Developing successful new products may sometimes involve luck, but more often it involves having a product that really meets a need and has significant points of difference over competitive products. The likelihood of success is improved by paying attention to the early steps of the new-product process described in the next section of the text.

CONCEPT CHECK

1. From a consumer's viewpoint, what kind of innovation would an improved electric toothbrush be?

2. What does "insignificant point of difference" mean as a reason for new-product failure?

■ ■ ■
THE NEW-PRODUCT PROCESS

new-product process
The stages a firm uses to identify business opportunities and convert them to a saleable good or service.

new-product strategy development
The stage of the new-product process that defines the role for a new product in terms of the firm's overall corporate objectives.

Such companies as General Electric, Sony, and Procter & Gamble take a sequence of steps before their products are ready for market. Figure 10–4 shows the seven stages of the **new-product process,** the stages a firm uses to identify business opportunities and convert them to a saleable good or service. This sequence begins with new-product strategy development and ends with commercialization.

New-Product Strategy Development

For companies, **new-product strategy development** is the stage of the new product process that defines the role for a new product in terms of the firm's overall corporate objectives. This step in the new-product process has been added by many companies recently to provide a needed focus for ideas and concepts developed in later stages.

Objectives of the Stage: Identify Markets and Strategic Roles   During this new-product strategy development stage, the company uses the environmental scanning process described in Chapter 3 to identify trends that pose either opportunities or threats. Relevant company strengths and weaknesses are also identified. The outcome of new-product strategy development is not only new-product ideas but also identifying markets for which new products will be developed and strategic roles new products might serve—the vital protocol activity explained earlier in the discussion of the Marketing NewsNet box on new-product winners and losers.

3M: Cross-Functional Teams, Six Sigma, and Lead Users   Key to 3M's success in new-product development is its use of *cross-functional teams*, a small number of people from different departments in an organization who are mutually accountable to a common set of performance goals. Today in 3M, teams are especially important in new-product development so that individuals from R&D, marketing, sales, manufacturing, and finance can simultaneously work together in a collaborative environment on new product and market opportunities. In the past, 3M and other firms often utilized these department people in sequence—possibly resulting in R&D designing new products that the manufacturing department could not produce economically and that the marketing department could not sell.

Six Sigma
A means to "delight the customer" by achieving quality through a highly disciplined process to focus on developing and delivering near-perfect products and services.

Important today in 3M's cross-functional teams is **Six Sigma**, a means to "delight the customer" by achieving quality through a highly disciplined process to focus on developing and delivering near-perfect products and services. "Near perfect" here means being 99.9997 percent perfect, or allowing 3.4 defects per million products produced or transactions processed—getting as close as possible to "zero

■ FIGURE 10–4 ■■
Stages in the new-product process

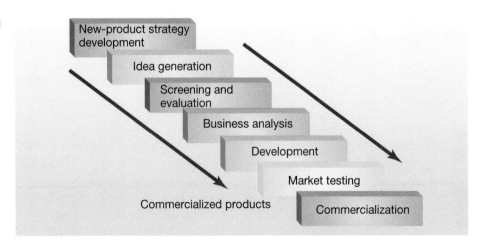

How listening to employees and co-workers matters in new product development: Volvo's innovative YCC and its design team.

defects." Six Sigma's success lies in determining what variables impact the results, measuring them, and making decisions based on data, not gut feeling.[10]

Idea Generation

idea generation
Developing a pool of concepts as candidates for new products.

Developing a pool of concepts as candidates for new products, or **idea generation**, must build on the previous stage's results. New-product ideas are generated by consumers, supplies, employees, basic R&D, and competitors.

Customer and Supplier Suggestions   Companies often analyze customer complaints or supplier ideas to discover new-product opportunities. Whirlpool, trying to reduce costs by cutting the number of different product platforms in half, got ideas from customers on ways to standardize components.[11] Business researchers now emphasize that firms must actively involve customers and suppliers in the product development process.[12] This often means focusing on what the new product will actually *do* for them rather than simply *what they want*.[13]

Employee and Co-Worker Suggestions   Employees may be encouraged to suggest new-product ideas through suggestion boxes or contests. The idea for Nature Valley Granola Bars from General Mills came when one of its marketing managers observed co-workers bringing granola to work in plastic bags.

As described at the start of Chapter 5, auto industry studies show that women buy about two-thirds of all vehicles and also influence about 85 percent of all sales. However, many auto manufacturers get ideas on new-car features by doing marketing research on gear-head guys who love cars. That is *exactly opposite* to what Volvo did recently in trying to bridge the gender gap. Volvo first obtained ideas on new-car features from all-female focus groups drawn from its Swedish workforce. It then named a five-woman team of Volvo managers to design a "concept car"—what the auto industry uses to test new designs, technical innovations, and consumer reactions. Shown in the photos above with its all-women design team are some features of Volvo's YCC (Your Concept Car) that appeared in auto shows recently:

- *Automatically opening doors.* Press a button on the car key and the gull-wing doors pop open, the chassis rises a few inches, and the steering pulls in to make a wide path in for the driver.
- *Ergovision system for automatic fit to the driver.* At a dealership, the driver's body is laser-scanned so that the car automatically sets the optimal positions for the seat belt, pedals, headrest, steering wheel, and seat—information saved in memory in the car key.
- *Parallel parking aid.* When the car stops in front of an empty spot, sensors confirm the space is big enough and the system automatically self-steers the car into the space while the driver controls the brake and gas.
- *Care and cleanliness.* The no-stick paint on body panels repels dirt, and customized seat covers can be removed and washed.

You may never see the YCC in your local Volvo showroom because its likely $65 000 price tag may be too high for the market. But you *will* see many of these women-designed features on future Volvos, testimony to the importance of listening to consumers in developing new products.[14]

Research and Development Breakthroughs   Another source of new products is a firm's basic research, but the costs can be huge. Sony is a world leader in new-product development in electronics. Sony's research and development breakthroughs have made it a legend in the electronics industry, popularizing VCRs, the Walkman, and—coming into your future?—flat-panel Organic Electroluminescence (OEL) monitors about the thickness of a credit card providing brighter images on large, 30-inch screens.

Not all R&D labs have Sony's genius for moving electronic breakthroughs into the marketplace. Take Xerox Corporation's Palo Alto Research Center (PARC). In what maybe the greatest electronic fumble of all time, by 1979, PARC had what is in your computer system now: graphical user interfaces, mice, windows and pull-down menus, laser printers, and distributed computing. Concerned with aggressive competition from Japan in its core photocopier business, Xerox did not even bother to patent these breakthroughs. Apple Computer's Steven Jobs visited PARC in 1979, adapted many of the ideas for the Macintosh, and the rest is history.

Professional R&D laboratories also provide new-product ideas. Laboratories at Arthur D. Little helped put the crunch in Cap'n Crunch cereal and the flavour in Carnation Instant Breakfast. As described in the WebLink box, IDEO is a world-class new-product development firm, having designed more than 4000 of them.

Brainstorming sessions run at IDEO can generate 100 new ideas in an hour. Its "shop-a-long" visits with managers of client firms let the managers experience firsthand what one of its customers does.[15]

Competitive Products   New-product ideas can also be found by analyzing the competition. A six-person intelligence team from the Marriott Corporation spent six months travelling around the United States staying at economy hotels. The team assessed the competition's strengths and weaknesses on everything from the soundproof qualities of the rooms to the softness of the towels. Marriott then budgeted $500 million for a new economy hotel chain, Fairfield Inns.

Screening and Evaluation

screening and evaluation
The stage of the new-product process that involves internal and external evaluations of the new-product ideas to eliminate those that warrant no further effort.

Screening and evaluation is the stage of the new-product process that involves internal and external evaluations of the new-product ideas to eliminate those that warrant no further effort.

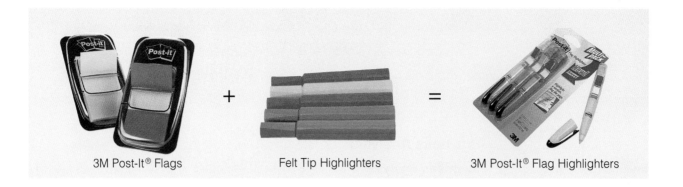

3M Post-It® Flags   +   Felt Tip Highlighters   =   3M Post-It® Flag Highlighters

For the creative way a student project helped lead to 3M's new Post-it® Flag Highlighter, see the text.

Atkins used product concept testing to develop and refine its brands of low-carb products for the Canadian market.

Internal Approach   Internally, the firm evaluates the technical feasibility of the proposal and whether the idea meets the objectives defined in the new-product strategy development step. In a recent project, 3M researcher David Windorski worked with a team of local university students to find new applications for Post-it® Flags in their studying activities. Student suggestions reinforced some ideas Windorski had been working on in his laboratory. Students said that combining Post-it® Flags with coloured felt-tip highlighters could be used as bookmarks on key pages in their textbooks that they highlighted. Windorski and the team worked on a few different prototypes: Post-it® Flags on top, on the side, and so on. He knew the basic idea was sound, but the designs were not.

Windorski then hit on his breakthrough idea: put small Post-it®® Flags *inside* pens and highlighters that students use! After much engineering, consumer testing, and evaluation, the result was the launch of 3M's Post-it® Flag Highlighter and Post-it® Flag Pen—a credit to global cross-functional collaboration among research, manufacturing, and marketing. In these two 3M products, the pen and highlighter components were sourced worldwide. The new product development team then coordinated the commercialization for a global introduction.

The final, marketable Post-it® Flag Highlighter version is shown in the photo above. But earlier prototypes were first mocked up in cardboard, then modelling clay, then components screwed together—a far cry from the final product you probably see in your student bookstore. By the end of 2004, 3M had sold over a million units of the two new products.[16]

External Approach   Concept tests are external evaluations that consist of preliminary testing of the new-product idea (rather than the actual, final product) with consumers. Generally, these tests are more useful with minor modifications of existing products than with new, innovative products that are not familiar to consumers.[17] Concept tests usually rely on written descriptions of the product but may be augments with sketches, mockups, or promotional literature. With food products, consumers may actually be asked to taste-test the products. Several key questions are asked during concept testing: How does the customer perceive the product? Who would buy it? How would it be used?

Frito-Lay spent a year interviewing 10 000 consumers about the concept of a multigrain snack chip before introducing its highly successful Sun Chips. Atkins, on the other hand, used product concept testing extensively before launching its low-carb food products in Canada, including its *Morning Start* cereals and breakfast bars and *Endulge* snack line. The goal for Atkins was to work with consumers to develop food products that were healthy but also tasted good.[18]

1. What step in the new-product process has been added in recent years?

2. What are the main sources of new-product ideas?

3. What is the difference between internal and external screening and evaluation approaches used by a firm in the new-product process?

Business Analysis

business analysis
The stage of the new-product process that involves specifying the product features and marketing strategy and making necessary financial projections needed to commercialize a product.

Business analysis is the stage of the new-product process that involves specifying the product features and marketing strategy and making necessary financial projections needed to commercialize a product. This is the last checkpoint before significant capital is invested in creating a *prototype,* a full-scale operating model of the product under development. Economic analysis, marketing strategy review, and legal examination of the proposed product are conducted at this stage. The product is also analyzed relative to the firm's marketing and technological synergies, two criteria noted in the Marketing NewsNet box earlier.

The marketing strategy review studies the new-product idea in relation to the marketing program to support it. The proposed product is assessed to determine whether it will help or hurt the sales of existing products. Likewise, the product is examined to assess whether it can be sold through existing channels or if new outlets will be needed. Profit projections involve estimating the number of units expected to be sold but also the costs of R&D, production, and marketing.

As an important aspect of the business analysis, the proposed new product is studied to determine whether it can be protected with a patent or copyright. An attractive new-product proposal is one in which the technology, product, or brand cannot easily be copied. All of these critical business issues emerge in huge research and development gambles on new drug compounds by pharmaceutical companies, such as Eli Lilly & Company, discussed in the next section.

Development

development
The stage of the new-product process that involves turning the idea on paper into a prototype.

Product ideas that survive the business analysis proceed to actual **development,** the stage of the new-product process that involves turning the idea on paper into a prototype. This results in a demonstrable, producible product in hand. Outsiders seldom understand the technical complexities of the development stage, which involves not only manufacturing the product but also performing laboratory and consumer tests to ensure that it meets the standards set. Design of the product becomes an important element.

Some new products can be so important and costly that the company is literally betting its very existence on success. And creative, out-of-the-box thinking can be critical. In the pharmaceutical industry, no more than one out of every 5000 to 10 000 new compounds developed in the laboratories emerges as an approved drug.[19]

With the success rate on new drug compounds so low, pharmaceutical giant Eli Lilly has initiated "failure parties" to recognize excellent scientific work that unfortunately resulted in products that failed anyway. But the failed drug compound does not end with the party. Instead, Lilly usually names a team of doctors and scientists to look back objectively at every compound that failed at any point in human clinical trials to learn the specific reasons for the failure.

This "failure analysis" has resulted in Lilly's sometimes finding ways to make the compound succeed in addressing the original disease for which it was designed. For example, in 1999 Lilly halted trials of Alimta, an experimental chemotherapy drug, when three patients died. Extensive failure analysis revealed that patients with the most severe side effects had reduced folic acid in their blood. The solution: simply give all patients suffering from a rare type of cancer caused by exposure to asbestos *both* Alimta *and* folic acid pills.

ETHICS AND SOCIAL RESPONSIBILITY ALERT

Sports Utilities versus Cars: Godzilla Meets a Chimp?

Make car wrecks safer. This sounds sort of stupid. But . . . the problem is death! The high and heavy pickups, vans, and sport utility vehicles (SUVs) are now involved in an increasing number of highway deaths. When one huge vehicle meets a bitty little car, the larger, higher one smashes the smaller one's passenger compartment, instead of going head-to-head at bumper level. The people in the cars, unfortunately, are more likely to be killed in such accidents.

The problem is also money. These mega-vehicles now account for a large percentage of Canadian automakers' sales and profits. Improving the smaller cars—with side air bags and steel supports—is cheaper than lowering the frame or adding a crumple zone for the frame of the bigger

vehicle. Nothing is easy. And consumers love the power of these hefty vehicles that are about 1000 kilograms heavier than a compact car.

But changes are on the way. Mercedes Benz has completely redesigned its M-class SUV. Mercedes engineers addressed the compatibility of their SUV with smaller cars so that the Mercedes SUV frame and bumper is as much as 20 centimetres lower than its competitor's SUV models. This makes the bumpers of Mercedes SUVs and those of small cars more likely to meet in a crash, dramatically increasing the safety for small-car passengers.

Who should address the problem here? The federal government? The insurance companies? The vehicle manufacturers? Consumers?

More surprisingly, a number of successful Eli Lilly drugs trace their origins back to trials that demonstrated the drug was a flop for the initial medical problem it was intended to address. Examples are a failed antidepressant drug now used in treating attention deficit/hyperactivity disorders and a drug that flopped in addressing asthma but works for cardiovascular diseases. Some of these breakthroughs come from researchers using an Eli Lilly "blue sky" fund that enables them to spend 10 to 20 percent of their time on projects with no clear immediate commercial value.[20]

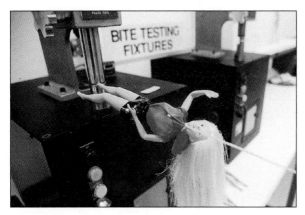

Eli Lilly's drug prototypes go through exhaustive laboratory and clinical tests to see if they meet design criteria set for them if used the way intended. But safety tests are also critical for when the product is not used as planned. To make sure seven-year-olds cannot bite Barbie's head off and choke, Mattel clamps her foot in steel jaws in a test stand and then pulls on her head with a wire. Similarly, car manufacturers have done extensive safety tests by crashing their cars into concrete walls. As mentioned in the Ethics and Social Responsibility Alert box, consumer groups are increasingly concerned about what happens when a pickup truck or sport utility vehicle hits a small car when their bumpers do not line up.[21] Auto industry tests are identifying some feasible, but costly, solutions.

Market Testing

market testing
Exposing actual products to prospective consumers under realistic purchase conditions to see if they will buy.

The **market testing** stage of the new-product process involves exposing actual products to prospective consumers under realistic purchase conditions to see if they will buy. Often, a product is developed, tested, refined, and then tested again to get consumer reactions through either test marketing or purchase laboratories.

Test Marketing Test marketing involves offering a product for sale on a limited basis in a defined area. This test is done to determine whether consumers will actually buy the product and to try different ways of marketing it. Only about a third of the products test-marketed do well enough to go on to the next phase. These market tests are usually conducted in cities that are viewed as being representative of

Canadian consumers. Test marketing gives the company an indication of potential sales volume and market share. Market tests are also used to check other elements of the marketing mix besides the product itself, such as price, level of advertising support, and distribution. Market tests are time consuming and expensive because production lines as well as promotion and sales programs must be set up. Costs can run to more than a million dollars. Market tests also reveal information to competitors, sometimes enabling them to get their products into national distribution first. Competitors can also try to sabotage test markets. With such problems, some firms skip test markets completely or use simulated test markets.

Simulated Test Markets   Because of the time, cost, and confidentiality problems of test markets, consumer packaged goods companies often turn to *simulated* (or *laboratory*) *test markets* (*STM*), a technique that simulates a full-scale test market but in a limited fashion. STMs are often run in shopping malls, where consumers are questioned to identify who uses the product class being tested. Willing participants are questioned on usage, reasons for purchase, and important product attributes. Qualified persons are then shown TV commercials or print ads for the test product along with competitors' advertising and are given money to make a decision to buy or not buy a package of the product (or the competitors') from a real or simulated store environment. STMs are used early in the development process to screen new-product ideas and later in the process to make sales projections.

When Test Markets Do Not Work   Test marketing is a valuable step in the new-product process, but not all products can use it. Testing a service beyond the concept level is very difficult because the service is intangible and consumers cannot see what they are buying. For example, how could Google easily have test marketed the mid-2004 launch of its Gmail, an e-mail service users get free in exchange for accepting ads with its Gmail?[22]

Similarly, test markets for expensive consumer products, such as cars or VCRs, or costly industrial products, such as jet engines or computers, are impractical. For these products, consumer reactions to mockup designs or one-of-a-kind prototypes are all that is feasible. Car makers test new style designs on early adopters (discussed in Chapter 11) who are more willing than the average customer to buy new designs or products.[23]

Commercialization

commercialization
The stage of the new-product process that involves positioning and launching a new product in full-scale production and sales.

Finally, the product is brought to the point of **commercialization**—the stage of the new-product process that involves positioning and launching a new product in full-scale production and sales. Companies proceed very carefully at the commercialization stage because this is the most expensive stage for most new products, especially consumer products. If competitors introduce a product that leapfrogs the firm's own new product or if cannibalization of its own existing products looks significant, the firm may halt the new-product launch permanently.[24] Large companies often use regional rollouts, introducing the product sequentially into certain geographical areas to allow production levels and marketing activities to build up gradually in order to minimize the risk of new-product failure. Grocery product manufacturers and some telecommunications service providers are two examples of firms that use this strategy.

slotting fee
A payment a manufacturer makes to place a new item on a retailer's shelf.

Grocery product manufacturers, in fact, are also exposed to other special commercialization problems. Because shelf space is so limited, many supermarkets require a **slotting fee** for new products, a payment a manufacturer makes to place a new item on a retailer's shelf. This can run to several million dollars for a single product. But there is yet another potential expense. If a new grocery product does not achieve a predetermined sales target, some retailers require a **failure fee**, a penalty payment a manufacturer makes to compensate a retailer for failed sales from its valuable shelf

failure fee
A penalty payment a manufacturer makes to compensate a retailer for failed sales from its valuable shelf space.

space. These costly slotting fees and failure fees are further examples of why large grocery product manufacturers use regional rollouts.

In recent years, companies have been trying to move very quickly from the idea generation or product concept stage to the commercialization stage of the new-product process. This is because speed or *time to market* (TtM) has been found to be correlated to new-product success. Recent studies, for example, have shown that high-tech products coming to market on time are far more profitable than those arriving late. So, some companies—such as Sony, Honda, 3M, and Hewlett-Packard—have overlapped the sequence of stages described in this chapter.

With this approach, termed *parallel development*, cross-functional team members, who conduct the simultaneous development of both the product and the product process, stay with the product from concept to production. This has enabled Hewlett-Packard (HP) to reduce the development time for computer printers from 54 months to 22. In software development, *fast prototyping* uses a "do it, try it, fix it" approach —encouraging continuous improvements after the initial design. One result: HP has been able to introduce many more new printer products to the market in substantially less time.[25]

HP's new-product success can be traced to its founders' innovative management style that shunned traditional rigid hierarchical structures. Instead, HP uses a decentralized system where the brainpower of its employees is freed so that they can get whoever is needed to get the job done.[26]

Figure 10–5 identifies the purpose of each stage of the new-product process and the kinds of marketing information and methods used. The third column of the figure

■ **FIGURE 10–5** ■

Marketing information and methods used in the new-product process

STAGE OF PROCESS	PURPOSE OF STAGE	MARKETING INFORMATION AND METHODS USED
New-product strategy development	Identify new-product niches to reach in light of company objectives	Company objectives; assessment of firm's current strengths and weaknesses in terms of market and product
Idea generation	Develop concepts for possible products	Ideas from employees and co-workers, consumers, R&D, and competitors; methods of brainstorming and focus groups
Screening and evaluation	Separate good product ideas from bad ones inexpensively	Screening criteria, concept tests, and weighted point systems
Business analysis	Identify the product's features and its marketing strategy, and make financial projections	Product's key features, anticipated marketing mix strategy; economic, marketing, production, legal, and profitability analyses
Development	Create the prototype product, and test it in the laboratory and on consumers	Laboratory and consumer tests on product prototypes
Market testing	Test product and marketing strategy in the marketplace on a limited scale	Test markets, simulated test markets (STMs)
Commercialization	Position and offer product in the marketplace	Perceptual maps, product positioning, regional rollouts

also suggests information that might help avoid some new-product failures. Although using the new-product process does not guarantee the success of products, it does increase a firm's success rate.

CONCEPT CHECK

1. How does the development stage of the new-product process involve testing the product inside and outside the firm?

2. What is a test market?

3. What is commercialization of a new product?

■ ■ ■
CHAPTER IN REVIEW

1 *Recognize the various terms that pertain to products and services.*

A product is a good, service, or idea consisting of a bundle of tangible and intangible attributes that satisfies consumers and is received in exchange for money or some other unit of value. Firms can offer a range of products, which involve decisions regarding the product item, product line, and product mix.

2 *Identify the ways in which consumer and business goods and services can be classified.*

Products can be classified by type of user and tangibility. By user, the major distinctions are consumer goods, which are products purchased by the ultimate consumer, and business goods, which are products that assist in providing other products for resale. By degree of tangibility, products may be classified as (*a*) nondurable goods, which are consumed in one or a few uses; (*b*) durable goods, which are items that usually last over an extended number of uses; or (*c*) services, which are activities, deeds, or other basic intangibles offered for sale.

Consumer goods can further be broken down on the basis of the effort involved in the purchase decision process, marketing mix attributes used in the purchase, and the frequency of purchase: (*a*) convenience goods are items that consumers purchase frequently and with a minimum of shopping effort, (*b*) shopping goods are items for which consumers compare several alternatives on selected criteria, (*c*) specialty goods are items that consumers make special efforts to seek out and buy, and (*d*) unsought goods are items that consumers do not either know about or initially want.

Business goods can further be broken down into (*a*) production goods, which are items used in the manufacturing process that become part of the final product, such as raw materials or component parts; and (*b*) support goods, which are items used to assist in producing other goods and services and include installations, accessory equipment, supplies, and services.

3 *Explain the implications of alternative ways of viewing "newness" in new products and services.*

A product may be defined as "new" if it (*a*) is functionally different from the firm's existing products; (*b*) falls within the Industry Canada definition; (*c*) is a product line extension, a significant innovation, or a revolutionary new product; or (*d*) affects the degree of learning that consumer's must engage in to use the product. With a continuous innovation, no new behaviours must be learned. With a dynamically continuous innovation, only minor behavioural changes are needed. With a discontinuous innovation, consumers must learn entirely new consumption patterns.

4 *Describe the factors contributing to a product's or service's failure.*

A new product often fails for these marketing reasons: (*a*) insignificant points of difference, (*b*) incomplete market and product definition before product development begins, (*c*) too little market attractiveness, (*d*) poor execution of the marketing mix, (*e*) poor product quality on critical factors, (*f*) bad timing, and (*g*) no economical access to buyers.

5 *Explain the purposes of each step of the new-product process.*

The new-product process consists of seven stages a firm uses to develop a salable good or service: (i) New-product strategy development involves defining the role for the new product within the firm's overall objectives. (ii) Idea generation involves developing a pool of concepts from consumers, employees, basic R&D, and competitors to serve as candidates for new products. (iii) Screening and evaluation involve evaluating new product ideas to eliminate those that are not feasible from a technical or consumer perspective. (iv) Business analysis involves defining the features of the new product, developing the marketing strategy and marketing program to introduce it, and making a financial forecast. (v) Development involves not only producing a prototype product but also testing it in the laboratory and on consumers to see that it meets the standards set for it. (vi) Market testing involves exposing actual products to prospective consumers under realistic purchasing conditions to see if they will buy the product. (vii) Commercialization involves positioning and launching a product in full-scale production and sales with a specific marketing program.

■ ■ ■
FOCUSING ON KEY TERMS

business analysis p. 270
business goods p. 257
commercialization p. 272
consumer goods p. 257
convenience goods p. 258
development p. 270
failure fee p. 272
idea generation p. 267
market testing p. 271
new-product process p. 266
new-product strategy development p. 266
product p. 256

product line p. 256
product mix p. 257
production goods p. 258
protocol p. 263
screening and evaluation p. 268
shopping goods p. 258
Six Sigma p. 266
slotting fee p. 272
specialty goods p. 258
support goods p. 259
unsought goods p. 258

■ ■ ■
DISCUSSION AND APPLICATION QUESTIONS

1 Products can be classified as either consumer or business goods. How would you classify the following products? (*a*) Johnson's baby shampoo, (*b*) a Black & Decker two-speed drill, and (*c*) an arc welder.

2 Are such products as Nature Valley Granola bars and Eddie Bauer hiking boots convenience, shopping, specialty, or unsought goods?

3 Based on your answer to question 2, how would the marketing actions differ for each product and the classification to which you assigned it?

4 In terms of the behavioural effect on consumers, how would a PC, such as an Apple PowerBook be classified? In light of this classification, what actions would you suggest to the manufacturers of these products to increase their sales in the market?

5 Several alternative definitions were presented for a new product. How would a company's marketing strategy be affected if it used (*a*) the legal definition, or (*b*) a behavioural definition?

6 What methods would you suggest to assess the potential commercial success for the following new products? (*a*) a new, improved ketchup, (*b*) a three-dimensional television system that took the company 10 years to develop, and (*c*) a new children's toy on which the company holds a patent.

7 Concept testing is an important step in the new-product process. Outline the concept tests for (*a*) an electrically powered car, and (*b*) a new loan payment system for automobiles that is based on a variable interest rate. What are the differences in developing concept tests for products as opposed to services?

GOING ONLINE	Jalapeño Soda, Anyone?

Jalapeño soda? Aerosol mustard? Fingos? These are just three of the more than 70 000 products (both successes and failures) on the shelves of the NewProduct-Works Showcase. Visit its new Web site (www.newproductworks.com). Study the "Hits & Misses" categories, such as "We Expect Them to Be Successes," which are those that probably will be commercial successes; "Jury Is Out," products whose future is in doubt; "Failures," which are recent products that have failed miserably; and "Favorite Failures," which are those that cause people to ask "What *were* they thinking?" Pick

two of the failed products and try to identify the reasons discussed earlier in the chapter that may have led to their failure. Contrast these failed products with those that are deemed successes to learn why the latter became "sure-fire winners."

VIDEO CASE 10   3M™ Greptile Grip™ Golf Glove: Great Gripping!

"Marketing is not brain surgery," says Dr. George Dierberger, Marketing and International Manager of 3M's Sports and Leisure Products Project. "We tend to make it a lot more difficult than it is. 3M wins with its technology. We're not in the 'me-too' business, and in marketing we've got to remember that."

3M'S MICRO-REPLICATION TECHNOLOGY AND ITS GREPTILE GOLF GLOVE

3M is a $20 billion global, diversified technology company. Among its well-known brands are Post-it Notes, Scotch tape, Scotch Brite scouring pads, and Nexcare bandages. The key to 3M's marketing successes is its commitment to innovation. For more than a century, 3M's management has given its employees the freedom to try new ideas. This "culture of creativity" has led to the commercialization of more than 50 000 products.

The Sports and Leisure Products Project is a business unit managed by Dierberger and his marketing staff. Recently, Dierberger and his staff changed the conventional thinking about golfing. Using 3M's proprietary "micro-replication" technology, and applying it to a golf glove, the new Greptile gripping material consists of thousands of tiny "gripping fingers" sewn into the upper palm and lower fingers of a golf glove. According to Dierberger, "It is the only glove on the market that actively improves a golfer's hold on the club by allowing a more relaxed grip, leading to greater driving distance with less grip pressure, even under wet conditions." Laboratory tests found that the Greptile material offers 610 percent greater gripping power than leather and 340 percent greater than tackified (sticky) grips. The result: on drives, the golf ball travels an average 10.5 feet farther![27]

Introduced in 2004, the new 3M Greptile Grip golf glove is made primarily of high-quality Cabretta sheep leather to give it a soft feel. Initially, 3M sold the Greptile Grip golf glove through Wal-Mart and other mass merchandisers for a suggested retail price of $11.95 to $15.95. And now it is also being stocked by golf retailers across the country, such as Nevada Bob's, Golfsmith, and Austad's. The golf glove is available in both men's and women's left hand versions and in small, medium, medium/ large, large, and extra-large

hand sizes. A right hand version for both genders appeared in 2005. 3M projected first-year sales of $1 million in the United States.

THE GOLF MARKET

Several socioeconomic and demographic trends impact the golf glove market favourably. First, the huge baby boomer population (those born between 1946 and 1964) has matured, reaching its prime earning potential. This allows for greater discretionary spending on leisure activities, such as golf. According to the National Golf Foundation (NGF), most spending on golf equipment (clubs, bags, balls, shoes, gloves, etc.) is by consumers 50 and older—today's baby boomers.[28] Second, according to the U.S. Census, the American population has shifted regionally from the East and North to the South and West, where golfing is popular year around due to the temperate weather. Third, the number of golf courses has been growing, totalling about 15 000 at the end of 2004.[29]

Finally, golf is becoming an increasingly popular leisure activity for all age groups and ethnic backgrounds. According to the NGF, golf participants in the United States totalled 37.9 million in 2003, an all-time high. Female golfers now account for about 25 percent of all golfers, while minority participation has increased to over 10 percent.[30] According to the National Sporting Goods Association, sales of golf equipment was $3.1 billion in 2004, an increase of 2 percent from 2003.[31]

THE GOLF GLOVE MARKET

The global market for golf gloves is estimated at $300 million, with the United States at $180 million or 60 percent of worldwide sales. Historically, about 80 percent of golf gloves are sold through public and private on- and off-course golf pro specialty shops, golf superstores, and sporting good superstores. However, mass merchandisers have recently increased their shares due to the typically lower prices offered by these retailers.[32] FootJoy (46 percent) and Titleist (9 percent), both owned by Acushnet, are the top two golf glove market share leaders. Nike, which recently entered the golf equipment market with Tiger Woods as its spokesperson, has vaulted to a 7-percent share of the golf glove market.[33] These golf glove marketers focus on technology and comfort to create points of difference from its competitors, such as the recently introduced FootJoy SciFlex™ glove ($18), the Titleist Perma-Tech™ glove ($19), and the Nike DriFit glove ($18).

3M'S NEW PRODUCT PROCESS

Since about half of 3M's products are less than five years old, the process used by 3M to develop new product innovations is critical to its success and continued growth. Every innovation must meet 3M's new product criteria: (1) be a patentable or trademarked technology; (2) offer a superior value proposition to consumers; and (3) change the basis of competition by achieving a significant point of difference.

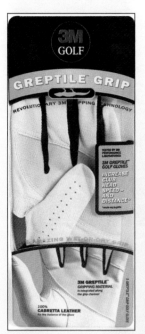

When developing a new product innovation, such as the 3M Greptile Grip golf glove, 3M uses a rigorous seven-step process: (1) ideas, (2) concept, (3) feasibility, (4) development, (5) scale-up, (6) launch, and (7) post-launch. "But innovation is not a linear path—not just A, then B, then C," says Dierberger. "It's the adjustments you make after you've developed the product that determines your success. And it's learning lessons from testing on real customers to make the final 'tweaks'—changing the price points, improving the benefits statement on the packaging, and sharpening the advertising appeals."

In the case of the 3M Greptile Grip golf glove, countless other examples of these adjustments appeared. Mike Kuhl, marketing coordinator at 3M, points out, "Consumer testing labs said the information on the back of our package was incomplete, so we had dozens of golfers hit drives using our glove and competitive gloves to compare driving distance." And 3M packaging engineer Travis Strom says, "Our first glove package 'pillowed'—bulked up—on the shelf, had hard-to-read text, and wasn't appealing to golfers, so we had to redesign it. After all, you only have a few seconds to capture the customer's attention with the package and make a sale."

THE FUTURE OF 3M GOLF AND GREPTILE

In 2005, 3M Golf launched a premium golf glove consisting of the highest quality Cabretta leather and selling for a suggested retail price of $16.95 to $19.95. On the drawing board: 3M Greptile Grip golf tape that can be applied to golf club grips and possibly a line of Greptile Grip golf grips to double the gripping power when used in conjunction with the Greptile Grip golf glove. In 2006, 3M intends to launch versions of its Greptile Grip golf gloves in Japan and Europe, the second and third largest golf markets behind the United States. Finally, 3M may develop and market baseball and softball batting gloves using the Greptile material in 2006 if the manufacturing and channels for golf gloves can been augmented.

QUESTIONS

1 What are the characteristics of the target market for the 3M Greptile Grip golf glove?

2 What are the key points of difference of the 3M Greptile Grip golf glove when compared with competitors' products, such as FootJoy and Nike? Substitute products, such as golf grips?

3 How does the Greptile Grip golf glove meet 3M's three criteria for new products?

4 Since 3M has no prior products for the golf market, what special promotion and distribution problems might 3M have?

5 How would you rate the 3M Greptile Grip golf glove on the following reasons for success and failure: (*a*) significant points of difference; (*b*) size and growth of the golf market; (*c*) product quality; (*d*) market timing; (*e*) execution of the marketing mix; (*f*) synergy or fit with 3M's R&D, manufacturing, and/or marketing capabilities; and (*g*) access to consumers?

MANAGING PRODUCTS AND BRANDS

CLEARLY CANADIAN: PRODUCT MANAGEMENT IN A COMPETITIVE ENVIRONMENT

Many industry experts credit Clearly Canadian Beverage Corporation of Vancouver, British Columbia, with pioneering the new-age or alternative beverage industry. In 1988, Clearly Canadian began marketing its premium-priced, single-serve sparkling flavoured water to North American consumers. To date, the company has sold more than 2.1 billion bottles of Clearly Canadian. Its goal now is to sell another billion bottles. To achieve that goal, the company is innovating in order to stay current with consumers' needs and ahead of its competition.

Like Clearly Canadian, the alternative beverage market has grown dramatically over the past decade and a half. The industry is currently valued at over $13 billion. Clearly Canadian Sparkling Flavoured Water, the product that started the whole phenomenon, continues to be a market leader in its category. But many products have also emerged to compete in this sector. Industry players now range from small, entrepreneurial firms, such as Clearly Canadian, to major beverage companies, such as Coca-Cola and PepsiCo, that use their marketing and distribution clout to garner share of the alternative beverage market.

Despite intense competition and crowded retail store shelves, Clearly Canadian is striving to remain competitive. According to Doug Mason, president and CEO of Clearly Canadian, innovation is a key success factor in this market. Accordingly, the company has diversified its product offerings. For example, it added O+2, an oxygen-enhanced beverage for active adults, and Tre Limone, a sparkling lemon-ginger drink, to its product portfolio.

Most importantly, the company is keeping in touch with market trends and consumer needs. After evaluating market trends and consumer needs, the company recently reformulated its flagship brand. Clearly Canadian Sparkling Flavoured Water now has half the carbs and half the calories while maintaining the same great taste. Mason suggests that the company simply had to respond to the heightened awareness for healthier food and beverage choices sweeping across Canada and the United States. The product comes in six flavours: blackberry, cherry, strawberry melon, peach, raspberry cream, and orange pineapple.

The company has also worked hard to improve its access to customers by establishing new distribution arrangements. One such arrangement is with Canada Dry, which will now distribute Clearly Canadian products in the New York area, giving Clearly Canadian access to over 15 million potential customers.

This chapter shows how actions taken by Clearly Canadian Beverage Corporation are typical of successful marketers in managing products and brands in competitive marketing environments.[1]

∎ ∎ ∎
PRODUCT LIFE CYCLE

product life cycle

The stages a new product goes through in the marketplace: introduction, growth, maturity, and decline.

Products, like people, have been viewed as having a life cycle. The concept of the **product life cycle** describes the stages a new product goes through in the marketplace: introduction, growth, maturity, and decline (Figure 11–1).[2] There are two curves shown in this figure: total industry sales revenue and total industry profit, which represent the sum of sales revenue and profit of all firms producing the product. The reasons for the changes in each curve and the marketing decisions involved are discussed on the following pages.

Introduction Stage

The introduction stage of the product life cycle occurs when a product is first introduced to its intended target market. During this period, sales grow slowly, and profit is minimal. The lack of profit is often the result of large investment costs in product development, such as the millions of dollars spent by Gillette to develop and launch the M3 power razor shaving system. The marketing objective for the company at this stage is to create consumer awareness and stimulate *trial*—the initial purchase of a product by a consumer.

Introducing
Gillette
M3 POWER
A MACH3 INNOVATION™

**FEEL THE POWER
OF THE WORLD'S BEST SHAVE.**

**The First Micro-Power™
Shaving System From Gillette.**

Just press the button to turn it on.   A motor sends micro-pulses to the blades.   New PowerGlide blades shave closer than ever

Gillette
The Best a Man Can Get

www.MACH3.com

Companies often spend heavily on advertising and other promotion tools to build awareness among consumers in the introduction stage. For example, Gillette budgeted millions in advertising alone to introduce the M3 power razor to consumers.[3] These expenditures are often made to stimulate *primary demand*, or desire for the product class, rather than for a specific brand, since there are few competitors with the same product. As more competitors introduce their own products and the product progresses along its life cycle, company attention is focused on creating *selective demand*, or demand for a specific brand.

Other marketing mix variables also are important at this stage. Gaining distribution can be a challenge because channel intermediaries may be hesitant to carry a new product. Moreover, in this stage, a company often restricts the number of variations of the product to ensure control of product quality. For example, Clearly Canadian Sparkling Water originally came in only one flavour.

During introduction, pricing can be either high or low. A high initial price may be used as part of a *skimming* strategy to help the company recover the costs of development as well as capitalize on the price insensitivity of early buyers. 3M is a master of this strategy. According to a 3M manager, "We hit fast, price high, and get the heck out when the me-too products pour in."[4] High prices also tend to attract competitors more eager to enter

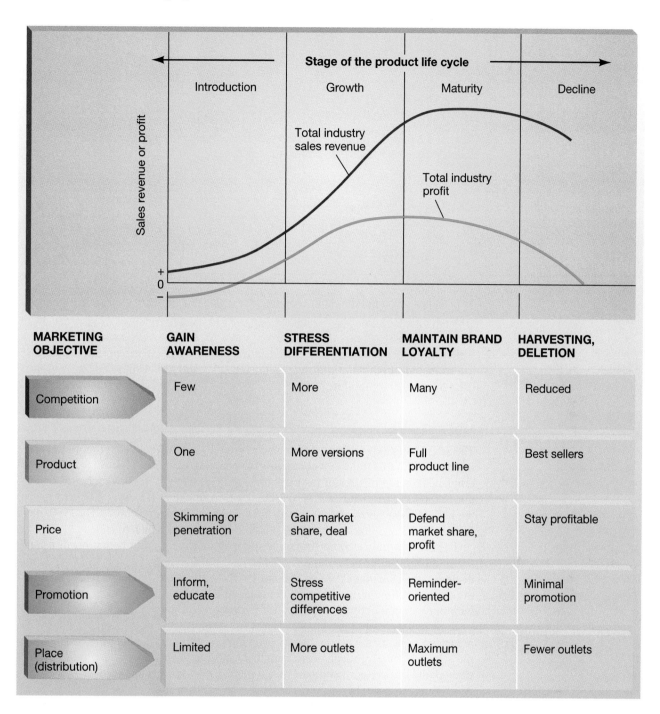

Stage of the product life cycle

| | Introduction | Growth | Maturity | Decline |

Sales revenue or profit

Total industry
sales revenue

Total industry
profit

+
0
−

MARKETING OBJECTIVE	GAIN AWARENESS	STRESS DIFFERENTIATION	MAINTAIN BRAND LOYALTY	HARVESTING, DELETION
Competition	Few	More	Many	Reduced
Product	One	More versions	Full product line	Best sellers
Price	Skimming or penetration	Gain market share, deal	Defend market share, profit	Stay profitable
Promotion	Inform, educate	Stress competitive differences	Reminder-oriented	Minimal promotion
Place (distribution)	Limited	More outlets	Maximum outlets	Fewer outlets

■ **FIGURE 11–1** ■

How stages of the product life cycle relate to a firm's marketing objectives and marketing mix actions

the market because they see the opportunity for profit. To discourage competitive entry, a company can price low, referred to as *penetration pricing*. This pricing strategy also helps build unit volume, but a company must closely monitor costs. These and other pricing techniques are covered in depth in Chapter 13.

Figure 11–2 charts the stand-alone fax machine product life cycle for business use from the early 1970s through 2006.[5] As shown, sales grew slowly in the 1970s and early 1980s after Xerox pioneered the first lightweight portable fax machine that sent and received documents. Fax machines were originally sold direct to businesses through company salespeople and were premium priced. The average price for a fax machine in 1980 was $12 700. By today's standards, those fax machines were primitive. They contained mechanical parts, not electronic circuitry, and offered few of the features seen in today's models.

■ FIGURE 11–2 ■

Product life cycle for the
stand-alone fax machine for
business use: 1970–2006

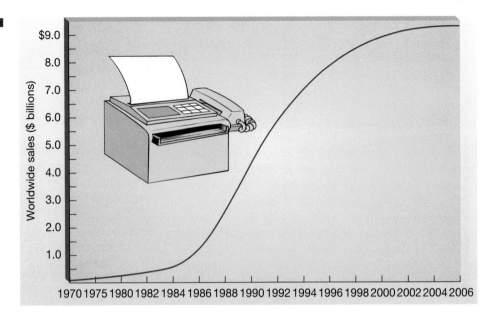

Several product classes are in the introductory stage of the product life cycle.
These include high-definition television (HDTV) and "hybrid" (gasoline-and-elec-
tric-powered) automobiles.

Growth Stage

The second stage of the product life cycle, growth, is characterized by rapid increases
in sales. It is in this stage that competitors appear. For example, Figure 11–2 shows the
dramatic increase in sales of fax machines from 1986 to 1995. The number of companies selling fax machines was also increasing, from one in the early 1970s to four in
the late 1970s to seven manufacturers in 1983, which sold nine brands. By 1990, there
were some 25 manufacturers and 60 possible brands from which to choose.

The result of more competitors and more aggressive pricing is that profit usually
peaks during the growth stage. For instance, the average price for a fax machine
declined from $3300 in 1985 to $500 in 1995. At this stage, the emphasis of advertising shifts to stimulating selective demand, in which product benefits are compared
with those of competitors' offerings for the purpose of gaining market share.

Product sales in the growth stage grow at an increasing rate because of new people trying or using the product and a growing proportion of *repeat purchasers*—people who tried the product, were satisfied, and bought again. As a product moves
through the life cycle, the ratio of repeat purchasers to trial purchasers grows. Failure
to achieve substantial repeat purchasers usually means an early death for a product.
Alberto-Culver introduced Mr. Culver's Sparklers, which were solid air fresheners
that looked like stained glass. The product moved quickly from the introduction to
the growth stage, but then sales plummeted. Why? The problem was that there were
almost no repeat purchasers because buyers treated the product like cheap window
decorations, left them there, and did not buy new ones. Durable fax machines meant
that replacement purchases were rare; however, it was common for more than one
machine to populate a business as their use became more widespread. By 1995, there
was one fax machine for every eight people in a business.

Changes start to appear in the product during the growth stage. To help differentiate a company's brand from those of its competitors, an improved version is created
or new features added to the original design, and product proliferation occurs.
Changes in fax machines included (1) models with built-in telephones; (2) models
that used plain, rather than thermal, paper for copies; (3) models that integrated telex

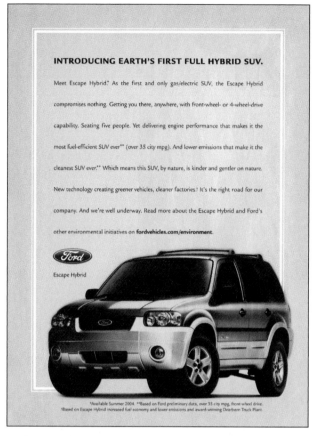

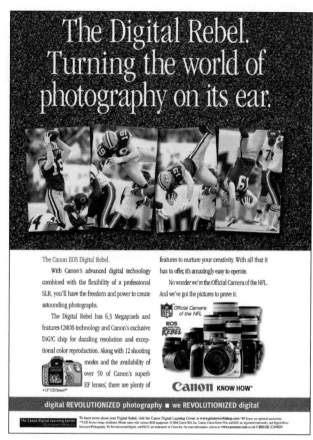

Hybrid automobiles made by Ford are in the introductory stage of the product life cycle. Digital cameras produced by Canon are in the growth stage. Each product as well as the company faces unique challenges based on its product life-cycle stage.

for electronic mail purposes; and (4) models that allowed for secure (confidential) transmissions. For Clearly Canadian, new flavours and package sizes were added during the growth stage.

In the growth stage, it is important to gain as much distribution for the product as possible. In the retail store, for example, this often means that competing companies fight for display and shelf space. Expanded distribution in the fax industry is an example. In 1986, early in the growth stage, only 11 percent of office machine dealers carried this equipment. By the mid-1990s, more than 70 percent of these dealers carried fax equipment, distribution was expanded to other stores selling electronic equipment, and the fight continues for market share.

Numerous product classes or industries are in the growth stage of the product life cycle. Examples include DVD players and digital cameras.

Maturity Stage

The third stage, maturity, is characterized by a slowing of total industry sales or product class revenue. Also, marginal competitors begin to leave the market. Most consumers who would buy the product are either repeat purchasers of the item or have tried and abandoned it. Sales increase at a decreasing rate in the maturity stage as fewer new buyers enter the market. Profit declines because there is fierce price competition among many sellers and the cost of gaining new buyers at this stage increases. By 2006, the average price for a fax machine had dropped to below $100.

Marketing attention in the maturity stage is often directed toward holding market share through further product differentiation and finding new buyers. Gillette, for example, differentiated its original MACH 3 razor through new product features specifically designed for women and then launched the Gillette Venus razor for women just as the original MACH 3 razor entered its maturity stage. Fax machine manufacturers

MARKETING NEWSNET

IDEAS AHEAD

Will E-Mail Spell Doom for the Familiar Fax?

Technological substitution often causes the decline stage in the product life cycle. Will the Internet and e-mail replace fax machines?

This question has caused heated debates. Even though sales of computers with Internet access are in the growth stage of the product life cycle, fax machine sales continue to grow as well. Industry analysts estimate that there are 1.5 billion e-mail mailboxes worldwide. However, the growth of e-mail has not affected faxing because the two technologies do not directly compete for the same messaging applications.

E-mail is used for text messages, and faxing is predominately used for communicating formatted documents by business users. Fax usage is expected to increase through 2007, even though unit sales of fax machines has plateaued on a worldwide basis. Internet technology may eventually replace facsimile technology, but not in the immediate future.

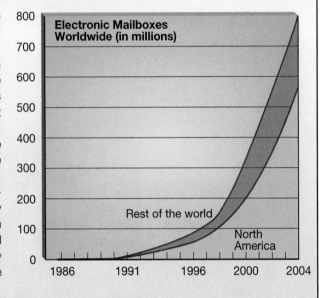

developed Internet-enabled multifunctional models that introduced product features suitable for small and home businesses, which today represent a substantial portion of industry sales. Still, a major consideration in a company's strategy in this stage is to reduce overall marketing costs by improving promotional and distribution efficiency.

Fax machines for business use entered the maturity stage in the late 1990s. By 2006, 90 percent of industry sales were captured by five producers (Hewlett-Packard, Matsushita, Lexmark, Brother, and Sharp), reflecting the departure of marginal competitors. By early 2006, 100 million stand-alone fax machines for business use were installed throughout the world.

Numerous product classes and industries are in the maturity stage of their product life cycle. These include soft drinks, automobiles, and conventional TVs.

Decline Stage

The decline stage occurs when sales and profits begin to drop. Frequently, a product enters this stage not because of any wrong strategy on the part of the company but because of environmental changes. Technological innovation often precedes the decline stage as newer technologies replace older technologies. The word-processing capability of personal computers pushed typewriters into decline. Compact discs did the same to cassette tapes in the prerecorded music industry.

Will Internet technology and e-mail spell doom for fax machines? The accompanying Marketing NewsNet box offers one perspective on this question.[6] Products in the decline stage tend to consume a disproportionate share of management time and financial resources relative to their potential future worth. A company will follow one of two strategies to handle a declining product: deletion or harvesting.

Deletion   Product *deletion*, or dropping the product from the company's product line, is the most drastic strategy. Because a residual core of consumers still consume or use a product even in the decline stage, product elimination decisions are not taken lightly. For example, Gillette continues to sell its Liquid Paper correction fluid for use in typewriters, even in the era of word-processing equipment.

Harvesting   A second strategy, *harvesting*, occurs when a company retains the product but reduces marketing support costs. The product continues to be offered, but salespeople do not allocate time in selling nor are advertising dollars spent. The purpose of harvesting is to maintain the ability to meet customer requests. Coca-Cola, for instance, still sells Tab, its first diet cola, to a small group of die-hard fans. According to Coke's CEO, "It shows you care. We want to make sure those who want Tab get Tab."[7]

Some Dimensions of the Product Life Cycle

Some important aspects of product life cycles are (1) their length, (2) the shape of their curves, and (3) how they vary with different levels of the products, and (4) the rate at which consumers adopt products.

Length of the Product Life Cycle   There is no exact time that a product takes to move through its life cycle. As a rule, consumer products have shorter life cycles than do business products. For example, many new consumer food products, such as Frito-Lay's WOW brand potato chips, move from the introduction stage to maturity in 18 months. The availability of mass communication vehicles informs consumers faster and shortens life cycles. Also, the rate of technological change tends to shorten product life cycles as new-product innovation replaces existing products.

The Shape of the Product Life Cycle   The product life-cycle curve shown in Figure 11–1 is the *generalized life cycle*, but not all products have the same shape to their curve. In fact, there are several different life-cycle curves, each type suggesting different marketing strategies. Figure 11–3 shows the shape of life-cycle curves for four different types of products: high-learning, low-learning, fashion, and fad products.

A *high-learning product* is one for which significant education of the customer is required and there is an extended introductory period (Figure 11–3A). It may surprise

■ **FIGURE 11–3** ■

Alternative product life cycles

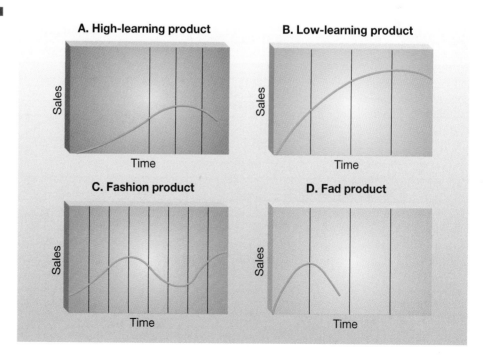

A. High-learning product

Sales / Time

B. Low-learning product

Sales / Time

C. Fashion product

Sales / Time

D. Fad product

Sales / Time

you, but personal computers had this type of life-cycle curve because consumers in the 1980s had to understand the benefits of purchasing the product or be educated in a new way of performing a familiar task. Convection ovens also necessitated that the consumer learn a new way of cooking and alter familiar recipes. As a result, these ovens spent years in the introductory period.

In contrast, for a *low-learning product*, sales begin immediately because little learning is required by the consumer, and the benefits of purchase are readily understood (Figure 11–3B). This product often can be easily imitated by competitors, and so the marketing strategy is to broaden distribution quickly. In this way, as competitors rapidly enter, most retail outlets already have the innovator's product. It is also important to have the manufacturing capacity to meet demand. A recent example of a successful low-learning product is Gillette's original MACH 3 razor. MACH 3 has already recorded close to $10 billion worldwide sales in less than give years.[8]

A *fashion product* (Figure 11–3C), such as hemline lengths on skirts or lapel widths on sports jackets, is introduced, declines, and then seems to return. Life cycles for fashion products most often appear in women's and men's clothing styles. The length of the cycles may be years or decades.

A *fad* experiences rapid sales on introduction and then an equally rapid decline (Figure 11–3D). These products are typically novelties and have a short life cycle. They include car tattoos (described as the first removable and reusable graphics for automobiles), vinyl dresses, fleece bikinis, and an AstroTurf miniskirt.[9]

The Product Level: Class and Form   The product life cycle shown in Figure 11–1 is a total industry or product class sales curve. Yet, in managing a product, it is important to often distinguish among the multiple life cycles (class and form) that may exist. **Product class** refers to the entire product category or industry, such as video game consoles and software shown in Figure 11–4.[10] **Product form** pertains to variations within the class. For video games, product form exists in the computing capability of game consoles such as 8-, 16-, 32/64-, and 128-bit machines, such as Sony's PlayStation 2, Nintendo's GameCube, and Microsoft's Xbox. Game consoles and software have life cycles of their own. They typically move from the introduction stage to maturity in five years. PlayStation 3 and rival game consoles and software arrived in 2005 on schedule.

The Life Cycle and Consumers   The life cycle of a product depends on sales to consumers. Not all consumers rush to buy a product in the introductory stage, and the

product class
The entire product category or industry.

product form
Variations of a product within the product class.

■ **FIGURE 11–4** ■
Video game console and software life cycles by product class and product form

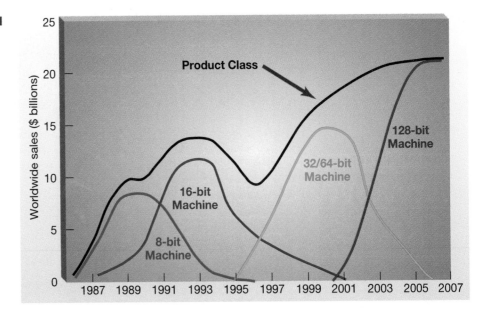

■ FIGURE 11–5 ■

Five categories and profiles
of product adopters

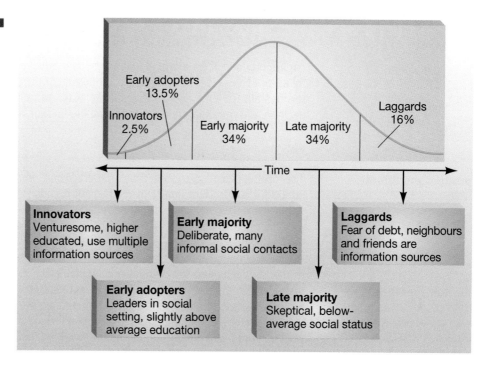

shapes of the life-cycle curves indicate that most sales occur after the product has
been on the market for some time. In essence, a product diffuses, or spreads, through
the population, a concept called the *diffusion of innovation*.[11]

Some people are attracted to a product early, while others buy it only after they see
their friends with the item. Figure 11–5 shows the consumer population divided into
five categories of product adopters based on when they adopt a new product. Brief profiles accompany each category. For any product to be successful, it must be purchased
by innovators and early adopters. This is why manufacturers of new pharmaceuticals try
to gain adoption by leading hospitals, clinics, and physicians that are widely respected
in the medical field. Once accepted by innovators and early adopters, the adoption of
new products moves on to the early majority, late majority, and laggard categories.

Several factors affect whether a consumer will adopt a new product. Common reasons for resisting a product in the introduction stage are usage barriers (the product is
not compatible with existing habits), value barriers (the product provides no incentive to change), risk barriers (physical, economic, or social), and psychological barriers (cultural differences or image).[12]

Companies attempt to overcome these barriers in numerous ways. They provide
warranties, money-back guarantees, extensive usage instructions, demonstrations, and
free samples to stimulate initial trial of new products. For example, software developers offer demonstrations downloaded from the Internet. Maybelline allows consumers
to browse through the Cover Girl Color Match system on its Web site to find out how
certain makeup products will look. Free samples are one of the most popular means to
gain consumer trial. For example, some Ontario winemakers from the Niagara region
believe that sampling (via taste testing) is critical in order for a new wine product to
be successful in the crowded and competitive Canadian market.[13]

**CONCEPT
CHECK**

1. Advertising plays a major role in the _____ stage of the product life
cycle, and _____ plays a major role in maturity.

2. How do high-learning and low-learning products differ?

3. What does the life cycle for a fashion product look like?

■ ■ ■
MANAGING THE PRODUCT LIFE CYCLE

An important task for a firm is to manage its products through the successive stages of their life cycles. This section discusses the role of the product manager, who is usually responsible for this, and analyzes three ways to manage a product through its life cycle: modifying the product, modifying the market, and repositioning the product.

Role of a Product Manager

product modification
Altering a product's characteristic, such as its quality, performance, appearance, features, or package to try to increase and extend the product's sales.

market modification
Strategy in which a company tries to find new customers, increase a product's use among existing customers, or create new-use situations.

The product manager (sometimes called *brand manager*) manages the marketing efforts for a close-knit family of products or brands.[14] Introduced by P&G in 1928, the product manager style of marketing organization is used by consumer goods firms, such as General Mills and PepsiCo, and by business firms, such as Intel and Hewlett-Packard. Pillsbury Canada and General Motors of Canada also use product managers. All product managers are responsible for managing existing products through the stages of the life cycle, and some are also responsible for developing new products. Product managers' marketing responsibilities include developing and executing a marketing program for the product line described in an annual marketing plan and approving ad copy, media selection, and package design. The role of product managers in planning, implementing, and controlling marketing strategy is covered in depth in Chapter 19.

Modifying the Product

Molson Kick—a modified beer product.

Product modification involves altering a product's characteristics, such as its quality, performance, or appearance, features, or package, to try to increase and extend the product's sales. Wrinkle-free cotton slacks sold by Levi Strauss revitalized sales of men's casual pants and now account for 60 percent of the men's cotton pants product class sales. Harley-Davidson modified its entry-level Sportster line of motorcycles by including smaller hand grips, a lower seat, and an easier-to-pull clutch lever to create a more comfortable rise for first-time motorcycle buyers. Heinz Canada modified its original red ketchup by adding a little food colouring to create new versions of ketchup called Blastin Green and Funky Purple.[15] And, Molson unveiled a new modified beer product, *Molson Kick*, which is a premium lager with the essence of guarana added. Guarana is a South American plant that is a natural source of caffeine. Molson Kick also comes in an innovative package, a 355-mL aluminum bottle that chills faster and is lighter than a traditional glass bottle.[16]

Modifying the Market

With **market modification** strategies, a company tries to find new customers, increase a product's use among existing customers, or create new-use situations.

Finding New Users   Produce companies have begun marketing and packaging prunes as "dried plums" for the purposes of attracting younger buyers. Sony has expanded its user base by developing PlayStation 2 video games specially designed for children under 13 years old.[17]

Increasing Use   Promoting more frequent usage has been a strategy of Campbell Soup Company. Since soup consumption rises in the winter and declines during the summer, the company now advertises more heavily in warm months to encourage consumers to think of soup as more than a cold-weather food. Similarly, The Florida Orange Growers Association advocates drinking orange juice throughout the day rather than for breakfast only. And the Canadian Turkey Marketing Agency is now telling Canadians that turkey meat is a good option for everyday meals not just for Thanksgiving and Christmas.

Nothing says barbeque quite like beef Turkey

BBQ Turkey Burgers

1 1/2 lb	fresh ground Turkey	750 g
1/2 cup	chopped onion	125 mL
1/2 cup	BBQ sauce	125 mL
1/2 cup	dried bread crumbs	125 mL
1/2 tsp	salt	2 mL
	ground black pepper, to taste	

Preparation Time: 5 minutes
Cooking Time: 12 minutes

Combine all ingredients in a large bowl. Mix thoroughly. Shape into 6 patties. Place on oiled grill. Grill over medium heat 4-6 minutes on each side, or until no longer pink in centre, basting with additional BBQ sauce if desired.

Turkey makes a good recipe taste better."

CTMA
CANADIAN TURKEY MARKETING AGENCY
turkeyfordinner.ca

© Canadian Turkey Marketing Agency 2004

Creating New-Use Situations   Finding new uses for an existing product has been the strategy behind Woolite, a laundry soap. Originally intended for hand washing of woollen fabric, Woolite now promotes itself for use with all fine clothing items. Mars, Inc. suggests a new-use situation when it markets its M&M's candy as a replacement for chocolate chips in baked goods.

Repositioning the Product

Often, a company decides to reposition its product or product line in an attempt to bolster sales. *Product repositioning* is changing the place a product occupies in a consumer's mind relative to competing products. A firm can reposition a product by changing one or more of the four marketing mix elements. Four factors that trigger a repositioning action are discussed next.

Reacting to a Competitor's Position   One reason to reposition a product is that a competitor's entrenched position is adversely affecting sales and market share. New Balance, Inc. successfully repositioned its athletic shoes to focus on fit and comfort rather than competing head-on against Nike and Reebok on fashion and sport. The company offers an expansive range of shoe widths with the message, "N is for fit," and it networks with podiatrists, not sport celebrities.[18]

Reaching a New Market   When Unilever introduced iced tea in the United Kingdom in the mid-1990s, sales were disappointing. British consumers viewed it as leftover hot tea, not suitable for drinking. The company made its tea carbonated and repositioned it as a cold soft drink to compete as a carbonated beverage, and sales improved. Johnson & Johnson effectively repositioned St. Joseph Aspirin from one for infants to an adult low-strength aspirin to reduce the risk of heart problems or strokes.[19]

Catching a Rising Trend   Changing consumer trends can also lead to repositioning. Growing consumer interest in foods that offer health and dietary benefits is an example, and many products have been repositioned to capitalize on this trend. Quaker Oats makes the claim that oatmeal, as part of a low-saturated-fat, low-cholesterol diet, may reduce the risk of heart disease. Calcium-enriched products, such as Uncle Ben's Calcium Plus rice, emphasize healthy bone structure for children and adults. Weight-conscious consumers have embraced low-carbohydrate diets in growing numbers. Today, every major consumer food and beverage company in Canada offers and advertises reduced-carbohydrate versions of its products.[20]

trading up
Adding value to a product (or line) through additional features or higher-quality materials.

trading down
Reducing the number of features, quality, or price.

Changing the Value Offered   In repositioning a product, a company can decide to change the value it offers buyers and trade up or down. **Trading up** involves adding value to the product (or line) through additional features or higher-quality materials. Michelin has done this with its "run-flat" tire, which can keep going up to 70 kilometres after suffering total air loss. Dog food manufacturers, such as Ralston Purina, also have traded up by offering super premium foods based on "life-stage nutrition." Mass merchandisers, such as Sears Canada, Zellers, and The Bay, can trade up by adding designer clothes sections to their stores.

Trading down involves reducing the number of features, quality, or price. For example, airlines have added more seats, thus reducing leg room, and eliminated

ETHICS AND SOCIAL RESPONSIBILITY ALERT

Consumer Economics of Downsizing: Get Less, Pay More

For more than 30 years, Starkist put 185 grams of tuna into its regular-sized can. Today, Starkist puts 175 grams of tuna into its can but charges the same price. Frito-Lay (Doritos and Lay's snack chips), Procter & Gamble (Pampers and Luvs disposable diapers), and Nestlé (Poland Spring and Calistoga bottled waters) have whittled away at package contents 5 to 10 percent while maintaining their products' package size, dimensions, and prices. Kimberly-Clark cut the retail price on its jumbo pack of Huggies diapers, but also reduced the number of diapers per pack from 48 to 42.

Consumer advocates charge that "downsizing" the content of packages while maintaining prices is a subtle and unannounced way of taking advantage of consumer buying habits. They also say downsizing is a price increase in disguise and deceptive, but legal. Manufacturers argue that this practice is a way of keeping prices from rising beyond the psychological barriers for their products.

Is downsizing an unethical practice if manufacturers do not inform consumers that the package contents are less than they were previously?

---

downsizing

Reducing the content of packages without changing package size and maintaining or increasing the package price.

extras, such as snack service and food portions. Trading down often exists when companies engage in **downsizing**—reducing the content of packages without changing package size and maintaining or increasing the package price. Firms have been criticized for this practice, as described in the accompanying Ethics and Social Responsibility Alert box.[21]

CONCEPT CHECK

1. How does a product manager help manage a product's life cycle?

2. What does "creating new-use situations" mean in managing a product's life cycle?

3. Explain the difference between trading up and trading down in repositioning.

BRANDING AND BRAND MANAGEMENT

branding

Activity in which an organization uses a name, phrase, design, or symbols, or combination of these, to identify its products and distinguish them from those of competitors.

brand name

Any word, device (design, shape, sound, or colour), or combination of these used to distinguish a seller's goods or services.

trade name

A commercial, legal name under which a company does business.

trademark

Identifies that a firm has legally registered its brand name or trade name so that the firm has its exclusive use.

A basic decision in marketing products is **branding**, in which an organization uses a name, phrase, design, symbols, or combination of these to identify its products and distinguish them from those of competitors. A **brand name** is any word, "device" (design, sound, shape, or colour), or combination of these used to distinguish a seller's goods or services. Some brand names can be spoken, such as Clearly Canadian or Bauer. Other brand names cannot be spoken, such as the rainbow-coloured apple (the *logotype* or *logo*) that Apple Computer puts on its machines and in its ads. A **trade name** is a commercial, legal name under which a company does business. The Campbell Soup Company is the trade name of that firm.

A **trademark** identifies that a firm has legally registered its brand name or trade name so that the firm has its exclusive use, thereby preventing others from using it. In Canada, trademarks are registered under the Trade-marks Act with Industry Canada. A well-known trademark can help a company advertise its offerings to customers and develop their brand loyalty.

Because a good trademark can help sell a product, *product counterfeiting*, which involves low-cost copies of popular brands not manufactured by the original producer, has been a growing problem. Counterfeit products can steal sales from the original manufacturer or hurt the company's reputation.[22]

Trademark protection is a significant issue in global marketing. For instance, the breaking up of the Soviet Union into individual countries has meant that many firms, such as Xerox, had to re-register trademarks in each of the republics to prohibit misuse and generic use ("xeroxing") of their trademarks by competitors and consumers.

Can you describe the personality traits for these two brands? Not sure? Try visiting their Web sites for more information.

got2b
www.got2b.com

Mambo
www.lizclaiborne.com/mambo

brand personality
A set of human characteristics associated with a brand name.

brand equity
The added value a given brand name gives to a product beyond the functional benefits provided.

Consumers may benefit most from branding. Recognizing competing products by distinct trademarks allows them to be more efficient shoppers. Consumers can recognize and avoid products with which they are dissatisfied while becoming loyal to other, more satisfying brands. As discussed in Chapter 5, brand loyalty often eases consumers' decision making by eliminating the need for an external search. CanWest Global TV System uses a single brand, "Global," which it says makes it easier for viewers to identify the network's stations and to find the schedule they have.

Brand Personality and Brand Equity

Product managers recognize that brands offer more than product identification and a means to distinguish their products from competitors. Successful and established brands take on a **brand personality**, a set of human characteristics associated with a brand name.[23] Research shows that consumers often assign personality qualities to products—traditional, romantic, rugged, sophisticated, rebellious—and choose brands that are consistent with their own or desired self-image. Marketers can and do imbue a brand with a personality through advertising that depicts a certain user or usage situation and conveys certain emotions or feelings to be associated with the brand. For example, the personality traits associated with Coca-Cola are *real* and *cool*; with Pepsi, *young*, *exciting*, and *hip*; and with Dr. Pepper, *nonconforming*, *unique*, and *fun*.

Brand name importance to a company has led to a concept called **brand equity**, the added value a given brand name gives to a product beyond the functional benefits provided. This value has two distinct advantages. First, brand equity provides a competitive advantage, such as the Sunkist label, which implies quality fruit, and the Disney name, which defines children's entertainment. A second advantage is that consumers are often willing to pay a higher price for a product with brand equity. Brand equity, in this instance, is represented by the premium a consumer will pay for

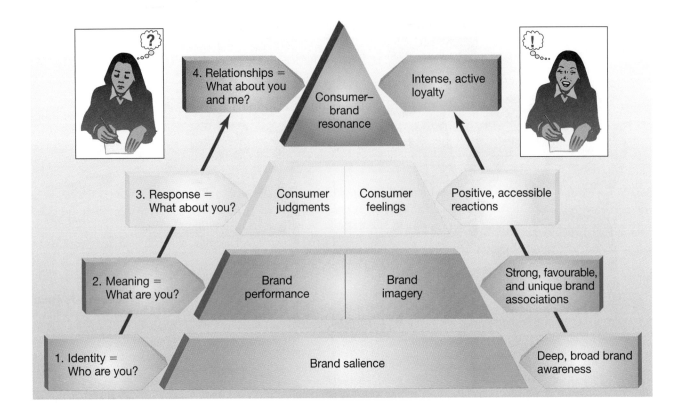

■ FIGURE 11–6 ■
Customer-based brand
equity pyramid

one brand over another when the functional benefits provided are identical. Intel microchips, Bose audio systems, Duracell batteries, Microsoft computer software, and Louis Vuitton luggage all enjoy a price premium arising from brand equity.

Creating Brand Equity   Brand equity does not just happen. It is carefully crafted and nurtured by marketing programs that forge strong, favourable, and unique consumer associations and experiences with a brand. Brand equity resides in the minds of consumers and results from what they have learned, felt, seen, and heard about a brand over time. Marketers recognize that brand equity is not easily or quickly achieved. Rather, it arises from a sequential building process consisting of four steps (Figure 11–6).[24]

- The first step is to develop positive brand awareness and an association of the brand in consumers' minds with a product class or need to give the brand an identity. Gatorade and Kleenex have done this in the sports drink and facial tissue product classes, respectively.
- Next, a marketer must establish a brand's meaning in the minds of consumers. Meaning arises from what a brand stands for and has two dimensions—a functional, performance-related dimension and an abstract, imagery-related dimension. Nike has done this through continuous product development and improvement and its links to peak athletic performance in its integrated marketing communications program.
- The third step is to elicit the proper consumer responses to a brand's identity and meaning. Here, attention is placed on how consumers think and feel about a brand. Thinking focuses on a brand's perceived quality, credibility, and superiority relative to other brands. Feeling relates to the consumer's emotional reaction to a brand. Michelin elicits both responses for its tires. Not only is Michelin thought of as a credible and superior-quality brand, but consumers also acknowledge a warm and secure feeling of safety, comfort, and self-assurance without worry or concern about the brand.

- The final, and most difficult, step is to create a consumer–brand resonance evident in an intense, active loyalty relationship between consumers and the brand. A deep psychological bond characterizes consumer–brand resonance and the personal identification consumers have with the brand. Examples of brands that have achieved this status include Harley-Davidson, Apple, and eBay.

Marketers of services also need to build their brand names and to create brand equity. Whether they market financial services or sports entertainment, the goal is the same. For example, Maple Leaf Sports & Entertainment Ltd. (MLS&E), which owns the Toronto Maple Leafs and the Toronto Raptors, markets its brand names diligently, focusing on building bonds between the fans and these sports teams. According to Tom Anselmi of MLS&E, "brand building is just as important in the business of sports as it is in selling laundry soap." Recent Canadian research on business start-ups suggests that building the brand is a key imperative for new venture success. In crowded and competitive markets, the entrepreneur must be able to develop a brand that resonates with the consumer.[25]

Maple Leaf Sports & Entertainment Ltd. focuses on building bonds between fans and its sports teams.

Valuing Brand Equity Brand equity also provides a financial advantage for the brand owner.[26] Successful, established brand names, such as Gillette, Nike, Gatorade, and Nokia, have an economic value in the sense that they are intangible assets. The recognition that brands are assets is apparent in the decision to buy and sell brands. For example, Triarc Companies bought the Snapple brand from Quaker Oats in 1997 for $300 million and sold it to Cadbury Schweppes in 2000 for $900 million. This example illustrates that brands, unlike physical assets that depreciate with time and use, can appreciate in value when effectively marketed. However, brands can lose value when they are not managed properly. Consider the purchase and sale of Lender's Bagels. Kellogg bought the brand for $466 million only to sell it to Aurora Foods for $275 million three years later following deteriorating sales and profits.

Financially lucrative brand licensing opportunities arise from brand equity. **Brand licensing** is a contractual agreement whereby one company (licensor) allows its brand name(s) or trademark(s) to be used with products or services offered by another company (licensee) for a royalty or fee. For example, Playboy earns more than $260 million licensing its name for merchandise ranging from wallpaper in

brand licensing
A contractual agreement whereby a company allows another firm to use its brand name, patent, trade secret, or other property for a royalty or fee.

General Motors is the worldwide leader in licensed product sales among automakers. A recent licensing arrangement is for Hummer® Footwear made by Roper Footwear & Apparel.

General Motors
www.hummer.com

Europe to cooking classes in Brazil. Disney makes billions of dollars each year licensing its characters for children's toys, apparel, and games. Licensing fees for Winnie the Pooh alone exceed $3 billion annually. General Motors sells more than $2 billion in licensed products each year.[27]

Successful brand licensing requires careful marketing analysis to assure a proper match between the licensor's brand and the licensee's products. World-renowned designer Ralph Lauren has built a $5 billion business licensing his Ralph Lauren, Polo, and Chaps brands for dozens of products, including paint by Sherwin-Williams, furniture by Hendredon, footwear by Rockport, and fragrances by Cosmair. Such mistakes as Kleenex diapers, Bic perfume, and Domino's fruit-favoured bubble gum represent a few examples of poor matches and licensing failures.

Picking a Good Brand Name

We take such brand names as Dial, Sanyo, Porsche, and Adidas for granted, but it is often a difficult and expensive process to choose a good name. Companies will spend between $25 000 and $100 000 to identify and test a new brand name. For instance, Intel spent $45 000 for the Pentium name given to its family of microchips. There are five criteria mentioned most often when selecting a good brand name.[28]

- The name should suggest the product benefits. For example, Accutron (watches), Easy Off (oven cleaner), Glass Plus (glass cleaner), Cling-Free (antistatic cloth for drying clothes), Powerbook (laptop computer), and Tidy Bowl (toilet bowl cleaner) all clearly describe the benefits of purchasing the product.
- The name should be memorable, distinctive, and positive. In the auto industry, when a competitor has a memorable name, others quickly imitate. When Ford named a car Mustang, others soon followed with Pintos, Colts, and Broncos. The Thunderbird name led to Phoenix, Eagle, Sunbird, and Firebird.
- The name should fit the company or product image. Sharp is a name that can apply to audio and video equipment. Excedrin, Anacin, and Nuprin are scientific-sounding names, good for an analgesic. However, naming a personal computer PCjr, as IBM did with its first computer for home use, fit neither the company nor the product. PCjr sounded like a toy and stalled IBM's initial entry into the home-use market.
- The name should have no legal or regulatory restrictions. Legal restrictions produce trademark infringement suits, and regulatory restrictions can arise through improper use of words. Increasingly, brand names need a corresponding address on the Internet. This further complicates name selection because millions of domain names are already registered.
- Finally, the name should be simple (such as Bold laundry detergent, Sure deodorant, and Bic pens) and should have emotional appeal (such as Joy and Obsession perfumes). In the development of names for international use, having a nonmeaningful brand name has been considered a benefit. A name such as Esso does not have any prior impressions or undesirable images among a diverse world population with different languages and cultures. The 7Up name is another matter. In Shanghai, China, the phrase means "death through drinking" in the local dialect, and sales have suffered as a result.

Do you have an idea for a brand name? If you do, check to see if the name has been registered with Industry Canada's trademark division. Visit its Web site, described in the accompanying WebLink box.

Branding Strategies

Companies can employ several different branding strategies, including multiproduct branding, multibranding, private branding, or mixed branding (Figure 11–7).

WEBLINK
HTTP://WWW.MCGRAWHILL.CA/
COLLEGE/CRANE

Have an Idea for a Brand or Trade Name? Check It Out!

There are thousands of brand names or trade names already registered with Industry Canada and its trademark division. More and more are being registered every day.

An important step in choosing a brand or trade name is to determine whether the name has already been registered. Industry Canada offers a valuable service by allowing individuals and companies to quickly check to see if a name has been registered.

Do you have an idea for a brand or trade name for a new snack, software package, retail outlet, or service? Check to see if the name has been registered by visiting www.strategis.gc.ca. Then, click on the trademark section under Industry Canada Services. You will be taken to the Canadian Intellectual Property Office section. Click on "trademark database." Enter your proposed brand name to find out if any person or organization has registered your chosen name.

multiproduct branding
Use by a company of one name for all its products in a product class.

Multiproduct Branding   With **multiproduct branding**, a company uses one name for all its products in a product class. This approach is sometimes called *family branding,* or *corporate branding* when the company's trade name is used. For example, General Electric, Gerber, and Sony engage in corporate branding—the company's trade name and brand name are identical. Church & Dwight employs the Arm & Hammer family brand name for all its products featuring baking soda as the primary ingredient.

There are several advantages to multiproduct branding. Capitalizing again on brand equity, consumers who have a good experience with the product will transfer this favourable attitude to other items in the product class with the same name. Therefore, this brand strategy makes possible *line extensions,* the practice of using a current brand name to enter a new market segment in its product class. Campbell Soup Company effectively employs a multiproduct branding strategy with soup line extensions. It offers regular Campbell soup, home-cooking style, and chunky varieties and more than 100 soup flavours. This strategy can also result in lower advertising and promotion costs because the same name is used on all products, thus raising the level of brand awareness. A risk with line extension is that sales of an extension may come at the expense of other items in the company's product line. Therefore, line extensions work best when they provide incremental company revenue by taking sales away from competing brands or attracting new buyers.

Some companies employ *sub-branding,* which combines a corporate or family brand with a new brand. For example, ThinkPad is a sub-brand to the IBM name.

■ FIGURE 11–7 ■
Alternative branding strategies

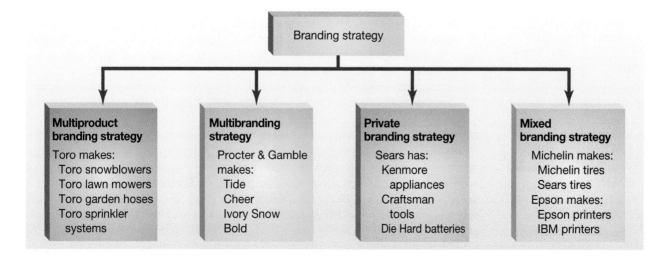

Black & Decker uses a multibranding strategy to reach different market segments. Black & Decker markets its line of tools for the do-it-yourselfer market with the Black & Decker name but uses the DeWalt name for its professional tool line.

Black & Decker
www.blackanddecker.com

co-branding
The pairing of two brand names of two manufacturers on a single product.

multibranding
A manufacturer's branding strategy giving each product a distinct name.

Gatorade has successfully used sub-branding with the introduction of Gatorade Frost, Gatorade Fierce, and Gatorade X-Factor, with unique flavours developed for each.

A strong brand equity also allows for *brand extension*, the practice of using a current brand name to enter a completely different product class. For instance, the equity in the Tylenol name as a trusted pain reliever allowed Johnson & Johnson to successfully extend this name to Tylenol Cold & Flu and Tylenol PM, a sleep aid. Honda's established name for motor vehicles has extended easily to snowblowers, lawn mowers, marine engines, and snowmobiles.

However, there is a risk with brand extensions. Too many uses for one brand name can dilute the meaning of a brand for consumers. Marketing experts claim this has happened to the Arm & Hammer brand given its use for toothpaste, laundry detergent, gum, cat litter, air freshener, carpet deodorizer, and antiperspirant.[29]

A recent variation on brand extensions is the practice of **co-branding**, the pairing of two brand names of two manufacturers on a single product.[30] Co-branding benefits firms by allowing them to enter new product classes, capitalize on an already established brand name in a product class, or reach new market segments. Second Cup of Toronto co-brands with Air Canada, and Rogers and AT&T Canada Inc. also co-brand, offering consumers seamless wireless telecommunications throughout North America.

Multibranding Alternatively, a company can engage in **multibranding**, which involves giving each product a distinct name. Multibranding is a useful strategy when each brand is intended for a different market segment. P&G makes Camay soap for those concerned about soft skin and Safeguard for those who want deodorant protection. Black & Decker markets its line of tools for the household do-it-yourselfer segment with the Black & Decker name but uses the DeWalt name for its professional tool line. Disney uses the Miramax and Touchstone Pictures names for films directed at adults and its Disney name for children's films.

Multibranding is applied in a variety of ways. Some companies array their brands on the basis of price–quality segments.[31] Marriott International offers 14 hotel and resort brands, each suited for a particular traveller experience and budget. To illustrate, Marriott Marquis hotels and Vacation Clubs offer luxury amenities at a premium price. Marriott and Renaissance hotels offer medium- to high-priced accommodations. Courtyard hotels and Town Place Suites appeal to economy-minded travellers, whereas the Fairfield Inn is for those on a very low travel budget. Other multibrand companies introduce new product brands as defensive moves to counteract competition. Called *fighting brands,* their chief purpose is to confront competitor brands. For instance, Frito-Lay introduced Santitas brand tortilla chip to go head-to-head against regional tortilla chip brands that were biting into the sales of its flagship Doritos and Tostitos brand tortilla chips. Mattel launched its Flava brand of hip-hop fashion dolls in response to the popularity of Bratz brand dolls sold by MGA Entertainment, which were attracting the 8- to 12-year-old-girl segment of Barbie brand sales.

Compared with the multiproduct approach, promotional costs tend to be higher with multibranding. The company must generate awareness among consumers and retailers for each new brand name without the benefit of any previous impressions. The advantages of this approach are that each brand is unique to each market segment, and there is no risk that one product's failure will affect other products in the line. Nevertheless, some large multibrand firms have found that the complexity and expense of implementing this strategy can outweigh the benefits. For example, Unilever recently pruned its brands from some 1600 to 400 through product deletion and sales to other companies.[32]

private branding

When a company manufactures products but sells them under the brand name of a wholesaler or retailer (often called *private labelling* or *reseller branding*).

Private Branding   A company uses **private branding**, often called *private labelling* or *reseller branding*, when it manufactures products but sells them under the brand name of a wholesaler or retailer. Radio Shack and Sears are large retailers that have their own brand names. Zellers also launched its Truly private brand hoping to foster the same customer loyalty as Loblaws' very successful President's Choice private brand. Other successful private brands in Canada include Sobeys' Smart Choice brand and Shoppers Drug Mart's Life brand.

Private branding is popular because it typically produces high profits for manufacturers and resellers. Consumers also buy these private brands with regularity.[33]

cohort brand management

The bundling of one company's multiple brands into a single marketing effort aimed at a common consumer group.

Cohort Brand Management   A recent innovation in brand management is the concept of **cohort brand management**—the bundling of one company's multiple brands into a single marketing effort aimed at a common consumer group. It is a collective approach to marketing in contrast to the traditional individualistic brand management approach. Cohort brand management is typically done through online marketing. For example, Proctor & Gamble uses cohort brand management via its Web site HomemadeSimple.com. The site offers an online guide to home and lifestyle issues while promoting several P&G brands, including Mr. Clean, Swiffer, and Febreze.

mixed branding

A firm markets products under its own name and that of a reseller because the segment attracted by the reseller is different from its own market.

Mixed Branding   A fourth branding strategy is **mixed branding**, where a firm markets products under its own name(s) and that of a reseller because the segment attracted to the reseller is different from its own market. Beauty and fragrance marketer Elizabeth Arden is a case in point. The company sells its Elizabeth Arden brand through department stores and a line of skincare products at Wal-Mart with the "skinsimple" brand name. Kodak uses a mixed branding approach in Japan to increase its sales of 35-mm film. In addition to selling its Kodak brand, the company now makes "COOP" private label film for the Japanese Consumer Cooperative Union, which is a group of 2500 stores. Priced significantly below its Kodak brand, the private label seeks to attract the price-sensitive Japanese consumer.[34]

MARKETING NEWSNET

Creating Customer Value through Packaging: Pez Heads Dispense More Than Candy

Customer value can assume numerous forms. For Pez Candy, Inc. (www.pez.com), customer value manifests itself in some 250 Pez character candy dispensers. Each 99-cent refillable dispenser ejects tasty candy tablets in a variety of flavours that delight preteens and teens alike.

Pez was formulated in 1927 by Austrian food mogul Edward Haas III and successfully sold in Europe as an adult breath mint. Pez, which comes from the German word for peppermint, *pfefferminz*, was originally packaged in a hygienic, headless plastic dispenser. Pez first appeared in North America in 1953 with a headless dispenser marketed to adults. After conducting extensive marketing research, Pez was repositioned with fruit flavours, repackaged with licensed character heads on top of the dispenser, and remarketed as a children's product in the mid-1950s. Since then, most top-level licensed characters and hundreds of other characters have become Pez heads. Consumers eat more than three billion Pez tablets annually, and company sales growth exceeds that of the candy industry as a whole.

The unique Pez package dispenses a "use experience" for its customers beyond the candy itself—namely, fun. And fun translates into a 98-percent awareness level for Pez among teenagers and 89 percent among mothers with children. Pez has not advertised its product for years. With that kind of awareness, who needs advertising?

PACKAGING AND LABELLING

packaging

Any container in which a product is offered for sale and on which label information is communicated.

label

An integral part of the package that typically identifies the product or brand, who made it, where and when it was made, how it is to be used, and package contents and ingredients.

The **packaging** component of a product refers to any container in which it is offered for sale and on which label information is conveyed. A **label** is an integral part of the package and typically identifies the product or brand, who made it, where and when it was made, how it is to be used, and package contents and ingredients. To a great extent, the customer's first exposure to a product is the package and label, and both are an expensive and important part of marketing strategy. For Pez Candy, Inc., the character-head-on-a-stick plastic container that dispenses a miniature brick candy is the central element of its marketing strategy, as described in the accompanying Marketing NewsNet box.[35]

Creating Customer Value through Packaging and Labelling

Today's packaging and labeling cost Canadian companies billions of dollars, and an estimated 15 cents of every dollar spent by a consumer goes to packaging.[36] Despite the cost, packaging and labelling are essential because both provide important benefits for the manufacturer, retailer, and ultimate consumer. Packaging and labelling can also provide a competitive advantage.

Communication Benefits   A major benefit of packaging is the label information on it conveyed to the consumer, such as directions on how to use the product and the composition of the product, which is needed to satisfy legal requirements of product disclosure. Other information consists of seals and symbols, either government-required or commercial seals of approval (such as the Good Housekeeping seal or the CSA seal). Packaging also can have brand equity benefits for a company. It has been

Which chip stacks up better? Frito-Lay's recent introduction of Lay's Stax potato crisps to compete against Procter & Gamble's Pringles illustrates the role of packaging in product and brand management.

Lay's Stax

www.laysstax.com

Pringles

www.pringles.com

shown that packaging can enhance brand recognition and facilitate the formation of strong, favourable, and unique brand associations.[37]

Functional Benefits   Packaging often plays an important functional role, such as storage, convenience, protection, or product quality. Storing food containers is one example, and beverage companies have developed lighter and easier ways to stack products on shelves and in refrigerators. Examples include Coca-Cola beverage packs designed to fit neatly into refrigerator shelves and Ocean Spray Cranberries' rectangular juice bottles that allow 10 units per package versus 8 of its former round bottles.[38]

The convenience dimension of packaging is becoming increasingly important. Kraft Miracle Whip salad dressing, Heinz ketchup, and Skippy Squeez'It peanut butter are sold in squeeze bottles; microwave popcorn has been a major market success; and Chicken of the Sea tuna and Folgers coffee are packaged in single-serving portions.

Consumer protection has become an important function of packaging, including the development of tamper-resistant containers. Today, companies commonly use safety seals or pop-tops that reveal previous opening. Nevertheless, no package is truly tamper resistant. There are now laws that provide for prison and fines for package tampering. Consumer protection through labelling also exists in "open dating," which states the expected shelf life of the product.

Functional features of packaging also can affect product quality. Procter & Gamble's Pringles, with its cylindrical packaging, offers uniform chips, minimal breakage, and, for some consumers, better value for the money than flex-bag packages for chips. Not to be outdone, Frito-Lay, the world's leading producer of snack chips recently decided to "stand up" to Pringles with its new line of Lay's Stax potato crisps.[39] The consumers will be the final judge of which chip stacks up better.

Can you name this soft drink brand?

Perceptual Benefits   A third component of packaging and labelling is the perception created in the consumer's mind. Just Born Inc., a candy manufacturer of such brands as Jolly Joes and Mike and Ike Treats, discovered the importance of this component of packaging. For many years, the brands were sold in old-fashioned black and white packages, but when the packaging was changed to four colour, with animated grape and cherry characters, sales increased 25 percent. Coca-Cola brought back its famous and universally recognized contoured bottle shape to further differentiate itself from competitors.

Because labels list a product's source, brands competing in the global marketplace can benefit from "country of origin or manufacture" perceptions as described in Chapter 7. Consumers tend to have stereotypes about country–product pairings that they judge "best"—English tea, French perfume, Italian leather, and Japanese electronics—which can affect a brand's image. Increasingly, Chinese firms are adopting the English language and Roman alphabet for their brands' labels. This is being done because of the perception in many Asian countries that "things Western are good," even if consumers do not understand the meaning of the English words![40]

Global Trends in Packaging

Two global trends in packaging originating in the mid-1990s will continue in the twenty-first century. One trend involves the environmental effects of packaging, and the other focuses on packaging health and safety concerns.

Environmental Sensitivity   Because of widespread worldwide concern about the growth of solid waste and the shortage of viable landfill sites, the amount, composition, and disposal of packaging material continues to receive much attention.[41] Recycling packaging material is a major thrust. Procter & Gamble now uses recycled cardboard in 70 percent of its paper packaging and is packaging Tide, Cheer, Era, and Dash detergents in jugs that contain 25 percent recycled plastic. Spic and Span liquid cleaner is packaged in 100-percent-recycled material. Other firms, such as the large British retailer Sainsbury, emphasize the use of less packaging material. Sainsbury examines every product it sells to ensure that each uses only the minimum material necessary for shipping and display.

European countries have been trendsetters in packaging guidelines and environmental sensitivity. Many of these guidelines now exist in provisions governing trade to and within the European Union. In Germany, for instance, 80 percent of packaging material must be collected, and 80 percent of this amount must be recycled or reused to reduce solid waste in landfills. Canadian firms marketing in Europe have responded to these guidelines, and this has ultimately benefitted Canadian consumers.

Increasingly, firms are using life-cycle analysis (LCA) to examine the environmental effects of their packaging at every stage, from raw material sources and production through distribution and disposal. A classic use of LCA was the decision by McDonald's to abandon the polystyrene clam-shells it used to package its hamburgers. LCA indicated that the environment would be better served if the amount of solid waste packaging were reduced than by recycling the polystyrene shells. McDonald's elected to package its hamburgers in a light wrap made of paper and polyethylene and eliminated the polystyrene package altogether.

Health and Safety Concerns   A second trend involves the growing health and safety concerns of packaging materials. Today, a majority of North American and European consumers believe that companies should make sure products and their packages are safe, regardless of the cost, and companies are responding to this view in numerous ways. Most butane lighters sold today, such as those made by Bic, contain a child-safety latch to prevent misuse and accidental fire. Childproof caps on pharmaceutical products and household cleaners and sealed lids on food packages are now common. New packaging technology and materials that extend a product's *shelf life* (the time a product can be stored) and prevent spoilage continue to be developed with special applications for the less developed countries.

■ ■ ■
PRODUCT WARRANTY

warranty
A statement indicating the liability of the manufacturer for product deficiencies.

A final component for product consideration is the **warranty**, which is a statement indicating the liability of the manufacturer for product deficiencies. There are various degrees of product warranties with different implications for manufacturers and customers.

Some companies offer *express warranties*, which are written statements of liabilities. In recent years, government has required greater disclosure on express warranties to indicate whether the warranty is a limited-coverage or full-coverage alternative. A *limited-coverage warranty* specifically states the bounds of coverage and, more importantly, areas of noncoverage, whereas a *full warranty* has no limits of noncoverage. Cadillac is a company that boldly touts its warranty coverage. Also, in an effort to improve its image with Canadian consumers, Hyundai offers what it claims to be the best automobile warranty in the industry.

With greater frequency, manufacturers are being held to *implied warranties*, which assign responsibility for product deficiencies to the manufacturer. Studies show that warranties are important and affect a consumer's product evaluation. Brands that have limited warranties tend to receive less positive evaluations compared with full-warranty items.

Warranties are important in light of increasing product liability claims. In the early part of the twentieth century, the courts protected companies, but the trend now is toward "strict liability" rulings, where a manufacturer is liable for any product defect, whether it followed reasonable research standards or not. This issue is hotly contested by companies and consumer advocates.

Warranties represent much more to the buyer than just protection from negative consequences—they can hold a significant marketing advantage for the producer. Sears has built a strong reputation for its Craftsman tool line with a simple warranty: if you break a tool, it is replaced with no questions asked. Zippo has an equally simple guarantee: "If it ever fails, we'll fix it for free."

CONCEPT CHECK

1. How does a generic brand differ from a private brand?

2. Explain the role of packaging in terms of perception.

3. What is the difference between an expressed warranty and an implied warranty?

■ ■ ■
CHAPTER IN REVIEW

1   *Explain the product life-cycle concept.*
The product life cycle describes the stages a new product goes through in the marketplace: introduction, growth, maturity, and decline. Product sales growth and profitability differ at each stage, and marketing managers have marketing objectives and marketing mix strategies unique to each stage based on consumer behaviour and competitive factors. In the introductory stage, the need is to establish primary demand, whereas the growth stage requires selective demand strategies. In the maturity stage, the need is to maintain market share; the decline stage necessitates a deletion or harvesting strategy. Some important aspects of product life cycles are (*a*) their length, (*b*) the shape of the sales curve, (*c*) how they vary by product classes and forms, and (*d*) the rate at which consumers adopt products.

2   *Identify ways that marketing executives manage a product's life cycle.*
Marketing executives manage a product's life cycle in three ways. First, they can modify the product itself by altering its characteristics, such as product quality, performance, or appearance. Second, they can modify the market by finding new customers for the product, increasing a product's use among existing customers, or creating new use situations for the product. Finally, they can reposition the product using any one or a combination of marketing mix elements. Four factors trigger a repositioning action. They include reacting to a competitor's position, reaching a new market, catching a rising trend, and changing the value offered to consumers.

3   *Recognize the importance of branding and alternative branding strategies.*
A basic decision in marketing products is branding, in which an organization uses a name, phrase, design, symbols, or a combination of these to identify its products and distinguish them from

those of its competitors. Product managers recognize that brands offer more than product identification and a means to distinguish their products from competitors. Successful and established brands take on a brand personality and acquire brand equity— the added value a given brand name gives to a product beyond the functional benefits provided—that is crafted and nurtured by marketing programs that forge strong, favourable, and unique consumer associations with a brand. A good brand name should suggest the product benefits, be memorable, fit the company or product image, be free of legal restrictions, and be simple and emotive. Companies can and do employ several different branding strategies. With multiproduct branding, a company uses one name for all its products in a product class. A multibranding strategy involves giving each product a distinct name. A company uses private branding when it manufactures products but sells them under the brand name of a wholesaler or retailer. A company can also employ mixed branding, where it markets products under its own name(s) and that of a reseller. Finally, a recent trend in brand management is cohort brand management, or the bundling of multiple brands into a single marketing effort aimed at a common consumer group.

4   *Describe the role of packaging, labelling, and warranties in the marketing of a product.*
Packaging, labelling, and warranties play numerous roles in the marketing of a product. The packaging component of a product refers to any container in which it is offered for sale and on which label information is conveyed. Manufacturers, retailers, and consumers acknowledge that packaging and labelling provide communication, functional, and perceptual benefits. Warranties indicate the liability of the manufacturer for product deficiencies and are an important element of product and brand management.

■ ■ ■
FOCUSING ON KEY TERMS

■ ■ ■
DISCUSSION AND APPLICATION QUESTIONS

1 Listed here are three different products in various stages of the product life cycle. What marketing strategies would you suggest to these companies? (*a*) Canon digital cameras —growth stage, (*b*) Panasonic high-definition television—introductory stage, and (*c*) handheld manual can openers—decline stage.

2 It has often been suggested that products are intentionally made to break down or wear out. Is this strategy a planned product modification approach?

3 The product manager of GE is reviewing the penetration of trash compactors in Canadian homes. After more than two decades in existence, this product is in relatively few homes.

What problems can account for this poor acceptance? What is the shape of the trash compactor life cycle?

4 For years, Ferrari has been known as the manufacturer of expensive luxury automobiles. The company plans to attract the major segment of the car-buying market of those who purchase medium-priced automobiles. As Ferrari considers this trading-down strategy, what branding strategy would you recommend? What are the tradeoffs to consider with your strategy?

5 The nature of product warranties has changed as the federal court system reassesses the meaning of warranties. How does the regulatory trend toward warranties affect product development?

| GOING ONLINE | | Brand News You Can Use |

Branding and brand management is a challenging task. Brandchannel.com seeks to inform its readers on the important issues facing brands now and in the future from a global perspective. Of particular interest are (1) "features," which discuss the success and failure of particular brands, and (2) "debate," which presents a point/counter-point discussion related to a brand's strategy.

Visit brandchannel.com (www.brandchannel.com) to complete the following assignment:

1 Pick a brand appearing in Chapter 11 and find a feature or debate pertaining to it either in the archives or from the current page. Summarize the views expressed in brandchannel.com.

2 Click the "papers" icon, and read a paper on a topic covered in Chapter 11. Compare and contrast the views in this paper with the coverage found in the chapter.

Do you want to get better grades and stay up to date with current issues in marketing? Visit the Online Learning Centre at www.mcgrawhill.ca/college/crane for practice tests, video cases, resources for building a marketing plan, *Globe and Mail* headlines, access to *Marketing Magazine*, and other learning and study tools.

VIDEO CASE 11   BMW: "Newness" and the Product Life Cycle

"We're fortunate right now at BMW in that all of our products are new and competitive," says Jim McDowell, vice-president of marketing at BMW, as he explains BMW's product life cycle. "Now, how do you do that? You have to introduce new models over time. You have to logically plan out the introductions over time, so you're not changing a whole model range at the same time you're changing another model range."

BMW's strategy is to keep its products in the introduction and growth stages by periodically introducing new models in each of its product lines. In fact, BMW does not like to have any products in the maturity or decline stage of the product life cycle. Explains McDowell, "If a product is declining, we would prefer to withdraw it from the market, as opposed to having a strategy for dealing with the declining product. We're kind of a progressive, go get 'em company, and we don't think it does our brand image any good to have any declining products out there. So, that's why we work so hard at managing the growth aspect."

BMW—THE COMPANY AND ITS PRODUCTS

BMW is one of the pre-eminent luxury car manufacturers in Europe, North America, and the world today. BMW produces several lines of cars, including the 3 series, the 5 series, the 7 series, the Z line (driven by Pierce Brosnan as James Bond in *Goldeneye*), and the new X line, BMW's "sport activity" vehicle line. In addition, BMW is now selling Rovers, a British car line anchored by the internationally popular Land Rover sport utility vehicle. It started selling Rolls Royce vehicles in 2003. Sales of all the BMW, Rover, and Land Rover vehicles have been on the rise globally. High-profile image campaigns (such as the James Bond promotion) and the award-winning BMW Web site (where users can design their own cars) continue to increase the popularity of BMW's products.

PRODUCT LIFE CYCLE

BMW cars typically have a product life cycle of seven years. To keep products in the introductory and growth stages, BMW regularly introduces new models for each of its series to keep the entire series "new." For instance, with the 3 series, it will introduce the new sedan model one year, the new coupe the next year, then the convertible, then the station wagon, and then the sport hatchback. That is a new product introduction for five of the seven years of the product life cycle.

McDowell explains, "So, even though we have seven-year life cycles, we constantly try and make the cars meaningfully different and new about every three years. And that involves adding features and other capabilities to the cars as well." How well does this strategy work? BMW often sees its best sales numbers in either the sixth or seventh year after the product introduction.

As global sales have increased, BMW has become aware of some international product-life-cycle differences. For example, it has discovered that some competitive products have life cycles that are shorter or longer than seven years. In Sweden and the United Kingdom, automotive product life cycles are eight years, while in Japan, they are typically only four years long.

BRANDING

"BMW is fortunate—we don't have too much of a dilemma as to what we're going to call our cars." McDowell is referring to BMW's trademark naming system that consists of the product line number and the motor type. For example, the designation "328" tells you the car is in the 3 series and the engine is 2.8 litres

visit us at www.mcgrawhill.ca/college/crane

in size. BMW has found this naming system to be clear and logical and can be easily understood around the world. The Z and X series do not quite fit in with this system. BMW had a tradition of building experimental, open-air cars and calling them Z's, and hence when the prototype for the Z3 was built, BMW decided to continue with the Z name. For the sport activity vehicle, BMW also used a letter name—the X series—since the four-wheel-drive vehicle did not fit with the sedan-oriented 3, 5, and 7 series. Other than the Z3 (the third in the Z series) and the X5 (named 5 to symbolize its mid-sized status within that series), the BMW branding strategy is quite simple, unlike the evocative names many car manufacturers choose to garner excitement for their new models.

MANAGING THE PRODUCT THROUGH THE WEB—THE WAVE OF THE FUTURE

One of the ways BMW is improving its product offerings even further is through its innovative Web site (www.bmw.com). At the site, customers can learn about the particular models, e-mail questions, and request literature or test-drives from their local BMW dealership. What really sets BMW's Web site apart from those of other car manufacturers, though, is the facility for customers to configure a car to their own specifications (interior choices, exterior choices, engine, packages, and

options) and then transfer that information to their local dealer. As Carol Burrows, product communications manager for BMW, explains, "The BMW Web site is an integrated part of the overall marketing strategy for BMW. The full range of products can be seen and interacted with online. We offer pricing options online. Customers can go to their local dealership via the Web site to further discuss costs for purchase of a car. And it is a distribution channel for information that allows people access to the information 24 hours a day at their convenience."

QUESTIONS

1 Compare the product life cycle described by BMW for its cars with the product life cycle shown in Figure 11–1. How are they (*a*) similar, and (*b*) dissimilar?

2 Based on BMW's typical product life cycle, what marketing strategies are appropriate for the 3 series? The X5?

3 Which of the three ways to manage the product life cycle does BMW utilize with its products—modifying the product, modifying the market, or repositioning the product?

4 How would you describe BMW's branding strategy (multiproduct branding, multibranding, private branding, or mixed branding)? Why?

5 Go to the BMW Web site (www.bmw.com), and design a car to your own specifications. How does this enable you as a customer to evaluate the product differently from what would otherwise be possible?

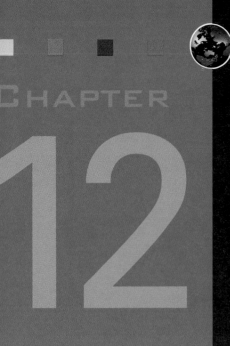

CHAPTER 12

MANAGING SERVICES

THE HARD ROCK CAFÉ KNOWS WHAT YOU WANT: AN EXCEPTIONAL EXPERIENCE!

Hard Rock Cafés "offer exciting nightlife, great food, and live entertainment," explains CEO and president Pete Beaudrault. In fact, the mission of Hard Rock Café International is "to spread the spirit of rock 'n' roll by delivering an exceptional entertainment and dining experience." If you have ever been to one of the cafés you will probably agree—they are designed to emphasize the rock 'n' roll theme and provide a unique and distinctive experience for customers.

It all started more than 30 years ago when Eric Clapton gave the original Hard Rock Café in London his guitar to be displayed at his favourite table. Soon another guitar arrived from The Who's Pete Townshend, and ever since the restaurants have displayed memorabilia from rock's favourite musicians and bands, including Elvis Presley, Jimi Hendrix, Aerosmith, The Red Hot Chili Peppers, Madonna, U2, Creed, and Matchbox Twenty. Today, there are more than 100 Hard Rock Cafés in 40 countries, including Canadian locations in Montreal and Toronto, and the music memorabilia collection is worth $32 million.

To add to the experience, the company is using digital streaming to bring local musical performances to all of its locations. According to Scott Little, Hard Rock's strategic planner, "we'll use the Web to create a forum for up-and-coming artists and to bring national bands that play our large concert venues into the smaller locations." There is also an e-commerce aspect to the experience now. as Hard Rock fans can use the Hard Rock Web page as an entertainment portal to listen to and purchase music, buy memorabilia through a special eBay auction service, and subscribe to digital music programming.[1]

The Hard Rock Café is one of many service organizations today competing for customers by offering enjoyable, memorable experiences rather than traditional service transactions. Walt Disney was one of the first to recognize the importance of sights, sounds, tastes, aromas, and textures to provide a unique experience when he created Disneyland. Chuck E. Cheese's uses a similar approach to sell birthday party experiences that include entertainment, food, music, and a fun environment. Companies that sell goods with a service element are also offering experiences. Nike, for example, offers fun activities and promotional events in its own store, Niketown, and Steinway provides a free concert, including a pianist, invitations, and hors d'oeuvres in its customers' homes. These businesses are increasing the value of their offering to customers by engaging them in experiential elements of their service.

Some experts believe we are on the verge of a new economic era driven by an *experience economy*.[2] Coffee can be purchased as a commodity in a grocery store and brewed at home at a cost of about 10 cents per cup. Coffee can also be purchased from 7-Eleven, where consumers pay for the convenience of the service, for a cost of about 75 cents per cup. But most of us have often paid about $3 per cup at a Starbucks, where the look of the shop, the jazz music, and the baristas' knowledge of the beans creates a "coffee experience" that is still a good value. ESPN Zone, Home Depot, Planet Hollywood, and many other companies are responding to consumers' preferences for compelling experiences.

As the actions of the Hard Rock Café and the other examples above illustrate, the marketing of services is dynamic and challenging. In this chapter, we discuss how services differ from traditional products (goods), how service consumers make purchase decisions, and the important aspects of developing and managing the marketing mix for services.

■ ■ ■
THE SERVICE ECONOMY

services

Intangible activities, benefits, or satisfactions that an organization provides to consumers in exchange for money or something else of value.

As defined in Chapter 1, **services** are activities, deeds, or other basic intangibles offered for sale to consumers in exchange for money or something else of value. One services-marketing expert suggests that services permeate every aspect of our lives.[3] We use transportation services, such as Via Rail, Air Canada, and Thrifty car rental, when we travel. We use restaurant services, such as McDonald's, to feed us and hotels, such as the Four Seasons, to put a roof over our heads when we are away from home. When we are at home, we rely on electricity providers, such as Ontario Power Generation, to keep the lights on, and telephone services from Bell Canada, to keep in touch with family. We also use Sympatico to keep us connected to the Net and Molly Maid to keep our houses clean.

At work, we rely on Canada Post to deliver our mail, and Purolator courier to get our urgent documents to their destinations overnight. And we use Servicemaster to keep our offices clean and Intercon Security services to keep them safe. Our employers use public relations firms, such as Edelman Public Relations, and advertising agencies, such as Cossette Communications, to maintain their corporate images, while we use the services of First Choice Haircutters to maintain our personal appearances. We use colleges and universities to improve our minds, and online employment services, such as Workopolis to find us better jobs. We use financial institutions, such as Scotiabank, to safeguard our money, and buy peace of mind with life insurance from Canada Life. We use lawyers to draw up our wills, and E*Trade.ca to trade our shares. In our leisure time, we pop in to Blockbuster Video to rent a DVD or stop by a Famous Players theatre to catch a flick. We might even visit one of the casinos run by the Great Canadian Gaming Corporation.

We might use an online travel service, such as Travelocity, to book our well-deserved vacation and stay and ski at Whistler Resort, run by Intrawest Corporation. While we are there, we might use the ING Direct card to pay for everything. Of course, we always need to stay in touch, and so the wireless telecommunications services provided by Rogers AT&T come in handy. Since Whistler Resort does not allow dogs, we have to use a boarding kennel or a personal pet watching service to care for our border collie. When we get home, we realize the car needs an oil change, and so we drive to Mr. Lube to get it done. The washing machine also sounds a little funny, and so we call the Maytag repair man. After a long day, we just might watch some digital cable and order in a pizza. Because the television looks a little blurry, we decide that it is time to get rid of our eyeglasses and contact TLC Laser Eye Centres to see if they might help. And because we believe in future planning, we have already decided on the nursing home for our parents and even pre-purchased their funerals and burial plots. Services: from the cradle to the grave, we rely on them.

Services have become one of the most important components of the Canadian as well as world economy. The services sector is now responsible for over 70 percent of Canada's total economic output as well as over 75 percent of its workforce. Moreover, the service sector generates 9 of 10 new jobs in Canada. At this rate, most experts predict that almost all Canadians will be working in services by 2025.[4] In other words, Canadians will simply be doing things (performing services) rather than making things (producing goods). And while Canada is still suffering a trade deficit in terms of service importation versus exportation, the country is experiencing greater growth in the export of services.

In terms of service job growth, much of it will be created by small- and medium-sized businesses, both business-to-consumer (B2C) and business-to-business (B2B). And according to the Canadian Franchise Association, many of these businesses which will be franchise-based will offer personal, professional, and informational services.[5] Many of these services companies will also rely heavily on technology to create and deliver their services, including online travel services, people locator services, information technology services, and financial services.

■ ■ ■
THE UNIQUENESS OF SERVICES

As we noted in Chapter 10, when consumers buy products they are purchasing a bundle of tangible and intangible attributes that deliver value and satisfaction. In general, it is very difficult to define a pure good or a pure service. A pure good implies that the consumer obtains benefits from the good alone without any added value from service; conversely, a pure service assumes there is no "goods" element to the service that the customer receives. In reality, most services contain some goods element. For example, at McDonald's you receive a hamburger; at the Royal Bank you are provided with a bank statement. And most goods offer some service—even if it is only delivery. In fact, many goods-producing firms are adding service offerings as a way to differentiate their products from those of their competitors.

But there are certain commonalities between *services as products* that set them apart from tangible goods. The four unique elements to services are intangibility, inconsistency, inseparability, and inventory. These elements are sometimes referred to as the **four I's of services**.

four I's of services
Four unique elements to services: intangibility, inconsistency, inseparability, and inventory.

Intangibility   Services are intangible; that is, they cannot be held, touched, or seen before the purchase decision. In contrast, before purchasing a traditional product, a consumer can touch a box of laundry detergent, kick the tire of an automobile, or sample a new breakfast cereal. A major marketing need for services is to make them tangible or to show the benefits of using a service. American Express emphasizes the gifts available to cardholders through its Membership Rewards program; a leading insurance company says, "You're in Good Hands with Allstate"; Fairmont Hotels tells business travellers that they will have the convenience of their offices away from their offices, including computer hookups and personal services.

Why do many services emphasize their tangible benefits? The answer appears in the text.

Fairmont Hotels & Resorts
www.fairmont.com

TOMORROW YOU'RE DUE TO MAKE THE BIGGEST PRESENTATION OF YOUR BUSINESS YEAR. AND MAGICALLY, THERE'S SOMEONE IN THE HOTEL WHO KNOWS IT.

Fairmont
HOTELS & RESORTS
Places in the heart.

Call your travel agent or 1 800 866 5577　www.fairmont.com

Inconsistency   Developing, pricing, promoting, and delivering services is challenging because the quality of a service is often inconsistent. Since services depend on the people who provide them, their quality varies with each person's capabilities and day-to-day job performance. Inconsistency is much more of a problem with services than it is with tangible goods. Tangible products can be good or bad in terms of quality, but with modern production lines, the quality will at least be consistent. On the other hand, the Toronto Maple Leafs hockey team may look like potential Stanley Cup winners on a particular day but lose by 10 goals the next day. Or a cello player with the Vancouver Symphony may not be feeling well and give a less-than-average performance. Whether the service involves tax assistance at Ernst & Young or guest relations at the Sheraton, organizations attempt to reduce inconsistency through standardization and training. Standardization through automation is becoming increasingly popular in many service industries, including banking.

Inseparability   A third difference between services and goods is inseparability. There are two dimensions to inseparability. The first is inseparability of production and consumption. Whereas goods are first produced, then sold, and then consumed, services are sold first, and then produced and consumed simultaneously. For example, you can buy a ticket at the Air Canada ticket office, then fly and consume in-flight service as it is being produced. The second dimension of inseparability is that, in most cases, the consumer cannot (and does not) separate the deliverer of the service from the service itself. For example, to receive an education, a person may attend a university. The quality of the education may be high, but if the student has difficulty interacting with instructors, finds counselling services poor, or does not receive adequate library or computer assistance, he or she may not be satisfied with the educational experience. In short, a student's evaluations of education will be influenced primarily by how the instructors, counsellors, librarians, and other people at the university responsible for delivering the education are perceived.

The amount of interaction between the consumer and the service deliverer or provider depends on the extent to which the consumer must be physically present to receive the service. Some services, such as golf lessons and medical diagnoses, require the customer to participate in the delivery process. Other services that process tangible objects, such as car repair or dry cleaning, require less involvement from the customer. Finally, many services, such as banking and insurance, can now

People play an important role in the delivery of many services.

Allstate

www.allstate.com

be delivered electronically, often requiring no face-to-face customer interaction, for example, Bank of Montreal's Web-based banking service.[6]

Inventory   Inventory of services is different from that of goods. Inventory problems exist with goods because many items are perishable and because there are costs associated with handling inventory. With services, inventory carrying costs are more subjective and are related to **idle production capacity**, which occurs when the service provider is available but there is no demand. The inventory cost of a service is the cost of paying the person used to provide the service along with any needed equipment. If a physician is paid to see patients but no one schedules an appointment, the fixed cost of the idle physician's salary is a high inventory-carrying cost. In some service businesses, however, the provider of the service is on commission (the Merrill Lynch stockbroker) or is a part-time employee (a counterperson at McDonald's). In these businesses, inventory-carrying costs can be significantly lower or nonexistent because the idle production capacity can be cut back by reducing hours or not having to pay salary because of the commission compensation system.

Figure 12–1 shows a scale of inventory-carrying costs, represented on the high end by airlines and hospitals and on the low end by real estate agencies. The inventory-carrying costs of airlines are high because of high-salaried pilots and very expensive equipment. In contrast, real estate agencies have employees who work on commission and need little expensive equipment to conduct business. One reason

idle production capacity

When the service provider is available but there is no demand.

■ **FIGURE 12–1** ■■

Inventory-carrying costs of services

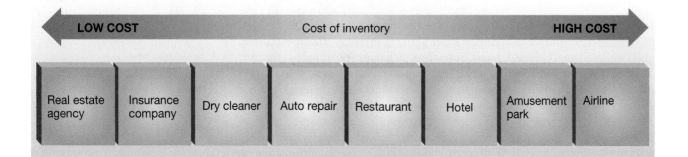

LOW COST			Cost of inventory				HIGH COST
Real estate agency	Insurance company	Dry cleaner	Auto repair	Restaurant	Hotel	Amusement park	Airline

why service providers must maintain production capacity is because of the importance of time to today's customers. People do not want to wait long for service.

The Service Continuum

The four I's differentiate services from goods in most cases, but as we mentioned earlier, most products sold cannot be defined as pure goods or pure services. For example, does IBM Canada sell goods or services? While the company sells computers and software, a major component of its business is information technology services, including consulting and training. Does Rogers Communications provide only goods when it publishes *Marketing Magazine*, or does it consider itself a service because it presents up-to-date Canadian business information? As companies look at what they bring to the market, there is a range from the tangible to the intangible or good-dominant to service-dominant offerings referred to as the **service continuum** (Figure 12–2).

service continuum
A range from the tangible to the intangible or goods-dominant to service-dominant offerings available in the marketplace.

Teaching, nursing, and the theatre are intangible, service-dominant activities, and intangibility, inconsistency, inseparability, and inventory are major concerns in their marketing. Salt, neckties, and dog food are tangible goods, and the problems represented by the four I's are not relevant in their marketing. However, some businesses are a mix of intangible-service and tangible-good factors. A clothing tailor provides a service but also a good, the finished suit. How pleasant, courteous, and attentive the tailor is to the customer is an important component of the service, and how well the clothes fit is an important part of the product. As shown in Figure 12–2, a fast-food restaurant is about half tangible goods (the food) and half intangible services (courtesy, cleanliness, speed, convenience).

For many businesses today, it is useful to distinguish between their core service and their supplementary services. A core service offering—a bank account, for example—also has supplementary services, such as deposit assistance, parking or drive-through availability, ATMs, and monthly statements. Supplementary services often allow service providers to differentiate their offering from competitors, and they may add value for consumers. While there are many potential supplementary services, key categories of supplementary services include information delivery, consultation, order taking, billing procedures, and payment options.[7]

■ FIGURE 12–2 ■
Service continuum

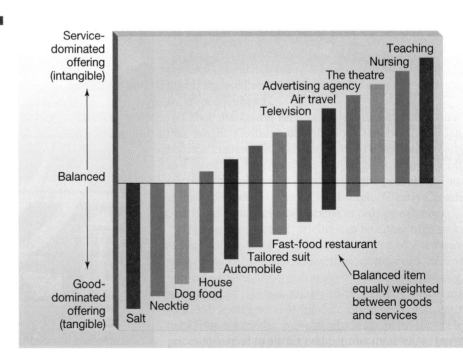

**CONCEPT
CHECK**

1. What are the four I's of services?

2. Would inventory-carrying costs for an accounting firm employing chartered accountants be (a) high, (b) low, or (c) nonexistent?

3. To eliminate inconsistencies, organizations rely on _____ and _____.

■ ■ ■ HOW CONSUMERS PURCHASE SERVICES

Universities, hospitals, hotels, and lawyers are facing an increasingly competitive environment. Successful service organizations, like successful goods-producing firms, must understand how the consumer makes a purchase decision and a postpurchase evaluation. Service companies will be better able to position themselves effectively if they understand why a consumer chooses to use a particular service. Moreover, by understanding the consumer's postpurchase evaluation process, service companies can identify sources of customer satisfaction or dissatisfaction.

Purchasing a Service

Because of their intangible nature, it is generally more difficult for consumers to evaluate services before purchase than it is to evaluate goods (Figure 12–3). Tangible goods, such as clothes, jewellery, and furniture, have *search* qualities, such as colour, size, and style, which can be determined before purchase. But rarely can a consumer inspect, try out, or test a service in advance. This is because some services, such as restaurants and child care, have *experience* qualities, which can be discerned only after purchase or consumption. Other services provided by specialized professionals, such as medical diagnosis and legal services, have *credence* qualities, or characteristics that the consumer may find impossible to evaluate even after purchase and consumption.[8]

The experience and credence qualities of services force consumers to make a prepurchase examination of the service by assessing the tangible characteristics that are part of, or surround, the service.[9] In other words, consumers will evaluate what they cannot see by what they can see. For example, you might consider the actual appearance of the dentist's office, or its physical location, when making a judgment about the possible quality of dental services that might be provided there. Many service organizations go

■ **FIGURE 12–3** ■ ■

Services are more difficult to evaluate than goods before a purchase

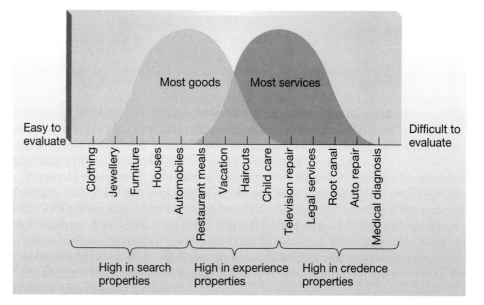

to great lengths to ensure that the tangible aspects of the services convey the appropriate image and serve as surrogate indicators of the intangible service to be provided.

Service marketers recognize that because of the uncertainty created by experience and credence qualities, consumers turn to personal sources of information, such as early adopters, opinion leaders, and reference group members, during the purchase decision process. Accordingly, services marketers work to ensure customer satisfaction in order to ensure positive word-of-mouth referral.

Customer Contact Audit

customer contact audit
A flowchart of the points of interaction between consumer and service provider.

To better understand the service purchasing process, service firms can develop a **customer contact audit**—a flowchart of the points of interaction between consumer and service provider.[10] These points of interaction are often referred to as *contact points* or *service encounter elements*. Constructing a customer contact audit is particularly important in high-contact services, such as educational institutions, health care, and even automobile rental agencies. Figure 12–4 illustrates a customer contact audit for renting a car from Hertz. The interactions identified in a customer contact audit often serve as the basis for developing better services and delivering them more efficiently and effectively.

When a customer decides to rent a car he or she (1) contacts the rental company (see Figure 12–4). (2) A customer service representative receives the information and checks the availability of the car at the desired location. (3) When a customer arrives at the rental site, (4) the reservation system is again accessed, and the customer provides information regarding payment, address, and driver's licence. (5) A car is assigned to the customer, (6) who proceeds by bus to the car pickup. (7) On return to the rental location, (8) the car is parked and the customer checks in, (9) providing information on mileage, gas consumption, and damages. (10) A bill is subsequently prepared.

■ **FIGURE 12–4** ■
Customer contact in car rental (green shaded boxes indicate customer activity)

Source: Adapted from W. Earl Sasser, R. Paul Olsen, and D. Daryl Wyckoff, Management of Service Operations: Text, Cases and Readings (Boston: Allyn & Bacon, 1978).

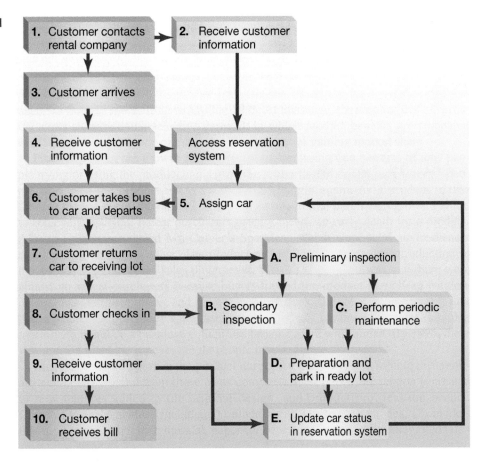

Each of the steps numbered 1 to 10 is a customer contact point where the tangible aspects of Hertz service are seen by the customer. Figure 12–4, however, also shows a series of steps lettered A to E that involve two levels of inspections on the automobile. These steps are essential in providing a car that runs, but they are not points of customer interaction. To be successful, Hertz must create a competitive advantage in the sequence of interactions with the customer. In essence, Hertz must attempt to deliver the car in a seamless and timely manner, limiting the amount of time and effort required on the part of the customer. The customer contact audit is one tool that may help create that competitive advantage for Hertz or any other service firm.

Postpurchase Evaluation

gap analysis
An evaluation tool that compares expectations about a service offering to the actual experience a consumer has with the service.

Once a consumer tries a service, how is it evaluated? The primary method is by comparing expectations about the service offering with the actual experience a consumer has with the service.[11] Differences between a consumer's expectations and experience are often identified through **gap analysis**. This type of analysis asks consumers to assess their expectations and experiences on various dimensions of service quality. Expectations are influenced by word-of-mouth communications, personal needs, past experience, and marketing communications activities, while actual experiences are determined by the way an organization delivers the service.

One popular instrument developed by researchers to measure service quality and to conduct gap analysis is called SERVQUAL.[12] Researchers measure consumers' expectations and their actual service experience using a multi-item instrument. Consumers are asked to rate the importance of various dimensions of service quality and to score the service in terms of their expectations and actual experience. SERVQUAL provides the services marketer with a consumer rating of service quality and an indication of where improvements can be made.

Using SERVQUAL, these researchers have found that consumers judge service quality along five key dimensions: tangibles, reliability, responsiveness, assurance, and empathy (Figure 12–5). However, the relative importance of these various dimensions of service quality has been found to vary by type of service.[13]

Service marketers must understand what dimensions consumers use in judging service quality, recognize the relative importance of each dimension, find out how they rate in terms of service quality, and take actions to deliver service quality that is consistent with consumer expectations. As a consumer, you play an important role in ensuring that service firms deliver high service quality. However, as the Ethics and

ETHICS AND SOCIAL RESPONSIBILITY ALERT

The Consumer's Role in Improving Service Quality

Research has shown that many consumers are reluctant to provide feedback to service firms about the quality of their services. In fact, current studies show that only 5 to 10 percent of service customers offered direct feedback to service firms that might be important in improving service quality.

Most services marketers want to know if customers are happy or satisfied with the services provided, and many try a variety of methods (e.g., customer response or comment cards) to obtain or encourage answers regarding perceived service quality. However, most consumers do not take the time to respond, even if they are dissatisfied. Instead, consumers, if unhappy, will simply not return and will switch providers. Moreover, while they will not take the time to tell the organization about their dissatisfaction, they will take the time to tell their friends and co-workers.

The question is, why? If you have a problem with a service firm—whether it is inconvenient hours or rude employees—wouldn't it be better to tell the firm? Is it ethical for you to complain to your friends without informing the firm?

■ FIGURE 12-5 ■
Dimensions of service
quality

Source: Adapted with the permission of
The Free Press, a Division of Simon &
Schuster Adult Publishing Group, from ON
GREAT SERVICE; A Framework for Action
by Leonard L. Berry. Copyright © 1995 by
Leonard L. Berry. All rights reserved.

DIMENSION	DEFINITION	EXAMPLES OF QUESTIONS AIRLINE CUSTOMERS MIGHT ASK
Tangibles	Appearance of physical facilities, equipment, personnel, and communications materials.	Are the plane, the gate, and the baggage area clean?
Reliability	Ability to perform the promised service dependably and accurately.	Is my flight on time?
Responsiveness	Willingness to help customers and provide prompt service.	Are the flight attendants willing to answer my questions?
Assurance	Respectful, considerate personnel who listen to customers and answer their questions.	Are the employees knowledgeable?
Empathy	Knowing the customer and understanding their needs. Approachable and available.	Do the employees know that I have special seating and meal requirements?

Social Responsibility Alert box points out, sometimes consumers do not provide the feedback necessary to improve service quality.[14]

There are benefits to the customer and the service provider when service quality is improved. Recent Canadian research indicated that for the customer, improved service quality is connected to customer satisfaction and increases the likelihood that the customer will return to the same provider, which, in effect, offers the benefits of continuity of a single provider, customized service potential, reduced stress due to repetitive purchase process, and an absence of switching costs.[15] For the service provider, retaining existing customers is much less costly than attracting new customers, and repeat customers are clearly more profitable over time.

Most importantly, service firms see service quality as a basis for customer relationship management (CRM). And, research indicates that customers are interested in having relationships with their service providers, but only if the relationship is balanced in terms of loyalty, benefits, and respect for privacy.[16]

CONCEPT CHECK

1. What are the differences between search, experience, and credence qualities?

2. What is gap analysis?

3. An instrument or approach used to measure service quality is _____.

■ ■ ■
MANAGING THE MARKETING OF SERVICES: THE EIGHT P'S

Just as the unique aspects of services necessitate changes in the consumer's purchase process, the marketing management process requires special adaptation. As we have seen in earlier chapters, the traditional marketing mix is composed of the Four P's: product, price, place, and promotion. Careful management of the Four P's is important when

Logos create service identities.

eight P's of service marketing
Product, price, place, and promotion, as well as people, physical evidence, process, and productivity that constitute the services marketing mix.

marketing services. However, the distinctive nature of services requires that other additional variables be effectively managed by service marketers. The concept of an expanded marketing mix for services has been adopted by many service-marketing organizations. In addition to the traditional Four P's, the services marketing mix includes people, physical evidence, process, and productivity, or the **Eight P's of services marketing**.[17] Let us now discuss the special nature of the marketing mix for services.

Product (Service)

To a large extent, the concepts of the product component of the marketing mix discussed in Chapters 10 and 11 apply equally to Cheerios (a good) and to Royal Bank Visa (a service). Managers of goods and services must design the product concept, whether a good or a service, with the features and benefits desired by customers. An important aspect of the product concept is branding. Because services are intangible and, therefore, more difficult to describe, the brand name or identifying logo of the service organization is particularly important when a consumer makes a purchase decision. Therefore, service organizations, such as banks, hotels, rental car companies, and restaurants, rely on branding strategies in order to distinguish themselves in the minds of the consumers. Strong brand names and symbols are important for service marketers, not only for differentiation purposes but also for conveying an image of quality. A service firm with a well-established brand reputation will also find it easier to market new services than firms without such brand reputation.[18]

Take a look at the figures at the top of the page to determine how successful some companies have been in branding their services by name, logo, or symbol.

Price

In service industries, price is often referred to in many ways. Hospitals refer to *charges*; consultants, lawyers, physicians, and accountants to *fees*; airlines to *fares*; hotels to *rates*; and colleges and universities to *tuition*. Because of the intangible nature of services, price is often perceived by consumers as a possible indicator of the quality of the service. For example, would you be willing to risk a $10 dental surgery? Or a $50 divorce lawyer? In many cases, there may be few other available cues for the customer to judge a service, and so price becomes very important as a quality indicator.[19]

Pricing of services also goes beyond the traditional tasks of setting the selling price. When customers buy services they consider nonmonetary costs, such as the time as well as the mental and physical efforts required to consume the service. Therefore, service marketers must also try to minimize the nonmonetary costs customers may bear in purchasing and using a service. Finally, as we will see later in this section, pricing also plays a role in balancing consumer demand for services.

Place (Distribution)

Place or distribution is a major factor in developing a service marketing strategy because of the inseparability of services from the producer. Rarely are intermediaries

Price influences perceptions of services.

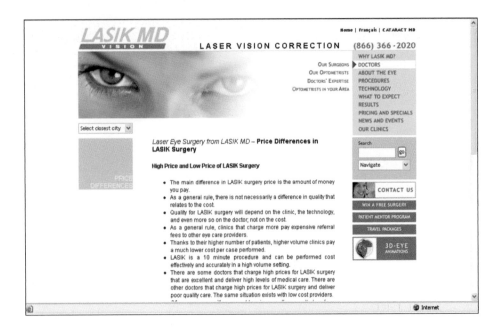

involved in the distribution of a service; the distribution site and the service deliverer are the tangible components of the service. And, until recently, customers generally had to go to the service provider's physical location to purchase the service. Increased competition has forced many service firms to consider the value of convenient distribution and to find new ways of distributing services to demanding customers. Hairstyling chains, such as First Choice Haircutters, legal firms, and accounting firms all use multiple locations for the distribution of services. Technology is also being used to deliver services beyond the provider's physical locations. For example, in the banking industry, customers of participating banks using the Interac system can access any one of thousands of automated teller machines across Canada and need not visit their own specific bank branch. The availability of electronic distribution of services over the Internet also allows for global reach and coverage for a variety of services, including travel services, banking, education, entertainment, and many other information-based services. With speed and convenience becoming increasingly important to customers when they select service providers, service firms can leverage the use of the Internet to deliver services on a 24/7 basis, in real time, on a global scale. In short, forward-looking firms no longer see face-to-face delivery of services as the only distribution option.[20]

Promotion

The value of promotion, especially advertising, for many services is to show consumers the benefits of purchasing the service. For example, advertising can be an effective way to demonstrate such attributes as availability, location, consistent quality, efficient and courteous service, and assurance of satisfaction.[21] While many service firms are using the Internet as an alternative distribution channel, they are also using it as an advertising or promotional medium. Many community colleges and universities, for example, have their own well-designed Web sites to convey their messages to prospective students. Tourism marketers are also finding the Internet a valuable tool in reaching their prospective target markets. Use the WebLink box to check out Nunavut Tourism's Web site.

Public relations is an important promotional tool for service firms. It is particularly useful in conveying a proper image and in helping to support a firm's positioning strategy. Public relations tools, such as event sponsorship or public-service activities, are very popular among service companies. This is particularly true for

professional service firms, which are often restricted in the use of advertising by their professional governing bodies.

Personal selling also plays an important role in services marketing. It has been said that when a consumer buys a service, he or she is buying the person selling the service. Personal selling is valuable not only in attracting customers but also in retaining them. Increasingly, many service marketers are following the path set by packaged-goods firms; that is, they are developing integrated marketing communications plans.[22]

People

Many services depend on people for the creation and delivery of services. In such cases, the service employee will play a central role in attracting, building, and maintaining relationships with customers.[23] The nature of the interaction between employees and customers strongly influences the customer's perceptions of service quality. In short, customers will often judge the quality of service they receive based on the performances of the people providing the service. This aspect of services marketing has led to a concept called internal marketing.[24]

internal marketing
The notion that in order for a service organization to serve its customers well, it must care for and treat its employees like valued customers.

Internal marketing is based on the notion that in order for a service organization to serve its customers well, it must care for and treat its employees like valued customers. In essence, it must focus on its employees (or its internal market) before successful marketing efforts can be directed at customers.[25] Internal marketing involves creating an organizational climate in general and jobs in particular, which will lead to the right service personnel performing the service in the right way. The organization must properly select, train, and motivate all of its employees to work together to provide service quality and customer satisfaction. Research has shown that service organizations that want to be truly customer oriented must be employee oriented.[26] Finally, customer behaviour influences not only their own service outcomes but also other customers. Whether at a hockey game or in a classroom, customers can influence the perceived quality of service by their actions. Therefore, the *people* element in services includes not only the employees and the customer but also other customers.

Physical Evidence

The appearance of the environment in which the service is delivered and where the firm and customer interact can influence the customer's perception of the service. The physical evidence of the service includes all the tangibles surrounding the service: the buildings, landscaping, vehicles, furnishings, signage, brochures, and equipment. Service firms need to manage physical evidence carefully and systematically in order to convey the proper impression of the service to the customer. This is sometimes referred to as *impression management*, or evidence management.[27] With highly tangible

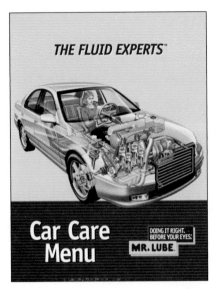

services, physical evidence provides an opportunity for the firm to send consistent and strong messages about the nature of the service to be delivered.

Process

In services marketing, *process* refers to the actual procedures, mechanisms, and flow of activities by which the service is created and delivered. The actual creation and delivery steps that the customer experiences provide customers with evidence on which to judge the service. In services marketing, process involves not only "what" gets created but also "how" it gets created. The customer contact audit discussed earlier in the chapter is relevant to understanding the service process discussed here. The customer contact audit—the flowchart of the points of interaction between customer and service provider—can serve as a basis for ensuring better service creation and delivery processes. Badly designed processes are likely to create unhappy customers, and poorly conceived operational processes can make it difficult for front-line employees to do their jobs well. Mr. Lube believes that it has the right process in the vehicle oil change and fluid exchange service business. Customers do not need appointments, most stores are open seven days a week, and customers are in and out in 15 to 20 minutes. While the service is being performed, customers can drink a coffee and read the newspaper.

Productivity

Most services have a limited capacity due to the inseparability of the service from the service provider and the perishable nature of the service. For example, a patient must be in the hospital at the same time as the surgeon to receive an appendectomy, and only one patient can be helped at that time. Similarly, no additional surgery can be conducted tomorrow because of an unused operating room or an available surgeon today—the service capacity is lost if it is not used. So, if service marketers have a relatively fixed capacity to produce a service, they must make that capacity as productive as possible without compromising service quality.[28] This is referred to as **capacity management**.

capacity management
Making service capacity as productive as possible without compromising service quality.

Service organizations must manage the availability of the offering so that (1) demand matches capacity over the duration of the demand cycle (e.g., one day, week, month, year), and (2) the organization's assets are used in ways that will maximize the return on investment.[29] Figure 12–6 shows how a hotel tries to manage its capacity during the high and low seasons. Differing price structures are assigned to each segment of consumers to help moderate or adjust demand for the service. Airline contracts fill a fixed number of rooms throughout the year. In the slow season, when more rooms are available, tour packages at appealing prices are used to attract groups or conventions, such as an offer for seven nights at a reduced price. Weekend packages are also offered to buyers. In high-demand season, groups are less desirable because more individual guests will be available and willing to pay higher prices. The use of **off-peak pricing**, which consists of charging different prices during different times of the day or days of the week to reflect variations in demand for the service, plays an important role in capacity management. For example, airlines offer discounts for weekend travel, movie theatres offer matinee pricing, and restaurants offer early-bird pricing in order to maintain the productivity of their service capacity.

off-peak pricing
Charging different prices during different times of the day or days of the week to reflect variations in demand for the service.

■ ■ ■
SERVICES IN THE FUTURE

What can we expect from the services industry in the future? New and better services, of course, and an unprecedented variety of choices. Many of the changes will be the result of technological development, an expanding scope in the global economy, changes in consumer interests, and a more competitive landscape.

■ FIGURE 12-6 ■

Managing capacity in a hotel

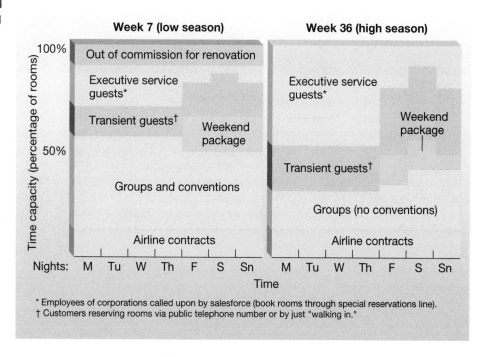

* Employees of corporations called upon by salesforce (book rooms through special reservations line).
† Customers reserving rooms via public telephone number or by just "walking in."

Technological advances are rapidly changing the service industry. New e-services now include voice-over-Internet telephone services; home video-conferencing, and new forms of security and identification services, such as retinal scanning. New Internet-based services also make it possible to obtain videos, movies, and e-text-books. What is one to the hottest trends in new services? Matchmaking. For example, firms like Lavalife.com and Match.com each claim to have millions of members who use their Internet sites to find their perfect soul mate. In Japan, the services are so popular that they are offered in I-mode so that clients can access their matches using wireless phone services.[30]

The expanding global economy is also changing the services industries landscape. Services have become the dominant part of the Canadian economy, and now global marketing of services has also increased at a dramatic rate. Technology is assisting this growth and consumers, around the globe, can consume services 24/7, in real time. In fact, many services experts predict that global economic exchange has shifted and will continue to shift away from tangible goods to intangible services, especially experiential services.[31]

Other changes in services will be driven by changes in consumer interests. Experts suggest that "time will be the currency of the future." Consumers are searching for new services that reduce the time needed to go to the post office, bank, or supermarket or to prepare food, clean clothes, or maintain their homes. Consumers are placing increased demand on service companies, expecting greater choice, convenience, information, responsiveness, and access to service. Technology is playing a key role in satisfying those demands. Many banking customers, for example, prefer to visit their banks as little as possible, and many are now doing more business by phone or over the Internet. Virtual banks, such as ING Direct, are available to Canadian banking customers, who now have the choice of doing everything electronically or dealing with a real person at a traditional brick-and-mortar bank.

Finally, as we mentioned in the chapter opener, consumers will be looking to purchase "experiences," not just basic goods and services. As a result of increased competition, many services have become commoditized or are seen by most consumers to be virtually identical. In that case, price often becomes the driver when making a service selection. But many consumers want something more than just a commoditized service and are prepared to pay for it. If a service firm can customize a service,

MARKETING NEWSNET   Marketing Experiences!

As we have discussed in this chapter, many services have become commoditized or are seen by most consumers to be virtually identical. In order for service firms to differentiate among themselves, many have turned to selling experiences and not just services. Service marketers believe that if they can customize a service for a customer, it can transform the service into an experience. Experts believe that services can be successfully transformed into experiences if (1) the service offering can be made memorable (it remains with the customer for a long time), (2) the customer is drawn into the offering such that they feel a real sensation (such as actually swimming with dolphins), and (3) highly skilled employees (actors) can dynamically personalize each experience for each customer.

Disney has long been recognized as offering experiences to its theme park visitors or guests. But now other services marketers are also in the experience business. For example, British Airways states "what we do is to go beyond the function (air passenger service) and compete on the basis of providing an experience. The aircraft and the flight is the stage for a distinctive en route experience." Experience-economy experts Pine and Gilmore suggest there are four types of experiences that marketers can offer customers: (1) entertainment, (2) educational, (3) esthetic, and (4) escapist. They suggest that service firms that can offer some or all of these experiences in the right combination will be successful experience marketers.

it turns it into an experience. For example, Pizza Hut can offer a customer more than a meal; it will host your child's birthday party and customize it the way you want it.[32] The Fairmont Southampton Princess Resort in Bermuda has plenty of competition on the tiny island. While prices for rooms at the Fairmont are competitive with other upscale resorts, it offers its guests a unique experience that others do not: a chance to swim with dolphins. And customers are lining up to pay for that experience. The price? About $150 per person for 45 minutes! Read the accompanying Marketing NewsNet box to see just how services marketers can create experiences, which are a distinct offering from services.[33]

The Fairmont Southampton Princess Resort markets more than a nice place to vacation in: it creates and markets experiences, such as swimming with dolphins.

CONCEPT CHECK

1. Matching demand with capacity is the focus of _____ management.

2. What factors will influence the services industries in the future?

■ ■ ■
CHAPTER IN REVIEW

1 *Describe the four unique elements of services.*
The four unique elements of services—the four I's—are intangibility, inconsistency, inseparability, and inventory. Intangibility refers to the tendency of services to be a performance that cannot be held or touched. Inconsistency is a characteristic of services because they depend on people to deliver them, and people vary in their capabilities and in their day-to-day performance. Inseparability refers to the difficulty of separating the deliverer of the service (hair stylist) from the service itself (hair cut). And services are produced and consumed simultaneously, requiring the consumer to be present for both the production and consumption processes. Inventory refers to the need to have service production capability when there is service demand.

2 *Explain the services continuum.*
Many organizations do not market pure services or pure goods. In general, companies market products that have tangible and intangible characteristics. As companies look at what they bring to market, there is a range from the tangible to the intangible or good-dominant to service-dominant offerings, referred to as a service continuum.

3 *Understand the ways in which consumers purchase and evaluate services.*
Because services are intangible, pre-purchase evaluation is difficult for consumers. To choose a service, consumers use search, experience, and credence qualities to evaluate the good and service elements of a service offering. Once the consumer tries a service, it is evaluated by comparing expectations with the actual service experience. Dimensions of quality often assessed by the consumer include reliability, tangibles, responsiveness, assurance, and empathy. Differences between expectations and experience are identified through gap analysis.

4 *Discuss the important role of internal marketing in service organizations.*
Because the employee plays a central role in creating the service experience and in building and maintaining relationships with customers, many services firms have adopted a concept called internal marketing. Internal marketing means the service organization will care for and treat its employees like valued customers. In essence, before successful marketing efforts can be directed to customers, the firm will first focus on its employees, or internal market, creating the right organizational climate and jobs in order to ensure the right personnel will perform the service in the right way.

5 *Explain the special nature of the marketing mix for services; the Eight Ps in services marketing.*
In addition to the traditional marketing mix (the four Ps), mentioned frequently throughout this text, the distinctive nature of services required that other variables be effectively managed by service marketers. These include people, physical evidence, process, and productivity. Collectively, the marketing mix for services is referred to as the eight Ps. Many services depend on people to create and deliver services, and thus people must be hired, trained, and motivated correctly. The physical environment (physical evidence) where the services are created must be managed to convey the proper impression to the customer. The process by which services are created and delivered must also be managed effectively in order for customers to receive the service in a timely and appropriate manner. And finally, because of the perishable nature of services, capacity management—managing productivity—of the services system is important.

■ ■ ■
FOCUSING ON KEY TERMS

capacity management p. 320
customer contact audit p. 314
eight P's of service marketing p. 317
four I's of services p. 309
gap analysis p. 315

idle production capacity p. 311
internal marketing p. 319
off-peak pricing p. 320
service continuum p. 312
services p. 308

■ ■ ■
DISCUSSION AND APPLICATION QUESTIONS

1 Explain how the four I's of services would apply to a branch office of the Royal Bank.

2 Idle production capacity may be related to inventory or capacity management. How would the pricing component of the marketing mix reduce idle production capacity for (a) a car wash, (b) stage theatre group, and (c) a university?

3 Look back at the service continuum in Figure 12–2. Explain how the following points on the continuum differ in terms of consistency: (a) salt, (b) automobile, (c) advertising agency, and (d) teaching.

4 What are the search, experience, and credence properties of an airline for the business traveller and pleasure traveller? What properties are most important to each group?

5 Outline the customer contact audit for a typical check-in at a local hotel.

6 The text suggests that internal marketing is necessary before a successful marketing program can be directed at consumers. Why is this particularly true for service organizations?

7 Outline the capacity management strategies that an airline must consider.

8 How does off-peak pricing influence demand for services?

9 Physical evidence of one of the eight Ps of services marketing. How would a physician go about managing the physical evidence of her practice to convey the proper image to her patients?

10 This chapter suggests that consumers judge service quality along five key dimensions: tangibles, reliability, responsiveness, assurance, and empathy. Which dimension is most important to you when you judge the following services: (a) a physician, (b) bank, (c) car rental, and (d) dry cleaning?

| GOING ONLINE | Reviewing the Latest Services Marketing Strategies |

The American Marketing Association provides a variety of useful services for anyone interested in the latest services marketing concepts and strategies. Go to AMA's home page (www.marketingpower.com), and type "services marketing" in the search engine to review the information and services available. If you click on "AMA info" and "publications," articles from a variety of publications, including *Marketing Health*

Services, can be reviewed. Another good site is www.emeraldinsight.com, where you can read abstracts of articles from *The Journal of Services Marketing.* Investigate a services marketing topic of interest to you.

1 What publications are available related to the topic you selected?

2 Describe two insights you obtained from the summaries of the publications.

Do you want to get better grades and stay up to date with current issues in marketing? Visit the Online Learning Centre at www.mcgrawhill.ca/college/crane for practice tests, video cases, resources for building a marketing plan, *Globe and Mail* headlines, access to *Marketing Magazine*, and other learning and study tools.

VIDEO CASE 12   National Hockey League

The National Hockey League (www.nhl.com) traces its beginnings to November 22, 1917, and, as such, is the second-oldest professional sports league of the four major team sports in North America. Only professional baseball predates it. Throughout its history, the NHL has been recognized for its ideas and innovations. For example, the NHL was the first major sports league to introduce a playoff system, which has been adopted by all other major sports.

However, historically the NHL and many of the team owners had a negative mindset toward marketing. Marketing was actually considered unseemly. The general approach was to simply open the doors of the arena and wait for customers to come. But with rising costs to operate the league, particularly player salaries, the NHL needed a bigger audience both at the games and on television. The league now fully embraces marketing—and it starts at the top. NHL Commissioner Gary Bettman, former vice-president of the NBA (National Basketball Association), leads the NHL's marketing effort.

In addition to trying to sell seats to fans at arenas and selling hockey to TV viewers, the league is also involved in product merchandising and product licensing. For example, it has an online store where fans can purchase official NHL merchandise. Fans can actually use their NHL MasterCard—complete with the logo of their favourite team—to purchase the merchandise. The league's highly interactive Web site allows fans to log on to find the latest scores and player statistics, and the Web site also offers NHL Broadband TV, NHL Game Radio, and an opportunity for fans to be directly involved in the NHL Fantasy Games programs. Corporate involvement and sponsorship is also a key priority with the league. Several teams have built new arenas and have attracted major corporate sponsors to be associated with the new complexes. For example, General Motors Place is home to the Vancouver Canucks, the Molson Centre is home to the Montreal Canadiens, the Air Canada Centre is home to the Toronto Maple Leafs, and the Corel Centre is home to the Ottawa Senators.

The NHL has also penetrated the European television market, with NHL games being broadcast on primetime Swedish TV. Europe is a good market for the NHL's product merchandising and licensing programs. In an effort to improve the entertainment value of the game for television viewers, the league has worked to improve how games are televised, including adding more cameras (e.g., cameras in the nets) and a variety of different camera angles from which fans can view the game.

Recently, marketing professional hockey in the United States has been a major focus for the NHL. While Canada was the birthplace of hockey, the NHL believes it is the United States that offers the best opportunity to ensure the long-term prosperity of the league. The NHL believes that strong franchises in major American cities will help sell the game to a larger and new generation of fans outside of Canada. In fact, strong fan support, media interest, and corporate sponsorship has led to an expansion of teams in the United States.

In 2005, the league consisted of 30 teams, with only 6 Canadian franchises and 24 U.S.–based franchises. The league is divided into two major Conferences (Eastern and Western), each with three divisions (see Figure 1). The teams play a regular season schedule of more than 80 games. The top eight teams in each conference advance to the playoff rounds. The eventual winner of the playoffs takes home the Stanley Cup, the world's oldest professional sports trophy.

Still, while other major sports leagues command massive broadcasting fees, the NHL collects comparatively modest fees from the networks that carry its games, including CBC, TSN, NBC, and OLN. The size of the NHL's product merchandising and product licensing program is also small compared with those of

FIGURE 1—NHL LEAGUE SETUP

EASTERN CONFERENCE	WESTERN CONFERENCE
Northeast Division	**Central Division**
Boston	Detroit
Toronto	Chicago
Ottawa	St. Louis
Montreal	Nashville
Buffalo	Columbus
Southeast Division	**Northwest Division**
Carolina	Colorado
Washington	Edmonton
Tampa Bay	Vancouver
Atlanta	Calgary
Florida	Minnesota
Atlantic Division	**Pacific Division**
Philadelphia	Los Angeles
NY Islanders	Dallas
NY Rangers	Phoenix
Pittsburgh	Anaheim

the other major-league sports. Most teams still generate more than 80 percent of their revenue at the gate. However, rising player salaries are putting a squeeze on many franchises. In order to pay for those high player salaries—some as high as $10 million per year—the teams basically need to fill the seats of their arenas for every single game. To do so, the teams need to offer fans a quality entertainment product. If not, the fans may not return. The home teams do not necessarily have to win every game, but fans need to feel they have received real entertainment value for the price of their admission. In addition, if the teams do not entertain the fans who are watching the games at home, viewership is likely to drop, and so will the league's ability to charge reasonable fees for broadcast rights.

The NHL realizes it must aggressively market professional hockey. It believes it must put great players on the ice with great teams, and it must offer wholesome and fun entertainment. If it does not, customers will not continue to support and patronize professional hockey. And without fan support, there will be no more *Hockey Night in Canada*—or anywhere else, for that matter.

In fact, in 2004–2005, there was no *Hockey Night in Canada*, at least no NHL hockey. The season was cancelled because the league and its players could not come to terms with regard to a new collective bargaining agreement. In essence, the owners of the teams suggested that they had lost, collectively, over $275 million during the 2003–2004 season because of rising costs and low revenues. However, the players were not prepared to accept salary caps proposed by owners. In the end, both parties walked away from the bargaining table and left the fans without a season. This action was analogous to a packaged-goods firm removing its product from the shelf. In such a case, the consumer would be forced to find an alternative. For the hockey fan, there was the issue of what other entertainment alternative would replace the NHL. Many turned to junior hockey and/or university hockey. Many sports experts had suggested that cancelling the 2004–2005 season would be catastrophic for the league and fans might not return if and when the NHL decided to commence business again.

However, the NHL and the players did end the labour dispute, signed a new collective agreement, and returned to the ice for the 2005–2006 season. In addition to the new collective agreement, the NHL also decided to make many rule changes in order to make the game more entertaining for fans. Some of the major rule changes included: (1) deciding tied games by a shootout, (2) making the two-line pass legal (with the long pass, defending the neutral zone is harder and the game has increased speed and more breakaways), (3) goaltender leg pads, blockers, catching gloves and jerseys were all cut down in size to increase chances for goal scoring, (4) more room inside the blue lines to help the offence and increase scoring opportunities, and (5) more fines and suspensions for fighting. The NHL wanted to improve the game's image and make the sport more family-friendly. However, some purists believe that fighting is part of the game and part of the entertainment value fans are looking for.

Ultimately, the NHL is hoping that with the new rule changes, new TV network agreements, and aggressive marketing, the League will be restored as a major team sport and entertainment product.

QUESTIONS

1 What is the "real product" that the NHL is marketing to prospective fans?

2 Who is the NHL competing with in terms of fan attendance?

3 How does marketing professional hockey differ from marketing a consumer product, such as breakfast cereal?

4 With the new rule changes, has the NHL altered its offering enough to revitalize the game and its fan base?

PRICING PRODUCTS AND SERVICES

LEARNING OBJECTIVES

After reading this chapter, you should be able to:

1 Understand the nature and importance of pricing products and services.

2 Recognize the constraints on a firm's pricing latitude and the objectives a firm has in setting prices.

3 Explain what a demand curve is and what price elasticity of demand means.

4 Perform a break-even analysis.

5 Understand approaches to pricing as well as factors considered to establish prices for products and services.

6 Describe basic laws and regulations affecting pricing practices.

HERE'S A PRICING PROBLEM FOR YOU!

Imagine you are part of the management team for Strait Crossing Bridge Ltd. (SCBL), a subsidiary company of Strait Crossing Development Inc. You know—the company that built the Confederation Bridge (www.confederation bridge.com), the bridge that joins Borden-Carleton, Prince Edward Island, and Cape Jourimain, New Brunswick? Yes, that one. It is 12.9 kilometres long and is the longest bridge over ice-covered waters in the world. And it just cost you $1 billion to build it. Now you must determine what price to charge users who might want to cross it.

Well, you have many things to ponder. First, you must consider what it is that you are offering customers. You have a pretty good handle on that. Your bridge carries two lanes of traffic 24 hours a day, seven days a week, and it takes approximately 10 minutes to cross at normal travelling speed, which is 80 km/hr. So, compared with ferry service, which often involves a wait and a much longer travel time to cross, you believe consumers will want to use the bridge. But how many customers and how often are two key questions. In this case, things are not so clear. You do know, however, that consumer demand for your product clearly affects the price that can be charged.

So, you hire a consulting firm that does some demand estimates for you. The problem is, you must consider the type of user for the bridge or, more specifically, the type of vehicle being driven across the bridge. Why? Because traffic volume is made up of a variety of different vehicles, from passenger cars and buses to recreational vehicles and motorcycles. Some vehicles, particularly heavy trucks, put more wear and tear on the bridge, and therefore you believe that these types of vehicles should pay more to use the bridge. So, now you try to crunch some numbers: traffic volume by type of vehicle.

But wait a minute. Before you can set prices to make some revenue projections, you must consult the federal government of Canada. The federal government, through its regulatory agency, Transport Canada, has the power to dictate the price you charge or, in this case, the toll users will pay. You are told that the base rate for tolls by vehicle type must be developed on the basis of previous ferry-service revenue data plus the rate of inflation. With all this information, you must come up with a pricing strategy for the bridge—a pricing strategy that will cover your capital and operating costs as well as provide some long-run profits for the firm. Wow, it is a pricing problem![1]

Welcome to the fascinating—and intense—world of pricing, where myriad forces come together in the specific price prospective buyers are asked to pay. This chapter covers important factors used in setting prices. By the way, the toll rate for a passenger vehicle, round trip, is $39 and is collected on exiting PEI. If you are riding a motorcycle, it is a little cheaper at $15.50. But if you are driving a tractor trailer, you pay $55.75. And if you are in a hurry, you can use the StraitPass Transportation System, an electronic poll and payment system. The transponder will cost you $40. And your toll charges are billed to your credit card.

NATURE AND IMPORTANCE OF PRICE

The price paid for goods and services goes by many names. You pay *tuition* for your education, *rent* for an apartment, *interest* on a bank credit card, and a *premium* for car insurance. Your dentist or physician charges you a *fee*, a professional or social organization charges *dues*, and operators of the Confederation Bridge charge you a *fare* or a *toll* to use their bridge. In business, a consultant may require a *retainer* for services rendered, an executive is given a *salary*, a salesperson receives a *commission*, and a worker is paid a *wage*. Of course, what you pay for clothes or a haircut is termed a *price*.

What Is a Price?

price
The money or other considerations (including other goods and services) exchanged for the ownership or use of a good or service.

These examples highlight the many varied ways that price plays a part in our daily lives. From a marketing viewpoint, **price** is the money or other considerations (including other goods and services) exchanged for the ownership or use of a good or service. For example, Shell Oil recently exchanged one million pest-control devices for sugar from a Caribbean country, and Wilkinson Sword exchanged some of its knives

for advertising used to promote its razor blades. This practice of exchanging goods and services for other goods and services rather than for money is called *barter*. These transactions account for billions of dollars annually in domestic and international trade.

For most products and services, money is exchanged, atlhough the amount is not always the same as the list or quoted price because of the discounts, allowances, and extra fees shown in Figure 13–1. Suppose you decide you want to buy the newly introduced Bugatti Veyron, the world's fastest production car, because its 8-litre, 1001-horsepower, V-16 engine moves you from 0 to over 100 km/hr in 2.9 seconds at a top speed of over 400 km/hr. The Veyron has a list price of $1.2 million, and only 300 are available. However, if you put $500 000 down now and finance the balance over the next year, you will receive a rebate of $100 000 off the list price and pay a finance chage of $26 317. To ship the car from France, you will pay a $5000 destination charge. For your 2000 Honda Civic DX four-door sedan that has 100 000 kilometres and is in fair condition, you are given a trade-in allowance of $5395.

Applying the price equation (as shown in Figure 13–1) to your purchase, your final price is:

Final price = List price − (Incentives + Allowances) + Extra fees
          = $1 200 000 − ($100 000 + $5395) + ($26 317 + $5000)
          = $1 135 922

Your monthly payment for the one-year loan of $600 000 is $52 192.06. Are you still interested? Figure 13–1 illustrates how the price equation applies to a variety of different products and services.

PRICE EQUATION

ITEM PURCHASED	PRICE	= LIST PRICE	INCENTIVES AND − ALLOWANCES	+ EXTRA FEES
New car bought by an individual	Final price	= List price	− Rebate Cash discount Old car trade-in	+ Financing charges Special accessories Destination charges
Term in university bought by a student	Tuition	= Published tuition	− Scholarship Other financial aid Discounts for number of credits taken	+ Special activity fees
Bank loan obtained by a small business	Principal and interest	= Amount of loan sought	− Allowance for collateral	+ Premium for uncertain creditworthiness
Merchandise bought from a wholesaler by a retailer	Invoice price	= List price	− Quantity discount Cash discount Seasonal discount Functional or trade discount	+ Penalty for late payment

■ FIGURE 13–1 ■

The price of four different purchases

Price as an Indicator of Value

From a consumer's perspective, price is often used to indicate value when it is compared with the benefits of the product. Specifically, *value* is defined as the ratio of perceived benefits to price.[3] At a given price, as perceived benefits increase, perceived value increases. For example, if you are used to paying $12.99 for a medium pizza from Pizza Pizza, wouldn't a large pizza at the same price be more valuable? Many marketers often engage in the practice of *value pricing*—increasing product or service benefits while maintaining or decreasing price. "Super-sizing" at fast-food restaurants is an example of value pricing.

But marketers must be careful when using price as an indicator of value. For example, for many consumers, a low price might imply possible poor quality, and ultimately, poor perceived value.[4] This is particularly true for service.[5] For example, what would be your perception of a dentist who charges only $25 for a checkup and cleaning when the average dentist charges between $100 and $150?[6]

This example also illustrates that consumers will often make comparative value assessments. That is, the consumer will judge one product or service against other alternatives or substitutes. In doing so, a "reference value" emerges, which involves comparing the prices and benefits of substitute items.

Price in the Marketing Mix

Pricing is also a critical decision made by a marketing executive because price has a direct effect on a firm's profits. This is apparent from a firm's **profit equation**:

profit equation
Profit = Total revenue − Total cost, or Profit = (Unit price × Quantity sold) − Total cost.

$$\text{Profit} = \text{Total revenue} - \text{Total cost}$$

or

$$\text{Profit} = (\text{Unit price} \times \text{Quantity sold}) - \text{Total cost}$$

What makes this relationship even more important is that price affects the quantity sold, as illustrated with demand curves later in this chapter. Furthermore, since the quantity sold sometimes affects a firm's costs because of efficiency of production,

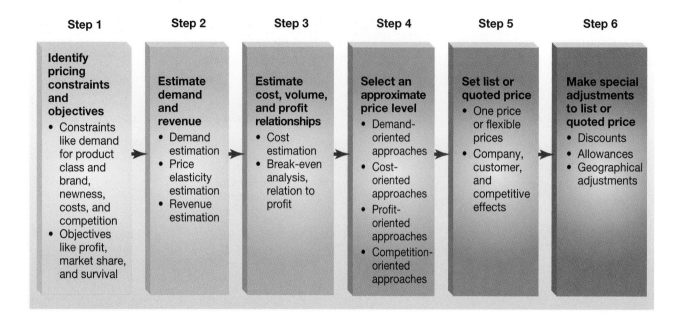

■ **FIGURE 13–2** ■■
Steps in setting price

price also indirectly affects costs. Thus, pricing decisions influence both total revenue and total cost, which makes pricing one of the most important decisions marketing executives face.

The importance of price in the marketing mix necessitates an understanding of six major steps involved in the process organizations go through in setting prices (Figure 13–2):

- Identifying pricing constraints and objectives
- Estimating demand and revenue
- Determining cost, volume, and profit relationships
- Selecting an approximate price level
- Setting list or quoted price
- Making special adjustments to list or quoted price

■ ■ ■
STEP 1: IDENTIFYING PRICING CONSTRAINTS AND OBJECTIVES

To define a problem, it is important to consider both the objectives and constraints that narrow the range of alternatives available to solve it. These same principles apply in solving a pricing problem. Let us first review the pricing constraints so that we can better understand the nature of pricing alternatives.

Identifying Pricing Constraints

pricing constraints
Factors that limit the latitude of price a firm may set.

Factors that limit the latitude of prices a firm may set are **pricing constraints**. Consumer demand for the product clearly affects the price that can be charged. Other constraints on price vary from factors within the organization to competitive factors outside the organization. Moreover, legal and regulatory factors, discussed at the end of this chapter, also restrict the prices an organization can set.

Demand for the Product Class, Product, and Brand   The number of potential buyers for the product class (such as cars), product (sports cars), and brand (Dodge Viper) clearly affects the price a seller can charge. So does the consideration whether the item is a luxury (a Viper) or a necessity (bread and a roof over your head). In fact, when a consumer is in urgent need of a particular necessity, a marketer may com-

ETHICS AND SOCIAL RESPONSIBILITY ALERT

Getting an Unfair Premium Price?

The drug Clozapine is one of the most significant advances in antipsychotic drugs in two decades. But few of the people who really need this drug get it, since the drug costs about $9000 a year. Phamaceutical companies have been accused of price gouging with respect to this drug and other critical life-saving drugs, such as those used in AIDS (acquired immune deficiency syndrome) treatment.

Some consumer advocates argue that many industries have a tendency to command premium prices for necessary products or services knowing that consumers usually have little choice but to pay them. Oil companies, for example, are often criticized for raising prices on home-heating oil during the cold Canadian winters. The oil companies argue it is simply a supply-and-demand issue. Many consumers, however, feel they are being gouged unfairly because oil companies realize the consumer has little choice but to pay the price. Price-gouging claims are also levied against major airlines during peak travel periods. Individual companies are sometimes accused of price gouging during shortages. For example, during water shortages, bottled water suppliers have sometimes increased the price of their product by two to three times its original price. University students often report paying high and unfair prices for off-campus housing when demand is high and supply is low.

The practice of commanding premium prices for luxuries and necessities appears to be gaining acceptability with marketers. In a recent survey of Canadian MBA students, 30 percent of them stated they would charge higher than normal prices if they believed the consumer would pay the higher price.

Is the use of premium pricing for necessities fair? Is it ethical? What should be done about this practice?

mand a premium price. In this case, there may be ethical issues involved (see the accompanying Ethics and Social Responsibility Alert box).[7]

Newness of the Product: Stage in the Product Life Cycle   The newer a product and the earlier it is in its life cycle, the higher the price that can usually be charged. Willing to spend up to $500 for a new electronic book? The high initial price is possible because of patents and limited competition early in its product life cycle. By the time you read this, the price will probably be much lower.

Single Product versus a Product Line   When Sony introduced its CD player, not only was it unique and in the introductory stage of its product life cycle but also it was the *only* CD player Sony sold, and so the firm had great latitude in setting a price. Now, with a wide range of Sony CD products and technologies, the price of individual models has to be consistent with the others based on features provided and meaningful price differentials that communicate value to consumers.

Cost of Producing and Marketing the Product   In the long run, a firm's price must cover all the costs of producing and marketing a product. If the price does not cover the cost, the firm will fail, and so in the long term, a firm's costs set a floor under its price. The operators of the Confederation Bridge are clearly conscious of the fact that the total cost of providing their bridge service must not exceed total revenue, as otherwise they cannot succeed.

Cost of Changing Prices and Time Period They Apply   If Air Canada asks General Electric (GE) to provide spare jet engines to power the new Boeing 737 it has just bought, GE can easily set a new price for the engines to reflect its latest information, since only one buyer has to be informed. But if Sears Canada decides that sweater prices are too low in its winter catalogues after thousands of catalogues have been mailed to customers, it has a big problem, and so it must consider the cost of changing prices and the time period for which they apply in developing the price list for its catalogue items. In actual practice, research indicates that most firms change the price for their major products once a year. But on a Web site, prices can change from minute to minute.

Type of Competitive Markets The seller's price is constrained by the type of market in which it competes. Economists generally delineate four types of competitive markets: pure monopoly, oligopoly, monopolistic competition, and pure competition. Figure 13–3 shows that the type of competition dramatically influences the latitude of price competition and, in turn, the nature of product differentiation and extent of advertising. A firm must recognize the general type of competitive market it is in to understand the latitude of both its price and nonprice strategies. For example, prices can be significantly affected by four competitive situations:

- *Pure monopoly*. In 1994, Johnson & Johnson (J&J) revolutionized the treatment of coronary heart diseases by introducing the "stent"—a tiny mesh tube "spring" that props clogged arteries open. Initially, a monopolist, J&J stuck with its early $2235 price and achieved $1.4 billion in sales and 91-percent market share in the category. But its reluctance to give price reductions for large-volume purchases antagonized hospitals. When competitors introduced an improved stent at lower prices, J&J's market share plummeted to 8 percent just two years later.[8]
- *Oligopoly*. The few sellers of aluminum (Alcan, Alcoa) or mainframe computers try to avoid price competition because it can lead to disastrous price wars in which all lose money. Yet, firms in such industries stay aware of a competitor's price cuts or increases and may follow suit. The products can be undifferentiated (aluminum) or differentiated (mainframe computers), and informative advertising that avoids head-to-head price competition is used.
- *Monopolistic competition*. Dozens of regional, private brands of peanut butter compete with national brands, such as Skippy and Jif. Both price competition (regional, private brands being lower than national brands) and nonprice competition (product features and advertising) exist.
- *Pure competition*. Hundreds of local grain elevators sell corn for which price per bushel is set by the marketplace. Within strains, the corn is identical, and so advertising only informs buyers that the seller's corn is available.

■ FIGURE 13–3 ■

Pricing, product, and advertising strategies available to firms in four types of competitive markets

TYPE OF COMPETITIVE MARKET

STRATEGIES AVAILABLE	PURE MONOPOLY (One seller who sets the price for a unique product)	OLIGOPOLY (Few sellers who are sensitive to each other's prices)	MONOPOLISTIC COMPETITION (Many sellers who compete on nonprice factors)	PURE COMPETITION (Many sellers who follow the market price for identical, commodity products)
Extent of price competition	None: sole seller sets price	Some: price leader or follower of competitors	Some: compete over range of prices	Almost none: market sets price
Extent of product differentiation	None: no other producers	Various: depends on industry	Some: differentiate products from competitors	None: products are identical
Extent of advertising	Little: purpose is to increase demand for product class	Some: purpose is to inform but avoid price competition	Much: purpose is to differentiate firm's products from competitors	Little: purpose is to inform prospects that seller's products are available

Competitors' Prices   Finally, a firm must know or anticipate what specific price its present and potential competitors are charging now or will charge in the future.

Identifying Pricing Objectives

pricing objectives
Expectations that specify the role of price in an organization's marketing and strategic plans.

Expectations that specify the role of price in an organization's marketing and strategic plans are **pricing objectives**. To the extent possible, these organizational pricing objectives are also carried to lower levels in the organization, such as in setting objectives for marketing managers responsible for an individual brand. These objectives may change depending on the financial position of the company as a whole, the success of its products, the target segments served by the company, or the competitive environment. For example, H.J. Heinz has specific pricing objectives for its ketchup, which vary by country.

Profit   Three different objectives relate to a firm's profit, usually measured in terms of return on investment (ROI) or return on assets. One objective is *managing for long-run profits*, which is followed by many Japanese firms that are willing to forgo immediate profit in cars, TV sets, or computers to develop quality products that can penetrate competitive markets in the future. A *maximizing current profit* objective, such as during this quarter or year, is common in many firms because the targets can be set and performance measured quickly. Canadian firms are sometimes criticized for this short-run orientation. A *target return* objective involves a firm, such as Irving Oil or Mohawk, setting a goal (such as 20 percent) for pretax ROI. These three profit objectives have different implications for a firm's pricing objectives.

Another profit consideration for such firms as movie studios and manufacturers is to ensure that those firms in their channels of distribution make adequate profits. Without profits for these channel members, the movie studio or manufacturer is cut off from its customers. For example, Figure 13–4 shows where each dollar of your movie ticket goes. The 51 cents the movie studio gets must cover both its production expenses and its profit. While the studio would like more than 51 cents of your dollar, it settles for this amount to make sure theatres and distributors are satisfied and willing to handle their movies. Still, with revenues close to $1 billion, the Canadian movie theatre industry has actually been raising ticket prices to increase its profitability.

Sales   Given that a firm's profit is high enough for it to remain in business, its objectives may be to increase sales revenue. The hope is that the increase in sales revenue will, in turn, lead to increases in market share and profit. Cutting price on one product in a firm's line may increase its sales revenue but reduce those of related products. Objectives related to sales revenue or unit sales have the advantage of being translated easily into meaningful targets for marketing managers responsible for a product line or brand—far more easily than with an ROI target, for example.

Market Share   Market share is the ratio of the firm's sales revenues or unit sales to those of the industry (competitors plus the firm itself). Companies often pursue a market share objective when industry sales are relatively flat or declining. The Molson and Labatt breweries have adopted this objective in the beer market, while Pepsi-Cola Canada and Coca-Cola Canada battle for market share in the soft drink category.[9] But although increased market share is the primary goal of some firms, others see it as a means to an end: increasing sales and profits.

Theatre
19¢

Distributor
30¢

Movie
studio
51¢

10¢ = Theatre expenses

9¢ = Left for theatre

6¢ = Misc. expenses

24¢ = Left for distributor

20¢ = Advertising and publicity expenses

8¢ = Actors' share of gross

23¢ = Left for movie studio

■ **FIGURE 13–4** ■
Where each dollar of your movie ticket goes

Unit Volume   Many firms use unit volume, the quantity produced or sold, as a pricing objective. These firms often sell multiple products at very different prices and need to match the unit volume demanded by customers with price and production capacity. Using unit volume as an objective can be counterproductive if a volume objective is achieved, say, by drastic price cutting that drives down company profitability.[10]

Survival   In some instances, profits, sales, and market share are less important objectives of the firm than mere survival. Continental Airlines has struggled to attract passengers with low fares, no-penalty advance-booking policies, and aggressive promotions to improve the firm's cash flow. This pricing objective has helped Continental to stay alive in the competitive airline industry.

demand curve
The summation of points representing the maximum number of products consumers will buy at a given price.

Social Responsibility   A firm may forgo higher profit on sales and follow a pricing objective that recognizes its obligations to customers and society in general. Medtronics followed this pricing policy when it introduced the world's first heart pacemaker. Gerber supplies a specially formulated product free of charge to children who cannot tolerate foods based on cow's milk. Government agencies, which set many prices for services they offer, use social responsibility as a primary pricing objective.

CONCEPT CHECK	**1.** What factors impact the list price to determine the final price? **2.** How does the type of competitive market a firm is in affect its latitude in setting price?

STEP 2: ESTIMATING DEMAND AND REVENUE

Basic to setting a product's price is the extent of customer demand for it. Marketing executives must also translate this estimate of customer demand into estimates of revenues the firm expects to receive.

Fundamentals of Estimating Demand

Newsweek decided to conduct a pricing experiment at newsstands in 11 cities.[11] In one city, newsstand buyers paid $2.25. In five cities, newsstand buyers paid the regular $2 price. In another city, the price was $1.50, and in four other cities it was only $1. By comparison, the regular newsstand price for *Time* was $1.95. Why did *Newsweek* conduct the experiment? According to a *Newsweek* executive, at that time, "We wanted to figure out what the demand curve for our magazine at the newsstand is." And you thought that demand curves only existed to confuse you on a test in basic economics!

The Demand Curve   A **demand curve** shows a maximum number of products consumers will buy at a given price. Demand curve D_1 in Figure 13–5 shows the newsstand demand for *Newsweek* under existing conditions. Note that as price falls, people buy more. But price is not the complete story in estimating demand. Economists stress three other key factors:

1. *Consumer tastes.* As we saw in Chapter 3, these depend on many factors, such as demographics, culture, and technology. Because consumer tastes can change quickly, up-to-date marketing research is essential.
2. *Price and availability of other products.* As the price of close substitute products falls (the price of *Time*) and their availability increases, the demand for a product declines (the demand for *Newsweek*).

■ FIGURE 13–5 ■
Illustrative demand curves
for *Newsweek* magazine

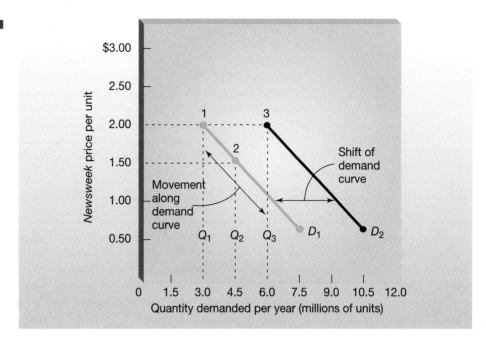

3. *Consumer income*. In general, as real consumer income (allowing for inflation) increases, demand for a product also increases.

The first of these two factors influences what consumers want to buy, and the third affects what they *can* buy. Along with price, these are often called *demand factors*, or factors that determine consumers' willingness and ability to pay for goods and services. As discussed earlier in Chapters 8 and 10, it is often very difficult to estimate demand for new products, especially because consumer likes and dislikes are often difficult to read clearly.

Movement Along versus Shift of a Demand Curve Demand curve D_1 in Figure 13–5 shows that as the price is lowered from $2 to $1.50, the quantity demanded increases from 3 million (Q_1) to 4.5 million (Q_2) units per year. This is an example of a movement along a demand curve and assumes that other factors (consumer tastes, price and availability of substitutes, and consumer income) remain unchanged.

What if some of the factors change? For example, if advertising causes more people to want *Newsweek*, newsstand distribution is increased, and when consumer incomes double, then the demand increases. This is shown in Figure 13–5 as a shift of the demand curve to the right, from D_1 to D_2. This increased demand means that more *Newsweek* magazines are wanted for a given price: at a price of $2, the demand is 6 million units per year (Q_3) on D_2 rather than 3 million units per year (Q_1) on D_1.

price elasticity of demand

The percentage change in quantity demanded relative to a percentage change in price.

Price Elasticity of Demand Marketing managers are especially interested in **price elasticity of demand**, or the percentage change in quantity demanded relative to a percentage change in price. Price elasticity is central to understanding a product's demand curve. It provides an indication of how sensitive consumer demand and the firm's revenues are to changes in the product's price.

For example, a product with elastic demand is one in which a slight decrease in price results in a relatively large increase in demand, or units sold. The reverse is also true. With elastic demand, a slight increase in price results in a relatively large decrease in demand. Typically, the more substitutes a product or service has, the more likely it is to be price elastic. For example, marketing experiments on soft drinks, coffee, and snack foods have been shown to have elastic demand. So, marketing managers may cut price to increase the demand of their products depending on what competitors' prices are.

In contrast, a product with inelastic demand means that slight increases or decreases in price will not significantly affect the demand, or units sold, for the product. Typically, products and services considered as necessities usually have inelastic demand, as do products or services with no competitive alternatives. For example, if you have to drive to class in your car and gasoline prices increase one cent per litre, you are probably not going to start using the bus instead. Therefore, gasoline has inelastic demand, which means the increase in price will have a relatively minor impact on the number of litres of gasoline sold and may actually increase the total revenue of your local Petro-Canada or Irving gasoline station.

Fundamentals of Estimating Revenue

total revenue
The total money received from the sale of a product.

While economists may talk about "demand curves," marketing executives are more likely to speak in terms of "revenues generated." Demand curves lead directly to an essential revenue concept critical to pricing decisions: **total revenue**—the total money received from the sale of a product. Total revenue (TR) equals the unit price (P) times the quantity sold (Q). Or $TR = P \times Q$. For example, assume a picture frame shop sets a price of $100 per picture and sells 400 pictures per year. In this case,

$$TR = P \times Q$$
$$= \$100 \times 400$$
$$= \$40\ 000$$

This combination of price and quantity sold annually shows total revenue of $40 000 per year. But, is that shop making a profit? Alas, total revenue is only part of the profit equation that we saw earlier:

Total profit = Total revenue − Total cost

In order to determine the profitability of the frame shop, we have to examine the costs of running the shop. The following section covers this other important part of the profit equation—the costs of doing business.

CONCEPT CHECK

1. What is the difference between a movement along and a shift of a demand curve?

2. What does it mean if a product has inelastic demand?

■ ■ ■
STEP 3: ESTIMATING COST, VOLUME, AND PROFIT RELATIONSHIPS

While revenues are the monies received by a firm from selling its products or services to customers, costs or expenses are the monies the firm pays out to its employees and suppliers. Marketing managers often use break-even analysis to relate revenues and costs, a topic covered in this section.

The Importance of Controlling Costs

total cost
The total expenses incurred by a firm in producing and marketing a product.

Understanding the role and behaviour of costs is critical to all marketing decisions, particularly pricing decisions. Many firms go bankrupt because their costs get out of control, causing their total costs to exceed their total revenues over an extended period of time. This is why smart marketing managers make pricing decisions that balance both their revenues and costs. Three cost concepts are important in pricing decisions: total cost, fixed cost, and variable cost. **Total cost** is the total expenses incurred by a firm in producing and marketing a product. It is the sum of fixed costs

fixed cost
The firm's expenses that are stable and do not change with the quantity of product that is produced and cost.

variable cost
The sum of the expenses of the firm that vary directly with the quantity of products that is produced and sold.

break-even analysis
A technique that analyzes the relationship between total revenue and total cost to determine profitability at various levels of output.

and variable costs. **Fixed cost** is the firm's expenses that are stable and do not change with the quantity of product that is produced and cost. These usually include salaries of executives and lease charges on a building. **Variable cost** is the sum of the expenses of the firm that vary directly with the quantity of products that is produced and sold. Variable costs can be direct labour and materials used in producing the product or sales commissions that are tied directly to the quantity sold.

Break-Even Analysis

Marketing managers often employ an approach that considers cost, volume, and profit relationships, based on the profit equations. **Break-even analysis** is a technique that analyzes the relationship between total revenue and total cost to determine profitability at various levels of output. The *break-even point* (BEP) is the quantity at which total revenue and total costs are equal. Profit comes from any units sold beyond the BEP.

Calculating a Break-Even Point

The break-even point (BEP) is calculated as follows:

$$BEP_{Quantity} = \frac{\text{Fixed cost}}{\text{Unit price} - \text{Unit variable cost}}$$

So, consider our frame shop example. Suppose the frame shop owner wanted to identify how many pictures must be sold to cover fixed costs at a given price. Also, assume that the average price a customer will pay for each picture is $100. Suppose the fixed cost (FC) for the business is $28 000 (for real estate rental, interest on a bank loan, and other fixed expenses) and unit variable cost (UVC) for a picture is $30 (for labour, glass, frame, matting). The break-even quanity (BEP_{Quantity}) is 400 pictures, as follows:

$$BEP_{Quantity} = \frac{\text{Fixed cost}}{\text{Unit price} - \text{Unit variable cost}}$$

$$= \frac{\$28\ 000}{\$100 - 30}$$

$$= 400 \text{ pictures}$$

■ **FIGURE 13–6** ■
Calculating a break-even point

The shaded row in Figure 13–6 shows the break-even quantity for the frame shop at a price of $100 per picture is 400 pictures. At less than 400 pictures, the frame shop incurs a loss, and at more than 400 pictures it makes a profit.

QUANTITY OF PICTURES SOLD (Q)	PRICE PER PICTURE (P)	TOTAL REVENUE (TR) = (P × Q)	UNIT VARIABLE COST (UVC)	TOTAL VARIABLE COST (TVC) = (UVC × Q)	FIXED COST (FC)	TOTAL COST (TC) = (FC + TVC)	PROFIT = (TR − TC)
0	$100	$ 0	$30	$ 0	$28 000	$28 000	−$28 000
200	100	20 000	30	6000	28 000	34 000	−14 000
400	100	40 000	30	12 000	28 000	40 000	0
600	100	60 000	30	18 000	28 000	46 000	14 000
800	100	80 000	30	24 000	28 000	52 000	28 000
1000	100	100 000	30	30 000	28 000	58 000	42 000
1200	100	120 000	30	36 000	28 000	64 000	56 000

■ FIGURE 13–7 ■

Break-even analysis chart for picture frame shop

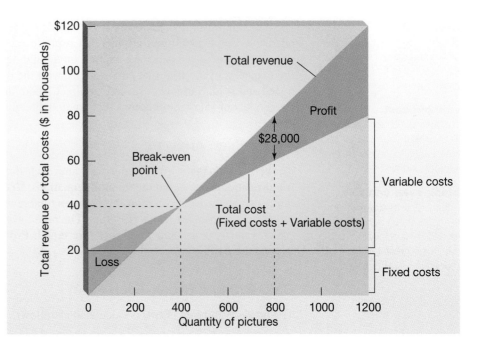

Figure 13–7 shows a graphic presentation of the break-even analysis, called a *break-even chart*. It shows that total revenue and total cost intersect and are equal at a quantity of 400 pictures sold, which is the break-even point at which profit is exactly $0. The frame shop owner would obviously want to do better. So, for example, if the frame shop owner could double the quantity sold annually to 800 pictures, the graph in Figure 13–7 shows an annual profit of $28 000 could be generated.

Application of Break-Even Analysis

Because of its simplicity, break-even analysis is used extensively in marketing, most frequently to study the impact of profit on changes in price, fixed cost, and variable cost. The mechanics of break-even analysis are the basis of the widely used electronic spreadsheets offered by such computer programs as Microsoft Excel that permit managers to answer hypothetical "what if" questions about the effect of changes in price and cost on their profit.

CONCEPT CHECK

1. What is the difference between fixed cost and variable cost?

2. What is a break-even point?

■ ■ ■

STEP 4: SELECTING AN APPROXIMATE PRICE LEVEL

A key to a marketing manager's setting a final price for a product is to find an "approximate price level" to use as a reasonable starting point. Four common approaches to finding this approximate price level are (1) demand-oriented, (2) cost-oriented, (3) profit-oriented, and (4) competition-oriented approaches (Figure 13–8). Although these approaches are discussed separately below, some of them overlap, and an effective marketing manager will consider several in searching for an approximate price level.

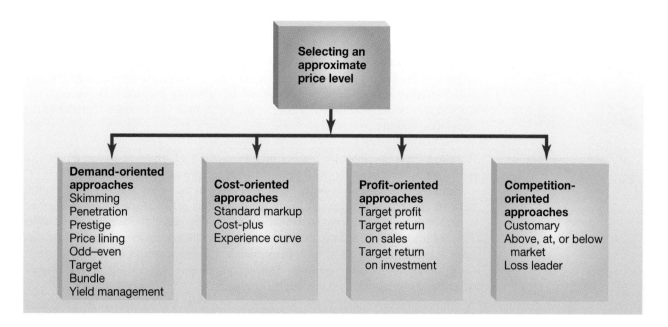

■ FIGURE 13–8 ■
Four approaches for
selecting an approximate
price level

Demand-Oriented Approaches

Demand-oriented approaches weigh factors underlying expected customer tastes and preferences more heavily than such factors as cost, profit, and competition when selecting a price level.

skimming pricing
The highest initial price that customers really desiring the product are willing to pay.

Skimming Pricing   A firm introducing a new or innovative product can use **skimming pricing**, setting the highest initial price that customers who really desire the product are willing to pay. These customers are not very price sensitive because they weigh the new product's price, quality, and ability to satisfy their needs against the same characteristics of substitutes. As the demand of these customers is satisfied, the firm lowers the price to attract another, more price-sensitive segment. Thus, skimming pricing gets its name from skimming successive layers of "cream," or customer segments, as prices are lowered in a series of steps.

Skimming pricing is an effective strategy when (1) enough prospective customers are willing to buy the product immediately at the high initial price to make these sales profitable, (2) the high initial price will not attract competitors, (3) lowering price has only a minor effect on increasing the sales volume and reducing the unit costs, and (4) customers interpret the high price as signifying high quality. These four conditions are most likely to exist when the new product is protected by patents or copyrights or its uniqueness is understood and valued by customers. Duracell adopted a skimming strategy for the Duracell Ultra alkaline battery because many of these conditions applied.

penetration pricing
Setting a low initial price on a new product to appeal immediately to the mass market.

Penetration Pricing   Setting a low initial price on a new product to appeal immediately to the mass market is **penetration pricing**, the exact opposite of skimming pricing. Nintendo consciously chose a penetration strategy when it introduced its GameCube video game console. GameCube was priced at substantially less than Microsoft's Xbox and Sony's PlayStation 2 consoles.[12]

The conditions favouring penetration pricing are the reverse of those supporting skimming pricing: (1) many segments of the market are price sensitive, (2) a low initial price discourages competitors from entering the market, and (3) unit production and marketing costs fall dramatically as production volumes increase. A firm using penetration pricing may (1) maintain the initial price for a time to gain profit lost from its low introductory level, or (2) lower the price further, counting on the new volume to generate the necessary profit.

In some situations, penetration pricing may follow skimming pricing. A company might initially price a product high to attract price-insensitive consumers and recoup initial research and development costs and introductory promotional expenditures. Once this is done, penetration pricing is used to appeal to a broader segment of the population and increase market share.

Prestige Pricing   *Prestige pricing* involves setting a high price so that quality- or status-conscious consumers will be attracted to the product and buy it.

Rolls-Royce cars, diamonds, perfumes, fine china, Swiss watches, and crystal have an element of prestige pricing in them and may sell worse at lower prices than at higher ones. When Swiss watchmaker TAG Heuer raised the average price of its watches from $250 to $1000, its sales volume increased sevenfold![13] Recently, Energizer learned that buyers of high-performance alkaline batteries tend to associate a lower price with lower quality. The accompanying Marketing NewsNet box describes the pricing lesson learned by Energizer.[14]

Price Lining   Often, a firm that is selling not just a single product but a line of products may price them at a number of different specific pricing points, which is called *price lining*. For example, a discount department store manager may price a line of women's dresses at $59, $79, and $99. In some instances, all the items might be purchased for the same cost and then marked up at different percentages to achieve these price points based on colour, style, and expected demand. In other instances, manufacturers design products for different price points, and retailers

---

MARKETING NEWSNET   **Energizer's Lesson in Price Perception: Value Lies in the Eye of the Beholder**

IDEAS AHEAD

Battery manufacturers are as tireless as a certain drum-thumping bunny in their efforts to create products that perform better, last longer, and, not incidentally, outsell the competition. The commercialization of new alkaline battery technology at a price that creates value for consumers is not always obvious or easy. Just ask the marketing executives at Energizer about their experience with pricing Energizer Advanced Formula and Energizer e2 AA alkaline batteries.

When Duracell launched its high-performance Ultra brand AA alkaline battery with a 25-percent price premium over standard Duracell batteries, Energizer quickly countered with its own high-performance battery—Energizer Advanced Formula. Believing that consumers would not pay the premium price, Energizer priced its Advanced Formula brand at the same price as its standard AA alkaline battery, expecting to gain market share from Duracell. It did not happen. Why not? According to industry analysts, consumers associated Energizer's low price with inferior quality in the high-performance segment. Instead of gaining market share, Energizer lost market share to Duracell and Rayovac, the number-three battery manufacturer.

Having learned its lesson, Energizer subsequently released its e2 high-performance battery, this time priced 4 percent higher than Duracell Ultra and about 50 percent higher than Advanced Formula. The result? Energizer recovered lost sales and market share. The lesson learned? Value lies in the eye of the beholder.

apply approximately the same markup percentages to achieve the three or four different price points offered to consumers.

Odd–Even Pricing   Sears Canada offers a Craftsman radial saw for $499.99, the suggested retail price for a MACH 3 razor set (razor and two blades) is $6.99, and Dollarama sells greeting cards for 99 cents. Why not simply price these items at $500, $7, and $1, respectively? These firms are using *odd–even pricing*, which involves setting prices a few dollars or cents under an even number. The presumption is that consumers see the Sears radial saw as priced at "something over $400" rather than "about $500." In theory, demand increases if the price drops from $500 to $499.99. There is some evidence to suggest that this does happen. However, research suggests that overuse of odd-ending prices tends to mute its effect on demand.[15]

Target Pricing   Manufacturers will sometimes estimate the price that the ultimate consumer would be willing to pay for a product. They then work backward through markups taken by retailers and wholesalers to determine what price they can charge wholesalers for the product. This practice, called *target pricing*, results in the manufacturer deliberately adjusting the composition and features of a product to achieve the target price to consumers. Canon uses this practice for pricing its cameras, and Heinz adopted target pricing for its complete line of pet foods.

Bundle Pricing   A frequently used demand-oriented pricing practice is *bundle pricing*—the marketing of two or more products in a single "package" price. For example, Air Canada offers vacation packages that include airfare, car rental, and lodging. Bundle pricing is based on the idea that consumers value the package more than the individual items. This is due to benefits received from not having to make separate purchases and due to enhanced satisfaction from one item given the presence of another. Moreover, bundle pricing often provides a lower total cost to buyers and lower marketing costs to sellers.[16] For example, Rogers AT&T offers an all-in-one wireless phone and service package that includes a Nokia phone and a calling plan for less than $20 a month.[17]

Yield Management Pricing   Have you noticed that seats on Air Canada flights are priced differently within the economy class? What you observed is *yield management pricing*—the charging of different prices to maximize revenue for a set amount of capacity at any given time.[18] As described in Chapter 12, service businesses engage in capacity management, and an effective way to do this is by varying price by time, day, week, or season. Yield management pricing is a complex approach that continually matches demand and supply to customize the price for a service. Airlines, hotels, cruise ships, and car rental companies use it. The airline industry reports that yield management pricing produces hundreds of millions of dollars of revenue each year that might not ordinarily be produced using traditional pricing practices.[19]

AIR CANADA ✦
vacations
aircanadavacations.com

Occidental Allegro Punta Cana • 4 ★

ALL-INCLUSIVE   FREE upgrade
Standard room   to VIP package!
September 3 – 25
1 week $879

PRICE INCLUDES ROUND-TRIP AIRFARE, ACCOMMODATION
AND AIRPORT TRANFERS AT DESTINATION

*PLUS TAXES OF $245, AND DEPARTURE TAX
OF USD$20 (CASH) PAID AT DESTINATION.

The **Dominican**Republic
a land of sensations

CONCEPT CHECK

1. What are the circumstances in pricing a new product that might support skimming or penetration pricing?

2. What is odd–even pricing?

Cost-Oriented Approaches

With cost-oriented approaches, the price setter stresses the supply or cost side of the pricing problem, not the demand side. Price is set by looking at the production and marketing costs and then adding enough to cover direct expenses, overhead, and profit.

Standard Markup Pricing   Managers of supermarkets and other retail stores have such a large number of products that estimating the demand for each product as a means of setting price is impossible. Therefore, they use *standard markup pricing*, which entails adding a fixed percentage to the cost of all items in a specific product class. This percentage markup varies depending on the type of retail store (such as furniture, clothing, or grocery) and on the product involved. High-volume products usually have smaller markups than do low-volume products. Supermarkets, such as Sobeys, Safeway, and Loblaws, have different markups for staple items and discretionary items. The markup on staple items, such as sugar, flour, and dairy products, varies from 10 to 23 percent, whereas markups on discretionary items, such as snack foods and candy, range from 27 to 47 percent. These markups must cover all the expenses of the store, pay for overhead costs, and contribute something to profits. For supermarkets, these markups, which may appear very large, result in only a 1-percent profit on sales revenue if the store is operating efficiently. By comparison, consider the markups on snacks and beverages purchased at your local movie theatre. The markup on soft drinks is 87 percent, 65 percent on chocolate bars, and a whopping 90 percent on popcorn! An explanation of how to compute a markup, along with operating statement data and other ratios, is given in Appendix B following this chapter.

Cost-Plus Pricing   Many manufacturing, professional services, and construction firms use a variation of standard markup pricing. *Cost-plus pricing* involves summing the total unit cost of providing a product or service and adding a specific amount to the cost to arrive at a price.

Cost-plus pricing is the most commonly used method to set prices for business products. But increasingly, this method is finding favour among business-to-business marketers in the service sector. For example, the rising cost of legal fees has prompted some law firms to adopt a cost-plus pricing approach. Rather than billing business clients on an hourly basis, lawyers and their clients agree on a fixed fee based on expected costs plus a profit for the law firm.[20] Many advertising agencies also use this approach. Here, the client agrees to pay the agency a fee based on the cost of its work plus some agreed-on profit, which is often a percentage of total cost.[21]

Experience Curve Pricing   The method of *experience curve pricing* is based on the learning effect, which holds that the unit cost of many products and services declines by 10 to 30 percent each time a firm's experience at producing and selling them doubles. This reduction is regular or predictable enough that the average cost per unit can be mathematically estimated. And, since prices often follow costs with experience curve pricing, a rapid decline in price is possible. Japanese firms in the electronics industry often adopt this pricing approach.

Profit-Oriented Approaches

A price setter may choose to balance both revenues and costs to set prices using profit-oriented approaches. These might involve either a target of a specific dollar volume of profit or express this target profit as a percentage of sales or investment.

Target Profit Pricing   A firm may set an annual target of a specific dollar volume of profit, which is called *target profit pricing*. Suppose our picture frame shop owner wishes to use target profit pricing to establish a price for a typical framed picture and assumes the following:

- Variable cost is a constant $22 per unit.
- Fixed cost is a constant $26 000.
- Demand is insensitive to price up to $60 per unit.
- A target profit of $7000 is sought at an annual volume of 1000 units (framed pictures).

The price can be calculated as follows:

$$\text{Profit} = \text{Total revenue} - \text{Total cost}$$
$$\text{Profit} = (P \times Q) - [FC + (UVC \times Q)]$$
$$\$7000 = (P \times 1000) - [\$26\,000 + (\$22 \times 1000)]$$
$$\$7000 = 1000P - (\$26\,000 + \$22\,000)$$
$$1000P = \$7000 + \$48\,000$$
$$P = \$55$$

Note that a critical assumption is that this higher average price of a framed picture will not cause the demand to fall.

Target Return-on-Sales Pricing A difficulty with target profit pricing is that although it is simple and the target involves only a specific dollar volume, there is no benchmark of sales or investment used to show how much of the firm's effort is needed to achieve the target. Such firms as supermarket chains often use *target return-on-sales pricing* to set typical prices that will give the firm a profit that is a specified percentage—say, 1 percent of the sales volume.

Target Return-on-Investment Pricing Such firms as GM and many public utilities set annual return-on-investment (ROI) targets, such as ROI of 20 percent. *Target return-on-investment pricing* is a method of setting prices to achieve this target.

Suppose the shop owner sets a target ROI of 10 percent, which is twice that achieved the previous year. She considers raising the average price of a framed picture to $54 or $58—up from last year's average of $50. To do this, she might improve product quality by offering better frames and higher-quality matting, which will increase the cost but will probably offset the decreased revenue from the lower number of units that can be sold next year.

Competition-Oriented Approaches

Rather than emphasize demand, cost, or profit factors, a price setter can stress what competitors (or "the market") are doing.

Customary Pricing For some products, when tradition, standardized channels of distribution, or other competitive factors dictate the price, *customary pricing* is used. Tradition prevails in the pricing of Swatch watches. The $40 customary price for the basic model has changed little in 10 years. Chocolate bars offered through standard vending machines have a customary price of 75 cents, and a significant departure from this price may result in a loss of sales for the manufacturer. Hershey typically has changed the amount of chocolate in its chocolate bars depending on the price of raw chocolate rather than vary its customary retail price so that it can continue selling through vending machines.

Above-, At-, or Below-Market Pricing For most products, it is difficult to identify a specific market price for a product or product class. Still, marketing managers often have a subjective feel for the competitor's price or market price. Using this benchmark, they then may deliberately choose a strategy of *above-, at-, or below-market pricing*.

Among watch manufacturers, Rolex takes pride in emphasizing that it makes one of the most expensive watches you can buy—a clear example of above-market pricing. Manufacturers of national brands of clothing, such as Alfred Sung and Christian Dior, and retailers, such as Holt Renfrew, deliberately set premium prices for their products.

Large mass-merchandise chains, such as Sears Canada and The Bay, generally use at-market pricing. These chains often establish the going market price in the minds of competitors. Similarly, Revlon generally prices its products "at market." These

Zellers uses a below-market price strategy for numerous products it retails.

companies also provide a reference price for competitors that use above- and below-market pricing.

In contrast, a number of firms, such as Zellers, use a strategy of below-market pricing. Also, manufacturers of all generic products and retailers who offer their own private brands of products deliberately set prices for their products about 8 to 10 percent below the prices of nationally branded competitive products. Below-market pricing also exists in business-to-business marketing.

Loss-Leader Pricing   For special promotions, many retail stores deliberately sell products below their customary prices to attract attention to them. For example, supermarkets will often use produce or paper goods as loss leaders. The purpose of *loss-leader pricing* is not to increase sales of that particular produce but to attract customers in the hope that they will buy other products as well, particularly discretionary items carrying large markups.

CONCEPT CHECK

1. What is standard markup pricing?

2. What is the purpose of loss-leader pricing when used by a retail firm?

■ ■ ■
STEP 5: SETTING THE LIST OR QUOTED PRICE

The first four steps in setting price result in an approximate price level for the product that appears reasonable. But it still remains for the manager to set a specific list or quoted price in light of all relevant factors.

One-Price Policy versus Flexible-Price Policy

A seller must decide whether to follow a one-price policy or a flexible-price policy. A *one-price policy*, also called *fixed pricing*, is setting one price for all buyers of a product or service. For example, when you buy a Wilson Sting tennis racquet from a discount store, you are offered the product at a single price. You can decide to buy it or not, but there is no variation in the price under the seller's one-price policy. Saturn Corporation uses this approach in its stores and features a "no haggle, one price" policy for its cars. Some retailers, such as Dollar Stores, have married this policy with a below-market approach and sell everything in their stores for $1 or less!

In contrast, a *flexible-price policy*, also called *dynamic pricing*, involves setting different prices for products and services depending on individual buyers and purchase situations. A flexible-price policy gives sellers considerable discretion in setting the final price in light of demand, cost, and competitive factors.

While most companies use the one-price policy, flexible pricing has grown in popularity because of increasingly sophisticated information technology. Today, many marketers have the ability to customize a price for an individual on the basis of his or her purchasing patterns, product preferences, and price sensitivity, all of which are stored in company data warehouses. Price customization is particularly prevalent for products and services bought online. Online marketers routinely adjust prices in response to purchase situations and past purchase behaviours of online buyers. Some online marketers monitor an online shopper's "clickstream"—the way that person navigates through its Web site. If the visitor behaves like a price-sensitive shopper—perhaps by comparing many different products—that person may be offered a lower price. However, as noted at the end of this chapter, flexible pricing carried to the extreme could be considered price discrimination and is a practice prohibited under the Competition Act.[22]

Company, Customer, and Competitive Effects

As the final list or quoted price is set, the effects on the company, customers, and competitors must be assessed.

Company Effects   For a firm with more than one product, a decision on the price of a single product must consider the price of other items in its product line or related product lines in its product mix. Within a product line or mix, there are usually some products that are substitutes for one another and some that complement each other. Frito-Lay recognizes that its tortilla chip product line consisting of Baked Tostitos, Tostitos, and Doritos brands are partial substitutes for one another and its bean and cheese dip line and salsa sauces complement the tortilla chip line.

A manager's challenge when marketing multiple products is *product-line pricing*, the setting of prices for all items in a product line. When setting prices, the manager seeks to cover the total cost and produce a profit for the complete line, not necessarily for each item.

Product-line pricing involves determining (1) the lowest priced product and price, (2) the highest priced product and price, and (3) price differentials for all other products in the line.[23] The lowest and highest priced items in the product line play important roles. The highest priced item is typically positioned as the premium item in quality and features. The lowest priced item is the traffic builder designed to capture the attention of the hesitant or first-time buyer. Price differentials between items in the line should make sense to customers and reflect the differences in their perceived values of the products offered. Behavioural research also suggests that the price differentials should get larger as one moves up the product line.

Customer Effects   In setting prices, retailers weigh factors heavily that satisfy the perceptions or expectations of ultimate consumers, such as the customary prices for a variety of consumer products. Retailers have found that they should not price their store brands 20 to 25 percent below manufacturers' brands. When they do, consumers often view the lower price as signalling lower quality and do not buy. This is also particularly true in marketing "intangible services," where low price can connote poor quality.[24]

Competitive Effects   A manager's pricing decision is immediately apparent to most competitors, who may retaliate with price changes of their own. Therefore, a manager who sets a final list or quoted price must anticipate potential price responses from competitors. Regardless of whether a firm is a price leader or follower, it wants to avoid cut-throat price wars in which no firm in the industry makes a satisfactory profit. A *price war* involves successive pricing by competitors to increase or maintain their unit sales or market share. For example, price wars in the airline industry usually result in losses for all players. Similarly, in the residential long-distance telephone industry, even price reductions as little as 1 percent can have a significant effect on company profitability.[25]

Frito-Lay recognizes that its tortilla chip products are partial substitutes for one another and its bean and cheese dips and salsa sauces complement tortilla chips. This knowledge is used in Frito-Lay product-line pricing.

Frito-Lay, Inc.

www.frito-lay.com

■ ■ ■
STEP 6: MAKING SPECIAL ADJUSTMENTS TO THE LIST OR QUOTED PRICE

When you pay 75 cents for a bag of M&Ms in a vending machine or receive a quoted price of $10 000 from a contractor to renovate your kitchen, the pricing sequence ends with the last step just described: setting the list or quoted price. But when you are a manufacturer of M&M candies or gas grills and sell your product to dozens or hundreds of wholesalers and retailers in your channel of distribution, you may need to make a variety of special adjustments to the list or quoted price. Wholesalers also must adjust list or quoted prices they set for retailers. Three special adjustments to the list or quoted price are (1) discounts, (2) allowances, and (3) geographical adjustments.

Discounts

Discounts are reductions from list price that a seller gives a buyer as a reward for some activity of the buyer that is favourable to the seller. Four kinds of discounts are especially important in marketing strategy: (1) quantity, (2) seasonal, (3) trade (functional), and (4) cash discounts.[26]

Toro uses seasonal discounts to stimulate consumer demand and smooth out seasonal manufacturing peaks and troughs.

The Toro Company
www.toro.com

Quantity Discounts   To encourage customers to buy larger quantities of a product, firms at all levels in the channel of distribution offer *quantity discounts*, which are reductions in unit costs for a larger order. For example, an instant photocopying service might set a price of 10 cents a copy for 1 to 25 copies, 9 cents a copy for 26 to 100, and 8 cents a copy for 101 or more. Because the photocopying service gets more of the buyer's business and has longer production runs that reduce its order-handling costs, it is willing to pass on some of the cost savings in the form of quantity discounts to the buyer.

Seasonal Discounts   To encourage buyers to stock inventory earlier than their normal demand would require, manufacturers often use seasonal discounts. For example, Toro, which manufactures lawn mowers and snow throwers, offers seasonal discounts to encourage wholesalers and retailers to stock up on lawn mowers in January and February and on snow throwers in July and August—five or six months before the seasonal demand by the ultimate consumers. This enables Toro to smooth out seasonal manufacturing peaks and troughs, thereby contributing to more efficient production. It also rewards wholesalers and retailers for the risk they accept in assuming increased inventory carrying costs and having supplies in stock at the time they are wanted by customers.

Trade (Functional) Discounts   To reward wholesalers and retailers for marketing functions they will perform in the future, a manufacturer often gives trade, or functional, discounts. These reductions off the list or base price are offered to resellers in the channel of distribution on the basis of (1) where they are in the channel, and (2) the marketing activities they are expected to perform in the future.

Traditional trade discounts have been established in various product lines, such as hardware, food, and pharmaceutical items. Although the manufacturer may suggest the trade discounts shown in the example just cited, the sellers are free to alter the discount schedule depending on their competitive situation.

Cash Discounts   To encourage retailers to pay their bills quickly, manufacturers offer them cash discounts. Suppose a retailer receives a bill quoted at $1000, 2/10 net 30. This means that the bill for the product is $1000, but the retailer can take a 2-percent discount ($1000 $\times$ 0.02 = $20) if payment is made within 10 days and send a cheque for $980. If the payment cannot be made within 10 days, the total amount of $1000 is due within 30 days. It is usually understood by the buyer that an interest charge will be added after the first 30 days of free credit.

Retailers also provide cash discounts to consumers as well to eliminate the cost of credit granted. These discounts take the form of discount-for-cash policies. Canadian Tire is famous for its discount-for-cash policy, where consumers receive 3 percent off for cash purchases in the form of cash-bonus coupons that can be used against future purchases. And if you order a computer from CanadaComputers.com, you will receive a 2-percent discount if you pay cash or by debit card.

Allowances

Allowances—like discounts—are reductions from list or quoted prices to buyers for performing some activity.

Trade-in Allowances   A new-car dealer can offer a substantial reduction in the list price of a new Toyota Camry by offering you a trade-in allowance of $500 for your Chevrolet. A trade-in allowance is a price reduction given when a used product is part of the payment on a new product. Trade-ins are an effective way to lower the price a buyer has to pay without formally reducing the list price.

Promotional Allowances   Sellers in the channel of distribution can qualify for *promotional allowances* for undertaking certain advertising or selling activities to promote a product. Various types of allowances include an actual cash payment or an extra amount of "free goods" (as with a free case of frozen pizzas to a retailer for every dozen cases purchased). Frequently, a portion of these savings is passed on to the consumer by retailers.

Some companies, such as Procter & Gamble, have chosen to reduce promotional allowances to retailers by using everyday low pricing. *Everyday low pricing* (EDLP) is the practice of replacing promotional allowances with lower manufacturer list prices. EDLP promises to reduce the average price to consumers while minimizing promotional allowances that cost manufacturers billions of dollars every year.

Geographical Adjustments

Geographical adjustments are made by manufacturers or even wholesalers to list or quoted prices to reflect the cost of transportation of the products from seller to buyer. The two general methods for quoting prices related to transportation costs are (1) FOB origin pricing, and (2) uniform delivered pricing.

- *FOB Origin Pricing*   FOB means "free on board" some vehicle at some location, which means the seller pays the cost of loading the product onto the vehicle that is used (such as a barge, railway car, or truck). *FOB origin pricing* usually involves the seller's naming the location of this loading as the seller's factory or warehouse (such as "FOB Toronto" or "FOB factory"). The title to the goods passes to the buyer at the point of loading, and so the buyer becomes responsible for picking the specific mode of transportation, for all the transportation costs, and for subsequent handling of the product. Buyers farthest from the seller face the big disadvantage of paying the higher transportation costs.
- *Uniform Devlivered Pricing*   When a *uniform delivered pricing* method is used, the price the seller quotes includes all transportation costs. It is quoted in a contract as "FOB buyer's location," and the seller selects the mode of transportation, pays the freight charges, and is responsible for any damage that may occur because the seller retains title to the goods until delivered to the buyer.

Legal and Regulatory Aspects of Pricing

Arriving at a final price is clearly a complex process. The task is further complicated by legal and regulatory restrictions. Five pricing practices receive the most scrutiny: (1) price fixing, (2) price discrimination, (3) deceptive pricing, (4) predatory pricing, and (5) delivered pricing.

Price Fixing   A conspiracy among firms to set prices for a product is termed *price fixing*. Price fixing is illegal *per se* (in and of itself) under the Competition Act. When two or more competitors explicitly or implicitly set prices, this practice is called *horizontal price fixing*.

Vertical price fixing involves controlling agreements between independent buyers and sellers (a manufacturer and a retailer) whereby sellers are required not to sell products below a minimum retail price. This practice, called *resale price maintenance*, is also illegal under the provisions of the Competition Act.

It is important to recognize that a manufacturer's "suggested retail price" is not illegal *per se*. The issue of legality arises only when manufacturers enforce such a practice by coercion.

Price Discrimination   The Competition Act prohibits *price discrimination*—the practice of charging different prices to different buyers for goods of like grade and quality. The Competition Act also covers promotional allowances. To legally offer promotional allowances to buyers, sellers must do so on a proportionally equal basis to all buyers distributing the seller's products. In general, this rule of reason is applied frequently in price discrimination cases and is often applied to cases involving flexible pricing policies of firms. It is not easy to prove price discrimination has actually taken place, especially when firms practise flexible-price policies.

Under the Competition Act, the legislation requires that there be a "practice" of price discrimination, implying more than one instance, or even two or three instances. However, some suggest that the use of flexible pricing may create the potential for some firms to engage in price discrimination. Even if the practice cannot be proven legally as price discrimination, there may be some ethical issues involved.

Deceptive Pricing   Price deals that mislead consumers fall into the category of deceptive pricing. Deceptive pricing is outlawed by the Competition Act. The five most common deceptive pricing practices are described in Figure 13–9. Over the past few years, companies from Newfoundland to British Columbia have been found guilty and fined for deceptive pricing practices. However, as you examine Figure 13–9, you should remember that it is often difficult for the government to police and enforce all of these laws. So, it is essential to rely on the ethical standards of those making and publicizing pricing decisions. A frequently used promotional practice is to offer goods or services "free." Check the accompanying WebLink box to see what the federal government says about the word "free."

Predatory Pricing   Two types of predatory pricing are defined within the Competition Act. The first is called *geographic predatory pricing*. Sellers are prohibited from engaging in a policy of selling products or services in one region in Canada at a price lower than in another region with the intent or effect of lessening competition or of eliminating a competitior.

The second type of predatory pricing offence is committed when a business engages in a policy of selling products or services at "unreasonably low" prices in an attempt to substantially lessen competition. In many cases, the very low prices are designed to drive competitiors out of business. Once competitors have been driven out, the firm raises its prices.

The offer of "free" goods or services as a promotional device is often used to attract customers. However, the Competition Bureau recognizes that such offers must be made with care to avoid any possibility that consumers will be misled or deceived.

The Competition Bureau has a publication called "Misleading Advertising Guidelines," which deals with the issue of the use of "free" as a promotional device. In this guide, many examples of the use of the word "free" are discussed. In some cases, the use of the word "free" is acceptable, while in other cases, it is considered deceptive. Go to www.strategis. ic.gc.ca/SSG.ct01299e.html#d, and check out Section 52(1)(d)–C to get an idea about the use of the word free from the government agency charged with the responsibility of protecting consumers against deceptive pricing practices.

■ FIGURE 13–9 ■

Five most common
deceptive pricing practices

Delivered Pricing   Delivered pricing is the practice of refusing a customer delivery of an article on the same trade terms as other customers in the same location. It is a noncriminal offence, but the Competition Tribunal can prohibit suppliers from engaging in such a practice.

DECEPTIVE PRACTICE	DESCRIPTION
Bait and switch	A deceptive practice exists when a firm offers a very low price on a product (the bait) to attract customers to a store. Once in the store, the customer is persuaded to purchase a higher-priced item (the switch) using a variety of tricks, including (1) downgrading the promoted item, and (2) not having the item in stock or refusing to take orders for the item.
Bargains conditional on other purchases	This practice may exist when a buyer is offered "1-Cent Sales," "Buy 1, Get 1 Free," and "Get 2 for the Price of 1." Such pricing is legal only if the first items are sold at the regular price, not a price inflated for the offer. Substituting lower-quality items on either the first or second purchase is also considered deceptive.
Comparable value comparisons	Advertising, such as "Retail Value $100.00, Our Price $85.00," is deceptive if a verified and substantial number of stores in the market area did not price the item at $100.
Comparisons with suggested prices	A claim that a price is below a manufacturer's suggested or list price may be deceptive if few or no sales occur at that price in a retailer's market area.
Former price comparisons	When a seller represents a price as reduced, the item must have been offered in good faith at a higher price for a substantial previous period. Setting a high price for the purpose of establishing a reference for a price reduction is deceptive.

CONCEPT CHECK

1. Why would a seller choose a flexible-price policy over a one-price policy?

2. Which pricing practices are covered by the Competition Act?

■ ■ ■
CHAPTER IN REVIEW

1 *Understand the nature and importance of pricing products and services.*

Price is the money or other considerations exchanged for the ownership or use of a product service. Although price typically involves money, the amount exchanged is often different from the list or quoted price because of allowances and extra fees.

2 *Recognize the constraints on a firm's pricing latitude and the objectives a firm has in setting prices.*

Pricing constraints, such as demand, product newness, costs, competitors, other products sold by the firm, and the type of competitive market, restrict a firm's pricing latitude. Pricing objectives may include profit, sales revenue, market share, unit volume, survival, or some socially responsible price level.

3 *Explain what a demand curve is and what price elasticity of demand means.*

A demand curve is a graph relating the quantity sold and price and shows the maximum number of product or service units that will be sold at given price. Three demand factors affect price: (a) consumer tastes, (b) price and availability of other products, and (c) consumer income. These demand factors determine consumers' willingness and ability to pay for products and services. Assuming these demand factors remain unchanged, when the price of a product is lowered or raised, the quantity demanded for it will increase or decrease, respectively. Price elasticity of demand measures the responsiveness of units of a product sold to a change in price, which is expressed as the percentage change in the quantity of a product demanded divided by the percentage change in price. It provides an indication of how sensitive consumer demand and the firm's revenue are to changes in the product's price.

4 *Perform a break-even analysis.*

Break-even analysis shows the relationship between total revenue and total cost at various quantities of output for given conditions of price, fixed cost, and variable cost. At the break-even point, total revenue and total cost are equal.

5 *Understand approaches to pricing as well as factors considered to establish prices for products and services.*

Four general approaches of finding an approximate price level for a product or service are demand-oriented, cost-oriented, profit-oriented, and competition-oriented pricing. Demand-oriented pricing stresses consumer demand; cost-oriented pricing emphasizes the costs aspects; profit-oriented pricing focuses on a balance between revenues and costs; and competition-oriented pricing stresses what competitors or the marketplace are doing. Demand, cost, profit, and competition influence the initial consideration of the price level for a product or service. To set list or quoted price, a marketer must also consider additional factors. First, the marketer must decide whether to follow a one-price policy or a flexible-price policy. And, second, the marketer must consider the effects the proposed price will have on the company, customer and competitors. Finally, list or quoted prices are often modified through discounts, allowances, and geographical adjustments.

6 *Describe basic laws and regulations affecting pricing practices.*

Legal and regulatory issues in pricing focus on price fixing, price discrimination, deceptive pricing, predatory pricing, and delivered pricing. The Competition Act in Canada prohibits such practices.

■ ■ ■
FOCUSING ON KEY TERMS

break-even analysis p. 339
demand curve p. 336
fixed cost p. 339
penetration pricing p. 341
price p. 330
price elasticity of demand p. 337
pricing constraints p. 332

pricing objectives p. 335
profit equation p. 331
skimming pricing p. 341
total cost p. 338
total revenue p. 338
variable cost p. 339

■ ■ ■
DISCUSSION AND APPLICATION QUESTIONS

1 How would the price equation apply to the purchase price of (a) gasoline, (b) an airline ticket, and (c) a chequing account?

2 What would be your response to the statement: "Profit maximization is the only legitimate pricing objective for the firm."

3 Touche Toiletries, Inc. has developed an addition to its Lizardman Cologne line tentatively branded Ode d'Toade

Cologne. Unit variable costs are 45 cents for a 60-mL bottle, and heavy advertising expenditures in the first year would result in total fixed costs of $900 000. Ode d'Toade Cologne is priced at $7.50 for a 60-mL bottle. How many bottles of Ode d'Toade must be sold to break even?

4 Suppose that marketing executives for Touche Toiletries reduced the price to $6.50 for a 60-mL bottle of Ode d'Toade and the fixed costs were $1 000 000. Suppose further that the unit variable cost remained at 45 cents for a 60-mL bottle. (a) How many bottles must be sold to break even? (b) What dollar profit level would Ode d'Toade achieve if 200 000 bottles were sold?

5 Under what conditions would a camera manufacturer adopt a skimming price approach for a new product? A penetration approach?

6 What are some similarities and differences between skimming pricing, prestige pricing, and above-market pricing?

7 Suppose executive estimate that the unit variable costs for their DVD is $100, the fixed cost related to the product is $10 million, and the target volume for next year is 100 000 units. What sales price will be necessary to achieve a target profit of $1 million?

GOING ONLINE   Checking Out Price Violations

As you know, the Competition Bureau is responsible for administrating the Competition Act in Canada. As you read in this chapter, competition can be lessened and/or consumers can be harmed by unfair pricing practices. Visit the Competition Bureau's home page at www.cb-bc.gc.ca. Go to the media room section on the site. Then, click on New Releases.

1 What are the types of pricing violations involving Canadian and international companies reported on the site?

2 What types of penalties were imposed?

3 What is your opinion regarding these pricing violations?

Do you want to get better grades and stay up to date with current issues in marketing? Visit the Online Learning Centre at www.mcgrawhill.ca/college/crane for practice tests, video cases, resources for building a marketing plan, *Globe and Mail* headlines, access to *Marketing Magazine*, and other learning and study tools.

VIDEO CASE 13   Washburn International, Inc.

"The relationship between musicians and their guitars is something really extraordinary—and is a fairly strange one," says Brady Breen in a carefully understated tone of voice. Breen has the experience to know. He is production manager of Washburn International (www.washburn.com), one of the most prestigious guitar manufacturers in the world. Washburn's instruments range from one-of-a-kind, custom-made acoustic and electric guitars and basses to less expensive, mass-produced ones.

THE COMPANY AND ITS HISTORY

The modern Washburn International started in 1977 when a small firm bought the century-old Washburn brand name and a small inventory of guitars, parts, and promotional supplies. At that time annual revenues of the company were $300 000 for the sale of about 2500 guitars. Washburn's first catalogue, appearing in 1978, told a frightening truth:

> Our designs are translated by Japan's most experienced craftsmen, assuring the consistent quality and craftmanship for which they are known.

At that time, the North American guitar-making craft was at an all-time low. Guitars made by Japanese firms, such as Ibane and Yamaha, were in use by an increasing number of professionals.

Times have changed for Washburn. Today, the company sells about 250 000 guitars a year. Annual sales exceed $50 million. All this resulted from Washburn's aggressive marketing strategies to develop product lines with different price points targeted at musicians in distinctly different market segments.

THE PRODUCTS AND MARKET SEGMENTS

Arguably the most trendsetting guitar developed by the modern Washburn company appeared in 1980. This was the Festival Series of cutaway, thin-bodied flattops, with built-in bridge pickups and controls, which went on to become the virtual standard for live performances. John Lodge of the Moody Blues endorsed the 12-string version—his gleaming white guitar appeared in both concerts and ads for years. In the time since the Festival Series appeared, countless rock and country stars, including Bob Dylan, Dolly Parton, Greg Allman, John Jorgenson, and George Harrison, have used these instruments.

Until 1991, all Washburn guitars were manufactured in Asia. That year, Washburn started building its high-end guitars in North America. Today, Washburn marketing executives divide its product line into four levels. From high-end to low-end, these are:

- One-of-a-kind, custom units
- Batch-custom units
- Mass-customized units
- Mass-produced units

The one-of-a-kind custom units are for the many stars that use Washburn instruments. The mass-produced units targeted at first-time buyers are still manufactured in Asian factories.

PRICING ISSUES

Setting prices for its various lines presents a continuing challenge for Washburn. Not only do the prices have to reflect the changing tastes of its various segments of musicians, but the prices must also be competitive with the prices set for guitars manufactured and marketed globally. In fact, Washburn and other well-known guitar manufacturers have a prestige-niche strategy. For Washburn this involves endorsements by internationally known musicians who play its instruments and lend their names to lines of Washburn signature guitars. This has the effect of reducing the price elasticity or price sensitivity for these guitars. Stars playing Washburn guitars, for example, Nuno Bettencourt, David Gilmour of Pink Floyd, Joe Perry of Aerosmith, and Darryl Jones of the Rolling Stones, have their own lines of signature guitars—the "batch-custom" units mentioned earlier.

Joe Baksha, Washburn's executive vice-president, is responsible for reviewing and approving prices for the company's lines of guitars. Setting a sales target of 2000 units for a new line of guitars, he is considering a suggested retail price of $329 per unit for customers at one of the hundreds of retail outlets carrying the Washburn line. For planning purposes, Baksha estimates half of the final retail price will be the price Washburn nets when it sells its guitar to the wholesalers and dealers in its channel of distribution.

Looking at Washburn's financial data for its present North American plant, Baksha estimates that this line of guitars must bear these fixed costs:

Rent and taxes	= $12 000
Depreciation of equipment	= $ 4 000
Management and quality control program	= $20 000

In addition, he estimates the variable costs for each unit to be:

Direct materials = $25/unit
Direct labour   = 8 hours/unit @ $14/hour

Carefully kept production records at Washburn's North American plant make Baksha believe that these are reasonable estimates. He explains, "Before we begin a production run, we have a good feel for what our costs will be. The North American-built N-4, for example, simply costs more than one of our foreign-produced Mercury or Wing series electrics."

Caught in the global competition for guitar sales, Washburn searches for ways to reduce and control costs. After much agonizing, the company decided to move to Nashville, Tennessee. In this home of country music, Washburn expects to lower its manufacturing costs because there are many skilled workers in the region, and its fixed costs will be reduced by avoiding some of the expenses of having a big-city location. Specifically, Washburn projects that it will reduce its rent and taxes expense by 40 percent and the wage rate it pays by 15 percent in relocating from its current plant to Nashville.

QUESTIONS

1 What factors are most likely to affect the demand for the lines of Washburn guitars bought by (*a*) a first-time guitar buyer, and (*b*) a sophisticated musician who wants a signature model signed by David Gilmour or Joe Perry?

2 For Washburn what are examples of (*a*) shifting the demand curve to the right to get a higher price for a guitar line (movement *of* the demand curve), and (*b*) pricing decisions involving moving *along* a demand curve?

3 In Washburn's current plant, what is the break-even point for the new line of guitars if the retail price is (*a*) $329, (*b*) $359, and (*c*) $299? Also, (*d*) if Washburn achieves the sales target of 2000 units at the $329 retail price, what will its profit be?

4 Assume that Washburn moves its production to Nashville and that the costs are reduced as projected in the case. Then, what will be the (*a*) new break-even point at a $329 retail price for this line of guitars, and (*b*) the new profit if it sells 2000 units?

5 If, for competitive reasons, Washburn eventually has to move all of its production back to Asia, (*a*) which specific costs might be lowered, and (*b*) what additional costs might it expect to incur?

FINANCIAL ASPECTS OF MARKETING

Basic concepts from accounting and finance provide valuable tools for marketing executives. This appendix describes an actual company's use of accounting and financial concepts and illustrates how they assist the owner in making marketing decisions.

THE CAPLOW COMPANY

An accomplished artist and calligrapher, Jane Westerlund, decided to apply some of her experience to the picture framing business. She bought an existing retail frame store, The Caplow Company, from a friend who owned the business and wanted to retire. She avoided the do-it-yourself end of the framing business and chose three kinds of business activities: (1) cutting the frame, mats, and glass for customers who brought in their own pictures or prints to be framed; (2) selling prints and posters that she had purchased from wholesalers; and (3) restoring high-quality frames and paintings.

To understand how accounting, finance, and marketing relate to each other, let us analyze (1) the operating statement for her frame shop, (2) some general ratios of interest that are derived from the operating statement, and (3) some ratios that pertain specifically to her pricing decisions.

The Operating Statement

The operating statement (also called an *income statement* or *profit-and-loss statement*) summarizes the profitability of a business firm for a specific time period, usually a month, quarter, or year. The title of the operating statement for The Caplow Company shows it is for a one-year period (Figure B–1). The purpose of an operating statement is to show the profit of the firm and the revenues and expenses that led to that profit. This information tells the owner or manager what has happened in the past and suggests actions to improve future profitability.

The left side of Figure B–1 shows that there are three key elements to all operating statements: (1) sales of the firm's goods and services, (2) costs incurred in making and selling the goods and services, and (3) profit or loss, which is the difference between sales and costs.

Sales Elements   The sales element of Figure B–1 has four terms that need explanation:

- *Gross sales* are the total amount billed to customers. Dissatisfied customers or errors may reduce the gross sales through returns or allowances.
- *Returns* occur when a customer gives the item purchased back to the seller, who either refunds the purchase price or allows the customer a credit on subsequent purchases. In any event, the seller now owns the item again.
- *Allowances* are given when a customer is dissatisfied with the item purchased and the seller reduces the original purchase price. Unlike returns, in the case of allowances the buyer owns the item.
- *Net sales* are simply gross sales minus returns and allowances.

The operating statement for The Caplow Company shows the following:

Gross sales	$80 500
Less: Returns and allowances	500
Net sales	$80 000

The low level of returns and allowances shows the shop generally has done a good job in satisfying customers, which is essential in building the repeat business necessary for success.

Cost Elements   The *cost of goods sold* is the total cost of the products sold during the period. This item varies according to the kind of business. A retail store purchases finished goods and resells them to customers without reworking them in any way. In contrast, a manufacturing

■ FIGURE B–1 ■

Example of an operating statement

THE CAPLOW COMPANY

Operating Statement
For the Year Ending December 31, 2005

Sales	Gross sales		$80 500
	Less: Returns and allowances		500
	Net sales		$80 000
Costs	Cost of goods sold:		
	Beginning inventory at cost		$ 6 000
	Purchases at billed cost	$21 000	
	Less: Purchase discounts	300	
	Purchases at net cost	20 700	
	Plus freight-in	100	
	Net cost of delivered purchases		20 800
	Direct labour (framing)		14 200
	Cost of goods available for sale		41 000
	Less: Ending inventory at cost		5 000
	Cost of goods sold		36 000
	Gross margin (gross profit)		$44 000
	Expenses:		
	Selling expenses:		
	Sales salaries	2 000	
	Advertising expense	3 000	
	Total selling expense		5 000
	Administrative expenses:		
	Owner's salary	18 000	
	Bookkeeper's salary	1 200	
	Office supplies	300	
	Total administrative expense		19 500
	General expenses:		
	Depreciation expense	1 000	
	Interest expense	500	
	Rent expense	2 100	
	Utility expenses (heat, electricity)	3 000	
	Repairs and maintenance	2 300	
	Insurance	2 000	
	Canada Pension Plan	2 200	
	Total general expense		13 100
	Total expenses		37 600
Profit or loss	Profit before taxes		$ 6 400

firm combines raw and semi-finished materials and parts, uses labour and overhead to rework these into finished goods, and then sells them to customers. All these activities are reflected in the cost of goods sold item on a manufacturer's operating statement. Note that the frame shop has some features of a pure retailer (prints and posters it buys that are resold without alteration) and some of a pure manufacturer (assembling the raw materials of moulding, matting, and glass to form a completed frame).

Some terms that relate to cost of goods sold need clarification:

- *Inventory* is the physical material that is purchased from suppliers, may or may not be reworked, and is available for sale to customers. In the frame shop, inventory includes moulding, matting, glass, prints, and posters.
- *Purchase discounts* are reductions in the original billed price for such reasons as prompt payment of the bill or the quantity bought.
- *Direct labour* is the cost of the labour used in producing the finished product. For the frame shop, this is the cost of producing the completed frames from the moulding, matting, and glass.

- *Gross margin (gross profit)* is the money remaining to manage the business, sell the products or services, and give some profit. Gross margin is net sales minus cost of goods sold.

The two right-hand columns in Figure B–1 between "Net sales" and "Gross margin" calculate the cost of goods sold:

Net sales		$80 000
Cost of goods sold		
Beginning inventory at cost	$ 6 000	
Net cost of delivered purchases	20 800	
Direct labour (framing)	14 200	
Cost of goods available for sale	41 000	
Less: ending inventory at cost	5 000	
Cost of goods sold		36 000
Gross margin (gross profit)		$44 000

This section considers the beginning and ending inventories, the net cost of purchases delivered during the year, and the cost of the direct labour going into making the frames. Subtracting the $36 000 cost of goods sold from the $80 000 net sales gives the $44 000 gross margin.

Three major categories of expenses are shown in Figure B–1 below the gross margin:

- *Selling expenses* are the costs of selling the product or service produced by the firm. For the Caplow Company, there are two such selling expenses: sales salaries of part-time employees waiting on customers and the advertising expense of simple newspaper ads and direct-mail ads sent to customers.
- *Administrative expenses* are the costs of managing the business and, for the Caplow Company, include three expenses: the owner's salary, a part-time bookkeeper's salary, and office supplies expense.
- *General expenses* are miscellaneous costs not covered elsewhere; for the frame shop, these include seven items: depreciation expense (on her equipment), interest expense, rent expense, utility expense, repair and maintenance expense, insurance expense, and employment insurance and Canada Pension Plan.

As shown in Figure B–1, selling, administrative, and general expenses total $37 600 for the Caplow Company.

Profit Element   What the company has earned, the *profit before taxes*, is found by subtracting cost of goods sold and expenses from net sales. For the Caplow Company, Figure B–1 shows that profit before taxes is $6400.

General Operating Ratios to Analyze Operations

Looking only at the elements of Caplow's operating statement that extend to the right column highlights the firm's performance on some important dimensions. Using operating ratios, such as *expense-to-sales ratios*, for expressing basic expense or profit elements as a percentage of net sales gives further insights:

ELEMENT IN OPERATING STATEMENT	DOLLAR VALUE	PERCENTAGE OF NET SALES
Gross sales	$80 500	
Less: Returns and allowances	500	
Net sales	80 000	100%
Less: Cost of goods sold	36 000	45
Gross margin	44 000	55
Less: Total expenses	37 600	47
Profit (or loss) before taxes	$ 6 000	8%

Westerlund can use this information to compare her firm's performance in one time period with that in the next. To do so, it is especially important that she keep the same definitions for each element of her operating statement, also a significant factor in using the electronic spreadsheets discussed in this chapter. Performance comparisons between periods are more difficult if she changes definitions for the accounting elements in the operating statement.

She can use either the dollar values or the operating ratios (the value of the element of the operating statement divided by net sales) to analyze the firm's performance. However, the operating ratios are more valuable than the dollar values for two reasons: (1) the simplicity of working with percentages rather than dollars, and (2) the availability of operating ratios of typical firms in the same industry, which are published by Dun & Bradstreet and trade associations. Thus, Westerlund can compare her firm's performance not only with that of *other* frame shops but also with that of *small* frame shops that have annual net sales, for example, of under $100 000. In this way, she can identify where her operations are better or worse than other similar firms. For example, if trade association data showed a typical frame shop of her size had a ratio of cost of goods sold to net sales of 37 percent, compared with her 45 percent, she might consider steps to reduce this cost through purchase discounts, reducing inbound freight charges, finding lower-cost suppliers, and so on.

Ratios to Use in Setting and Evaluating Price

Using the Caplow Company as an example, we can study four ratios that relate closely to setting a price: (1) markup, (2) markdown, (3) stockturns, and (4) return on investment. These terms are defined in Figure B–2 and explained below.

Markup   Both markup and gross margin refer to the amount added to the cost of goods sold to arrive at the selling price, and they may be expressed either in dollar or percentage terms. However, the term *markup* is more commonly used in setting retail prices. Suppose the average price Westerlund charges for a framed picture is $80. Then, in terms of the first two definitions in Figure B–2 and the earlier information from the operating statement,

ELEMENT OF PRICE	DOLLAR VALUE
Cost of goods sold	$36
Markup (or gross margin)	44
Selling price	$80

The third definition in Figure B–2 gives the percentage markup on selling price:

$$\text{Markup on selling price (\%)} = \frac{\text{Markup}}{\text{Selling price}} \times 100$$

$$= \frac{44}{80} \times 100 = 55\%$$

And the percentage markup on cost is obtained as follows:

$$\text{Markup on cost (\%)} = \frac{\text{Markup}}{\text{Cost of goods sold}} \times 100$$

$$= \frac{44}{36} \times 100 = 122.2\%$$

Inexperienced retail clerks sometimes fail to distinguish between the two definitions of markup, which (as the preceding calculations show) can represent a tremendous difference, and so it is essential to know whether the base is cost or selling

NAME OF FINANCIAL ELEMENT OR RATIO	WHAT IT MEASURES	EQUATION
Selling price ($)	Price customer sees	Cost of goods sold (COGS) + Markup
Markup ($)	Dollars added to COGS to arrive at selling price	Selling price − COGS
Markup on selling price (%)	Relates markup to selling price	$\dfrac{\text{Markup}}{\text{Selling price}} \times 100 = \dfrac{\text{Selling price} - \text{COGS}}{\text{Selling price}} \times 100$
Markup on cost (%)	Relates markup to cost	$\dfrac{\text{Markup}}{\text{COGS}} \times 100 = \dfrac{\text{Selling price} - \text{COGS}}{\text{COGS}} \times 100$
Markdown (%)	Ability of firm to sell its products at initial selling price	$\dfrac{\text{Markdowns}}{\text{Net Sales}} \times 100$
Stockturn rate	Ability of firm to move its inventory quickly	$\dfrac{\text{COGS}}{\text{Average inventory at cost}}$ or $\dfrac{\text{Net sales}}{\text{Average inventory at selling price}}$
Return on investment (%)	Profit performance of firm compared with money invested in it	$\dfrac{\text{Net profit after taxes}}{\text{Investment}} \times 100$

■ **FIGURE B–2** ■
How to calculate selling price, markup, markdown, stockturn, and return on investment

price. Marketers generally use selling price as the base for talking about "markups" unless they specifically state that they are using cost as a base.

Retailers and wholesalers that rely heavily on markup pricing (discussed in the next chapter) often use standardized tables that convert markup on selling price to markup on cost, and vice versa. The two equations below show how to convert one to the other:

$$\text{Markup on selling price (\%)} = \frac{\text{Markup on cost (\%)}}{100\% + \text{Markup on cost (\%)}}$$

$$\text{Markup on cost (\%)} = \frac{\text{Markup on selling price (\%)}}{100\% - \text{Markup on selling price (\%)}}$$

Using the data from the Caplow Company gives the following:

$$\text{Markup on selling price (\%)} = \frac{\text{Markup on cost (\%)}}{100\% + \text{Markup on cost (\%)}} \times 100$$

$$= \frac{122.2}{100 + 122.2} \times 100 = 55\%$$

$$\text{Markup on cost (\%)} = \frac{\text{Markup on selling price (\%)}}{100\% - \text{Markup on selling price (\%)}} \times 100$$

$$= \frac{55}{100} - 55 \times 100 = 122.2\%$$

The use of an incorrect markup base is shown in Westerlund's business. A markup of 122.2 percent on her cost of goods sold for a typical frame she sells gives 122.2% × $36 = $44 of markup. Added to the $36 cost of goods sold, this gives her a selling price of $80 for the framed picture. However, a new clerk working for her who erroneously priced the framed picture at 55 percent of cost of goods sold set the final price at $55.80 ($36 of cost of goods sold plus 55% × $36 = $19.80). The error, if repeated, can be disastrous: frames would be mistakenly sold at $55.80, or $24.20 below the intended selling price of $80.

Markdown A markdown is a reduction in a retail price that is necessary if the item will not sell at the full selling price to which it has been marked up. The item might not sell for a variety of reasons: the selling price was set too high or the item is out of style or has become soiled or damaged. The seller "takes a markdown" by lowering the price to sell it, thereby converting it to cash to buy future inventory that will sell faster.

The markdown percentage cannot be calculated directly from the operating statement. As shown in the fifth item of Figure B–2, the numerator of the markdown percentage is the total dollar markdowns. Markdowns are reductions in the prices of goods that are purchased by customers. The denominator is net sales.

Suppose the Caplow Company had a total of $700 in markdowns on the prints and posters that are stocked and available for sale. Since the frames are custom made for individual customers, there is little reason for a markdown there. Caplow's markdown percentage then is as follows:

$$\text{Markdown}(\%) = \frac{\text{Markdowns}}{\text{Net sales}} \times 100$$

$$= \frac{\$700}{\$80\,000} \times 100$$

$$= 0.875\%$$

Other kinds of retailers often have markdown ratios several times this amount. For example, women's dress stores have markdowns of about 25 percent, and menswear stores have markdowns of about 2 percent.

Stockturn Rate A business firm is anxious to have its inventory move quickly, or "turn over." Stockturn rate, or simply stockturns, measures this inventory movement. For a retailer, a slow stockturn rate may show it is buying merchandise customers do not want, and so this is a critical measure of performance. When a firm sells only a single product, one convenient way to measure stockturn rate is simply to divide its cost of goods sold by average inventory at cost. The sixth item in Figure B–2 shows how to calculate stockturn rate using information in the following operating statement:

$$\text{Stockturn rate} = \frac{\text{Cost of goods sold}}{\text{Average inventory at cost}}$$

The dollar amount of average inventory at cost is calculated by adding the beginning and ending inventories for the year and dividing by 2 to get the average. From Caplow's operating statement, we have the following:

$$\text{Stockturn rate} = \frac{\text{Cost of goods sold}}{\text{Average inventory at cost}}$$

$$= \frac{\text{Cost of goods sold}}{\dfrac{\text{Beginning inventory} + \text{Ending inventory}}{2}}$$

$$= \frac{\$36\,000}{\dfrac{\$6000 + \$5000}{2}}$$

$$= \frac{\$36\,000}{\$5500}$$

$$= 6.5 \text{ stockturns per year}$$

What is considered a "good stockturn" varies by the kind of industry. For example, supermarkets have limited shelf space for thousands of new products from manufacturers each year, and so they watch stockturn carefully by product line. The stockturn

Jane Westerlund (left) and an
assistant assess the restoration of
a gold frame for reguilding.

rate in supermarkets for breakfast foods is about 17 times per year, for pet food about 22 times, and for paper products about 25 times per year.

Return on Investment   A better measure of the performance of a firm than the amount of profit it makes in a year is its ROI, which is the ratio of net income to the investment used to earn that net income. To calculate ROI, it is necessary to subtract income taxes from profit before taxes to obtain net income, then divide this figure by the investment that can be found on a firm's balance sheet (another accounting statement that shows the firm's assets, liabilities, and net worth). While financial and accounting experts have many definitions for "investment," an often-used definition is "total assets."

For our purposes, let us assume that Westerlund has total assets (investment) of $20 000 in the Caplow Company, which covers inventory, store fixtures, and framing equipment. If she pays $1000 in income taxes, her store's net income is $5400, and so her ROI is given by the seventh item in Figure B–2:

$$\text{Return on investment} = \text{Net income/investment} \times 100$$
$$= \$5400/\$20\ 000 \times 100$$
$$= 27\%$$

If Westerlund wants to improve her ROI next year, the strategies she might take are found in this alternative equation for ROI:

$$\text{ROI} = \text{Net sales/investment} \times \text{Net income/net sales}$$
$$= \text{Investment turnover} \times \text{Profit margin}$$

This equation suggests that the Caplow Company's ROI can be improved by raising turnover or increasing profit margin. Increasing stockturns will accomplish the former, whereas lowering cost of goods sold to net sales will cause the latter.

MANAGING MARKETING CHANNELS AND SUPPLY CHAINS

CHAPTER 14

APPLE STORES: ADDING HIGH-TOUCH TO HIGH-TECH MARKETING CHANNELS

Apple Computer thrives on innovation. Apple ignited the personal computer revolution in the 1970s with the Apple II, reinvented the personal computer in the 1980s with the Macintosh, and captured the imagination of personal computer buyers worldwide in the 1990s with the introduction of the iMac, a design and technological breakthrough. Today, Apple's hot-selling iPod digital music players and popular online music store, iTunes, plus ongoing development projects promise to revolutionize digital entertainment.

But there's more. Apple Computer is changing the way consumer electronics are distributed and marketed with its company-owned Apple Stores. The thinking behind Apple Stores was to create an atmosphere where consumers can experience the thrill of owning and using Apple's complete line of products including computers, digital cameras, the entire iPod family, and more with the assistance of knowledgeable Apple personnel. Apple has been opening stores at a rate of about 25 stores per year. The company has Apple Stores across the United States, as well as in Canada, the U.K., and Japan. Apple is locating these stores mostly in upscale shopping malls, like the Yorkdale Shopping Centre, in Toronto, so customers can have easy access to the Apple experience. These new stores are part of Apple's marketing efforts to ensure that Apple products will be available at the right place, at the right time, and in the right quantity, form, and condition that the customers want them.

Has Apple's decision to open its own stores a wise move? So far, yes. Apple Stores have achieved more than $1 billion in sales faster than any retail business in history, taking just three years to reach that mark. About 40 percent of the people purchasing items at Apple Stores are new customers. Equally important, Apple Stores are profitable.[1]

This chapter focuses in marketing channels of distribution and supply chains and their importance for marketing success. You will discover that it makes no sense to have good products, like those found in the Apple Store, if they are not accessible to the customer where and when they want them.

■ ■ ■
NATURE AND IMPORTANCE OF MARKETING CHANNELS

Reaching prospective buyers, either directly or indirectly, is a prerequisite for successful marketing. At the same time, buyers benefit from distribution systems used by firms.

Defining Marketing Channels of Distribution

You see the results of distribution every day. You may have purchased Lay's Potato Chips at the 7-Eleven store, a book through Chapters-Indigo.ca, and Levi's jeans at Sears. Each of these items was brought to you by a marketing channel of distribution, or simply a **marketing channel**, which consists of individuals and firms involved in the process of making a product or service available for use or consumption by consumers or industrial users.

Marketing channels can be compared with a pipeline through which water flows from a source to a terminus. Marketing channels make possible the flow of goods from a producer, through intermediaries, to a buyer. Intermediaries go by various names (Figure 14–1) and perform various functions.[2] Some intermediaries actually purchase items from the seller, store them, and resell them to buyers. For example, Sunshine Biscuits produces cookies and sells them to food wholesalers. The wholesalers then sell the cookies to supermarkets and grocery stores, which, in turn, sell them to consumers. Other intermediaries, such as brokers and agents, represent sellers but do not actually take title to products—their role is to bring a seller and buyer together. Century 21 real estate agents are examples of this type of intermediary. The importance of intermediaries is made even clearer when we consider the functions they perform and the value they create for buyers.

marketing channel
Individuals and firms involved in the process of making a product or service available for use or consumption by consumers or industrial users.

■ **FIGURE 14–1** ■
Terms used for marketing intermediaries
Source: American Marketing Association. Used by permission.

Value Created by Intermediaries

Few consumers appreciate the value created by intermediaries; however, producers recognize that intermediaries make selling goods and services more efficient because

TERM	DESCRIPTION
Intermediary	Any intermediary between manufacturer and end-user markets
Agent or broker	Any intermediary with legal authority to act on behalf of the manufacturer
Wholesaler	An intermediary who sells to other intermediaries, usually to retailers; usually applies to consumer markets
Retailer	An intermediary who sells to consumers
Distributor	An imprecise term, usually used to describe intermediaries who perform a variety of distribution functions, including selling, maintaining inventories, extending credit, and so on; a more common term in business markets but may also be used to refer to wholesalers
Dealer	An even more imprecise term that can mean the same as distributor, retailer, wholesaler, and so forth

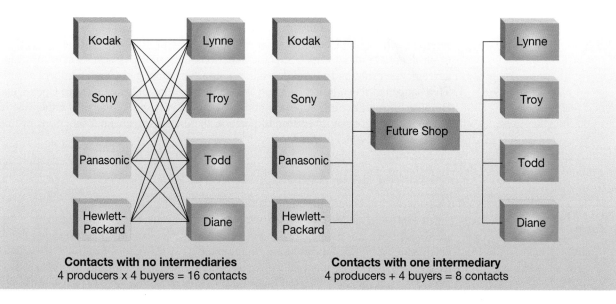

Contacts with no intermediaries
4 producers x 4 buyers = 16 contacts

Contacts with one intermediary
4 producers + 4 buyers = 8 contacts

■ **FIGURE 14–2** ■
How intermediaries minimize transactions

they minimize the number of sales contacts necessary to reach a target market. Figure 14–2 shows a simple example of how this comes about in the digital camera industry. Without a retail intermediary (such as Future Shop), Kodak, Sony, Panasonic, and Hewlett-Packard would each have to make four contacts to reach the four buyers shown who are in the target market. However, each producer has to make only one contact when Future Shop acts as an intermediary. Equally important from a macromarketing perspective, the total number of industry transactions is reduced from 16 to 8, which reduces producer cost and hence benefits the consumer.

Functions Performed by Intermediaries   Intermediaries make possible the flow of products from producers to buyers by performing three basic functions (Figure 14–3). Most prominently, intermediaries perform a transactional function that involves buying, selling, and risk taking because they stock merchandise in anticipation of sales. Intermediaries perform a logistical function evident in the gathering, storing, and dispersing of products. Finally, intermediaries perform facilitating functions, which assist producers in making goods and services more attractive to buyers.

■ **FIGURE 14–3** ■
Marketing channel functions performed by intermediaries

TYPE OF FUNCTION   **ACTIVITIES RELATED TO FUNCTION**

Transactional function
- *Buying*: Purchasing products for resale or as an agent for supply of a product
- *Selling*: Contacting potential customers, promoting products, and soliciting orders
- *Risk taking*: Assuming business risks in the ownership of inventory that can become obsolete or deteriorate

Logistical function
- *Assorting*: Creating product assortments from several sources to serve customers
- *Storing*: Assembling and protecting products at a convenient location to offer better customer service
- *Sorting*: Purchasing in large quantities and breaking into smaller amounts desired by customers
- *Transporting*: Physically moving a product to customers

Facilitating function
- *Financing*: Extending credit to customers
- *Grading*: Inspecting, testing, or judging products, and assigning them quality grades
- *Marketing information and research*: Providing information to customers and suppliers, including competitive conditions and trends

All three groups of functions must be performed in a marketing channel, even though each channel member may not participate in all three. Channel members often negotiate about which specific functions they will perform. Sometimes, disagreements result, and a breakdown in relationships among channel members occurs. This happened recently when PepsiCo's bottler in Venezuela switched to Coca-Cola. Because all marketing channel functions had to be performed, PepsiCo either had to set up its own bottling operation to perform the marketing channel functions or find another bottler, which it did.[3]

Consumer Benefits from Intermediaries

Consumers also benefit from intermediaries. Having the goods and services you want, when you want them, where you want them, and in the form you want them is the ideal result of marketing channels. For example, FedEx provides next-morning delivery; Esso offers gas stations along highways. Compaq Computer delivers unfinished PCs to dealers, which then add memory, chips, modems, and other parts, based on consumer specifications. And airlines allow tickets to be delivered by a travel agency.

CONCEPT CHECK

1. What is meant by a marketing channel?

2. What are the three basic functions performed by intermediaries?

■ ■ ■
CHANNEL STRUCTURE AND ORGANIZATION

A product can take many routes on its journey from a producer to buyers, and marketers search for the most efficient route from the many alternatives available.

Marketing Channels for Consumer Goods and Services

Figure 14–4 shows the four most common marketing channels for consumer goods and services. It also shows the number of levels in each marketing channel, as evidenced by the number of intermediaries between a producer and ultimate buyers. As

■ **FIGURE 14–4** ■

Common marketing channels for consumer goods and services

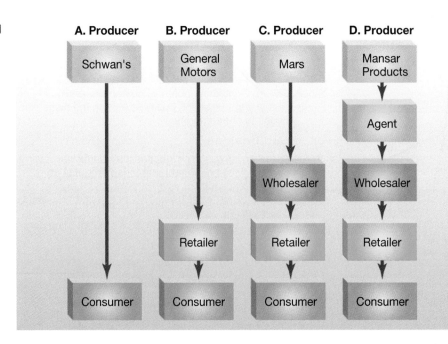

the number of intermediaries between a producer and buyer increases, the channel is viewed as increasing in length. Thus, the producer → wholesaler → retailer → consumer channel is longer than the producer → consumer channel.

direct channel

A marketing channel where a producer and ultimate consumer deal directly with each other.

Channel A represents a **direct channel** because a producer and ultimate consumers deal directly with each other. Many products and services are distributed this way. A number of insurance companies sell their financial services using a direct channel and branch sales offices, and World Book Educational Products sells its encyclopedias direct to consumers. Schwan's Sales Enterprises markets a full line of frozen foods using door-to-door salespeople who sell from refrigerated trucks. Because there are no intermediaries with a direct channel, the producer must perform all channel functions.

indirect channel

A marketing channel where intermediaries are inserted between the producer and consumers and perform numerous channel functions.

The remaining three channel forms are considered **indirect channels** because intermediaries are inserted between the producer and consumers and perform numerous channel functions. Channel B, with a retailer added, is most common when a retailer is large and can buy in large quantities from a producer or when the cost of inventory makes it too expensive to use a wholesaler. Such manufacturers as General Motors, Ford, and DaimlerChrysler use this channel, and a local car dealer acts as a retailer. Why is there no wholesaler? So many variations exist in the product that it would be impossible for a wholesaler to stock all the models required to satisfy buyers; in addition, the cost of maintaining an inventory would be too high. However, large retailers, such as Sears Canada, 7-Eleven, and The Bay, buy in sufficient quantities to make it cost-effective for a producer to deal with only a retail intermediary.

Adding a wholesaler in Channel C is most common for low-cost, low-unit-value items that are frequently purchased by consumers, such as candy, confectionary items, and magazines. For example, Mars sells its line of candies to wholesalers in case quantities; they can then break down (sort) the cases so that individual retailers can order in boxes or much smaller quantities.

Channel D, the most indirect channel, is employed when there are many small manufacturers and many small retailers and an agent is used to help coordinate a large supply of the product. Mansar Products, Ltd. is a Belgian producer of specialty jewellery that uses agents to sell to wholesalers, which then sell to many small retailers.

Marketing Channels for Business Goods and Services

The four most common channels for business goods and services are shown in Figure 14–5. In contrast to channels for consumer products, business channels typically are shorter and rely on one intermediary or none at all because business users are fewer in number, tend to be more concentrated geographically, and buy in larger quantities (see Chapter 6).

Channel A, represented by IBM's large, mainframe computer business, is a direct channel. Firms using this channel maintain their own salesforce and perform all channel functions. This channel is employed when buyers are large and well defined, the sales effort requires extensive negotiations, and the products are of high unit value and require hands-on expertise in terms of installation or use.

business distributor

Performs a variety of marketing channel functions, including selling, stocking, delivering a full product assortment, and financing for business goods and services.

Channels B, C, and D are indirect channels with one or more intermediaries to reach industrial users. In Channel B, a **business distributor** performs a variety of marketing channel functions, including selling, stocking, and delivering a full product assortment and financing. In many ways, business distributors are like wholesalers in consumer channels. Caterpillar relies on industrial distributors to sell its construction and mining equipment in almost 200 countries. In addition to selling, Caterpillar distributors stock 40 000 to 50 000 parts and service equipment using highly trained technicians.[4]

Channel C introduces a second intermediary, an *agent*, who serves primarily as the independent selling arm of producers and represents a producer to industrial users. For example, Stake Fastener Company, a producer of industrial fasteners, has an agent call on industrial users rather than employing its own salesforce.

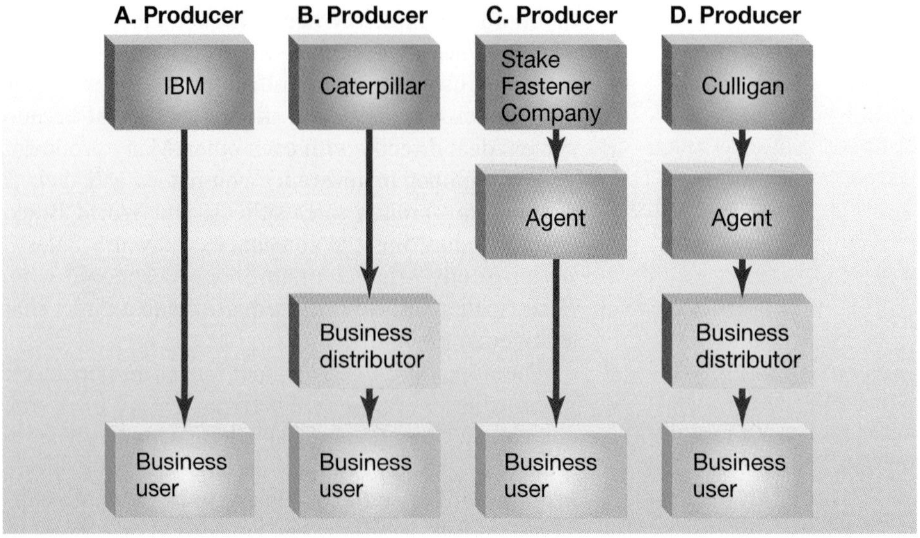

FIGURE 14–5 Common marketing channels for business goods and services

Channel D is the longest channel and includes both agents and distributors. For instance, Culligan, a producer of water treatment equipment, uses agents to call on distributors, who sell to industrial users.

Electronic Marketing Channels

These common marketing channels for consumer and business goods and services are not the only routes to the marketplace. Advances in electronic commerce have opened new avenues for reaching buyers and creating customer value.

electronic marketing channels Employ the Internet to make goods and services available for consumption or use by consumers or business buyers.

Interactive electronic technology has made possible **electronic marketing channels** that employ the Internet to make goods and services available for consumption or use by consumers or business buyers. A unique feature of these channels is that they combine electronic and traditional intermediaries to create value for buyers.[5]

Figure 14–6 shows the electronic marketing channels for books (Amazon.ca), automobiles (Autobytel.ca), reservation services (Travelocity.ca), and personal computers (Dell.ca). Are you surprised that they look a lot like the common marketing channels? An important reason for the similarity resides in channel functions detailed in Figure 14–3. Electronic intermediaries can and do perform transactional and facil-

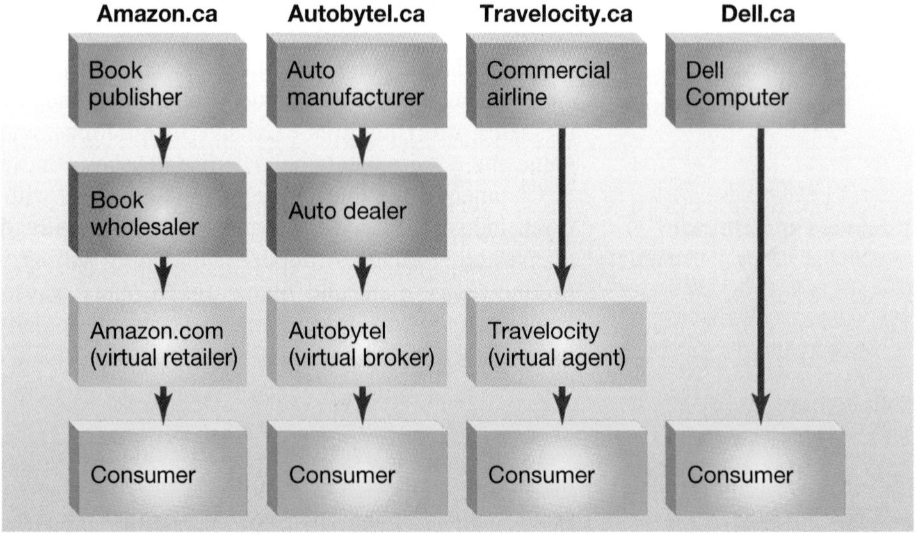

FIGURE 14–6 Representative electronic marketing channels

itating functions effectively and at a relatively lower cost than traditional intermediaries because of efficiencies made possible by information technology. However, electronic intermediaries are incapable of performing elements of the logistical function, particularly for such products as books and automobiles. This function remains with traditional intermediaries or with the producer, as evident with Dell Computer Corporation and its direct channel.

Many services can be distributed through electronic marketing channels, such as travel reservation marketed by Travelocity.ca, financial securities by e.trade.ca, and insurance by MetLife.ca. Software, too, can be marketed this way. However, many other services, such as health care and auto repair, still involve traditional intermediaries.

Direct Marketing Channels

direct marketing channels
Allow consumers to buy products by interacting with various advertising media without a face-to-face meeting with a salesperson.

Many firms also use direct marketing channels to reach buyers. **Direct marketing channels** allow consumers to buy products by interacting with various advertising media without a face-to-face meeting with a salesperson. Direct marketing includes mail-order selling, direct-mail sales, catalogue sales, telemarketing, interactive media, and televised home shopping.[6]

Some firms sell products almost entirely through direct marketing channels. These firms include L.L. Bean (apparel), Sharper Image (expensive gifts and novelties), and Egghead.com (personal computers). Such manufacturers as Nestlé and Sunkist, in addition to using traditional channels composed of wholesalers and retailers, employ direct marketing through catalogues and telemarketing to reach more buyers. At the same time, such retailers as Sears Canada use direct marketing techniques to augment conventional store merchandising activities. Some experts believe that direct marketing accounts for 20 percent of all retail transactions in North America and 10 percent of retail transactions in Europe. Direct marketing is covered in greater depth in Chapter 16.

Multiple Channels and Strategic Alliances

multichannel distribution
An arrangement whereby a firm reaches buyers by employing two or more different types of marketing channels.

Historically, most organizations used a single channel of distribution to reach their customers. Today, however, many firms engage in **multichannel distribution**—an arrangement whereby a firm reaches buyers by employing two or more different types of marketing channels. This is sometimes referred to as *hybrid marketing channels*. Multichannel distribution can be used to reach similar customers with the same basic product; different customers with the same basic product; or different customers with different products. For example, as the chapter opener pointed out, Avon sells its products through independent representatives, while its Web site, kiosks, and some outlet and department stores reach similar customers with the same products. On the other hand, GE sells certain appliances directly to home and apartment builders but uses retail stores to sell to other appliances to regular homeowners. Finally, Hallmark sells its Hallmark greeting cards through Hallmark stores and select department stores, and its Ambassador brand of cards through discount and drugstore chains, thus reaching different customers with different brands. This is typical of firms that use a multibrand strategy (see Chapter 11), since they wish to minimize cannibalization of the firms' family brand and differentiate the channels.

Many large and small Canadian firms distribute through multiple channels. In fact, multichannel distribution is very common at the manufacturing and retail levels. Retailers that use multiple channels to reach their customers, labelled as *multichannel retailers*, will be discussed in detail in Chapter 15.

strategic channel alliances
A practice whereby one firm's marketing channel is used to sell another firm's products.

Another innovation in marketing channels is the use of **strategic channel alliances**, whereby one firm's marketing channel is used to sell another firm's products. An alliance between Kraft Foods and Starbucks is an example. Kraft distributes

IDEAS
AHEAD

Nestlé and General Mills: Cereal Partners Worldwide

Can you say Nestlé Cheerios *miel amandes*? Millions of French start their day with this European equivalent of General Mills' Honey Nut Cheerios, made possible by Cereal Partners Worldwide (CPW). CPW is the food industry's first strategic alliance designed to be a global business; it joined the cereal manufacturing and marketing capability of General Mills with the worldwide distribution clout of Nestlé.

From its headquarters near Lake Geneva, Switzerland, CPW first launched General Mills cereals under the Nestlé label in France, the United Kingdom, Spain, and Portugal in 1991. Today, CPW competes in 75 markets worldwide.

The General Mills–Nestlé strategic alliance is also likely to increase the ready-to-eat worldwide market share of these companies, which are already rated as the two best-managed firms in the world. CPW is on track to reach its goal of a 20-percent worldwide share.

Starbucks coffee in supermarkets. Strategic alliances are popular in global marketing, where the creation of marketing and channel relationships is expensive and time-consuming. For example, General Motors distributes the Swedish Saab through Saturn dealers in Canada. General Mills and Nestle have an extensive alliance that spans 75 markets worldwide. Read the accompanying Marketing NewsNet box so that you will not be surprised when you are served Nestlé (not General Mills) Cheerios in Europe, South America, and parts of Asia.[7]

A Closer Look at Channel Intermediaries

Channel structures for consumer and business products assume various forms based on the number and type of intermediaries. Knowledge of the roles played by these intermediaries is important for understanding how channels operate in practice.

The terms *wholesaler*, *agent*, and *retailer* have been used in a general fashion consistent with the meanings given in Figure 14–1. However, on closer inspection, a variety of specific types of intermediaries emerges. These intermediaries engage in wholesale activities—those activities involved in selling products and services to those who are buying for the purposes of resale or business use. Intermediaries engaged in retailing activities are discussed in detail in Chapter 15.

merchant wholesalers
Independently owned firms that take title to the merchandise they handle.

Merchant Wholesalers   Merchant wholesalers are independently owned firms that take title to the merchandise they handle. They go by various names, including industrial distributor (described earlier). About 83 percent of the firms engaged in wholesale activities are merchant wholesalers.

Merchant wholesalers are classified as either full-service or limited-service wholesalers, depending on the number of functions performed. Two major types of full-service wholesalers exist. *General merchandise* (or *full-line*) *wholesalers* carry a broad assortment of merchandise and perform all channel functions. This type of wholesaler is most prevalent in the hardware, drug, and clothing industries. However, these wholesalers do not maintain much depth of assortment within specific product lines. *Specialty merchandise* (or *limited-line*) *wholesalers* offer a relatively narrow range of products but have an extensive assortment within the product lines carried. They perform all channel functions and are found in the health foods, automotive parts, and seafood industries.

Four major types of limited-service wholesalers exist. *Rack jobbers* furnish the racks or shelves that display merchandise in retail stores, perform all channel functions, and sell on consignment to retailers, which means they retain the title to the products displayed and bill retailers only for the merchandise sold. Familiar products, such as hosiery, toys, housewares, and health and beauty aids, are sold by rack jobbers. *Cash-and-carry wholesalers* take title to merchandise but sell only to buyers who call on them, pay cash for merchandise, and furnish their own transportation for merchandise. They carry a limited product assortment and do not make deliveries, extend credit, or supply market information. This wholesaler is common in electric supplies, office supplies, hardware products, and groceries. *Drop shippers*, or *desk jobbers*, are wholesalers that own the merchandise they sell but do not physically handle, stock, or deliver it. They simply solicit orders from retailers and other wholesalers and have the merchandise shipped directly from a producer to a buyer. Drop shippers are used for bulky products, such as coal, lumber, and chemicals, which are sold in extremely large quantities. *Truck jobbers* are small wholesalers that have a small warehouse from which they stock their trucks for distribution to retailers. They usually handle limited assortments of fast-moving or perishable items that are sold for cash directly from trucks in their original packages. Truck jobbers handle such products as bakery items, dairy products, and meat.

Agents and Brokers   Unlike merchant wholesalers, agents and brokers do not take title to merchandise and typically provide fewer channel functions. They make their profit from commissions or fees paid for their services, whereas merchant wholesalers make their profit from the sale of the merchandise they own.

Manufacturer's agents and selling agents are the two major types of agents used by producers. **Manufacturer's agents**, or *manufacturer's representatives*, work for several producers and carry noncompetitive, complementary merchandise in an exclusive territory. Manufacturer's agents act as a producer's sales arm in a territory and are principally responsible for the transactional channel functions, primarily selling. They are used extensively in the automotive supply, footwear, and fabricated steel industries. However, Swank Jewelry and Japanese computer firms have used manufacturer's agents as well. By comparison, **selling agents** represent a single producer and are responsible for the entire marketing function of that producer. They design promotional plans, set prices, determine distribution policies, and make recommendations on product strategy. Selling agents are used by small producers in the textile, apparel, food, and home furnishing industries.

Brokers are independent firms or individuals whose principal function is to bring buyers and sellers together to make sales. Brokers, unlike agents, usually have no continuous relationship with the buyer or seller but negotiate a contract between two parties and then move on to another task. Brokers are used extensively by producers of seasonal products (such as fruits and vegetables) and in the real estate industry.

A unique broker that acts in many ways like a manufacturer's agent is a food broker, representing buyers and sellers in the grocery industry. Food brokers differ from conventional brokers because they act on behalf of producers on a permanent basis and receive a commission for their services. For example, Nabisco uses food brokers to sell its candies, margarine, and Planters peanuts, but it sells its line of cookies and crackers directly to retail stores.

Manufacturer's Branches and Offices   Unlike merchant wholesalers, agents, and brokers, manufacturer's branches and sales offices are wholly owned extensions of the producer that perform wholesale activities. Producers assume wholesale functions when there are no intermediaries to perform these activities, customers are few

manufacturer's agents
Work for several producers and carry noncompetitive, complementary merchandise in an exclusive territory; also called *manufacturer's representatives*.

selling agents
Represent a single producer and are responsible for the entire marketing function of that producer.

brokers
Independent firms or individuals whose principal function is to bring buyers and sellers together to make sales.

in number and geographically concentrated, or orders are large or require significant attention. A *manufacturer's branch office* carries a producer's inventory and performs the functions of a full-service wholesaler. A *manufacturer's sales office* does not carry inventory, typically performs only a sales function, and serves as an alternative to agents and brokers.

Vertical Marketing Systems and Channel Partnerships

The traditional marketing channels described so far represent a loosely knit network of independent producers and intermediaries brought together to distribute goods and services. However, new channel arrangements have emerged for the purpose of improving efficiency in performing channel functions and achieving greater marketing effectiveness. These new arrangements are called vertical marketing systems and channel partnerships. **Vertical marketing systems** are professionally managed and centrally coordinated marketing channels designed to achieve channel economies and maximum marketing impact.[8] Figure 14–7 depicts the major types of vertical marketing systems: corporate, contractual, and administered.

Corporate Systems   The combination of successive stages of production and distribution under a single ownership is a *corporate vertical marketing system.* For example, a producer might own the intermediary at the next level down in the channel. This practice, called *forward integration*, is exemplified by Irving Oil, which refines gasoline and also operates retail gasoline stations. Other examples of forward integration include Good Year, Singer, Sherwin Williams, and the building materials division of Boise Cascade. Alternatively, a retailer might own a manufacturing operation, a practice called *backward integration*. For example, Safeway supermarkets operate their own bakeries; Tim Horton's operates its own coffee roasting facilities.

Contractual Systems   Under a *contractual vertical marketing system*, independent production and distribution firms integrate their efforts on a contractual basis to obtain greater functional economies and marketing impact than they could achieve

vertical marketing systems
Professionally managed and centrally coordinated marketing channels designed to achieve channel economies and maximum marketing impact.

■ **FIGURE 14–7** ■
Types of vertical marketing systems

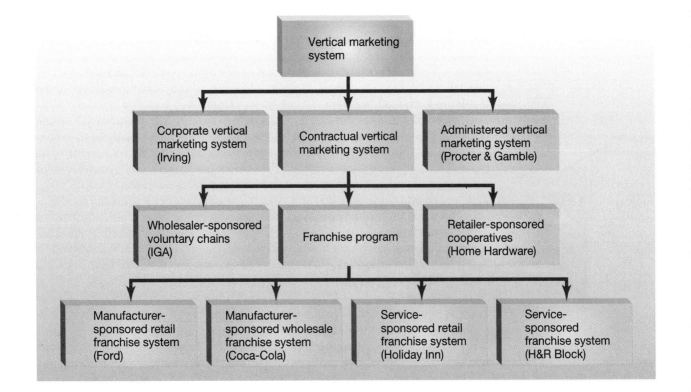

Sherwin-Williams and Home Hardware represent two different types of vertical marketing systems.

Sherwin-Williams
www.sherwin-williams.com

alone. Contractual systems are the most popular among the three types of vertical marketing systems. They account for about 40 percent of all retail sales.

Three variations of contractual systems exist. *Wholesaler-sponsored voluntary chains* involve a wholesaler that develops a contractual relationship with small, independent retailers to standardize and coordinate buying practices, merchandising programs, and inventory management efforts. With the organization of a large number of independent retailers, economies of scale and volume discounts can be achieved to compete with chain stores. IGA stores represent wholesaler-sponsored voluntary chains. *Retailer-sponsored cooperatives* exist when small, independent retailers form an organization that operates a wholesale facility cooperatively. Member retailers then concentrate their buying power through the wholesaler and plan collaborative promotional and pricing activities. Home Hardware is an example of a retailer-sponsored cooperative.

The most visible variation of contractual systems is **franchising**, a contractual arrangement between a parent company (a franchisor) and an individual or firm (a franchisee) that allows the franchise to operate a certain type of business under an established name and according to specific rules. Four types of franchise arrangements are most popular. Manufacturer-sponsored retail franchise systems are prominent in the automobile industry, where a manufacturer, such as Ford, licenses dealers to sell its cars subject to various sales and service conditions. Manufacturer-sponsored wholesale systems are evident in the soft-drink industry, where Pepsi-Cola licenses wholesalers (bottlers) that purchase concentrate from Pepsi-Cola and then carbonate, bottle, promote, and distribute its products to supermarkets and restaurants. Service-sponsored retail franchise systems are provided by firms that have designed a unique approach for performing a service and wish to profit by selling the franchise to others. Holiday Inn, Avis, and McDonald's represent this franchising approach. Service-sponsored franchise systems exist when franchisors license individuals or firms to dispense a service under a trade name and specific guidelines. An example is H&R Block tax services. Service-sponsored franchise arrangements are the fastest-growing type of franchise. Franchising is discussed further in Chapter 15.

Administered Systems   In comparison, *administered vertical marketing systems* achieve coordination at successive stages of production and distribution by the size and influence of one channel member rather than through ownership. Procter & Gamble, given its broad product assortment ranging from disposable diapers to detergents, is able to obtain cooperation from supermarkets in displaying, promoting, and pricing its products. Wal-Mart can obtain cooperation from manufacturers in terms of product specifications, price levels, and promotional support, given its position as the world's largest retailer.

franchising

Contractual arrangement between a parent company (a franchisor) and an individual or firm (a franchisee) that allows the franchise to operate a certain type of business under an established name and according to specific rules.

1. What is the difference between a direct channel and an indirect channel?

2. What is the principal distinction between a corporate vertical marketing system and an administered vertical marketing system?

CHANNEL CHOICE AND MANAGEMENT

Marketing channels not only link a producer to its buyers but also provide the means through which a firm implements various elements of its marketing strategy. Therefore, choosing a marketing channel is a critical decision.

Factors Affecting Channel Choice and Management

The final choice of a marketing channel by a producer depends on a number of factors that often interact with each other.

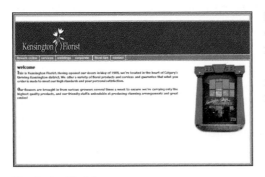

Kensington Florist
www.kensingtonflorist.com

Environmental Factors The changing environment described in Chapter 3 has an important effect on the choice and management of a marketing channel. For example, the Fuller Brush Company, a name synonymous with door-to-door selling, now uses catalogues and telemarketing to reach customers. Rising employment among women, resulting in fewer being at home during working hours, prompted this action. Advances in the technology of growing, transporting, and storing perishable cut flowers has allowed many retailers, such as Calgary's Kensington Florist, to eliminate flower wholesalers and buy direct from flower growers. Additionally, the Internet has created new marketing channel opportunities for online marketing of flowers as well as consumer electronics, books, and music and video products.

Consumer Factors Consumer characteristics have a direct bearing on the choice and management of a marketing channel. Determining which channel is most appropriate is based on answers to some fundamental questions, such as: Who are potential customers? Where do they buy? When do they buy? How do they buy? What do they buy? The answers also indicate the type of intermediary best suited to reaching target buyers. For example, Ricoh Company, Ltd. studied the serious (as opposed to recreational) camera user and concluded that a change in marketing channels was necessary. The company terminated its contract with a wholesaler that sold to mass merchandise stores and began using manufacturer's agents that sold to photo specialty stores. These stores agreed to stock and display Ricoh's full line and promote it prominently. Sales volume tripled within 18 months. Recognizing that car buyers now comparison shop on the Internet, automakers now have their own Web sites to provide price and model information.

Product Factors In general, highly sophisticated products, such as large, scientific computers, unstandardized products, such as custom-built machinery, and products of high unit value are distributed directly to buyers. Unsophisticated, standardized products with low unit value, such as table salt, are typically distributed through indirect channels. A product's stage in the life cycle also affects marketing channels.

Company Factors A firm's financial, human, or technological capabilities affect channel choice. For example, firms that are unable to employ a salesforce might use manufacturer's agents or selling agents to reach wholesalers or buyers. If a firm has multiple products for a particular target market, it might use a direct channel, whereas firms with a limited product line might use intermediaries of various types to reach buyers.

Channel Design Considerations

Recognizing that numerous routes to buyers exist and also recognizing the factors just described, marketing executives typically consider three questions when choosing a marketing channel and intermediaries:

1. Which channel and intermediaries will provide the best coverage of the target market?
2. Which channel and intermediaries will best satisfy the buying requirements of the target market?
3. Which channel and intermediaries will be the most profitable?

Target Market Coverage   Achieving the best coverage of the target market requires attention to the density and type of intermediaries to be used at the retail level of distribution. Three degrees of distribution density exist: intensive, exclusive, and selective. *Intensive distribution* means that a firm tries to place its products and services in as many outlets as possible. Intensive distribution is usually chosen for convenience products or services; for instance, candy, fast food, newspapers, and soft drinks. Increasingly, medical services are distributed in this fashion. Cash—yes, cash—is also distributed intensively by Visa. Visit Visa's Web site described in the WebLink box to locate the nearest Visa automated teller machine.

Exclusive distribution is the extreme opposite of intensive distribution because only one retail outlet in a specified geographical area carries the firm's product. Exclusive distribution is typically chosen for specialty products or services; for example, automobiles, some women's fragrances, men's suits, and yachts. Sometimes, retailers sign exclusive distribution agreements with manufacturers. Gucci, one of the world's leading luxury goods companies, uses exclusive distribution.[9]

Selective distribution lies between these two extremes and means that a firm selects a few retail outlets in a specific geographical area to carry its products. Selective distribution weds some of the market coverage benefits of intensive distribution to the control over resale evident with exclusive distribution. For this reason, selective distribution is the most common form of distribution intensity and is usually associated with shopping goods or services, such as Rolex watches and Ping golf clubs.

WEBLINK
HTTP://WWW.MCGRAWHILL.CA/ COLLEGE/CRANE

Need Cash Fast? Check the Visa ATM Locator

Short of cash? Visa offers a valuable Web resource in its ATM Locator, which can be accessed at www.visa.com. Visa has some 750 000 automated teller machines in 120 countries. One is probably in your neighbourhood, wherever that is in the world! To find the nearest Visa ATM, follow the easy ATM Locator directions and request a site map. You will be in the money in no time. Here is the map for the McGraw-Hill Ryerson Ltd. neighbourhood.

Satisfying Buyer Requirements   A second consideration in channel design is gaining access to channels and intermediaries that satisfy at least some of the interests buyers might want fulfilled when they purchase a firm's products or services. These interests fall into four categories: (1) information, (2) convenience, (3) variety, and (4) attendant services.

Information is an important requirement when buyers have limited knowledge or desire specific data about a product or service. Properly chosen intermediaries communicate with buyers through in-store displays, demonstrations, and personal selling. Personal computer manufacturers, such as Gateway and Apple Computer, have opened their own retail outlets staffed with highly trained personnel to inform buyers how their products can better meet each customer's needs.

Convenience has multiple meanings for buyers, such as proximity or driving time to a retail outlet. For example, 7-Eleven stores with outlets nationwide satisfy this interest for buyers, and candy and snack food firms benefit by gaining display space in these stores. For other consumers, convenience means a minimum of time and hassle. Jiffy Lube and Mr. Lube, which promise to change engine oil and filters quickly, appeal to this aspect of convenience. For those who shop on the Internet, convenience means that Web sites must be easy to locate and navigate, and image downloads must be fast.

Variety reflects buyers' interest in having numerous competing and complementary items from which to choose. Variety is evident in both the breadth and depth of products and brands carried by intermediaries, which enhances their attraction to buyers. Thus, manufacturers of pet food and supplies seek distribution through pet superstores, such as Petco and Petsmart, which offer a wide array of pet products.

Services provided by intermediaries are an important buying requirement for such products as large household appliances that require delivery, installation, and credit. Therefore, Whirlpool seeks dealers that provide such services.

Profitability   The third consideration in designing a channel is profitability, which is determined by the margins earned (revenues minus cost) for each channel member and for the channel as a whole. Channel cost is the critical dimension of profitability. These costs include distribution, advertising, and selling expenses associated with different types of marketing channels. The extent to which channel members share these costs determines the margins received by each member and by the channel as a whole.

Global Dimensions of Marketing Channels

Marketing channels around the world reflect traditions, customs, geography, and the economic history of individual countries and societies. Even so, the basic marketing channel functions must be performed. But differences do exist and are illustrated by highlighting marketing channels in Japan.

Intermediaries outside Western Europe and North America tend to be small, numerous, and often owner-operated. Japanese marketing channels tend to include many intermediaries based on tradition and lack of storage space. As many as five intermediaries are involved in the distribution of soap in Japan compared with one or two in North America.

Understanding marketing channels in global markets is often a prerequisite to successful marketing. For example, Gillette attempted to sell its razors and blades through company salespeople in Japan as it does in North America, thus eliminating wholesalers traditionally involved in marketing toiletries. Warner-Lambert Company sold its Schick razors and blades through the traditional Japanese channel involving wholesalers. The result? Schick achieved a commanding lead over Gillette in the Japanese razor and blade market.[10]

Channel relationships also must be considered. In Japan, the distribution *keiretsu* (translated as "alignments") bonds producers and intermediaries together. The bond, through vertical integration and social and economic ties, ensures that each channel

For the answer to how Schick became a razor and blade market share leader in Japan, read the text.

Warner Lambert Company
www.warner-lambert.com

member benefits from the distribution alignment. The dominant member of the distribution *keiretsu*, which is typically a producer, has considerable influence over channel member behaviour, including which competing products are sold by other channel members. Well-known Japanese companies, such as Matsushita (electronics), Nissan and Toyota (automotive products), Nippon Gakki (musical instruments), and Kirin (and other brewers and distillers), employ the distribution *keiretsu* extensively. Shiseido and Kanebo, for instance, influence the distribution of cosmetics through Japanese department stores.

Channel Relationships: Conflict, Cooperation, and Law

Unfortunately, because channels consist of independent individuals and firms, there is always potential for disagreements concerning who performs which channel functions, how profits are allocated, which products and services will be provided by whom, and who makes critical channel-related decisions. These channel conflicts necessitate measures for dealing with them. Sometimes, they result in legal action.

channel conflict
Arises when one channel member believes another channel member is engaged in behaviour that prevents it from achieving its goals.

Conflict in Marketing Channels **Channel conflict** arises when one channel member believes another channel member is engaged in behaviour that prevents it from achieving its goals. Two types of conflict occur in marketing channels: vertical conflict and horizontal conflict.[11]

Vertical conflict occurs between different levels in a marketing channel; for example, between a manufacturer and a wholesaler or retailer or between a wholesaler and a retailer. Three sources of vertical conflict are most common. First, conflict arises when a channel member bypasses another member and sells or buys products direct, a practice called **disintermediation**. This conflict emerged when Jenn-Air, a producer of kitchen appliances, decided to terminate its distributors and sell direct to retailers. Second, disagreements over how profit margins are distributed among channel members produce conflict. This happened when Compaq Computer Corporation and one of its dealers disagreed over how price discounts were applied in the sale of Compaq's products. Compaq Computer stopped selling to the dealer for 13 months until the issue was resolved. A third conflict situation arises when manufacturers believe wholesalers or retailers are not giving their products adequate attention. For example, H. J. Heinz Company found itself in a conflict situation with its supermarkets in the United Kingdom when the supermarkets promoted and displayed private brands at the expense of Heinz brands.

disintermediation
Channel conflict that arises when a channel member bypasses another member and sells or buys products direct.

Horizontal conflict occurs between intermediaries at the same level in a marketing channel, such as between two or more retailers (Zellers and Wal-Mart) or two or more wholesalers that handle the same manufacturer's brands. Two sources of horizontal conflict are common. First, horizontal conflict arises when a manufacturer increases its distribution coverage in a geographical area. For example, a franchised Cadillac dealer might complain to General Motors that another franchised Cadillac dealer has located too close to its dealership. Second, multi-channel distribution causes conflict when different types of retailers carry the same brands. For instance, the launch of Elizabeth Taylor's Black Pearls fragrance by Elizabeth Arden was put on hold when some upscale department store chains refused to stock the item once they learned that mass merchants would also carry the brand. Elizabeth Arden subsequently introduced the brand only through department stores.[12]

Cooperation in Marketing Channels Conflict can have destructive effects on the workings of a marketing channel, and so it is necessary to secure cooperation among channel members. One means is through a *channel captain*, a channel member that coordinates, directs, and supports other channel members. Channel captains can be producers, wholesalers, or retailers. P&G assumes this role because it has a strong consumer following in such brands as Crest, Tide, and Pampers. Therefore, it can set policies or terms that supermarkets will follow. Wal-Mart and Home Depot are retail channel captains because of their strong consumer image, number of outlets, and purchasing volume.

A firm becomes a channel captain because it is typically the channel member with the ability to influence the behaviour of other members.[13] Influence can take four forms. First, economic influence arises from the ability of a firm to reward other members given its strong financial position or customer franchise. Microsoft Corporation and Toys "Я" Us have such influence. Expertise is a second source of influence over other channel members. Third, identification with a particular channel member may also create influence for that channel member. For instance, retailers may compete to carry the Ralph Lauren line, or clothing manufacturers may compete to be carried by well-known retailers. In both instances, the desire to be associated with a channel member gives that firm influence over others. Finally, influence can arise from the legitimate right of one channel member to direct the behaviour of other members. This situation would occur under contractual vertical marketing systems where a franchisor could legitimately direct how a franchisee behaves. Other means for securing cooperation in marketing channels rest in the different variations of vertical marketing systems.

Channel influence can be used to gain concessions from other channel members. For instance, some large supermarket chains expect manufacturers to pay allowances, in the form of cash or free goods, to stock and display their products. Some manufacturers call these allowances "extortion," as described in the Ethics and Social Responsibility Alert box.[14]

Legal Considerations Conflict in marketing channels is typically resolved through negotiation or the exercise of influence by channel members. Sometimes, conflict produces legal action. Therefore, knowledge of legal restrictions affecting channel strategies and practices is important. Some restrictions were described in Chapter 13, namely, vertical price fixing and price discrimination. However, other legal considerations unique to marketing channels warrant attention.

In general, suppliers have the right to choose the intermediaries that carry or represent their products. However, suppliers can run into legal difficulty over *refusing to deal* with customers who can meet the usual trade terms offered by the supplier. The Competition Act looks seriously at cases where a supplier withholds or withdraws products from a customer if such behaviour will adversely affect the customer.

Dual distribution is a situation where a manufacturer distributes through its own vertically integrated channel in direct competition with wholesalers and retailers that

---

ETHICS AND SOCIAL RESPONSIBILITY ALERT

The Ethics of Slotting Allowances

Have you ever wondered why your favourite cookies are no longer to be found at your local supermarket? Or why that delicious tortilla chip you like to serve at parties is missing from the shelves and replaced by another brand?

Blame it on slotting allowances. Some large supermarket chains demand slotting allowances from food manufacturers, paid in the form of money or free goods, to stock and display products. These allowances can run up to $25 000 per item for a supermarket chain. Not surprisingly, slotting allowances have been labelled "ransom," "extortional allowances," and "commercial bribery" by manufacturers because they already pay supermarkets "trade dollars" to promote and discount their products. Small food manufacturers, in particular, view slotting allowances as an economic barrier to the distribution of their products. Supermarket operators see these allowances as a reasonable cost of handling business for manufacturers.

Is the practice of charging slotting allowances unethical behaviour?

also sell its products. If the manufacturer's behaviour is viewed as an attempt to unduly lessen competition by eliminating wholesalers or retailers, then such action may violate the Competition Act and would be examined by the Competition Bureau.

Vertical integration is viewed in a similar light. Like dual distribution, it is not illegal, but the practice could be subject to legal action if such integration were designed to eliminate or lessen competition unduly.

Exclusive dealing and tied selling are prohibited under the Competition Act if they are found to unduly lessen competition or create monopolies. *Exclusive dealing* exists when a supplier requires channel members to sell only its products or restricts distributors from selling directly competitive products. *Tied selling* occurs when a supplier requires a distributor purchasing some products to buy others from the supplier. These arrangements often arise in franchising. Tied selling would be investigated by the Competition Bureau if the tied products could be purchased at fair market value from other suppliers at desired standards of the franchisor and if the arrangements were seen as restricting competition. Full-line forcing is a special kind of tied selling. This is a supplier's requiring that a channel member carry its full line of products to sell a specific item in the supplier's line.

Resale or market restrictions refer to a supplier's attempt to stipulate to whom distributors may resell the supplier's products and in what specific geographical areas or territories they may be sold. These practices could be subject to review under the Competition Act if such restrictions were deemed to be restraining or lessening competition.

logistics

Those activities that focus on getting the right amount of the right products to the right place at the right time at the lowest possible cost.

CONCEPT CHECK

1. What are the three degrees of distribution density?

2. What are the three questions marketing executives consider when choosing a marketing channel and intermediaries?

3. What is meant by "exclusive dealing"?

■ ■ ■
LOGISTICS AND SUPPLY CHAIN MANAGEMENT

logistics management

The practice of organizing the cost-effective flow of raw materials, in-process inventory, finished goods, and related information from point of origin to point of consumption to satisfy customer requirements.

supply chain

A sequence of firms that perform activities required to create and deliver a good or service to consumers or industrial users.

supply chain management

The integration and organization of information and logistics activities across firms in a supply chain for the purpose of creating and delivering goods and services that provide value to customers.

A marketing channel relies on logistics to actually make products available to consumers and business users—a point emphasized earlier in this chapter. **Logistics** involves those activities that focus on getting the right amount of the right products to the right place at the right time at the lowest possible cost. The performance of these activities is **logistics management**, the practice of organizing the *cost-effective flow* of raw materials, in-process inventory, finished goods, and related information from point of origin to point of consumption to satisfy *customer requirements*. This perspective is represented in the concept of a supply chain and the practice of supply chain management.

A **supply chain** is a sequence of firms that perform activities required to create and deliver a good or service to consumers or industrial users. It differs from a marketing channel in terms of membership. A supply chain includes suppliers who provide raw material inputs to a manufacturer as well as the wholesalers and retailers who deliver finished goods to you. The management process is also different. **Supply chain management** is the integration and organization of information and logistics activities *across firms* in a supply chain for the purpose of creating and delivering goods and services that provide value to consumers. The relationship among marketing channels, logistics management, and supply chain management is shown in Figure 14–8. An important feature of supply chain management is its application of sophisticated information technology, which allows companies to share and operate systems for order processing, transportation scheduling, and inventory and facility management.

■ **FIGURE 14–8** ■

Logistics management and
supply chain management

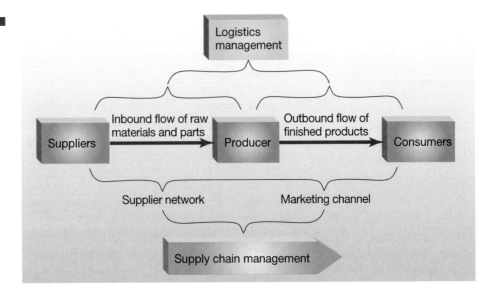

Sourcing, Assembling, and Delivering a New Car: The Automotive Supply Chain

All companies are members of one or more supply chains. A supply chain is essentially a sequence of linked suppliers and customers in which every customer is, in turn, a supplier to another customer until a finished product reaches the final consumer. Even the simplified supply chain diagram for car makers shown in Figure 14–9 illustrates how complex a supply chain can be.[15] A car maker's supplier network includes thousands of firms that provide the 5000 or so parts in a typical automobile. They provide items ranging from raw materials, such as steel and rubber, to components, including transmissions, tires, brakes, and seats, to complex subassemblies and assemblies evident in chassis and suspension systems that make for a smooth, stable ride. Coordinating and scheduling material and component flows for their assembly into actual automobiles by car makers is heavily dependent on logistical activities, including transportation, order processing, inventory control, materials handling, and information technology. A central link is the car maker supply chain manager, who is responsible for translating customer requirements into actual orders and arranging for delivery dates and financial arrangements for automobile dealers. This is not an easy task, given the different consumer preferences and the amounts consumers are willing to pay.

Logistical aspects of the automobile marketing channel are also an integral part of the supply chain. Major responsibilities include transportation, which involves the selection and oversight of external carriers (trucking, airline, railroad, and shipping companies) for cars and parts to dealers, the operation of distribution centres, the

■ **FIGURE 14–9** ■

The automotive supply chain

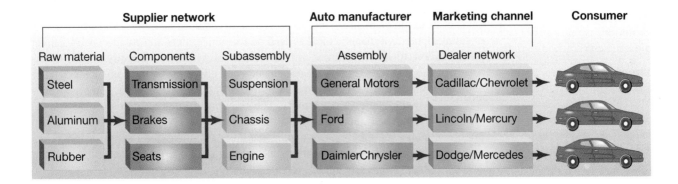

management of finished goods inventories, and order processing for sales. Supply chain managers also play an important role in the marketing channel. They work with extensive car dealer networks to ensure that the right mix of automobiles are delivered to different locations. In addition, they make sure that spare and service parts are available so that dealers can meet the car maintenance and repair needs of consumers. All of this is done with the help of information technology that links the entire automotive supply chain. What does all of this cost? It is estimated that logistics costs represent 25 to 30 percent of the retail price of a typical new car.

Supply Chain Management and Marketing Strategy

The automotive supply chain illustration shows how information and logistics activities are integrated and organized across firms to create and deliver a car for you. What is missing from this illustration is the link between a specific company's supply chain and its marketing strategy. Just as companies have different marketing strategies, they also manage supply chains differently. More specifically, the goals to be achieved by a firm's marketing strategy determine whether its supply chain needs to be more responsive or efficient in meeting customer requirements.

Aligning a Supply Chain with Marketing Strategy   There are a variety of supply chain configurations, each which is designated to perform a different task well. Marketers today recognize that the choice of a supply chain follows from a clearly defined marketing strategy and involves three steps:[16]

1. *Understand the customer.* To understand the customer, a company must identify the needs of the customer segment being served. These needs, such as a desire for a low price or convenience of purchase, help a company define the relative importance of efficiency and responsiveness in meeting customer requirements.
2. *Understand the supply chain.* Second, a company must understand what a supply chain is designed to do well. Supply chains range from those that emphasize being responsive to customer requirements and demand to those that emphasize efficiency with a goal of supplying products at the lowest possible delivered cost.
3. *Harmonize the supply chain with the marketing strategy.* Finally, a company needs to ensure that what the supply chain is capable of doing well is consistent with the targeted customer's needs and its marketing strategy. If a mismatch exists between what the supply chain does particularly well and a company's marketing strategy, the company will either need to redesign the supply chain to support the marketing strategy or change the marketing strategy. The bottom line is that a poorly designed supply chain can do serious damage to an otherwise brilliant marketing strategy.

How are these steps applied, and how are efficiency and responsive considerations built into a supply chain? Let us briefly look at how two market leaders—Dell Computer Corporation and Wal-Mart, Inc.—have harmonized their supply chain and marketing strategies.[17]

Dell Computer Corporation: A Responsive Supply Chain   The Dell marketing strategy targets customers who wish to have the most up-to-date personal computer equipment customized to their needs. These customers are also willing to (1) wait to have their customized personal computer delivered in a few days rather than picking out a model at a retail store, and (2) pay a reasonable, though not the lowest, price in the marketplace. Given Dell's customer segment, the company has the option of adopting an efficient or responsive supply chain. An efficient supply chain may use inexpensive but slower modes of transportation, emphasize economies of scale in its production process by reducing the variety of PC configurations offered, and limit its

World-class marketers Dell Computer and Wal-Mart emphasize responsiveness and efficiency in their supply chains.

assembly and inventory storage facilities to a single location. If Dell opted only for efficiency in its supply chain, it would be difficult, if not impossible, to satisfy its target customer's desire for rapid delivery and a wide variety of customizable products. Dell, instead, has opted for a responsive supply chain. It relies on more expensive express transportation for receipt of components from suppliers and delivery of finished products to customers. The company achieves product variety and manufacturing efficiency by designing common platforms across several products and using common components. Dell operates manufacturing facilities in various countries to ensure rapid delivery. Moreover, Dell has invested heavily in information technology to link itself with suppliers and customers.

Wal-Mart, Inc.: An Efficient Supply Chain   Now, let us consider Wal-Mart. Wal-Mart's marketing strategy is to be a reliable, lower-price retailer for a wide variety of mass-consumption consumer goods. This strategy favours an efficient supply chain designed to deliver products to consumers at the lowest possible cost. Efficiency is achieved in a variety of ways. For instance, Wal-Mart keeps relatively low inventory levels, and most inventory is stocked in stores available for sale, not in warehouses gathering dust. The low inventory arises from Wal-Mart's innovative use of *cross-docking*—a practice that involves unloading products from suppliers, sorting products for individual stores, and quickly reloading products onto trucks for a particular store. No warehousing or storing of products occurs, except for a few hours or at most a day. Cross-docking allows Wal-Mart to operate only a small number of distribution centres to service its vast network of Wal-Mart stores, Supercentres, and Sam's Clubs, which contributes to efficiency. On the other hand, the company runs its own fleet of trucks to service its stores. This does increase cost and investment, but the benefits in terms of responsiveness justify the cost, in Wal-Mart's case. Wal-Mart has invested significantly more than its competitors have in information technology to operate its supply chain. The company feeds information about customer requirements and demand from its stores back to its suppliers, which manufacture only what is being demanded. This large investment has improved the efficiency of Wal-Mart's supply chain and made it responsive to customer needs.

Three lessons can be learned from these two examples. First, there is no one best supply chain for every company. Second, the best supply chain is the one that is consistent with the needs of the customer segment being served and complements a company's marketing strategy. And finally, supply chain managers are often called upon to make tradeoffs between efficiency and responsiveness on various elements of a company's supply chain.

CONCEPT CHECK

1. What is the principal difference between a marketing channel and a supply chain?

2. That three steps does the choice of a supply chain involve?

INFORMATION AND LOGISTICS MANAGEMENT OBJECTIVE IN A SUPPLY CHAIN

The objective of information and logistics management in a supply chain is to minimize logistics costs while delivering maximum customer service. The Dell Computer and Wal-Mart examples highlight how two market leaders have realized this objective by different means. An important similarity between these two companies is that both use information to leverage logistics activities, reduce logistics costs, and improve customer service.

Information's Role in Supply Chain Responsiveness and Efficiency

Information consists of data and analysis regarding inventory, transportation, distribution facilities, and customers throughout the supply chain.[18] Continuing advances in information technology make it possible to track logistics activities and customer service variables and manage them for efficiency and responsiveness. For example, information on customer demand patterns allows pharmaceutical companies, such as Eli Lilly and Smithkline Beecham, to produce and stock medicines in anticipation of customer needs. This improves supply chain responsiveness because customers will find the medicines when and where they want them. Demand information improves supply chain efficiency because pharmaceutical firms are better able to forecast customer needs and produce, transport, and store the required amount of inventory.

A variety of technologies are used to transmit and manage information in a supply chain. *Electronic data interchanges (EDI)* combine proprietary computer and telecommunication technologies to exchange electronic invoices, payments, and information between suppliers, manufacturers, and retailers. When linked with store scanning equipment and systems, EDI provides a seamless electronic link from a retail checkout counter to suppliers and manufacturers. Wal-Mart and Procter & Gamble actually pioneered the use of EDI. EDI is commonly used in the retail, apparel, transportation, pharmaceutical, grocery, health care, and insurance industries, as well as by local, provincial, and federal government agencies. About 95 percent of the companies listed in the *Fortune 1000* use EDI, as do most of the Canadian companies listed in the *Financial Post 500*. At Hewlett-Packard, for example, one million EDI transactions are made every month.

Another technology is the *extranet*, which is an Internet/Web-based network that permits secure business-to-business communication between a manufacturer and its suppliers, distributors, and sometimes other partners (such as advertising agencies). Extranets are less expensive and more flexible to operate than EDI because of their connection to the public Internet. This technology is prominent in private electronic exchanges described in Chapter 6. For example, WhirlpoolWebWorld.com allows Whirlpool to fulfill retailer orders quickly and inexpensively and better match appliance demand and supply.

Whereas EDI and extranets transmit information, other technologies help manage information in a supply chain. Enterprise resource planning (ERP) technology and supply chain management software track logistics cost and customer service variables, both of which are described next.

Total Logistics Cost Concept

total logistics cost
Expenses associated with transportation, materials handling and warehousing, inventory, stockouts, order processing, and return goods handling.

For our purposes, **total logistics cost** includes expenses associated with transportation, materials handling and warehousing, inventory, stockouts (being out of inventory), order processing, and return goods handling. Note that many of these costs are interrelated, and so changes in one will impact the others. For example, as the firm attempts to minimize its transportation costs by shipping in larger quantities, it will also experience an increase in inventory levels. Larger inventory levels will not only increase inventory costs but should also reduce stockouts. It is important, therefore, to study the impact on all of the logistics decision areas when considering a change.

Customer Service Concept

customer service
The ability of logistics management to satisfy users in terms of time, dependability, communication, and convenience.

Because a supply chain is a *flow*, the end of it—or *output*—is the service delivered to customers. Within the context of a supply chain, **customer service** is the ability of logistics management to satisfy users in terms of time, dependability, communication, and convenience. As suggested by Figure 14–10, a supply chain manager's key task is to balance these four customer service factors against total logistics cost factors.

Time   In a supply chain setting, time refers to *lead time* for an item, which means the lag from ordering an item until it is received and ready for use or sale. This is also referred to as *order cycle time* or *replenishment time* and may be more important to retailers or wholesalers than consumers. The various elements that make up the typical order cycle include recognition of the need to order, order transmittal, order processing, documentation, and transportation. A current emphasis in supply chain management is to reduce lead time so that the inventory levels of customers may be minimized. Another emphasis is to make the process of reordering and receiving products as simple as possible, often through electronic data and inventory systems called *quick response* and *efficient consumer response* delivery systems. These inventory management systems are designed to reduce the retailer's lead time for receiving merchandise, thereby lowering a retailer's inventory investment, improving customer service levels, and reducing logistics expense.

Dependability   Dependability is the consistency of replenishment. This is important to all firms in a supply chain and to consumers. It can be broken into three elements: consistent lead time, safe delivery, and complete delivery. Consistent service allows planning (such as appropriate inventory levels), whereas inconsistencies create surprises. Intermediaries may be willing to accept longer lead times if they know about them in advance and can thus make plans.

■ **FIGURE 14–10** ■
Supply chain managers balance total logistics cost factors against customer service factors

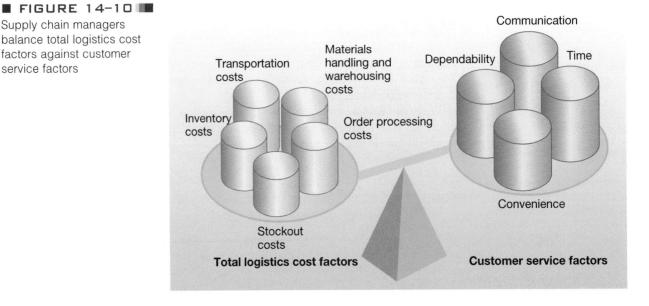

Total logistics cost factors   **Customer service factors**

Communication   Communication is a two-way link between buyer and seller that helps in monitoring service and anticipating future needs. Status reports on orders are a typical example of improved communication between buyer and seller.

Convenience   The concept of convenience for a supply chain manager means that there should be a minimum of effort on the part of the buyer in doing business with the seller. Is it easy for the customer to order? Are the products available from many outlets? Does the buyer have to buy huge quantities of the product? Will the seller arrange all necessary details, such as transportation? The seller must concentrate on removing unnecessary barriers to customer convenience.

| CONCEPT CHECK | **1.** The objective of information and logistics management in a supply chain is to _____.
2. How does consumer demand information increase supply chain responsiveness and efficiency? |
| --- | --- |

■ ■ ■
KEY LOGISTICS FUNCTIONS IN A SUPPLY CHAIN

FedEx and Emery Worldwide are two third-party logistics providers that perform most or all of the logistics functions that manufacturers, suppliers, and distributors would normally perform.

FedEx

The four key logistic functions in a supply chain include (1) transportation, (2) warehousing and materials handling, (3) order processing, and (4) inventory management. These functions have become so complex and interrelated that many companies have outsourced them to third-party logistics providers. *Third-party logistics providers* are firms that perform most or all of the logistics functions that manufacturers, suppliers, and distributors would normally perform themselves.[19] Today, many of Canada's top manufacturers outsource one or more logistics functions, at least on a limited basis. UPS Logistics, FedEx, Roadway Logistics, Emery Worldwide, Global Logistics, and

Penske are just a few of the companies that specialize in handling logistics functions for their clients.

The four major logistics functions and the involvement of third-party logistics providers are described in detail next.

Transportation

Transportation provides the movement of goods necessary in a supply chain. There are five basic modes of transportation: railroads, motor carriers, air carriers, pipelines, and water carriers, and modal combinations involving two or more modes, such as highway trailers on a rail flatcar.

All transportation modes can be evaluated on six basic service criteria:

- *Cost*. Charges for transportation.
- *Time*. Speed of transit.
- *Capability*. What can be realistically carried with this mode.
- *Dependability*. Reliability of service regarding time, loss, and damage.
- *Accessibility*. Convenience of the mode's routes (such as pipeline availability).
- *Frequency*. Scheduling.

Figure 14–11 summarizes service advantages and disadvantages of five of the modes of transportation available.[20]

Warehousing and Materials Handling

Warehouses may be classified in one of two ways: (1) storage warehouses, and (2) distribution centres. In *storage warehouses* the goods are intended to come to rest for some period of time, as in the aging of products or in storing household goods. *Distribution centres*, on the other hand, are designed to facilitate the timely movement of goods and represent a very important part of a supply chain. They represent the second most significant cost in a supply chain after transportation.

Distribution centres not only allow firms to hold their stock in decentralized locations but also are used to facilitate sorting and consolidating products from different

■ **FIGURE 14–11** ■

Advantages and disadvantages of five modes of transportation

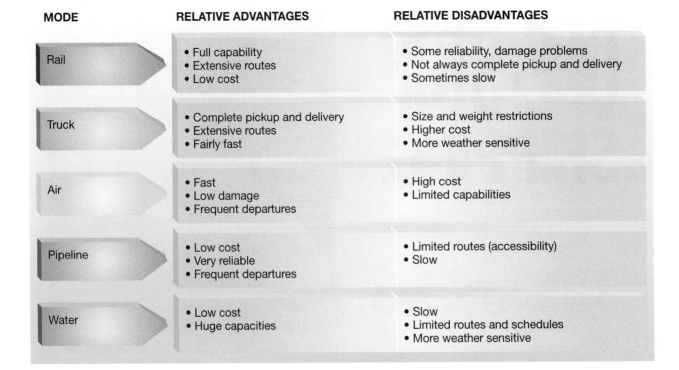

MODE	RELATIVE ADVANTAGES	RELATIVE DISADVANTAGES
Rail	• Full capability • Extensive routes • Low cost	• Some reliability, damage problems • Not always complete pickup and delivery • Sometimes slow
Truck	• Complete pickup and delivery • Extensive routes • Fairly fast	• Size and weight restrictions • Higher cost • More weather sensitive
Air	• Fast • Low damage • Frequent departures	• High cost • Limited capabilities
Pipeline	• Low cost • Very reliable • Frequent departures	• Limited routes (accessibility) • Slow
Water	• Low cost • Huge capacities	• Slow • Limited routes and schedules • More weather sensitive

plants or different suppliers. Some physical transformation can also take place in distribution centres, for example, mixing or blending different ingredients, labelling, and repackaging. Paint companies, such as Sherwin-Williams and Benjamin Moore, use distribution centres for this purpose. In addition, distribution centres may serve as manufacturer sales offices and order processing centres.

materials handling
Moving goods over short distances into, within, and out of warehouses and manufacturing plants.

Materials handling, which involves moving goods over short distances into, within, and out of warehouses and manufacturing plants, is a key part of warehouse operations. The two major problems with this activity are high labour costs and high rates of loss and damage. Every time an item is handled, there is a chance for loss or damage. Common materials handling equipment includes forklifts, cranes, and conveyors. Today, materials handling in warehouses is automated by using computers and robots to reduce the cost of holding, moving, and recording inventories.

Order Processing

There are several stages in the processing of an order, and a failure at any one of them can cause a problem with the customer. The process starts with transmitting the order by a variety of means, such as the Internet, an extranet, or electronic data interchange (EDI). This is followed by entering the order in the appropriate databases and sending the information to those who need it. For example, a regional warehouse is notified to prepare an order. After checking inventory, a new quantity may need to be reordered from the production line, or purchasing may be requested to reorder from a vendor. If the item is currently out of stock, a "backorder" is created, and the whole process of keeping track of a small part of the original order must be managed. In addition, credit may have to be checked for some customers, all documentation for the order must be prepared, transportation must be arranged, and an order confirmation must be sent. Order processing systems are evaluated in terms of speed and accuracy.

Electronic order processing has replaced manual processing for most large companies.[21] For example, IBM soon expects to be doing business electronically with all of its suppliers, either on the Internet or through EDI. Kiwi Brands, the marketer of Kiwi shoe polish, Endust, and Behold, receives 75 percent of its retailers' purchase orders via EDI. The company has also implemented financial EDI, sending invoices to retailers and receiving payment order/remittance advice documents and electronic

Materials handling through automation is now common in distribution centres.

The key to Saturn's JIT system: a Ryder truck driver downloads a key-shaped floppy disk from an onboard computer to get delivery instructions.

Ryder System, Inc.

www.ryder.com

funds transfer (EFT) payments. Shippers as well are linked to the system, allowing Kiwi to receive shipment status messages electronically.

Inventory Management

Inventory management is one of the primary responsibilities of the supply chain manager. The major problem is maintaining the delicate balance between too little and too much. Too little inventory may result in poor service, stockouts, brand switching, and loss of market share; too much leads to higher costs because of the money tied up in inventory and the risk that it may become obsolete.

Reasons for Inventory   Traditionally, carrying inventory has been justified on several grounds: (1) to offer a buffer against variations in supply and demand, often caused by uncertainty in forecasting demand; (2) to provide better service for those customers who wish to be served on demand; (3) to promote production efficiencies; (4) to provide a hedge against price increases by suppliers; (5) to promote purchasing and transportation discounts; and (6) to protect the firm from such contingencies as strikes and shortages. However, companies today view inventory as something to be moved, not stored, and more of a liability than an asset. The traditional justification for inventory has resulted in excessive inventories that have proven costly to maintain. Consider the North American automobile industry. Despite efforts to streamline its supply chain, industry analysts estimate that more than $230 billion worth of excess inventory piles up annually in the form of unused raw materials, parts waiting to be delivered, and vehicles sitting on dealers' lots.[22]

Inventory Costs   Specific inventory costs are often hard to detect because they are difficult to measure and occur in many different parts of the firm. A classification of inventory costs includes the following:

- *Capital costs*. The opportunity costs resulting from tying up funds in inventory instead of using them in other, more profitable investments; these are related to interest rates.
- *Inventory service costs*. Such items as insurance and taxes that are present in many provinces.
- *Storage costs*. Warehousing space and materials handling.
- *Risk costs*. Possible loss, damage, pilferage, perishability, and obsolescence.

Storage costs, risk costs, and some service costs vary according to the characteristics of the items inventoried. For example, perishable products or highly seasonal items have higher risk costs than a commodity-type product, such as lumber. Capital costs are always present and are proportional to the *values* of the item and prevailing interest rates. The costs of carrying inventory vary with the particular circumstances but quite easily could range from 10 to 35 percent for different firms.

Supply Chain Inventory Strategies   Conventional wisdom a decade ago was that a firm should protect itself against uncertainty by maintaining a reserve inventory at

just-in-time (JIT) concept

An inventory supply system that operates with very low inventories and requires fast, on-time delivery.

each of its production and stocking points. This has been described as a "just-in-case" philosophy of inventory management and led to unnecessarily high levels of inventory. In contrast is the **just-in-time (JIT) concept**, which is an inventory supply system that operates with very low inventories and requires fast, on-time delivery. When parts are needed for production, they arrive from suppliers "just in time," which means neither before nor after they are needed. Note that JIT is used in situations where demand forecasting is reliable, such as when supplying an automobile production line, and is not suitable for inventories that are to be stored over significant periods of time.

Saturn uses a sophisticated JIT system. A central computerized system directs trucks to deliver pre-inspected parts at specific times 21 hours a day, six days a week to one of the plant's 56 receiving docks. Incredibly, the JIT system must coordinate Saturn's suppliers, many of whom are located hundreds of kilometres from the Saturn facility. Does the JIT system work for Saturn? The answer is a resounding yes. The Saturn production line has been shut down only once—for 18 minutes!—because the right part was not delivered at the right place and time.

Ryder Integrated Logistics is charged with making Saturn's JIT system work smoothly. Ryder long-haul trucks and their drivers are the most expensive part of the system. The key—very literally—to this JIT system is a computer disk in the form of a plastic key that drivers plug into an on-truck computer. The computer screen then tells the driver where to go, the route to use, and how much time to spend getting there.

Electronic data interchange and electronic messaging technology coupled with the constant pressure for faster response time in replenishing inventory have also changed the way suppliers and customers do business in a supply chain. The approach, called **vendor-managed inventory** (VMI), is an inventory-management system whereby the *supplier* determines the product amount and assortment a customer (such as a retailer) needs and automatically delivers the appropriate items.

vendor-managed inventory

An inventory management system whereby the supplier determines the product amount and assortment a customer (such as a retailer) needs and automatically delivers the appropriate items.

Campbell Soup's system illustrates how VMI works.[23] Campbell first establishes EDI links with retailers. Every morning, retailers electronically inform the company of their demand for all Campbell products and the inventory levels in their distribution centres. Campbell uses that information to forecast future demand and determine which products need replenishment based on upper and lower inventory limits established with each retailer. Trucks leave the Campbell shipping plant that afternoon and arrive at the retailer's distribution centres with the required replenishments the same day.

Closing the Loop: Reverse Logistics

reverse logistics

A process of reclaiming recyclable and reusable materials, returns, and reworks from the point of consumption or use for repair, remanufacturing, redistribution, or disposal.

The flow of goods in a supply chain does not end with the consumer or industrial user. Companies today recognize that a supply chain can work in reverse. **Reverse logistics** is a process of reclaiming recyclable and reusable materials, returns, and reworks from the point of consumption or use for repair, remanufacturing, redistribution, or disposal. The effect of reverse logistics can be seen in the reduced waste in landfills and lowered operating costs for companies.

Such companies as Eastman Kodak (reusable cameras), Hewlett-Packard (printer toner cartridges returned for filling), Xerox, and IBM (remanufacturing and recycling equipment parts) have implemented acclaimed reverse logistics programs.[24] Other firms have enlisted third-party logistics providers to handle this process along with other supply chain functions.

CONCEPT CHECK

1. What are the basic tradeoffs among the modes of transportation?

2. What types of inventory should use storage warehouses, and which types should use distribution centres?

3. What are the strengths and weaknesses of a just-in-time system?

■ ■ ■
CHAPTER IN REVIEW

1 *Explain what is meant by a marketing channel of distribution and why intermediaries are often needed.*

A marketing channel of distribution, or simply a marketing channel, consists of individuals and firms involved in the process of making a product or service available for use or consumption by consumers and business users. Intermediaries make possible the flow of products from producers to buyers by performing three basic functions. The transactional function involves buying, selling, and risk taking because intermediaries stock merchandise in anticipation of sales. The logistics function involves the gathering, storing, and dispensing of products. The facilitating function assists producers in making products and services more attractive to buyers.

2 *Distinguish among traditional marketing channels, electronic marketing channels, multichannel distribution, and different types of vertical marketing systems.*

Traditional marketing channels describe the route taken by products and services from producers to buyers. This route can range from a direct channel with no intermediaries, because a producer and ultimate consumers deal directly with each other, to indirect channels where intermediaries (agents, wholesalers, distributors, or retailers) are inserted between a producer and consumer and perform numerous channel functions. Electronic marketing channels employ the Internet to make products and services available for consumption and use by consumer or business buyers. Today, many firms engage in multichannel distribution—an arrangement whereby a firm reaches buyers by employing two or more different types of marketing channels. Vertical marketing systems (VMS) are professionally managed and centrally coordinated marketing channels designed to achieve channel economics and maximum marketing impact. There are three types of VMS; corporate, contractual, and administered.

3 *Describe factors considered by marketing executives when selecting and managing a marketing channel.*

Four factors affect a company's choice and management of a marketing channel: environmental factors, consumer factors, product factors, and company factors. Recognizing that numerous routes to buyers exist and also recognized the factors just described, marketers consider three questions when choosing and managing a marketing channel. Which channel and intermediaries will provide the best coverage of the target market? Marketers typically choose one of three levels of coverage: intensive, selective, and exclusive distribution. Which channel and intermediaries will best satisfy the buying requirements of the target market? These buying requirements include information, convenience, variety, and attendant services. Which channel and intermediaries will be the most profitable?

4 *Recognize how conflict, cooperation, and legal considerations affect marketing channels relationships.*

Because marketing channels consist of independent individuals and firms, there is the potential for conflict. Two types of conflict can occur: vertical and horizontal. Vertical conflict occurs between different levels of a marketing channel while horizontal conflict occurs between intermediaries at the same level in a marketing channel. One way to reduce the prospect of conflict is to have a channel captain—a channel member that coordinates, directs, and supports other channel members. However, sometimes channel conflict can result in legal action. Such legal action arises from channel practices that are perceived to restrain competition or to create monopolies.

5 *Recognize the relationship between marketing channels, logistics, and supply chain management and how a company's supply chain aligns with its marketing strategy.*

A marketing channel relies on logistics to make products available to consumers and business users. Logistics involves those activities that focus on getting the right amount of the right products to the right place at the right time at the lowest possible cost. The performance of these activities is logistics management—the practice of organizing the cost-effective flow of raw materials, in-process inventory, finished goods, and related information from point of origin to point of consumption to satisfy customer requirements.

A supply chain is a sequence of firms that perform activities required to create and deliver a product or service to consumers or business users. It differs from a marketing channel in terms of membership. A supply chain includes suppliers that provide raw material inputs to a manufacturer as well as the wholesalers and retailers that deliver products and services. The management process is also different. Supply chain management is the integration and organization of information and logistics activities across firms in a supply chain for the purpose of creating and delivering products and services that provide value to consumers.

A company's supply chain follows from its defined marketing strategy. The alignment of a company's supply chain with its marketing strategy involves three steps: (1) a supply chain must reflect the needs of the customer being served, (2) a company must understand what a supply chain is designed to do well, and (3) a supply chain must be consistent with the customer's needs and the company's marketing strategy.

6 *Identify the major logistics costs and customer service factors that managers consider when making supply chain decisions.*

Companies strive to provide superior customer service while controlling logistics costs. The major customer service factors include the time between orders and deliveries, dependability in replenishing inventory, communication between buyers and sellers, and convenience in buying from the seller. Logistics cost factors include transportation, materials handling and warehousing, order processing, inventory, and stockouts.

7 *Describe the key logistics functions in a supply chain.*

The four logistics functions in a supply chain include transportation, warehousing and materials handling, order processing, and inventory management. Transportation provides the movement of goods necessary in a supply chain. Five major transport modes are railroads, motor carriers, air carriers, pipelines, and water carriers. Warehousing and materials handling include the storing, sorting, and handling of products at storage warehouse or distribution centres. Order processing includes order receipt, delivery, invoicing, and collection from customers. Inventory management involves minimizing inventory-carrying costs while maintaining sufficient stocks of products to satisfy customer needs. Two popular inventory management practices are just-in-time (JIT) and vendor-managed inventory (VMI) systems.

■ ■ ■

FOCUSING ON KEY TERMS

■ ■ ■

DISCUSSION AND APPLICATION QUESTIONS

1 Suppose the president of a carpet manufacturing firm has asked you to look into the possibility of bypassing the firm's wholesalers (who sell to carpet, department, and furniture stores) and sell direct to these stores. What caution would you voice on this matter, and what type of information would you gather before making this decision?

2 How does the channel captain idea differ among corporate, administered, and contractual vertical marketing systems with particular reference to the use of different forms of influence available to firms?

3 How do specialty, shopping, and convenience goods generally relate to intensive, selective, and exclusive distribution? Give a brand name that is an example of each goods–distribution matchup.

4 List several companies to which logistical activities might be unimportant. Also list some whose focus is only on the inbound or outbound side.

5 List the logistics customer service factors that would be important to buyers in the following types of companies: (a) manufacturing, (b) retailers, (c) hospitals, and (d) construction.

6 The auto industry is a heavy user of just-in-time concept. Why? What other industries would be good candidates for its application? What do they have in common?

7 What are some types of business in which order processing may be among the most important success factors in terms of logistics management?

| GOING ONLINE | | Checking Out Unfair Pricing Practices |

Companies define "bullwhip" as too much or too little inventory to satisfy customer needs, missed production schedules, and ineffective transportation or delivery causes by miscommunication among material suppliers, manufacturers, and resellers of consumer and business goods. Its sting is poor customer service and lost revenue and profit opportunities. The bullwhip effect is a common problem in supply chains.

The Quick MBA, at www.quickmba.com/scm, provides an overview of supply chain management, and insights into the bullwhip effect. Visit QuickMBA, and answer the following questions:

1 What are the principal contributors to the bullwhip effect?

2 How have companies reduced the sting of the bullwhip?

Do you want to get better grades and stay up to date with current issues in marketing? Visit the Online Learning Centre at www.mcgrawhill.ca/college/crane for practice tests, video cases, resources for building a marketing plan, *Globe and Mail* headlines, access to *Marketing Magazine*, and other learning and study tools.

VIDEO CASE 14

Amazon: Delivering the Goods . . .
Millions of Times Each Day!

"The new economy means that the balance of power has shifted toward the consumer," explains Jeff Bezos, CEO of Amazon.com, Inc. The global online retailer is a pioneer of fast, convenient, low-cost virtual shopping that has attracted millions of consumers. Of course, while Amazon has changed the way many people shop, the company still faces the traditional and daunting task of creating a seamless flow of deliveries to its customers—often millions of times each day!

THE COMPANY

Bezos started Amazon.com with a simple idea: to use the Internet to transform book buying into the fastest, easiest, and most enjoyable shopping experience possible. The company was incorporated in 1994 and opened its virtual doors in July 1995. At the forefront of a huge growth of dot-com businesses, Amazon pursued a get-big-fast business strategy. Sales grew rapidly and Amazon began adding products and services other than books. In fact, Amazon soon set its goal on being the world's most customer-centric company, where customers can find and discover anything they might want to buy online!

Today, Amazon claims to have the "Earth's Biggest Selection™" of products and services, including books, CDs, videos, toys and games, electronics, kitchenware, computers, free electronic greeting cards, and auctions. Other services allow customers to:

- search for books, music, and videos with any word from the title or any part of the artist's name,
- browse hundreds of product categories, and
- receive personalized recommendations, based on past purchases, through e-mail or when they log on.

These products and services have attracted millions of people in more than 220 countries and made Amazon.com, along with its international sites in the United Kingdom, Germany, Japan, and France, the leading online retailer.

Despite its incredible success with consumers and continuing growth in sales to more than $3 billion annually, Amazon.com found it difficult to be profitable. Many industry observers questioned the viability of online retailing and Amazon's business model. Then, Amazon shocked many people by announcing its first profit in the fourth quarter of 2001. There are a variety of explanations for the turnaround. Generally, Bezos suggests that "efficiencies allow for lower prices, spurring sales growth across the board, which can be handled by existing facilities without much additional cost." More specifically, the facilities Bezos is referring to are the elements of its supply chain—which are one of the most complex and expensive aspects of the company's business.

SUPPLY CHAIN AND LOGISTICS MANAGEMENT AT AMAZON.COM

What happens after an order is submitted on Amazon's Web site but before it arrives at the customer's door? A lot! Amazon.com maintains seven huge distribution, or "fulfillment," centres, where it keeps inventory of more than 2.7 million products. This is one of the key differences between Amazon.com and some of its competitors—it actually stocks products. So, Amazon must manage the flow of products from its suppliers to its distribution centres and the flow of customer orders from the distribution centres to individuals' homes or offices.

The process begins with the suppliers. "Amazon's goal is to collaborate with our suppliers to increase efficiencies and improve inventory turnover," explains Jim Miller, vice-president of supply chain at Amazon.com. "We want to bring to suppliers the kind of interactive relationship that has inspired customers to shop with us," he adds. For example, Amazon is using software to more accurately forecast purchasing patterns by region, which allows it to give its suppliers better information about delivery dates and volumes. Prior to the development of this software, 12 percent of incoming inventory was sent to the wrong location, leading to lost time and delayed orders. Now, only 4 percent of the incoming inventory is mishandled.

At the same time, Amazon has been improving the part of the process that sorts the products into the individual orders. Jeffrey Wilke, Amazon's senior vice-president of operations, says, "We spent the whole year really focused on increasing productivity." Again, technology has been essential. "The speed at which telecommunications networks allow us to pass information back and forth has enabled us to do the real-time work that we keep talking about. In the past, it would have taken too long to get this many items through a system," explains Wilke. Once the order is in the system, computers ensure that all items are included in the box before it is taped and labelled. A network of trucks and regional postal hubs then conclude the process with delivery of the order.

The success of Amazon's logistics and supply chain management activities may be most evident during the year-end holiday shopping season. Amazon received orders for 37.9 million items between November 9 and

December 21, including orders for 450 000 Harry Potter books and products and orders for 36 000 items placed just before the holiday delivery deadline. Well over 99 percent of the orders were shipped and delivered on time!

AMAZON'S CHALLENGES

Despite all of Amazon's recent improvements, logistics experts estimate that the company's distribution centres are operating at approximately 40 percent of their capacity. This situation suggests that Amazon must reduce its capacity or increase its sales.

Several sales growth options are possible. First, Amazon can continue to pursue growth through sales of books, CDs, and videos. Expanded lists of books, music, and movies from throughout the world and convenient selection services may appeal to current and potential customers. Second, Amazon can continue its expansion into new product and service categories. This approach would prevent Amazon from becoming a niche merchant of books, music, and movies, and position it as an online department store. Finally, Amazon

can pursue a strategy of providing access to its existing operations to other retailers. For example, Amazon took over the Toys "Я" Us Web site, adding it as a store on Amazon's site. Borders, Expedia, and Circuit City have begun similar partnerships.

Amazon.com has come a long way toward proving that online retailing can work. As the company strives to maintain profitability and continue its growth, its future success is likely to depend on the success of its logistics and supply chain management activities!

QUESTIONS

1 How do Amazon.com's logistics and supply chain management activities help the company create value for its customers?

2 What systems did Amazon develop to improve the flow of products from suppliers to Amazon distribution centres? What systems improved the flow of orders from the distribution centres to customers?

3 Why will logistics and supply chain management play an important role in the future success of Amazon.com?

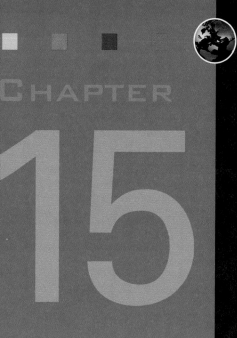

RETAILING

LEARNING OBJECTIVES

After reading this chapter, you should be able to:

1 Explain the alternative ways to classify retail outlets.

2 Describe the many methods of nonstore retailing.

3 Classify retailers in terms of the retail positioning matrix.

4 Develop retailing mix strategies over the life cycle of a retail store.

TIM HORTONS—"ALWAYS FRESH" AND "A FRIEND ALONG THE WAY"

What began as a single donut shop in an Ontario steel town has grown into Canada's top food-service retail chain. With 2500 locations coast-to-coast and $2.9 billion in revenues, Tim Horton's has become "the people's restaurant." In fact, Tim's now holds 70 percent market share of the coffee and fresh-baked-goods segment in Canada. In 2004, Tim's Horton's celebrated its 40th anniversary and was also named *Marketing Magazine*'s Marketer of the Year. It received this award because of its product innovation, unpretentious advertising, smart partnerships, and its status as a national icon. As Rob Wilson, marketing professor at Ryerson University notes, "People don't go for coffee at Tim Horton's, they go for a Tim's."[1]

When NHL great, Tim Horton, opened his first namesake location in Hamilton in 1964, it was simply a coffee and donut shop. Today, Tim Horton's has grown into a fast-casual and drive-thru retail giant that offers convenient, great-tasting options for breakfast, lunch, and dinner. In addition to the original coffee-and-donut cornerstone products, the menu now consists of a variety of sandwiches, soups, stews, and a wide variety of baked goods, such as Timbits, muffins, and cookies. To ensure the quality of its products, Tim's now operates its own coffee-roasting facility in Rochester, New York. It also runs a 300 000 square foot bakery, known as Maidstone Bakery in Brantford, Ontario. This facility allows the company to produce fresh baked goods delivered in just a few minutes at Tim Horton stores.

In addition to these vertical integration efforts, Tim Horton's is also embarking on an expansion plan that will result in over 3500 Canadian locations in the next five to seven years. It is also expanding south of the border, where there are already over 250 Tim Horton's in New York, Ohio, Michigan, and New England. The company plans to have over 500 stores in the United States by the end of 2007. As a wholly owned subsidiary of Wendy's International, Tim Horton's now accounts for 45 percent of Wendy's total profits while generating just 25 percent of Wendy's total revenues.

Professor Wilson attributes Tim Horton's retail success to its superb strategy and unbelievable execution. He insists that Tim's has provided quality products, great pricing, excellent locations, and promotions. Importantly, he argues, that Tim Horton's delivers what it says it will deliver! Doug Fisher, president of FHG International, a food-service consultancy firm, believes that Tim Horton's success is also tied to the fact that it has associated itself with Canada—that it is down-home Canadiana!

David McMullen, vice-president of regional marketing and national promotions at Tim Horton's, adds that the company's success is also based on the tenets of good and friendly service as well as community involvement. Currently, Tim sponsors the Brier—the Canadian Curling Championship, as well as Timbit hockey and soccer programs involving more than 100 000 kids across the country.[2]

retailing
All activities involved in selling, renting, and providing goods and services to ultimate consumers for personal, family, or household use.

Tim Horton's is just one example of many dynamic and exciting retailers you may encounter today in the Canadian marketplace. This chapter examines the concept of **retailing**, which includes all activities involved in selling, renting, and providing goods and services to ultimate consumers for personal, family, or household use. We will look at the critical role of retailing in the marketplace and the challenging decisions retailers face as they strive to create value and customer satisfaction. In the channel of distribution, retailing is where the customer meets the product.

■ ■ ■
THE VALUE OF RETAILING

Retailing is an important marketing activity. Not only do producers and consumers meet through retailing actions, but retailing also creates customer value and has a significant impact on the economy. In fact, retailing is critically important to the Canadian and global economies. Retail sales in Canada are expected to surpass $350 billion in 2006. And the retail sector also employs over two million people in Canada, making it the second-largest labour force in the country.[3] Major retail categories in Canada include automotive, food, furniture, and clothing.

The magnitude of retail sales is hard to imagine. Some of Canada's top retailers have annual sales revenues that surpass the gross domestic product (GDP) of several nation-states. For example, Canada's top three grocery store rivals (Loblaws, Sobeys, and A&P Dominion) have combined sales greater than the GDP of North Korea; Canada's largest department store companies (The Hudson's Bay Company, Wal-Mart Canada, and Sears Canada) have combined sales greater than the GDP of both Iceland and Honduras.

Outside of Canada, large retailers include Daiei in Japan, Pinault-Printemps in France, Karstadtquelle in Germany, and Marks & Spencer in the United Kingdom. In emerging economies, such as China and Mexico, a combination of local and global retailers are evolving. Wal-Mart, for example, now has stores in China, Germany, Mexico, and the United Kingdom.

form of ownership
Distinguishes retail outlets based on whether individuals, corporate chains, or contractual systems own the outlet.

level of service
The degree of service provided to the customer by self-, limited-, and full-service retailers.

merchandise line
How many different types of products a store carries and in what assortment.

Classifying Retail Outlets

For manufacturers, consumers, and the economy, retailing is an important component of marketing that has several variations. Because of the large number of alternative forms of retailing, it is easier to understand the differences among retail institutions by recognizing that outlets can be classified in several ways. First, **form of ownership** distinguishes retail outlets based on whether individuals, corporate chains, or contractual systems own the outlet. Second, **level of service** is used to describe the degree of service provided to the customer. Finally, the type of **merchandise line** describes how many different types of products a store carries and in what assortment. A more in-depth discussion of the alternative types of outlets follows.

Form of Ownership

Independent Retailer   One of the most common forms of retail ownership is the independent business, owned by an individual. The independent retailer accounts for over 60 percent of total retail trade in Canada. Small retailers tend to dominate in bakeries, sporting goods, jewellery, and gift stores. They are also popular retailers of auto supplies, books, paint, flowers, and women's accessories. The advantage of this form of ownership for the owner is that he or she can be his or her own boss. For customers, the independent store can offer convenience, quality, personal service, and lifestyle compatibility.

Corporate Chain   A second form of ownership, the corporate chain, involves multiple outlets under common ownership. If you have ever shopped at The Bay, Zellers, or Loblaws, you have shopped at a chain outlet.

In a chain operation, centralization in decision making and purchasing is common. Chain stores have advantages in dealing with manufacturers, particularly as the size of the chain grows. A large chain can bargain with a manufacturer to obtain good service or volume discounts on orders. The buying power of chains allows them to offer consumers competitive prices on merchandise. Wal-Mart's large volume makes it a strong negotiator with manufacturers of most products. Consumers also benefit in dealing with chains because there are multiple outlets with similar merchandise and consistent management policies.

Retailing has become a high-tech business for many large chains. Wal-Mart, for example, has developed a sophisticated inventory management and cost-control system that allows rapid price changes for each product in every store. In addition, such stores as Wal-Mart and Target are implementing pioneering new technologies, such as radio frequency identification (RFID) tags, to improve the quality of information available about products. The accompanying Marketing NewsNet box describes the trend.[4]

Contractual System   Contractual systems involve independently owned stores that band together to act like a chain. The three kinds described in Chapter 14 are retailer-sponsored cooperatives, wholesaler-sponsored voluntary chains, and franchises. One retailer-sponsored cooperative is Guardian Drugs, which consists of neighbourhood pharmacies that all agree to buy their products from the same wholesaler. In this way, members can take advantage of volume discounts commonly available to chains and also give the impression of being a large chain, which may be

---

MARKETING NEWSNET ⚠ **IDEAS AHEAD**   Say Good-Bye to Bar Codes!

New technologies are continually changing the marketing and retailing environment. The next big thing, however, may be tiny microchips known as radio frequency identification (RFID) tags, which are so small and inexpensive that they can be attached to pallets, cases, cartons, or even individual items. The new technology allows manufacturers, distributors, and retailers to collect detailed information about a product's origin, distribution path, and price, eliminating the need for the current bar codes used to track goods. Wal-

Mart and Target have already mandated that their top vendors begin using RFID tags, and some manufacturers, such as Gillette, Procter & Gamble, Nestlé, and Unilever, are actively involved in implementing the technology. Some companies, such as Hewlett-Packard and Sun Microsystems, are also getting involved, offering consulting services to companies that are developing RFID technology strategies. Experts predict that RFID could soon be used in driver's licences, passports, and even money.

viewed more favourably by some consumers. Wholesaler-sponsored voluntary chains, such as Ace Hardware and Independent Grocers' Alliance (IGA), try to achieve similar benefits.

As noted in Chapter 14, in a franchise system an individual or firm (the franchisee) contracts with a parent company (the franchisor) to set up a business or retail outlet. The franchisor usually assists in selecting the location, setting up the store or facility, advertising, and training personnel. The franchisee usually pays a one-time franchise fee and an annual royalty, usually tied to the franchise's sales. There are two general types of franchises: *business-format franchises,* such as McDonald's, Radio Shack (now Source), and Blockbuster, and *product-distribution franchises,* such as a Ford dealership or a Coca-Cola distributor. In business-format franchising, the franchisor provides step-by-step procedures for most aspects of the business and guidelines for the most likely decisions a franchisee will face.

Franchising is attractive because it offers an opportunity for people to enter a well-known, established business for which managerial advice is provided. Also, the franchise fee may be less than the cost of setting up an independent business.

Franchise fees paid to the franchisor can range from $10 000 for a Subway franchise to $45 000 for a McDonald's restaurant franchise. When the fees are combined with other costs, such as real estate and equipment, however, the total investment can be much higher. Figure 15–1 shows the top five franchises in North America, as rated by *Entrepreneur* magazine, based on such factors as size, financial strength, stability, years in business, and costs.[5] By selling franchises, an organization reduces the cost of expansion but loses some control. A good franchisor, however, will maintain strong control of the outlets in terms of delivery and presentation of merchandise and try to enhance recognition of the franchise name. Canadian entrepreneurs have plenty of franchise opportunities, from automotive care to wine making. You can check it out at the Canadian Franchise Association Web site (www.cfa.ca). Or visit CanadianFranchisees.com for the latest news on hot franchises in Canada.

Level of Service

Even though most customers perceive little variation in retail outlets by form of ownership, differences among retailers are more obvious in terms of level of service. In some department stores, very few services are provided. Some warehouse grocery stores have customers bag the food themselves. Other retail outlets, such as Holt Renfrew, provide a wide range of customer services from gift wrapping to wardrobe consultation.

■ **FIGURE 15–1** ■
The top five franchises in North America

FRANCHISE	TYPE OF BUSINESS	TOTAL STARTUP COST	NUMBER OF FRANCHISES
Subway	Sandwich restaurant	$86 000–213 000	21 000
Curves	Women-only fitness centre	$36 000–43 000	7500
Quizno's	Sandwich restaurant	$208 000–244 000	3500
7-Eleven	Convenience store	$65 000–227 000	25 800
Jackson Hewitt Tax Service	Income tax preparation	$47 000–75 000	4900

Self-Service

Self-service is at the extreme end of the level of service continuum because the customer performs many functions and little is provided by the outlet. Home building supply outlets and gas stations are often self-service. Warehouse stores, usually in buildings several times larger than a conventional store, are self-service with all nonessential customer services eliminated. Similarly, many gas stations are self-service. New forms of self-service are being developed in grocery stores, airlines, and hotels. For example, when you fly, you can often choose to use self-service kiosks to check in, find a seat, and print a boarding pass without the help of an attendant.

Limited Service   Limited-service outlets provide some services, such as return of credit and merchandise, but not others, such as return of custom-made clothes. General merchandise stores, such as Wal-Mart and Zellers, are usually considered limited-service outlets. Customers are responsible for most shopping activities, although salespeople are available in such departments as consumer electronics, jewellery, and lawn and garden.

Full-Service   Full-service retailers, which include most specialty stores and some department stores, provide many services to their customers. Services can include more salespeople on the floor or delivering purchases to customers' homes. Often, this full-service strategy is a competitive advantage for such stores.[6]

Merchandise Line

depth of product line
The store carries a large assortment of each item.

breadth of product line
The variety of different items a store carries.

Retail outlets also vary by their merchandise lines, the key distinction being the breadth and depth of the items offered to customers (Figure 15–2). **Depth of product line** means that the store carries a large assortment of each item, such as a shoe store that offers running shoes, dress shoes, and children's shoes. **Breadth of product line** refers to the variety of different items a store carries.

Depth of Line   Stores that carry a considerable assortment (depth) of a related line of items are limited-line stores. Black's photography stores carry considerable depth in photography equipment. Stores that carry tremendous depth in one primary line of merchandise are single-line stores. Victoria's Secret carries great depth in women's lingerie. Both limited- and single-line stores are often referred to as *specialty outlets*.

Specialty discount outlets focus on one type of product, such as electronics, business supplies, or books, at very competitive prices. These outlets are referred to in the trade as *category killers* because they often dominate the market.

■ FIGURE 15–2 ■
Breadth versus depth of merchandise lines

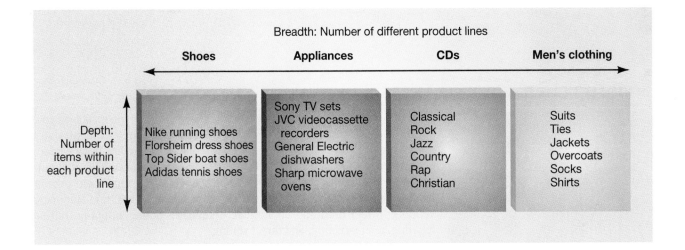

Breadth: Number of different product lines

	Shoes	Appliances	CDs	Men's clothing
Depth: Number of items within each product line	Nike running shoes Florsheim dress shoes Top Sider boat shoes Adidas tennis shoes	Sony TV sets JVC videocassette recorders General Electric dishwashers Sharp microwave ovens	Classical Rock Jazz Country Rap Christian	Suits Ties Jackets Overcoats Socks Shirts

scrambled merchandising
Offering several unrelated product lines in a single retail store.

hypermarket
A large store (more than 200 000 square feet) offering consumers everything in a single outlet.

Breadth of Line   Stores that carry a broad product line, with limited depth, are referred to as *general merchandise stores*. For example, large department stores carry a wide range of different types of products but not unusual sizes. The breadth and depth of merchandise lines are important decisions for a retailer. Traditionally, outlets carried related lines of goods. Today, however, **scrambled merchandising**, offering several unrelated product lines in a single store, is common. The modern drugstore carries food, camera equipment, magazines, paper products, toys, small hardware items, and pharmaceuticals. Supermarkets rent video tapes, develop film, and sell flowers.

A form of scrambled merchandising, the **hypermarket**, has been successful in Europe. These hypermarkets are large stores (more than 200 000 square feet) based on a simple concept: Offer consumers everything in a single outlet, eliminating the need to stop at more than one location. The stores provide variety, quality, and low price for food and groceries and general merchandise. In France, the concept is so successful that hypermarkets maintain a 51-percent share of the grocery market. Carrefour, one of the largest hypermarket retailers, is introducing private-label items to help keep prices low, while it also adds upscale touches, such as in-store butchers and extensive cheese selections.[7]

In North America, retailers discovered that many shoppers were uncomfortable with the huge size of hypermarkets. So, they developed a variation of the hypermarket called the *supercentre*, which combines a typical merchandise store with a full-size grocery. These supercentres tend to range in size between 100 000 and 200 000 square feet. Loblaws, one of Canada's top retail grocery chains, uses the supercentre concept very successfully. Its McCowan Market in Markham, Ontario, is 115 000 square feet and offers its traditional grocery line along with other merchandise selection, including housewares, office supplies, cosmetics, and electronics. Wal-Mart is also a major player in the supercentre category.

Scrambled merchandising is convenient for consumers because it eliminates the number of stops required in a shopping trip. However, for the retailer, this merchandising policy means there is competition between very dissimilar types of retail outlets, or **intertype competition**. A local bakery may compete with a department store, discount outlet, or even a local gas station. Scrambled merchandising and intertype competition make it more difficult to be a retailer.

intertype competition
Competition between very dissimilar types of retail outlets.

CONCEPT CHECK

1. Centralized decision making and purchasing are an advantage of _____ ownership.

2. What are some examples of new forms of self-service retailers?

3. Would a shop for big men's clothes carrying pants in sizes 40 to 60 have a broad or deep product line?

■ ■ ■
NONSTORE RETAILING

Most of the retailing examples discussed earlier in the chapter, such as corporate chains, department stores, and limited- and single-line specialty stores, involve store retailing. Many retailing activities today, however, are not limited to sales in a store. Nonstore retailing occurs outside a retail outlet through activities that involve varying levels of customer and retailer involvement. Figure 15–3 shows six forms of nonstore retailing: automatic vending, direct mail and catalogues, television home shopping, online retailing, telemarketing, and direct selling.

■ FIGURE 15-3 ■

Forms of nonstore retailing

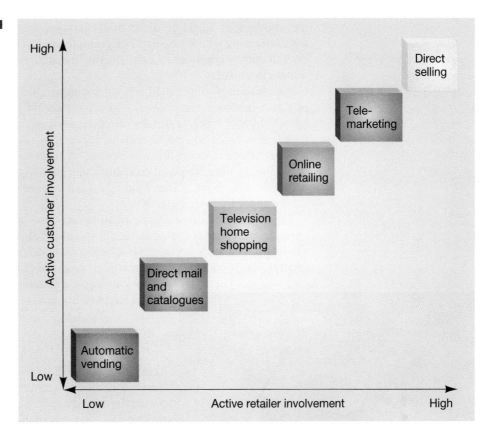

Automatic Vending

Nonstore retailing includes vending machines, which make it possible to serve customers when and where stores cannot. Maintenance and operating costs are high, and so product prices in vending machines tend to be higher than those in stores. Typically, small convenience products are available in vending machines. In fact, most of the machines in use in Canada are soft-drink machines.

Improved technology is making vending machines easier to use by reducing the need for cash. Many machines already accept credit cards, and cashless purchases using cell phones are likely in the near future. Japan's largest mobile phone company, DoCoMo, is working with Sony to introduce cell phones equipped with an electronic cash system called Edy (*e*uro, *d*ollar, *y*en), which will allow consumers to charge vending machine purchases to their cell phone accounts. Another improvement in vending machines is the use of wireless technology to notify vendors when their machines are empty. Nestlé, for example, is installing hundreds of ice cream vending machines in France and England that send wireless messages to supply-truck drivers. Finally, one of the biggest developments in vending is being tested by Vision Inc.—it is experimenting with huge vending machines for parking lots that will be fully automated convenience stores.[8]

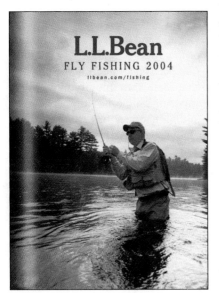

Direct Mail and Catalogues

Direct mail and catalogue retailing is attractive because it eliminates the cost of a store and clerks. In addition, it improves marketing efficiency through segmentation and targeting and creates customer value by providing a fast and convenient means of making a purchase. Canadians have been increasing the amount they spend on direct mail catalogue merchandise. Internationally, catalogue shopping is also popular. For example, Swedish furniture retailer IKEA delivers 130 million copies of its catalogue to 36 countries in 28 languages, including five million to Canada.[9]

As consumers' direct mail and catalogue purchases have increased, the numbers of direct mailings, catalogues, and products sold have also increased. A typical household now receives dozens of catalogues per year. The competition, combined with higher paper and postal costs, however, has caused direct retailers to focus on proven customers rather than "prospects." A successful approach now used by many catalogue retailers is to send specialty catalogues to market niches identified in their databases. L.L. Bean, a longstanding catalogue retailer, has developed an individual catalogue for fly fishing enthusiasts.

Creative forms of catalogue retailing are also being developed. Hallmark, for example, offers cards for businesses in its colourful 32-page "Business Expressions" catalogue. Victoria's Secret mails as many as 45 catalogues a year to its customers to generate mail-order and 800-number business and to increase traffic in its 900 stores.

Many catalogue retailers, such as Sharper Image, now accept telephone orders, mail orders, and online orders!

Television Home Shopping

Television home shopping is possible when consumers watch a shopping channel on which products are displayed; orders are then placed over the telephone or on the Internet. Two popular programs, the Canadian Home Shopping Network and QVC, reach millions of Canadian households. Because these programs have traditionally attracted women over 35, other such programs as MTV Network's "House of Style," with host Molly Sims, are designed to attract a younger audience. A limitation of TV shopping has been the lack of buyer–seller interaction and the inability of consumers to control the items they see. But new Internet technologies now allow consumers to simultaneously shop, chat, and interact with their favourite show host while watching TV.

Online Retailing

Online retailing allows consumers to search for, evaluate, and order products through the Internet. For many consumers, the advantage of this form of retailing, sometimes called *e-tailing*, are 24-hour access, the ability to comparison shop, in-home privacy, and variety. Studies of online shoppers indicated that men were initially more likely than women to buy something online. As the number of online-buying households increased, however, the profile of the Canadian online shopper has changed. Currently, the online buyer is far more likely to be female, married, and with kids.[10] Many Internet-only businesses, or pure-play online retailers, have actually failed or consolidated. Today, there has been a melding of traditional and online retailers—"bricks and clicks"—that are using experiences from both approaches to provide the customer better value, better experiences, and increased satisfaction. Average annual online spending in Canada is $1200 per capita and total online sales in Canada are currently estimated at $4 billion.[11]

Online retail purchases can occur in several ways. Consumers can pay a fee to become a member of an online discount service. Or, they can use a shopping "bot," such as MySimon (www.mysimon.com). Or, they can go directly to online malls or online shopping directories (portals), such as www.retailcanada.com, which features more than 7000 Canadian merchants. Online retailing can also be done via auction on such sites as www.ebay.ca. And, finally, you could simply go to a specific online retailer's site. Currently, 25 percent of all Canadian retailers have a Web site and over 85 percent of large Canadian retailers sell via the Internet.[12] As the Marketing News-Net box points out, a popular online retail phenomenon is the Canadian online pharmacy. Internet sales of prescription drugs to American consumers is now a major retailing industry.[13]

Online retailers are working hard at improving the online retailing experience by adding experiential or interactive activities on their Web sites. Research shows that almost 75 percent of Canadians treasure the social aspect of shopping, and so e-tailers are integrating their online experiences with the real thing.[14] For example, the WebLink box describes how apparel stores use virtual models to involve consumers in the purchase process and help with product selection.[15] Similarly, car manufacturers, such as BMW, Mercedes, and Jaguar, encourage Web site visitors to "build" a vehicle by selecting interior and exterior colours, packages, and options and then view the customized virtual car. In addition, the merger of television home shopping and online retailing is possible through TV-based Web platforms, such as Microsoft's MSN TV. Finally, owning a computer is not a necessity for online retailing. There are 15 000 Internet cafes in 171 countries that provide guests with access to the Internet.

MARKETING NEWSNET

Canada's New Retail Industry: Online Pharmacies

Hundreds of thousands of American consumers now buy their prescription drugs online from Canadian online pharmacies. Business is booming because American consumers are attracted by lower Canadian drug prices and the lower Canadian dollar. It is estimated that the online pharmacy industry is valued at $700 million to $1 billion, with Americans receiving more than two million packages of prescription drugs last year from these Canadian online retail pharmacies. There are now over 100 online pharmacies in Canada, with more than one-half based in Manitoba, including such firms as RxNorth.com and Crossborderpharmacy.com. It is estimated that between 10 and 20 percent of Manitoba's pharmacists now work for an Internet or online pharmacy.

Buying through Canadian online pharmacies can mean substantial cost savings for the American consumer. For example, Zoloft, a popular depression medication can cost over $233 for 100 tablets in the United States but only $165 in Canada, saving over $67. Zocor, a cholesterol medication, would cost over $383 dollars for 100 tablets in the United States, but in Canada, it costs only $205. There are several reasons for the price differentials.

First, the exchange rate plays a role. Second, Canadian drug companies cannot sell their products directly to consumers. In the United States, however, drug companies spend billions of dollars on direct-to-consumer advertising, and that cost gets passed along to the American consumer. Third, there are drug price controls in Canada. The Patented Medicine Prices Review Board reviews drug prices and enacts price caps for patented drugs and medicines.

However, while American consumers love our online pharmacies, many government officials, on both sides of the border, as well as the pharmaceutical companies vehemently oppose them. In fact, some major drug companies have curtailed their supplies to Canadian pharmacies. And Canadian Health Minister Ujjal Dosanjh is attempting to enact new legislation that would block the online pharmacies from selling to American citizens. Part of the legislation would prevent Canadian doctors from co-signing prescriptions for American patients without examining them. If this legislation were enacted, it would seriously hurt the viability of this new industry. It remains to be seen whether or not this new industry has a future.

Shopping online has many advantages: the convenience of 24-hour access, easy price comparisons, no parking hassles, and trying clothes on in the privacy of your home. That's right, now you can "build" a virtual model that reflects your body

type and try on any clothing combination to see how it would look and fit. Want to try it? Go to www.landsend.com, click on My Model, answer a few questions, and pick out some clothes. So . . . how do you look?!

Telemarketing

telemarketing

Using the telephone to interact with and sell directly to consumers.

Another form of nonstore retailing, called **telemarketing**, involves using the telephone to interact with and sell directly to consumers. Compared with direct mailing, telemarketing is often viewed as a more efficient means of targeting consumers. Insurance companies, brokerage firms, and newspapers have often used this form of retailing as a way to cut costs but still maintain access to their customers. According to the Canadian Marketing Association, annual telemarketing sales exceed $16 billion.[16]

The telemarketing industry has gone through some changes as a result of past and proposed legislation related to telephone solicitations. Such issues as consumer privacy, industry standards, and ethical guidelines have encouraged discussion among consumer groups, government, and businesses. New legislation and regulation are evolving to provide a balance between consumer privacy and the right to engage in ethical business practices.

Direct Selling

Direct selling, sometimes called door-to-door retailing, involves direct sales of goods and services to consumers through personal interactions and demonstrations in their homes or offices. A variety of companies, including familiar names, such as Fuller Brush, Avon, World Book, and Mary Kay Cosmetics, have created a multi-billion-dollar industry by providing consumers with personalized service and convenience. In Canada, however, sales have been declining as retail chains, such as Wal-Mart, begin to carry similar products at discount prices and as the increasing number of dual-career households reduces the number of potential buyers at home.

In response to the changes, many direct-selling retailers are expanding into other markets. Avon, for example, already has four million sales representatives in 137 countries, including Mexico, Poland, Argentina, and China.[17] Similarly, other retailers, such as Amway, Herbalife, and Electrolux, are rapidly expanding. More than 70 percent of Amway's $7 billion in sales now comes from outside North America, and sales in Japan alone exceed sales in North America.[18] Direct selling is likely to continue to grow in markets where the lack of effective distribution channels increases the importance of door-to-door convenience and where the lack of consumer knowledge about products and brands will increase the need for a person-to-person approach.[19]

CONCEPT CHECK

1. Successful catalogue retailers often send _____ catalogues to _____ markets identified in their databases.

2. How are retailers increasing consumer interest and involvement in online retailing?

3. Where are direct selling retail sales growing? Why?

■ ■ ■
RETAILING STRATEGY

This section identifies how a retailer develops and implements a retailing strategy by positioning the store and taking specific retailing mix actions. Figure 15–4 identifies the relationship between positioning and the retailing mix.

Positioning a Retail Store

The classification alternatives presented in the previous sections help determine one store's position relative to its competitors.

retail positioning matrix
Positions retail outlets on two dimensions: breadth of product line and value added.

Retail Positioning Matrix   The **retail positioning matrix** was developed by the MAC Group, Inc., a management consulting firm.[20] This matrix positions retail outlets on two dimensions: breadth of product line and value added. As defined previously, breadth of product line is the range of products sold through each outlet. The second dimension, *value added*, includes such elements as location (as with 7-Eleven stores), product reliability (as with Holiday Inn or McDonald's), or prestige (as with Birks).

The retail positioning matrix in Figure 15–5 shows four possible positions. An organization can be successful in any position, but unique strategies are required within each quadrant. Consider the four stores shown in the matrix:

1. The Bay has high value added and a broad product line. Retailers in this quadrant pay great attention to store design and product lines. Merchandise often has a high margin of profit and is of high quality. The stores in this position typically provide high levels of service.

■ **FIGURE 15–4** ■

Elements of a retailing strategy

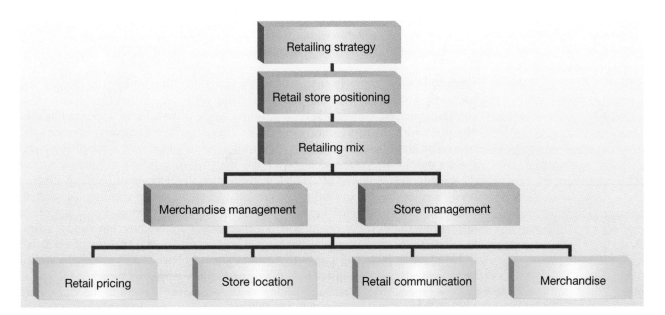

■ FIGURE 15-5 ■

Retail positioning matrix

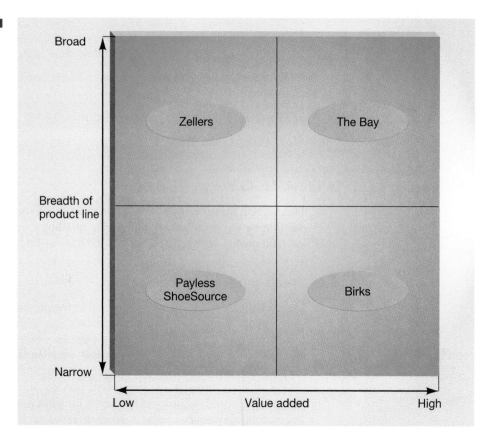

2. Zellers has low value added and a broad line. Zellers and similar firms typically trade a lower price for increased volume in sales. Retailers in this position focus on price with low service levels and an image of being a place for good buys.

3. Birks has high value added and a narrow line. Retailers of this type typically sell a very restricted range of products that are of high-status quality. Customers are also provided with high levels of service.

4. Payless ShoeSource has low value added and a narrow line. Such retailers are specialty mass merchandisers. Payless, for example, carries attractively priced shoes for the entire family. These outlets appeal to value-conscious consumers. Economies of scale are achieved through centralized advertising, merchandising, buying, and distribution. Stores are usually the same in design, layout, and merchandise; hence, they are often referred to as "cookie-cutter" stores.

Keys to Positioning   To successfully position a store, it must have an identity that has some advantages over the competitors and yet is recognized by consumers. A company can have outlets in several positions on the matrix, but this approach is usually done with different store names. The Hudson's Bay Company, for example, owns The Bay department stores (with high value added and a broad line) and Zellers stores (low value added and a broad line). Shifting from one box in the retail positioning matrix to another is also possible, but all elements of retailing strategy must be re-examined. In fact, as the competitive landscape in retailing has shifted, Zellers has now responded and adjusted its positioning by altering several aspects of its retailing strategy. For example, new Zellers stores are brighter, have wider aisles, have tasteful cosmetic counters, take-out at in-store diners, and an array of exclusive fashion brands, including a new line of furniture and home décor products by Alfred Sung Home Brand. So, instead of occupying the low value and broad line space as seen in Figure 15–5, Zellers is adding value. Moreover, Zellers at the Cloverdale Mall in Toronto, at approximately 100 000 square feet, is supersized like its competitor Wal-mart and has a grocery section, just like Wal-mart. Hudson's Bay Company, the parent of Zellers, says it plans to operate a slimmed-down fleet of renovated stores designed to the 100 000 square feet prototype at Cloverdale.[21]

Retailing Mix

retailing mix
Activities related to managing the store and the merchandise in the store—including retail pricing, store location, retail communication, and merchandise.

In developing retailing strategy, managers work with the **retailing mix**, which includes activities related to managing the store and the merchandise in the store. The retailing mix is similar to the marketing mix and includes retail pricing, store location, retail communication, and merchandise.

Retail Pricing   In setting prices for merchandise, retailers must decide on the markup, markdown, and timing for markdowns. As mentioned in the appendix to Chapter 13 (Appendix B), the *markup* refers to how much should be added to the cost the retailer paid for a product to reach the final selling price. Retailers decide on the *original markup*, but by the time the product is sold, they end up with a *maintained markup*. The original markup is the difference between retailer cost and initial selling price. When products do not sell as quickly as anticipated, their price is reduced. The difference between the final selling price and retailer cost is the maintained markup, which is also called the *gross margin*.

Discounting a product, or taking a *markdown*, occurs when the product does not sell at the original price and an adjustment is necessary. Often, new models or styles force the price of existing models to be marked down. Discounts may also be used to increase demand for complementary products.[22] For example, retailers might take a markdown on stereos to increase sales of CDs or reduce the price of cake mix to generate frosting purchases. The *timing* of a markdown can be important. Many retailers take a markdown as soon as sales fall off to free up valuable shelf space and cash. However, other stores delay markdowns to discourage bargain hunters and maintain an image of quality. There is no clear answer, but retailers must consider how the timing might affect future sales.

Although most retailers plan markdowns, many retailers use price discounts as part of their regular merchandising policy. Wal-Mart and Home Depot, for example, emphasize consistently low prices and eliminate most markdowns with a strategy often called *everyday low pricing*. Because consumers often use price as an indicator of product quality, however, the brand name of the product and the image of the store become important decision factors in these situations. Another strategy, *everyday fair pricing*, is advocated by retailers that may not offer the lowest price but try to create value for customers through service and the total buying experience.[23] A special issue for retailers trying to keep prices low is **shrinkage**, or theft of merchandise by customers and employees.[24]

shrinkage
Breakage and theft of merchandise by customers and employees.

off-price retailing
Selling brand-name merchandise at lower than regular prices.

Off-price retailing is a retail pricing practice that has become quite common. **Off-price retailing** involves selling brand-name merchandise at lower than regular prices. The difference between the off-price retailer and a discount store is that off-price merchandise is bought by the retailer from manufacturers with excess inventory at prices below wholesale prices, while the discounter buys at full wholesale price (but takes less of a markup than do traditional department stores). Because of this difference in the way merchandise is purchased by the retailer, selection at an off-price retailer is unpredictable, and searching for bargains has become a popular activity for many consumers. Savings to the consumer at off-price retailers are reported as high as 70 percent off the prices of a traditional department store.[25]

There are several variations of off-price retailing. One is the warehouse club. These large stores (more than 100 000 square feet) began as rather stark outlets with no elaborate displays, customer service, or home delivery. They require an annual membership fee (usually $25) for the privilege of shopping there. While a typical Zellers store stocks 30 000 items, warehouse clubs carry about 3500 items and usually stock just one brand name of appliance or food product. Service is minimal, and customers usually must pay by cash or cheque. However, the extremely competitive pricing of merchandise makes warehouse clubs attractive. Some major warehouse clubs you may be familiar with include Wal-Mart's Sam's Club, BJ's Wholesale Club, and Costco. Sales of these off-price retailers have grown dramatically over the past decade.

A second variation is the outlet store. Factory outlets, such as Van Heusen Factory Store, Bass Shoe Outlet, and Oneida Factory Store, offer products for 25 to 30 percent off the suggested retail price. Manufacturers use the stores to clear excess merchandise and to reach consumers who focus on value shopping. Some retail outlets, such as Brooks Brothers Outlet Store, allow retailers to sell excess merchandise and still maintain an image of offering merchandise at full price in their primary store. Experts expect the next trend to combine the various types of off-price retailers in "value-retail centres."[26]

A third variation of off-price retailing is offered by single-price, or extreme value, retailers, such as Family Dollar, Dollar General, and Dollar Tree. These stores average about 6000 square feet in size and attract customers who want value and a "corner store" environment rather than a large supercentre experience. Some experts predict extraordinary growth of these types of retailers.[27]

Store Location   A second aspect of the retailing mix involves deciding where to locate the store and how many stores to have. Department stores, which started downtown in most cities, have followed customers to the suburbs, and in recent years, more stores have been opened in large regional malls. Most stores today are near several others in one of five settings: the central business district, the regional centre, the community shopping centre, the strip, or the power centre.

The **central business district** is the oldest retail setting, the community's downtown area. Until the regional outflow to suburbs, it was the major shopping area, but the suburban population has grown at the expense of the downtown area. However, recently, there has been some downtown revitalization, with even some "big box " retailers, such as Home Depot and Costco, locating in the downtown core. But some consumers are put off by big-box stores and large department stores. So, some downtowns are revitalizing themselves by offering smaller boutiques where product quality and customer service are the focus.

Regional shopping centres consist of 50 to 150 stores that typically attract customers who live or work within an 8- to 16-km range. These large shopping areas often contain two or three anchor stores, which are well-known national or regional stores, such as Sears and The Bay. The largest variation of a regional centre is the West Edmonton Mall in Alberta. This shopping centre is a conglomerate of 600 stores, six amusement centres, 110 restaurants, and a 355-room Fantasyland Hotel.

Another new concept in regional shopping centres is Vaughan Mills, a 1.2 million square foot complex with more than 200 retailers and a unique merchandising concept. It is the first new enclosed regional shopping centre built in Canada in more than a decade. It is distinctive in that it is organized into six "themed neighbourhoods" each emphasizing an aspect of Ontario's cultures. One focuses on urban cities and contains urban youth-oriented retailers, such as Bluenotes and West 49. Another focuses on fashion and houses stores, such as Aritzia and BCBG Max Azria Outlet. The complex also houses Bass Pro Shops Outdoor World—which features an indoor trout pond, NASCAR Speedpark go-cart track, and the largest Tommy Hilfiger outlet in the world.

A more limited approach to retail location is the **community shopping centre**, which typically has one primary store (usually a department store branch) and often about 20 to 40 smaller outlets. Generally, these centres serve a population of consumers who are within a 10- to 20-minute drive.

Not every suburban store is located in a shopping mall. Many neighbourhoods have clusters of stores, referred to as a **strip location**, to serve people who are

---

central business district
The oldest retail setting, the community's downtown area.

regional shopping centres
Consist of 50 to 150 stores that typically attract customers who live within an 8- to 16-km range, often containing two or three anchor stores.

community shopping centre
A retail location that typically has one primary store (usually a department store branch) and 20 to 40 smaller outlets, serving a population of consumers who are within a 10- to 20-minute drive.

strip location
A cluster of stores serving people who live within a 5- to 10-minute drive.

power centre
A huge shopping strip with
multiple anchor (or national)
stores, a convenient location,
and a supermarket.

within a 5- to 10-minute drive. Gas station, hardware, laundry, grocery, and pharmacy outlets are commonly found in a strip location. Unlike the larger shopping centres, the composition of these stores is usually unplanned. A variation of the strip shopping location is called the **power centre**, which is a huge shopping strip with multiple anchor (or national) stores. Power centres are seen as having the convenient location found in many strip centres and the additional power of national stores. These large strips often have two to five anchor stores and usually contain a supermarket, which brings the shopper to the power centre on a weekly basis.

Another trend in Canada is "off-mall retailing." It this case, retailers who traditionally locate in malls are building on stand-alone sites. For example, Sears Canada, a common anchor at malls has opened new-format stores across Canada away from the malls, while Hudson's Bay Company has also its launched Designer Depot outlets as free-standing stores.

Several new types of retail locations include carts, kiosks, (including electronic kiosks) and wall units. These forms of retailing have been popular in airports and mall common areas because they provide consumers with easy access and also provide rental income for the property owner. Retailers benefit from the relatively low cost compared with a regular store.

Retail Communication   A retailer's communication activities can play an important role in positioning a store and creating its image. While the traditional elements of communication and promotion are discussed in Chapter 17 (advertising) and Chapter 18 (personal selling), the message communicated by the many other elements of the retailing mix are also important.

Deciding on the image of a retail outlet is an important retailing mix factor that has been widely recognized and studied since the late 1950s. Pierre Martineau described image as "the way in which the store is defined in the shopper's mind," partly by its functional qualities and partly by an aura of psychological attributes.[28] In this definition, *functional* refers to mix such elements as price ranges, store layouts, and breadth and depth of merchandise lines. The psychological attributes are the intangibles, such as a sense of belonging, excitement, style, or warmth. Image has been found to include impressions of the corporation that operates the store, the category or type of store, the product categories in the store, the brands in each category, merchandise and service quality, and the marketing activities of the store.[29]

Closely related to the concept of image is the store's atmosphere or ambiance. Many retailers believe that sales are affected by layout, colour, lighting, and music in the store, as well as by how crowded it is. In addition, the physical surroundings that influence customers may affect the store's employees.[30] In creating the right image and atmosphere, a retail store tries to attract its target audience with what those consumers seek from the buying experience, and so the store will fortify the beliefs and the emotional reactions buyers are seeking.[31] Sears, for example, is attempting to shift from its appliance and tool image with advertising that speaks to all members of a family, emphasizing a broad range of brand-name merchandise and one-stop shopping.[32]

category management
An approach that assigns a
manager with the responsibility
for selecting all products
that consumers in a market
segment might view as
substitutes for each other,
with the objective of
maximizing sales and profits
in the category.

Merchandise   A final element of the retailing mix is the merchandise offering. Managing the breadth and depth of the product line requires retail buyers who are familiar with the needs of the target market and the alternative products available from the many manufacturers that might be interested in having a product available in the store. A popular approach to managing the assortment of merchandise today is called **category management**. This approach assigns a manager with the responsibility for selecting all products that consumers in a market segment might view as substitutes for each other, with the objective of maximizing sales and profits in the category. For example, a category manager might be responsible for shoes in a department store or paper products in a grocery store.

Many retailers are developing an advanced form of category management called *consumer marketing at retail* (CMAR). Recent surveys show that as part of their

CMAR programs, retailers are conducting research, analyzing the data to identify shopper problems, translating the data into retailing mix actions, executing shopper-friendly in-store programs, and monitoring the performance of the merchandise. Wal-Mart, for example, has used the approach to test baby-product and dollar-product categories. Some grocery stores, such as Safeway and Kroger, use the approach to determine the appropriate mix of brand name and private label products. Specialty retailer Barnes & Noble recently won a best practice award for its application of the approach to the selection, presentation, and promotion of magazines.[33]

CONCEPT CHECK

1. What are the two dimensions of the retail positioning matrix?

2. How does original markup differ from maintained markup?

3. A huge shopping strip with multiple anchor stores is a _____ centre.

■ ■ ■
THE CHANGING NATURE OF RETAILING

Retailing is the most dynamic aspect of a channel of distribution. Such stores as factory outlets show that new retailers are always entering the market, searching for a new position that will attract customers. The reason for this continual change is explained by two concepts: the wheel of retailing and the retail life cycle.

The Wheel of Retailing

wheel of retailing
A concept that describes how new retail outlets enter the market as low-status, low-margin stores and gradually add embellishments that raise their prices, and status. They now face a new low-status, low-margin operator, and the cycle starts to repeat itself.

The **wheel of retailing** describes how new forms of retail outlets enter the market.[34] Usually, they enter as low-status, low-margin stores, such as a drive-through hamburger stand with no indoor seating and a limited menu (Figure 15–6, box 1). Gradually, these outlets add fixtures and more embellishments to their stores (in-store seating, plants, and chicken sandwiches as well as hamburgers) to increase the

---

■ **FIGURE 15–6** ■■
The wheel of retailing

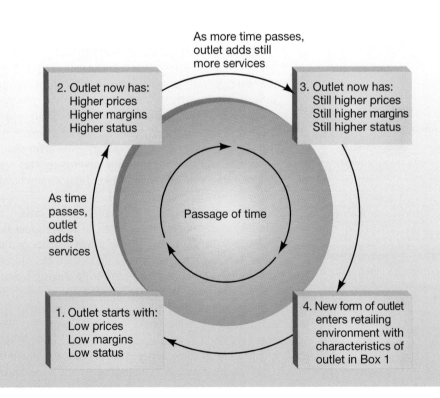

attractiveness for customers. With these additions, prices and status rise (see box 2). As time passes, these outlets add still more services, and their prices and status increase even further (see box 3). These retail outlets now face some new form of retail outlet that again appears as a low-status, low-margin operator (see box 4), and the wheel of retailing turns as the cycle starts to repeat itself.

In the 1950s, McDonald's and Burger King had very limited menus of hamburgers and french fries. Most stores had no inside seating for customers. Over time, the wheel of retailing for fast-food restaurants has turned. These chains have changed by altering their stores and expanding their menus. Today, McDonald's is testing new products, such as its all-white-meat Chicken McNuggets, chicken breast strips called Big Dippers, and the Go Active Happy Meal for adults; new fomats, such as its coffee, pastry, and sandwich outlets called McCafe; and new service options, such as wireless Internet connections.[35] These changes are leaving room for new forms of outlets that offer only the basics—burgers, fries, and cola, a drive-through window, and no inside seating. For still others, the wheel has come full circle. Taco Bell is now opening small, limited-offering outlets in gas stations, discount stores, or "wherever a burrito and a mouth might possibly intersect."

Discount stores were a major new retailing form in the 1960s and priced their products below those of department stores. As prices in discount stores rose, in the 1980s, they found themselves overpriced compared with a new form of retail outlet—the warehouse retailer. Today, off-price retailers and factory outlets are offering prices even lower than warehouses!

The Retail Life Cycle

retail life cycle
The process of growth and decline that retail outlets, like products, experience.

The process of growth and decline that retail outlets, like products, experience is described by the **retail life cycle**.[36] Figure 15–7 shows the retail life cycle and the position of various current forms of retail outlets on it. *Early growth* is the stage of

■ FIGURE 15–7 ■
The retail life cycle

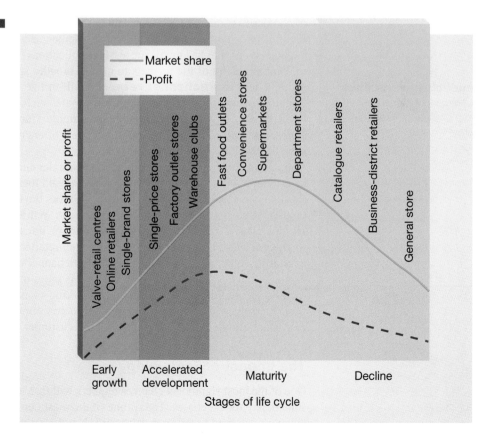

emergence of a retail outlet, with a sharp departure from existing competition. Market share rises gradually, although profits may be low because of startup costs. In the next stage, *accelerated development*, both market share and profit achieve their greatest growth rates. Usually, multiple outlets are established as companies focus on the distribution element of the retailing mix. In this stage, some later competitors may enter. Wendy's, for example, appeared on the hamburger chain scene almost 20 years after McDonald's had begun operation. The key goal for the retailer in this stage is to establish a dominant position in the fight for market share.

The battle for market share is usually fought before the *maturity* phase, and some competitors drop out of the market. New retail forms enter in the maturity phase, stores try to maintain their market share, and price discounting occurs. For example, when McDonald's introduced its Extra Value Meal, a discounted package of burger, fries, and drink, Wendy's followed with its 99¢ Value Menu.

The challenge facing retailers is to delay entering the *decline* stage, in which market share and profit fall rapidly. Specialty apparel retailers, such as The Gap, Benetton, and Ann Taylor, have noticed a decline in market share after a decade of growth. To prevent further decline, these retailers will need to find ways of discouraging their customers from moving to low-margin, mass-volume outlets or high-price, high-service boutiques.

■ ■ ■
FUTURE CHANGES IN RETAILING

Three exciting trends in retailing—the growth of multichannel retailing, the increasing impact of technology, and the dramatic changes in the way we shop—are likely to lead to many changes for retailers and consumers in the future.

Multichannel Retailing

The retailing formats described previously in this chapter represent an exciting menu of choices for creating customer value in the marketplace. Each format allows retailers to offer unique benefits and meet particular needs of various customer groups. While each format has many successful applications, retailers in the future are likely to combine many of the formats to offer a broader spectrum of benefits and experiences. These **multichannel retailers** will utilize and integrate a combination of traditional store formats and nonstore formats, such as catalogues, television, electronic kiosks, and online retailing.[37] For example, Canadian Tire markets via its retail stores, catalogues, and online, while Chapters offers customers both traditional retail stores as well as online shopping.

Integrated channels can make shopping simpler and more convenient. A consumer can research choices online or in a catalogue and then make a purchase online, over the telephone, or at the closest store. In addition, the use of multiple channels allows retailers to reach a broader profile of customers. While online retailing may cannibalize catalogue business to some degree, an online transaction costs about half as much to process as a catalogue order. Multichannel retailers also benefit from the synergy of sharing information among the different channel operations. Online retailers, for example, have recognized that the Internet is more of a transactional medium than a relationship-building medium and are working to find ways to complement traditional customer interactions. Importantly, to stay competitive, retailers must create a consistent cross-channel experience for the customer.[38]

The Impact of Technology

One of the most significant changes retailers will face in the future will be the way consumers pay for purchases. Today, one of the most convenient and popular methods of payment is a credit card or a debit card. However, these are being replaced by *smart*

multichannel retailers
Utilize and integrate a combination of traditional store formats and nonstore formats, such as catalogues, television, and online retailing.

cards, which store information on computer chips instead of magnetic strips. They hold information about bank accounts and amounts of available funds, and they even contain customer purchase information, such as airline seat preferences, clothing sizes, and even health information. Smart cards are already very popular in Europe and Asia with more than 35 million already in use. Benefits for consumers include faster service—a smart card transaction is much faster than having a cheque or credit card approved—and they are a convenient method of payment for small-dollar-amount-transactions.

Merchants also benefit because they save the 5 to 7 percent usually paid to credit card companies or funds lost in handling. New versions of smart cards are now available for use in the memory slot in cellphones, PDAs, and computers. But another new technology is also now available, called *biometric payment systems*, which use either thumbprint, fingerprint, or iris scanning as a way to identify a customer, and make a payment automatically from an established account. Read the Ethics and Social Responsibility Alert box about how biometric payments work and the possible dark side of this new technology.[39]

Changing Shopping Behaviour

In recent years, there has been a trend toward two types of shopping behaviour: chore shopping versus pleasure shopping. Chore shoppers are precision shoppers. They tend to be time-strapped and demand convenient hours and locations as well as the facility to do one-stop shopping. These shoppers are also tired of the old concept of putting the milk and eggs at the back of the store to force you to walk all the way back. Accordingly, some stores, such as Sobey's Metro Market, are catering to these chore shoppers. Metro Market is a 15 000 square foot market compared with a traditional 40 000 square foot Sobey's store. The store has fresh-prepared meals at the front, soup bar, bakery, and deli to appeal to the time-starved shopper.

On the other hand, there are the pleasure shoppers who want a "shopping experience," shopping that is emotionally satisfying. For example, the Liquor Control

---

ETHICS AND SOCIAL RESPONSIBILITY ALERT

Biometric Payment Systems: The Possible Dark Side

Makers of biometric payment systems assert that this technology has a big advantage over other payment systems: speed at the checkout counter. Here is how a biometric system works: (1) To enroll, a customer gives the retailer a blank cheque and valid ID to scan into a computer. (2) The customer then places each index finger on a tennis-ball-sized reader that captures fingerprints. (Other systems will use thumbprints or even scan your iris) (3) The customer selects a code to authorize debits from a checking account and to verify age. (4) Once enrolled, the customer makes purchases by placing a finger on the reader and entering a code (or PIN ID).

The finger scan biometric payment system is already being used in convenience stores and supermarket chains in the United States. Some experts predict these payment systems will be ubiquitous because they offer speed and convenience, two key things retail customers are looking for. Biometric technology, reportedly, can complete a transaction in less than 15 seconds, compared with the 65 seconds it takes to process a cheque and the 50 seconds to process a credit card. And retailers will have the added benefit of saving the fees they normally pay to credit card companies.

However, many people are concerned about possible abuses and privacy concerns revolving around this technology. For some people, a fingerprint only means one thing: a police record. And this is making people wary of the technology. In fact, Dollar Rent a Car used fingerprinting in the past to combat theft of its cars but had to stop this practice after widespread complaints by customers. Moreover, many privacy experts suggest that the biometric systems may be compromised and expose customers to identity theft. Some insist that you might be able to get a new social insurance card, but you cannot get new fingerprints!

What are your thoughts on biometric payment systems? Do the benefits outweigh the possible downside?

Board of Ontario (LCBO) is trying to create an emotional envelope around what it sells. Rather than simply selling liquor, LCBO tries to go further by marketing enjoyment to the customer. An outgrowth of this trend toward pleasure shopping is the retail concept of *lifestyle centres*—clusters of specialty retailers, along with theatres, restaurants, fountains, play areas, and green spaces. A lifestyle centre called Park Place in Barrie, Ontario, is trying to appeal to these pleasure shoppers who are seeking a total shopping experience.

A form of co-branding where two retailers share a location can actually cater to either type of shopper. For example, a chore shopper can shop at Wal-Mart and get a McDonald's meal on site, while a pleasure shopper can sip a Statrbuck's coffee while reading a book at Chapters. Either way, in Canada's competitive retail environment, the customer is king or queen. To survive and prosper, a retailer must cater to the customer by not only offering the right products at the right price, but they may also have to be time-savers, lifestyle gurus, entertainment experts, inspiration givers, or pleasure providers.

CONCEPT CHECK

1. According to the wheel of retailing, when a new retail form appears, how would you characterize its image?

2. Market share is usually fought out before the _____ stage of the retail life cycle.

3. What is a smart card?

■ ■ ■
CHAPTER IN REVIEW

1 *Explain the alternative ways to classify retail outlets.*
Retail outlets can be classified by form of ownership, level of service, and type of merchandise line. The forms of ownership include independent retailers, corporate chains, and contractual systems that include retailer-sponsored cooperatives, wholesaler-sponsored voluntary chains, and franchises. The levels of service include self-service, limited-service, and full-service outlets. Stores classified by their merchandise line include stores with depth, such as sporting good specialty stores, and stores with breadth, such as large department stores.

2 *Describe the many methods of nonstore retailing.*
Nonstore retailing includes automatic vending, direct mail and catalogues, television home shopping, online retailing, telemarketing, and direct selling. The methods of nonstore retailing vary by the level of involvement of the retailer and the level of involvement of the customer. Vending, for example, has low involvement, whereas both the consumer and the retailer have high involvement in direct selling.

3 *Classify retailers in terms of the retail positioning matrix.*
The retail positioning matrix positions retail outlets on two dimensions: breadth of product line and value added. There are four possible positions in the matrix. Such stores as The Bay have a broad product line and high value added. Such stores as Zellers also have a broad product line but have low value added because they offer fewer services. Birks represents a narrow product line and high value added. Finally, such stores as Payless ShoeSource offer a narrow product line and low value added.

4 *Develop retailing mix strategies over the life cycle of a retail store.*
The retail life cycle describes the process of growth and decline for retail outlets through four stages: early growth, accelerated development, maturity, and decline. The retail mix—pricing, store location, communication, and merchandise—can be managed to match the retail strategy with the stage of the life cycle. The challenge facing retailers is to delay entering the decline stage, where market share and profit fall rapidly.

■ ■ ■
FOCUSING ON KEY TERMS

breadth of product line p. 401
category management p. 411
central business district p. 410
community shopping centre p. 410

depth of product line p. 401
form of ownership p. 398
hypermarket p. 402
intertype competition p. 402

■ ■ ■

DISCUSSION AND APPLICATION QUESTIONS

1 Discuss the impact of the growing number of dual-income households on (*a*) nonstore retailing, and (*b*) the retail mix.

2 How does value added affect a store's competitive position?

3 In retail pricing, retailers often have a maintained markup. Explain how this maintained markup differs from original markup and why it is so important.

4 What are the similarities and differences between product and retail life cycles?

5 How would you classify Zellers in terms of its position on the wheel of retailing versus that of an off-price retailer?

6 Develop a chart to highlight the role of each of the three main elements of the retailing mix across the four stages of the retail life cycle.

7 In Figure 15–5, Payless was placed on the retail positioning matrix. What strategies should Payless follow to move itself into the same position as Birks?

8 Breadth and depth are two important components in distinguishing among types of retailers. Discuss the breadth and depth implications of the following retailers discussed in this chapter: (*a*) Levi Strauss, (*b*) Wal-Mart, (*c*) L.L. Bean, and (*d*) Future Shop.

9 According to the wheel of retailing and the retail life cycle, what will happen to factory outlet stores?

10 The text discusses the development of online retailing. How does the development of this retailing form agree with the implications of the retail life cycle?

| GOING ONLINE | Welcome to the Retail Council of Canada |

Founded in 1963, Retail Council of Canada is the Voice of Retail. RCC is a not-for-profit association, whose more than 9000 members represent all retail formats, including national and regional department stores, mass merchants, specialty chains, independent stores, and online merchants. It speaks for an industry that touches the daily lives of Canadians in every corner of the country—by providing jobs; consumer value; world-class product selection; and the colour, sizzle and entertainment of the marketplace. RCC promotes retail as a career; as an economic driver; and as a barometer of consumer tastes and confidence. Go to its Web site www.retailcouncil.org. On the homepage, go to the heading "Media." Click on Press Releases, and then click on Current Releases. Read about the latest developments in retailing in Canada.

Do you want to get better grades and stay up to date with current issues in marketing? Visit the Online Learning Centre at www.mcgrawhill.ca/college/crane for practice tests, video cases, resources for building a marketing plan, *Globe and Mail* headlines, access to *Marketing Magazine*, and other learning and study tools.

VIDEO CASE 15   Vaughan Mills Shopping Centre

INTRODUCTION

Vaughan Mills Shopping Centre was the first enclosed shopping centre to be built in Canada in more than 14 years and the first Mills Shopping Centre developed in Canada (there are three dozen other Mills centres across the United States and in Europe). Vaughan Mills opened on November 4, 2004. It is located 32 kilometres north of downtown Toronto, in the City of Vaughan. It contains 1.2 million square feet of gross leasable space. It combines manufacturers' outlets, top brand-name retailers, and entertainment offerings, including theme restaurants, live entertainment, and interactive retailers. In its first month of operation, more than one million shoppers visited Vaughan Mills. Vaughan Mills is a joint venture project between Montreal-based Ivanhoe Cambridge and The Mills Corporation, Arlington, VA, and represents the first foray into the Canadian market for Mills, which owns, develops, manages, and markets a portfolio of more than three dozen retail and entertainment destinations in the United States and Europe.

RETAIL OFFERINGS

Vaughan Mills features more than 200 anchor and in-line retailers. Some of the anchor retailers include: the first Bass Pro Shops Outdoor World in Canada, H&M, Hudson's Bay Company's new designer depot concept, LaSenza/LaSenza Girl (their largest store in Canada), Linens 'N Things, The Children's Place Outlet, the largest Tommy Hilfiger Outlet in the world, Urban Behavior, Winners and Home Sense, and the first Burlington Coat Factory in Canada.

A sample of the in-line retailers include: the first Tommy Bahama Outlet in Canada, the first Town Shoes Outlet in Canada, the first Benetton Outlet in Canada; Aldo Outlet, American Outfitters, Aritzia, BCBG Max Azria Outlet, Buffalo Outlet, Build-A-Bear Workshop, Danier Outlet, Ecco Outlet, Eggspectations, Esprit Outlet, Fial Outlet, Fiorio Salon and Spa, Guess Outlet, HMV, Jacob Annex, Johnny Rockets, La Vie en Rose Outlet, Music World, Mexx Outlet, Nike Factory Store, Nine West Shoes Outlet, Purdy's Chocolates, The Sony Store, Timberland Outlet, and West 49.

The complex also has entertainment offerings, including the first Lucky Strike Lanes in Canada, and the first NASCAR Speedpark in Canada, and numerous restaurants designed to appeal to every shopper's taste. According to Carol Hyams, general manager, Vaughan Mills, "Only at Vaughan Mills will you be able to find fabulous designer deals at brand name outlet stores, drive a go cart, and enjoy a great meal, all under one roof."

INTENDED SHOPPERS

Research by The Mills Corporation showed that Vaughan Mills would draw shoppers from more than a 100-kilometre radius, which includes 60 percent of Ontario's population—or about 7.5 million people and nearly one-quarter of the entire Canadian population. Vaughan Mills would also draw shoppers from across the border from such areas as Buffalo and Niagara Falls, New York.

The targeted shoppers are diverse in terms of culture and socio-economic status. But, a major commonality among the shoppers is that they can be labelled recreational shoppers or pleasure shoppers who are seeking a "shopping experience." Accordingly, Vaughan Mills has been positioned as a destination shopping centre and as a "retailtainment" or "shoppertainment" concept intended to produce an experience for the shoppers, including entire families.

THE NEIGHBOURHOOD CONCEPT

Vaughan Mills's six unique neighbourhoods based on the design theme "Discover Ontario" celebrate the beauty, diversity, and icons of the Province of Ontario. The six themed neighbourhoods are punctuated by six transition courts that connect the neighbourhoods with each other, and each neighbourhood has its own key outside entry point as well. The six neighbourhoods include: (1) Fashion, which houses mid- to higher-end fashion retailers, such as UpCountry, RK Outlet, and Town Shoes; (2) Small Towns, which houses the centre's main entertainment attractions, including Lucky Strike Lanes and NASCAR Speedpark; (3) City, which features retailers geared toward Generation Y, such as H&M, Danier Leather, and BCBG Outlet; (4) Rural, which includes a number of outlets and moderately priced stores, such as Suzy Shier, Benix, and The Shoe Company; (5) Nature, which comprises lifestyle-oriented retailers, such as Build-A-Bear Workshop, Tommy Hilfiger, and Aritzia; and (6) The Lakes, which features classics, such as Bass Pro Shops Outdoor World, Home Company, and Esprit. There is also a 1000-seat food court in the complex.

Additionally, Vaughan Mills has involved corporations to sponsor the neighbourhoods. For example, Visa sponsors the "Fashion" neighbourhood. The sponsorship deal includes signage and promotion opportunities for Visa. The *Toronto Star* sponsors the "Small Towns" neighbourhood. The *Star* chose that neighbourhood because it appeals to local residents, who are most likely to read the newspaper.

SUCCESS TO DATE

Vaughan Mills's 1.2 million square foot shopping space has been almost fully leased. Its grand opening was the most successful among all Mills shopping centres and was the most successful shopping centre opening ever in Canada. More than 81 000 people attended the grand opening, and a total of over 300 000 attended during the weekend of grand opening celebrations. In just its first month of operation, Vaughan Mills welcomed more than one million shoppers. Vaughan Mills and its retail partners also employ more than 3500 individuals on a full- or part-time basis.

QUESTIONS

1 What consumer and retail trends gave rise to the development and success of Vaughan Mills?

2 Chapter 15 discusses the trend toward two types of shoppers: chore shoppers and pleasure shoppers. Which type of shopper is Vaughan Mills targeting?

3 What criteria should Vaughan Mills use when adding new stores or facilities to its complex?

4 What specific marketing actions would you propose that Vaughan Mills take to ensure its continuing success in attracting and keeping shoppers?

VSC

CORNER GAS

SEASON ONE

corner gas

CORNER GAS

SEASON ONE

DVD
VIDEO

CTV1526

2
DISC
SET

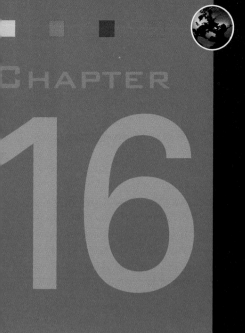

INTEGRATED MARKETING COMMUNICATIONS AND DIRECT MARKETING

LEARNING OBJECTIVES

After reading this chapter, you should be able to:

1. Discuss integrated marketing communications and the communication process.

2. Describe the promotional mix and the uniqueness of each component.

3. Select the promotional approach appropriate to a product's lifecycle and characteristics.

4. Discuss the characteristics of push and pull strategies.

5. Describe the elements of the promotion decision process.

6. Explain the value of direct marketing for consumers and sellers.

CTV ACHIEVES SUCCESS WITH *CORNER GAS* USING AN INTEGRATED MARKETING COMMUNICATIONS STRATEGY

According to Susanne Boyce, president, CTV Programming, "Canadians produce great television. But getting audiences to watch is another matter." Programs such as *Canadian Idol* prove that a home-grown series can be successful. But *Canadian Idol* came with a predeveloped brand. This was not the case for *Corner Gas*, Canada's hottest sitcom. In fact, *Corner Gas* is so successful that it is the first time in a generation that the highest-rated sitcom on primetime TV in Canada is Canadian, and not American. How did it happen?

Boyce insists that it started with a great concept, a solid cast, great writing, and polished production. Still, when the series first aired on CTV, very few noticed. And, as you know, without an audience, shows get cancelled. So, how did CTV go about building awareness for the series and building this new brand called *Corner Gas*? Their solution: integrated marketing communications (IMC).

CTV executives believed that if *Corner Gas* was to be successful, viewers had to not only become aware of the series, they had to make a connection with the series. CTV launched a major integrated marketing communications campaign designed to do just that. The entire promotional campaign was produced in-house at CTV and included a focused public relations and publicity campaign, pre-series promotions, intensive on-air advertising, an integrated Web site with interactive promotions, and a cross-country standup comedy tour. Additionally, the kick-start for the promotional activities was buzz generation. The show was put into as many hands as possible. CTV sent out preview screeners not only to members of the media but to a select group of connectors (remember connectors from Chapter 5?)—or buzz generators.

CTV utilized its full resources to increase the profile of the series. For example, CTV's *etalk Daily* profiled the series, and the cast appeared on some CTV shows, such as *Canadian AM*, *Vicki Gabereau*, and *Off The Record*. Premiums, such as branded ice scrapers, air fresheners, and a car safety kit, were also given away to consumers. There was even a free-gas campaign at a Toronto Canadian Tire gas bar. In return for the free gas, consumers were asked to pledge to watch the premiere of the program.

Television advertising on other key CTV programs, supported by a print campaign in major daily newspapers was also used to generate awareness for the series and to build a relationship with a potential audience. CTV also took the series star, Brent Butt, on the road on a standup comedy tour. The tour provided another promotional push as additional advertising spots ran to promote the tour, and free ticket give-aways were used by CTV affiliates.

A unique tool to build an affinity between the audience and the series was the *Corner Gas* Web site (Cornergas.com). The Web site is an online replica of Dog River, the fictional town in which *Corner Gas* is set. Visitors become "virtual residents," collecting Dog River dollars, to earn points and win prizes. Numerous online promotions were used on the Web site, including an opportunity to win a walk-on guest appearance on the show and a chance to win a piece of land in Climax, Sask. The Web site has thousands of registered users and has over 30 000 visitors per month.

The results? Well, according to Boyce, "remarkable." Since *Corner Gas* launched with 1.15 million viewers, the series has continued to attract more and more viewers, with over 1.5 million tuning in regularly, placing the series in the top 15 of all programs watched on Canadian television. And the program has now hit nearly two million viewers making it the highest-rated sitcom in primetime television in Canada. Another gauge of success, according to Boyce, is "the buzz at dinner conversations and the testimonials the show receives daily supporting *Corner Gas*."[1]

The many types of promotional tools used by CTV to market *Corner Gas* demonstrate the opportunity for creativity in communication with potential customers (in this case, potential audience members) and the importance of integrating the various elements in a marketing communications program. Promotion represents the fourth element in the marketing mix. The promotional element consists of specific communications tools, including advertising, personal selling, sales promotion, public relations, and direct marketing. The combination of one or more of these communication tools is called the **promotional mix**. All of these tools can be used to (1) inform prospective buyers about the benefits of the product, (2) persuade them to try it, and (3) remind them later about the benefits they enjoyed by using the product.

In the past, marketers often viewed the communications tools as separate and independent. The advertising department, for example, often designed and managed its activities without consulting departments or agencies that had responsibility for sales promotion or public relations. The result was often an overall communication effort that was uncoordinated and, in some cases, inconsistent. Today, the concept of designing marketing communications programs that coordinate all promotional activities—advertising, personal selling, sales promotion, public relations, and direct marketing—to provide a consistent message across all audiences and to maximize the promotional budget and impact of the communications is referred to as **integrated marketing communications** (IMC).

This chapter provides an overview of the communications process, a description of the promotional mix elements, several tools for integrating the promotional mix, and a process for developing a comprehensive promotion program. One of the promotional mix elements, direct marketing, is also discussed in this chapter. Chapter 17 covers advertising, sales promotion, and public relations, and Chapter 18 discusses personal selling.

THE COMMUNICATION PROCESS

Communication is the process of conveying a message to others and requires six elements: a source, a message, a channel of communication, a receiver, and the processes of encoding and decoding[2] (Figure 16–1). The **source** may be a company or person who has information to convey. The information sent by a source, such as a description of a new wireless telephone, forms the **message**. The message is conveyed by means of a **channel of communication**, such as a salesperson, adver-

---

promotional mix
The combination of one or more of these communication tools, including advertising, personal selling, sales promotion, public relations, and direct marketing.

integrated marketing communications
The concept of designing marketing communications programs that coordinate all promotional activities—advertising, personal selling, sales promotion, public relations, and direct marketing—to provide a consistent message across all audiences and to maximize the promotional budget and impact of the communications.

communication
The process of conveying a message to others, which requires six elements: a source, a message, a channel of communication, a receiver, and the processes of encoding and decoding.

source
A company or person who has information to convey.

message
The information sent by a source to a receiver in the communication process.

channel of communication
The means of conveying a message to a receiver.

■ FIGURE 16-1 ■

The communication process

receivers
Consumers who read, hear, or see the message sent by a source in the communication process.

encoding
The process of having the sender transform an abstract idea into a set of symbols.

decoding
The process of having the receiver take a set of symbols, the message, and transform them back to an abstract idea.

A source and a message.

BMW
www.bmw.ca.

tising media, or public relations tools. Consumers who read, hear, or see the message are the **receivers**.

Encoding and Decoding

Encoding and decoding are essential to communication. **Encoding** is the process of having the sender transform an abstract idea into a set of symbols. **Decoding** is the reverse, or the process of having the receiver take a set of symbols, the message, and transform them back to an abstract idea. Look at the accompanying automobile advertisement: Who is the source, and what is the message?

Decoding is performed by the receivers according to their own frame of reference: their attitudes, values, and beliefs.[3] In the ad below, BMW is the source, and the message is this advertisement, which appeared in a magazine (the channel). How would you interpret (decode) this advertisement? The picture and text in the advertisement show that the source's intention is to generate interest in a BMW Sports Activity Vehicle designed for "Any corner. Any pace. Any passion."—a statement the source believes will appeal to the readers of the magazine.

The process of communication is not always a successful one. Errors in communication can happen in several ways. The source may not adequately transform the abstract idea into an effective set of symbols, a properly encoded message may be sent through the wrong channel and never make it to the receiver, the receiver may not properly transform the set of symbols into the correct abstract idea, or finally, feedback may be so delayed or distorted that it is of no use to the sender. Although communication appears easy to perform, truly effective communication can be very difficult.

For the message to be communicated effectively, the sender and receiver must have a mutually shared **field of experience**—similar understanding and knowledge. Figure 16–1 shows two circles representing the fields of experience of the sender and receiver, which overlap in the message. Some of the better-known communication problems have occurred when Canadian companies have taken their messages to cultures with different fields of experience. Many misinterpretations are merely the result of bad translations. For example, KFC made a mistake when its "finger-lickin' good" slogan was translated into Mandarin Chinese as "eat your fingers off"![4]

Feedback

Figure 16–1 shows a line labelled *feedback loop*, which consists of a response and feedback. A **response** is the impact the message had on the receiver's knowledge, attitudes, or behaviours. **Feedback** is the sender's interpretation of the response and indicates whether the message was decoded and understood as intended. Chapter 17 reviews approaches called *pretesting* that ensure that messages are decoded properly.

Noise

Noise includes extraneous factors that can work against effective communication by distorting a message or the feedback received (see Figure 16–1). Noise can be a simple error, such as a printing mistake that affects the meaning of a newspaper advertisement, or using words or pictures that fail to communicate the message clearly. Noise can also occur when a salesperson's message is misunderstood by a prospective buyer, such as when a salesperson's accent, use of slang terms, or communication style makes hearing and understanding the message difficult.

field of experience
Similar understanding and knowledge; to communicate effectively, a sender and a receiver must have a mutually shared field of experience.

response
The impact the message had on the receiver's knowledge, attitudes, or behaviours.

feedback
The communication flow from receiver back to the sender that helps the sender know whether the message was decoded and understood as intended.

noise
Extraneous factors that can work against effective communication by distorting a message or the feedback received.

CONCEPT CHECK

1. What are the six elements required for communication to occur?

2. A difficulty for Canadian companies advertising in foreign markets is that the audience does not share the same _____.

3. A misprint in a newspaper ad is an example of _____.

■ ■ ■

THE PROMOTIONAL ELEMENTS

To communicate with consumers, a company can use one or more of five promotional alternatives: advertising, personal selling, public relations, sales promotion, and direct marketing. Figure 16–2 summarizes the distinctions among these five elements. Three of these elements—advertising, sales promotion, and public relations—are often said to use *mass selling* because they are used with groups of prospective buyers. In contrast, personal selling uses *customized interaction* between a seller and

PROMOTIONAL ELEMENT	MASS VERSUS CUSTOMIZED	PAYMENT	STRENGTHS	WEAKNESSES
Advertising	Mass	Fees paid for space or time	• Efficient means for reaching large numbers of people	• High absolute costs • Difficult to receive good feedback
Personal selling	Customized	Fees paid to salespeople as either salaries or commissions	• Immediate feedback • Very persuasive • Can select audience • Can give complex information	• Extremely expensive per exposure • Messages may differ between salespeople
Public relations	Mass	No direct payment to media	• Often most credible source in the consumer's mind	• Difficult to get media cooperation
Sales promotion	Mass	Wide range of fees paid, depending on promotion selected	• Effective at changing behaviour in short run • Very flexible	• Easily abused • Can lead to promotion wars • Easily duplicated
Direct marketing	Customized	Cost of communication through mail, telephone, or online	• Messages can be prepared quickly • Facilitates relationship with customer	• Declining customer response • Database management is expensive

■ FIGURE 16–2 ■

The promotional mix

advertising

Any paid form of nonpersonal communication about an organization, good, service, or idea by an identified sponsor.

An attention-getting advertisement.

a prospective buyer. Personal selling activities include face-to-face, telephone, and interactive electronic communication. Direct marketing also uses messages customized for specific customers.

Advertising

Advertising is any paid form of nonpersonal communication about an organization, good, service, or idea by an identified sponsor. The *paid* aspect of this definition is important because the space for the advertising message normally must be bought. An occasional exception is the public service announcement, where the advertising time or space is donated. A full-page, four-colour ad in *Canadian Living* magazine, for example, costs over $33 000, and over $15 000 in *Viola*. The *nonpersonal* component of advertising is also important. Advertising involves mass media (such as TV, radio, and magazines), which are nonpersonal and do not have an immediate feedback loop as does personal selling. So, before the message is sent, marketing research plays a valuable role; for example, it determines that the target market will actually see the medium chosen and that the message will be understood.

There are several advantages to a firm using advertising in its promotional mix. It can be attention-getting—as with this Best Buy ad—and also can communicate specific product benefits to prospective buyers. By paying for the advertising space, a company can control *what* it wants to say and, to some extent, to *whom* the message is sent. If an electronics company wants university students to receive its message about MP3 players, advertising space is purchased in a campus newspaper. Advertising also allows the company to decide *when* to send its message (which includes how often). The nonpersonal aspect of advertising also has its advantages. Once the message is created, the same message is sent to all receivers in a market segment. If the message is properly pretested, an advertiser can ensure the ad's ability to capture consumers' attention and trust that the same message will be decoded by all receivers in the market segment.[5]

Advertising has some disadvantages. As shown in Figure 16–2 and discussed in depth in Chapter 17, the costs to produce and place a message are significant, and the lack of direct feedback makes it difficult to know how well the message was received.

Personal Selling

personal selling
The two-way flow of communication between a buyer and seller, often in a face-to-face encounter, designed to influence a person's or group's purchase decision.

The second major promotional alternative is **personal selling**, defined as the two-way flow of communication between a buyer and seller, designed to influence a person's or group's purchase decision. Unlike advertising, personal selling is usually face-to-face communication between the sender and receiver (although telephone and electronic sales are growing). Why do companies use personal selling?

There are important advantages to personal selling, as summarized in Figure 16–2. A salesperson can control to *whom* the presentation is made. Some control is available in advertising by choosing the medium, for example, some people who are not in the target audience for MP3 players may read the campus newspaper. For the MP3-player manufacturer, those readers outside the target audience are *wasted coverage*. Wasted coverage can be reduced with personal selling. The personal component of selling has another advantage over advertising in that the seller can see or hear the potential buyer's reaction to the message. If the feedback is unfavourable, the salesperson can modify the message.

The flexibility of personal selling can also be a disadvantage. Different salespeople can change the message so that no consistent communication is given to all customers. The high cost of personal selling is probably its major disadvantage. On a cost-per-contact basis, it is generally the most expensive of the five promotional elements.

Public Relations

public relations
A form of communication management that seeks to influence the feelings, opinions, or beliefs held by customers, prospective customers, shareholders, suppliers, employees, and other publics about a company and its products or services.

publicity
A nonpersonal, indirectly paid presentation of an organization, good, or service.

Public relations is a form of communication management that seeks to influence the feelings, opinions, or beliefs held by customers, prospective customers, shareholders, suppliers, employees, and other publics about a company and its products or services. Many tools, such as special events sponsorship, lobbying efforts, annual reports, and image management, may be used by a public relations department, although publicity often plays the most important role. **Publicity** is a nonpersonal, indirectly paid presentation of an organization, good, or service. It can take the form of a news story, editorial, or product announcement. A difference between publicity and both advertising and personal selling is the "indirectly paid" dimension. With publicity, a company does not pay for space in a mass medium (such as television or radio) but attempts to get the medium to run a favourable story on the company. In this sense, there is an indirect payment for publicity in that a company must support a public relations staff.

An advantage of publicity is credibility. When you read a favourable story about a company's product (such as a glowing restaurant review), there is a tendency to believe it. Travellers throughout the world have relied on Arthur Frommer's guides, such as *Ireland from $80 a Day*. These books outline out-of-the-way, inexpensive restaurants, hotels, inns, and bed-and-breakfast rooms, giving invaluable publicity to these establishments. Such businesses do not (nor can they) buy a mention in the guides, which in recent years have sold millions of copies.

The disadvantages of publicity relate to the lack of the user's control over it. A company can invite a news team to preview its innovative exercise equipment and hope for a favourable mention on the 6 P.M. newscasts. But without buying advertis-

Frommer's
IRELAND
FROM $80 A DAY

Plan Your Trip Online at Frommers.com

ing time, there is no guarantee of any mention of the new equipment or that it will be aired when the target audience is watching. The company representative who calls the station and asks for a replay of the story may be told, "Sorry, it's only news once." With publicity, there is little control over what is said, to whom, or when. As a result, publicity is rarely the main component of a promotional campaign.

Sales Promotion

sales promotion
A short-term inducement of value offered to arouse interest in buying a good or service.

A fourth promotional element is **sales promotion**, a short-term inducement of value offered to arouse interest in buying a good or service. Used in conjunction with advertising or personal selling, sales promotions are offered to intermediaries as well as to ultimate consumers. Coupons, rebates, samples, and sweepstakes are just a few examples of sales promotions discussed in Chapter 17.

The advantage of sales promotion is that the short-term nature of these programs (such as a coupon or sweepstakes with an expiration date) often stimulates sales for their duration. Offering value to the consumer in terms of a cents-off coupon or rebate may increase store traffic from consumers who are not store-loyal.[6]

Sales promotions cannot be the sole basis for a campaign because gains are often temporary and sales drop off when the deal ends.[7] Advertising support is needed to convert the customer who tried the product because of a sales promotion into a long-term buyer.[8] If sales promotions are conducted continuously, they lose their effectiveness. Customers begin to delay purchase until a coupon is offered, or they question the product's value. Some aspects of sales promotions also are regulated by the federal government. These issues are reviewed in detail later in Chapter 17.

Direct Marketing

direct marketing
Promotional element that uses direct communication with consumers to generate a response in the form of an order, a request for further information, or a visit to a retail outlet.

Another promotional alternative, **direct marketing**, uses direct communication with consumers to generate a response in the form of an order, a request for further information, or a visit to a retail outlet.[9] The communication can take many forms including face-to-face selling, direct mail, catalogues, telephone solicitations, direct response advertising (on television and radio and in print), and online marketing. Like personal selling, direct marketing often consists of interactive communication. It also has the advantage of being customized to match the needs of specific target markets. Messages can be developed and adapted quickly to facilitate one-to-one relationships with customers.

While direct marketing has been one of the fastest-growing forms of promotion, it has several disadvantages. First, most forms of direct marketing require a comprehensive and up-to-date database with information about the target market. Developing and maintaining the database can be expensive and time-consuming. In addition, growing concern about privacy has led to a decline in response rates among some customer groups. Companies with successful direct marketing programs are sensitive to these issues and often use a combination of direct marketing alternatives together, or direct marketing combined with other promotional tools, to increase value for customers.

CONCEPT CHECK

1. Explain the difference between advertising and publicity when both appear on television.

2. Which promotional element should be offered only on a short-term basis?

3. Cost per contact is high with the _____ element of the promotional mix.

■ ■ ■

INTEGRATED MARKETING COMMUNICATIONS—
DEVELOPING THE PROMOTIONAL MIX

A firm's promotional mix is the combination of one or more of the promotional elements it chooses to use. In putting together the promotional mix, a marketer must consider several issues. First, the balance of the elements must be determined. Should advertising be emphasized more than personal selling? Should a promotional rebate be offered? Would public relations activities be effective? Several factors affect such decisions: the target audience for the promotion,[10] the stage of the product's life cycle, characteristics of the product, decision stage of the buyer, and even the channel of distribution. Second, because the various promotional elements are often the responsibility of different departments, coordinating a consistent promotional effort is necessary. A promotional planning process designed to ensure integrated marketing communications can facilitate this goal.

The Target Audience

Promotional programs are directed to the ultimate consumer, to an intermediary (retailer, wholesaler, or industrial distributor), or to both. Promotional programs directed to buyers of consumer products often use mass media because the number of potential buyers is large. Personal selling is used at the place of purchase, generally the retail store. Direct marketing may be used to encourage first-time or repeat purchases. Combinations of many media alternatives are a necessity for some target audiences today. The Marketing NewsNet box describes how Generation Y consumers give media only partial attention but can be reached through integrated programs.[11]

MARKETING NEWSNET

Gen Y Applies Multi-tasking to Media Consumption—29 Hours per Day!

Consumers are increasingly multi-tasking, or doing many things at the same time. The concept of multi-tasking applied to communication—watching TV while surfing the Internet, or reading a magazine while listening to the radio—has led to the term *simultaneous media usage* (SIMM). Generation Y seems to be particularly adept at SIMM as recent research found that 75 percent of the age group does something else while watching TV. In fact, SIMM has created 29.8 hour "media days" for this group. One reason is that media are pervasive—the average student may be exposed to 5000 messages each day—but other reasons are the desire to be informed and the desire to keep in touch. As a result, consumers in this group probably do not give full attention to any single message. Instead, they use continuous partial attention to scan the media.

Marketers can still communicate with Gen Y by utilizing a variety of promotional tools—from advertising to packaging to word-of-mouth communication—with an integrated message. Which media work particularly well with Gen Y? The most popular television channel is MTV. The most popular magazines are *Sports Illustrated* and *Seventeen*. Favourite Web sites include anything with content related to their interests: celebrities, music, sports, and games. Another approach growing in popularity is "buzz," marketing. When BMW dealers started selling the new Mini convertible, for example, they held contests to see how long drivers could go before putting the top up. The drivers and potential buyers started talking about the contests and the new car, for at least part of the 29.8 hour day.

The Expanding World of
Specialty Fencing
CFIA's Montreal Show Preview

Advertising directed to business buyers is used selectively in trade publications, such as *Fence Industry* magazine for buyers of fencing material. Because business buyers often have specialized needs or technical questions, personal selling is particularly important. The salesperson can provide information and the necessary support after sales.

Intermediaries are often the focus of promotional efforts. As with business buyers, personal selling is the major promotional ingredient. The salespeople assist intermediaries in making a profit by coordinating promotional campaigns sponsored by the manufacturer and by providing marketing advice and expertise. Intermediaries' questions often pertain to the allowed markup, merchandising support, and return policies.

The Product Life Cycle

All products have a product life cycle (see Chapter 11), and the composition of the promotional mix changes over the four life-cycle stages, as shown for Purina Dog Chow in Figure 16–3.

Introduction Stage Informing consumers in an effort to increase their level of awareness is the primary promotional objective in the introduction stage of the product life cycle. In general, all the promotional mix elements are used at this time, although the use of specific mix elements during any stage depends on the product and situation. News releases about Purina's new nutritional product are sent to veterinary magazines, trial samples are sent to registered dog owners, advertisements are placed in *Dog World* magazine, and the salesforce begins to approach supermarkets to get orders. Advertising is particularly important as a means of reaching as many people as possible to build up awareness and interest. Publicity may even begin slightly before the product is commercially available.

Growth Stage The primary promotional objective of the growth stage is to persuade the consumer to buy the product—Purina Dog Chow—rather than substitutes, and so the marketing manager seeks to gain brand preference and solidify distribution. Sales promotion assumes less importance in this stage, and publicity is not a factor because it depends on novelty of the product. The primary promotional

■ FIGURE 16–3 ■

Promotional tools used over the product life cycle of Purina Dog Chow

	Introduction	Growth	Maturity	Decline
Stage of product life cycle				
Promotional objective	To inform	To persuade	To remind	
Promotional activity	• Publicity in veterinary magazines • Advertising • Salesforce calling on intermediaries • Sales promotion in form of free samples	• Personal selling to intermediaries • Advertising to differentiate Dog Chow attributes from those of competing brands	• Reminder advertising • Sales promotion in form of discounts and coupons • Limited personal selling • Direct-mail or online reminders	• Little money spent on promotion

element is advertising, which stresses brand differences. Personal selling is used to solidify the channel of distribution. For consumer products, such as dog food, the salesforce calls on wholesalers and retailers in hopes of increasing inventory levels and gaining shelf space. For industrial products, the salesforce often tries to get contractual arrangements to be the sole source of supply for the buyer.

Maturity Stage   In the maturity stage, the need is to maintain existing buyers, and advertising's role is to remind buyers of the product's existence. Sales promotion, in the form of discounts and coupons offered to both ultimate consumers and intermediaries, is important in maintaining loyal buyers. In a test of one mature consumer product, it was found that 80 percent of the product's sales at this stage resulted from sales promotions.[12] For the past eight years, Purina has sponsored the Incredible Dog Challenge, which is now covered by ESPN.[13] Direct marketing actions, such as direct mail, are used to maintain involvement with existing customers and to encourage repeat purchases. Price cuts and discounts can also significantly increase a mature brand's sales. The salesforce at this stage seeks to satisfy intermediaries. An unsatisfied customer who switches brands is hard to replace.

Decline Stage   The decline stage of the product life cycle is usually a period of phaseout for the product, and little money is spent in the promotional mix. The rate of decline can be rapid, when a product is replaced by an improved or lower cost product, for example, or slow, if there is a loyal group of customers.

Purina Dog Chow: a product in the maturity stage of its life cycle.

Product Characteristics

The proper blend of elements in the promotional mix also depends on the type of product. Three specific characteristics should be considered: complexity, risk, and ancillary services. *Complexity* refers to the technical sophistication of the product and hence the amount of understanding required to use it. It is hard to provide much information in a one-page magazine ad or 30-second television ad; so, the more complex the product, the greater is the emphasis on personal selling. Gulfstream asks potential customers to call their senior vice-president in its ads. No information is provided for simple products, such as Heinz ketchup.

How do Gulfstream aircraft and Heinz ketchup differ on complexity, risk, and ancillary services?

Gulfstream
www.gulfstreamvsp.com

Heinz
www.heinz.com

A second element is the degree of *risk* represented by the product's purchase. Risk for the buyer can be assessed in terms of financial risk, social risk, and physical risk. A private jet, for example, might represent all three risks—it is expensive, employees and customers may see and evaluate the purchase, and safety and reliability are important. Although advertising helps, the greater the risk, the greater is the need for personal selling. Consumers are unlikely to associate any of these risks with, say, cereal.

The level of ancillary services required by a product also affects the promotional strategy. *Ancillary services* pertain to the degree of service or support required after the sale. This characteristic is common to many business products and consumer purchases. Who will provide maintenance for the plane? Advertising's role is to establish the seller's reputation. Direct marketing can be used to describe how a product or service can be customized to individual needs. However, personal selling is essential to build buyer confidence and provide evidence of customer service.

Stages of the Buying Decision

Knowing the customer's stage of decision making can also affect the promotional mix. Figure 16–4 shows how the importance of the promotional elements varies with the three stages in a consumer's purchase decision.

Prepurchase Stage In the prepurchase stage, advertising is more helpful than personal selling because advertising informs the potential customer of the existence of the product and the seller. Sales promotion in the form of free samples also can play an important role to gain low-risk trial. When the salesperson calls on the customer after heavy advertising, there is some recognition of what the salesperson represents. This is particularly important in business settings in which sampling of the product is usually not possible.

Purchase Stage At the purchase stage, the importance of personal selling is highest, whereas the impact of advertising is lowest. Sales promotion in the form of coupons, deals, point-of-purchase displays, and rebates can be very helpful in encouraging demand. In this stage, although advertising is not an active influence on the purchase, it is the means of delivering the coupons, deals, and rebates that are often important.

■ **FIGURE 16–4** ■

How the importance of promotional elements varies during the consumer's purchase decision

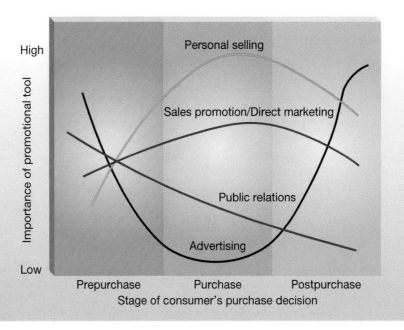

Postpurchase Stage   In the postpurchase stage, the salesperson is still important. In fact, the more personal contact after the sale, the more the buyer is satisfied. Advertising is also important to assure the buyer that the right purchase was made. Advertising and personal selling help reduce the buyer's postpurchase anxiety.[14] Sales promotion in the form of coupons and direct marketing reminders can help encourage repeat purchases from satisfied first-time users. Public relations plays a small role in the postpurchase stage.

Channel Strategies

Chapter 14 discussed the channel flow from producer to intermediaries to consumer. Achieving control of the channel is often difficult for the manufacturer, and promotional strategies can assist in moving a product through the channel of distribution. This is where a manufacturer has to make an important decision about whether to use a push strategy, a pull strategy, or both in its channel of distribution.[15]

push strategy

Directing the promotional mix to channel members to gain their cooperation in ordering and stocking a product.

Push Strategy   Figure 16–5A shows how a manufacturer uses a **push strategy**, directing the promotional mix to channel members to gain their cooperation in ordering and stocking the product. In this approach, personal selling and sales promotions play major roles. Salespeople call on wholesalers to encourage orders and provide sales assistance. Sales promotions, such as case discount allowances (20 percent off the regular case price), are offered to stimulate demand. By pushing the product through the channel, the goal is to get channel members to push it to their customers.

Canadian firms, such as Pepsi-Cola Canada and Molson's, spend a significant amount of their marketing resources on maintaining their relationships with their distributors and, through them, with retailers. In general, Canadian consumer goods firms are allocating greater percentages of their promotional budgets toward intermediaries. In some cases, as much as 60 percent of the promotional budget is being allocated to personal selling and sales promotions designed to reach intermediaries, while 40 percent is spent on promotional activities directed toward ultimate consumers.[16]

■ **FIGURE 16–5** ■

A comparison of push and pull promotional strategies

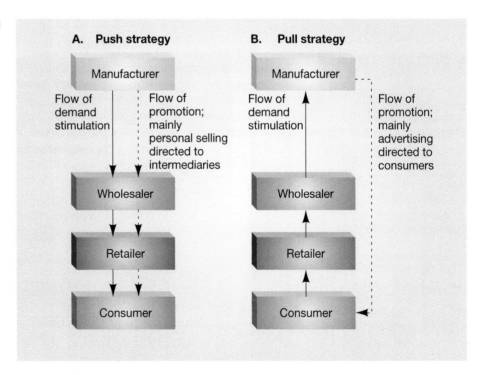

Pull Strategy   In some instances, manufacturers face resistance from channel members who do not want to order a new product or increase inventory levels of an existing brand. As shown in Figure 16–5B, a manufacturer may then elect to implement a **pull strategy** by directing its promotional mix at ultimate consumers to encourage them to ask the retailer for the product. Seeing demand from ultimate consumers, retailers order the product from wholesalers and thus the item is pulled through the intermediaries. Such firms as Procter & Gamble and Heinz Canada, use pull strategies, including e-mail marketing campaigns, directed at ultimate consumers to create consumer pull. The Pampers Parenting Institute Web site at www.pampers.ca is also an example of how P&G engages in pull strategy activities.[17]

A novel pull strategy is one being used by B.C. hemlock producers and their Coastal Forest and Lumber Association as they seek greater market share in Japan. B.C. hemlock, now rebranded as Canada Tsuga, uses a Japanese sumo wrestler in its advertising that is directed toward home builders, who are now, in turn, demanding the product from lumber suppliers. The product is now the preferred product in post-and-beam construction, and the Japanese consumer now views the Canadian Tsuga very positively.[18]

pull strategy
Directing the promotional mix at ultimate consumers to encourage them to ask the retailer for the product.

CONCEPT CHECK

1. Describe the promotional objective for each stage of the product life cycle.

2. At what stage of the consumer purchase decision is the importance of personal selling highest? Why?

3. Explain the differences between a push strategy and a pull strategy.

■ ■ ■
DEVELOPING THE PROMOTION PROGRAM

Because media costs are high, promotion decisions must be made carefully, using a systematic approach. Paralleling the planning, implementation, and control steps described in the strategic marketing process (Chapter 2), the promotion decision process is divided into (1) developing, (2) executing, and (3) evaluating the promotion program (Figure 16–6). Development of the promotion program focuses on the four *W*s:

- *Who* is the target audience?
- *What* are (1) the promotion objectives, (2) the amounts of money that can be budgeted for the promotion program, and (3) the kinds of promotion to use?
- *Where* should the promotion be run?
- *When* should the promotion be run?

■ FIGURE 16–6 ■
The promotion decision process

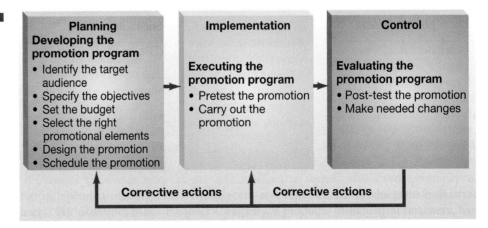

| Planning
Developing the promotion program
• Identify the target audience
• Specify the objectives
• Set the budget
• Select the right promotional elements
• Design the promotion
• Schedule the promotion | Implementation

Executing the promotion program
• Pretest the promotion
• Carry out the promotion | Control

Evaluating the promotion program
• Post-test the promotion
• Make needed changes |

Corrective actions   Corrective actions

Identifying the Target Audience

The first decision in developing the promotion program is identifying the *target audience*, the group of prospective buyers toward which a promotion program is directed. To the extent that time and money permit, the target audience for the promotion program is the target market for the firm's product, which is identified from marketing research and market segmentation studies. The more a firm knows about its target audience's profile—including their lifestyle, attitudes, and values—the easier it is to develop a promotion program. If a firm wanted to reach you with television and magazine ads, for example, it would need to know what TV shows you watch and what magazines you read.

Specifying Promotion Objectives

After the target audience is identified, a decision must be reached on what the promotion should accomplish. Consumers can be said to respond in terms of a **hierarchy of effects**, which is the sequence of stages a prospective buyer goes through from initial awareness of a product to eventual action (either trial or adoption of the product).[19]

hierarchy of effects
The sequence of stages a prospective buyer goes through from initial awareness of a product to eventual action (either trial or adoption of the product). The stages include awareness, interest, evaluation, trial, and adoption.

- *Awareness.* The consumer's ability to recognize and remember the product or brand name.
- *Interest.* An increase in the consumer's desire to learn about some of the features of the product or brand.
- *Evaluation.* The consumer's appraisal of the product or brand on important attributes.
- *Trial.* The consumer's actual first purchase and use of the product or brand.
- *Adoption.* Through a favourable experience on the first trial, the consumer's repeated purchase and use of the product or brand.

For a totally new product, the sequence applies to the entire product category, but for a new brand competing in an established product category, it applies to the brand itself. These steps can serve as guidelines for developing promotion objectives.

Although sometimes an objective for a promotion program involves several steps in the hierarchy of effects, it often focuses on a single stage. Regardless of what the specific objective might be, from building awareness to increasing repeat purchases,[20] promotion objectives should possess three important qualities. They should (1) be designed for a well-defined target audience, (2) be measurable, and (3) cover a specified time period.

Setting the Promotion Budget

After setting the promotion objectives, a company must decide on how much to spend. The promotion expenditures needed to reach millions of Canadian households are enormous. Canadian companies spent over $10 billion in 2006 on advertising and billions more on sales promotion and direct marketing to reach these households.[21] Some companies, such as McDonald's Canada, Procter & Gamble, General Motors of Canada, and the Royal Bank, spend hundreds of millions of dollars each year.

Determining the ideal amount for the budget is difficult because there is no precise way to measure the exact results of spending promotion dollars. However, several methods are used to set the promotion budget.[22]

percentage of sales budgeting
Allocating funds to advertising as a percentage of past or anticipated sales, in terms of either dollars or units sold.

Percentage of Sales   In the **percentage of sales budgeting** approach, funds are allocated to promotion as a percentage of past or anticipated sales, in terms of either dollars or units sold. A common budgeting method,[23] this approach is often stated in such terms as, "Our promotion budget for this year is 3 percent of last year's gross sales." The advantage of this approach is obvious: it is simple and provides a financial safeguard by tying the promotion budget to sales. However, there is a major fallacy in this approach, which implies that sales cause promotion. Using this method, a company may reduce its promotion budget because of a downturn in past sales or an anticipated downturn in future sales—situations where it may need promotion the most.

competitive parity budgeting

Matching the competitors' absolute level of spending or the proportion per point of market share.

Competitive Parity   A second common approach, **competitive parity budgeting**, is matching the competitor's absolute level of spending or the proportion per point of market share. This approach has also been referred to as *matching competitors* or *share of market*. It is important to consider the competition in budgeting.[24] Consumer responses to promotion are affected by competing promotional activities; thus, if a competitor runs 30 radio ads each week, it may be difficult for another firm to get its message across with only five messages.[25] The competitor's budget level, however, should not be the only determinant in setting a company's budget. The competition might have very different promotional objectives, which require a different level of promotion expenditures.

all-you-can-afford budgeting

Allocating funds to promotion only after all other budget items are covered.

All You Can Afford   Common to many small businesses is **all-you-can-afford budgeting**, in which money is allocated to promotion only after all other budget items are covered. As one company executive said in reference to this budgeting process, "Why, it's simple. First, I go upstairs to the controller and ask how much they can afford to give us this year. She says a million and a half. Later, the boss comes to me and asks how much we should spend, and I say 'Oh, about a million and a half.' Then we have our promotion appropriation."[26]

Fiscally conservative, this approach has little else to offer. Using this budgeting philosophy, a company acts as though it does not know anything about a promotion–sales relationship or what its promotion objectives are.

objective and task budgeting

A budgeting approach whereby the company (1) determines its promotion objectives, (2) outlines the tasks to accomplish these objectives, and (3) determines the promotion cost of performing these tasks.

Objective and Task   The best approach to budgeting is **objective and task budgeting**, whereby the company (1) determines its promotion objectives, (2) outlines the tasks to accomplish these objectives, and (3) determines the promotion cost of performing these tasks.[27]

This method takes into account what the company wants to accomplish and requires that the objectives be specified.[28] Strengths of the other budgeting methods are integrated into this approach because each previous method's strength is tied to the objectives. For example, if the costs are beyond what the company can afford, objectives are reworked and the tasks revised. The difficulty with this method is the judgment required to determine the tasks needed to accomplish objectives. Would two or four insertions in *Time* magazine be needed to achieve a specific awareness level? Figure 16–7 shows a sample media plan with objectives, tasks, and budget outlined. The total amount to be budgeted is $430 000. If the company can afford only $300 000, the objectives must be reworked, tasks redefined, and the total budget recalculated.

■ **FIGURE 16–7** ■■
The objective and task approach

OBJECTIVE	
To increase awareness among university students for a new video game. Awareness at the end of one semester should be 20 percent of all students from the existing 0 percent today.	
TASKS	**COSTS**
Advertisements once a week for a semester in 500 university papers	$280 000
Direct-mail samples to student leaders on 500 university campuses	50 000
Sponsor a national contest for video-game players	100 000
Total budget	$430 000

Selecting the Right Promotional Tools

Once a budget has been determined, the combination of the five basic integrated marketing communications (IMC) tools—advertising, personal selling, sales promotion, public relations, and direct marketing—can be specified. While many factors provide direction for selection of the appropriate mix, the large number of possible combinations of the promotional tools means that many combinations can achieve the same objective. Therefore, an analytical approach and experience are particularly important in this step of the promotion decision process. The specific mix can vary from a simple program using a single tool to a comprehensive program using all forms of promotion. The Olympics have become a very visible example of a comprehensive IMC program. Because the Games are repeated every two years, the promotion is almost continuous. Included in the program are advertising campaigns; personal selling efforts by the Olympic committee and organizers; sales promotion activities, such as product tie-ins and sponsorships; public relations programs managed by the host cities; and direct marketing efforts targeted at a variety of audiences, including governments, organizations, firms, athletes, and individuals.[29] At this stage, it is also important to assess the relative importance of the various tools. While it may be desirable to utilize and integrate several forms of promotion, one may deserve emphasis. The Olympics, for example, place exceptional importance on public relations and publicity.

Designing the Promotion

The central element of a promotion program is the promotion itself. Advertising consists of advertising copy and the artwork that the target audience is intended to see or hear. Personal selling efforts depend on the characteristics and skills of the salesperson. Sales promotion activities consist of the specific details of inducements, such as coupons, samples, and sweepstakes. Public relations efforts are readily seen in tangible elements, such as news releases; and direct marketing actions depend on written, verbal, and electronic forms of delivery. The design of the promotion will play a primary role in determining the message that is communicated to the audience. This design activity is frequently viewed as the step requiring the most creativity. In addition, successful designs are often the result of insight regarding consumers' interests and purchasing behaviour. All of the promotion tools have many design alternatives. Advertising, for example, can utilize fear, humour, or other emotions in its appeal.[30] Similarly, direct marketing can be designed for varying levels of personal or customized appeals. One of the challenges of IMC is to design each promotional activity to communicate the same message.

Scheduling the Promotion

Once the designs of all of the promotional program elements are complete, it is important to determine the most effective timing of their use. The promotion schedule describes the order in which each promotional tool is introduced and the frequency of its use during the campaign. New Line Cinema, for example, developed one of the longest promotion schedules on record for its *Lord of the Rings* movie trilogy. To generate interest in each movie before its release, a movie "trailer" was shown on television and in theatres. Then, movie-related products were released, followed by special promotions by Burger King, General Mills, and the NBA. Now that all three movies have been released, New Line is running a 30-second ad with high-definition footage to promote the DVD sales.[31]

Overall, the scheduling of the various promotions was designed to generate interest, bring consumers into theatres, and then encourage additional purchases after seeing the movie. Several other factors, such as seasonality and competitive promotion activity, can also influence the promotion schedule. Such businesses as ski resorts, airlines, and professional sports teams are likely to reduce their promotional activity during the "off" season. Similarly, restaurants, retail stores, and health clubs are likely to increase their promotional activities when new competitors enter the market.

■ ■ ■
EXECUTING AND EVALUATING THE PROMOTION PROGRAM

Carrying out the promotion program can be expensive and time-consuming. One researcher estimates that "an organization with sales less than $10 million can successfully implement an IMC program in one year, one with sales between $200 million and $500 million will need about three years, and one with sales between $2 billion and $5 billion will need five years." To facilitate the transition, there are hundreds of IMC agencies, large and small, all across Canada that are available to assist companies that are making the shift to IMC. Moreover, some of the largest global agencies have also adopted approaches that embrace "total communications solutions." While many agencies still have departments dedicated to advertising, direct marketing, and other specialties, the trend is clearly toward a long-term perspective in which all forms of promotion are integrated.[32] Cossette Communications, one of Canada's largest marketing communications companies, offers its clients complete IMC services, including strategic research. Check out the WebLink box to learn more about their approach to integrated marketing communications.

An important factor in developing successful IMC programs is to create a process that facilitates their design and use. A tool used to evaluate a company's current process is the *IMC audit*. The audit analyzes the internal communication network of the company; identifies key audiences; evaluates customer databases; assesses messages in recent ads, public relations releases, packaging, video news releases, signage, sales promotion programs, direct mail, and online Web sites; and determines the IMC expertise of the company and agency personnel. Still, although many organizations are interested in improving their IMC processes, they have not been successful at implementing them because of lack of expertise, lack of budget, and lack of management approval.

As shown earlier in Figure 16–6, the ideal execution of a promotion program involves pretesting each design before its actual use to allow for changes and modifications which improve its effectiveness. Similarly, post-tests are recommended to evaluate the impact of each communication and the contribution it makes in achieving

---

WEBLINK
HTTP://WWW.MCGRAWHILL.CA/ COLLEGE/CRANE

A Look at One Agency's Approach to IMC

Cossette Communication Group is one of Canada's largest marketing communications firms. It has over 1400 employees working in offices in Halifax, Montreal, Toronto, and Vancouver as well as other locations across Canada and in the United States. Cossette has a unique approach to providing IMC services to its clients. It is called Convergent Communication. The company has specialized business units that can offer clients a total solution to IMC, including strategic research, advertising, media planning and buying, direct marketing, database management, public relations, and interactive technologies.

Go to their Web site, www.cossette.com. Click on "Enter Here." Then, select "Convergent Disciplines." Take a look at their approach to IMC. Then, click on one of their service offerings, for example, "Direct Marketing." Note that service is offered by the specialized business unit called Blitz. Click on "Blitz." Then, select "Our Work," and examine some of the work performed by this specialized unit.

What do you think about Cossette's approach to IMC? What do you think about the work performed by Blitz?

program objectives. The most sophisticated pretest and post-test procedures have been developed for advertising and are discussed in Chapter 19. Testing procedures for sales promotion and direct marketing efforts currently focus on comparisons of different designs and/or responses to programs by the target audience and even different segments within the target audience. To fully benefit from IMC programs, companies must create and maintain a test-result database that allows comparisons of the relative impact of the promotional tools and their execution options in varying situations. Information from the database allow informed design and execution decisions and provide support for IMC activities during internal reviews by financial or administrative personnel.

Currently, about one-fourth of all businesses assess promotion program effectiveness by measuring "most of their communication tactics."[33] For most organizations, the assessment focuses on trying to determine which element of promotion works better or which ones work best in combination. In an integrated program, for example, media advertising might be used to build awareness, sales promotion to generate trial, direct marketing to generate additional information on individual prospects, and personal sales to complete a transaction. These tools are obviously used for different reasons to achieve specific objectives, but their combined use creates a synergy that should be the focus of the assessment. Another level of assessment is necessary when firms have global IMC programs.

CONCEPT CHECK

1. What are the characteristics of good promotion objectives?

2. What is the weakness of the percentage of sales budgeting approach?

3. How have advertising agencies changed to facilitate the use of IMC programs?

■ ■ ■

DIRECT MARKETING

Direct marketing has many forms and utilizes a variety of media. Several forms of direct marketing—direct mail and catalogues, television home shopping, telemarketing, and direct selling—were discussed as methods of nonstore retailing in Chapter 15. In addition, although advertising is discussed in Chapter 17, a form of advertising—direct response advertising—is an important form of direct marketing, as is direct mail advertising, also discussed in Chapter 17. Finally, online advertising, especially interactive online advertising, is also discussed in Chapter 17 and is now an important part of many Canadian companies' direct marketing activities. In this section, the growth of direct marketing, its value to consumers and sellers, and key global, technological, and ethical issues are discussed.

The Growth of Direct Marketing

The increasing interest in customer relationship management (CRM) is reflected in the dramatic growth of direct marketing in Canada. The ability to customize communication efforts and create one-to-one interactions is appealing to most marketers, particularly those with IMC programs. While direct marketing methods are not new (e.g., direct mail), the ability to design and use them has increased with the availability of databases. In recent years, direct marketing growth—in terms of spending, revenue generation, and employment—has outpaced total economic growth. The Canadian Marketing Association (CMA) reports that $51 billion in annual sales are generated through direct marketing activities in Canada and that the direct marketing industry employees over 480 000 Canadians.[34] Telemarketing, including call-centre-based direct marketing is responsible for about one-half of that employment.

However, a major component of the growth in direct marketing is due to the increasing popularity of the newest direct marketing channel—the Internet. As discussed in Chapter 15, online sales have risen from close to nothing in the mid-1990s to over $4 billion. Continued growth is expected as more and more Canadians gain Internet access and the number of businesses with Web sites and electronic commerce offerings increase. According to the CMA, the fastest growing direct marketing medium in Canada is *e-mail marketing*.[35] E-mail marketing is considered a fast and easy way to stay in touch with customers. Marketers use e-mail to promote special offers and announce new products and upgrades. E-mail is also often used as a component of well-designed IMC programs and as a powerful tool for CRM programs. For example, The Hudson's Bay Company utilizes e-mail marketing as part of its IMC program, which is focused CRM. Many Canadian companies are also using e-mail newsletters, or *ezines*, as a way to increase their contact points with customers, while others communicate with customers through text messaging via cellphones and PDAs.

Just about any offer communicated through traditional direct marketing methods can be promoted through the e-mail channel. However, the key to success with e-mail programs include making it permission-based and having excellent technology to ensure that the campaigns are focused, tracked, and analyzed. In order to avoid SPAM (unsolicited e-mail), which draws the ire of recipients, successful e-mail marketing should be permission-based. Research shows that over 75 percent of Canadians prefer to deal with companies that use permission-based e-mail marketing. In essence, obtaining a consumer's explicit or opt-in consent to engage in e-mail marketing is imperative. Moreover, since the standard in Canada is "opt-out" with regard to not contacting customers via direct marketing, all e-mail recipients who have not given a company permission to contact them must be able to reply to the marketers and request no further contact.[36]

The Value of Direct Marketing

One of the most visible indicators of the value of direct marketing for consumers is the level of use of the various forms of direct marketing. For example, over one-half of the Canadian population has ordered merchandise or services by phone or mail; millions purchase items from television offers; the average Canadian household places about seven online shopping orders per year; and about 20 percent of Canadian adults purchase from a catalogue each year.[37] Consumers report many benefits purchasing via direct marketing, including the following: they do not have to go to a store; they can usually shop 24/7; buying direct saves time; they avoid hassles with salespeople; they can save money, it is fun and entertaining; and direct marketing offers more privacy than does in-store shopping. Many consumers also believe that direct marketing companies provide excellent customer service. Toll-free telephone numbers, customer service representatives with access to information regarding purchase preferences, overnight delivery services, and unconditional guarantees all help create value for direct marketing customers.

direct orders
The result of offers that contain all the information necessary for a prospective buyer to make a decision to purchase and complete the transaction.

lead generation
The result of an offer designed to generate interest in a product or service and a request for additional information.

traffic generation
The outcome of an offer designed to motivate people to visit a business.

The value of direct marketing for marketers can be described in terms of the responses it generates.[38] **Direct orders** are the result of offers that contain all the information necessary for a prospective buyer to make a decision to purchase and complete the transaction. Club Med, for example, uses e-mail marketing to sell "last-minute specials" to people in its database. The messages, which are sent midweek, describe rooms and air transportation available at 30 to 40 percent discount if the customer can make the decision to travel on such short notice. **Lead generation** is the result of an offer designed to generate interest in a product or service and a request for additional information. Finally, **traffic generation** is the outcome of an offer designed to motivate people to visit a business. Mitsubishi mailed a sweepstakes offer to prospective buyers to encourage them to visit a Mitsubishi dealer and test drive the new vehicles. The names of prospects who took test drives were entered in the sweepstakes to win cars, trips, and plasma TVs.

Technological, Global, and Ethical Issues in Direct Marketing

The information technology and databases described in Chapter 8 are key elements of any direct marketing program. Databases are the result of organizations' efforts to collect demographic, media, and consumption profiles of customers so that direct marketing tools, such as catalogues, direct mail, and telemarketing, can be directed at specific customers.

While most companies try to keep records of their customers' past purchases, many other types of data are needed in direct marketing to develop one-to-one relationships with customers. Data, however, have little value by themselves. To translate data into information, the data must be unbiased, timely, pertinent, accessible, and organized in a way that helps the marketing manager make decisions that lead to direct marketing actions. Some data, such as lifestyles, media use, and consumption behaviour, must be collected from consumers. Other types of data can be collected from the stores where purchases are made. Today, such technology as the optical scanner helps collect data with as little intrusion on the customer as possible. Safeway supermarkets, for example, use scanners to capture and track customer purchases in its database. Other marketers capture online customer data, including clickstream behaviour (how someone navigates a Web site), and some direct marketers rely on cookies to focus their direct marketing efforts. *Cookies* are computer files that a marketer can upload onto the computer of an online shopper who visits the marketer's Web site. Cookies allow the marketer to record a user's visit, track visits to other Web sites, and store and retrieve this information in the future. Cookies can also contain information provided by the visitors, such as expressed product preferences, personal data, passwords, and financial information. Clearly, cookies make it possible for customized direct marketing. But there is some controversy over the use of cookies as the accompanying Ethics and Social Responsibility Alert box discusses.[39]

ETHICS AND SOCIAL RESPONSIBILITY ALERT

Cookies Are a Concern to Canadians

Canadian research reveals that we are concerned about our privacy online. We appear to be uneasy about providing our personal information online and having it stored online. In fact, many Canadians abandon Web sites and forgo purchases online because of privacy concerns. The privacy concern has also become more acute as consumers have became familiar with the concept of cookies, where a marketer can capture Web visits by downloading files onto consumers' computers. One expert suggests that "at best a cookie makes for a user-friendly Web world: like a doorman or salesclerk who knows who you are. At worst, cookies represent a potential loss of privacy."

The Canadian Marketing Association (CMA) has responded to consumers' online privacy concerns by introducing guidelines for all its members to follow. We briefly noted this issue of privacy when the CMA Codes of Ethics were presented in Chapter 4. In short, the CMA tells its members that a privacy policy must be presented on a member's Web site that articulates the organization's policy with respect to the collection, use, and disclosure of personal information gathered from the consumer and that the consumer can opt out from having this information collected and stored for use.

What do you think about the concept of cookies? Are you concerned about your privacy and/or the safety of your personal information captured by marketers through cookie technology?

Technology may also prove to be important in the global growth of direct marketing. Compared with Canada, many other countries' direct marketing systems are underdeveloped. The mail and telephone systems in many countries are likely to improve, however, creating many new direct marketing opportunities. Developments in global marketing research and database management will also facilitate global growth in direct marketing.

Global and domestic direct marketers also face ethical challenges. For example, considerable attention has been given to some annoying direct marketing activities, such as telephone solicitations during dinner and evening hours. And concerns about consumer privacy have also been raised. In fact, the Canadian government established The Office of Privacy Commissioner of Canada and enacted legislation, including the *Personal Information Protection and Electronic Documents Act* (www.privcom.gc.ca), as a way of protecting the privacy of Canadians. Industry associations, such as the CMA, have also developed guidelines for their members to follow when it comes to consumer privacy, including online privacy.

CONCEPT CHECK

1. The ability to design and use direct marketing programs has increased with the availability of _____ and _____.

2. The fastest growing direct market medium in Canada is _____.

3. What are the three types of responses generated by direct marketing activities?

■ ■ ■

CHAPTER IN REVIEW

1 *Discuss integrated marketing communication and the communication process.*
Integrated marketing communication is the concept of designing marketing communications programs that coordinate all promotional activities—advertising, personal selling, sales promotion, public relations, and direct marketing—to provide a consistent message across all audiences and to maximize the promotional budget and impact of communication. The communication process conveys messages with six elements: a source, a message, a channel of communication, a receiver, and encoding and decoding. The communication process also includes a feedback loop and can be distorted by noise.

2 *Describe the promotional mix and the uniqueness of each component.*
There are five promotional alternatives. Advertising, sales promotion, and public relations are mass selling approaches, whereas personal selling and direct marketing use customized messages. Advertising can have high absolute costs but reaches large numbers of people. Personal selling has a high cost per contact but provides immediate feedback. Public relations is often difficult to obtain but is very credible. Sales promotion influences short-term consumer behaviour. Direct marketing can help develop customer relationships, although maintaining a database can be very expensive.

3 *Select the promotional approach appropriate to a product's life-cycle stage and characteristics.*
The promotional mix changes over the four product life-cycle stages. During the introduction stage, all the promo-tional mix elements are used. In the growth stage, the primary promotional element is advertising. The maturity stage utilizes sales promotion and direct marketing. During the decline stage, little money is spent on the promotional mix.

4 *Discuss the characteristics of push and pull strategies.*
A push strategy directs the promotional mix to channel members to gain their cooperation in ordering and stocking the product. Personal selling and sales promotion are commonly used in push strategies. A pull strategy directs the promotional mix at ultimate customers to encourage them to ask the retailer for the product. Direct-to-consumer advertising is typically used in pull strategies.

5 *Describe the elements of the promotion decision process.*
The promotion decision process consists of three steps: planning, implementation, and control. The planning step consists of six elements: identifying the target audience, specifying the objectives, setting the budget, selecting the right promotional elements, designing the promotion, and scheduling the promotion. The implementation step includes pretesting. The control step includes post-testing.

6 *Explain the value of direct marketing for consumers and sellers.*
The value of direct marketing for consumers is indicated by its level of use. The value of direct marketing for sellers can be measured in terms of three types of responses: direct orders, lead generation, and traffic generation. Growth in electronic forms of direct marketing, including e-mail marketing, is evident in Canada.

■ ■ ■

FOCUSING ON KEY TERMS

advertising p. 425
all-you-can-afford budgeting p. 435
channel of communication p. 422
communication p. 422
competitive parity budgeting p. 435
decoding p. 423
direct marketing p. 427
direct orders p. 439
encoding p. 423
feedback p. 424
field of experience p. 424
hierarchy of effects p. 434
integrated marketing communications (IMC) p. 422
lead generation p. 439
message p. 422

noise p. 424
objective and task budgeting p. 435
percentage of sales budgeting p. 434
personal selling p. 426
promotional mix p. 422
public relations p. 426
publicity p. 426
pull strategy p. 433
push strategy p. 432
receivers p. 423
response p. 424
sales promotion p. 427
source p. 422
traffic generation p. 439

■ ■ ■

DISCUSSION AND APPLICATION QUESTIONS

1 After listening to a recent sales presentation, Mary Smith signed up for membership at the local health club. On arriving at the facility, she learned there was an additional fee for racquetball court rentals. "I don't remember that in the sales talk; I thought they said all facilities were included with the membership fee," complained Mary. Describe the problem in terms of the communication process.

2 Develop a matrix to compare the five elements of the promotional mix on three criteria—to *whom* you deliver the message, *what* you say, and *when* you say it.

3 Explain how the promotional tools used by an airline would differ if the target audience were (*a*) consumers who travel for pleasure, and (*b*) corporate travel departments that select the airlines to be used by company employees.

4 Suppose you introduced a new consumer food product and invested heavily both in national advertising (pull strategy) and in training and motivating your field salesforce to sell the product to food stores (push strategy). What kinds of feedback would you receive from both the advertising and your salesforce? How could you increase both the quality and quantity of each?

5 Fisher-Price Company, long known as a manufacturer of children's toys, has introduced a line of clothing for children. Outline a promotional plan to get this product introduced in the marketplace.

6 Many insurance companies sell health insurance plans to companies. In these companies, the employees pick the plan, but the set of offered plans is determined by the company. Recently Blue Cross–Blue Shield, a health insurance company, ran a television ad stating, "If your employer doesn't offer you Blue Cross–Blue Shield coverage, ask why." Explain the promotional strategy behind the advertisement.

7 Identify the sales promotion tools that might be useful for (*a*) Tastee Yogurt, a new brand introduction, (*b*) 3M self-sticking Post-it notes, and (*c*) Wrigley's Spearmint Gum.

8 Design an integrated marketing communications program—using each of the five promotional elements—for Music Boulevard, the online music store.

9 BMW introduced the activity vehicle, the X5, to compete with other popular 4 × 4 vehicles, such as the Mercedes-Benz M-class and Jeep Grand Cherokee. Design a direct marketing program to generate (*a*) leads, (*b*) traffic in dealerships, and (*c*) direct orders.

10 Develop a privacy policy for database managers that provides a balance of consumer and seller perspectives. How would you encourage voluntary compliance with your policy? What methods of enforcement would you recommend?

GOING ONLINE   Canadian Agencies Adopt IMC Approaches

Many traditional ad agencies in Canada have shifted their approach away from offering clients only strict advertising solutions to comprehensive marketing communications solutions, including an IMC approach. Zig is one such Canadian firm. It offers its Canadian clients a host of marketing communications solutions, many of which combine the promotional elements discussed in this chapter. Go to Zig's Web site at www.zig.ca. Click on "Zigging" which will reveal many of Zig's latest campaigns, ranging from work done for nonprofit organizations to that for several of Canada's well-known packaged goods brands.

1   Examine the campaigns Zig has developed for its clients. What are your thoughts on Zig's communications solutions?

2   Which campaigns seem to embrace an IMC approach?

3   How effective do you think these campaigns are? How should they be evaluated in terms of success?

Do you want to get better grades and stay up to date with current issues in marketing? Visit the Online Learning Centre at www.mcgrawhill.ca/college/crane for practice tests, video cases, resources for building a marketing plan, *Globe and Mail* headlines, access to *Marketing Magazine*, and other learning and study tools.

VIDEO CASE 16

UPS: Repositioning a Business with IMC

"As a business, we have, for decades, been primarily in the business of small package transportation and delivery," observes Paul Meyer, group manager of UPS Brand Communications, "which is how the vast majority of our customers and the population at large know us today." Now, UPS is undertaking the challenge of expanding into new businesses, and it must change the perceptions of the services it provides. As Meyers explains, the question he faces is: "How do we position UPS as an enterprise . . . into a new space that we can define?"

THE COMPANY

UPS was founded by 19-year-old James Casey in 1907 as a messenger service. As the use of telephones and automobiles increased, the demand for message delivery declined, and Casey began to focus his business on package delivery for retail stores. In 1919, the company expanded and adopted its present name, United Parcel Service. The expansion continued to the East coast and Canada, necessitating the development of air and ground delivery routes. As retail stores moved to large suburban shopping centres with large parking lots, however, the demand for retail package delivery began to decline and UPS decided to expand its delivery service to include all possible customers, both private and commercial.

Today, UPS has grown into a $33 billion corporation and the world's largest package delivery service. The company consists of 357 000 employees, 88 000 package cars, vans, and motorcycles, and 269 airplanes which operate in 200 countries and territories worldwide. UPS now ships more than 13.6 million packages and documents each day to more than 7.9 million customers!

REPOSITIONING UPS

During the late 1990s, UPS began to evaluate its core business—the distribution and delivery of goods—and the possibility of expanding into new services. Managers at UPS realized that commerce consisted of more than the flow of goods; it also included the flow of information and capital, and so they began to build a network of services to help UPS customers with all three components. UPS began a series of acquisitions which created UPS Supply Chain Solutions, UPS Capital, UPS Mail Innovations, and UPS Consulting. In addition, it acquired the Mail Boxes Etc. franchise. UPS hoped that these new offerings would reposition UPS into a marketspace the company called "synchronized commerce."

Through its acquisitions, UPS had the potential to be a comprehensive enabler of global commerce. It hoped to offer customized supply chain, information, and financial product solutions for each individual customer. Despite its new services, however, the company was challenged by the perception that it only provided package delivery. "We found that we needed to help our customers, and the different decision makers that we engage," explains Meyers. "We had to find a way to build a bridge for them from what they knew us to be as a small package transportation company into something larger than that. We do more than just deliver packages was the basic proposition," he says.

THE UPS–IMC CAMPAIGN

UPS needed to convey its new capabilities, and its transformation to the "synchronized" commerce positioning, to current and potential customers. An integrated marketing communications campaign was needed. UPS started by conducting two years of strategic research and planning to guide the new communication activities. The result was a comprehensive campaign that included advertising, public relations, personal selling, and promotional efforts.

The first announcement was the new logo. UPS had utilized four logos in its history. The first logo was adopted in 1916 and featured an eagle carrying a package on a shield with the words "Safe, Swift, Sure." The second logo retained the shield, added the letters "UPS" and the phrase "The Delivery System for Stores of Quality." The third logo, simplified UPS's identity by adding a bow-tied package above the shield and the letters UPS, and eliminating all words and phrases. This logo was used without change for 42 years! Finally, the new logo removed the bow-tied package to underscore the company's expanded services, and simply retained the shield and the letters "UPS." The new logo now appears on all UPS vehicles and aircraft, and its 45 000 drop-off boxes and one million uniform pieces.

Another element of the communication campaign was to rename Mail Boxes Etc. as *The UPS Store*—with the new logo prominent in the new store signage. The retail presence gave UPS the world's largest and fastest-growing shipping and business services outlet and access to a variety of small businesses, sales personnel, and retail consumers. In response, competitor FedEx purchased Kinko's 1200 retail outlets for $2.4 billion dollars in the hope that it would add new locations to pick up packages.

Advertising also supports the changes at UPS. The company's largest national campaign "What Can Brown Do for You?" emphasizes the colour that was selected by one of the company's founders because it

reflected class, elegance, and professionalism. The colour is viewed as a creative platform that ties all pieces of the campaign together. It is part of the presentation of all vehicles, planes, uniforms, and packaging. In addition, although brown will remain the primary colour representing UPS, other new complementary colours will become part of new designs of company assets. The advertising also emphasizes the theme of "synchronizing the world of commerce."

UPS has identified five segments it tries to reach with its advertising. They are shipping decision makers, front office decision makers, small business owners, senior level managers, and retail consumers. Each campaign has a specific context and emphasizes benefits important to that segment. All campaigns, however, utilize the colour brown theme as a means of integration.

The colour brown is such an important part of the UPS image that UPS registered two trademarks on the colour brown which prevent other delivery companies from using the colour for vehicles or clothing if it creates confusion in the marketplace. It takes more than 142 000 gallons of brown paint to keep UPS's fleet of vehicles brown, and 1 673 000 yards of brown cloth to make the 188 000 hats, 459 000 shirts, 303 000 pants, and 192 000 pairs of shorts needed to keep all UPS drivers in uniform.

Another element of the integrated program is the Web page (www.ups.com), which now receives 115 million hits per day, including 9.1 million online tracking requests. UPS's new CampusShip service allows consumers to operate a virtual post office. From any location, customers can build an online address list, print labels, track a package, and e-mail shipping notifications. UPS even uses its online capabilities to manage online orders for such companies as Jockey International. Apparel bought on the Jockey Web site is boxed by UPS employees managing the Jockey warehouse and delivered by UPS drivers.

Other elements of the campaign include promotions, personal selling activities, and public relations efforts that influence executives' public appearances and copy in popular business press, such as *The Wall Street Journal* and *Fortune*.

Future Strategy

How can UPS managers assess the success of their campaign? There are several measures that give an indication of the impact of the various message activities. First, there have been a variety of awards. For example, the "What Can Brown Do for You?" advertising was selected for an EFFIE award, and *BtoB Magazine* cited the campaign as one of the best integrated advertising campaigns. Meyer explains, "People across all of our target audiences have such a powerful association of the colour brown with the company UPS, and the brand UPS, that we can use the colour to personify the brand without even mentioning the brand and still get nearly 100 percent recall on all of our messaging."

Another measure of success is the new revenue being generated by logistics customers—a market growing at a rate of about 20 percent. In addition, some experts estimate that the new logistics business generates an additional $2 billion in shipping volume. Finally, a growing number of businesses, such as Ford and Birkenstock Footprint Sandals, have given UPS complete responsibility for their distribution networks. At Ford, UPS cut the time it takes a car to move from product to factory dealer by 40 percent, from 14 to 10 days; and at Birkenstock, UPS cut the time it takes shoes to get to stores by 50 percent.

For UPS, it is all about helping customers effectively operate their supply chains by simultaneously managing the flow of goods, information, and money. In the future, UPS will need to continue to evolve by developing new capabilities and by continuing to ask "What Can Brown Do for You?"

QUESTIONS

1 What information about consumer perceptions of UPS led the company to pursue an integrated marketing communications campaign? What was UPS's promotional objective as it repositioned itself in the "synchronized commerce" marketspace?

2 Which of the promotional elements described in Figure 16–2 were used by UPS in its integrated campaign? Describe how UPS might use different media or promotional elements to reach each of its five segments.

3 Why does the colour brown provide a useful "creative platform" for UPS's IMC campaign? What is your first reaction to the advertising theme "What Can Brown Do for You?"

4 As UPS has expanded throughout the world, it has chosen to use a global marketing strategy, as defined in Chapter 7. What are the advantages and disadvantages of this strategy for UPS?

ADDITION.   DIVISION.

MULTIPLICATION.

THEY'RE   SMARTER   THAN

WE   THINK.

The way dandelion has taken over western Canada, you'd think they planned it. Especially in reduced tillage where less-disturbed soil can provide ideal conditions for infestations. In ten years, this puff ball has exploded into a significant problem for growers.

For instance, in 2002, in Manitoba, dandelion was present in 19.8 percent of wheat fields and 20.3 percent of canola fields, and is now #12 of the over 62 weeds found during the survey. These surveys are conducted after

growers have sprayed, so hard-to-kill weeds like dandelion tend to show up more.

What's more, dandelion that grow past six inches become very resistant to control by any herbicides. And dandelion infestation providing 50% ground cover can cause between 39% and 64% yield loss, meaning even a patchy infestation of dandelion could warrant control. Suddenly, spending a little extra on Spectrum* seems pretty smart.

This year, find out how Spectrum can keep dandelion and other broadleaf weeds from blowing away your yields in wheat, barley and oats. Call your retailer, Dow AgroSciences Sales Representative or the Solutions Center at 1-800-667-3852.

Dow AgroSciences

ADVERTISING, SALES PROMOTION, AND PUBLIC RELATIONS

LEARNING OBJECTIVES

After reading this chapter, you should be able to:

1 Explain the differences between product advertising and institutional advertising and the variations with each type.

2 Describe the steps used to develop, execute, and evaluate an advertising program.

3 Explain the advantages and disadvantages of alternative advertising media.

4 Discuss the strengths and weaknesses of consumer-oriented and trade-oriented sales promotions.

5 Recognize public relations as an important form of communication.

SO, HOW WOULD YOU LIKE TO BE A CANADIAN ADFARMER?

Although you may see, hear, or read hundreds of advertisements daily, you might not be fully aware of the industry behind these ads. For many students, the advertising business evokes images of glamour, expense accounts, and an exciting lifestyle. This may be partially true. But the advertising business is also demanding, challenging, and a lot of hard work. To be successful in the advertising business requires a mix of personal abilities, considerable business skills, and an ability to work under pressure to meet deadlines. And compared with other industries, there are actually few entry-level positions available in Canadian advertising agencies. Also, the competition for those jobs is very intense, as there are only a few hundred advertising agencies in Canada. One of the most unique agencies in the business is called AdFarm.

AdFarm is Canada's largest agricultural marketing communications firm. It has also been recognized as one of the 50 Best Managed Companies in Canada. It focuses exclusively on providing communications solutions for companies and organizations operating in the agriculture sector. It has offices in Calgary and Guelph as well as in Fargo, ND, and Kansas City, MO. In 2002, it set what it called its BHAG—Big Hairy Audacious Goal, a 30-year goal to become the world's most respected agricultural marketing communications firm. It operates under a novel "one-agency matrix model" involving functions and teams and has no head office per se. It believes that this model allows AdFarm to create and deliver consistently excellent work for its clients, which includes some of the industry's leading players: Bayer Cropscience (seed and crop protection), RBC Royal Bank (the largest bank serving agriculture in North America), Case New Holland (farm equipment), Novartis (animal health), Alberta Beef Producers, and Ontario Pork Producers.

AdFarm is a full service agency offering a complete range of marketing communications services, including advertising, public relations, issue management, media relations, direct marketing, and online marketing. One of the other unique aspects of the organization is its focus on its employees, which the agency refers to as AdFarmers. All AdFarmers must meet a strict set of hiring criteria including being able to meet and live the AdFarm Values such as integrity, excellence, and fun. They must also possess excellent knowledge and skills within their respective functional area—creative, public relations, strategy, account services, media, and administration. Moreover, AdFarmers must be totally focused and passionate about the agriculture industry. Finally, the AdFarmers must also be willing to commit to ongoing training to refine their skills and obtain new knowledge. AdFarm, in fact, supports its AdFarmers who wish to continue their studies through additional university and college courses.

How successful is AdFarm? Its growth and financial performance is higher than the majority of competing firms; it has received numerous awards for its work; has achieved high levels of client satisfaction; and employee retention and work satisfaction are higher than the agency industry average. You will read more about AdFarm in the end-of-chapter case.

So, do you think you have what it takes to become an AdFarmer? Or to work in advertising industry, in general? If you are skilled, bright, articulate, creative, and personable and if you have a well-rounded education and a good business sense, you might. If you want to learn more about working in the Canadian advertising industry, go to the Institute of Communications and Advertising's Web site (www.ica-ad.com), Canada's national association of advertising agencies, and click on "Careers." You will find an interesting publication called, "*So....You Want to be in an Advertising Agency.*" You might also want to check out AdFarm's Web site ([www.adfarm online.com](www.adfarmonline.com)) just to see how unique this agency is in the overall Canadian advertising agency landscape. You never know, maybe some day you will get to become a Canadian AdFarmer after all![1]

advertising
Any *paid* form of nonpersonal communication about an organization, good, service, or idea by an identified sponsor.

This chapter introduces you to **advertising**—any *paid* form of nonpersonal communication about an organization, good, service, or idea by an identified sponsor. It will also detail the alternative types of advertisement and the advertising decision process as well as introduce you to the concepts of sales promotion and public relations.

■ ■ ■ TYPES OF ADVERTISEMENTS

As you look through any magazine or watch television, listen to the radio, or browse the Internet, many advertisements you see or hear may give you the impression that they have few similarities. Advertisements are prepared for different purposes, but they basically consist of two types: product and institutional. These two types of ads can also be classified on the basis of whether they are intended to get the consumer to take immediate action (*direct-response advertising*) or to influence future purchase or actions (*delayed-response advertising*).

Product Advertisements

product advertisements
Advertisements that focus on selling a good or service and take three forms:
(1) pioneering (or informational),
(2) competitive (or persuasive), and (3) reminder.

Focused on selling a good or service, **product advertisements** take three forms: (1) pioneering (or informational), (2) competitive (or persuasive), and (3) reminder. Look at the ads on the next page by Verizon, Allegra, and FTD, and determine the type and objective of each ad.

Used in the introductory stage of the product life cycle, *pioneering* advertisements tell people what a product is, what it can do, and where it can be found. The key objective of a pioneering advertisement (such as the ad for Verizon's new Mobile IM service) is to inform the target market. Informative ads have been found to be interesting, convincing, and effective.[2]

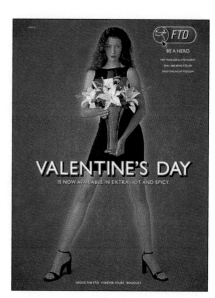

Advertisements serve varying purposes. Which ad would be considered (1) pioneering, or (2) competitive, and which is used as (3) a reminder?

Advertising that promotes a specific brand's features and benefits is *competitive*. The objective of these messages is to persuade the target market to select the firm's brand rather than that of a competitor. An increasingly common form of competitive advertising is *comparative* advertising, which shows one brand's strengths relative to those of competitors.[3] The Allegra ad, for example, highlights the competitive advantage of Allegra over its primary competitors Benadryl, Tylenol, and Chlor-Trimeton. Studies indicate that comparative ads attract more attention and increase the perceived quality of the advertiser's brand.[4] Firms that use comparative advertising need market research to provide legal support for their claims.[5]

Reminder advertising is used to reinforce previous knowledge of a product. The FTD ad shown reminds consumers about the association between its product and a special event—in this case, Valentine's Day. Reminder advertising is good for products that have achieved a well-recognized position and are in the mature phase of their product life cycle. Another type of reminder ad, *reinforcement*, is used to assure current users they made the right choice. One example: "Aren't you glad you use Dial? Don't you wish everybody did?"

institutional advertisements

Advertisements designed to build goodwill or an image for an organization, rather than promote a specific good or service.

Institutional Advertisements

The objective of **institutional advertisements** is to build goodwill or an image for an organization, rather than promote a specific good or service. Institutional advertising has been used by such companies as the Royal Bank, Pfizer, and IBM Canada to build confidence in the company name.[6] Often, this form of advertising is used to support the public relations plan or counter adverse publicity. Four alternative forms of institutional advertisements are often used:

1. *Advocacy* advertisements state the position of a company on an issue. For example, Molson's "Take Care" ads encourage the responsible use of alcohol.

2. *Pioneering institutional* advertisements, like the pioneering ads for products discussed earlier, are used for announcement about what a company is, what it can do, or where it is located. Recent Bayer ads stating "We cure more headaches than you think" are intended to inform consumers that the company produces many products in addition to Aspirin.

Dial soap uses reinforcement ads to encourage consumers to keep using the product.

3. *Competitive institutional* advertisements promote the advantages of one product class over another and are used in markets where different product classes compete for the same buyers. The Steel Alliance, for example, made up of major North American steel producers, including Stelco, Dofasco, and Ipsco, spend millions on advertising promoting steel's advantages over alternative products like wood, plastic, and aluminum.

4. *Reminder institutional* advertisements, like the product form, simply bring the company's name to the attention of the target market again.

As mentioned earlier, advertising can also be classified as either direct-response advertising or delayed-response advertising. *Direct-response advertising* seeks to motivate the customer to take immediate action, such as a television ad asking you to phone a toll-free telephone number and place an order immediately. *Delayed-response advertising*, on the other hand, presents images and/or information designed to influence the consumer in the near future when making purchases or taking other actions. Direct marketers often rely on direct-response advertising as part of their direct marketing efforts. However, even traditional marketers are using this form of advertising as they attempt to obtain an immediate return on their advertising dollar and measured response in terms of advertising effectiveness.

CONCEPT CHECK

1. What is the difference between pioneering and competitive ads?

2. What is the purpose of an institutional advertisement?

3. What is direct-response advertising?

DEVELOPING THE ADVERTISING PROGRAM

The promotion decision process described in Chapter 16 can be applied to each of the promotional elements. Advertising, for example, can be managed by following the three steps (developing, executing, and evaluating) of the process.

Identifying the Target Audience

To develop an effective advertising program, advertisers must identify the target audience. All aspects of an advertising program are likely to be influenced by the characteristics of the prospective consumer. Understanding the lifestyles, attitudes, and demographics of the target market is essential. Mary Quinlan, vice-chairman of the MacManus Group advertising agency, suggests that when women are the target, it is important that the ad content reflects that women "like to see other women who are diverse, confident, and naturally beautiful," and that "women respond to emotional truth and real-life experience."[7] Similarly, the placement of ads depends on the audience. When Hummer, the biggest and most expensive sport-utility vehicle in the market, began its $3-million campaign targeted at "rugged individualists" with incomes above $200 000, it selected *Wired, Spin, Red Herring, Business Week, Skiing*, and *Cigar Aficionado* to carry the ads.[8] Even scheduling can depend on the audience. Claritin, the nation's most prescribed allergy medication, schedules its use of brochures, in-store displays, coupons, and advertising to coincide with the allergy season, which varies by geographic region.[9] To eliminate possible bias that might result from subjective judgments about some population segments, advertising program decisions should be based on market research about the target audience.[10]

Specifying Advertising Objectives

The guidelines for setting promotion objectives described in Chapter 16 also apply to setting advertising objectives. This step helps advertisers with other choices in the promotion decision process, such as selecting media and evaluating a campaign. Advertising with an objective of creating awareness, for example, would be better matched with a magazine than a directory, such as the Yellow Pages.[11] Similarly, an advertiser looking to induce consumers to trial or to take other direct action, such as visit a store location, would use a direct-response form of advertising, such as direct mail. The Association of Canadian Advertisers believes that establishing advertising objectives is so important that it established the CASSIE Awards, whereby advertisers are recognized for achieving ad campaign objectives. Experts believe that such factors as product category, brand, and consumer involvement in the purchase decision may change the importance—and, possibly, the sequence—of the stages of the hierarchy of effects. Snickers, for example, knew that its consumers were unlikely to engage in elaborate information processing when it designed a recent campaign. The result was ads with simple humorous messages rather than extensive factual information.

Setting the Advertising Budget

The methods used to set the overall promotion budget as outlined in Chapter 16 can be used to establish a specific advertising budget. As with the promotional or integrated marketing communications (IMC) budget, the best approach to setting the ad budget is the objective and task approach. There are numerous advertising options available to the advertiser, and most of the alternatives require substantial financial commitments. A formal budgeting process that involves matching the target audience to the available advertising options, evaluating the ability of those options to achieve specified objectives, and weighing the relative costs of the advertising options is definitely a requirement for effective advertising.

Designing the Advertisement

An advertising message usually focuses on the key benefits of the product that are important to a prospective buyer in making trial and adoption decisions. The message depends on the general form or appeal used in the ad and the actual words included in the ad.

Message Content   Most advertising messages are made up of both informational and persuasional elements. These two elements, in fact, are so intertwined that it is sometimes difficult to tell them apart. For example, basic information contained in many ads, such as the product name, benefits, features, and price, is presented in a way that tries to attract attention and encourage purchase. On the other hand, even the most persuasive advertisements must contain at least some basic information to be successful.

Information and persuasive content can be combined in the form of an appeal to provide a basic reason for the consumer to act. Although the marketer can use many different types of appeals, common advertising appeals include fear appeals,[12] sex appeals, and humorous appeals.

Fear appeals suggest to the consumer that he or she can avoid some negative experience through the purchase and use of a product or service, a change in behaviour, or a reduction in the use of a product. Examples with which you may be familiar include fire or smoke detector ads that depict a home burning or social cause ads warning of the serious consequences of drug and alcohol use or high-risk sexual behaviour. Insurance companies often try to show the negative effects of premature death on the relatives of those who do not carry enough life or mortgage insurance.

Get tested.

Not all sexually transmitted infections are this easy
to spot. Many have no symptoms. You may be at risk.
Between 13 and 25? Get a fast, free and confidential
test by calling the House Community Health Centre.

416.927.7171   ppt.on.ca

An example of the use of humour
in advertising.

The use of celebrity spokespersons
is popular in Canadian advertising.

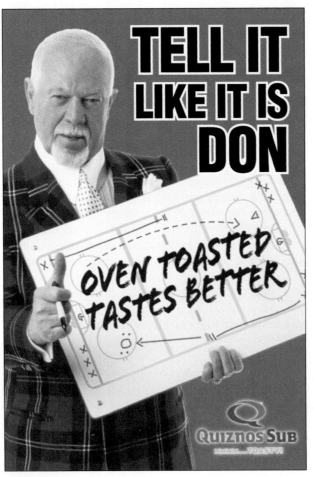

TELL IT LIKE IT IS DON

OVEN TOASTED TASTES BETTER

QuiznosSub

Food producers encourage the purchase of low-carb, low-fat, and high-fibre products
as a means of reducing weight, cholesterol levels, and the risk of a heart attack.[13]
When using fear appeals, the advertiser must be sure that the appeal is strong enough
to get the audience's attention and concern but not so strong that it will cause them to
tune out the message. In fact, recent research on antismoking ads indicates that
stressing the severity of long-term health risks may actually enhance smoking's
allure among youth.[14]

In contrast, *sex appeals* suggest to the audience that the product will increase the
attractiveness of the user. Sex appeals can be found in almost any product category,
from automobiles to toothpaste. Unfortunately, many commercials that use sex
appeals are successful only at gaining the attention of the audience; they have
little impact on how consumers think, feel, or act. Some
advertising experts even argue that such appeals get in
the way of successful communication by distracting the
audience from the purpose of the ad.

Humorous appeals imply either directly or more sub-
tly that the product is more fun or exciting than competitors' offerings. As with fear and sex appeals, the use of
humour is widespread in Canadian advertising and can
be found in many product categories. In fact, no product
sector appears immune. For example, typically conservative accounting firms, including PriceWaterhouseCoop-
ers, have used humour in advertising. The MS Society
also used humour to promote its Super Cities Walk for
MS. And Planned Parenthood of Toronto used humour in
its transit advertising designed to encourage young males
(17 to 25 years of age) to become more aware of sexually
transmitted infections and to seek testing, if necessary.
Their "spotted banana" program was very successful in
achieving this objective.[15] However, humour has to be
used with care. Jokes tend to wear out quickly, eventually boring the consumer. Sometimes, the humour may
offend the target audience, and humorous appeals tend
not to travel well across cultures.[16]

Creating the Actual Message   The "creative people"
in an advertising agency—copywriters and art directors—have the responsibility to turn appeals and such
features as quality, style, dependability, economy, and
service into attention-getting, believable advertisements.
Translating creative ideas into actual advertisements is a

complex process. Designing quality artwork, layout, and production for the advertisements is also often costly and time-consuming. High-quality TV commercials typically cost more than $200 000 to produce a 30-second ad. High-visibility integrated ad campaigns can even be more expensive. Other costs can include paying celebrity spokespersons to appear in the ads. In fact, Canadians are seeing many celebrities featured in advertising today, including sports heroes and entertainers. For example, Tourisme Quebec used Celine Dion as their celebrity spokeperson to promote tourism in Quebec. Don Cherry is another spokesperson used by different Canadian firms, including Quiznos, to increase the visibility of their ads. Finally, The Yellow shoe store chain used MusiquePlus VJs Réjean Laplanche and Izabelle Desjardins as the spokespersons for their ad campaign urging Quebec teens to stay in school in a campaign with the tag line "Laisse ta trace, gagne ta place (Leave your mark, earn your place)."[17]

CONCEPT CHECK

1. What are the three common advertising appeals?

2. Who is responsible for turning appeals and product features into attention-getting advertising?

Selecting the Right Media

Every advertiser must decide where to place its advertisements. The alternatives are the *advertising media*, the means by which the message is communicated to the target audience. Newspapers, magazines, radio, and TV are examples of advertising media. This "media selection" decision is related to the target audience, type of product, nature of the message, campaign objectives, available budget, and the costs of the alternative media. Figure 17–1 shows the distribution of the more than $10 billion spent on advertising in Canada among the many media alternatives.[18] Some of Canada's leading advertisers include General Motors of Canada, Sears Canada, BCE (Bell Canada Enterprises), the Government of Canada, Procter & Gamble, Rogers Communications, The Hudson's Bay Co., and Ford Motor Co. of Canada.

Choosing a Medium and a Vehicle within That Medium   In deciding where to place advertisements, a company has several media to choose from and a number of

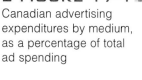

■ FIGURE 17–1 ■

Canadian advertising expenditures by medium, as a percentage of total ad spending

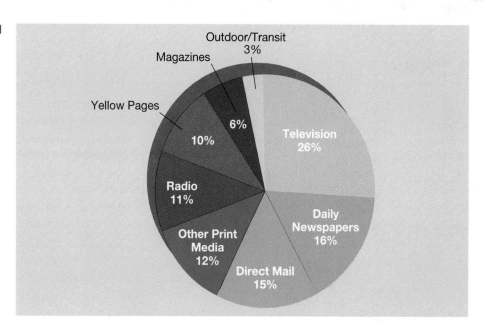

alternatives, or vehicles, within each medium. Often, advertisers use a mix of media forms and vehicles to maximize the exposure of the message to the target audience while time minimizing costs. These two conflicting goals of (1) maximizing exposure and (2) minimizing costs are of central importance to media planning.

Basic Terms   Media buyers speak a language of their own, and so every advertiser involved in selecting the right media for their campaigns must be familiar with some common terms used in the advertising industry. Figure 17–2 shows the most common terms used in media decisions.

Because advertisers try to maximize the number of individuals in the target market exposed to the message, they must be concerned with reach. **Reach** is the number of different people or households exposed to an advertisement. The exact definition of reach sometimes varies among alternative media. Newspapers often use reach to describe their total circulation or the number of different households that buy the paper. Television and radio stations, in contrast, describe their reach using the term **rating**—the percentage of households in a market that are tuned to a particular TV show or radio station. In general, advertisers try to maximize reach in their target market at the lowest cost.

Like greater reach, greater frequency has been historically viewed as desirable.[19] This was because it was believed that consumers often do not pay close attention to the advertising message. Therefore, many advertisers wanted to expose the same audience more than once to their message. This involves **frequency**, or the average number of times a person in the target audience is exposed to a message or advertisement. In fact, the traditional 3+ effective-frequency model (exposing the target audience 3+ times to an ad) has dominated the advertising industry for years. Now, however, there is evidence that this model is flawed. Many Canadian advertisers have turned to a new approach called *recency*—delivering media messages in a way that increases the likelihood of reaching more people with a message close to the time of their purchase. This is sometimes called just-in-time communications. The Marketing NewsNet box outlines the rationale for recency over frequency.[20]

When reach (expressed as a percentage of the total market) is multiplied by frequency, an advertiser will obtain a commonly used reference number called **gross rating points** (GRPs). To obtain the appropriate number of GRPs to achieve an advertising campaign's objectives, the media planner must balance reach and frequency. The balance will also be influenced by cost. **Cost per thousand** (CPM) refers to the cost of reaching 1000 individuals or households with the advertising message in a given medium (*M* is the Roman numeral for 1000).

Margin glossary

reach
The number of different people or households exposed to an advertisement.

rating
The percentage of households in a market that are tuned to a particular TV show or radio station.

frequency
The average number of times a person in the target audience is exposed to a message or advertisement.

gross rating points (GRPs)
A reference number for advertisers, created by multiplying reach (expressed as a percentage of the total market) by frequency.

cost per thousand (CPM)
The cost of reaching 1000 individuals or households with an advertising message in a given medium.

■ **FIGURE 17–2** ■
The language of the media buyer

TERM	WHAT IT MEANS
Reach	The number of different people or households exposed to an advertisement.
Rating	The percentage of households in a market that are tuned to a particular TV show or radio station.
Frequency	The average number of times an individual is exposed to an advertisement.
Gross rating points (GRPs)	Reach (expressed as a percentage of the total market) multiplied by frequency.
Cost per thousand (CPM)	The cost of advertising divided by the number of thousands of individuals or households who are exposed.

MARKETING NEWSNET   Recency versus Frequency

It had been widely held that advertising could only be effective if one achieved the effective frequency threshold—exposing the target audience three or more times to the advertising message. But, recent research from Canada, the United States, and the United Kingdom shows that this traditional 3+ effective-frequency model for planning and buying advertising is not valid. An different model has been proposed and is now taking root in the advertising business. "Recency" is the concept of delivering media messages in a way that increases the likelihood of reaching more people with a message close to the time of their purchase decision. Recency is sometimes described as just-in-time communications. It has been found that when properly executed with good creativity, a single impression can influence behaviour if delivered at the right time. In short, close to the time of purchase, one exposure to an ad message can be effec-

tive. Experts who argue in favour of recency over frequency suggest that advertising effectiveness can be improved if money spent on delivering excessive frequency is redirected to disperse messages more widely, to run more often "just-in-time."

And while Canada has been lagging behind the United States and the United Kingdom in implementing the recency ad planning and buying discipline, more and more Canadian advertisers are adopting the recency model as an alternative to the traditional frequency model. They are discovering that money does not have to be spent on excessive frequency. And, excessive frequency, which can often result in ad wearout, can be avoided with recency. Canadian advertisers are also discovering that recency, executed correctly, results in greater reach and continuity. To learn more about recency, visit Lowell Lunden's (President of Lunden & Associates Ltd.) Web site at www.recency.ca.

Different Media Alternatives

Figure 17–3[21] summarizes the advantages and disadvantages of the important advertising media, which are described in more detail below.

Television Television is a valuable medium because it communicates with sight, sound, and motion. Print advertisements alone could never give you the sense of a new sports car accelerating from a stop or cornering at high speed. In addition, network television is the only medium that can reach 99 percent of the homes in Canada.[22] And 85 percent of Canadian households are cable- or satellite-equipped. *Out-of-home* TV also reaches millions of Canadians in bars, hotels, and college campuses each week.

Television's major disadvantage is cost: the average price of a prime-time 30-second spot on a Canadian national network can be $80 000.[23] Because of these high charges, many advertisers have reduced the length of their commercials from 30 seconds to 15 seconds. This practice, referred to as *splitting 30s*, reduces costs but severely restricts the amount of information and emotion that can be conveyed. Research indicates, however, that two different versions of a 15-second commercial, run back-to-back, will increase recall over long intervals.[24]

Another problem with television is the likelihood of *wasted coverage*—having people outside the market for the product see the advertisement. In recent years, the cost and wasted-coverage problems of TV have been reduced through the introduction of specialized digital or cable and direct broadcast (satellite) channels. Advertising time is often less expensive on cable and direct broadcast channels than on the major networks. There are currently many channel options—such as CMT, Much Music, HGTV, Canadian Learning, and CNN—that reach very narrowly defined audiences. Other forms of television are changing television advertising also. Pay-per-view movie services and DVRs, for example, offer the potential of commerical-free viewing.

MEDIUM	ADVANTAGES	DISADVANTAGES
Television	Reaches extremely large audience; uses picture, print, sound, and motion for effect; can target specific audiences	High cost to prepare and run ads; short exposure time and perishable message; difficult to convey complex information
Radio	Low cost; can target specific local audiences; ads can be placed quickly; can use sound, humour, and intimacy effectively	No visual element; short exposure time and perishable message; difficult to convey complex information
Magazines	Can target specific audiences; high-quality colour; long life of ad; ads can be clipped and saved; can convey complex information	Long time needed to place ad; relatively high cost; competes for attention with other magazine features
Newspapers	Excellent coverage of local markets; ads can be placed and changed quickly; ads can be saved; quick consumer response; low cost	Ads compete for attention with other newspaper features; short life span; poor colour
Yellow Pages	Excellent coverage of geographic segments; long use period; available 24 hours/365 days	Proliferation of competitive directories in many markets; difficult to keep up-to-date
Direct mail	High selectivity of audience; can contain complex information and personalized messages; high-quality graphics	High cost per contact; poor image (junk mail)
Internet	Video and audio capabilities; animation can capture attention; ads can be interactive and link to advertiser	Animation and interactivity require large files and more time to load; effectiveness is still uncertain
Outdoor	Low cost; local market focus; high visibility; opportunity for repeat exposures	Message must be short and simple; low selectivity of audience; criticized as a traffic hazard

■ **FIGURE 17–3** ■

Advantages and disadvantages of major advertising media

Source: William F. Arens, *Contemporary Advertising*, 9th ed. Copyright © 2004 by The McGraw-Hill Companies; Figure 17.3 from William G. Nickels, James M. McHugh, and Susan M. McHugh, *Understanding Business*, 7th ed. © 2005 by The McGraw-Hill Companies.

infomercials

Program-length (30-minute) advertisements that take an educational approach to communication with potential customers.

Another popular form of television advertising is the infomercial. **Infomercials** are program-length (30-minute) advertisements that take an educational approach to communication with potential customers. Volvo, Club Med, General Motors, Mattel, Revlon, and many other companies are using infomercials as a means of providing information that is relevant, useful, and entertaining to prospective customers. In many cases, marketers are using infomericals for direct-response purposes, asking customers to order products and/or to request further information during the airing. About $20 million is spent on infomercials in Canada.[25]

Radio There are over 900 radio stations in Canada. The major advantage of radio is that it is a segmented medium. There are jazz stations, classical music stations, all-talk shows, and hard rock stations, all catering to different market segments. The average radio listener spends 3+ hours listening to the radio.

The disadvantage of radio is that it has limited use for products that must be seen. Another problem is the ease with which consumers can tune out a commercial by switching stations. Radio is also a medium that competes for people's attention as do other activities, such as driving, working, or relaxing. Peak radio listening time, for example, is during peak-hour commuting (6 to 10 A.M. and 4 to 7 P.M.).

And now, radio listeners have another radio listening option—satellite radio services that offer digital-quality radio channels for a monthly subscription. Sirius Radio and XM Satellite Radio offer commercial-free channels and channels with only 6 minutes of advertising per hour compared with 15 to 20 minutes on "free" channels. Recent research shows that over 30 percent of Canadians are interested in subscribing to satellite radio and that over 2 percent already subscribe to US-based services. Canadian Satellite Radio has partnered with XM Satellite Radio of the United States to offer Canadians satellite radio services in Canada.[26]

Magazines   Magazines have become a very specialized medium. There are about 500 consumer magazines in Canada.[27] The marketing advantage of this medium is the great number of special-interest publications that appeal to narrowly defined segments. Runners read *Runner's World*, sailors buy *Sail*, gardeners subscribe to *Gardening Life*, and children peruse *Sports Illustrated for kids*. Each magazine's readership often represents a unique profile. Take the *Rolling Stone* reader, who tends to travel, backpack, and ski more than do most people—and so a manufacturer of ski equipment that places an ad in *Rolling Stone* knows it is reaching the desired target audience. In addition to the distinct audience profiles of magazines, good colour production is an advantage that allows magazines to create strong images.

The cost of advertising in national magazines is a disadvantage, but many national publications, such as *Canadian Living*, publish regional and even metro editions, which reduce the absolute cost and wasted coverage. In addition to cost, a limitation to magazines is their infrequency. At best, magazines are printed on a weekly basis, with many specialized publications appearing only monthly or less often.

Newspapers   Newspapers are an important local medium with excellent reach potential. There are over 100 daily newspapers in Canada, including 12 French language papers. There are also over 1100 community newspapers. Because of the daily publication of most papers, they allow advertisements to focus on specific current events, such as a "24-hour sale." Local retailers often use newspapers as their sole advertising medium.

Newspapers, however, are rarely saved by the purchaser, and so companies are generally limited to ads that call for an immediate customer response (although customers can clip and save the ads they are interested in). Companies also cannot depend on newspapers for the same colour reproduction quality as that in most magazines.

National advertising campaigns rarely include this medium except in conjunction with local distributors of their products. In these instances, both parties often share the advertising costs using a cooperative advertising program, which is described later in this chapter. Another exception is the use of newspapers, such as *The Globe and Mail*, which has national distribution.

In an effort to deliver timely news coverage, many newspapers are delivering online or digital newspapers. For example, *The Globe and Mail* and *The National Post* both offer online or digital papers and are expecting to make them interactive as well. This concept is opening up new advertising potential for such newspapers.

Yellow Pages   Yellow Pages represent an alternative advertising medium comparable with radio in terms of expenditures in Canada. Over $1 billion is spent on Yellow Pages advertising in Canada and over $25 billion is spent globally.[28] Yellow Pages directories reach almost every household in Canada and are a *directional* medium because they help consumers know where purchases can be made after other media have created awareness and demand.

Yellow Pages have several other advantages. First, they are available 24 hours each day and 365 days each year. In addition, Yellow Pages have a long life span—directories are typically published once each year and provide advertisers with many advertising size options. A disadvantage of Yellow Pages advertising is the proliferation of similar directories. Many markets now have competing directories for specific neighbourhoods and even ethnic groups. Another disadvantage is the lack of timeliness because Yellow Pages can only be updated with new information once each year. Yellow pages are typically used for local advertising—more than 80 percent of all Yellow Pages expenditures are local—because of the difficulty of coordinating a nationwide campaign in Yellow Pages directories.

Direct Mail Direct mail advertising is often considered the cornerstone of many direct marketers (see Chapters 15 and 16) efforts to reach consumers. But any advertiser looking for good audience selectivity can find direct mail advertising effective. Also, direct mail advertising allows the marketers to provide more information to the customer than is possible in a television or radio spot. In many cases, direct mail advertising is being used in conjunction with other media, particularly broadcast, as part of an integrated marketing communications solution. Mass media are used to create awareness, while direct mail advertising is used to build a relationship and facilitate a purchase.

One disadvantage of direct mail advertising is its rising costs due to postal rate increases. Another limitation is that people often view direct mail advertising as junk mail and are reluctant to open such mail. A novel approach to overcome that problem is the use of *self-mailers*—simple white envelopes without any promotional messaging—that consumers are more likely to open. Also, the availability of robust databases now allows the advertiser to send mail only to well-defined targets with very specific and appealing offers, which is helping to improve consumer response rates.

Internet The Internet is a relatively new medium for advertising. But with 75 percent of Canadians now having Internet access, it is attracting advertisers from a variety of industries. Online or Web advertising is similar to print advertising in that is offers a visual message. It has additional advantages, however, because it can also use the audio and visual capabilities of the Internet. Sound and movement may attract more attention or make the message more entertaining. Online advertising also has the unique feature of being interactive. Interactive online advertising, called *rich media*, have drop-down menus, built-in games, or search engines to engage viewers. Online advertising, particularly interactive ads, has grown substantially in Canada over the past few years. Current expenditures on this medium is expected to exceed $400 million.[29]

There are a variety of venues to advertise online, including (1) portal sites, such as www.sympatico.com, or www.canoe.ca; (2) network buys through multi-site vendors, such as 24/7 Canada; (3) individual site advertising; (4) search engines, such as Google.ca or AskJeeves. Advertisers also have a choice of the type of online ads that wish to present to the customer. The most common is the banner ad. Other forms of online advertising include skyscrapers, pop-ups, interstitials, and mini-sites, which use streaming video and audio and are very similar to traditional television advertising.

One disadvantage of online advertising is that because the medium is new, technical and administrative standards for the various formats are still evolving. The Interactive Advertising Bureau of Canada provides some guidance regarding online advertising standards and makes recommendations for formatting. Another disadvantage of online advertising is the difficulty in measuring effectiveness or impact. Online advertising currently lags behind other media, such as radio, TV, and print, in offering proof of effectiveness. Several companies are now involved in attempting to measure online advertising effectiveness. For example, Nielsen Media Research measures click-by-click behaviour through meters installed on the computers of 225 000 individuals in 26 countries both at home and at work (see www.nielsen

<u>netratings.com</u> for recent ratings). Another method being tested to provide some indication of the effectiveness of online advertising is *permission-based* advertising, where viewers agree to watch a commercial online in exchange for points, samples, or access to premium content and advertisers only pay for completed views. The Interactive Advertising Bureau of Canada is also working to advance the use and effectiveness of online advertising. For example, it has a research program called the Canadian Media Optimization (CMOST) designed to measure the impact of online advertising. It has already conducted research for Molson, RBC Insurance, General Motors, Canadian Tire, and AIM Trimark. For example, it discovered that when Canadian Tire combined its radio campaign with online advertising, its awareness levels among its customers went up by 6 percent. Check out these and other findings after reading the accompanying WebLink box.[30]

Outdoor   A very effective medium for reminding consumers about your product is outdoor advertising. Outdoor and transit advertising expenditures in Canada are estimated at over $290 million.[31] The most common form of outdoor advertising, called *billboards*, often results in good reach and frequency. The visibility of this medium is good supplemental reinforcement for well-known products, and it is a relatively low-cost, flexible alternative. A company can buy space just in the desired geographical market. A disadvantage of billboards, however, is that no opportunity exists for long advertising copy. Also, the effectiveness of a billboard site depends on traffic patterns and sight lines. In many areas, environmental laws have limited the use of this medium.

If you have ever lived in a metropolitan area, chances are you might have seen another frequently used form of outdoor advertising, transit advertising. This medium includes messages on the interior and exterior of buses, subway cars, taxis, and transit shelters. In fact, the advertiser can actually purchase an entire bus, called a superbus for about $100 000 and place its message over the entire vehicle. If selectivity is important, space can be bought in specific neighbourhoods or even transit routes. One disadvantage to this medium is that anxious travel times, when audiences are largest, are not conducive to reading advertising copy. People are standing shoulder to shoulder, hoping not to miss their stop, and little attention is paid to the advertising.

Captivate TV Network offers "TV in Elevators."

Other Media   As traditional media have become more expensive and cluttered, advertisers have been attracted to a variety of nontraditional advertising options, called *place-based media*. Messages are placed in locations that attract a specific target audience, such as airports, doctors' offices, health clubs, theatres (where ads are played on the screen before the movies are shown), even bathrooms of bars, colleges, restaurants, and nightclubs! You have probably also seen advertising on video screens on gas pumps, ATMs, and in elevators! Another new form of advertising is called advergaming, as the accompanying Marketing NewsNet box discusses.

WEBLINK

HTTP://WWW.MCGRAWHILL.CA/
COLLEGE/CRANE

GLOBAL ACCESS

IAB of Canada and Internet/Online Advertising

The Interactive Advertising Bureau (IAB) of Canada is a not-for-profit association with membership composed of publishers, advertisers, advertising agencies, and service associates in the Canadian online/interactive marketing industry. IAB Canada is dedicated to establishing and communicating interactive advertising best practices that opti-mize advertising investment, leading to increased stakeholder value. Go to its Web site (<u>www.iabcanada.com</u>). Select "Standards" on the main menu. Click on "Best Practices White Papers." Select "Online Ad Campaign Measuring" paper. Read about what has been learned so far about online ad measurement.

MARKETING NEWS NET — Advergaming—A New Venue for Advertising

The popularity of video games and the growing interest in massive multi-player games (MMPs) has led to the concept of *advergaming*, or the integration of advertising messages in the virtual world of game settings. Nike and Levi Strauss, for example, are included in a popular game called *There*, which allows players to use Therebucks to purchase in-game products. Some manufacturers, such as Atari, are now designing video games with predetermined spots in the games, such as billboards along the track in a driving game, and so advertisers can send messages into the game over the Internet in real time.

According to some experts, advergaming will become much more sophisticated than signs. For example, such games as Tony Hawk Underground might be designed so that a skateboarder has to do a trick off a Jeep Liberty to accomplish a goal in the game. Advergaming is predicted to be just one of many exciting changes taking place in the field of advertising. Of course, like any other form of advertising, advertisers are going to want to know if advergaming will be effective and provide a return on their advertising dollar investment.

Selection Criteria   Choosing among these alternative media is difficult and depends on several factors. First, knowing the media habits of the target audience is essential. Second, occasionally, product attributes necessitate that certain media be used. For example, if colour is a major aspect of product appeal, radio is excluded. Newspapers allow advertising for quick actions to confront competitors, and magazines are more appropriate for complicated messages because the reader can spend more time reading the message. The final factor in selecting a medium is cost. When possible, alternative media are compared using a common denominator that reflects both reach and cost—a measure such as CPM.

Scheduling the Advertising

There is no correct schedule to advertise a product, but three factors must be considered. First is the issue of *buyer turnover*, which is how often new buyers enter the market to buy the product. The higher the buyer turnover, the greater the amount of advertising required. A second issue in scheduling is the *purchase frequency*; the more frequently the product is purchased, the less repetition is required. Finally, companies must consider the *forgetting rate*, the speed with which buyers forget the brand in the absence of advertising.

Setting schedules requires an understanding of how the market behaves. Most companies tend to follow one of three basic approaches:

1. *Continuous (steady) schedule.* When seasonal factors are unimportant, advertising is run at a continuous or steady schedule throughout the year.
2. *Flighting (intermittent) schedule.* Periods of advertising are scheduled between periods of no advertising to reflect seasonal demand.
3. *Pulse (burst) schedule.* A flighting schedule is combined with a continuous schedule because of increases in demand, heavy periods of promotion, or introduction of a new product.

For example, such products as dry breakfast cereals have a stable demand throughout the year and would typically use a continuous schedule of advertising. In contrast, such products as snow skis and suntan lotions have seasonal demands and receive flighting-schedule advertising during the seasonal demand period. Some products, such as toys or automobiles, require pulse-schedule advertising to facilitate sales throughout the year and during special periods of increased demand (such as holidays or new car introductions). Some evidence suggests that pulsing schedules are superior to other advertising strategies. In addition, findings indicate that the effectiveness of a particular ad "wears out" quickly and, therefore, many alternative forms of an advertisement may be more effective, particularly in light of new evidence concerning "recency," discussed earlier.

CONCEPT CHECK	**1.** You see the same ad in *Time* and *Maclean's* magazines and on billboards and TV. Is this an example of reach or frequency? **2.** Why has the Internet become a popular advertising medium? **3.** What factors must be considered when choosing among alternative media?

■ ■ ■
EXECUTING THE ADVERTISING PROGRAM

Executing the advertising program involves pretesting the advertising copy and actually carrying out the advertising program. An advertiser once remarked, "I know half my advertising is wasted, but I don't know what half." By evaluating advertising efforts, marketers can try to ensure that their advertising expenditures are not wasted. Evaluation is done usually at two separate times: before and after the advertisements are run in the actual campaign. Several methods used in the evaluation process at the stages of idea formulation and copy development are discussed below. Post-testing methods are reviewed in the section on evaluation.

Pretesting the Advertising

pretests
Tests conducted before an advertisement is placed to determine whether it communicates the intended message or to select among alternative versions of an advertisement.

To determine whether the advertisement communicates the intended message or to select among alternative versions of the advertisement, **pretests** are conducted before the advertisements are placed in any medium.

Portfolio Tests   Portfolio tests are used to test copy alternatives. The test ad is placed in a portfolio with several other ads and stories, and consumers are asked to read through the portfolio. Subsequently, subjects are asked for their impressions of the ads on several evaluative scales, such as from "very informative" to "not very informative."

Jury Tests   Jury tests involve showing the ad copy to a panel of consumers and having them rate how they liked it, how much it drew their attention, and how attractive they thought it was. This approach is similar to the portfolio test in that consumer reactions are obtained. However, unlike the portfolio test, a test advertisement is not hidden within other ads.

Theatre Tests   Theatre testing is the most sophisticated form of pretesting. Consumers are invited to view new television shows or movies in which test commercials are also shown. Viewers register their feelings about the advertisements either on handheld electronic recording devices used during the viewing or later on questionnaires.

Carrying Out the Advertising Program

full-service agency
An advertising agency providing the most complete range of services, including market research, media selection, copy development, artwork, and production.

The responsibility for actually carrying out the advertising program can be handled in one of three ways, as shown in Figure 17–4. The **full-service agency** provides the most complete range of services, including market research, media selection, copy development, artwork, and production. Some of Canada's leading full-service ad agencies include Cossette Communications, MDC Partners, Maritz Canada, Carlson Marketing, and Nerun. But as we saw in Chapter 16, many clients are looking to

■ FIGURE 17–4 ■

Alternative structures of advertising agencies used to carry out the advertising program

TYPE OF AGENCY	SERVICES PROVIDED
Full-service agency	Does research, selects media, develops copy, and produces artwork; also coordinates integrated companies with all marketing efforts
Limited-service specialty agency	Specializes in one aspect of creative process; usually provides creative production work; buys previously unpurchased media space
In-house agency	Provides range of services, depending on company needs

limited-service agency
Specializes in one aspect of the advertising process, such as providing creative services to develop the advertising copy or buying previously unpurchased media space.

in-house agency
A company's own advertising staff, which may provide full services or a limited range of services.

develop and execute IMC programs. Almost all of the major full-service agencies in Canada now offer totally integrated marketing communications capabilities, including AdFarm, our featured agency in the chapter opener.

Limited-service agencies specialize in one aspect of the advertising process, such as providing creative services to develop the advertising copy or buying previously unpurchased media space. Limited-service agencies that deal in creative work are compensated by a contractual agreement for the services performed. Finally, **in-house agencies** made up of the company's own advertising staff may provide full services or a limited range of services.

■ ■ ■
EVALUATING THE ADVERTISING PROGRAM

The advertising decision process does not stop with executing the advertising program. The advertisements must be post-tested to determine whether they are achieving their intended objectives, and results may indicate that changes must be made in the advertising program.

post-tests
Tests conducted after an advertisement has been shown to the target audience to determine whether it has accomplished its intended purpose.

Post-testing the Advertising

An advertisement may go through **post-tests** after it has been shown to the target audience to determine whether it accomplished its intended purpose. Five approaches common in post-testing are discussed here.[32]

Aided Recall (Recognition-Readership) After being shown an ad, respondents are asked whether their previous exposure to it was through reading, viewing, or listening. The Starch test shown in the accompanying photo uses aided recall to determine the percentage (1) who remember seeing a specific magazine ad (*noted*), (2) who saw or read any part of the ad identifying the product or brand (*seen-associated*), and (3) who read at least half of the ad (*read most*). Elements of the ad are then tagged with the results, as shown in the picture.

Unaided Recall Such questions as, "What ads do you remember seeing yesterday?" are asked of respondents without any prompting to determine whether they saw or heard advertising messages.

Attitude Tests Respondents are asked questions to measure changes in their attitudes after an advertising campaign, such as whether they have a more favourable attitude toward the product advertised.

Starch scores an advertisement.

Inquiry Tests   Additional product information, product samples, or premiums are offered to an ad's readers or viewers. Ads generating the most inquiries are presumed to be the most effective.

Sales Tests   Sales tests involve such studies as controlled experiments (e.g., using radio ads in one market and newspaper ads in another and comparing the results) and consumer purchase tests (measuring retail sales that result from a given advertising campaign). The most sophisticated experimental methods today allow a manufacturer, a distributor, or an advertising agency to manipulate an advertising variable (such as schedule or copy) through cable systems and observe subsequent sales effects by monitoring data collected from checkout scanners in supermarkets.

Making Needed Changes

Results of post-testing the advertising copy are used to reach decisions about changes in the advertising program. If the post-test results show that an advertisement is doing poorly in terms of awareness or cost efficiency, it may be dropped and other ads run in its place in the future. Sometimes, advertisers drop their ads as a result of complaints they receive from consumers. Sometimes, the ads are dropped as a result of Advertising Standards Canada (ASC) receiving complaints about the ads. ASC is the body that administers the industry's self-regulatory code, the Canadian Code of Advertising Standards. In the past year, the ASC received over 1500 complaints about advertising, of which over 60 percent involved TV advertisements. Most of the complaints focused on the sexually explicit nature of the ads or that the ads were inaccurate or misleading.[33]

CONCEPT CHECK	**1.** Explain the difference between pretesting and post-testing advertising copy.
	2. What is the difference between aided and unaided recall post-tests?

■ ■ ■
SALES PROMOTION

The Importance of Sales Promotion

At one time, sales promotion was considered by many to be a supplemental ingredient of the promotional mix. But more recently, the use of sales promotion has increased, and so has its perceived importance to marketers. In fact, in Canada, more money is now spent on sales promotion than on advertising.[34]

There are several reasons for the growth in importance of sales promotion. For one, many marketers are looking for measurable results from their promotional efforts. Sales promotion is viewed as an effective tool in this regard. Second, consumers and the trade (e.g., retailers) have become more value-conscious and thus more responsive to sales promotion activities. Third, some suggest that the use of sales promotion has grown because it has become contagious. In short, many marketers are simply responding to the increased use of sales promotion by competitors. Finally, the availability of information technology, such as computerized scanning equipment, has also served as a stimulus for the growth of sales promotion.

While sales promotion techniques have grown in use and in stature, they are rarely used in isolation or as a stand-alone promotional tool. With the trend toward IMC, sales promotion techniques are used more commonly in conjunction with other promotional activities. However, the selection and integration of the many sales promotion techniques requires a good understanding of the relative advantages and disadvantages of each kind of sales promotion.

Consumer-Oriented Sales Promotions

consumer-oriented sales promotions

Sales tools used to support a company's advertising and personal selling efforts directed to ultimate consumers; examples include coupons, sweepstakes, and samples.

Directed to ultimate consumers, **consumer-oriented sales promotions**, or simply consumer promotions, are sales tools used to support a company's advertising and personal selling efforts. Consumer-oriented sales promotion tools include coupons, deals, premiums, contests, sweepstakes, samples, loyalty programs, point-of-purchase displays, rebates, and product placement (Figure 17–5).

Coupons   Coupons are typically printed certificates that give the bearer a saving or a stated price reduction when they purchase a specific product. Coupons can be used to stimulate demand for mature products or promote the early trial of a new brand. Billions of direct-to-consumer coupons are distributed annually in Canada. Canadians redeem

millions of these coupons resulting in savings of over $100 million on products as a result of using coupons.[35]

Studies show that when coupons are used, a company's market share does increase during the period immediately after they are distributed.[36] There are indications, however, that couponing can reduce gross revenues by lowering the price paid by already-loyal consumers.[37] Therefore, manufacturers and retailers are particularly interested in coupon programs directed at potential first-time buyers. One means of focusing on these potential buyers is through electronic in-store coupon machines that match coupons to your most recent purchases.

Deals   Deals are short-term price reductions, commonly used to increase trial among potential customers or to retaliate against a competitor's actions. There are two basic types of deals: cents-off deals and price-pack deals. Cents-off deals offer a brand at less than a regular price, and the reduced prices are generally marked directly on the label or package. Cents-off deals can be very effective, even more so than coupons in stimulating short-term sales.

Price-pack deals offer consumers something extra, such as "20 percent more for the same price," or "Two packages for the price of one." Price-pack deals can be very effective in retaliating against or pre-empting a competitor's actions. For example, if a rival manufacturer introduces a new cake mix, the company could respond with the price-pack deal (e.g., 2 for 1), building up the stock on the kitchen shelves of cake mix buyers and making the competitor's introduction more difficult. Marketers must be careful, however, of overusing deals. If consumers expect a deal, they may delay a purchase until the deal occurs. Moreover, frequent deals may erode the perceived value of the brand to the consumer.

Premiums   Premiums are items offered free or at significant savings as incentives to buy a product. A premium offered at below its normal price is known as *self-liquidating* because the cost charged to the consumers covers the cost of the item. McDonald's used a free premium in a promotional partnership with Disney during the release of the movie *The Incredibles*; collectable toys that portrayed movie characters were given away free with the purchase of a Happy Meal. Offering premiums at no cost or at low cost encourages customers to return frequently or to use more of the product. However, the company must be careful that the consumer does not just buy the premium.

Contests   In the fourth sales promotion shown in Figure 17–5—the contest—consumers apply their analytical or creative thinking to try to win a prize. Most often, a consumer submits an entry to be judged by a panel. Many companies use contests not only to increase consumer purchases but also to obtain the names and addresses of consumers for use in database marketing purposes. For example, Gillette's Cavalcade of Sports 25-week hockey pool contest awarded a $1-million cash prize to each week's winner.

KIND OF SALES PROMOTION	OBJECTIVES	ADVANTAGES	DISADVANTAGES
Coupons	Stimulate demand	Encourage retailer support	Consumers delay purchases
Deals	Increase trial; retaliate against competitor's actions	Reduce consumer risk	Consumers delay purchases; reduce perceived product value
Premiums	Build goodwill	Consumers like free or reduced-price merchandise	Consumers buy for premium, not product
Contests	Increase consumer purchases; build business inventory	Encourage consumer involvement with product	Require creative or analytical thinking
Sweepstakes	Encourage present customers to buy more; minimize brand switching	Get customer to use product and store more often	Sales drop after sweepstakes
Samples	Encourage new-product trial	Low risk for consumer	High cost for company
Loyalty programs	Encourage repeat purchases	Help create loyalty	High cost for company
Point-of-purchase displays	Increase product trial; provide in-store support for other promotions	Provide good product visibility	Hard to get retailer to allocate high-traffic space
Rebates	Encourage customers to purchase; stop sales decline	Effective at stimulating demand	Easily copied; steal sales from future; reduce perceived product value
Product placement	Introduce new products; demonstrate product use	Positive message in a noncommercial setting	Little control over presentation of product

■ FIGURE 17–5 ■■
Sales promotion alternatives

Sweepstakes   Sweepstakes require participants to submit some kind of entry forms but are purely games of chance requiring no analytical or creative effort from the consumer. *Reader's Digest* and Publisher's Clearing House are two of the better-known sweepstakes. Canada has federal and provincial regulations covering sweepstakes, contests, and games regarding fairness, to ensure that the chance of winning is represented honestly and to guarantee that the prizes are awarded.

Samples   Another common consumer sales promotion is sampling, or offering the product free or at a greatly reduced price. Often used for new products, sampling puts the product in the consumer's hands: a trial size is generally offered that is smaller than the regular package size. If consumers like the sample, it is hoped they will remember and buy the product. Many Canadian firms have successfully used sampling as part of their marketing strategy. For example, Campbell Company of Canada used sampling for its frozen meal line, Ignite; Coca-Cola introduced Canadians to Diet Coke with Lime through an extensive sampling program in theatres, video stores, and malls; and Gillette launched its men's fragrance Tag through a sampling program, in which attractive females hired by the company picked some men from a crowd and sprayed them with the fragrance.

Loyalty Programs   Loyalty programs are a sales promotion tool used to encourage and reward repeat purchases by acknowledging each purchase made by a consumer and offering a premium as purchases accumulate. The most popular loyalty programs today are frequent-flyer and frequent traveller programs used by airlines, hotels, and car rental companies to reward loyal customers. Some programs are free, while others require the customer to pay an annual membership fee. Chapters Inc.

offers a loyalty program that provides discounts and gift certificates to its customers. The Royal Bank has a loyalty program called "Ultimix" which gives its Visa cardholders the opportunity to gain points to redeem for gifts and to also win prizes instantly. But perhaps the most famous and most successful loyalty program in Canada is the Canadian Tire money program. Now, in addition to receiving your Canadian Tire money at the checkout when you make your purchases, you can also collect "virtual" money through the use of a Canadian Tire credit card, and even through the use of the company's Web site.

Point-of-Purchase Displays   In a store aisle, you often encounter a sales promotion called a *point-of-purchase display*. These product displays take the form of

advertising signs, which sometimes actually hold or display the product, and are often located in high-traffic areas near the cash register or the end of an aisle. The accompanying picture shows a point-of-purchase display for Nabisco's annual Back-to-School program. The display is designed to maximize the consumer's attention to lunch-box and after-school snacks and to provide storage for the products.

Some studies estimate that two-thirds of a consumer's buying decisions are made in the store. This means that grocery product manufacturers want to get their message to you at the instant you are next to their brand in your supermarket aisle—perhaps through a point-of-purchase display.

Rebates   Another consumer sales promotion in Figure 17–5—the cash rebate—offers the return of money based on proof of purchase. This tool has been used heavily by car manufacturers facing increased competition. When the rebate is offered on lower-priced items, the time and trouble of mailing in a proof-of-purchase to get the rebate cheque means that many buyers— attracted by the rebate offer—never take advantage of it. However, this "slippage" is less likely to occur with frequent users of rebate promotions.

product placement
Using a brand-name product in a movie, television show, video, or a commercial for another product.

Can you identify this product placement?

Product Placement   A final consumer promotion, **product placement**, involves the use of a brand-name product in a movie, television show, video, or commercial for another product. It was Steven Spielberg's placement of Hershey's Reese's Pieces in *E.T.* that first brought a lot of interest to the candy. Similarly, when Tom Cruise wore Bausch and Lomb's Ray-Ban sunglasses in *Risky Business* and its Aviator sunglasses in *Top Gun*, sales skyrocketed from 100 000 pairs to seven million pairs in five years. More recently, you might remember seeing participants in the television show *Survivor* eating Doritos and drinking Mountain Dew, actors in the movie *Matrix* using Samsung cell phones, and Shirley MacLaine and Cameron Diaz driving Jaguars in *In Her Shoes*. Another form of product placement uses new digital technology, which can make "virtual" placements in any existing program. Reruns of *Seinfeld*, for example, could insert a Pepsi on a desktop, a Lexus parked on the street, or a box of Tide on Jerry's kitchen countertop!

Companies are usually eager to gain exposure for their products, and the studios believe that product placements add authenticity to the film or program. The studios receive fees—Sears paid $1 million for product placements in six episodes of ABC's *Extreme Makeover: Home Edition*—in exchange for the in-program exposure.

Trade-Oriented Sales Promotions

trade-oriented sales promotions

Sales tools used to support a company's advertising and personal selling efforts directed to wholesalers, distributors, or retailers. Three common approaches are allowances and discounts, cooperative advertising, and salesforce training.

Trade-oriented sales promotions, or simply trade promotions, are sales tools used to support a company's advertising and personal selling directed to wholesalers, retailers, or distributors. Some of the sales promotions just reviewed are used for this purpose, but there are three other common approaches targeted uniquely to these intermediaries: (1) allowances and discounts, (2) cooperative advertising, and (3) training of distributors' salesforces.

Allowances and Discounts   Trade promotions often focus on maintaining or increasing inventory levels in the channel of distribution. An effective method for encouraging such increased purchases by intermediaries is the use of allowances and discounts. However, overuse of these "price reductions" can lead to retailers changing their ordering patterns in the expectation of such offerings. Although there are many variations that manufacturers can use with discounts and allowances, three common approaches include the merchandise allowance, the case allowance, and the finance allowance.[38]

Reimbursing a retailer for extra in-store support or special featuring of the brand is a *merchandise allowance*. Performance contracts between the manufacturer and trade member usually specify the activity to be performed, such as a picture of the product in a newspaper with a coupon good at only one store. The merchandise allowance then consists of a percentage deduction from the list case price ordered during the promotional period. Allowances are not paid by the manufacturer until it sees proof of performance (such as a copy of the ad placed by the retailer in the local newspaper).

A second common trade promotion, a *case allowance*, is a discount on each case ordered during a specific time period. These allowances are usually deducted from the invoice. A variation of the case allowance is the "free goods" approach whereby retailers receive some amount of the product free based on the amount ordered, such as one case free for every 10 cases ordered.

A final trade promotion, the *finance allowance*, involves paying retailers for financing costs or financial losses associated with consumer sales promotions. This trade promotion is regularly used and has several variations. One type is the floor stock protection program—manufacturers give retailers a case allowance price for products in their warehouses, which prevents shelf stock from running down during promotional periods. Also common are freight allowances, which compensate retailers that transport orders from the manufacturer's warehouse.

cooperative advertising

Advertising programs by which a manufacturer pays a percentage of the retailer's local advertising expense for advertising the manufacturer's products.

Cooperative Advertising   Resellers often perform the important function of promoting the manufacturer's products at the local level. One common sales promotional activity is to encourage both better quality and greater quantity in the local advertising efforts of resellers through **cooperative advertising**. These are programs by which a manufacturer pays a percentage of the retailer's local advertising expense for advertising the manufacturer's products.

Usually, the manufacturer pays a percentage, often 50 percent, of the cost of advertising up to a certain dollar limit, which is based on the amount of the purchases the retailer makes of the manufacturer's products. In addition to paying for the advertising, the manufacturer often furnishes the retailer with a selection of different ad executions, sometimes suited for several different media. A manufacturer may provide, for example, several different print layouts as well as a few broadcast ads for the retailer to adapt and use.

Training of Distributors' Salesforces   One of the many functions the intermediaries perform is customer contact and selling for the producers they represent. Both retailers and wholesalers employ and manage their own sales personnel. A manufacturer's success often rests on the ability of the reseller's salesforce to represent its products.

Thus, it is in the best interests of the manufacturer to help train the reseller's salesforce. Because the reseller's salesforce is often less sophisticated and less knowledgeable about the products than the manufacturer might like, training can increase their sales performance. Training activities include producing manuals and brochures to educate the reseller's salesforce. The salesforce then uses these aids in selling situations. Other activities include national sales meetings sponsored by the manufacturer and field visits to the reseller's location to inform and motivate the salesperson to sell the products. Manufacturers also develop incentive and recognition programs to motivate reseller's salespeople to sell their products.

CONCEPT CHECK

1. Which sales promotional tool is most common for new products?

2. What's the difference between a coupon and a deal?

3. Which trade promotion is used on an ongoing basis?

■ ■ ■
PUBLIC RELATIONS

As noted in Chapter 16, public relations is a form of communication management that seeks to influence the feelings, opinions, or beliefs held by various publics about a company and its products or services. PR efforts may utilize a variety of tools and may be directed at many distinct audiences. While public relations personnel usually focus on communicating the positive aspects of the business, they may also be called on to minimize the negative impact of a problem or crisis, sometimes called crisis management.

Public Relations Tools

In developing a public relations campaign, several tools and tactics are available to the marketer. The most frequently used public relations tool is publicity, which we defined in Chapter 16 as a nonpersonal, indirectly paid presentation of an organization, good, or service. Publicity usually takes the form of a *news release*, consisting of an announcement regarding changes in the company, or the product line.

The objective of a news release is to inform a newspaper, radio station, or other medium of an idea for a story. A study found that more than 40 percent of all free mentions of a brand name occur during news programs.[39] A second common publicity tool is the *news conference*. Representatives of the media are invited to an informational meeting, and advance materials regarding the content are sent. This tool is often used when negative publicity requires a company response.

Nonprofit organizations rely heavily on publicity to spread their messages. PSAs (*public service announcements*), for which free space or time is donated by the media, are a common mode of publicity for these organizations. The Canadian Red Cross, for example, depends on PSAs on radio and television to announce its needs.

A growing area of public relations is event or cause sponsorship, sometimes referred to as *sponsorship marketing*. The goal of sponsorship marketing is to create a forum to disseminate company information and/or to create brand identification for the company or its product with members of the target audience. For example, CIAU sports championships are sponsored by some of Canada's leading companies. Hudson's Bay Company is an official sponsor and the official outfitter for the Vancouver

ETHICS AND SOCIAL RESPONSIBILITY ALERT

Is PETA's PR Believable?

Many organizations realize that most consumers view public relations, particularly news-oriented publicity, as more credible than advertising per se. As such, organizations have turned to well-managed public relations programs in order to influence the perceptions that relevant segments of the public have toward them or their causes. Many organizations disseminate information that will cast them only in the best possible light or to ensure that their view on a particular issue is conveyed to the public. However, there is growing concern about the public relations activities of organizations that may or may not be presenting all of the relevant information or facts surrounding a particular issue. One organization that is viewed with some skepticism by some is the People for the Ethical Treatment of Animals (PETA).

PETA has had a history of using PR to win the hearts of minds of Canadians concerning their views on the treatment of animals. It has clashed with the Canadian Cattlemen's Association making claims that eating meat causes impotence. The medical community discredited this claim. PETA has also run a PR campaign claiming that Jesus was a vegetarian and encouraged Christians to give up eating meat. Now, PETA is drawing fire for claiming that drinking milk can result in impotence. Again, experts have counterclaimed that there is no evidence that milk can cause impotence. PETA has also issued PR releases stating that eating meat causes cancer. Again, experts have suggested that PETA is overstating acknowledged scientific facts and omitting relevant information about the subject.

What are the relevant concerns regarding ethics and social responsibility here? Should the media release such claims made by PETA or any other organization when there may be some question as to the validity of the information being released to the public?

2010 Olympics, and many Canadian firms, including Petro-Canada, are official sponsors of the Trans Canada Trail project. CIBC is the official sponsor for the Run for Life campaign, and Ciba-Geigy Canada sponsors Health & Welfare Canada's Quit-4-Life Program. Sponsorship marketing has become so popular that there is now a national organization that has been created to help enhance the development of this concept. Check out the Sponsorship Marketing Council of Canada at www.sponsorshipmarketing.ca.

Finally, the development of *collateral materials,* such as annual reports, brochures, newsletters, corporate Web sites, or videos about the company and its product, are also basic public relations tools. These materials provide information to target publics and often generate good publicity.

Good public relations activities, however, should always be carefully planned and made part of an organization's IMC effort. However, public relations activities must be used wisely and in an ethical and socially responsible manner (see the accompanying Ethics and Social Responsibility Alert box).[40]

CONCEPT CHECK

1. What is a new release?

2. A growing area of public relations is _____

■ ■ ■
CHAPTER IN REVIEW

1 *Explain the differences between product advertising and institutional advertising and the variations within each type.*
Product advertisements focus on selling a good or service and take three forms: Pioneering advertisements tell people what a product is, what it can do, and where it can be found; competitive advertisements persuade the target market to select the firm's brand rather than a competitor's; and reminder advertisements reinforce previous knowledge of a product. Institutional advertisements are use to build good-will or an image for an organization. They include advocacy advertisements, which state the position of a company on an issue, and pioneering, competitive, and reminder advertisements, which are similar to the product ads but focused on the institution.

2 *Describe the steps used to develop, execute, and evaluate an advertising program.*
The promotion decision process can be applied to each of the advertising elements. The steps to develop an advertising program include identify the target audience, specify the advertising objectives, set the advertising budget, design the advertisement, create the message, select the media, and schedule the advertising. Executing the program requires pretesting, and evaluating the program requires post-testing.

3 *Explain the advantages and disadvantages of alternative advertising media.*
Television advertising reaches large audiences and uses picture, print, sound, and motion; its disadvantages, however, are that it is expensive and ephemeral. Radio advertising is inexpensive and can be placed quickly, but it has no visual element and is also ephemeral. Magazine advertising can target specific audiences and can convey complex information, but it takes a long time to place the ad and is relatively expensive. Newspapers provide excellent coverage of local markets and can be changed quickly, but they have a short life span and poor colour. Yellow Pages advertising has a long use period and is available 24 hours per day; its disadvantages, however, are that there is a proliferation of directories and they cannot be updated frequently. Internet advertising can be interactive, but its effectiveness is difficult to measure. Outdoor advertising provides repeat exposures, but its message must be very short and simple. Direct mail can be targeted at very selective audiences, but its cost per contact is high.

4 *Discuss the strengths and weaknesses of consumer-oriented and trade-oriented sales promotions.*
Coupons encourage retailer support but may delay consumer purchases. Deals reduce consumer risk but also reduce perceived value. Premiums offer consumers additional merchandise they want, but they may be purchasing only for the premium. Contests create involvement but require creative thinking. Sweepstakes encourage repeat purchases, but sales drop after the sweepstakes. Samples encourage product trial but are expensive. Loyalty programs help create loyalty but are expensive to run. Displays provide visibility but are difficult to place in retail space. Rebates stimulate demand but are easily copied. Product placement provides a positive message in a noncommercial setting but is difficult to control. Trade-oriented sales promotions include (*a*) allowances and discounts, which increase purchases but may change retailer ordering patterns, (*b*) cooperative advertising, which encourages local advertising, and (*c*) salesforce training, which helps increase sales by providing the salespeople with product information and selling skills.

5 *Recognize public relations as an important form of communication.*
Public relations activities usually focus on communicating positive aspects of the business. A frequently used public relations tool is publicity, which includes new releases and news conferences or public service announcements. A growing area of public relations is sponsorship marketing.

■ ■ ■
FOCUSING ON KEY TERMS

advertising p. 448
consumer-oriented sales promotions p. 464
cooperative advertising p. 467
cost per thousand (CPM) p. 454
frequency p. 454
full-service agency p. 461
gross rating points (GRPs) p. 454
in-house agency p. 462
infomercials p. 456

institutional advertisements p. 449
limited-service agency p. 462
post-tests p. 462
pretests p. 461
product advertisements p. 448
product placement p. 466
rating p. 454
reach p. 454
trade-oriented sales promotions p. 467

■ ■ ■
DISCUSSION AND APPLICATION QUESTIONS

1 How does competitive product advertising differ from competitive institutional advertising?

2 Suppose you are the advertising manager for a new line of children's bath products. Which form of media would you use for this new product?

3 You have recently been promoted to be director of advertising for the Timkin Tool Company. In your first meeting with Mr. Timkin, he says, "Advertising is a waste! We've been advertising for six months now and sales haven't increased. Tell me why we should continue." Give your answer to Mr. Timkin.

4 A large life insurance company has decided to switch from using a strong fear appeal to a humorous approach. What are the strengths and weaknesses of such a change in message strategy?

5 Which medium has the lowest cost per thousand?

MEDIUM	COST	AUDIENCE
TV show	$5 000	25 000
Magazine	2 200	6 000
Newspaper	4 800	7 200
FM radio	420	1 600

6 Some national advertisers have found that they can have more impact with their advertising by running a large number of ads for a period and then running no ads at all for a period. Why might such a flighting schedule be more effective than a continuous or steady schedule?

7 Each year, managers at Bausch and Lomb evaluate the many advertising media alternatives available to them as they develop their advertising program for contact lenses. What advantages and disadvantages of each alternative should they consider? Which media would you recommend to them?

8 What are two advantages and two disadvantages of the advertising post-tests described in the chapter?

9 The Royal Bank is interested in consumer-oriented sales promotions that would encourage senior citizens to direct deposit their Canada Pension cheques with the bank. Evaluate the sales promotion options, and recommend two of them to the bank.

GOING ONLINE		Advertising on the Internet

Most Web sites accept some form of advertising. If you were to advise your college or university to advertise on the Internet, what three sites would you recommend? You should use pricing information from each Web site to calculate a CPM and to help make your recommendation.

1 What is the monthly rate for a full banner ad at each of the Web sites?

2 Describe the profile of the audience for each of the Web sites.

3 Calculate the CPM for each Web site.

Do you want to get better grades and stay up to date with current issues in marketing? Visit the Online Learning Centre at www.mcgrawhill.ca/college/crane for practice tests, video cases, resources for building a marketing plan, *Globe and Mail* headlines, access to *Marketing Magazine*, and other learning and study tools.

VIDEO CASE 17   AdFarm

INTRODUCTION

AdFarm is Canada's largest agricultural marketing communications firm and has been recognized as one of 50 Best Managed Companies in Canada. It focuses exclusively on providing marketing communications solutions for companies and organizations operating in the agriculture sector. AdFarm is a full service agency offering a complete range of marketing communications services, including advertising, public relations, issue management, media relations, direct marketing, and online marketing.

AdFarm is a collection of four successful regional agricultural marketing communications agencies that saw the opportunity to respond to the changing needs and expectations of industry leaders operating in a highly competitive, global market. These four firms believed that a combined organization operating with a single focus could compete successfully in serving the multi-billion dollar, global agricultural industry. AdFarm has offices in Calgary and Guelph as well as in Fargo, ND, and Kansas City, MO. AdFarm's past and current clients include some of the world's premiere agricultural leaders, such as Bayer CropScience, Dow Agro-Sciences, RBC Royal Bank (the largest bank serving agriculture in North America), Case New Holland, Merial, Novartis, Bayer Animal Health, Nitragin, Alberta Beef Producers, and Ontario Pork Producers.

THE ADFARM BUSINESS MODEL

The AdFarm business model is somewhat unique for the agency business because of its single industry focus and the "matrix model" in which it operates. AdFarm operates a "one-agency matrix model" involving *Functions* and *Teams* and no head office per se. This model ensures greater consistency and excellence across all office locations and enables greater business growth. A key to this model's success is communication technology made possible today as a result of the Internet, video conferencing, and collaborative tool technology.

THE ADFARM BRAND PROMISE

Branding is a key part of the marketing communications services that AdFarm offers its clients. AdFarm has a director of brand, who is assigned the responsibility for leading and monitoring this important task. AdFarm expresses its brand in a variety of ways, including its Web site (www.adfarmonline.com), logo, stationery, promotional materials, sponsorships, and even offices. Most importantly, the AdFarm brand is expressed and experienced through its people.

The AdFarm brand promise centres around three strategic anchors:

- Total focus on agriculture (they like to say they are "Crazy about Farming").
- Commitment to "go deeper" and provide greater insights and value to its clients as a result of its specialized knowledge of agriculture and marketing communications.
- Connections within the industry that enable it to open doors and gain greater insights that are of value to its clients.

ADFARM'S VISION

AdFarm has articulated its vision and communicated it to all its employees and clients:

- To be the world's most respected agricultural marketing communications firm within 30 years; what it calls its BHAG (Big Hairy Audacious Goal).
- To be the second largest North American agency within three years as reported by *AgriMarketing* magazine.
- To have a solid and respected client portfolio in the United States and Canada.
- To be conducting business and providing services throughout North America as well as in two other continents.
- To be the industry's most respected employer.

AdFarm has also outlined its strategy to achieve and fulfill this vision:

- Continue to follow the BHAG journey.
- Grow revenue—through existing clients, by attracting new clients, and through acquisition/mergers that meet the AdFarm acquisition/merger policy.
- Grow service offering—by adapting to the continual changing needs of clients and the market with new product/service offering, including public affairs, consulting, and traceability/transparency technology.

ATTRACTING AND RETAINING QUALITY PEOPLE

The marketing communications business is an idea business and a service business. Quality people are imperative to attract clients, retain clients, create products and services that resonate with consumers, and differentiate AdFarm from competitors. The challenge, therefore, is to attract and retain exceptional people with the proper balance of "age-ness" and "ad-ness" and do this in a manner that is rewarding to the employee, profitable to shareholders, and of value to AdFarm's clients.

In terms of hiring, the first criterion that all AdFarmers must meet relates to the AdFarm values. These values include: the desire for relationships, excellence, passion, integrity, fun, personal accountability, and "thinking outside the box." The next screen involves the individual's demonstrated ability to provide excellence in his or her respective function area—creative, public relations, strategy, account service, media, or finance and administration. Adfarm wants to attract people that are committed to and passionate about delivering excellence within their chosen field or profession. And because AdFarm is totally focused on agriculture, it wants people with a knowledge and appreciation of this industry and its potential.

AdFarm then utilizes a combination of internal and external training initiatives to ensure peak employee performance. For example, it holds an annual Farm Days, which provides hands-on experience for all AdFarmers on real working farms.

Adfarm also operates its own real farms; one outside Calgary and one outside Fargo, North Dakota. AdFarmers are invited to purchase shares in one or both of these farms and to participate in the management of the farms. While the company retains a farm manager, AdFarmers make the decisions on what crop to grow, what inputs to use, and how and when they will market the crops.

In terms of external training—AdFarmers also participate in a variety of external training programs specific to their professional requirements. The firm supports employees taking university and college programs as well as training offered by the Institute of Communications and Advertising.

Another method of attracting and retaining quality people involves flexibility. Not only does AdFarm offer flexible hours, it also has something called "the summertime option." This provides AdFarmers who have gained the support of their teammates to cover for them, the opportunity to take a period of time off during the slower summer months. Also, because of technology, AdFarm has been able to retain key AdFarmers who might have left its employ for family reasons. AdFarm also believes in sharing the profits of its efforts proportionately with shareholders and employees. This focus on employees has led to employee retention rates that are considerably higher than the agency industry average. Morale is excellent, and contribution per employee is considerably higher than industry average.

PERFORMANCE

AdFarm is the largest agency serving the Canadian agricultural industry, the largest agency in Alberta, and probably the largest agency between Toronto and Vancouver. And its performance, to date, has been outstanding on a number of measures. For example:

1. Growth and Financial Performance—its growth and financial performance are substantially greater than the majority of marketing communications agencies operating in Canada.
2. Market Share—AdFarm has a dominant position and is estimated to be involved in approximately 40 percent of the agricultural communications spending in Canada.
3. Corporate Reputation—AdFarm has developed an excellent corporate reputation within its industry.
4. Awards—AdFarm has received numerous local, national, and international creative and public relations awards for its work.
5. Employee Pride—this is measured by employee involvement in firm events, their inputs and ideas for growth and performance, the number of people they invite to visit their unique offices, and the enthusiasm they convey to people in both the agricultural and marketing communications communities.

FUTURE GROWTH

AdFarm's strategic plan calls for continued growth. It is pursuing new business in high growth areas, such as the horticulture markets of California, the cotton markets of southern United States, the public affairs markets in both Canada and the United States, and the rapidly emerging food safety and traceability technology field. It is also carefully pursuing new opportunities and requests for business expansion outside North America, but in the short term, this will only occur at the request of its clients who are asking AdFarm to grow with them.

QUESTIONS:

1 Comment on the rationale for AdFarm's focus of its business 100 percent on agriculture. What are the pros and cons of this decision?

2 What do you think about AdFarm's corporate culture and focus on employees? Why does it emphasize the importance of attracting and retaining excellent employees?

3 Many people argue that the advertising business is an "idea business." How does AdFarm reinforce this notion?

PERSONAL SELLING AND SALES MANAGEMENT

SELLING THE WAY CUSTOMERS WANT TO BUY

Anne Mulcahy has a challenging assignment. As the chairman of the board and chief executive officer at Xerox Corporation, she is in the midst of successfully implementing one of the greatest feats in the annals of business history: restoring Xerox's legendary marketing and financial vitality. Her success can be attributed to staying in sync with Xerox customers and employees. "I believe strongly that my success as a leader is driven by my commitment to understanding and meeting customers' requirements, as well as developing and nurturing a motivated and proud workforce," says Mulcahy (shown on the opposite page). "With the right amount of focus, the two have the potential to drive exceptional results."

Mulcahy is ideally suited to the task. She began her 28-year career in Xerox as a field sales representative and assumed increasingly responsible management and executive positions. These included chief staff officer, president of Xerox's General Markets Operations, and president and chief operating officer of Xerox. As chairman and CEO, Mulcahy has to muster the knowledge and experience gained from this varied background. Not surprisingly, her sales background has played a pivotal role.

"We will win back market share one customer at a time, one sale at a time," Mulcahy says. "We'll do that by providing greater value than our competitors—and that means selling the way customers want to buy." She adds that Xerox must offer a broad range of products and services at competitive prices through direct, indirect, Internet, and telephone sales, and customer support. Her approach to sales, coupled with her considerable management experience, has already borne fruit as Xerox positions itself for future sales and profit growth.[1]

This chapter examines the scope and significance of personal selling and sales management in marketing. It first highlights the many forms of personal selling and outlines the selling process. Sales management functions are then described, including recent advances in salesforce automation and customer relationship management (CRM).

SCOPE AND SIGNIFICANCE OF PERSONAL SELLING AND SALES MANAGEMENT

Chapter 16 described personal selling and management of the sales effort as being part of the firm's promotional mix. Although it is important to recognize that personal selling is a useful vehicle for communicating with present and potential buyers, it is much more. Take a moment to answer the questions in the personal selling and sales management quiz in Figure 18–1. As you read on, compare your answers with those in the text.

Nature of Personal Selling and Sales Management

personal selling
The two-way flow of communication between a buyer and seller, often in a face-to-face encounter, designed to influence a person's or group's purchase decision.

sales management
Planning the selling program and implementing and controlling the personal selling effort of the firm.

Personal selling involves the two-way flow of communication between a buyer and seller, often in a face-to-face encounter, designed to influence a person's or group's purchase decision. However, with advances in telecommunications, personal selling also takes place over the telephone, through video teleconferencing, and through Internet-enabled links between buyers and sellers.

Personal selling remains a highly human-intensive activity despite the use of technology. Accordingly, the people involved must be managed. **Sales management** involves planning the selling program and implementing and controlling the personal selling effort of the firm. The tasks involved in managing personal selling include setting objectives; organizing the salesforce; recruiting, selecting, training, and compensating salespeople; and evaluating the performance of individual salespeople.

Pervasiveness of Selling

"Everyone lives by selling something," wrote author Robert Louis Stevenson a century ago. His observation still holds true today. In Canada, more than one million people are employed in sales positions.[2] Included in this number are manufacturing sales personnel, real estate brokers, stockbrokers, and salesclerks who work in retail stores. In reality, however, virtually every occupation that involves customer contact has an element of personal selling. For example, lawyers, accountants, bankers, and company personnel recruiters perform sales-related activities, whether or not they acknowledge it.

Many executives in major companies, like Anne Mulcahy at Xerox, have held sales positions at some time in their careers. Selling often serves as a stepping-stone to top management, as well as being a career path in itself.

Personal Selling in Marketing

Personal selling serves three major roles in a firm's overall marketing effort. First, salespeople are the critical link between the firm and its customers. This role requires

■ FIGURE 18–1 ■■
Personal selling and sales management quiz

1. About how much does it cost for a field sales representative to make a single personal sales call on a business customer? (check one)

   $150 _____ $200 _____ $300 _____
   $175 _____ $250 _____ $350 _____

2. "A salesperson's job is finished when a sale is made." True or false? (circle one)

   True   False

3. About what percentage of companies include customer satisfaction as a measure of salesperson performance? (check one)

   10% _____   30% _____   50% _____
   20% _____   40% _____   60% _____

Could this be a salesperson in the operating room? Read the text to find why Medtronic salespeople visit hospital operating rooms.

Medtronic

www.medtronic.com

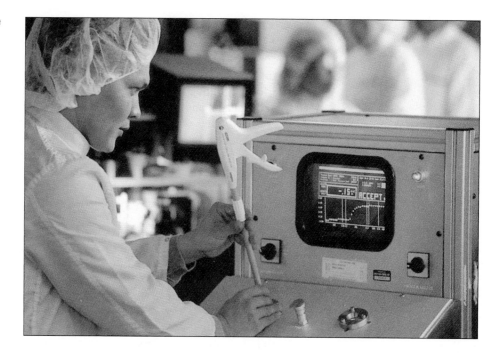

that salespeople match company interests with customer needs to satisfy both parties in the exchange process. Second, salespeople *are* the company in a consumer's eyes. They represent what a company is or attempts to be and are often the only personal contact a customer has with the company. For example, the "look" projected by Gucci salespeople is an important factor in communicating the style of the company's apparel line. Third, personal selling may play a dominant role in a firm's marketing program. This situation typically arises when a firm uses a push marketing strategy, described in Chapter 16. Avon, for example, pays almost 40 percent of its total sales dollars for selling expenses. Pharmaceutical firms and office and educational equipment manufacturers also rely heavily on personal selling in the marketing of their products.

Creating Customer Value through Salespeople: Relationship and Partnership Selling

As the critical link between the firm and its customers, salespeople can create customer value in many ways. For instance, by being close to the customer, salespeople can identify creative solutions to customer problems. Salespeople at Medtronic, Inc., the world leader in the heart pacemaker market, are in the operating room for more than 90 percent of the procedures performed with their product, and are on call, through pagers, 24 hours a day. "It reflects the willingness to be there in every situation, just in case a problem arises—even though nine times out of ten the procedure goes just fine," notes a satisfied customer.[3] Salespeople can create value by easing the customer buying process. This happened at AMP, Inc., a producer of electrical products. Salespeople and customers had a difficult time getting product specifications and performance data on AMP's 70 000 products quickly and accurately. The company now records all information on CD-ROMs that can be scanned instantly by salespeople and customers. Customer value is also created by salespeople who follow through after the sale. At Jefferson Smurfit Corporation, a multi-billion dollar supplier of packaging products, one of its salespeople juggled production from three of the company's plants to satisfy an unexpected demand for boxes from General Electric. This person's action led to the company being given GE's "Distinguished Supplier Award."

relationship selling

The practice of building ties to customers based on a salesperson's attention and commitment to customer needs over time.

Customer value creation is made possible by **relationship selling**, the practice of building ties to customers based on a salesperson's attention and commitment to customer needs over time. Relationship selling involves mutual respect and trust among buyers and sellers. It focuses on creating long-term customers, not a one-time sale.[4] A survey of senior sales executives revealed that 96 percent consider "building long-term relationships with customers" to be the most important activity affecting sales performance. Such companies as Merck Frosst Canada, IBM Canada, National Bank, Bell Canada, and Kraft Canada have made relationship building a core focus of their sales effort.

Some companies have taken relationship selling a step further and forged partnerships between buyer and seller organizations. With **partnership selling**, sometimes called *enterprise selling*, buyers and sellers combine their expertise and resources to create customized solutions; commit to joint planning; and share customer, competitive, and company information for their mutual benefit, and ultimately the customer. As an approach to sales, partnership selling relies on cross-functional business specialists who apply their knowledge and expertise to achieve higher productivity, lower cost, and greater customer value. Partnership selling complements supplier and channel partnering described in Chapters 6 and 14. This practice is embraced by such companies as IBM Canada, 3M, DuPont, and Honeywell, which have established partnerships with their customers, such as Air Canada, Ford, and McDonald's.

Relationship and partnership selling represent another dimension of customer relationship management (CRM). Both emphasize the importance of learning about customer needs and wants and tailoring solutions to customer problems as a means to create customer value.

partnership selling
The practice whereby buyers and sellers combine their expertise and resources to create customized solutions; commit to joint planning; and share customer, competitive, and company information for their mutual benefit, and ultimately the customer; sometimes called *enterprise selling*.

CONCEPT CHECK

1. What is personal selling?

2. What is involved in sales management?

THE MANY FORMS OF PERSONAL SELLING

Personal selling assumes many forms based on the amount of selling done and the amount of creativity required to perform the sales task. Broadly speaking, three types of personal selling exist: order taking, order getting, and sales support activities. While some firms use only one of these types of personal selling, others use a combination of all three.

Order Taking

order taker
Processes routine orders or reorders for products that have already been sold by the company.

Typically, an **order taker** processes routine orders or reorders for products that have already been sold by the company. The primary responsibility of order takers is to preserve an ongoing relationship with existing customers and maintain sales. Two types of order takers exist. *Outside order takers* visit customers and replenish inventory stocks of resellers, such as retailers or wholesalers. For example, Frito-Lay salespeople call on supermarkets, neighbourhood grocery stores, and other establishments to ensure that the company's line of snack products is in adequate supply. In addition, outside order takers often provide assistance in arranging displays. *Inside order takers*, also called *order clerks* or *salesclerks*, typically answer simple questions, take orders, and complete transactions with customers. Many retail clerks are inside order takers. Inside order takers are often employed by companies that use *inbound telemarketing*, the use of toll-free telephone numbers that customers can call to obtain information about products or services and make purchases. In business-to-business settings, order taking arises in straight rebuy situations. Order takers generally do little selling in a conventional sense and engage in only modest problem solving with

A Frito-Lay salesperson takes inventory of snacks for the store manager to sign. In this situation, the manager will make a straight rebuy decision.

Frito-Lay, Inc.

www.fritolay.com

customers. They often represent products that have few options, such as confectionary items, magazine subscriptions, and highly standardized industrial products. Inbound telemarketing is also an essential selling activity for more "customer service" driven firms, such as Dell Computer. Order takers in such firms undergo extensive training so that they can better assist callers with their purchase decisions.

Order Getting

order getter
A salesperson who sells in a conventional sense and identifies prospective customers, provides customers with information, persuades customers to buy, closes sales, and follows up on customers' use of a product or service.

An **order getter** sells in a conventional sense and identifies prospective customers, provides customers with information, persuades customers to buy, closes sales, and follows up on customers' use of a product or service. Like order takers, order getters can be inside (an automobile salesperson) or outside (a Xerox salesperson). Order getting involves a high degree of creativity and customer empathy and is typically required for selling complex or technical products with many options, and so considerable product knowledge and sales training are necessary. In modified-rebuy or new-buy purchase situations in organizational selling, an order getter acts as a problem solver who identifies how a particular product may satisfy a customer's need. Similarly, in the purchase of a service, such as insurance, a Metropolitan Life insurance agent can provide a mix of plans to satisfy a buyer's needs depending on income, stage of the family's life cycle, and investment objectives.

Order getting is not a 40-hour-per-week job. Industry research indicates that outside order getters, or field service representatives, work about 48 hours per week. As shown in Figure 18–2, 54 percent of their time is spent selling, and another 13 percent is devoted to customer service calls. The remainder of their work time is occupied by getting to customers and performing numerous administrative tasks.[5]

Order getting by outside salespeople is also expensive. It is estimated that the average cost of a single field sales call on a business customer is about $350, factoring in salespeople compensation, benefits, and travel and entertainment expenses. (What amount did you check for question 1 in Figure 18–1?) This cost illustrates why outbound telemarketing is so popular today. *Outbound telemarketing* is the practice of using the telephone rather than personal visits to contact customers. A significantly lower cost per sales call (in the range of $20 to $25) and little or no field expense accounts for its widespread appeal. Accordingly, outbound telemarketing has grown significantly.

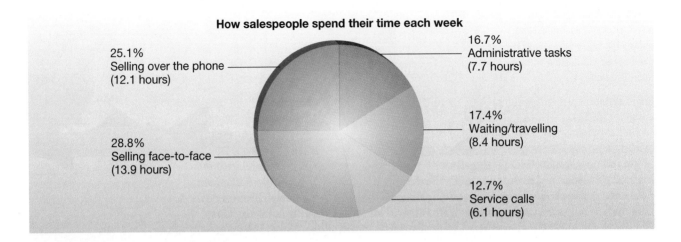

How salespeople spend their time each week

25.1%
Selling over the phone
(12.1 hours)

16.7%
Administrative tasks
(7.7 hours)

17.4%
Waiting/travelling
(8.4 hours)

28.8%
Selling face-to-face
(13.9 hours)

12.7%
Service calls
(6.1 hours)

■ **FIGURE 18–2** ■

How outside order-getting salespeople spend their time each week

missionary salespeople
Sales support personnel who do not directly solicit orders but rather concentrate on performing promotional activities and introducing new products.

sales engineer
A salesperson who specializes in identifying, analyzing, and solving customer problems and who brings know-how and technical expertise to the selling situations but does not actually sell goods and services.

team selling
Using an entire team of professionals in selling to and servicing major customers.

Customer Sales Support Personnel

Customer sales support personnel augment the selling effort of order getters by performing a variety of services. For example, **missionary salespeople** do not directly solicit orders but rather concentrate on performing promotional activities and introducing new products. They are used extensively in the pharmaceutical industry, where they persuade physicians to prescribe a firm's product. Actual sales are made through wholesalers or directly to pharmacists who fill prescriptions. A **sales engineer** is a salesperson who specializes in identifying, analyzing, and solving customer problems and brings know-how and technical expertise to the selling situation but often does not actually sell products and services. Sales engineers are popular in selling industrial products, such as chemicals and heavy equipment.

In many situations, firms engage in cross-functional **team selling**, the practice of using an entire team of professionals in selling to and servicing major customers.[6] Team selling is used when specialized knowledge is needed to satisfy the different interests of individuals in a customer's buying centre. For example, a selling team might consist of a salesperson, a sales engineer, a service representative, and a financial executive, each of whom would deal with a counterpart in the customer's firm. Selling teams have grown in popularity due to partnering and take different forms. In *conference selling*, a salesperson and other company resource people meet with buyers to discuss problems and opportunities. In *seminar selling*, a company team conducts an educational program for a customer's technical staff, describing state-of-the-art developments. IBM and Xerox pioneered cross-functional team selling in working with prospective buyers. Other firms have embraced this practice and created and sustained value for their customers.[7]

CONCEPT CHECK

1. What is the principal difference between an order taker and an order getter?

2. What is team selling?

■ ■ ■
THE PERSONAL SELLING PROCESS: BUILDING RELATIONSHIPS

personal selling process
Sales activities occurring before and after the sale itself, consisting of six stages: (1) prospecting, (2) preapproach, (3) approach, (4) presentation, (5) close, and (6) follow-up.

Selling, and particularly order getting, is a complicated activity that involves building buyer–seller relationships. Although the salesperson–customer interaction is essential to personal selling, much of a salesperson's work occurs before this meeting and continues after the sale itself. The **personal selling process** consists of six stages: (1) prospecting, (2) preapproach, (3) approach, (4) presentation, (5) close, and (6) follow-up (Figure 18–3).

■ FIGURE 18-3 ■■

Stages and objectives of the
personal selling process

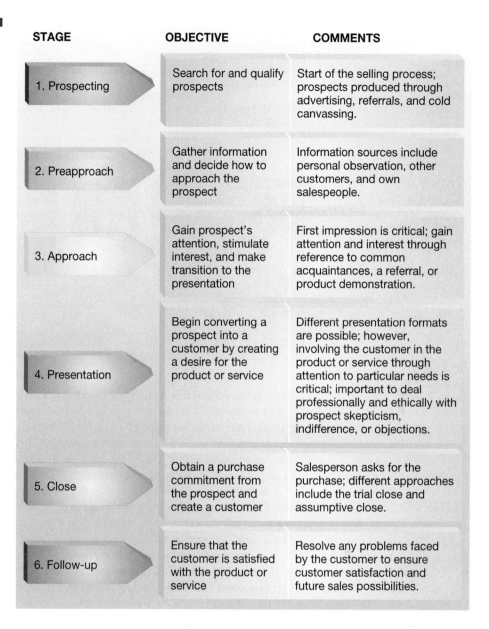

STAGE	OBJECTIVE	COMMENTS
1. Prospecting	Search for and qualify prospects	Start of the selling process; prospects produced through advertising, referrals, and cold canvassing.
2. Preapproach	Gather information and decide how to approach the prospect	Information sources include personal observation, other customers, and own salespeople.
3. Approach	Gain prospect's attention, stimulate interest, and make transition to the presentation	First impression is critical; gain attention and interest through reference to common acquaintances, a referral, or product demonstration.
4. Presentation	Begin converting a prospect into a customer by creating a desire for the product or service	Different presentation formats are possible; however, involving the customer in the product or service through attention to particular needs is critical; important to deal professionally and ethically with prospect skepticism, indifference, or objections.
5. Close	Obtain a purchase commitment from the prospect and create a customer	Salesperson asks for the purchase; different approaches include the trial close and assumptive close.
6. Follow-up	Ensure that the customer is satisfied with the product or service	Resolve any problems faced by the customer to ensure customer satisfaction and future sales possibilities.

Prospecting

Personal selling begins with *prospecting*—the search for and qualification of potential customers. For some products that are one-time purchases, such as encyclopedias, continual prospecting is necessary to maintain sales. There are three types of prospects. A *lead* is the name of a person who may be a possible customer. A *prospect* is a customer who wants or needs the product. If an individual wants the product, can afford to buy it, and is the decision maker, this individual is a *qualified prospect*.

Leads and prospects are generated using several sources. For example, advertising may contain a coupon or a toll-free number to generate leads. Some companies use exhibits at trade shows, professional meetings, and conferences to generate leads or prospects. Staffed by salespeople, these exhibits are used to attract the attention of prospective buyers and disseminate information. Others use lists and directories or the Internet for generating leads and prospects. Web sites, e-mail, bulletin boards, and newsgroups are used by salespeople to connect with individuals and companies that may be prospects. Another approach for generating leads is through *cold canvassing* in person or by telephone. This approach simply means that a salesperson may open a directory, pick a name, and visit or call that individual or business.

Trade shows are a popular source
for leads and prospects.

Although the refusal rate is high with cold canvassing, this approach can be successful. For example, 41 brokers at a major brokerage firm identified 18 004 prospects, qualified 1208 of them, made 659 sales presentations, and opened 40 new accounts in four working days.[8] However, cold canvassing is frowned upon in most Asian and Latin American societies. Personal visits, based on referrals, are expected.

Cold canvassing is also often criticized by Canadian consumers. Many consumers see cold canvassing as an intrusion into their privacy, and many find it simply distasteful.[9] Many trade associations, including the Canadian Marketing Association, have codes of ethics for dealing with this issue, such as adhering to consumers' "do not call," "do not mail," or "do not visit" requests. The Canadian government has also attempted to more closely regulate cold canvassing with the Canadian Radio-television and Telecommunications Commission (CRTC) requiring telemarketers to inform consumers that they have the right to say no to such solicitations.

Preapproach

Once a salesperson has identified a qualified prospect, preparation for the sale begins with the preapproach. The *preapproach* stage involves obtaining further information on the prospect and deciding on the best method of approach. Knowing how the prospect prefers to be approached, and what the prospect is looking for in a product or service, is essential regardless of cultural setting. For example, a Merrill Lynch stockbroker will need information on a prospect's discretionary income, investment objectives, and preference for discussing brokerage services over the telephone or in person. For business product companies, such as Texas Instruments, the preapproach involves identifying the buying role of a prospect (for example, influencer or decision maker), important buying criteria, and the prospect's receptivity to a formal or informal presentation. Identifying the best time to contact a prospect is also important. For example, insurance companies have discovered the best times to call on people in different occupations: dentists before 9:30 A.M., lawyers between 11:00 A.M. and 2:00 P.M., and university professors between 7:00 and 8:00 P.M.

This stage is very important in global selling where customs dictate appropriate protocol. In many South American countries, for example, buyers expect salespeople to be punctual for appointments. However, prospective buyers are routinely 30 minutes late. South Americans take negotiating seriously and prefer straightforward presentations, but a hard-sell approach will not work.[10]

Successful salespeople recognize that the preapproach stage should never be shortchanged. Their experience coupled with research on customer complaints indicates that failure to learn as much as possible about the prospect is unprofessional and the ruin of a sales call.

Approach

The *approach* stage involves the initial meeting between the salesperson and prospect, where the objectives are to gain the prospect's attention, stimulate interest,

and build the foundation for the sales presentation itself and the basis for a working relationship. The first impression is critical at this stage, and it is common for salespeople to begin the conversation with a reference to common acquaintances, a referral, or even the product or service itself. Which tactic is used will depend on the information obtained in the prospecting and preapproach stages.

The approach stage is very important in international settings. In many societies outside Canada, considerable time is devoted to nonbusiness talk designed to establish a rapport between buyers and sellers. For instance, it is common for two or three meetings to occur before business matters are discussed in the Middle East and Asia. Gestures are also very important. The initial meeting between a salesperson and a prospect in Canada customarily begins with a firm handshake. Handshakes also apply in France, but they are gentle, not firm. Forget the handshake in Japan. A bow is appropriate. What about business cards? Business cards should be printed in English on one side and the language of the prospective customer on the other. Knowledgeable Canadian salespeople know that their business cards should be handed to Asian customers using both hands, with the name facing the receiver. In Asia, anything involving names demands respect.[11]

Presentation

The *presentation* is at the core of the order-getting selling process, and its objective is to convert a prospect into a customer by creating a desire for the product or service. Three major presentation formats exist: (1) stimulus-response format, (2) formula selling format, and (3) need-satisfaction format.

stimulus-response presentation

A selling format that assumes the prospect will buy if given the appropriate stimulus by a salesperson.

Stimulus-Response Format   The **stimulus-response presentation** format assumes that given the appropriate stimulus by a salesperson, the prospect will buy. With this format, the salesperson tries one appeal after another, hoping to "hit the right button." A counter clerk at McDonald's is using this approach when he or she asks whether you would like an order of french fries or a dessert with your meal. The counter clerk is engaging in what is called *suggestive selling*. Although useful in this setting, the stimulus-response format is not always appropriate, and for many products, a more formalized format is necessary.

formula selling presentation

Providing information in an accurate, thorough, and step-by-step manner to inform the prospect.

Formula Selling Format   A more formalized presentation, the **formula selling presentation** format, is based on the view that a presentation consists of information that must be provided in an accurate, thorough, and step-by-step manner to inform the prospect. A popular version of this format is the *canned sales presentation*, which is a memorized, standardized message conveyed to every prospect. Used frequently by firms in telephone and door-to-door selling of consumer products (for example, Hoover vacuum cleaners), this approach treats every prospect the same, regardless of differences in needs or preference for certain kinds of information. Canned sales presentations can be advantageous when the differences between prospects are unknown or with novice salespeople who are less knowledgeable about the product and the selling process than are experienced salespeople. Although it guarantees a thorough presentation, it often lacks flexibility and spontaneity and, more importantly, does not provide for feedback from the prospective buyer—a critical component in the communication process and the start of a relationship.

Need-Satisfaction Format   The stimulus-response and formula selling formats share a common characteristic: the salesperson dominates the conversation. By comparison, the **need-satisfaction presentation** format emphasizes probing and listening by the salesperson to identify the needs and interests of prospective buyers. Once these are identified, the salesperson tailors the presentation to the prospect and highlights product benefits that may be valued by the prospect. The need-satisfaction format, which emphasizes problem solving, is the most consistent with the marketing concept and relationship building.

Two selling styles are associated with this format.[12] **Adaptive selling** involves adjusting the presentation to fit the selling situation, such as knowing when to offer solutions and when to ask for more information. Sales research and practice show that knowledge of the customer and sales situation are key ingredients for adaptive selling. Many consumer service firms, such as brokerage and insurance firms (e.g., ING Canada) and consumer product firms (e.g., Gillette), effectively apply this selling style. **Consultative selling** focuses on problem identification, where the salesperson serves as an expert on problem recognition and resolution. With consultative selling, problem solution options are not simply a matter of choosing from an array of existing products or services. Rather, novel solutions often arise thereby creating unique value for the customer. Consultative selling is prominent in business-to-business marketing. IBM Canada is often recognized for its consultative selling style.

Handling Objections   A critical concern in the presentation stage is handling objections. *Objections* are excuses for not making a purchase commitment or decision. Some objections are valid and are based on the characteristics of the product or service or price. However, many objections reflect prospect skepticism or indifference. Whether valid or not, experienced salespeople know that objections do not put an end to the presentation. Rather, techniques can be used to deal with objections in a courteous, ethical, and professional manner. The following six techniques are the most common:[13]

1. *Acknowledge and convert the objection.* This technique involves using the objection as a reason for buying. For example, a prospect might say, "The price is too high." The reply: "Yes, the price is high because we use the finest materials. Let me show you . . . ."
2. *Postpone.* The postpone technique is used when the objection will be dealt with later in the presentation: "I'm going to address that point shortly. I think my answer would make better sense then."
3. *Agree and neutralize.* Here, a salesperson agrees with the objection, then shows that it is unimportant. A salesperson would say, "That's true, and others have said the same. However, they concluded that this issue was outweighed by the other benefits."
4. *Accept the objection.* Sometimes, the objection is valid. Let the prospect express such views, probe for the reason behind it, and attempt to stimulate further discussion on the objection.
5. *Denial.* When a prospect's objection is based on misinformation and clearly untrue, it is wise to meet the objection head on with a firm denial.

need-satisfaction presentation
A selling format that emphasizes probing and listening by the salesperson to identify the needs and interests of prospective buyers.

adaptive selling
A need-satisfaction sales presentation that involves adjusting the presentation to fit the selling situation.

consultative selling
Focuses on problem definition, where the salesperson serves as an expert on problem recognition and resolution.

6. *Ignore the objection.* This technique is used when it appears that the objection is a stalling mechanism or is clearly not important to the prospect.

Each of these techniques requires a calm, professional interaction with the prospect and is most effective when objections are anticipated in the preapproach stage. Handling objections is a skill requiring a sense of timing, appreciation for the prospect's state of mind, and adeptness in communication. Objections also should be handled ethically. Lying or misrepresenting product or service features are grossly unethical practices.

Close

The *closing* stage in the selling process involves obtaining a purchase commitment from the prospect. This stage is the most important and the most difficult because the salesperson must determine when the prospect is ready to buy. Telltale signals indicating a readiness to buy include body language (prospect re-examines the product or contract closely), statements ("This equipment should reduce our maintenance costs"), and questions ("When could we expect delivery?").

The close itself can take several forms. Three closing techniques are used when a salesperson believes a buyer is about ready to make a purchase: (1) trial close, (2) assumptive close, and (3) urgency close. A *trial close* involves asking the prospect to make a decision on some aspect of the purchase: "Would you prefer the blue or grey model?" An *assumptive close* entails asking the prospect to consider choices concerning delivery, warranty, or financing terms under the assumption that a sale has been finalized. An *urgency close* is used to commit the prospect quickly by making reference to the timeliness of the purchase: "The low-interest financing ends next week" or "That is the last model we have in stock." Of course, these statements should be used only if they accurately reflect the situation; otherwise, such claims would be unethical. When a prospect is clearly ready to buy, the final close is used, and a salesperson asks for the order.

Knowing when the prospect is ready to buy becomes even more difficult in cross-cultural buyer–seller negotiations where societal customs and language play a large role. Read the accompanying Marketing NewsNet box to understand the multiple meanings of *yes* in Japan and other societies in East Asia.[14]

MARKETING NEWSNET **The Subtlety of Saying Yes in East Asia**

The economies of East Asia—spanning from Japan to Indonesia—closely rival the North American and EU economies. The marketing opportunities in East Asia are great, but effective selling in these countries requires a keen cultural ear. Seasoned global marketers know that in many Asian societies, it is impolite to say *no*, and *yes* has multiple meanings.

Yes in Asian societies can have at least four meanings. It can mean that listeners are simply acknowledging that a speaker is talking to them, even though they do not understand what is being said; or it can mean that a speaker's words are understood, but that they are not agreed with. A third meaning of *yes* conveys that a presentation is understood, but other people must be consulted before any commitment is possible. Finally, *yes* can also mean that a proposal is understood and accepted. However, experienced negotiators also note that this *yes* is subject to change if the situation changes.

This example illustrates why savvy salespeople are sensitive to cultural underpinnings when engaged in cross-cultural sales negotiations.

Follow-Up

The selling process does not end with the closing of a sale; rather, professional selling requires customer follow-up. One marketing authority equated selling and follow-up with courtship and marriage, by observing ". . . the sale merely consummates the courtship. Then the marriage begins. How good the marriage is depends on how well the relationship is managed."[15] The *follow-up stage* includes making certain that the customer's purchase has been properly delivered and installed and that any difficulties experienced with the use of the item are addressed. Attention to this stage of the selling process solidifies the buyer–seller relationship. Moreover, research shows that the cost and effort to obtain repeat sales from a satisfied customer is roughly half of that necessary to gain a sale from a new customer.[16] In short, today's satisfied customers become tomorrow's qualified prospects or referrals. (What was your answer to question 2 in the quiz?)

<table>
<tr>
<td>

CONCEPT CHECK

</td>
<td>

1. What are the six stages in the personal selling process?

2. What is the distinction between a lead and a qualified prspect?

3. Which presentation format is most consistent with the marketing concept? Why?

</td>
</tr>
</table>

■ ■ ■
THE SALES MANAGEMENT PROCESS

Selling must be managed if it is going to contribute to a firm's overall objectives. Although firms differ in the specifics of how salespeople and the selling effort are managed, the sales management process is similar across firms. Sales management consists of three interrelated functions: (1) sales plan formulation, (2) sales plan implementation, and (3) evaluation and control of the salesforce (Figure 18–4).

Sales Plan Formulation: Setting Direction

Formulating the sales plan is the most basic of the three sales management functions. According to the vice-president of the Harris Corporation, a global communications company, "If a company hopes to implement its marketing strategy, it really needs a detailed sales planning process."[17] The **sales plan** is a statement describing what is to be achieved and where and how the selling effort of salespeople is to be deployed. Formulating the sales plan involves three tasks: (1) setting objectives, (2) organizing the salesforce, and (3) developing account management policies.

sales plan
A statement describing what is to be achieved and where and how the selling effort of salespeople is to be deployed.

Setting Objectives   Setting objectives is central to sales management because this task specifies what is to be achieved. In practice, objectives are set for the total salesforce and for each salesperson. Selling objectives can be output related and focus on dollar or unit sales volume, number of new customers added, and profit. Alternatively,

■ **FIGURE 18–4** ■
The sales management process

they can be input related and emphasize the number of sales calls and selling expenses. Output- and input-related objectives are used for the salesforce as a whole and for each salesperson. A third type of objective that is behaviourally related is typically specific for each salesperson and includes his or her product knowledge, customer service, and selling and communication skills. Increasingly, firms are also emphasizing knowledge of competition as an objective, since salespeople are calling on customers and should see what competitors are doing.[18] But should salespeople explicitly ask their customers for information about competitors? Read the accompanying Ethics and Social Responsibility Alert box to see how salespeople view this practice.[19]

Whatever objectives are set, they should be precise and measurable and specify the time period over which they are to be achieved. Once established, these objectives serve as performance standards for the evaluation of the salesforce—the third function of sales management.

Organizing the Salesforce   Establishing a selling organization is the second task in formulating the sales plan. Three questions are related to organization. First, should the company use its own salesforce, or should it use independent agents, such as manufacturer's representatives? Second, if the decision is made to employ company salespeople, then should they be organized according to geography, customer type, or product or service? Third, how many company salespeople should be employed?

The decision to use company salespeople or independent agents is made infrequently. However, recently, Coca-Cola's Food Division replaced its salesforce with independent agents (food brokers). The Optoelectronics Division of Honeywell, Inc. has switched back and forth between agents and its own salesforce over the last 25 years and now uses both. The decision is based on an analysis of economic and behavioural factors. An economic analysis examines the costs of using both types of salespeople and is a form of break-even analysis.

Consider a situation in which independent agents would receive a 5-percent commission on sales, and company salespeople would receive a 3-percent commission, salaries, and benefits. In addition, with company salespeople, sales administration costs would be incurred for a total fixed cost of $500 000 per year. At what sales level would independent or company salespeople be less costly? This question can be answered by setting the costs of the two options equal to each other and solving for the sales level amount, as shown in the following equation:

$$\frac{\text{Total cost of company salespeople}}{0.03(X) + \$500,000} = \frac{\text{Total cost of independent agents}}{0.05(X)}$$

where X = sales volume. Solving for X, sales volume equals $25 million, indicating that below $25 million in sales, independent agents would be cheaper, but above $25 million, a company salesforce would be cheaper. This relationship is shown in Figure 18–5.

Economics alone does not answer this question, however. A behavioural analysis is also necessary and should focus on issues related to the control, flexibility, effort, and availability of independent and company salespeople.[20] An individual firm must weigh the pros and cons of the economic and behavioural considerations before making this decision.

If a company elects to employ its own salespeople, then it must choose an organizational structure based on (1) geography, (2) customer, or (3) product (Figure 18–6). A geographical structure is the simplest organization, where Canada or, indeed, the globe is first divided into regions and each region is divided into districts or territories. Salespeople are assigned to each district with defined geographical boundaries and call on all customers and represent all products sold by the company. The principal advantage of this structure is that it can minimize travel time, expenses, and duplication of selling effort. However, if a firm's products or customers require specialized knowledge, then a geographical structure is not suitable.

When different types of buyers have different needs, a customer sales organizational structure is used. In practice, this means that a different salesforce calls on each separate type of buyer or marketing channel. For example, Kodak recently switched from a geographical to a marketing channel structure, with different sales teams serving specific retail channels: mass merchandisers, photo specialty outlets, and food and drug stores. The rationale for this approach is that more effective, specialized customer support and knowledge are provided to buyers. However, this structure often leads to higher administrative costs and some duplication of selling effort because two separate salesforces are used to represent the same products.

A variation of the customer organizational structure is **major account management**, or *key account management*, the practice of using team selling to focus on important customers so as to build mutually beneficial, long-term, cooperative relationships.[21] Major account management involves teams of sales, service, and often technical personnel who work with purchasing, manufacturing, engineering,

major account management

The practice of using team selling to focus on important customers so as to build mutually beneficial, long-term, cooperative relationships. Also called *key account management*.

■ FIGURE 18–5 ■■

Break-even chart for comparing independent agents and a company salesforce

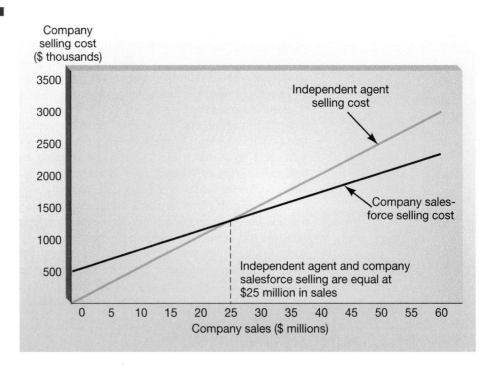

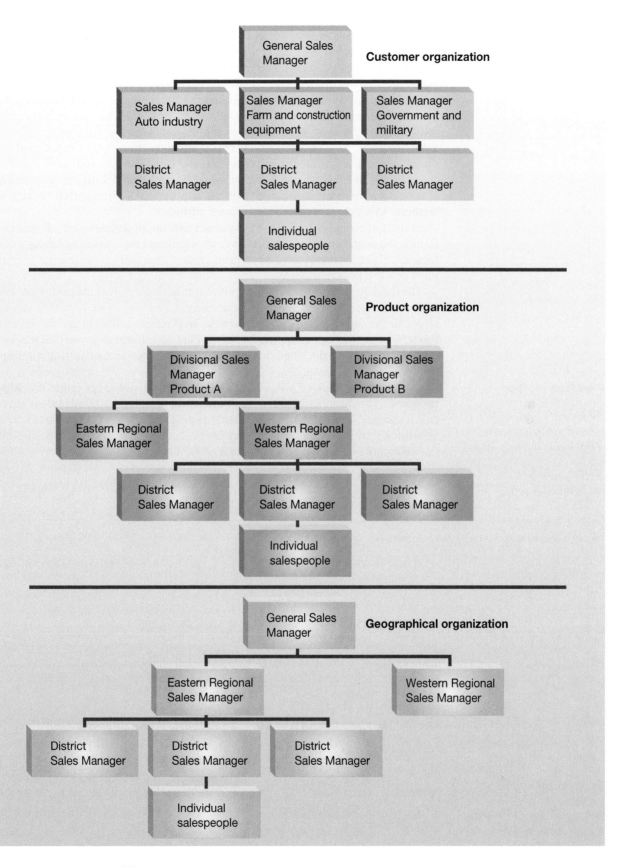

Customer organization

Product organization

Geographical organization

■ FIGURE 18–6 ■

Organizing the salesforce
by customer, product, and
geography

logistics, and financial executives in customer organizations. This approach, which often assigns company personnel to a customer account, results in "customer specialists" who can provide exceptional service. Procter & Gamble uses this approach with Wal-Mart, as does Black & Decker with Home Depot.

When specific knowledge is required to sell certain types of products, then a product sales organization is used. For example, a steel manufacturer has a salesforce that sells drilling pipe to oil companies and another that sells specialty steel products to manufacturers. The primary advantage of this structure is that salespeople can develop expertise with technical characteristics, applications, and selling methods associated with a particular product or family of products. However, this structure also produces high administrative costs and duplication of selling effort because two company salespeople may call on the same customer.

In short, there is no one best sales organization for all companies in all situations. Rather, the organization of the salesforce should reflect the marketing strategy of the firm. Each year, about 10 percent of firms change their sales organizations to implement new marketing strategies.

The third question related to salesforce organization involves determining the size of the salesforce. For example, why does Frito-Lay have about 17 500 salespeople who call on supermarkets, grocery stores, and other establishments to sell snack foods? The answer lies in the number of accounts (customers) served, the frequency of calls on accounts, the length of an average call, and the amount of time a salesperson can devote to selling.

workload method

A formula-based method for determining the size of a salesforce that integrates the number of customers served, call frequency, call length, and available selling time to arrive at a salesforce size.

A common approach for determining the size of a salesforce is the **workload method**. This formula-based method integrates the number of customers served, call frequency, call length, and available selling time to arrive at a figure for the salesforce size. For example, Frito-Lay needs about 17 500 salespeople according to the following workload method formula:

$$NS = \frac{NC \times CF \times CL}{AST}$$

where:

NS = Number of salespeople

NC = Number of customers

CF = Call frequency necessary to service a customer each year

CL = Length of an average call

AST = Average amount of selling time available per year

Frito-Lay sells its products to 350 000 supermarkets, grocery stores, and other establishments. Salespeople should call on these accounts at least once a week, or 52 times a year. The average sales call lasts an average of 81 minutes (1.35 hour). An average salesperson works 2000 hours a year (50 weeks × 40 hours a week), but 12 hours a week are devoted to nonselling activities, such as travel and administration, leaving 1400 hours a year. Using these guidelines, Frito-Lay would need:

$$NS = \frac{350\,000 \times 52 \times 1.35}{1400} = 17\,550 \text{ salespeople}$$

account management policies

Policies that specify whom the salespeople should contact, what kinds of selling and customer service activities should be engaged in, and how these activities should be carried out.

The value of this formula is apparent in its flexibility; a change in any one of the variables will affect the number of salespeople needed. Changes are determined, in part, by the firm's account management policies.

Developing Account Management Policies   The third task in formulating a sales plan involves developing **account management policies** specifying whom the salespeople should contact, what kinds of selling and customer service activities should be engaged in, and how these activities should be carried out. These

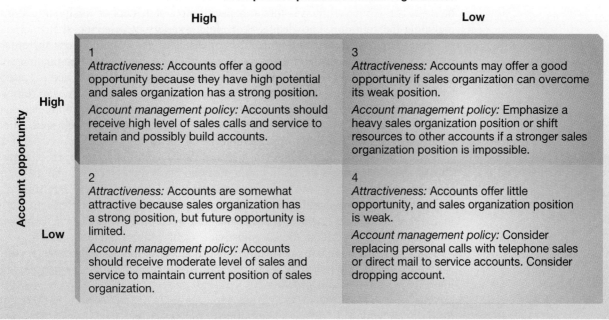

Competitive position of sales organization

	High	**Low**
High *(Account opportunity)*	**1** *Attractiveness:* Accounts offer a good opportunity because they have high potential and sales organization has a strong position. *Account management policy:* Accounts should receive high level of sales calls and service to retain and possibly build accounts.	**3** *Attractiveness:* Accounts may offer a good opportunity if sales organization can overcome its weak position. *Account management policy:* Emphasize a heavy sales organization position or shift resources to other accounts if a stronger sales organization position is impossible.
Low	**2** *Attractiveness:* Accounts are somewhat attractive because sales organization has a strong position, but future opportunity is limited. *Account management policy:* Accounts should receive moderate level of sales and service to maintain current position of sales organization.	**4** *Attractiveness:* Accounts offer little opportunity, and sales organization position is weak. *Account management policy:* Consider replacing personal calls with telephone sales or direct mail to service accounts. Consider dropping account.

■ **FIGURE 18–7** ▥

Account management policy grid

policies might state which individuals in a buying organization should be contacted, the amount of sales and service effort that different customers should receive, and the kinds of information that the salespeople should collect before or during a sales call.

An example of an account management policy in Figure 18–7 shows how different accounts or customers can be grouped according to level of opportunity and the firm's competitive sales position.[22] When specific account names are placed in each cell, salespeople clearly see which accounts should be contacted, with what level of selling and service activity, and how to deal with them. Accounts in cells 1 and 2 might have high frequencies of personal sales calls and increased time spent on a call. Cell 3 accounts will have lower call frequencies, and cell 4 accounts might be contacted through telemarketing or direct mail rather than in person.[23]

Sales Plan Implementation: Putting the Plan into Action

The sales plan is put into practice through the tasks associated with sales plan implementation. Whereas sales plan formulation focuses on "doing the right things," implementation emphasizes "doing things right." The three major tasks involved in implementing a sales plan are (1) salesforce recruitment and selection, (2) salesforce training, and (3) salesforce motivation and compensation.

Salesforce Recruitment and Selection   Effective recruitment and selection of salespeople is one of the most crucial tasks of sales management. It entails finding people who match the type of sales position required by a firm. Recruitment and selection practices would differ greatly between order-taking and order-getting sales positions, given the differences in the demands of these two jobs. Therefore, recruitment and selection begin with a carefully crafted job analysis and job description followed by a statement of job qualifications.[24]

A *job analysis* is a study of a particular sales position, including how the job is to be performed and the tasks that make up the job. Information from a job analysis is used to write a *job description*, a written document that describes job relationships and requirements that characterize each sales position. It explains (1) to whom a salesperson reports, (2) how a salesperson interacts with other company personnel, (3) the customers to be called on, (4) the specific activities to be carried out, (5) the physical and mental demands of the job, and (6) the types of products and services to be sold. The job description is then translated into a statement of job qualifications, including the aptitudes, knowledge, skills, and a variety of behavioural characteristics considered necessary to perform the job successfully. Qualifications for order-getting sales positions often mirror the expectations of buyers: (1) imagination and problem-solving ability, (2) honesty, (3) intimate product knowledge, and (4) attentiveness reflected in responsiveness to buyer needs and customer loyalty and follow-up.[25] Firms use a variety of methods for evaluating prospective salespeople. Personal interviews, reference checks, and background information provided on application forms are the most frequently used methods.

emotional intelligence

The ability to understand one's own emotions and the emotions of people with whom one interacts on a daily basis.

Successful selling also requires a high degree of emotional intelligence. **Emotional intelligence** is the ability to understand one's own emotions and the emotions of people with whom one interacts on a daily basis. These qualities are important for adaptive selling and may spell the difference between effective and ineffective order-getting salespeople.[26] Are you interested in what your emotional intelligence might be? Read the accompanying WebLink box and test yourself.

The search for qualified salespeople has produced an increasingly diverse salesforce in Canada. Women now represent half of all professional salespeople, and minority representation is growing.

Salesforce Training   Whereas recruitment and selection of salespeople is a one-time event, salesforce training is an ongoing process that affects both new and seasoned salespeople. Sales training covers much more than selling practices. For example, IBM Global Services salespeople, who sell consulting and various information technology services, take at least two weeks of in-class and Web-based training on both consultative selling and the technical aspects of business.

On-the-job training is the most popular type of training, followed by individual instruction provided by experienced salespeople. Formal classes and seminars conducted by sales trainers and computer-based training are also popular.

Two areas with regard to salesforce training in Canada are: training salespeople to respect and connect with female buyers, and training salespeople for their new roles in enterprise-wide customer relationship management (CRM). Evidence suggests that many Canadian companies are failing to do both.[27] Read the accompanying Marketing NewsNet box about some insight into the state of salesforce training when it comes to female Canadian consumers.[28]

Salesforce Motivation and Compensation   A sales plan cannot be successfully implemented without motivated salespeople. Research on salesperson motivation suggests that (1) a clear job description, (2) effective sales management practices, (3) a personal need for achievement, and (4) proper compensation, incentives, or rewards will produce a motivated salesperson.[29]

WEBLINK

HTTP://WWW.MCGRAWHILL.CA/
COLLEGE/CRANE

What Is Your Emotional Intelligence?

A person's success at work depends on many talents, including intelligence and technical skills. Recent research indicates that an individual's emotional intelligence is also important, if not more important! Emotional intelligence (E-IQ) has five dimensions: (1) self-motivation skills; (2) self-awareness, or knowing one's own emotions; (3) the ability to manage one's emotions and impulses; (4) empathy, or the ability to sense how others are feeling; and (5) social skills, or the ability to handle the emotions of other people.

What is your E-IQ? Visit the Web site at http://ei.hay group.com, and go to the "Learn More" header. Answer the questions to learn what your E-IQ is and obtain additional insights.

MARKETING NEWSNET

Sales Training Should Include Gender Intelligence

A recent study asked Canadian women to name a company that actually markets or sells well to women. Twenty-five percent of respondents could not come up with an answer. Morever, respondents then went on to fail all 22 industries examined in the study based on their inability to satisfy women's needs. Women gave poor marks, for example, to the banking, investment, and insurance industries, citing the poor treatment they received because of their gender. Additionally, they ranked car dealers at 21 out of 22 industry categories in terms of meeting their needs as buyers.

Many experts are suggesting that Canadian companies should start focusing their efforts on training their salespeople to become more gender intelligent. Fortunately, some companies are heeding the call and are investing in gender intelligent salesforces. For example, RBC Financial

Group trained 1500 account managers on how to meet the specific requirements of female clients. The results? After just one year, RBC reported a 10-point jump in market share and a 29-percent increase in customer satisfaction levels of women entrepreneurs with their account managers. Toyota Canada also created a new sales process called Access, designed specifically to meet the needs of women consumers. All salespeople are trained to be gender sensitive and to understand and approach women in such a way as to ensure a satisfying car-shopping experience. According to Toyota Canada, Access has been a major success, and its women-friendly program has driven market share and customer satisfaction numbers. Finally, Rona has also seen close to a 40-percent annual compounded growth rate in revenue since they implemented their gender-intelligent sales strategies.

The importance of compensation as a motivating factor means that close attention must be given to how salespeople are financially rewarded for their efforts. Salespeople are paid using one of three plans: (1) straight salary, (2) straight commission, or (3) a combination of salary and commission. Under a *straight salary compensation plan*, a salesperson is paid a fixed fee per week, month, or year. With a *straight commission compensation plan*, a salesperson's earnings are directly tied to the sales or profit generated. For example, an insurance agent might receive a 2-percent commission of $2000 for selling a $100 000 life insurance policy. A *combination compensation plan* contains a specified salary plus a commission on sales or profit generated.

Each compensation plan has its advantages and disadvantages.[30] A straight salary plan is easy to administer and gives management a large measure of control over

Mary Kay Cosmetics recognizes a top salesperson at its annual sales meeting.

Mary Kay Cosmetics, Inc.
www.marykay.com

how salespeople allocate their efforts. However, it provides little incentive to expand sales volume. This plan is used when salespeople engage in many nonselling activities, such as account servicing. A straight commission plan provides the maximum amount of selling incentive but can detract salespeople from providing customer service. This plan is common when nonselling activities are minimal. Combination plans are most preferred by salespeople and attempt to build on the advantages of salary and commission plans while reducing the potential shortcomings of each. Today, a majority of companies use combination plans.

Nonmonetary rewards are also given to salespeople for meeting or exceeding objectives. These rewards include trips, honour societies, distinguished salesperson awards, and letters of commendation. Some unconventional rewards include the new pink Cadillacs and Pontiacs, fur coats, and jewellery given by Mary Kay Cosmetics to outstanding salepeople. Mary Kay, with 10 000 cars, has the largest fleet of General Motors cars in the world![31]

Effective recruitment, selection, training, motivation, and compensation programs combine to create a productive salesforce. Ineffective practices often lead to costly salesforce turnover. Canadian and American firms experience an annual 11.6 percent turnover rate, which means that more than 1 of every 10 salespeople are replaced each year.[32] The expense of replacing a salesperson and training a new one, including the cost of lost sales, can be high. Moreover, new recruits are often less productive than established salespeople.

Salesforce Evaluation and Control

The final function in the sales management process involves evaluating and controlling the salesforce. It is at this point that salespeople are assessed as to whether sales objectives were met and account management policies were followed. Both quantitative and behavioural measures are used to tap different selling dimensions.[33]

Quantitative Assessments   Quantitative assessments, called quotas, are based on input- and output-related objectives set forth in the sales plan. Input-related measures focus on the actual activities performed by salespeople, such as those involving sales calls, selling expenses, and account management policies. The number of sales calls made, selling expense related to sales made, and the number of reports submitted to superiors are frequently used input measures.

sales quota
Contains specific goals assigned to a salesperson, sales team, branch sales office, or sales district for a stated time period.

Output measures often appear in a sales quota. A **sales quota** contains specific goals assigned to a salesperson, sales team, branch sales office, or sales district for a stated time period. Dollar or unit sales volume, last year/current year sales ratio, sales of specific products, new accounts generated, and profit achieved are typical goals. The time period can range from one month to one year.

Behavioural Evaluation   Behavioural measures are also used to evaluate salespeople. These include assessments of a salesperson's attitude, attention to customers, product knowledge, selling and communication skills, appearance, and professional demeanour. Even though these assessments are sometimes subjective, they are frequently considered and, in fact, inevitable, in salesperson evaluation. Moreover, these factors are often important determinants of quantitative outcomes.

Almost 60 percent of companies now include customer satisfaction as a behavioural measure of salesperson performance.[34] (What percentage did you check for question 3 in Figure 18–1?) IBM Canada has been the most aggressive in using this behavioural measure. Forty percent of an IBM salesperson's evaluation is linked to customer satisfaction; the remaining 60 percent is linked to profits achieved. Eastman Chemical Company surveys its customers with eight versions of its customer satisfaction questionnaire printed in nine languages. Some 25 performance items are studied, including on-time and correct delivery, product quality, pricing practice, and sharing of market information. The survey is managed by the salesforce, and salespeople review the results with customers. Eastman salespeople know that "the second most important thing they have to do is get their customer satisfaction surveys out to and back from customers," says Eastman's sales training director. "Number one, of course, is getting orders."

Salesforce Automation and Customer Relationship Management

salesforce automation
The use of technology to make the sales function more effective and efficient.

Personal selling and sales management are undergoing a technological revolution with the integration of salesforce automation into customer relationship management (CRM) processes. In fact, the convergence of computer, information, communication, and Internet/technologies has transformed the sales function in many companies and made the promise of CRM a reality. Computer software packages by PeopleSoft, Siebel, and Oracle enable salespeople to manage customer data and track customer needs. **Salesforce automation** (SFA) is the use of these technologies to make the sales function more effective and efficient. SFA applies to a wide range of activities, including each stage in the personal selling process and management of the salesforce itself.

Salesforce automation exists in many forms. Examples of SFA applications include computer hardware and software for account analysis, time management, order processing and follow-up, sales presentations, proposal generation, and product and sales training. Each application is designed to ease the administrative task and free up time for salespeople to be with customers building relationships and providing service.[35]

Salesforce Computerization   Computer technology has become an integral part of field selling through innovations, such as laptop, notebook, palmtop, pad, and tablet computers. Today, most Canadian companies supply their field salespeople with laptop computers. For example, salespeople for Godiva Chocolates use their laptop computers to process orders, plan time allocations, forecast sales, and communicate with Godiva personnel and customers. While in a department store candy buyer's office, such as Neiman Marcus, a salesperson can calculate the order cost (and discount), transmit the order, and obtain a delivery date within minutes from Godiva's order processing department.[36]

Toshiba Medical System salespeople now use laptop computers with built-in CD-ROM capabilities to provide interactive presentations for their computed tomography (CT) and magnetic resonance imaging (MRI) scanners. In these presentations, the customer sees elaborate three-dimensional animations, high-resolution scans, and video clips of the company's products in operation as well as narrated testimonials from satisfied customers. Toshiba has found this application to be effective both for sales presentations and for training its salespeople.[37]

Salesforce Communication   Technology also has changed the way salespeople communicate with customers, other salespeople and sales support personnel, and management. Facsimile (fax), electronic mail, and voice mail are three common communication technologies used by salespeople today. Wireless phone technology, which now allows salespeople to exchange data as well as voice transmissions, is equally popular. Whether travelling or in a customer's office, these technologies provide information at the salesperson's fingertips to answer customer questions and solve problems.

Advances in communication and computer technologies have made possible mobile and home sales offices. Some salespeople now equip minivans with a fully functional desk, swivel chair, light, computer, printer, fax machine, wireless phone, and satellite dish. If a salesperson cannot see the prospect right away, he or she can go outside to work in the mobile office until the prospect is available.[38] Home offices are now common. Hewlett-Packard is a case in point. The company shifted its salesforce into home offices, closed three regional sales offices, and saved $10 million in staff salaries and office rent. A fully equipped home office for each salesperson costs

Toshiba America Medical System salespeople have found computer technology to be an effective sales tool and training device.

Toshiba America Medical Systems
www.toshiba.com

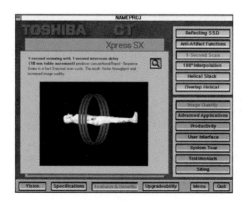
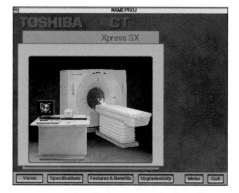

Computer and communication technologies have made it possible for Compaq Computer salespeople to work out of their homes.

Compaq Computer Corporation

www.compaq.com

the company about $8000 and includes a laptop computer, fax/copier, cellular phone, two phone lines, and office furniture.[39]

Perhaps the greatest impact on salesforce communication is the application of Internet technology. Today, salespeople are using their company's intranet for a variety of purposes. At EDS, a professional services firm, salespeople access its intranet to download client material, marketing content, account information, technical papers, and competitive profiles. In addition, EDS offers 7000 training classes that salespeople can take anytime, anywhere.[40]

Salesforce automation is clearly changing how selling is done and how salespeople are managed. Its numerous applications promise to boost selling productivity, improve customer relationships, and decrease selling cost. As applications increase, SFA has the potential to transform selling and sales management.

CONCEPT CHECK

1. What are the three types of selling objectives?

2. What three factors are used to structure sales organizations?

3. How does emotional intelligence tie to adaptive selling?

CHAPTER IN REVIEW

1 *Discuss the nature and scope of personal selling and sales management in marketing.*
Personal selling involves the two-way flow of communication between a buyer and seller, often in a face-to-face encounter, designed to influence a person's or group's purchase decision. Sales management involves planning the selling program and implementing and controlling the personal selling effort of the firm. The scope of selling and sales management is apparent in three ways. First, virtually every occupation that involves customer contact has an element of personal selling. Second, selling plays a significant role in a

company's overall marketing effort. Salespeople occupy a boundary position between buyers and sellers; they *are* the company to many buyers and account for a major cost of marketing in a variety of industries; and they can create value for customers. Finally, through relationship and partnership selling, salespeople play a central role in tailoring solutions to customer problems as a means to customer value creation.

2 *Identify the different types of personal selling.*
Three types of personal selling exist: (*a*) order taking, (*b*) order getting, and (*c*) customer sales support activities. Each type differs from the others in terms of actual selling done

and the amount of creativity required to perform the sales task. Order takers process routine orders or reorders for products that were already sold by the company. They generally do little selling in a conventional sense and engage in only modest problem solving with customers. Order getters sell in a conventional sense and identify prospective customers, provide customers with information, persuade customers to buy, close sales, and follow up on customers' use of a product or service. Order getting involves a high degree of creativity and customer empathy and is typically required for selling complex or technical products with many options. Customer sales support personnel augment the sales effort of order getters by performing a variety of services. Sales support personnel are prominent in cross-functional team selling, the practice of using an entire team of professionals in selling to and servicing major customers.

3 *Explain the stages in the personal selling process.*
The personal selling process consists of six stages: (*a*) prospecting, (*b*) preapproach, (*c*) approach, (*d*) presentation, (*e*) close, and (*f*) follow-up. Prospecting involves the search for and qualification of potential customers. The preapproach stage involves

obtaining further information on the prospect and deciding on the best method of approach. The approach stage involves the initial meeting between the salesperson and prospect. The presentation stage involves converting a prospect into a customer by creating a desire for the product or service. The close involves obtaining a purchase commitment from the prospect. The follow-up stage involves making certain that the customer's purchase has been properly delivered and installed and difficulties experienced with the use of the item are addressed.

4 *Describe the major functions of sales management.*
Sales management consists of three interrelated functions: (*a*) sales plan formulation, (*b*) sales plan implementation, and (*c*) evaluation and control of the salesforce. Sales plan formulation involves setting objectives, organizing the salesforce, and developing account management policies. Sales plan implementation involves salesforce recruitment, selection, training, motivation, and compensation. Finally, evaluation and control of the salesforce focuses on quantitative assessments of sales performance and behavioural measures, such as customer satisfaction that are linked to selling objectives and account management policies.

■ ■ ■

FOCUSING ON KEY TERMS

account management policies p. 490
adaptive selling p. 484
consultative selling p. 484
emotional intelligence p. 492
formula selling presentation p. 483
major account management p. 488
missionary salespeople p. 480
need-satisfaction presentation p. 484
order getter p. 479
order taker p. 478
partnership selling p. 478

personal selling p. 476
personal selling process p. 480
relationship selling p. 477
sales engineer p. 480
sales management p. 476
sales plan p. 486
sales quota p. 494
salesforce automation p. 494
stimulus-response presentation p. 483
team selling p. 480
workload method p. 490

■ ■ ■

DISCUSSION AND APPLICATION QUESTIONS

1 Jane Dawson is a new sales representative for the Charles Schwab brokerage firm. In searching for clients, Jane purchased a mailing list of subscribers to *The Financial Post* and called them all regarding their interest in discount brokerage services. She asked if they had any stocks and if they had a regular broker. Those people without a regular broker were asked about their investment needs. Two days later, Jane called back with investment advice and asked if they would like to open an account. Identify each of Jane Dawson's actions in terms of the personal selling process.

2 For the first 50 years of business, the Johnson Carpet Company produced carpets for residential use. The salesforce was structured geographically. In the past five years, a large percentage of carpet sales has been to industrial users, hospitals, schools, and architects. The company also has broadened its product line to include area rugs, Oriental carpets,

and wall-to-wall carpeting. Is the present salesforce structure appropriate, or would you recommend an alternative?

3 Where would you place each of the following sales jobs on the order-taker/order-getter continuum shown below? (*a*) Tim Horton's counter clerk, (*b*) automobile insurance salesperson, (*c*) IBM salesperson, (*d*) life insurance salesperson, and (*e*) shoe salesperson.

Order taker	**Order getter**

4 Listed here are two different firms. Which compensation plan would you recommend for each firm, and what reasons would you give for your recommendations? (*a*) A newly formed company that sells lawn care equipment on a door-to-door basis directly to consumers; and (*b*) the Nabisco Company, which sells heavily advertised products in supermarkets by having the salesforce call on these stores and arrange shelves, set up displays, and make presentations to store buying committees.

5 The TDK tape company services 1000 audio stores throughout the United States. Each store is called on 12 times a year, and the average sales call lasts 30 minutes. Assuming a salesperson works 40 hours a week, 50 weeks a year, and devotes 75 percent of the time to actual selling, how many salespeople does TDK need?

6 A furniture manufacturer is currently using manufacturer's representatives to sell its line of living room furniture.

These representatives receive an 8-percent commission. The company is considering hiring its own salespeople and has estimated that the fixed cost of managing and paying their salaries would be $1 million annually. The salespeople would also receive a 4-percent commission on sales. The company has sales of $25 million dollars, and sales are expected to grow by 15 percent next year. Would you recommend that the company switch to its own salesforce? Why, or why not?

7 Suppose someone said to you, "The only real measure of a salesperson is the amount of sales produced." How might you respond?

GOING ONLINE   Selling News You Can Use

A unique resource for the latest developments in personal selling and sales management is the Sales Marketing Network (SMN) at www.info-now.com. SMN provides highly readable reports on a variety of topics, including many discussed in this chapter, such as telemarketing, motivation, sales training, and sales management. These reports contain concise overviews, definitions, statistics, and reviews of critical issues. They also include references to additional information and links to related material elsewhere on the SMN site. Registration (at no cost) is required to view some of the reports.

Visit the SMN site, and do the following:

1 Select a chapter topic, and update the statistics for, say, sales training costs or the popularity of different salesforce incentives.

2 Select a topic covered in the chapter, such as telemarketing, and summarize the critical issues identified for this practice.

Do you want to get better grades and stay up to date with current issues in marketing? Visit the Online Learning Centre at www.mcgrawhill.ca/college/crane for practice tests, video cases, resources for building a marketing plan, *Globe and Mail* headlines, access to *Marketing Magazine*, and other learning and study tools.

VIDEO CASE 18 — Reebok: Relationship Selling and Customer Value

"I think face-to-face selling is the most important and exciting part of this whole job. It's not writing the sales reports. It's not analyzing trends and forecasting. It's the two hours that you have to try to sell the buyer your products in a way that's profitable for both you and the retailer," relates Robert McMahon, key account sales representative. McMahon's job encompasses myriad activities, from supervising other sales representatives to attending companywide computer training sessions to monitoring competitors' activities. But it is the actual selling that is most appealing to McMahon. "That's the challenging, stimulating part of the job. Selling to the buyer is a different challenge every day. Every sales call, as well as you may have preplanned it, can change based on shifts and trends in the market. So, you need to be able to react to those changes and really think on your feet in front of the buyer."

REEBOK—HOT ON NIKE'S HEELS IN THE ATHLETIC SHOE AND APPAREL MARKET

Reebok is the second-largest athletic shoe manufacturer behind the market leader Nike. In addition to its athletic shoes, Reebok also sells Rockport, Greg Norman Collection, and Ralph Lauren Footwear shoes. The Reebok sporting goods line remains the flagship brand, though, and distinguishes itself on the market through the DMX cushioning technology in its footwear. Reebok concentrates its resources on getting its footwear and sporting goods gear into a diversified mix of distribution channels, such as athletic footwear specialty stores, department stores, and large sporting goods stores. Reebok is unique in that it emphasizes relationships with the retailers as an integral part of its marketing strategy. As an employee at one of Reebok's major retailers puts it, "Reebok is the only company that comes in on a regular basis and gives us information. Nike comes in once in a great while. New Balance comes in every six months. Saucony has come in twice. That's been it. Reebok comes in every month to update us on new information and new products. They tell us about the technology so we can tell the customers." Says Laurie Sipples, "vector" representative for Reebok, "There's a partnership that exists between Reebok and an account like this sporting goods store that sets us apart. That relationship is a great asset that Reebok has because the retailer feels more in touch with us than other brands."

THE SELLING PROCESS AT REEBOK

Selling at Reebok includes three elements—building trust between the salesperson and the retailer, providing enough information to the retailer for them to be successful selling Reebok products, and finally supporting the retailer after the sale. Sean Neville, senior vice-president and general manager of Reebok North America, explains, "Our goal is not to sell to the retailer; our goal is ultimately to sell to the consumer, and so we use the retailer as a partner. The salespeople are always keeping their eyes open and thinking like the retailer and selling to the consumer."

Reebok sells in teams that consist of the account representatives, who do the actual selling to the retailer, and the vector representatives, who spend their time in the stores training the store salespeople and reporting trends back to the account manager. The selling teams are organized geographically so that the salespeople live and work in the area where they are selling. This allows the sales team to understand the consumer intuitively. Neville explains, "If you have someone from one city fly to another and try to tell someone on the streets of that city what's happening from a trends standpoint and what products to purchase, it's very difficult."

On average, Reebok salespeople spend 70 percent of their time preparing for a sale and 30 percent of their time actually selling. The sales process at Reebok typically follows the six steps of the personal selling process identified in Figure 18–3: (1) Reebok identifies the outlets it would like to carry its athletic gear; (2) the salesforce prepares for the a presentation by familiarizing themselves with the store and its customers; (3) a Reebok representative approaches the prospect and suggests a meeting and presentation; (4) as the presentation begins, the salesperson summarizes relevant market conditions and consumer trends to demonstrate Reebok's commitment to a partnership with the retailer, states what he or she hopes to get out of the sales meeting, explains how the products work, and reinforces the benefits of Reebok products; (5) the salesperson engages in an action close (gets a signed document or a firm confirmation of the sale); and (6) later, various members of the salesforce frequently visit the retailer to provide assistance and monitor consumer preferences.

THE SALES MANAGEMENT PROCESS AT REEBOK

The sales teams at Reebok are organized on the basis of Reebok's three major distribution channels: athletic

visit us at www.mcgrawhill.ca/college/crane

specialty stores, sporting goods stores, and department stores. The smaller stores have sales teams assigned to them based on geographical location. The salesforce is then further broken down into footwear and apparel teams. The salesforce is primarily organized by distribution channel because this is most responsive to customer needs and wants. The salesforce is compensated on both short-term and long-term bases. In the short term, salespeople are paid based on sales results and profits for the current quarter as well as forecasting. In the long term, salespeople are compensated based on their teamwork and team building efforts. As Neville explains, "Money is typically fourth or fifth on the list of pure motivation. Number one is recognition for a job well done. And that drives people to succeed." Management at Reebok is constantly providing feedback to the salesforce acknowledging their success, not just during annual reviews, and Neville feels this is the key to the high level of motivation, energy, and excitement that exists in the salesforce at Reebok.

WHAT'S NEW ON THE HORIZON FOR THE SALESFORCE AT REEBOK?

Reebok has recently issued laptop computers to its entire salesforce, which enables the salespeople to check inventories in the warehouses, make sure orders are being shipped on time, and even enter orders while they are out in the field. Reebok is also focusing more on relationship selling. McMahon describes his relationship with a major buyer as "one of trust and respect. It's gotten to the point now where we're good friends. We go to a lot of sporting events together, which I think really helps." Another recent innovation is for the salesforce to incentivize the stores' sales clerks. For instance, whoever sells the most pairs of Reebok shoes in a month will get tickets to a concert or a football game.

QUESTIONS

1 How does Reebok create customer value for its major accounts through relationship selling?

2 How does Reebok utilize team selling to provide the highest level of customer value possible to its major accounts?

3 Is Reebok's salesforce organized on the basis of geography, customer, or product?

4 What are some ways Reebok's selling processes are changing due to technical advancements?

PART

5

MANAGING THE MARKETING PROCESS

HOW PART 5 FITS INTO THE BOOK

The final chapter of the text shows how marketing managers weave a myriad controllable and uncontrollable factors into successful marketing programs using the strategic marketing process.

CHAPTER 19

PULLING IT ALL TOGETHER: THE STRATEGIC MARKETING PROCESS

LEARNING OBJECTIVES

After reading this chapter, you should be able to:

1. Explain how marketing managers allocate their limited resources.

2. Describe three marketing planning frameworks: Porter's generic strategies, profit enhancement options, and market–product synergies.

3. Explain what makes an effective marketing plan and some problems that often exist with it.

4. Describe the alternatives for organizing a marketing department and the role of a product manager.

5. Explain how sales and profitability analyses and ROI marketing are used to evaluate and control marketing programs.

WESTJET: CRAFTING STRATEGY IN AN EVOLVING MARKETING ENVIRONMENT

WestJet was founded in 1996 by four Calgary entrepreneurs led by Clive Beddoe. WestJet's original strategy was simple: offer low-fare air travel across Western Canada. The WestJet founders studied the success of Southwest Airlines' and determined that a similar concept could be successful in western Canada. The team developed a business plan and raised the capital to start the business. The airline started flight operations with 220 employees and three 737 aircraft to the cities of Vancouver, Kelowna, Calgary, Edmonton, and Winnipeg. The company then added Victoria, Regina, and Saskatoon to its route network. In 1997, WestJet began service to Abbotsford/Fraser Valley, and in 1999, WestJet added Thunder Bay, Prince George, and Grande Prairie to its service area.

In July 1999, WestJet became a publicly traded company and extended its airline service across Canada. In June 2000, the company added service to the eastern Canadian cities of Hamilton, Moncton, and Ottawa, creating an eastern network with Hamilton as the hub. In 2001, WestJet added new service to Fort McMurray, Comox, and Brandon. In 2001, WestJet also added its first four Next-Generation Boeing 737-700 aircraft. In 2002, WestJet added service to two new Ontario destinations, London and Toronto. In February 2002, the corporation successfully offered three million common shares yielding net proceeds of $78.9 million. The proceeds were used to fund aircraft additions, spare parts, and a third flight simulator. In 2003, WestJet added service to the new markets of Halifax, Windsor, Montréal, St. John's, and Gander. As the Canadian airline market evolved, WestJet looked to continue its growth and found an opportunity to expand its routes into the United States. Cross-border service commenced in the fall of 2004 to the cities of Los Angeles, San Francisco, Phoenix, Fort Lauderdale, Tampa, Orlando, and New York, and service to Palm Springs began in January 2005. To date, WestJet has offered service to more than 32.5 million passengers whom they refer to as "guests."

So, what are the ingredients to WestJet's success? Well, as you will discover in this chapter, four basic business practices are fundamental to business success: strategy, execution, culture, and structure. From the beginning, WestJet had a clear and focused strategy, and it executed it well. The company also developed a strong organizational and entrepreneurial culture with its employees (who are shareholders) as key architects to its success. The company has built and maintains a flat, flexible organization, with its employees empowered to make corporate decisions and solve problems.

However, as market conditions change and organizations evolve, many companies cannot stay wedded to their original strategies. WestJet's original low-price, no frills, point-to-point regional air travel model was successful in driving the growth of the company. But WestJet is now a national airline with $1 billion in revenue competing head-to-head against some major competitors, including Air Canada. In fact, Air Canada is now taking the battle to WestJet, pushing hard to compete in regional markets originally built by WestJet. While WestJet intends to defend those markets, it believes that future growth lies in the United States. This has forced the company to rethink some of its original strategies. For example, the low-cost or discount carrier market in the United States is stratified with some consumers demanding the lowest price, while others want an additional level of comfort, such as leather seats and free seatback TV. JetBlue, an American value-based carrier, has targeted the segment wanting higher comfort levels. WestJet seems to have noticed this and is now offering similar amenities.

The American market is, however, extremely competitive, and WestJet has to continue to be able to differentiate itself. It seems that WestJet will focus on offering low-cost fares but with some comfort features. But a pivotal aspect of its competitive strategy will be its cross-border travel, which is, in fact, an emerging travel trend. WestJet is hoping this will allow it to compete successfully and to help propel it into a world-class brand. There is even strategic thought being given to further expansion into Europe.[1]

Chapter 19 discusses issues and techniques related to the planning, implementation, and control phases of the strategic marketing process, the kind of topics marketing managers and executives deal with every day. Throughout the chapter, you will be able to obtain insights into the marketing strategies used by many successful Canadian and global companies.

MARKETING BASICS: DOING WHAT WORKS AND ALLOCATING RESOURCES

As noted in Chapter 2, corporate and marketing executives search continuously to find a competitive advantage—a unique strength relative to competitors. Having identified this competitive advantage, they must figure out how to exploit it.[2] This involves (1) finding and using what works for their organization and industry, and (2) allocating resources effectively.

Finding and Using What Really Works

In a five-year study, researchers conducted in-depth analysis of 160 companies and more than 200 management tools and techniques, such as supply chain management, customer relationship management (CRM), or the use of an intranet. The result? Individual management tools and techniques had no direct relationship to superior business performance.[3]

What did matter? The researchers concluded that what matters are four basic business and management practices—"what really works"—to use a phrase. These are (1) strategy, (2) execution, (3) culture, and (4) structure. Firms with excellence in all four of these areas are likely to achieve superior business performance. And in terms of individual tools and techniques, the researchers concluded that the firm's choice of a tool or technique is less important than the flawless execution of it.

Industry leaders, such as Wal-Mart, Home Depot, and Dell, do all four of the basic practices extremely well, not just two or three, and are vigilant to keep doing them well even when conditions change. And as the chapter opener indicated, WestJet also performs well on all four dimensions. However, Coca-Cola,[4] and Kodak,[5] superstars a decade ago, are struggling today to get these basics right and regain past success. But let us look at some other companies that stand out today in each of the four basics:

Costco achieves excellence in what really matters.

- *Strategy: Devise and maintain a clearly stated, focused strategy.* While Wal-Mart may be the unstoppable force in mass-merchandise retailing, among warehouse clubs, its Sam's Club is not. The winner, to date, is Costco, with 60 percent as many stores as Sam's Club but almost twice the sales revenue. A key reason is Costco's focused strategy based on the knowledge that of all retail channels, warehouse clubs attract the largest proportion of affluent shoppers. Costco's strategy: sell a limited selection of branded high-end merchandise at low prices.[6]
- *Execution: Develop and maintain flawless operational execution.* Toyota is generally acknowledged as the best in the world in revolutionizing the design and manufacture of autos. Toyota managers created the doctrine of *kaizen*, or continuous improvement. For example, by speeding up decisions, Toyota reduced the time to get the Solara from the drawing board to the showroom in 19 months, about half the industry average.[7]
- *Culture: Develop and maintain a performance-oriented culture.* Several high-performing companies point to their culture as central to their success. Janssen-Ortho, for example, promotes leadership development and innovation teams as part of its organizational culture. Flight Centre keeps its organization performing well by promoting from within, thus motivating its employees and perpetuating its winning culture. Spinmaster Toys promotes a fun and positive environment that keeps its company humming along, while Dofasco leverages employee profit-sharing to promote a performance-oriented culture.
- *Structure: Build and maintain a fast, flexible, flat organization.* Successful small organizations often grow into bureaucratic large ones with layers of managers and red tape that slow down the decision-making process. High-performing firms, on the other hand, empower their employees to make decisions and provide an environment where internal communications are encouraged as is active problem-solving, all within simple and flat organizational structures.

Of course, in practice, a firm cannot allocate unlimited resources to achieving each of these business basics. It must make choices on where its resources can give the greatest return, the topic of the next section.

Allocating Marketing Resources Using Sales Response Functions

sales response function
Relates the expense of marketing effort to the marketing results obtained.

A **sales response function** relates the expense of marketing effort to the marketing results obtained.[8] For simplicity, in the examples that follow, only the effects of annual marketing effort on annual sales revenue will be analyzed, but the concept applies to other measures of marketing success—such as profit, units sold, or level of awareness—as well.

Maximizing Incremental Revenue Minus Incremental Cost   Economists give managers a specific guideline for optimal resource allocation: allocate the firm's marketing, production, and financial resources to the markets and products where the excess of incremental revenues over incremental costs is greatest.

Figure 19–1 illustrates the resource allocation principle that is inherent in the sales response function. The firm's annual marketing effort, such as sales and advertising expenses, is plotted on the horizontal axis. As the annual marketing effort increases, so does the resulting annual sales revenue, which is plotted on the vertical axis. The relationship is assumed to be S-shaped, showing that an additional $1 million of marketing effort from $3 million to $4 million results in far greater increases of sales revenue in the midrange ($20 million) of the curve than at either end (an increase from $2 million to $3 million in spending yields an increase of $10 million in sales; an increase from $6 million to $7 million in spending leads to an increase of $5 million in sales).

A Numerical Example of Resource Allocation   Suppose Figure 19–1 shows the situation for a new General Mills product, such as Berry Burst Cheerios®, an extension of the Cheerios brand targeted at "the grocery shopper," who is typically a 35- to 54-year-old woman. Berry Burst Cheerios contains berries that plump up when milk is added, a technical challenge for scientists.[9]

Also, assume that the sales response function does not change through time as a result of changing consumer tastes and incomes. Point A shows the position of the firm in year 1, whereas Point B shows it three years later in year 4. Suppose General Mills decides to launch new advertising and sales promotions that, say, increase its marketing effort for the brand from $3 million to $6 million a year. If the relationship in Figure 19–1 holds true and is a good picture of consumer purchasing behaviour, the sales revenues of Berry Burst Cheerios should increase from $30 million to $70 million a year.

Let us look at the major resource allocation question: what are the probable increases in sales revenue for Berry Burst Cheerios in year 1 and year 4 if General Mills were to spend an additional $1 million in marketing effort? As Figure 19–1 reveals:

Year 1

Increase in marketing effort from $3 million to $4 million = $1 million

Increase in sales revenue from $30 million to $50 million = $20 million

Ratio of incremental sales revenue to effort = $20 000 000:$1 000 000 = 20:1

Year 4

Increase in marketing effort from $6 million to $7 million = $1 million

Increase in sales revenue from $70 million to $73 million = $3 million

Ratio of incremental sales revenue to effort = $3 000 000:$1 000 000 = 3:1

■ FIGURE 19–1 ■

Sales response function showing the situation for two different years

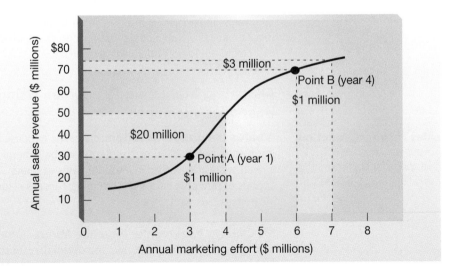

Thus, in year 1, a dollar of extra marketing effort returned $20 in sales revenue, whereas in year 4, it returned only $3. If no other expenses are incurred, it might make sense to spend $1 million in year 4 to gain $3 million in incremental sales revenue. However, it may be far wiser for General Mills to invest the money in products in one of its other business units, such as its new Yoplait Nouriche Light. The essence of resource allocation is simple: put incremental resources where the incremental returns are greatest over the foreseeable future.

share points

Percentage points of market share; often used as the common basis of comparison to allocate marketing resources effectively.

Allocating Marketing Resources in Practice   General Mills, like many firms in these businesses, does extensive analysis using **share points**, or percentage points of market share, as the common basis of comparison to allocate marketing resources effectively for different product lines within the same firm. This allows it to seek answers to the question, "How much is it worth to us to try to increase our market share by another 1 (or 2, or 5, or 10) percentage point?"

This analysis enables higher-level managers to make resource allocation tradeoffs among different kinds of business units owned by the company. To make these resource allocation decisions, marketing managers must estimate (1) the market share for the product, (2) the revenues associated with each point of market share (a share point in breakfast cereals may be five times what it is in cake mixes), (3) the contribution to overhead and profit (or gross margin) of each share point, and (4) possible cannibalization effects on other products in the line (for example, new Berry Burst Cheerios might reduce the sales of regular Cheerios).[10]

The resource allocation process helps General Mills choose wisely from among the many opportunities that exist in its various products and markets. In the case of Berry Burst Cheerios, it was the most successful launch in General Mills' history, achieving almost $100 million in retail sales its first year.[11]

Resource Allocation and the Strategic Marketing Process   Company resources are allocated effectively in the strategic marketing process by converting marketing information into marketing actions. Figure 19–2 on the next page summarizes the strategic marketing process introduced in Chapter 2, along with some details of the marketing actions and information that comprise it. Figure 19–2 is really a simplification of the actual strategic marketing process: while the three phases of the strategic marketing process have distinct separations in the figure and the marketing actions are separated from the marketing information, in practice, these blend together and interact.

The upper half of each box in Figure 19–2 highlights the actions involved in that part of the strategic marketing process, and the lower half summarizes the information and reports used. Note that each phase has an output report:

PHASE	OUTPUT REPORT
Planning	Marketing plans (or programs) that define goals and the marketing mix strategies to achieve them
Implementation	Results (memos or computer outputs) that describe the outcomes of implementing the plans
Control	Corrective action memos, triggered by comparing results with plans, that (1) suggest solutions to problems, and (2) take advantage of opportunities

The corrective action memos become feedback loops in Figure 19–2 that help improve decisions and actions in the earlier phases of the strategic marketing process.

■ **FIGURE 19–2** ■■

The strategic marketing process: actions and information

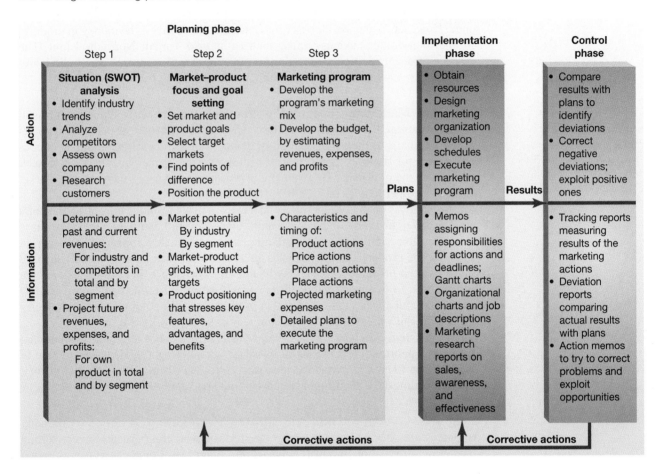

THE PLANNING PHASE OF THE STRATEGIC MARKETING PROCESS

Three aspects of the strategic marketing process deserve special mention: (1) the varieties of marketing plans, (2) marketing planning frameworks that have proven useful, and (3) some marketing planning and strategy lessons.

The Variety of Marketing Plans

The planning phase of the strategic marketing process usually results in a marketing plan that sets the direction for the marketing activities of an organization. As noted earlier in Appendix A, a marketing plan is the heart of a business plan. Like business plans, marketing plans are not all from the same mould; they vary with the length of the planning period, the purpose, and the audience. Let us look briefly at two kinds: long-range plans and annual marketing plans.

Long-Range Marketing Plans

Typically, long-range marketing plans cover marketing activities from two to five years into the future. Except for firms in such industries as autos, steel, or forest products, marketing plans rarely go beyond five years into the future because the tremendous number of uncertainties present make the benefits of planning less than

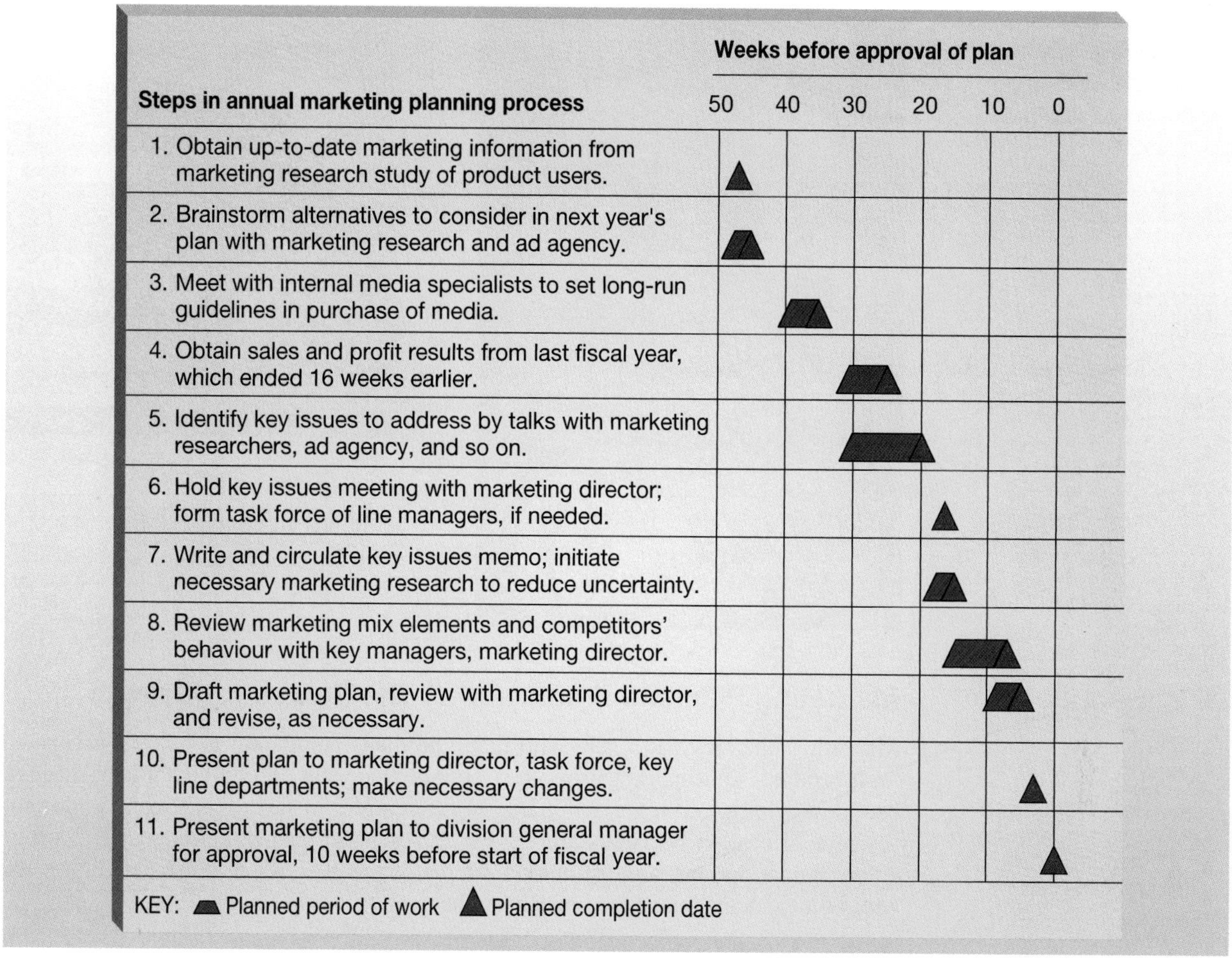

Steps in annual marketing planning process	Weeks before approval of plan					
	50	40	30	20	10	0
1. Obtain up-to-date marketing information from marketing research study of product users.	▲					
2. Brainstorm alternatives to consider in next year's plan with marketing research and ad agency.	◣▲					
3. Meet with internal media specialists to set long-run guidelines in purchase of media.		◣▲				
4. Obtain sales and profit results from last fiscal year, which ended 16 weeks earlier.			◣▲			
5. Identify key issues to address by talks with marketing researchers, ad agency, and so on.			◣▲			
6. Hold key issues meeting with marketing director; form task force of line managers, if needed.				▲		
7. Write and circulate key issues memo; initiate necessary marketing research to reduce uncertainty.				▲		
8. Review marketing mix elements and competitors' behaviour with key managers, marketing director.					◣▲	
9. Draft marketing plan, review with marketing director, and revise, as necessary.					◣▲	
10. Present plan to marketing director, task force, key line departments; make necessary changes.						▲
11. Present marketing plan to division general manager for approval, 10 weeks before start of fiscal year.						▲

KEY: ◣ Planned period of work   ▲ Planned completion date

■ **FIGURE 19–3** ■

Steps a large consumer packaged goods firm takes in developing its annual marketing plan

Source: Reprinted with permission from *Journal of Marketing*, published by the American Marketing Association, Summer 1980, p. 82.

the effort expended. Such plans are often directed at top-level executives and the board of directors.

Annual Marketing Plans   Usually developed by a marketing or product manager (discussed later in the chapter) in a consumer products firm, such as General Mills, annual marketing plans deal with marketing goals and strategies for a product, product line, or entire firm for a single year. Typical steps that such firms as Kellogg's, Coca-Cola, and Johnson & Johnson take in developing their annual marketing plans for their existing products are shown in Figure 19–3.[12] This annual planning cycle typically starts with a detailed marketing research study of current users and ends after 48 weeks, with the approval of the plan by the division general manager—10 weeks before the fiscal year starts. Between these points, there are continuing efforts to uncover new ideas through brainstorming and key-issues sessions with specialists both inside and outside the firm. The plan is fine-tuned through a series of often-excruciating reviews by several levels of management, which leaves few surprises and very little to chance.

CONCEPT CHECK

1. What is the significance of the S-shape of the sales response function in Figure 19–1?

2. What are the main output reports from each phase of the strategic marketing process?

3. What are two kinds of marketing plans?

Which of Porter's generic strategies are Wal-Mart and Volkswagen using? For the answer and a discussion of the strategies, see the text.

Marketing Planning Frameworks: The Search for Growth

Marketing planning for a firm with many products competing in many markets—a multiproduct, multimarket firm—is a complex process. Three techniques that are useful in helping corporate and marketing executives in such a firm make important resource allocation decisions are (1) Porter's generic business strategies, (2) profit enhancement options, and (3) market–product synergies. All of these techniques are based on elements introduced in earlier chapters.

generic business strategy

Strategy that can be adopted by any firm, regardless of the product or industry involved, to achieve a competitive advantage.

Porter's Generic Business Strategies   As shown in Figure 19–4, Michael E. Porter has developed a framework in which he identifies four basic, or "generic," strategies.[13] A **generic business strategy** is one that can be adopted by any firm, regardless of the product or industry involved, to achieve a competitive advantage.

Although all of the techniques discussed here involve generic strategies, the phrase is most often associated with Porter's framework. In this framework, the columns identify the two fundamental alternatives firms can use in seeking competitive advantage: (1) becoming the low-cost producer within the markets in which it competes, or (2) differentiating itself from competitors through developing points of difference in its product offerings or marketing programs. In contrast, the rows identify the competitive scope: (1) a broad target by competing in many market segments, or (2) a narrow target by competing in only a few segments or even a single segment. The columns and rows result in four generic business strategies, any one

■ **FIGURE 19–4** ■

Porter's four generic business strategies

Source: Adapted with permission from The Free Press, a Division of Simon & Schuster Group, from COMPETITIVE ADVANTAGE: Creating and Sustaining Superior Performance by Michael E. Porter. Copyright © 1985, 1998 by Michael E. Porter. All rights reserved.

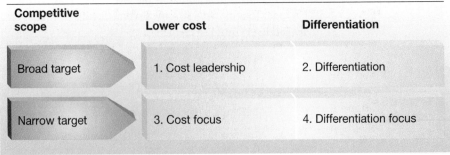

	SOURCE OF COMPETITIVE ADVANTAGE	
Competitive scope	**Lower cost**	**Differentiation**
Broad target	1. Cost leadership	2. Differentiation
Narrow target	3. Cost focus	4. Differentiation focus

of which can provide a competitive advantage among similar business units in the same industry:

cost leadership strategy

Focuses on reducing expenses and lowering produce prices while targeting a broad array of market segments.

1. A **cost leadership strategy** (cell 1) focuses on reducing expenses and lowering product prices while targeting a broad array of market segments. One way is by securing raw materials from a lower-cost supplier. Also, significant investments in capital equipment may be necessary to improve the production or distribution process and achieve these lower unit costs. The cost leader still must have adequate quality levels. Wal-Mart's sophisticated systems of regional warehouses and electronic data interchange with its suppliers have led to huge cost savings and its cost leadership strategy.

differentiation strategy

Requires products to have significant points of difference in product offerings, brand image, higher quality, advanced technology, or superior service to charge a higher price while targeting a broad array of market segments.

2. A **differentiation strategy** (cell 2) requires products to have significant points of difference in product offerings, brand image, higher quality, advanced technology, or superior service to charge a higher price while targeting a broad array of market segments. This allows the firm to charge a price premium. Delphi Automobile Systems has used this strategy to use satellite communications to connect car and driver to 24-hour-a-day emergency services, directions to a destination, and the opportunity to order a movie while on the road.

cost-focus strategy

Involves controlling expenses and, in turn, lowering product prices targeting a narrow range of market segments.

3. A **cost-focus strategy** (cell 3) involves controlling expenses and, in turn, lowering product prices, targeting a narrow range of market segments. Retail chains targeting only a few market segments in a restricted group of products—such as Office Depot in office supplies—have used a cost-focus strategy successfully. Similarly, some airlines have been very successful in offering low fares between very restricted pairs of cities.

differentiation-focus strategy

Requires products to have significant points of difference to target one or only a few market segments.

4. Finally, a **differentiation-focus strategy** (cell 4) requires products to have significant points of difference to target one or only a few market segments. Volkswagen has achieved spectacular success by targeting the "nostalgia segment," 35- to 55-year-old baby boomers, with its technology-laden Beetle. It is also using a differentiation flow for its luxury Phaeton brand.

These strategies also form the foundation for Michael Porter's theory about what makes a nation's industries successful, as was discussed in Chapter 7.

Profit Enhancement Options   If a business wants to increase, or "enhance," its profits, it can (1) increase revenues, (2) decrease expenses, or (3) do both. Among these "profit enhancement options," let us look first at the strategy options of increasing revenues and then at those for decreasing expenses.

The strategy option of increasing revenues can be achieved only by using one or a combination of four ways to address present or new markets and products (Figure 19–5): (1) market penetration, (2) product development, (3) market development, and (4) diversification (which were described in Chapter 2).

Procter & Gamble has followed a successful strategy of market penetration (present markets, present products) by concentrating its effort on becoming the market leader in each of its more than 30 product categories. It is currently first in market share in more than half these product categories. Efforts to increase customer satisfaction have also helped increase market penetration. It has also increased its market share in 19 of its 20 largest core brands by introducing product improvements and trimming retail prices.[14]

In contrast, Johnson & Johnson has succeeded with a product development strategy—finding new products for its present markets—to complement popular brands, such as Tylenol pain reliever and Accuvue contact lenses. To compete with Bristol-Meyers and other companies, Johnson & Johnson developed Tylenol PM—a combination pain killer and sleeping pill—and Surevue—a longer-lasting disposable contact lens.

Walt Disney Co. pursued a market development strategy (new market, present product) following the success of the original Disneyland in Anaheim, California.

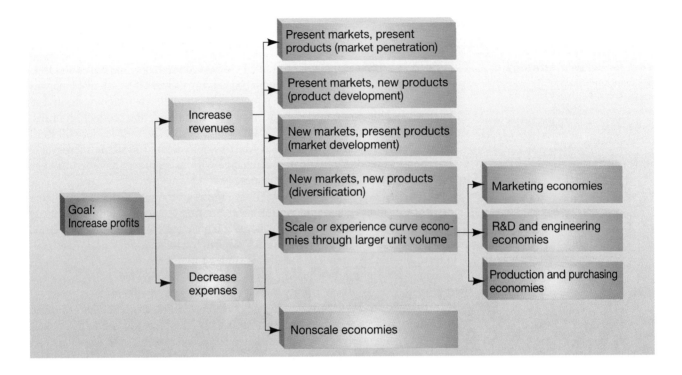

■ **FIGURE 19–5** ■

Profit enhancement options for increasing a firm's profits

The first market expansion was to Orlando, Florida, and then Tokyo and Paris. Disney has also pursued a diversification strategy by entering into the motion picture business with the development of Touchstone Pictures: buying and operating an NHL franchise, the Mighty Ducks, (now divested); and operating a cruise line.

Canadian Tire has pursued a multipronged strategy, including increased market penetration in existing markets, market development (geographic expansion), introducing new products to expand its current product line, and diversification through the acquisition of Mark's Work Wearhouse, establishment of a car wash division, and participation in the financial services business. In fact, Canadian Tire Financial Services is the only nonbank institution in Canada that has a MasterCard licence.

Strategy options for decreasing expenses fall into two broad categories (see Figure 19–5). One is relying on scale economies or experience curve benefits from an increased volume of production to drive unit costs down and gross margins up, the best-known examples being electronic devices, such as fax or voice-mail machines whose prices fell by half in a few years. Scale economies may occur in marketing, as well as in R&D, engineering, production, and purchasing.

The other strategy option to decrease expenses is simply finding other ways to reduce costs, such as cutting the number of managers, increasing the effectiveness of the salesforce through more training, or reducing product rejects by improving quality. Procter & Gamble concluded that the world did not really need 31 varieties of Head & Shoulders shampoo, and so it cut the number of packages, sizes, and formulas and thereby reduced expenses and increased profits.

Market–Product Synergies Using the market–product grid framework introduced in Chapter 9, we can see two kinds of synergy that are critical in developing corporate and marketing strategies: (1) marketing synergy, and (2) R&D–manufacturing synergy. While the following example involves external synergies through mergers and acquisitions, the concepts apply equally well to internal synergies sought in adding new products or seeking new markets.

A critical step in the external analysis is to assess how these merger and acquisition strategies provide the organization with synergy—the increased customer value achieved through performing organizational functions more efficiently. The "increased customer value" can take many forms: more products, improved quality

MARKETING NEWSNET

A Key Strategy Issue: Finding Synergies

The Molson–Coors merger created the fifth largest brewing company in the world. It also created synergy—with expectations to generate $175 million a year in cost savings and new revenues. This merger follows Molson's acquisition of Kaiser in Brazil and Coors' acquisition of British Carling brands. The companies believe the new merger will result in a stronger company in a consolidating global beer industry. Another major merger creating plenty of synergy is the Procter & Gamble–Gillette merger which has resulted in one of the largest packaged goods companies in the world. Finally, Toronto-Dominion Bank (TD) acquired BankNorth of New England to achieve synergy and obtain a presence in the lucrative American retail banking market. The newly merged firm will result in cost-savings, technology sharing, and increased revenues.

To try your hand in this synergy game, assume you are a vice-president of marketing for Great Lawns Corp., which markets a line of nonpowered and powered walking and riding lawnmowers. A market–product grid for your business is shown here. You distribute your nonpowered mowers in all three market segments shown and powered walking mowers only in suburban markets. However, you do not offer powered riding mowers for any of the three markets.

Here are your strategy dilemmas:

1. Where are the marketing synergies (efficiencies)?
2. Where are the R&D and manufacturing synergies (efficiencies)?
3. What would a market–product grid look like for an ideal company that Great Lawns could merge with for it to achieve both marketing and R&D/manufacturing synergies (efficiencies)?

For answers to these questions, read the text and study Figures 19–6 and 19–7.

Market segments	P_1 Nonpowered	P_2 Powered, walk	P_3 Powered, ride
City market M_1	■		
Suburban market M_2	■	■	
Rural market M_3	■		

on existing products, lower prices, improved distribution, and so on. But the ultimate criterion is that customers should be better off as a result of the increased synergy. The firm, in turn, should be better off by gaining more satisfied customers.

A market–product grid helps identify important tradeoffs in the strategic marketing process. As noted in the Marketing NewsNet box,[15] assume you are vice-president of marketing for Great Lawns Corporation's line of nonpowered lawnmowers and powered walking mowers sold to the consumer market. You are looking for new product and new market opportunities to increase your revenues and profits.

You conduct a market segmentation study and develop a market–product grid to analyze future opportunities. You identify three major segments in the consumer market based on geography: (1) city, (2) suburban, and (3) rural households. These market segments relate to the size of lawn a consumer must mow. The product clusters are (1) nonpowered, (2) powered walking, and (3) powered riding mowers. Five alternative marketing strategies are shown in the market–product grids in Figure 19–6. The important marketing efficiencies—or synergies—run horizontally across the rows in Figure 19–6. Conversely, the important R&D and production efficiencies—or synergies—run vertically down the columns. Let us look at the synergy effects for the five combinations in Figure 19–6:[16]

> **A.** *Market–product concentration.* The firm benefits from "focus" on a single product line and market segment, but it loses opportunities for significant synergies in both marketing and R&D–manufacturing.
>
> **B.** *Market specialization.* The firm gains marketing synergy through providing a complete product line, but R&D–manufacturing have the difficulty of developing and producing two new products.

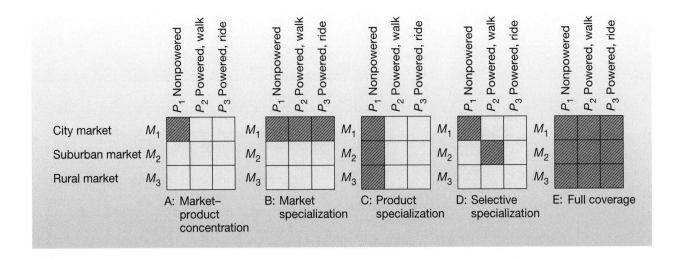

■ FIGURE 19–6 ■

Market–product grid of alternative strategies for a lawnmower manufacturer

Source: Kotler, Philip, *Marketing Management*, 11th Ed., © 2003. Adapted by permission of Pearson Education, Inc., Upper Saddle River, N.J.

C. *Product specialization.* The firm gains R&D–manufacturing synergy through production economies of scale, but gaining market distribution in the three different geographic areas will be costly.

D. *Selective specialization.* The firm does not get either marketing or R&D–manufacturing synergies because of the uniqueness of the market–product combinations.

E. *Full coverage.* The firm has the maximum potential synergies in both marketing and R&D–manufacturing. The question is: is it spread too thin due to the resource requirements needed to reach all market–product combinations?

The Marketing NewsNet box posed the question of what the ideal partner for Great Lawns would be if it merged with another firm, given the market–product combinations shown in the box. If, as vice-president of marketing, you want to follow a full-coverage strategy, then the ideal merger partner is shown in Figure 19–7. This would give the maximum potential synergies—if you are not spreading your merged companies too thin. Marketing gains by having a complete product line in all regions, and R&D–manufacturing gains by having access to new markets that can provide production economies of scale through producing larger volumes of its existing products.

CONCEPT CHECK

1. Describe Porter's four generic business strategies.

2. What are four alternative ways to increase a firm's profit when considering profit enhancement options and strategies?

3. Where do (a) marketing synergies, and (b) R&D–manufacturing synergies appear in a market–product grid framework?

■ FIGURE 19–7 ■

An ideal merger for Great Lawns to obtain full market–product coverage

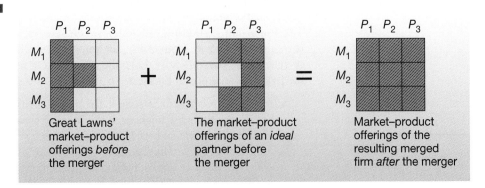

Great Lawns' market–product offerings *before* the merger

The market–product offerings of an *ideal* partner before the merger

Market–product offerings of the resulting merged firm *after* the merger

Some Planning and Strategy Lessons

Applying these frameworks is not automatic but requires a great deal of managerial judgment. Common-sense requirements of an effective marketing plan are discussed next, followed by problems that can arise.

Guidelines for an Effective Marketing Plan   Dwight D. Eisenhower, when he commanded Allied armies in World War II, made his classic observation, "Plans are nothing; planning is everything." It is the process of careful planning that focuses an organization's efforts and leads to success. The plans themselves, which change with events, are often secondary. Effective planning and plans are inevitably characterized by identifiable objectives, specific strategies or courses of action, and the means to execute them. Here are some guidelines in developing effective marketing plans:

Marketing 101 final exam: What is the common feature of these brands that explains General Mills focus on one-handedness? For the answer and its significance, see the Marketing NewsNet box.

- *Set measurable, achievable goals.* Ideally, goals should be quantified and measurable in terms of what is to be accomplished and by when. So, "Increase market share from 18 to 22 percent by December 31, 2008" is preferable to "Maximize market share given our available resources." Also, to motivate people, the goals must be achievable.
- *Use a base of facts and valid assumptions.* The more a marketing plan is based on facts and valid assumptions, rather than guesses, the less are the uncertainty and risk associated with executing it. Good marketing research helps. For example, General Mills' research indicates a basic fact that busy consumers on the go want very convenient food products—ones they can eat with one hand. So, when Steve Sanger, CEO of General Mills, receives plans for a new food product from his employees, he asks one question: does it have the "one-handedness" feature that consumers want? Without that feature, the marketing plan for that product is not likely to be successful (see the Marketing NewsNet box).
- *Utilize simple but clear and specific plans.* Effective execution of plans requires that people at all levels in the firm understand what, when, and how they are to accomplish their tasks.
- *Have complete and feasible plans.* Marketing plans must incorporate all the key marketing mix factors and be supported by adequate resources.
- *Make plans controllable and flexible.* Marketing plans must enable results to be compared with planned targets, which allows replanning—the flexibility to update the original plans.

Problems in Marketing Planning and Strategy   From postmortems on company plans that did work and on those that did not work, a picture emerges of where problems occur in the planning phase of a firm's strategic marketing process. The following list explores these problems:

1. Plans may be based on very poor assumptions about environmental factors, especially changing economic conditions and competitors' actions. Canadians used to equate the name Listerine with mouthwash. But Scope started an anti-Listerine campaign and successfully convinced Canadians that mouthwash did not have to taste bad to work. The result? Listerine lost its position as market leader.
2. Planners and their plans may have lost sight of their customers' needs. The "better ingredients, better pizza" slogan makes the hair stand up on the back of the necks of Pizza Hut executives. The reason is that this slogan of Papa John's International pizza chain reflects the firm's obsessive attention to detail, which is stealing market share from the five-times-bigger Pizza Hut! Sample detail: if the cheese on the pizza shows a single air bubble or the crust is not golden brown, the offending pizza is not served to the customer!

MARKETING NEWSNET

Keeping Planning Simple at Big G: "One-Handed" Convenience plus Cover All the Bases

What do you do if you are the chief executive officer of a firm in the low-growth food industry? This is the problem facing Steve Sanger, CEO of General Mills. His remarkable answer: one-handedness and covering all the bases, both built on a focus on today's consumers and keeping marketing planning simple and clear.

One-Handedness

When Steve Sanger gets proposals for a new food product or a way to reposition an old one, he asks one question, "Can we make it 'one-handed'?" This does not mean *build* it one-handed but being able to *eat* it one-handed! This lets consumers of the product have a free hand while typing or driving. A Go-Bag pouch of Cinnamon Toast Crunch, a Yoplait Nouriche Light yogurt smoothie, and Big G Milk 'n Cereal Bars are examples of Sanger's one-handed strategy.

Cover All the Bases

Big G responds to changing consumer tastes and covers all bases using market and product strategies, such as those with the brands shown below. This also involves joint ventures with other firms with special expertise, such as Nestlé, to reach Polish consumers or Du Pont to develop 8th Continent Soymilk.

PRODUCTS

Markets	Current		New	
	Market Penetration		**Product Development**	
Current		Finding ways to make current products appeal to current customers: Go-Bags, six-to-a-carton pouches of breakfast cereal for snacking		Reaching current customers with a new product: Yoplait Nouriche, a healthy yogurt smoothie with 20 vitamins and minerals
	Market Development		**Diversification**	
New		Reaching new customers with a current product: Cini Minis for Polish consumers—known as Cinnamon Toast Crunch in the U.S.		Reaching new customers with a new product: 8th Continent Soymilk, for consumers who cannot drink milk or are health conscious

3. Too much time and effort may be spent on data collection and writing the plans. Westinghouse has cut its planning instructions for operating units "that looked like an auto repair manual" to five or six pages.

4. Line operating managers often feel no sense of ownership in implementing the plans. Andy Grove, when he was CEO of Intel, observed, "We had the very ridiculous system . . . of delegating strategic planning to strategic planners. The strategies these [planners] prepared had no bearing on anything we actually did."[17] The solution is to assign more planning activities to line operating managers—the people who actually carry them out.

Balancing Value and Values in Strategic Marketing Plans   Two important trends are likely to influence the strategic marketing process in the future. The first, *value-based planning*, combines marketing planning ideas and financial planning techniques to assess how much a division or strategic business unit (SBU) contributes to the price of a company's shares (or shareholder wealth). Value is created when the financial return of a strategic activity exceeds the cost of the resources allocated to the activity.

The second trend is the increasing interest in *value-driven strategies*, which incorporate concerns for ethics, integrity, employee health and safety, and environmental safeguards with more common corporate values, such as growth, profitability, customer service, and quality. Some experts have observed that although many corporations cite broad corporate values in advertisements, press releases, and company newsletters, they have not yet changed their strategic plans to reflect the stated values. Canadian firms are increasingly called on to be good global citizens and so support sustainable development.[18]

Finally, remember that it is easier to talk about planning than to do it well. Try your hand as a consultant to help Trevor's Toys make some strategic decisions, as described in the WebLink box.

THE IMPLEMENTATION PHASE OF THE STRATEGIC MARKETING PROCESS

The Monday-morning diagnosis of a losing football coach often runs something like "We had an excellent game plan: we just didn't execute it."

Is Planning or Implementation the Problem?

The planning-versus-execution issue applies to the strategic marketing process as well: a difficulty when a marketing plan fails is determining whether the failure is due to a poor plan or poor implementation.[19]

Effective managers tracking progress on a struggling plan first try to identify whether the problems involve: (1) the plan and strategy, (2) its implementation, or (3) both, and then they try to correct the problems. But as discussed earlier in the chapter, research on what really works shows that successful firms have excellence on both the planning and strategy side and the implementation and execution side. For example, General Electric's continuing leadership in lighting combines strong innovative products (planning and strategy) with excellent advertising and distribution (implementation and execution). Figure 19–8 shows the outcomes of (1) good and bad marketing planning, and (2) good and bad marketing implementation.

■ **FIGURE 19–8** ■

Results of good and bad
marketing planning and
implementation

MARKETING PLANNING AND STRATEGY

Marketing implementation	Good (appropriate)	Bad (inappropriate)
Good (effective)	1. *Success:* Marketing program achieves its objectives.	2. *Trouble:* Solution lies in recognizing that only the strategy is at fault and correcting it.
Bad (ineffective)	3. *Trouble:* Solution lies in recognizing that only implementation is at fault and correcting it.	4. *Failure:* Marketing program flounders and fails to achieve its objectives.

Increasing Emphasis on Marketing Implementation

The implementation phase of the strategic marketing process has emerged as a key factor to success by moving many planning activities away from the duties of planners to those of line managers.

General Electric's Jack Welch has become a legend in making GE far more efficient and far better at implementation. When Welch became CEO in 1981, he faced an organization mired in red tape, turf battles, and slow decision making. Further, Welch saw GE bogged down with 25 000 managers and close to a dozen layers between him and the factory floor. In his "delayering," he sought to cut GE's levels in half and to speed up decision making and implementation by building an atmosphere of trust and autonomy among his managers and employees. Although there are debates on some Welch strategies, businesses around the world are using his focus on implementation as a benchmark. One measure of GE's global impact: in 2000, *Fortune* magazine named General Electric "the world's most admired company."[20]

General Electric's innovative lights
have benefited from having both
good planning and implementation
of their marketing programs.

General Electric Company
www.gc.com

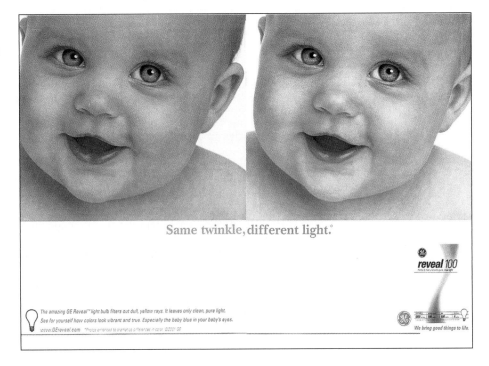

Improving Implementation of Marketing Programs

No magic formula exists to guarantee effective implementation of marketing plans. In fact, the answer seems to be equal parts of good management skills and practices, from which have come some guidelines for improving program implementation.

Communicate Goals and the Means to Achieving Them   Those called on to implement plans need to understand both the goals sought and how they are to be accomplished. Everyone in Papa John's—from founder John Schnatter to telephone order takers and make-line people—is clear on what the firm's goal is: to deliver better pizzas using better ingredients. The firm's orientation packet for employees lists its six "core values," which executives are expected to memorize. Sample: Core value no. 4 is "PAPA," or "People Are Priority No. 1, Always."[21]

**product (or program)
champion**

A person who is able and
willing to cut red tape and
move the program forward.

Have a Responsible Program Champion Willing to Act   Successful programs almost always have a **product (or program) champion** who is able and willing to cut red tape and move the program forward. Such people often have the uncanny ability to move back and forth between big-picture strategy questions and specific details when the situation calls for it. Program champions are notoriously brash in overcoming organizational hurdles. In many cases, they adhere to the axiom "Better to ask forgiveness than permission." Using this strategy, 3M's Art Fry championed Post-it Notes to success, an idea he got when looking for a simple way to mark places in his hymnal while singing in his church choir.

Reward Successful Program Implementation   When an individual or a team is rewarded for achieving the organization's goal, they have maximum incentive to see a program implemented successfully because they have personal ownership and a stake in its success. At a General Electric surge protector plant, employees receive a bonus for each quarter that the facility meets plantwide performance goals.

Take Action and Avoid "Paralysis by Analysis"   Management experts warn against paralysis by analysis, the tendency to excessively analyze a problem instead of taking action. To overcome this pitfall, they call for a "bias for action" and recommend a "do it, fix it, try it" approach.[22] Conclusion: Perfectionists finish last, so getting 90-percent perfection and letting the marketplace help in the fine-tuning makes good sense in implementation.

Lockheed Martin's Skunk Works got its name from the comic strip *L'il Abner* and its legendary reputation from achieving superhuman technical feats with a low budget and ridiculously short deadlines by stressing teamwork. Under the leadership of Kelly Johnson, Skunk Works turned out a series of world-class aircraft, from the world's fastest (the SR-71 Blackbird) to the nation's most untrackable aircraft (the F-117 Stealth fighter). Two of Kelly Johnson's basic tenets: (1) make decisions promptly, and (2) avoid paralysis by analysis. In fact, one study showed that Johnson's Skunk Works could carry out a program on schedule with 126 people, whereas a competitor in a comparable program was behind schedule with 3750 people.[23]

Foster Open Communication to Surface the Problems   Success often lies in fostering a work environment that is open enough so that employees are willing to speak out without fear of recrimination when they see problems. The focus is placed on trying to solve the problem as a group rather than finding someone to blame. Solutions are solicited from anyone who has a creative idea to suggest—from the caretaker to the president—without regard to status or rank in the organization.

Two more Kelly Johnson axioms from Lockheed Martin's Skunk Works apply here: (1) when trouble develops, surface the problem immediately, and (2) get help; do not keep the problem to yourself. This latter point is important even if it means getting ideas from competitors.

For the unusual way General Motors avoided the "NIH syndrome" to help develop the Saturn, see the text.

The Chose His Car Over His Girlfriend **Guy**   The 205-horsepower **Saturn ION Red Line**

People first.

Saturn is General Motors' attempt to create a new company where participatory management and improved communications lead to a successful product. For example, to encourage discussion of possible cost reductions, each employee receives 100 to 750 hours of training, including balance sheet analysis. To avoid "NIH syndrome"—the reluctance to accept ideas "not invented here" or not originated inside one's own firm—Saturn engineers bought 70 import cars to study them for product design ideas and selected options that would most appeal to their target market.

Schedule Precise Tasks, Responsibilities, and Deadlines Successful implementation requires that people know the tasks for which they are responsible and the deadline for completing them. To implement the tasks required to carry out its marketing plans, the Royal Canadian Mint prepares an **action item list** that has three columns: (1) the task, (2) the name of the person responsible for accomplishing that task, and (3) the date by which the task is to be finished. Action item lists are forward looking, clarify the targets, and put strong pressure on people to achieve their designated tasks by the deadline.

Related to the action item lists are formal *program schedules*, which show the relationships through time of the various program tasks. Scheduling an action program involves (1) identifying the main tasks, (2) determining the time required to complete each, (3) arranging the activities to meet the deadline, and (4) assigning responsibilities to complete each task.

Scheduling program activities can be done efficiently with *Gantt charts* developed by Henry L. Gantt. This method is the basis for the scheduling techniques used today, including elaborate computerized methods. The key to all scheduling techniques is to distinguish tasks that *must* be done sequentially from those that *can* be done concurrently. Scheduling tasks concurrently often reduces the total time required for a program. Software programs, such as Microsoft Project, simplify the task of developing a schedule or a Gantt chart.

action item list

An aid to implementing a market plan, consisting of three columns: (1) the task, (2) the name of the person responsible for completing that task, and (3) the date by which the task is to be finished.

CONCEPT CHECK

1. Why is it important to include line operating managers in the planning process?

2. What is the meaning and importance of a program champion?

3. Explain the difference between sequential and concurrent tasks in a Gantt chart.

line positions
People in line positions, such as senior marketing managers, have the authority and responsibility to issue orders to the people who report to them, such as product managers.

staff positions
People in staff positions have the authority and responsibility to advise people in the line positions but cannot issue direct orders to them.

product line groupings
Organizational groupings in which a unit is responsible for specific product offerings.

functional groupings
Organizational groupings, such as manufacturing, marketing, and finance, which are the different business activities within a firm.

■ **FIGURE 19–9** ■
Organization of a Pillsbury business unit, showing product or brand groups

Organizing for Marketing

A marketing organization is needed to implement the firm's marketing plans. Basic issues in today's marketing organizations include understanding (1) how line versus staff positions and divisional groupings interrelate to form a cohesive marketing organization, and (2) the role of the marketing or product manager.

Line versus Staff and Divisional Groupings   Although simplified, Figure 19–9 shows the organization of a typical business unit in a consumer packaged goods firm, such as Kraft Canada. This business unit consists of Dinner Products, Baked Goods, and Desserts. It highlights the distinction between **line** and **staff positions** in marketing. People in line positions, such as senior marketing manager for Biscuits, have the authority and responsibility to issue orders to the people who report to them, such as the two product managers shown in Figure 19–9.

In this organizational chart, line positions are connected with solid lines. Those in staff positions (shown by dotted lines) have the authority and responsibility to advise people in line positions but cannot issue direct orders to them.

Most marketing organizations use divisional groupings—such as product line, functional, geographical, and market-based—to implement plans and achieve their organizational objectives. Some of these appear in some form in the organizational chart in Figure 19–9. The top of the chart shows organization by **product line groupings**, in which a unit is responsible for specific product offerings, such as Dinner Products or Baked Goods.

At levels higher than those shown in Figure 19–9, firms may be organized by **functional groupings**, such as manufacturing, marketing, and finance, which are the different business activities within a firm.

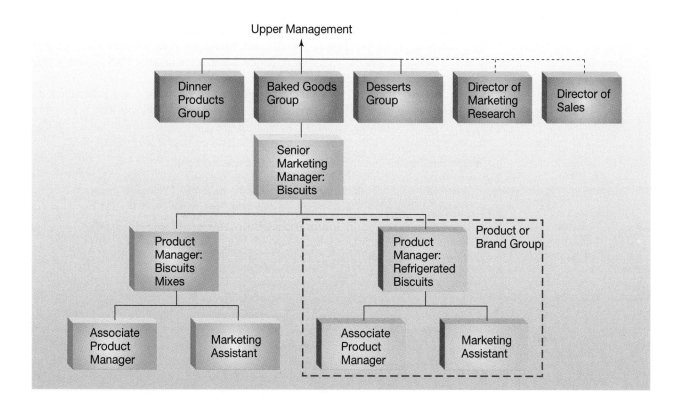

geographical groupings
Organizational groupings in which a unit is subdivided according to geographical location.

market-based groupings
Organizational groupings that utilize specific customer segments.

Many packaged goods firms use **geographical groupings**, in which sales territories are subdivided according to geographic location. Each director of sales has several regional sales managers reporting to him or her, such as Western, Eastern, and so on. These, in turn, have district managers reporting to them, with the field sales representatives at the lowest levels.

A fourth method of organizing a company is to use **market-based groupings**, which utilize specific customer segments, such as the banking, health care, or manufacturing segments. When this method of organizing is combined with product groupings, the result is a *matrix organization*.

A relatively new position in consumer products firms is the *category manager* (senior marketing manager in Figure 19–9). Category managers have profit-and-loss responsibility for an entire product line—all biscuit brands, for example. They attempt to reduce the possibility of one brand's actions hurting another brand in the same category. Procter & Gamble uses category managers to organize by "global business units," such as baby care and beauty care. Cutting across country boundaries, these global business units implement standardized worldwide pricing, marketing, and distribution.[24]

Role of the Product Manager   The key person in the product or brand group shown in Figure 19–10 is the manager who heads it. This person is often called the *product manager* or *brand manager*. This person and the assistants in the product group are the basic building blocks in the marketing department of most consumer and industrial product firms. The function of a product manager is to plan, implement, and control the annual and long-range plans for the products for which he or she is responsible.

There are both benefits and dangers to the product manager system. On the positive side, product managers become strong advocates for the assigned products, cut red tape to work with people in various functions both inside and outside the organization (see Figure 19–10), and assume profit-and-loss responsibility for the performance of the product line. On the negative side, even though product managers have major responsibilities, they have relatively little direct authority, and so most groups and functions shown in Figure 19–10 must be coordinated to meet the product's goals.[25] To coordinate the many units, product managers must use persuasion rather than orders.

But as Canadian firms move toward more customer-intimacy and customer relationship management (CRM) strategies, product managers are no longer the only

■ **FIGURE 19–10** ■
Units with which the product manager and product group work

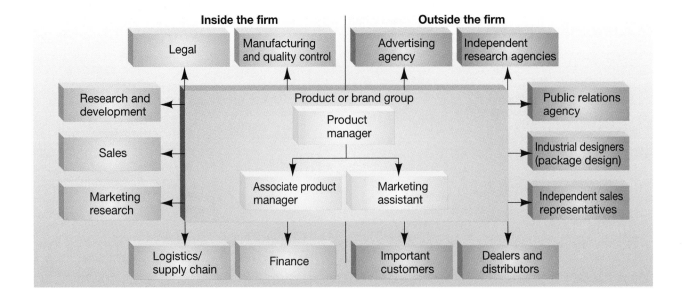

ones responsible for managing the product or customer base. Some Canadian firms have created new positions, such as "manager of student segment" or "VP of financial services clients," which shadow the traditional product manager roles. These firms have divided their organizations into "customer-facing roles" (such as segment managers). More and more often, it is the segment managers, not the product managers, who make the final decisions on product, price, promotion, and place (distribution).

THE CONTROL PHASE OF THE STRATEGIC MARKETING PROCESS

The essence of control, the final phase of the strategic marketing process, is to compare results with planned goals for the marketing program in order to take necessary corrective actions.

The Marketing Control Process

Ideally, quantified goals from the marketing plans developed in the planning phase have been accomplished by the marketing actions taken in the implementation phase (Figure 19–11) and measured as results in the control phase. A marketing manager then uses *management by exception*, which means identifying results that deviate from plans to diagnose their causes and take new actions. Often, results fall short of plans, and a corrective action is needed. For example, after enjoying 50 years of profits, Caterpillar found itself with accumulated losses of $1.4 billion. To correct the problem, Caterpillar focused its marketing efforts on core products and reduced its manufacturing costs. At other times, the comparison shows that performance is far better than anticipated, in which case the marketing manager tries to identify the reason and move quickly to exploit the unexpected opportunity.

Measuring Results   Without some quantitative goal, no benchmark exists with which to compare actual results. Manufacturers of both consumer and business products are increasingly trying to develop marketing programs that have not only specific action programs but also specific procedures for monitoring key measures of performance. Today, marketing executives are measuring not only tangible financial targets, such as sales revenues and profits, but also less tangible ones, such as customer satisfaction, time-to-market, and salesforce motivation.

■ **FIGURE 19–11** ■
The control phase of the strategic marketing process

Taking Marketing Actions   When results deviate significantly from plans, some kind of action is essential. Deviations can be the result of the process used to specify goals or can be due to changes in the marketplace. Beaten badly for years in the

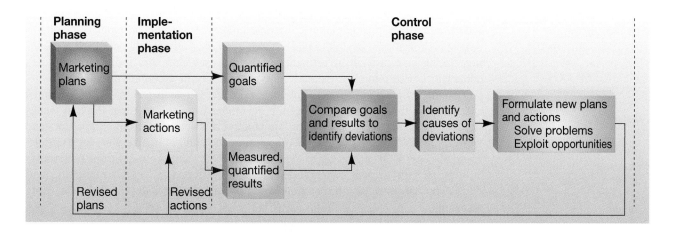

Strange. It's only breakfast and your
toothpaste has already called it a day.

Unless you use Colgate Total.

Colgate Total

12-Hour Protection

Canadian toothpaste market by P&G's Crest, Colgate went on the offensive. It took aggressive marketing action to introduce its Total toothpaste. Not only does Total clean teeth, but it also helps heal gingivitis, a gum disease of increasing concern to aging baby boomers. For the first time in 30 years, Colgate usurped P&G's Crest to take the number-one spot.[26]

Sales Analysis

sales analysis
A tool for controlling marketing programs using sales records to compare actual results with sales goals and to identify strengths and weaknesses.

For controlling marketing programs, **sales analysis**—using the firm's sales records to compare actual results with sales goals and identify areas of strength and weakness—is critical. All the variables that might be used in market segmentation may be used in **sales component analysis** (also called *microsales analysis*), which traces sales revenues to their sources, such as specific products, sales territories, or customers. Common breakdowns include the following:

sales component analysis
A tool for controlling marketing programs that traces sales revenues to their sources, such as specific products, sales territories, or customers. Also called *microsales analysis*.

- Customer characteristics: demographics, NAICS, size, reason for purchase, and type of reseller (retailer or wholesaler).
- Product characteristics: model, package size, and colour.
- Geographical region: sales territory, city, province, and region.
- Order size.
- Price or discount class.
- Commission to the sales representative.

Today's computers can easily produce these breakdowns, provided the input data contain these classifications. Therefore, it is critical that marketing managers specify the breakdowns they require from the accounting and information systems departments so that they get the needed information while avoiding information overload.

Profitability Analysis and ROI Marketing

profitability analysis
A tool for controlling marketing programs using the profit attributable to the firm's products, customer groups, sales territories, channels of distribution, and promotions.

To their surprise, marketing managers often discover the 80/20 rule the hard way—on the job. **Profitability analysis** is a tool for controlling marketing programs using the profit attributable to the firm's products, customer groups, sales territories, channels of distribution, and promotions. This leads to decisions to expand, maintain, reduce, or eliminate specific products, customer groups, channels, or promotions.

For example, following the 80/20 rule, a marketing manager will try to find the common characteristics among the 20 percent of the customers (or products, brands, sales districts, salespeople, or kinds of orders) that generate 80 percent (or the bulk) of revenues and profits to find more like them in order to exploit competitive advantages. Conversely, the 80 percent of customers, products, brands, and so on that generate few revenues and profits may need to be reduced or even dropped entirely unless a way is found to make them more profitable.

ROI marketing
The application of modern measurement technologies and contemporary organizational design to understand, quantify, and optimize marketing spending.

Obtaining the detailed data to do this kind of profitability analysis and knowing how to analyze these data are difficult. To bridge these gaps, researchers developed **ROI marketing**, the application of modern measurement technologies and contemporary organizational design to understand, quantify, and optimize marketing spending.[27] ROI, or return on investment, marketing uses computer models on the data collected to determine, for example, the profitability of a coupon directed at a specific market segment. The analysis takes into account such factors as the coupon's cost to reach the segment, the revenue generated from the segment the two weeks following the coupon's distribution, the amount of sales taken from competitors and from cannibalizing the company's other products, and so on. WestJet, for example, could also use ROI marketing to determine the costs and profitability of new routes as it pursues its growth strategies. Widespread acceptance of ROI marketing will depend on the impact on the demonstrated profitability of its use in key marketing decisions.[28]

CONCEPT CHECK

1. What is the difference between line and a staff positions in a marketing organization?

2. What are four groupings used within a typical marketing organization?

3. What two components of the strategic marketing process are compared to control a marketing program?

■ ■ ■

CHAPTER IN REVIEW

1 *Explain how marketing managers allocate their limited resources.*

Marketing managers use the strategic marketing process and marketing information, such as marketing plans, sales reports, and action memos, to effectively allocate their scarce resources to exploit the competitive advantages of their products. Marketers may use either sales response functions or market share (share point) analysis to help them assess what the market's response will be to additional marketing efforts.

2 *Describe three marketing planning frameworks: Porter's generic strategies, profit enhancement options, and market-product synergies.*

Three useful frameworks to improve marketing planning are: (*a*) Porter's generic business strategies; (*b*) profit enhancement options; and (*c*) market–product synergies. Porter identifies four generic business strategies that firms can adopt: a cost leadership strategy, which focuses on reducing expenses to lower product prices while targeting a broad array of market segments; a differentiation strategy, which requires products to have significant points of difference to charge a premium price while targeting a broad array of market segments; a cost-focus strategy, which involves controlling costs to lower prices of products targeted at a narrow range of market segments; and a differentiation-focus strategy, which requires products to have significant points of difference to reach one or only a few market segments.

A second marketing planning framework is to use profit enhancement options to increase sales revenues, decrease costs, or both. To increase revenues, marketers can use one or a combination of four strategies to focus on present or new products or markets: market penetration (selling more of a product to existing markets); market development (selling an existing product to new markets); product development (selling a new product to existing markets); and diversification (selling new products to new markets). To reduce expenses, marketers can (*a*) generate additional economies of scale in marketing and production costs, and (*b*) reduce personnel and other nonmarketing costs, product rejects through improved quality, and so forth.

The third framework is to use a market–product grid that results in two kinds of synergies: marketing synergies (efficiencies), which run horizontally across the row of the various products offered by the firm to a single market segment; and R&D–manufacturing synergies (efficiencies), which run vertically down a column of the various market segments targeted for a given product or product class. The interactions or synergy effects of these marketing and production efficiencies results in five alternative combinations: market–product concentration, market specialization, product specialization, selective specialization, and full coverage.

3 *Explain what makes an effective marketing plan and some problems that often exist with it.*

An effective marketing plan has measurable, achievable goals; uses facts and valid assumptions; is simple, clear, and specific; is complete and feasible; and is controllable and flexible. Some problems that arise with marketing plans are that marketers (*a*) base them on poor assumptions about the marketing environment; (*b*) lose sight of their customers' needs; (*c*) spend too much time and effort on data collection for and writing the actual plan; and (*d*) do not seek ownership of the plan by operating managers and others charged with its implementation.

4 *Describe the alternatives for organizing a marketing department and the role of a product manager.*

A marketing department must be organized to effectively implement a marketing plan. First, marketing organizations must distinguish between line positions, those individuals in the marketing organization who have the authority and responsibility to issue orders to people that report to them to carry out a particular aspect of the marketing plan, and staff positions, those individuals who have the authority and responsibility to advise but not directly order people in line positions to do something.

Second, marketing organizations use one of four divisional groupings to implement marketing plans: product line groupings, responsible for specific product offerings; functional groupings that represent the different departments and business activities (marketing, manufacturing, finance, and so on) within a firm; geographical groupings, in which sales territories are subdivided according to geographical location; and market-based groupings, which utilize specific customer segments.

The role of the product manager is to interact with numerous people and groups both inside and outside the firm to coordinate the planning, implementation, and control of the marketing plan and its budget on an annual and long-term basis for the products responsible.

5 *Explain how sales and profitability analyses and ROI marketing are used to evaluate and control marketing programs.*

The control phase of the strategic marketing process involves measuring the results of the actions from the implementation phase and comparing them with goals set in the planning phase. Sales analysis uses the firm's sales records to compare actual sales with sales objectives. Profitability analysis uses the profit attributable to the firm's products, customer groups, sales territories, distribution channels, and promotions.

A specific kind of profitability analysis is ROI marketing, which is the application of modern measurement technologies and contemporary organizational design to understand, quantify, and optimize marketing spending.

■ ■ ■

FOCUSING ON KEY TERMS

action item list p. 522
cost leadership strategy p. 513
cost-focus strategy p. 513
differentiation strategy p. 513
differentiation-focus strategy p. 513
functional groupings p. 523
generic business strategy p. 512
geographical groupings p. 524
line positions p. 523
market-based groupings p. 524

product line groupings p. 523
product (or program) champion p. 521
profitability analysis p. 526
ROI marketing p. 526
sales analysis p. 526
sales component analysis p. 526
sales response function p. 507
share points p. 509
staff positions p. 523

■ ■ ■

DISCUSSION AND APPLICATION QUESTIONS

1 Assume a firm faces an S-shaped sales response function. What happens to the ratio of incremental sales revenue to incremental marketing effort at the (*a*) bottom, (*b*) middle, and (*c*) top of this curve?

2 What happens to the ratio of incremental sales revenue to incremental marketing effort when the sales response function is an upward-sloping straight line?

3 In 2006, General Mills invested millions of dollars in expanding its cereal and yogurt businesses. To allocate this money between these two businesses, what information would General Mills like to have?

4 Suppose your Great States lawn mower company has the market-product concentration situation shown in Figure 19–6A. What are both the synergies and potential pitfalls of

following expansion strategies of (*a*) market specialization, and (*b*) product specialization?

5 Are value-driven strategies inconsistent with value-based planning? Give an example that supports your position.

6 The first Domino's Pizza restaurant was near a college campus. What implementation problems are (*a*) similar, and (*b*) different for restaurants near a college campus versus a military base?

7 A common theme among managers who succeed repeatedly in program implementation is fostering open communication. Why is this so important?

8 Why are quantified goals in the planning phase of the strategic marketing process important for the control phase?

GOING ONLINE	Strategic Actions of Three CEOs

Because of General Electric's reputation for developing good managers, executive search firms often tap its talent to lead other organizations. Three GE executives were the leading candidates to replace Jack Welch, GE's CEO, when he retired in mid-2001.

Today, all three are now CEOs of major corporations: Jeffrey Immelt (General Electric), James McNerney (3M),

and Robert Nardelli (Home Depot). Go to the Web sites of these three companies (www.ge.com, www.3m.com, and www.homedepot.com). Look at the most recent quarterly press or news release or annual report to identify any strategic actions each CEO initiated to improve the company's performance, such as acquisitions, new products or services, new markets, and so forth.

Do you want to get better grades and stay up to date with current issues in marketing? Visit the Online Learning Centre at www.mcgrawhill.ca/college/crane for practice tests, video cases, resources for building a marketing plan, *Globe and Mail* headlines, access to *Marketing Magazine*, and other learning and study tools.

VIDEO CASE 19   WestJet: Canada's Low-Cost Airline is on the Fly

COMPANY OVERVIEW

Founded in 1996 by a team of Calgary entrepreneurs led by Clive Beddoe, WestJet Airlines Ltd.'s original strategy was simple: offer low-fare, point-to-point air travel on Boeing 737 jet aircraft to customers across Western Canada. With 220 employees and three aircraft, WestJet originally offered service to five cities: Vancouver, Kelowna, Calgary, Edmonton, and Winnipeg. The company then added Victoria, Regina, and Saskatoon to its route network. In 1997, WestJet began service to Abbotsford/Fraser Valley, and in 1999, WestJet added Thunder Bay, Prince George, and Grande Prairie to its service area.

In July 1999, WestJet became a publicly traded company and extended its airline service across Canada. In June 2000, the company added service to the eastern Canadian cities of Hamilton, Moncton, and Ottawa, creating an eastern network with Hamilton as the hub. In 2001, WestJet added new service to Fort McMurray, Comox, and Brandon. In 2001, WestJet also added its first four Next-Generation Boeing 737-700 aircraft. In 2002, WestJet added service to two new Ontario destinations, London and Toronto (its new eastern hub).

In February of 2002, the corporation successfully offered three million common shares, yielding net proceeds of $78.9 million. The proceeds were used to fund aircraft additions, spare parts, and a third flight simulator. In 2003, WestJet added service to the new markets of Halifax, Windsor, Montréal, St. John's, and Gander. As the Canadian airline market evolved, WestJet looked to continue its growth and found an opportunity to expand its routes into the United States. Transborder service commenced in the fall of 2004 to the cities of Los Angeles, San Francisco, Phoenix, Fort Lauderdale, Tampa, Orlando, and New York, and service to Palm Springs began in January 2005.

With its focus on safety, high-efficiency structure, motivated personnel, and customer service, WestJet, in less than one decade, has evolved into Canada's leading low-cost airline, serving Canadians coast-to-coast and with scheduled service to the United States. To date, WestJet has offered service to more than 33 million passengers, whom they refer to as guests, and has surpassed the $1 billion level in annual revenue. No longer the "little airline that could," WestJet now competes on the national and international stages in a highly competitive industry that is sensitive to numerous external factors in the marketing environment.

THE INDUSTRY

The Canadian airline industry market (passenger service) is estimated to be worth $4.5 billion. Transborder and sun-destination markets are estimated to be worth $5.5 billion. Total potential for WestJet is thus $10 billion. WestJet has achieved 10 percent market share, or $1 billion of that total market. The industry is a landscape characterized by intense competition, few barriers to entry, restrictive taxes and fees on travelers, seasonality, and geographic dispersion. The industry is also sensitive to other factors in the external marketing environment, including the threat of terrorism, epidemics such as SARS (severe acute respiratory syndrome), and changes in economic conditions that can affect the costs of operation as well as passenger demand.

Deregulation of the industry in Canada has also allowed for a reduction of the barriers for new competitors. However, the high-risk nature of the airline industry has deterred many new entrants. Since 2001, the Canadian airline industry has witnessed failures, mergers, and births of airlines. In 2003, the largest carrier in Canada, and the only remaining legacy carrier, Air Canada, underwent bankruptcy protection but emerged again in 2004. However, it wound down its two low-fare airline-within-an-airline concepts, Tango and Zip. In 2005, another competitor, Jetsgo, also ceased operation after just a few years in operation. CanJet, purchased by the now-defunct Canada 3000 in 2001, revived its business model and restarted operations in 2002. Zoom Airlines, based in Ottawa, sprouted as a charter airline offering service to international destinations only.

THE COMPETITION

Within the Canadian domestic market, WestJet competes with scheduled airlines, such as Air Canada, and its regional subsidiary carrier, Jazz, which operates turbo-prop and regional aircraft designed to provide feed traffic to Air Canada's hub network. WestJet also competes with another regional carrier, CanJet, and, to a lesser degree, charter airlines. Airlines also compete with surface transportation alternatives in short-haul markets and even in some medium- to long-haul markets. Surface transportation primarily consists of automobiles, bus, and rail transportation. When travellers choose their preferred mode of transportation, price is often a factor that influences their decision and is a competitive factor when contending with surface transportation alternatives. Frequency, speed, convenience of scheduling, facilities, safety, and customer service are aspects that are also considered by travellers when making their travel choices. In the transborder (U.S.) market, WestJet also competes with Air Canada, CanJet, and numerous American carriers, including American Airlines and Northwest Airlines.

WESTJET'S STRATEGY AND COMPETITIVE ADVANTAGES

WestJet's original low-price, no frills, point-to-point regional air travel model was successful in driving the early growth of the company. WestJet used (and continues to use) one aircraft type (737) to reduce maintenance and training costs and realize bulk purchasing benefits. It also leveraged technology to lower its operating costs. It created and maintained simplified route structures and used secondary airports, where available. It focused on strategic hiring, training, and rewarding service-oriented employees while maintaining a lean organizational structure. In doing so, it was able to leverage cost efficiencies (its costs are 33 percent below its main competitors), which, in turn, allowed it to offer its guests (passengers) low fares and convenient point-to-point air travel.

However, WestJet is now a national airline with $1 billion in revenue competing head-to-head against some major competitors, including Air Canada. And, in fact, Air Canada is now taking the battle to WestJet, pushing hard to compete in regional markets originally built by WestJet. While WestJet intends to defend those markets, it believes that its future growth lies in the United States. This has forced the company to rethink some of its original strategies. For example, the low-cost or discount carrier market in the United States is stratified, with some consumers demanding the lowest price and others demanding an additional level of comfort, such as leather seats and free seatback TV. JetBlue, an American value-based carrier, has targeted the segment wanting higher comfort levels. WestJet seems to have noticed this and is now offering similar amenities.

The American market is, however, extremely competitive, and WestJet has to continue to be able to distinguish itself. It seems that WestJet will focus on offering low-cost fares but with some comfort features. A pivotal aspect of its competitive strategy will be exploiting the growth in transborder travel, which is, in fact, an emerging travel trend. WestJet is hoping this will allow it to compete successfully and to help propel it into a world-class brand. There is even strategic thought given to further expansion into Europe.

GROWTH STRATEGY

In short, WestJet's future growth strategy will include (1) increasing the passenger load on existing flights in existing markets, as well as increase the frequency of flights in those existing markets; and (2) increasing the number of new markets served, including the United States. At the same time, the company will continue to focus on keeping its costs low in order to continue to offer the low fares that its customers have come to expect and at the same time upgrading the creature comforts now demanded by many customers.

QUESTIONS

1 Relate WestJet's success to the four basic business practices discussed in the chapter and found to be connected to business performance (strategy, execution, culture, and structure).

2 Review Porter's generic business strategies (see Figure 19–4). Which cell does WestJet fit into? Why?

3 Review the profit enhancement options discussed in this chapter (see Figure 19–5). Which strategies is WestJet pursuing to increase its profitability?

4 What other opportunities for growth are available to WestJet?

GLOSSARY

account management policies   Policies that specify whom salespeople should contact, what kinds of selling and customer service activities should be engaged in, and how these activities should be carried out. p. 490

action item list   An aid to implementing a market plan, consisting of three columns: (1) the task, (2) the name of the person responsible for completing that task, and (3) the date by which the task is to be finished. p. 522

adaptive selling   A need-satisfaction sales presentation that involves adjusting the presentation to fit the selling situation. p. 484

advertising   Any paid form of nonpersonal communication about an organization, good, service, or idea by an identified sponsor. pp. 425, 448

all-you-can-afford budgeting   Allocating funds to promotion only after all other budget items are covered. p. 435

attitude   A learned predisposition to respond to an object or class of objects in a consistently favourable or unfavourable way. p. 124

baby boomers   The generation of children born between 1946 and 1964. p. 71

back translation   Retranslating a word or phrase into the original language by a different interpreter to catch errors. p. 177

balance of trade   The difference between the monetary value of a nation's exports and imports. p. 165

barriers to entry   Business practices or conditions that make it difficult for new firms to enter the market. p. 81

beliefs   A consumer's subjective perception of how well a product or brand performs on different attributes; these are based on personal experience, advertising, and discussions with other people. p. 124

benchmarking   Discovering how others do something better than your own firm so you can imitate or leapfrog competition. p. 32

bidders' list   A list of firms believed to be qualified to supply a given item. p. 153

blended family   Formed by the merging into a single household of two previously separated units. p. 72

blog   A Web site that contains an online personal journal that contains reflections, comments, and often hyperlinks provided by the writer. p. 115

brand equity   The added value a given brand name gives to a product beyond the functional benefits provided. p. 291

brand licensing   A contractual agreement whereby a company allows another firm to use its brand name, patent, trade secret, or other property for a royalty or fee. p. 293

brand loyalty   A favourable attitude toward and consistent purchase of a single brand over time. p. 123

brand name   Any word, device (design, shape, sound, or colour), or combination of these used to distinguish a seller's goods or services. p. 290

brand personality   A set of human characteristics associated with a brand name. p. 291

branding   Activity in which an organization uses a name, phrase, design, or symbols, or combination of these, to identify

its products and distinguish them from those of competitors. p. 290

breadth of product line   The variety of different items a store carries. p. 401

break-even analysis   A technique that analyzes the relationship between total revenue and total cost to determine profitability at various levels of output. p. 339

brokers   Independent firms or individuals whose principal function is to bring buyers and sellers together to make sales. p. 373

business analysis   Involves specifying the features of the product and the marketing strategy needed to commercialize it and making necessary financial projections. p. 270

business distributor   Performs a variety of marketing channel functions, including selling, stocking, delivering a full product assortment, and financing. p. 369

business goods   Products that assist directly or indirectly in providing products for resale (also known as *B2B goods*, *industrial goods*, or *organizational goods*). p. 257

business marketing   The marketing of goods and services to commercial enterprises, governments, and other profit and not-for-profit organizations for use in the creation of goods and services that they then produce and market to other business customers as well as individuals and ultimate consumers. p. 142

business unit   An organization that markets a set of related products to a clearly defined group of customers. p. 27

business unit level   Level at which business unit managers set the direction for their products and markets. p. 27

buy classes   Three types of organizational buying situations: new buy, straight rebuy, and modified rebuy. p. 150

buying centre   The group of people in an organization who participate in the buying process and share common goals, risks, and knowledge important to a purchase decision. p. 149

capacity management   Making service capacity as productive as possible without compromising service quality. p. 320

category management   An approach that assigns a manager with the responsibility for selecting all products that consumers in a market segment might view as substitutes for each other, with the objective of maximizing sales and profits in the category. p. 411

cause marketing   Occurs when the charitable contributions of a firm are tied directly to the customer revenues produced through the promotion of one of its products. p. 102

caveat emptor   The legal concept of "let the buyer beware" that was pervasive in Canadian business culture before the 1960s. p. 96

census metropolitan area (CMA)   Geographic labour market areas having a population of 100 000 persons or more. p. 73

central business district   The oldest retail setting, the community's downtown area. p. 410

channel of communication   The means of conveying a message to a receiver. p. 422

channel conflict   Arises when one channel member believes another channel member is engaged in behaviour that prevents it from achieving its goals. p. 379

co-branding The pairing of two brand names of two manufacturers on a single product. p. 296

code of ethics A formal statement of ethical principles and rules of conduct. p. 97

cognitive dissonance The feeling of postpurchase psychological tension or anxiety a consumer often experiences. p. 116

cohort brand management The bundling of one company's multiple brands into a single marketing effort aimed at a common consumer group. p. 297

commercialization Positioning and launching a new product in full-scale production and sales. p. 272

communication The process of conveying a message to others, which requires six elements: a source, a message, a channel of communication, a receiver, and the processes of encoding and decoding. p. 422

community shopping centre A retail location that typically has one primary store (usually a department store branch) and 20 to 40 smaller outlets, serving a population of consumers who are within a 10- to 20-minute drive. p. 410

company forecast The total sales of a product that a firm expects to sell during a specified time period under specified environmental conditions and its own marketing efforts. p. 245

competencies An organization's special capabilities, including skills, technologies, and resources that distinguish it from other organizations. p. 31

competition The alternative firms that could provide a product to satisfy a specific market's needs. p. 80

Competition Act The key legislation designed to protect competition and consumers in Canada. p. 82

competitive advantage A unique strength relative to competitors, often based on quality, time, cost, innovation, or customer intimacy. p. 31

competitive parity budgeting Matching the competitors' absolute level of spending or the proportion per point of market share. p. 435

consideration set The group of brands that a consumer would consider acceptable from among all the brands which he or she is aware of. p. 115

consultative selling Focuses on problem definition, where the salesperson serves as an expert on problem recognition and resolution. p. 484

consumer behaviour The actions a person takes in purchasing and using products and services, including the mental and social processes that precede and follow these actions. p. 114

consumer ethnocentrism The tendency to believe that it is inappropriate, indeed immoral, to purchase foreign-made products. p. 178

consumer goods Products purchased by the ultimate consumer. p. 257

consumer socialization The process by which people acquire the skills, knowledge, and attitudes necessary to function as consumers. p. 129

consumer-oriented sales promotions Sales tools used to support a company's advertising and personal selling efforts directed to ultimate consumers; examples include coupons, sweepstakes, and samples. p. 464

consumerism A grassroots movement started in the 1960s to increase the influence, power, and rights of consumers in dealing with institutions. p. 83

convenience goods Items that the consumer purchases frequently and with a minumum of shopping effort. p. 258

cooperative advertising Advertising programs by which a manufacturer pays a percentage of the retailer's local advertising expense for advertising the manufacturer's products. p. 467

corporate level Level at which top management directs overall strategy for the entire organization. p. 26

cost leadership strategy Using a serious commitment to reducing expenses that, in turn, lowers the price of the items sold in a relatively broad array of market segments. p. 513

cost per thousand (CPM) The cost of reaching 1000 individuals or households with an advertising message in a given medium. (M is the Roman numeral for 1000.) p. 454

cost-focus strategy Involves controlling expenses and, in turn, lowering prices, in a narrow range of market segments. pp. 454, 513

countertrade The practice of using barter rather than money for making international sales. p. 164

cross-cultural analysis The study of similarities and differences among consumers in two or more nations or societies. p. 175

cross-functional teams A small number of people from different departments in an organization who are mutually accountable to a common set of performance goals. p. 27

cultural symbols Things that represent ideas and concepts. p. 176

culture The set of values, ideas, and attitudes of a homogeneous group of people that are transmitted from one generation to the next. p. 73

currency exchange rate The price of one country's currency expressed in terms of another country's currency. p. 181

customer contact audit A flowchart of the points of interaction between consumer and service provider. p. 314

customer lifetime value (CLV) The profit generated by the customer's purchase of an organization's product or service over the customer's lifetime. p. 17

customer relationship management (CRM) The process of identifying prospective buyers, understanding them intimately, and developing favourable long-term perceptions of the organization and its offerings so that buyers will choose them in the marketplace. p. 17

customer satisfaction The match between customer expectations of the product and the product's actual performance. p. 17

customer service The ability of logistics management to satisfy users in terms of time, dependability, communication, and convenience. p. 386

customer value The unique combination of benefits received by targeted buyers that includes quality, price, convenience, on-time delivery, and both before-sale and after-sale service. p. 17

customs Norms and expectations about the way people do things in a specific country. p. 176

data mining The extraction of hidden predictive information from large databases. p. 219

decoding The process of having the receiver take a set of symbols, the message, and transform them back to an abstract idea. p. 423

demand curve The summation of points representing the maximum number of products consumers will buy at a given price. p. 336

demographics   Describing the population according to selected characteristics such as their age, gender, ethnicity, income, and occupation. p. 70

depth interview   A detailed, individual interview with a person relevant to the research project. p. 206

depth of product line The store carries a large assortment of each item. p. 401

derived demand   Demand for industrial products and services driven by, or derived from, demand for consumer products and services. p. 146

development   The stage of the new-product process that involves turning the idea on paper into a prototype. p. 270

differentiation strategy   Requires innovation and significant points of difference in product offerings, brand image, higher quality, advanced technology, or superior service in a relatively broad array of market segments. p. 513

differentiation-focus strategy   Using significant points of difference in the firm's offerings to reach one or only a few market segments. p. 513

direct channel   A marketing channel where a producer and ultimate consumer deal directly with each other. p. 369

direct forecast   Estimating the value to be forecast without any intervening steps. p. 246

direct investment   A domestic firm actually investing in and owning a foreign subsidiary or division. p. 185

direct marketing   Promotional element that uses direct communication with consumers to generate a response in the form of an order, a request for further information, or a visit to a retail outlet. p. 427

direct marketing channels   Allow consumers to buy products by interacting with various advertising media without a face-to-face meeting with a salesperson. p. 371

direct orders   The result of direct marketing offers that contain all the information necessary for a prospective buyer to make a decision to purchase and complete the transaction. p. 439

discretionary income   The money that remains after paying for taxes and necessities. p. 76

disintermediation   Channel conflict that arises when a channel member bypasses another member and sells or buys products direct. p. 379

disposable income   The money a consumer has left after paying taxes to use for necessities such as food, shelter, and clothing. p. 76

downsizing   Reducing the content of packages without changing package size and maintaining or increasing the package price. p. 290

dumping   When a firm sells a product in a foreign country below its domestic price or below its actual cost. p. 188

e-marketplaces   Online trading communities that bring together buyers and supplier organizations. p. 156

economic espionage   The clandestine collection of trade secrets or proprietary information about a company's competitors. p. 96

economy   The income, expenditures, and resources that affect the cost of running an organization or a household. p. 75

eCRM   A Web-centric, personalized approach to managing customer relationships electronically. p. 18

eight P's of service marketing   Product, price, place, and promotion, as well as people, physical evidence, process, and productivity that constitute the services marketing mix. p. 317

80/20 rule   A concept that suggests 80 percent of a firm's sales are obtained from 20 percent of its customers. p. 234

electronic commerce   Any activity that uses some form of electronic communication in the inventory, exchange, advertisement, distribution, and payment of goods and services. p. 79

electronic marketing channels   Employ the Internet to make goods and services available for consumption or use by consumers or business buyers. p. 370

emotional intelligence   The ability to understand one's own emotions and the emotions of people with whom one interacts on a daily basis. p. 492

encoding   The process of having the sender transform an abstract idea into a set of symbols. p. 423

environmental factors   The uncontrollable factors involving social, economic, technological, competitive, and regulatory forces. p. 13

environmental scanning   The process of continually acquiring information on events occurring outside the organization to identify and interpret potential trends. p. 68

ethics   The moral principles and values that govern the actions and decisions of an individual or group. pp. 19, 92

ethnographic research   Observational approach to discover subtle emotional reactions as consumers encounter products in their "natural use environment." p. 213

evaluative criteria   Factors that represent both the objective attributes of a brand and the subjective ones a consumer uses to compare different products and brands. p. 115

experiment   Obtaining data by manipulating factors under tightly controlled conditions to test cause and effect. p. 211

exporting   Producing goods in one country and selling them in another country. p. 183

extranet   A network that uses Internet-based technologies to permit communication between an organization and its suppliers, distributors, and other partners. p. 79

failure fee   A penalty payment made by a manufacturer to compensate the retailer for sales its valuable shelf space never made. p. 272

family life cycle   The distinct phases that a family progresses through from formation to retirement, each phase bringing with it identifiable purchasing behaviours. p. 129

feedback   The communication flow from receiver back to the sender that helps the sender know whether the message was decoded and understood as intended. p. 424

field of experience   Similar understanding and knowledge; to communicate effectively, a sender and a receiver must have a mutually shared field of experience. p. 424

fixed cost   The sum of expenses of the firm that are stable and do not change with the quantity of product that is produced and sold. p. 339

focus group   An informal session of 6 to 10 past, present, or prospective customers in which a discussion leader, or moderator, asks their opinions about the firm's and its competitors' products. p. 206

form of ownership   Distinguishes retail outlets based on whether individuals, corporate chains, or contractual systems own the outlet. p. 398

formula selling presentation   Providing information in an accurate, thorough, and step-by-step manner to inform the prospect. p. 483

four I's of services Four unique elements to services: intangibility, inconsistency, inseparability, and inventory. p. 309

franchising Contractual arrangement between a parent company (a franchisor) and an individual or firm (a franchisee) that allows the franchise to operate a certain type of business under an established name and according to specific rules. p. 375

frequency The average number of times a person in the target audience is exposed to a message or advertisement. p. 454

full-service agency An advertising agency providing the most complete range of services, including market research, media selection, copy development, artwork, and production. p. 461

functional groupings Organizational groupings, such as manufacturing, marketing, and finance, which are the different business activities within a firm. p. 523

functional level Level at which groups of specialists actually create value for the organization. p. 27

gap analysis An evaluation tool that compares expectations about a service offering to the actual experience a consumer has with the service. p. 315

Generation X Those born between 1965 and 1976. p. 71

Generation Y The population of those born between 1976 and 1995. p. 72

generic business strategy Strategy that can be adopted by any firm, regardless of the product or industry involved, to achieve a competitive advantage. p. 512

geographical groupings Organizational groupings in which a unit is subdivided according to geographical location. p. 524

global brand A brand marketed under the same name in multiple countries with similar and centrally coordinated marketing programs. p. 174

global competition Exists when firms originate, produce, and market their products and services worldwide. p. 172

global consumers Customer groups living in many countries or regions of the world who have similar needs or seek similar features and benefits from products or services. p. 174

global marketing strategy The practice of standardizing marketing activities when there are cultural similarities and adapting them when cultures differ. p. 173

goals or **objectives** Convert the mission into targeted levels of performance to be achieved. p. 29

government units The federal, provincial, and local agencies that buy goods and services for the constituents they serve. p. 143

green marketing Marketing efforts to produce, promote, and reclaim environmentally sensitive products. p. 101

grey market A situation where products are sold through unauthorized channels of distribution; also called *parallel importing*. p. 189

gross domestic product The monetary value of all goods and services produced in a country during one year. p. 165

gross income The total amount of money made in one year by a person, household, or family unit. p. 76

gross rating points (GRPs) A reference number for advertisers, created by multiplying reach (expressed as a percentage of the total market) by frequency. p. 454

hierarchy of effects The sequence of stages a prospective buyer goes through from initial awareness of a product to eventual action (either trial or adoption of the product). The stages include awareness, interest, evaluation, trial, and adoption. p. 434

hypermarket A large store (more than 200 000 square feet) offering a mix of 40 percent food products and 60 percent general merchandise. p. 402

ISO 14001 Worldwide standards for environmental quality and green marketing practices. p. 102

ISO 9000 standards Registration and certification of a manufacturer's quality management and quality assurance system. p. 148

idea generation Developing a pool of concepts as candidates for new products. p. 267

idle production capacity When the service provider is available but there is no demand. p. 311

in-house agency A company's own advertising staff, which may provide full services or a limited range of services. p. 462

indirect channel A marketing channel where intermediaries are inserted between the producer and consumers and perform numerous channel functions. p. 369

industrial firm An organizational buyer that in some way reprocesses a good or service it buys before selling it again to the next buyer. p. 142

industry potential The maximum total sales of a product by all firms to a segment during a specified time period under specified environmental conditions and marketing efforts of the firms. p. 245

infomercials Program-length (30-minute) advertisements that take an educational approach to communication with potential customers. p. 456

information technology Designing and managing computer and communication networks to provide a system to satisfy an organization's needs for data storage, processing, and access. p. 218

institutional advertisements Advertisements designed to build goodwill or an image for an organization, rather than promote a specific good or service. p. 449

integrated marketing communications The concept of designing marketing communications programs that coordinate all promotional activities—advertising, personal selling, sales promotion, public relations, and direct marketing—to provide a consistent message across all audiences and to maximize the promotional budget. p. 422

internal marketing The notion that a service organization must focus on its employees, or internal market, before successful programs can be directed at customers. p. 319

intertype competition Competition between very dissimilar types of retail outlets. p. 402

intranet An Internet/Web-based network used within the boundaries of an organization. p. 79

involvement The personal, social, and economic significance of the purchase to the consumer. p. 116

joint venture An arrangement in which a foreign company and a local firm invest together to create a local business, sharing ownership, control, and profits of the new company. p. 185

just-in-time (JIT) concept An inventory supply system that operates with very low inventories and requires fast, on-time delivery. p. 391

label An integral part of the package that typically identifies the product or brand, who made it, where and when it was made, how it is to be used, and package contents and ingredients. p. 298

laws Society's values and standards that are enforceable in the courts. p. 92

lead generation The result of a direct marketing offer designed to generate interest in a product or a service, and a request for additional information. p. 439

learning Those behaviours that result from (1) repeated experience and (2) thinking. p. 123

level of service The degree of service provided to the customer by self-, limited-, and full-service retailers. p. 398

lifestyle A mode of living that is identified by how people spend their time and resources (activities), what they consider important in their environment (interests), and what they think of themselves and the world around them (opinions). p. 124

limited-service agency Specializes in one aspect of the advertising process such as providing creative services to develop the advertising copy or buying previously unpurchased media space. p. 462

line positions People in line positions, such as senior marketing managers, have the authority and responsibility to issue orders to the people who report to them, such as product managers. p. 523

linear trend extrapolation The pattern is described with a straight line. p. 246

logistics Those activities that focus on getting the right amount of the right products to the right place at the right time at the lowest possible cost. p. 381

logistics management The practice of organizing the cost-effective flow of raw materials, in-process inventory, finished goods, and related information from point of origin to point of consumption to satisfy customer requirements. p. 381

lost-horse forecast Starting with the last known value of the item being forecast, listing the factors that could affect the forecast, assessing whether they have a positive or negative impact, and making the final forecast. p. 246

macromarketing The study of the aggregate flow of a nation's goods and services to benefit society. p. 19

major account management The practice of using team selling to focus on important customers so as to build mutually beneficial, long-term, cooperative relationships. Also called *key account management*. p. 488

make-buy decision An evaluation of whether components and assemblies will be purchased from outside suppliers or built by the company itself. p. 153

manufacturer's agents Work for several producers and carry noncompetitive, complementary merchandise in an exclusive territory; also called *manufacturer's representatives*. p. 373

market People with the desire and with the ability to buy a specific product. p. 8

market modification Strategy in which a company tries to find new customers, increase a product's use among existing customers, or create new-use situations. p. 288

market orientation Focusing organizational efforts on (1) continuously collecting information about customers' needs and competitors' capabilities, (2) sharing this information across departments, and (3) using the information to create customer value. p. 16

market potential Maximum total sales of a product by all firms to a segment during a specified time period under specified environmental conditions and marketing efforts of the firms (also called *industry potential*). p. 245

market segmentation Aggregating prospective buyers into groups, or segments, that (1) have common needs and (2) will respond similarly to a marketing action. p. 39

market segments The groups that result from the process of market segmentation; these groups ideally (1) have common needs and (2) will respond similarly to a marketing action. p. 227

market share The ratio of sales revenue of the firm to the total sales revenue of all firms in the industry, including the firm itself. p. 29

market testing Exposing actual products to prospective consumers under realistic purchase conditions to see if they will buy. p. 271

market-based groupings Organizational groupings that utilize specific customer segments. p. 524

market-product grid Framework to relate the segment of a market to products offered or potential marketing actions by the firm. p. 228

marketing The process of planning and executing the conception, pricing, promotion, and distribution of ideas, goods, and services to create exchanges that satisfy individual and organizational objectives. p. 7

marketing channel Individuals and firms involved in the process of making a product or service available for use or consumption by consumers or industrial users. p. 366

marketing concept The idea that an organization should (1) strive to satisfy the needs of consumers (2) while also trying to achieve the organization's goals. p. 16

marketing mix The marketing manager's controllable factors; the marketing actions of product, price, promotion, and place that he or she can take to solve a marketing problem. p. 13

marketing plan A road map for the marketing activities of an organization for a specified future period of time, such as one year or five years. p. 36

marketing program A plan that integrates the marketing mix to provide a good, service, or idea to prospective buyers. p. 14

marketing research The process of defining a marketing problem and opportunity, systematically collecting and analyzing information, and recommending actions to improve an organization's marketing activities. p. 199

marketing strategy The means by which a marketing goal is to be achieved, usually characterized by a specified target market and a marketing program to reach it. p. 42

marketing tactics The detailed day-to-day operational decisions essential to the overall success of marketing strategies. p. 42

marketspace An information- and communication-based electronic exchange environment mostly occupied by sophisticated computer and telecommunication technologies and digitized offerings. p. 79

materials handling Moving goods over short distances into, within, and out of warehouses and manufacturing plants. p. 389

merchandise line How many different types of products a store carries and in what assortment. p. 398

merchant wholesalers Independently owned firms that take title to the merchandise they handle. p. 372

message The information sent by a source to a receiver in the communication process. p. 422

micromarketing How an individual organization directs its marketing activities and allocates its resources to benefit its customers. p. 19

mission A statement of the organization's scope. p. 28

missionary salespeople Sales support personnel who do not directly solicit orders but rather concentrate on performing promotional activities and introducing new products. p. 480

mixed branding A firm markets products under its own name and that of a reseller because the segment attracted by the reseller is different from its own market. p. 297

moral idealism A personal moral philosophy that considers certain individual rights or duties as universal, regardless of the outcome. p. 99

motivation The energizing force that causes behaviour that satisfies a need. p. 119

multibranding A manufacturer's branding strategy giving each product a distinct name. p. 296

multichannel distribution An arrangement whereby a firm reaches buyers by employing two or more different types of marketing channels. p. 371

multichannel retailers Utilize and integrate a combination of traditional store formats and nonstore formats such as catalogues, television, and online retailing. p. 414

multicultural marketing Combinations of the marketing mix that reflect the unique attitudes, ancestry, communication preferences, and lifestyles of ethnic Canadians. p. 73

multidomestic marketing strategy A multinational firm's offering as many different product variations, brand names, and advertising programs as countries in which it does business. p. 173

multiproduct branding A company uses one name for all products; also called *blanket* or *family branding*. p. 295

national character A distinct set of personality characteristics common among people of a country or society. p. 120

need-satisfaction presentation A selling format that emphasizes probing and listening by the salesperson to identify needs and interests of prospective buyers. p. 484

new-product process The sequence of activities a firm uses to identify business opportunities and convert them to a salable good or service. p. 266

new-product strategy development Defining the role for a new product in terms of the firm's overall corporate objectives. p. 266

noise Extraneous factors that can work against effective communication by distorting a message or the feedback received. p. 424

nonprobability sampling Using arbitrary judgments to select the sample so that the chance of selecting a particular element may be unknown or zero. p. 215

North American Industry Classification System (NAICS) Provides common industry definitions for Canada, Mexico, and the United States, which facilitate the measurement of economic activity in the three member countries of NAFTA. p. 144

objective and task budgeting A budgeting approach whereby the company (1) determines its promotion objectives, (2) outlines the tasks to accomplish these objectives, and (3) determines the promotion cost of performing these tasks. p. 33; p. 435

observation Watching, either mechanically or in person, how people behave. p. 212

off-peak pricing Charging different prices during different times of the day or days of the week to reflect variations in demand for the service. p. 320

off-price retailing Selling brand-name merchandise at lower than regular prices. p. 409

opinion leaders Individuals who exert direct or indirect social influence over others. p. 127

order getter A salesperson who sells in a conventional sense and identifies prospective customers, provides customers with information, persuades customers to buy, closes sales, and follows up on customers' use of a product or service. p. 479

order taker Processes routine orders or reorders for products that were already sold by the company. p. 478

organizational buyers Those manufacturers, wholesalers, retailers, and government agencies that buy goods and services for their own use or for resale. pp. 9, 142

organizational buying behaviour The decision-making process that organizations use to establish the need for products and services and identify, evaluate, and choose among alternative brands and suppliers. p. 146

organizational buying criteria The objective attributes of the supplier's products and services and the capabilities of the supplier itself. p. 147

organizational culture A set of values, ideas, and attitudes that is learned and shared among the members of an organization. p. 28

packaging Any container in which a product is offered for sale and on which label information is communicated. p. 298

partnership selling The practice whereby buyers and sellers combine their expertise and resources to create customized solutions; commit to joint planning; and share customer, competitive, and company information for their mutual benefit, and ultimately the customer. Sometimes called *enterprise selling*. p. 478

penetration pricing Setting a low initial price on a new product to appeal immediately to the mass market. p. 341

perceived risk The anxieties felt because the consumer cannot anticipate the outcomes of a purchase but believes that there may be negative consequences. p. 122

percentage of sales budgeting Allocating funds to advertising as a percentage of past or anticipated sales, in terms of either dollars or units sold. p. 434

perception The process by which an individual selects, organizes, and interprets information to create a meaningful picture of the world. p. 121

perceptual map A means of displaying or graphing in two dimensions the location of products or brands in the minds of consumers to enable a manager to see how consumers perceive competing products or brands relative to its own and then take marketing actions. p. 243

personal selling The two-way flow of communication between a buyer and seller, often in a face-to-face encounter, designed to influence a person's or group's purchase decision. pp. 426, 476

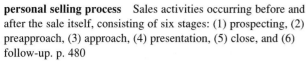

personal selling process   Sales activities occurring before and after the sale itself, consisting of six stages: (1) prospecting, (2) preapproach, (3) approach, (4) presentation, (5) close, and (6) follow-up. p. 480

personality   A person's consistent behaviours or responses to recurring situations. p. 120

points of difference   Those characteristics of a product that make it superior to competitive substitutes. p. 39

post-tests   Tests conducted after an advertisement has been shown to the target audience to determine whether it has accomplished its intended purpose. p. 462

power centre   A huge shopping strip with multiple anchor (or national) stores, a convenient location, and a supermarket. p. 411

pretests   Tests conducted before an advertisement is placed to determine whether it communicates the intended message or to select among alternative versions of an advertisement. p. 461

price   The money or other considerations (including other goods and services) exchanged for the ownership or use of a good or service. p. 330

price elasticity of demand   The percentage change in quantity demanded relative to a percentage change in price. p. 337

pricing constraints   Factors that limit the latitude of price a firm may set. p. 332

pricing objectives   Expectations that specify the role of price in an organization's marketing and strategic plans. p. 335

primary data   Facts and figures that are newly collected for the project. p. 204

private branding   When a company manufactures products but sells them under the brand name of a wholesaler or retailer (often called *private labelling* or *reseller branding*). p. 297

probability sampling   Using precise rules to select the sample such that each element of the population has a specific known chance of being selected. p. 215

product   A good, service, or idea consisting of a bundle of tangible and intangible attributes that satisfies consumers and is received in exchange for money or some other unit of value. p. 256

product advertisements   Advertisements that focus on selling a good or service and take three forms: (1) pioneering (or informational), (2) competitive (or persuasive), and (3) reminder. p. 448

product (or program) champion   A person who is able and willing to cut red tape and move the program forward. p. 521

product class   The entire product category or industry. p. 286

product differentiation   Strategy involves a firm's using different marketing mix activities, such as product features and advertising, to help consumers perceive the product as being different from and better than competing products. p. 227

product form   Variations of a product within the product class. p. 286

product life cycle   The stages a new product goes through in the marketplace: introduction, growth, maturity, and decline. p. 280

product line   A group of products that are closely related because they satisfy a class of needs, are used together, are sold to the same customer group, are distributed through the same outlets, or fall within a given price range. p. 256

product line groupings   Organizational groupings in which a unit is responsible for specific product offerings. p. 523

product mix   The number of product lines offered by a company. p. 257

product modification   Altering a product's characteristic, such as its quality, performance, or appearance, to try to increase and extend the product's sales. p. 288

product placement   Using a brand-name product in a movie, television show, video, or a commercial for another product. p. 466

product positioning   The place an offering occupies in consumers' minds on important attributes relative to competitive offerings. p. 243

product repositioning   Changing the place an offering occupies in a consumer's mind relative to competitive products. p. 243

production goods   Items used in the manufacturing process that become part of the final product. p. 258

profit   The reward to a business firm for the risk it undertakes in offering a product for sale; the money left over after a firm's total expenses are subtracted from its total revenues. p. 26

profit equation   Profit = Total revenue − Total cost, or Profit = (Unit price × Quantity sold) = Total cost. p. 331

profitability analysis   A means of measuring the profitability of the firm's products, customer groups, sales territories, channels of distribution, and order sizes. p. 526

promotional mix   The combination of one or more of the promotional elements a firm uses to communicate with consumers. The promotional elements include advertising, personal selling, sales promotion, public relations, and direct marketing. p. 422

protectionism   The practice of shielding one or more sectors of a country's economy from foreign competition through the use of tariffs or quotas. p. 168

protocol   A statement that, before product development begins, identifies (1) a well-defined target market; (2) specific customers' needs, wants, and preferences; and (3) what the product will be and do. p. 263

public relations   A form of communication management that seeks to influence the feelings, opinions, or beliefs held by customers, prospective customers, shareholders, suppliers, employees, and other publics about a company and its products or services. p. 426

publicity   A nonpersonal, indirectly paid presentation of an organization, good, or service. p. 426

pull strategy   Directing the promotional mix at ultimate consumers to encourage them to ask the retailer for the product. p. 433

purchase decision process   The stages a buyer passes through in making choices about which products and services to buy. p. 114

push strategy   Directing the promotional mix to channel members to gain their cooperation in ordering and stocking a product. p. 432

quality   Those features and characteristics of a product that influence its ability to satisfy customer needs. p. 32

quota   A restriction placed on the amount of a product allowed to enter or leave a country. p. 168

ROI marketing   The application of modern measurement technologies and contemporary organizational design to understand, quantify, and optimize marketing spending. p. 526

rating   The percentage of households in a market that are tuned to a particular TV show or radio station. p. 454

reach   The number of different people or households exposed to an advertisement. p. 454

receivers   Consumers who read, hear, or see the message sent by a source in the communication process. p. 423

reciprocity   An industrial buying practice in which two organizations agree to purchase each other's products and services. p. 149

reference groups   People to whom an individual looks as a basis for self-appraisal or as a source of personal standards. p. 129

regional shopping centres   Consist of 50 to 150 stores that typically attract customers who live within an 8- to 16-km range, often containing two or three anchor stores. p. 410

regulation   Restrictions the provincial and federal laws place on business with regard to the conduct of its activities. p. 82

relationship selling   The practice of building ties to customers based on a salesperson's attention and commitment to customer needs over time. p. 477

reseller   A wholesaler or retailer that buys physical products and resells them again without any processing. p. 143

response   The impact the message had on the receiver's knowledge, attitudes, or behaviours. p. 424

retail life cycle   The process of growth and decline that retail outlets, like products, experience. p. 413

retail positioning matrix   Positions retail outlets on two dimensions: breadth of product line and value added. p. 407

retailing   All activities involved in selling, renting, and providing goods and services to ultimate consumers for personal, family, or household use. p. 398

retailing mix   In retailing strategy, the (1) goods and services, (2) physical distribution, and (3) communications tactics chosen by a store. p. 409

reverse auction   A buyer communicates a need for a product or service and would-be suppliers are invited to bid in competition with each other. p. 157

reverse logistics   A process of reclaiming recyclable and reusable materials, returns, and reworks from the point of consumption or use for repair, remanufacturing, redistribution, or disposal. p. 391

reverse marketing   The deliberate effort by organizational buyers to build relationships that shape suppliers' products, services, and capabilities to fit a buyer's needs and those of its customers. p. 148

SWOT analysis   An acronym describing an organization's appraisal of its internal strengths and weaknesses and its external opportunities and threats. p. 37

sales analysis   A tool for controlling marketing programs using sales records to compare actual results with sales goals and to identify strengths and weaknesses. p. 526

sales component analysis   A tool for controlling marketing programs that traces sales revenues to their sources, such as specific products, sales territories, or customers. Also called *microsales analysis*. p. 526

sales engineer   A salesperson who specializes in identifying, analyzing, and solving customer problems and who brings know-how and technical expertise to the selling situations, but does not actually sell goods and services. p. 480

sales forecast   The maximum total sales of a product that a firm expects to sell during a specified time period under specified environmental conditions and its own marketing efforts (also called *company forecast*). p. 245

sales management   Planning the selling program and implementing and controlling the personal selling effort of the firm. p. 476

sales plan   A statement describing what is to be achieved and where and how the selling effort of salespeople is to be deployed. p. 486

sales promotion   A short-term inducement of value offered to arouse interest in buying a good or service. p. 427

sales quota   Contains specific goals assigned to a salesperson, sales team, branch sales office, or sales district for a stated time period. p. 494

sales response function   Relates the expense of marketing effort to the marketing results obtained. Measures of marketing results include sales revenue, profit, units sold, and level of awareness. p. 507

salesforce automation   The use of technology to make the sales function more effective and efficient. p. 494

salesforce survey forecast   Asking the firm's salespeople to estimate sales during a coming period. p. 246

sampling   The process of selecting subsets from a population. p. 215

scrambled merchandising   Offering several unrelated product lines in a single retail store. p. 402

screening and evaluation   The third stage of the new-product process, which involves internal and external evaluations of the new-product ideas to eliminate those that warrant no further effort. p. 268

secondary data   Facts and figures that have already been recorded before the project at hand. p. 203

self-concept   The way people see themselves and the way they believe others see them. p. 120

self-regulation   An alternative to government control where an industry attempts to police itself. p. 83

selling agent   Represents a single producer and is responsible for the entire marketing function of that producer. p. 373

semiotics   The field of study that examines the correspondence between symbols and their role in the assignment of meaning for people. p. 176

service continuum   A range from the tangible to the intangible or goods-dominant to service-dominant offerings available in the marketplace. p. 312

services   Intangible activities, benefits, or satisfactions that an organization provides to consumers in exchange for money or something else of value. p. 308

share points   Percentage points of market share; often used as the common basis of comparison to allocate marketing resources effectively. p. 509

shopping goods   Items for which the consumer compares several alternatives on criteria such as price, quality, or style. p. 258

shrinkage   Breakage and theft of merchandise by customers and employees. p. 409

situation analysis   Taking stock of where the firm or product has been recently, where it is now, and where it is headed in terms of the organization's plans and the external factors and trends affecting it. p. 36

situational influences The purchase situation affects the purchase decision process through five situational influences: (1) the purchase task, (2) social surroundings, (3) physical surroundings, (4) temporal effects, and (5) antecedent states. p. 118

Six Sigma A means to "delight the customer" by achieving quality through a highly disciplined process to focus on developing and delivering near-perfect products and services. p. 266

skimming pricing The highest initial price that customers really desiring the product are willing to pay. p. 341

slotting fee The payment a manufacturer makes to place a new item on a retailer's shelf. p. 272

social audit A systematic assessment of a firm's objectives, strategies, and performance in the domain of social responsibility. p. 103

social class The relatively permanent, homogeneous divisions in a society into which people sharing similar values, lifestyles, interests, and behaviour can be grouped. p. 131

social forces The demographic characteristics of the population and its values in the environment. p. 70

social marketing Marketing designed to influence the behaviour of individuals in which the benefits of the behaviour accrue to those individuals or to the society in general and not to the marketer. p. 9

social responsibility The idea that organizations are part of a larger society and are accountable to that society for their actions. pp. 19, 100

societal marketing concept The view that an organization should discover and satisfy the needs of its consumers in a way that also provides for society's well-being. p. 19

source A company or person who has information to convey. p. 422

specialty goods Items that a consumer makes a special effort to search out and buy. p. 258

staff positions People in staff positions have the authority and responsibility to advise people in the line positions but cannot issue direct orders to them. p. 523

stakeholders Individuals or groups, either within or outside an organization, that relate to it in what it does and how well it performs. p. 28

stimulus-response presentation A selling format that assumes the prospect will buy if given the appropriate stimulus by a salesperson. p. 483

strategic alliances Agreements among two or more independent firms to cooperate for the purpose of achieving common goals. p. 172

strategic channel alliances A practice whereby one firm's marketing channel is used to sell another firm's products. p. 371

strategic marketing process The approach whereby an organization allocates its marketing mix resources to reach its target markets. p. 36

strip location A cluster of stores serving people who live within a 5- to 10-minute drive. p. 410

subcultures Subgroups within the larger, or national, culture with unique values, ideas, and attitudes. p. 132

subliminal perception Means that you see or hear messages without being aware of them. p. 122

supply chain A sequence of firms that perform activities required to create and deliver a good or service to consumers or industrial users. p. 381

supply chain management The integration and organization of information and logistics activities across firms in a supply chain for the purpose of creating and delivering goods and services that provide value to customers. p. 381

supply partnership A relationship that exists when a buyer and its supplier adopt mutually beneficial objectives, policies, and procedures for the purpose of lowering the cost and/or increasing the value of products and services delivered to the ultimate consumer. p. 149

support goods Items used to assist in producing other goods and services. p. 259

survey A research technique used to generate data by asking people questions and recording their responses on a questionnaire. p. 208

survey of buyers' intentions forecast Asking prospective customers whether they are likely to buy the product during some future time period. p. 246

sustainable development Conducting business in a way that protects the natural environment while making economic progress. p. 103

synergy The increased customer value achieved through performing organizational functions more efficiently. p. 231

target market One or more specific groups of potential consumers toward which an organization directs its marketing program. p. 12

tariff A government tax on goods or services entering a country primarily serving to raise prices on imports. p. 168

team selling Using an entire team of professionals in selling to and servicing major customers. p. 480

technology Inventions or innovations from applied science or engineering research. p. 77

telemarketing Using the telephone to interact with and sell directly to consumers. p. 406

total cost (1) The total expense incurred by a firm in producing and marketing a product. Total cost is the sum of fixed cost and variable cost. (2) In physical distribution decisions, the sum of all applicable costs for logistical activities. p. 338

total logistics cost Expenses associated with transportation, materials handling and warehousing, inventory, stockouts, order processing, and return goods handling. p. 385

total revenue The total money received from the sale of a product. p. 338

trade feedback effect A country's imports affect its exports and exports affect its imports. p. 165

trade name A commercial, legal name under which a company does business. p. 290

trade-oriented sales promotions Sales tools used to support a company's advertising and personal selling efforts directed to wholesalers, distributors, or retailers. Three common approaches are allowances and discounts, cooperative advertising, and salesforce training. p. 467

trademark Identifies that a firm has legally registered its brand name or trade name so the firm has its exclusive use. p. 290

trading down Reducing the number of features, quality, or price. p. 289

trading up Adding value to a product (or line) through additional features or higher-quality materials. p. 289

traditional auction A seller puts an item up for sale and would-be buyers are invited to bid in competition with each other. p. 156

traffic generation The outcome of a direct marketing offer designed to motivate people to visit a business. p. 439

trend extrapolation Extending a pattern observed in past data into the future. p. 246

ultimate consumers People—whether 80 years or 8 months old—who use the goods and services purchased for a household. p. 9

unsought goods Items that the consumer either does not know about or knows about but does not initially want. p. 258

usage rate Quantity consumed or patronage—store visits— during a specific period; varies significantly among different customer groups. p. 234

utilitarianism A personal moral philosophy that focuses on the "greatest good for the greatest number" by assessing the costs and benefits of the consequences of ethical behaviour. p. 99

value analysis A systematic appraisal of the design, quality, and performance of a product to reduce purchasing costs. p. 153

value consciousness The concern for obtaining the best quality, features, and performance of a product or service for a given price. p. 75

values (1) Personally or socially preferable modes of conduct or states of existence that are enduring. (2) The ratio of perceived quality to price. p. 124

variable cost The sum of the expenses of the firm that vary directly with the quantity of product that is produced and sold. p. 339

vendor-managed inventory An inventory management system whereby the supplier determines the product amount and assortment a customer (such as a retailer) needs and automatically delivers the appropriate items. p. 391

vertical marketing systems Professionally managed and centrally coordinated marketing channels designed to achieve channel economies and maximum marketing impact. p. 374

warranty A statement indicating the liability of the manufacturer for product deficiencies. p. 300

wheel of retailing A concept that describes how new retail outlets enter the market as low-status, low-margin stores and gradually add embellishments that raise their prices, and status. They now face a new low-status, low-margin operator, and the cycle starts to repeat itself. p. 412

whistle-blowers Employees who report unethical or illegal actions of their employers. p. 99

word of mouth People influencing each other during their face-to-face conversations. p. 127

workload method A formula-based method for determining the size of a salesforce that integrates the number of customers served, call frequency, call length, and available selling time to arrive at a salesforce size. p. 490

World Trade Organization A permanent institution that sets rules governing trade between its members through a panel of trade experts who (1) decide on trade disputes between members and (2) issue binding decisions. p. 169

CHAPTER NOTES

CHAPTER 1

1. Amy Luft, "Ahead of the Curve," *The New Canadian Magazine* (Jan/Feb 2004), pp. 31–34.
2. Regis McKenna, "Marketing Is Everything," *Harvard Business Review* (Jan/Feb 1991), pp. 65–79.
3. "AMA Adopts New Definition of Marketing," *Marketing News* (September 15, 2004), p. 1.
4. Philip Kotler and Sidney J. Levy, "Broadening the Concept of Marketing," *Journal of Marketing* (January 1969), pp. 10–15.
5. Adapted from George G. Brenkert, "Ethical Challenges in Social Marketing," *Journal of Public Policy & Marketing* (Spring 2002), pp. 14–25; and Alan R. Andreasen, "Marketing Social Marketing in the Social Change Marketplace," *Journal of Public Policy & Marketing* (Spring 2002), pp. 3–13.
6. Robert M. McMath and Thom Forbes, *What Were They Thinking?* (New York: Times Business, 1998), pp. 3–22.
7. McMath and Forbes, pp. 181–82.
8. "Cereal and Junk Food Advertising," October 1, 2004; and "Watching for Weasel Words," October 1, 2004, www.media-awaress.ca (downloaded October 5, 2004).
9. E. Jerome McCarthy, *Basic Marketing: A Managerial Approach* (Homewood, IL: Richard D. Irwin, 1960); and Walter van Waterschoot and Christophe Van den Bulte, "The 4P Classification of the Marketing Mix Revisited," *Journal of Marketing* (October 1992), pp. 83–93.
10. Amy Luft, pp. 31–34.
11. Robert F. Keith, "The Marketing Revolution," *Journal of Marketing* (January 1960), pp. 35–38.
12. *Annual Report* (New York: General Electric Company, 1952), p. 21.
13. Michael Treacy and Fred D. Wiersema, *The Discipline of Market Leaders* (Reading, MA: Addison-Wesley, 1995); Michael Treacy and Fred Wiersema, "How Market Leaders Keep Their Edge," *Fortune* (February 6, 1995), pp. 88–89; and Michael Treacy, "You Need a Value Discpline—But Which One?" *Fortune* (April 17, 1995), p. 195.
14. Frederick G. Crane and Jeffrey E. Sohl, "Imperatives for Venture Success: Entrepreneurs Speak," *International Journal of Entrepreneurship and Innovation* (May 2004), pp. 99–106.
15. "What's a Loyal Customer Worth?" *Fortune*, December 11, 1995, p.182; and Lauren Keller Johnson, "The Real Value of Customer Loyalty," *MIT Sloan Management Review* (Winter 2002), pp. 14–17.
16. G.R. Iyer and David Bejou, *Customer Relationship Management in Electronic Markets* (New York: The Haworth Press Inc. 2004).
17. Mark Whitmore and Jonathan Copulsky, "CRM R.I.P.?" *Marketing Magazine*, April 7, 2003, www.marketingmag.ca (downloaded June 10, 2005); Jay Curry and Adam Curry, *The Customer Marketing Method: How to Implement and Profit from Customer Relationship Management* (New York: The Free Press, 2000); Jim Berkowitz, "A Customer-Centric Philosophy," www.showcasecorp.com (downloaded April 25, 2002); and www.crmguru.com (downloaded April 27, 2002).
18. Whitmore and Copulsky, "CRM R.I.P.?"
19. Lesley Young, "Cutting through All the Hype about CRM," *Marketing Magazine* February 12, 2001, www.marketingmag.ca (downloaded, June 10, 2005).
20. The Hudson's Bay Company. www.hbc.ca.
21. Elliot Ettenberg, "Goodbye CRM, Hello Concierge Marketing," *Marketing Magazine*, August 25, 2003, www.marketingmag.ca (downloaded June 10, 2005).
22. Andrew Crane and John Desmond, "Societal Marketing and Morality," *European Journal of Marketing* (Spring 2002), pp. 548–570.
23. Shelby D. Hunt and John Burnett, "The Macromarketing/ Micromarketing Dichotomy: A Taxonomical Model," *Journal of Marketing* (Summer 1982), pp. 9–26.

Case: Courtesy of Curves International.

CHAPTER 2

1. Information supplied by Bombardier, Inc., May 1, 2005.
2. Roger A. Kerin, Vijay Mahajan, and P. Rajan Varadarajan, *Contemporary Perspectives on Strategic Marketing Planning* (Boston: Allyn & Bacon, 1990), chap. 1; and Orville C. Walker, Jr., Harper W. Boyd, Jr., and Jean-Claude Larreche, *Marketing Strategy* (Burr Ridge, IL: Richard D. Irwin, 1992), chaps. 1 and 2.
3. Theodore Levitt, "Marketing Myopia," *Harvard Business Review* (July–August 1960), pp. 45–56.
4. Katherine Ellison, "The Bottom Line Redefined," *Nature Conservancy* (Winter 2002), pp. 45–50.
5. George Stalk, Phillip Evans, and Lawrence E. Shulman, "Competing on Capabilities. The New Rules of Corporate Strategy," *Harvard Business Review* (March–April 1992), pp. 57–69.
6. Roger A. Kerin and Robert A. Peterson, *Strategic Marketing Problems: Cases and Comments,* 10th ed. (Englewood Cliffs, NJ: Prentice Hall, 2004), pp. 2–3; and Derek F. Abell, *Defining the Business* (Englewood Cliffs, NJ: Prentice Hall, 1980), p. 18.
7. Adapted from "The Experience Curve Reviewed, IV. The Growth Share Matrix of the Product Portfolio" (Boston: The Boston Consulting Group, 1973).
8. Kerin, Mahajan, and Vardarajan, *Contemporary Perspectives on Strategic Marketing Planning* (Boston: Allyn & Bacon, 1990), p. 52.
9. William C. Symonds, "The Kodak Revolt Is Short-Sighted," *BusinessWeek* (November 3, 2003), p. 38.
10. Jefferson Graham, "Kodak Gives Film Cameras Heave-Ho," *USA Today* (January 14, 2004), p. 5B.
11. "Has Kodak Missed the Moment?" *The Economist* (January 3, 2004), pp. 46–47.
12. James Bandler, "Kodak to Cut Staff Up to 21%, EasyShare up 81% Amid Digital Push," *The Wall Street Journal*, January 23, 2004, pp. A1, A7.
13. Faith Keenan and Cathy Schottenstein, "Big Yellow's Digital Dilemma," *BusinessWeek* (March 24, 2003), pp. 80–81.
14. Ben Dobbin, "Kodak Unveils Photo Kiosk to Develop Film in Minutes," *Star Tribune,* February 9, 2004, startribune.com.
15. Strengths and weaknesses of the BCG technique are based on Derek F. Abell and John S. Hammond, *Strategic Market Planning: Problem and Analytic Approaches* (Englewood Cliffs, NJ: Prentice Hall, 1979); Yoram Wind, Vijay Mahajan, and Donald Swire, "An Empirical Comparison of Standardized Portfolio Models," *Journal of Marketing* (Spring 1983), pp. 89–99; and J. Scott Armstrong and Roderick J. Brodie, "Effects of Portfolio Planning Methods on Decision Making: Experimental Results," *International Journal of Research in Marketing* (Winter 1994), pp. 73–84.
16. H. Igor Ansoff, "Strategies for Diversification," *Harvard Business Review* (September–October 1957), pp. 113–24.
17. Linda Swenson and Kenneth E. Goodpaster, *Medtronic in China (A)* (Minneapolis, MN: University of St. Thomas, 1999), pp. 4–5.
18. Joseph Nocera, "Kodak: The CEO vs. the Gadfly," *Fortune* (January 12, 2004), pp. 85–92.

19. Bandler, "Kodak to Cut Staff," pp. A1, A7.
20. Todd Wasserman, "The Mercenary" (a.k.a 'Super') CMO, *BrandWeek* (June 21, 2004), pp. S6–S18.
21. "Has Kodak Missed the Moment?" *The Economist,* January 3, 2004, pp. 46–47.
22. Ibid.

Specialized Bicycle Components, Inc.: This case was written by Giana Eckhardt and Steven Hartley. Sources: "Industry Overview 2003–04," National Bicycle Dealers Association (see http://nbda.com); Nancy Bouchard, "Above the Rim," *Sporting Goods Business* (October 1, 2003); "A Passion For Cycling Guides Specialized to Repeated New Breakthroughs," Specialized press release (see www.specialized.com); "Humble Origins Set Customer Service Standards" Specialized press release (see www.specialized.com).

APPENDIX A

1. Personal interview with Authur R. Kydd, St. Croix Management Group.
2. Examples of guides to writing marketing plans include William A. Cohen, *The Marketing Plan* (New York: Wiley, 1995); Mark Nolan, *The Instant Marketing Plan* (Santa Maria, CA: Puma Publishing Company, 1995); and Roman G. Hiebing, Jr., and Scott W. Cooper, *The Successful Marketing Plan,* 2nd ed. (Lincolnwood, IL: NTC Business Books, 1997).
3. Examples of guides to writing business plans include the following Rhonda M. Abrahms, *The Successful Business Plan: Secrets & Strategies,* 3rd ed. (Grants Pass, OR: Oasis Press/PSI Research, 2000); Joseph A. Covello and Brian J. Hazelgren, *The Complete Book of Business Plans* (Naperville, IL: Sourcebooks, 1995); Joseph A. Covello and Brian J. Hazelgren, *Your First Business Plan,* 3rd ed. (Naperville, IL: Sourcebooks, 1998); and Angela Shupe, ed., *Business Plans Handbook,* vols. 1–4 (Detroit: Gale Research, 1997).
4. Abrahms, *The Successful Business Plan*, p. 30.
5. Some of these points are adapted from Abrahms, pp. 30–38; others are adapted from William Rudelius, *Guidelines for Technical Report Writing* (Minneapolis: University of Minnesota, undated). See also William Strunk, Jr., and E. B. White, *The Elements of Style* (New York, Macmillan, 1979).

CHAPTER 3

1. Peter Burrows, "Show Time!" *BusinessWeek* (February 2, 2004), pp. 57–64; and Devine Leonard, "Songs in the Key of Steve," *Fortune* (May 12, 2003), pp. 52–62.
2. "Coffee Shops in the U.S.," press release from Mintel Group, February 2004; "Java's Hot, Bagels Not," *Restaurant Business* (April 1, 2003); Stephanie Thompson, "Coffee Brands Think Outside of the Can," *Advertising Age* (July 28, 2003), p. 26; and Rebecca Gardyn, "Grounds for a New Strategy," *American Demographics* (June 2001), pp. 115–17.
3. "Starbucks Automates Espresso Preparation," *Restaurant Business* (March 12, 2004); and Jeff Cioletti and Sherry Petersen, "Soda Shakeout," *Convenience Store News Online* (February 9, 2004).
4. Fred Vogelstein, "10 Tech Trends to Bet On," *Fortune* (February 23, 2004), pp. 76–88; Alison Stein Wellner, "The Next 25 Years," *American Demographics* (April 2003), pp. 24–27; Stephen B. Shepard, "You Read It Here First," *BusinessWeek* (March 15, 2004), p. 16; Catherine Arnold, "Anti-Smoking Trend Hits Asia," *Marketing News* (January 15, 2004), p. 4; Arundhati Parmar, "Outlook 2004: Competitive Intelligence," *Marketing News* (January 15, 2004), pp. 16–17; and Steve Jarvis, "Internet Privacy at the Plate, Net Names, Taxes on Deck Too," *Marketing News* (January 1, 2001), pp. 12–14.

5. *World Population Prospects: The 2002 Revision* (2003), United Nations, table A4; and Carl Haub, "2003 World Population Data Sheet," Population Reference Bureau.
6. Haub, "2003 World Population Data Sheet"; "World Population at a Glance: 1998 and Beyond," "Global Demographics: The Group of Seven's Senior Moment," *BusinessWeek Online* (March 17, 2003); and "New Facts on Globalization, Poverty, and Income Distribution," International Chamber of Commerce, (January 15, 2003).
7. Statistics Canada, CANSIM 052-001.
8. Statistics Canada, "Population Projections for Canada, Provinces and Territories 2000-2026, 91-520-KPB.
9. Michael J. Weiss, "To Be about to Be," *American Demographics* (September 2003), pp. 29–36; Peter Francese, "Ahead of the Next Wave," *American Demographics* (September 2003), pp. 42–43; and Don O'Briant, "Millenials: The Next Generation," *Atlanta Journal-Constitution* (August 11, 2003), p. 1D.
10. "EU's Future Consumers: 3 Groups to Watch," *Marketing News* (June 4, 2001), p. 9.
11. Statistics Canada, "Population Projections of Visible Minority Groups in Canada, 91-541-XIE (March 22, 2005).
12. Laura Pratt, " Ethnic Marketing Just Good Business for HSBC Bank," *Strategy Magazine* (February 12, 2001), p. B7; and Lucy Saddleton, "Mainstream Retail Spices It Up," *Strategy Magazine* (April 19, 2004), p. 4.
13. "Food Makers Designing Menus for Dashboard Diners," *Portland Press Herald* (August 26, 2004), p. A4.
14. Terry Poulton, "Canada's New Fashion Leader: The Plus-size Woman," *Strategy Magazine* (April 5, 2004), p. 1.
15. Lisa D'Innocenzo, "Unconventional $3.5 million Jays Campaign Borrows from Retail Playbook: Value and Affordability,' *Strategy Magazine* (March 8, 2004), p. 3.
16. Statistics Canada, CANSIM 2003-001 (January 2005).
17. John Carey, "Tiny Smart Bombs vs. Cancer?" *BusinessWeek* (March 1, 2004), p. 115; Stephen H. Wildstrom, "Get Ready for an Innovative New Year," *BusinessWeek* (December 29, 2003), p. 28; Herve Gallaire, "Can New Technology Recharge Xerox?" *BusinessWeek* (December 22, 2003), p. IM2; and Fred Vogelstein, "10 Tech Trends to Bet On," *Fortune* (February 23, 2004), pp. 75–88.
18. Michael Krauss, "Young Net Entrepreneurs Leverage Web Anew," *Marketing News* (February 1, 2004), p. 6.
19. Leon Jaroff, "Smart's the Word in Detroit," *Time* (February 6, 1995), pp. 50–52.
20. Clint Willis, "25 Cool Things You Wish You Had and Will," *Forbes ASAP* (June 1, 1998), pp. 49–60.
21. Canadian Plastics Industry Association, http://www.cpia.ca, December 12, 2005.
22. Nyla Matuk, "Green Roofing," Canadian Architect, vol. 46(10), October 2001, p. 25.
23. Jim Carlton, "Recycling Redefined," *The Wall Street Journal* (March 6, 2001), pp. B1, B4; Stephanie Anderson, "There's Gold in Those Hills of Soda Bottles," *BusinessWeek* (September 11, 1995), p. 48; Maxine Wilkie, "Asking Americans to Use Less Stuff," *American Demographics* (December 1994), pp. 11–12; and Jacquelyn Ottman, "New and Improved Won't Do," *Marketing News* (January 30, 1995), p. 9.
24. Chris Anderson, "The Wi-Fi Revolution," *Unwired,* supplement to *Wired* (2003).
25. Michael Porter, *Competitive Advantage* (New York: Free Press, 1985); and Michael Porter, *Competitive Strategy* (New York: Free Press, 1980).
26. Canadian Federation of Independent Business, www.cfib.ca (downloaded March 25, 2005).
27. www.ic.gc.ca
28. Lisa D'Innocenzo, "What Privacy Law," *Strategy Magazine* (January 12, 2004), p. 4.

29. Amanda Maltby, "Adapting to Canada's New Privacy Rules," *Marketing Magazine* (November 3, 2003); www.marketingmag.ca (downloaded June 10, 2005).

Flyte Time Productions, Inc.: This case was written by William Rudelius based on personal interviews with Jimmy Jam and Terry Lewis, and the following sources: Jon Bream, "Flyte Tyme Is Still Ticking After 20 Years of Hits," Star Tribune (April 29, 2001), pp. F1, F7; "Jimmy Jam and Terry Lewis Make Flyte Tyme Studios No. 1," Business Wire (August 21, 2001).

CHAPTER 4

1. www.generalmotors.ca, www.ford.ca, www.nissan.ca, and www.toyota.ca (downloaded June 5, 2005).
2. Eugene R. Lazniak and Patrick E. Murphy, *Ethical Marketing Decisions: The Higher Road* (Boston: Allyn & Bacon, 1993), chapter 1.
3. Verne E. Henderson, "The Ethical Side of Enterprise," *Sloan Management Review* (Spring 1982), pp. 37–47. See also, Joseph L. Badaracco, Jr., *Defining Moments: When Managers Must Choose Between Right and Right* (Boston: Harvard Business School Press, 1997).
4. M. Bommer, C. Gratto, J. Grauander, and M. Tuttle, "A Behavioral Model of Ethical and Unethical Decision Making," *Journal of Business Ethics*, vol. 6 (1987), pp. 265–80.
5. F. G. Crane, "What's Ethical and What's Not with Canadian Business Students," Working Paper, 2001.
6. F. G. Crane, "Teaching Business Ethics in B-Schools: A Cross-Cultural Examination," *Journal of the Academy of Business Education* (2006).
7. N. Craig Smith, "Marketing Strategies for the Ethics Era," *Sloan Management Review* (Summer 1995), pp. 85–97; Kenneth Labich, "The New Crisis in Business Ethics," *Fortune* (April 29, 1992), pp. 167ff.
8. www.ethicscan.on.ca (downloaded November 20, 2004).
9. Lawrence B. Chonko, *Ethical Decision Making in Marketing* (Thousand Oaks, CA: Sage, 1995).
10. William Beaver, "Levi's Is Leaving China," *Business Horizons* (March–April 1995), pp. 35–40.
11. Barry R. Shapiro, "Economic Espionage," *Marketing Management* (Spring 1998), pp. 56–58; and Dan T. Swartwood and Richard J. Hefferman, *Trends in Intellectual Property Loss, Survey Report* (Alexandria, VA: American Society for Industrial Security, 1998).
12. "Five years: $59.2 Billion Lost," *Software & Information Industry Association Press Release* (May 2000); Bryan W. Husted, "The Impact of National Culture on Software Piracy," *Journal of Business Ethics*, vol. 26 (2000), pp. 197–211.
13. Vern Terpstra and Kenneth David, *The Cultural Environment of International Business*, 3rd ed. (Cincinnati: South-Western Publishing, 1991), p. 12.
14. For an extended treatment of ethics in the exchange process, see Gregory T. Gundlach and Patrick E. Murphy, "Ethical and Legal Foundations in Relational Marketing Exchanges," *Journal of Marketing* (October 1993), pp. 35–46.
15. "Carnivore in the Cabbage Patch," *U.S. News & World Report* (January 20, 1997), p. 69.
16. "The Battle over Web Privacy," *The Wall Street Journal* (March 21, 2001), pp. B1, B4.
17. For an extensive examination on slotting fees, see Paul N. Bloom, Gregory T. Gundlach, and Joseph P. Cannon, "Slotting Allowances and Fees: Schools of Thought and Views of Practicing Managers," *Journal of Marketing* (April 2000), pp. 92–109.
18. This discussion contains statistics reported in Carolyn F. Siegel, "Introducing Marketing Students to Business Intelligence Using Project-Based Learning on the World Wide Web," *Journal of Marketing Education* (August 2000), pp. 90–98.

19. "P&G Expected to Get About $120 Million in Settlement of Chewy-Cookie Lawsuit," *The Wall Street Journal* (September 11, 1989), p. B10.
20. www.transparency.de (downloaded January 25, 2005).
21. *KPMG Business Ethics Survey*, KPMG Canada, 1999, www.kpmg.ca/ethics; and *Management Ethics*, The Canadian Centre for Ethics and Corporate Policy, www.ethicscentre.com (downloaded August 21, 2001).
22. "Simon Says, 'Behave'," *Success* (January 2000), p. 21; and Savior L.S. Nwachukwu and Scott J. Vitell, Jr., "The Influence of Corporate Culture on Managerial Ethical Judgments," *Journal of Business Ethics*, vol. 17 (1997), pp. 757–76.
23. "Workers Who Blow the Whistle on Bosses Often Pay a High Price," *The Wall Street Journal* (July 18, 1995), p. B1.
24. R. Eric Reidenbach and Donald P. Robin, *Ethics and Profits* (Englewood Cliffs, NJ: Prentice Hall, 1989); Chonko, *Ethical Decision Making*; Laziniak and Murphy, *Ethical Marketing Decisions*.
25. James Q. Wilson, "Adam Smith on Business Ethics," *California Management Review* (Fall 1989), pp. 59–72; and George M. Zinkham, Michael Bisesi, and Mary Jane Saxon, "MBAs: Changing Attitudes Toward Marketing Dilemmas," *Journal of Business Ethics*, vol. 8 (1989), pp. 963–74.
26. www.nestlecanada.ca (downloaded April 25, 2001).
27. Robert B. Reich, "The New Meaning of Corporate Social Responsibility," *California Management Review* (Winter 1998), pp. 8–17.
28. Harvey S. James and Farhad Rassekh, "Smith, Friedman, and Self-Interest in Ethical Society," *Business Ethics Quarterly* (July 2000), pp. 659–74.
29. "Beating the Odds in Biotech," *Newsweek* (October 12, 1992), p. 63.
30. For an extended description of the Perrier decision, see "Perrier— Overresponding to a Crisis," in Robert F. Hartley, *Marketing Mistakes and Successes*, 8th ed. (New York: Wiley, 2001), pp. 127–37.
31. Harvey Meyer, "The Greening of Corporate America," *Journal of Business Strategy* (January–February 2000), pp. 38–43; Irina Maslennikova and David Foley, "Xerox's Approach to Sustainability," *Interfaces* (May–June 2000), pp. 226–33. Also see Philemon Oyewale, "Social Costs of Environmental Justice Associated with the Practice of Green Marketing," *Journal of Business Ethics*, vol. 29 (2001), pp. 239–51; and Ajay Menon and Anil Menon, "Environpreneurial Marketing Strategy: The Emergence of Corporate Environmentalism as Market Strategy," *Journal of Marketing* (January 1997), pp. 51–67.
32. The ISO Survey of ISO 9000 and ISO 14000 Certificates (Geneva, Switzerland: International Organization for Standardization, 2004).
33. For an extended discussion on this topic, see P. Rajan Varadarajan and Anil Menon, "Causes-Related Marketing: A Coalignment of Marketing Strategy and Corporate Philanthropy," *Journal of Marketing* (July 1988), pp. 58–74. The examples given are found in "The Socially Correct Corporation," *Fortune* (July 24, 2000), special section; and "The Wider Benefits of Backing a Good Cause," *Marketing* (September 2, 1999), pp. 18–22.
34. "Reinventing Cause Marketing," *Brandweek* (October 27, 1997), p. 17.
35. These steps are adapted from J. J. Carson and G. A. Steiner, *Measuring Business Social Performance: The Corporate Social Audit* (New York: Committee for Economic Development, 1974). See also Sandra Waddock and Neil Smith, "Corporate Responsibility Audits: Doing Well by Doing Good," *Sloan Management Review* (Winter 2000), pp. 75–84.
36. D.A. Rondinelli and G. Vastag, "International Standards and Corporate Policies: An Integrated Framework," *California Management Review* (November 9, 1998), p. 14.
37. "Sweatshops: Finally, Airing the Dirty Linen," *Business Week* (June 23, 2003), pp. 100–01.
38. "Corporate America's Social Conscience," *Fortune* (May 26, 2003), p. 147ff.

39. This discussion is based on Wayne D. Hoyer and Deborah J. MacInnis, *Consumer Behavior,* 3rd ed. (New York: Houghton Mifflin Company, 2004), pp. 535–37; "Factoids," *Research Alert,* December 8, 2002, p. 5; and "Penny for Your Thoughts," *American Demographics* (September 2000), pp. 8–9.

40. M. Laroche, Jasmin Bergeron, Marc-Alexandre Tomiuk, and Guido Barbaro-Forleo, "Cultural Differences in Environmental Knowledge, Attitudes, and Behaviors of Canadian Consumers," *Canadian Journal of Administrative Sciences,* vol. 8 (2002).

41. "Schism on the Green," *Brandweek* (February 26, 2001), p. 18.

42. Jason MacDonald, "Not So Easy Being Green," www.marketingmag.ca (downloaded June 4, 2001).

Starbucks Corporation: This case is based on information on the company Web site (www.starbucks.com) and the following sources: "Living Our Values," *2003 Corporate Social Responsibility Annual Report;* "Starbucks Annual Shareholder Meeting," Starbucks press release (March 30, 2004); Ranjay Gulati, Sarah Huffman, and Gary Neilson, "The Barista Principle: Starbucks and the Rise of Relational Capital," *Strategy and Business* (3rd Quarter 2002), pp. 58–69; and Andy Serwer, "Hot Starbucks to Go," *Fortune* (January 12, 2004), p. 52ff.

CHAPTER 5

1. "This Volvo Is Not a Guy Thing," *BusinessWeek,* March 15, 2004, pp. 84–86; and "Volvo for Wife," www.forbes.com, downloaded April 1, 2004.

2. Roger D. Blackwell, Paul W. Miniard, and James F. Engel, *Consumer Behavior,* 9th ed. (Mason, OH: South-Western Publishing, 2001).

3. For thorough descriptions of consumer expertise, see Joseph W. Alba and J. Wesley Hutchinson, "Knowledge Calibration: What Consumers Know and What They Think They Know," *Journal of Consumer Research* (September 2000), pp. 123–57.

4. For in-depth studies on external information search patterns, see Sridhar Moorthy, Brian T. Ratchford, and Debabrata Tulukdar, "Consumer Information Search Revisited: Theory and Empirical Analysis," *Journal of Consumer Research* (March 1997), pp. 263–77; Joel E. Urbany, Peter R. Dickson, and William L. Wilkie, "Buyer Uncertainty and Information Search," *Journal of Consumer Research* (March 1992), pp. 452–63.

5. Samson Okalow, "Marketers Retool Sites to Exploit Web Research Boom," *Strategy Magazine* (May 3, 2004), p. 11.

6. For an extended discussion on evaluative criteria, see Del J. Hawkins, Roger J. Best, and Kenneth A. Coney, *Consumer Behavior,* 9th ed. (Burr Ridge, IL: McGraw-Hill/Irwin, 2004), pp. 562–79.

7. John A. Howard, *Buyer Behavior in Marketing Strategy,* 2nd ed. (Englewood Cliffs, NJ: Prentice Hall, 1994), pp. 101, 128–89. For an extended discussion on consumer choice sets, see Allan D. Shocker, Moshe Ben-Akiva, Bruno Boccara, and Prakesh Nedungadi, "Consideration Set Influences on Consumer Decision Making and Choice: Issues, Models, and Suggestions." *Marketing Letters* (August 1991), pp. 181–98.

8. William J. McDonald, "Time Use in Shopping: The Role of Personal Characteristics," *Journal of Retailing* (Winter 1994, pp. 345–66; Robert J. Donovan, John R. Rossiter, Gillian Marcoolyn, and Andrew Nesdale, "Store Atmosphere and Purchasing Behavior," *Journal of Retailing* (Fall 1994), pp. 283–94; and Eric A. Greenleaf and Donald R. Lehman, "Reasons for Substantial Delay in Consumer Decision Making," *Journal of Consumer Research* (September 1995), pp. 186–99.

9. Ruth N. Bolton, "A Dynamic Model of the Duration of the Customer's Relationship with a Continuous Service Provider: The Role of Satisfaction," *Marketing Science* 17 (1998), pp. 45–65.

10. Jagdish N. Sheth, Banwari Mitral, and Bruce Newman, *Consumer Behavior* (Fort Worth: Dryden Press, 1999), p. 22.

11. Frederick F. Reichheld and Thomas Teal, *The Loyalty Effect* (Boston: Harvard Business School Press, 1996); "What's a Loyal Customer Worth?" *Fortune* (December 11, 1995), p. 182; and Patricia Sellers, "Keeping the Buyers You Already Have," *Fortune* (Autumn–Winter 1993), p. 57. For an in-depth examination of this topic, see Werner J. Reinartz and V. Kumar, "On the Profitability of Long-Life Customers in a Noncontractual Setting: An Empirical Investigation and Implications for Marketing," *Journal of Marketing* (October 2000), pp. 17–35.

12. For an overview of research on involvement, see John C. Mowen and Michael Minor, *Consumer Behavior,* 5th ed. (Upper Saddle River, NJ: Prentice Hall, 1998), pp. 64–68; and Wayne D. Hoyer and Deborah J. MacInnis, *Consumer Behavior,* 3rd ed. (Boston: Houghton Mifflin Co., 2004), pp. 57–59.

13. For an overview on the three problem-solving variations, see Hawkins, Best, and Coney, *Consumer Behavior,* pp. 500–04.

14. Russell Belk, "Situational Variables and Consumer Behavior," *Journal of Consumer Research* (December 1975), pp. 157–63.

15. A.H. Maslow, *Motivation and Personality* (New York: Harper & Row, 1970). Also see Richard Yalch and Frederic Brunel, "Need Hierarchies in Consumer Judgments of Product Design: Is It Time to Reconsider Maslow's Hierarchy?" in Kim Corfman and John Lynch, eds., *Advances in Consumer Research* (Provo, UT: Association for Consumer Research, 1996), pp. 405–10.

16. Joel B. Cohen, "An Interpersonal Orientation to the Study of Consumer Behavior," *Journal of Marketing Research* (August 1967), pp. 270–78; and Rena Bartos, *Marketing to Women around the World* (Cambridge, MA: Harvard Business School, 1989).

17. Terry Clark, "International Marketing and National Character: A Review and Proposal for an Integrative Theory," *Journal of Marketing* (October 1990), pp. 66–79; and John-Benedict E. M. Steenkamp, "The Role of National Culture in International Marketing Research," *International Marketing Review* 18, no. 1 (2001), pp. 30–44.

18. Myron Magnet, "Let's Go for Growth," *Fortune* (March 7, 1994), p. 70.

19. This example provided in Michael R. Solomon, *Consumer Behavior,* 4th ed. (Upper Saddle River, NJ: Prentice Hall, 1999), p. 59.

20. For further reading on subliminal perception, see Anthony G. Greenwald, Sean C. Draine, and Richard L. Abrams, "Three Cognitive Markers of Unconscious Semantic Activation," *Science* (September 1996), pp. 1699–701; Dennis L. Rosen and Surendra N. Singh, "An Investigation of Subliminal Embedded Effect on Multiple Measures of Advertising Effectiveness," *Psychology & Marketing* (March–April 1992), pp. 157–73; and Kathryn T. Theus, "Subliminal Advertising and the Psychology of Processing Unconscious Stimuli: A Review of the Research," *Psychology & Marketing* (May–June 1994), pp. 271–90.

21. August Bullock, *The Secret Sales Pitch* (San Jose, CA: Norwich Publishers, 2004); "GOP Commercial Resurrects Debate on Subliminal Ads," *The Wall Street Journal* (September 13, 2000), p. B10; "I Will Love This Story," *U.S. News & World Report* (May 12, 1997), p. 12; and "Firm Gets Message Out Subliminally," *Dallas Morning News* (February 2, 1997), pp. 1H, 6H.

22. "CPG Brand Loyalty Is up for Grabs," www.forrester.com, downloaded December 2002; and "Customer Loyalty: Going, Going . . . ," *American Demographics* (September 1997), pp. 20–23.

23. Martin Fishbein and I. Aizen, *Belief, Attitude, Intention and Behavior: An Introduction to Theory and Research* (Reading, MA: Addison-Wesley 1975), p. 6.

24. Richard J. Lutz, "Changing Brand Attitudes through Modification of Cognitive Structure," *Journal of Consumer Research* (March 1975), pp. 49–59. See also Mowen and Minor, *Consumer Behavior,* pp. 287–88.

25. www.mbgoldfarb.com (downloaded January 25, 2005).

26. This discussion is based on Ed Keller and Jon Berry, *The Influentials* (New York: Simon and Schuster, 2003).

27. "Word of Mouth Is Where It's At," *BrandWeek* (June 2, 2003), p. 26; F.G. Crane and T.K. Clarke, "The Identification of Evaluative Criteria and Cues Used in Selecting Services," *Journal of Services Marketing* (Spring 1988), pp. 53–59.

28. Lyn Fletcher, "The Buzz on Buzz," *Marketing Magazine* (August 23, 2004); Susanne Boyce, "Cooking with Gas," *Marketing Magazine* (May 10, 2004), www.marketingmag.ca (downloaded June 10, 2005); and Linda Tischler, "What's the Buzz," *Fast Company* (May 2004), pp. 76–77.

29. For an extensive review on consumer socialization of children, see Deborah Roedder John, "Consumer Socialization of Children: A Retrospective Look at Twenty-Five Years of Research," *Journal of Consumer Research* (December 1999), pp. 183–213.

30. "Get 'Em While They're Young," *Marketing News* (November 10, 1997), p. 2.

31. This discussion is based on "Marriage Drain's Big Cost," *American Demographics* (April 2004), pp. 40–41; James Morrow, "A Place for One," *American Demographics* (November 2003), pp. 25–31; and J. Paul Peter and Jerry C. Olson, *Consumer Behavior and Marketing Strategy*, 7th ed. (Burr Ridge, IL: McGraw Hill/Irwin, 2005), pp. 342–44.

32. "Co-Masters of Their Domain," *BrandWeek* (September 8, 2003), p. 20; and "Tailor-Made," *Advertising Age* (September 23, 2002), p. 14.

33. "He's in Fashion," *American Demographics* (November 2002), p. 10; and "Look Who's Shopping," *Progressive Grocer* (January 2001), p. 18.

34. "Kids Gaining Voice in How Home Looks," *Advertising Age* (March 29, 2004), p. S4; "Coming of Age in Consumerdom," *American Demographics* (April 2004), p. 14; and www.teenresearch.com (downloaded January 15, 2004).

35. Harold R. Kerbo, *Social Stratification and Inequality* (Burr Ridge, IL: McGraw-Hill, 2000). For an extensive discussion on social class, see Eric Arnould, Linda Price, and George Zinkhan, *Consumers,* 2nd ed. (Burr Ridge, IL: McGraw Hill/Irwin, 2004), chap. 6.

36. Jason Gondziolo, "If You're Happy and You Know It, You're Canadian," *The New Canadian Magazine* (January/February 2004), pp. 42–44; and "Proof You're Canadian," *The New Canadian Magazine* (January/February 2004), p. 64.

37. Astrid Van Den Broek, "Fighting Cultural Fade," *Strategy Magazine* (February 11, 2004), p. 21.

38. Adapted from Eric Blais, "The 36 Keys of the Quebecois Revisited," *Marketing Magazine* (November 2004). With statistics cited coming from the following sources: *Creative Research International,* "The Yankelovich Monitor in Canada, 1998"; *Goldfarb Consultants* for Bank of Nova Scotia, in *The Globe and Mail* (December 19, 1996); *Ipsos-Reid,* "2nd Annual Tainted Love Poll," January 2003, "A Reader's Digest Poll: Marriage in Canada," March 2003, "God and Other Mysteries: A look into the religious and spiritual beliefs of Canadians," November 2003; *Leger Marketing:* "Canadian Perceptions of Homosexuality," June 2001, "How Canadians Perceive Euthanasia," June 2001, "A Study of How Canadians Perceive Canada–U.S. Relations," August 2001, "Canadians and Advertising," October 2001, "Canadians and Canada," March 2002, "Canadians and Immigration," February 2002, "Canadians and Immorality," January 2002; *PMB 2004,* Two-Year Readership Database. Andrea Zoe Aster, Portals Cozy Up to French Market, *Marketing Magazine* (December 4, 2000); Nicolette Fleming, "The True Meaning of Profitez," *Marketing Magazine* (June 10, 2002); and www.environics.ca, PRIZM_CE (downloaded June 10, 2005).

39. Jo Marney, "Counting Ethnic Canadians In," *Marketing* (June 4, 2001), p. 32.

40. Sara Minogue, "Reaching New Canadians," *Strategy Magazine* (September 22, 2003), p. 16.

The Consumer on the Couch: This case was prepared by Barry Potyondi, Context Inc. Sources: Paco Underhill, *Why We Buy: The Science of Shopping* (New York: Simon and Schuster), 1999; "Retail Trade: Service Industries Overviews Series," *Industry Canada* (March 2001). p. 1 (sales figure from 2000 and employment statistic from 1999); Julie McCann, "Design that makes you buy: the tricks and techniques retailers use to separate you from your money," *National Post Business* (May 2001), pp. 62–68; "Canadian retail ripe for picking, Underhill says: Global competitors are coming, top consultant warns," *Financial Post-National Post* (March 9, 2002), p. FP5; Hollie Shaw, "Space: female shoppers' frontier: buying differences. Women more likely to spend time in an uncluttered store," *Financial Post-National Post* (October 23, 2000), p. C3; Hilary Davidson, "6 ways to sell more. Your one-stop shopping guide to today's best retail business opportunities," *Profit Magazine* (April 2002) (www.profitguide.com/magazine/issues_article.asp?ID=884); ABCNEWS.com, "Chat Transcript: Learning About The Science of Shopping with Paco Underhill." www.abcnews.go.com/onair/DailyNews/chat_990511underhill.html; Elizabeth Razzi, "Retailers' Siren Song. Merchants use psychology to entice you into spending more. Knowing what they know will make you a smarter shopper," *Kiplinger's Personal Finance* (November 2000); (www.kiplinger.com/magazine/archives/2000/November/spending/SHOPPING.html); "Retail anthropologist tracks time and money: Canadian malls 'frumpy'," *Canadian Press Newswire* (June 23, 2000); Scott S. Smith, "Attention, shoppers! Paco Underhill knows what they look at, what they buy and why, so get ready to put a huge dent in the concept of customers' free will," *Entrepreneur* (December 2001) entrepreneur.com/magazines/masegarticle/0,1539,294668.

CHAPTER 6

1. Information provided by Dofasco, Inc. 2005.

2. Statistics Canada, www.statcan.ca, CANSIM, 304-0014, January 3, 2005.

3. Statistics Canada, www.statcan.ca, CANSIM, 380-0002 and 13-001 XIB, January 3, 2005.

4. http://stds.statcan.ca/english/naics/2002/naics02-title-search.asp?criteria=51 (downloaded January 10, 2005).

5. An argument that consumer buying and organizational buying do not have important differences is found in Edward F. Fern and James R. Brown, "The Industrial/Consumer Marketing Dichotomy: A Case of Insufficient Justification," *Journal of Marketing* (Spring 1984), pp. 68–77. However, most writers on the subject do draw distinctions between the two types of buying. See, for example, Michael D. Hutt and Thomas W. Speh, *Business Marketing Management,* 7th ed. (Fort Worth, TX: Dryden Press, 2001); and H. Michael Hayes, Per V. Jenster, and Nils-Erik Aaby, *Business Marketing: A Global Perspective* (Chicago: Richard D. Irwin, 1996).

6. This listing and portions of the following discussion are based on F. Robert Dwyer and John F. Tanner, Jr., *Business Marketing,* 2nd ed. (Burr Ridge, IL: McGraw-Hill/Irwin, 2002; Edward G. Brierty, Robert W. Eckles, and Robert R. Reeder, *Business Marketing,* 3rd ed. (Upper Saddle River, NJ: Prentice Hall, 1998); Frank G. Bingham, Jr., *Business Marketing Management* (Lincolnwood, IL: NTC, 1998).

7. F. Robert Dwyer and John Tanner, *Business Marketing* (Burr Ridge, ILL: McGraw-Hill, 2002).

8. "Latin Trade Connection," *Latin Trade* (June 1997), p. 72.

9. "Boise Cascade Turns Green," *The Wall Street Journal* (September 3, 2003), p. B6.

10. For a study of buying criteria used by industrial firms, see Daniel H. McQuiston and Rockney G, Walters, "The Evaluative Criteria of Industrial Buyers: Implications for Sales Training," *Journal of*

Business & Industrial Marketing (Summer/Fall 1989), pp. 65–75. See also "What Buyers Look For," *Sales & Marketing Management* (August 1995), p. 31.

11. For an overview on ISO 9000 certification, see Thomas H. Stevenson and Frank C. Barnes, "What Industrial Marketers Need to Know about ISO 9000 Certification: A Review, Update, and Integration with Marketing," *Industrial Marketing Management* (November 2002), pp. 695–703.

12. Michael R. Leenders and David L. Blenkhorn, *Reverse Marketing: The New Buyer-Supplier Relationship* (New York: Free Press, 1996).

13. This example is found in Sandy D. Jap and Jakki J. Mohr, "Leverage Internet Technologies in B2B Relationships," *California Management Review* (Summer 2002), pp. 24–38.

14. "Harley-Davidson Company," *Purchasing Magazine Online* (September 4, 2003).

15. "IBM Plans New Supercomputers," *Dallas Morning News* (November 19, 2002), p. 8D.

16. www.ibm.com/procurement/html/principles_practices (downloaded March 10, 2004); and Hayes, Jenster, and Aaby, *Business Marketing: A Global Perspective.*

17. Pratibha A. Dabholkar, Wesley J. Johnston, and Amy S. Cathey, "The Dynamics of Long-Term Business-to-Business Exchange Relationships," *Journal of Academy of Marketing Science*, vol. 22, 2 (1994), pp. 130–45.

18. www.internationaldelivers.com/news_room, April 26, 2002.

19. James C. Anderson and James A. Narus, *Business Market Management* (Upper Saddle River, NJ: Prentice Hall, 1999); and Neil Rackham, Lawrence Friedman and Richard Ruff, *Getting Partnering Right* (New York: McGraw-Hill, 1996); and Joseph P. Cannon and Christian Homburg, "Buyer-Supplier Relationships and Customer Firm Costs, *Journal of Marketing* (January 2001), pp. 29–43.

20. Thomas V. Bonoma, "Major Sales: Who Really Does the Buying?" *Harvard Business Review* (May–June 1982), pp. 11–19. For recent research on buying centres, see Morry Ghinghold and David T. Wilson, "Buying Center Research and Business Marketing Practices: Meeting the Challenge of Dynamic Marketing," *Journal of Business & Industrial Marketing*, vol. 13, no. 2 (1998), pp. 96–108; and Philip L. Dawes, Don Y. Lee, and Grahame R. Dowling, "Information Control and Influence in Emerging Buying Centers," *Journal of Marketing* (July 1998), pp. 55–68.

21. Paul A. Herbig, *Handbook of Cross-Cultural Marketing* (New York: The Halworth Press, 1998).

22. Jule M. Bristor, "Influence Strategies in Organizational Buying: The Importance of Connections to the Right People in the Right Places," *Journal of Business-to-Business Marketing*, vol. 1 (1993), pp. 63–98.

23. These definitions are adapted from Frederick E. Webster, Jr., and Yoram Wind, *Organizational Buying Behavior* (Englewood Cliffs, NJ: Prentice Hall, 1972), p. 6.

24. "Can Corning Find Its Optic Nerve?" *Fortune* (March 19, 2001), pp. 148–50.

25. Representative studies on the buy-class framework that document its usefulness include Erin Anderson, Wujin Chu, and Barton Weitz, "Industrial Purchasing: An Empirical Exploration of the Buy-Class Framework," *Journal of Marketing* (July 1987), pp. 71–86; Morry Ghingold, "Testing the 'Buy-Grid' Buying Process Model," *Journal of Purchasing and Materials Management* (Winter 1986), pp. 30–36; P. Matthyssens and W. Faes, "OEM Buying Process for New Components: Purchasing and Marketing Implications," *Industrial Marketing Management* (August 1985), pp. 145–57; and Thomas W. Leigh and Arno J. Ethans, "A Script-Theoretic Analysis of Industrial Purchasing Behavior," *Journal of Marketing* (Fall 1984), pp. 22–32. Studies not supporting the buy-class framework include Joseph A. Belizzi and Philip McVey, "How Valid Is the

Buy-Grid Model?" *Industrial Marketing Management* (February 1983), pp. 57–62; and Donald W. Jackson, Janet E. Keith, and Richard K. Burdick, "Purchasing Agents' Perceptions of Industrial Buying Center Influences: A Situational Approach," *Journal of Marketing* (Fall 1984), pp. 75–83.

26. See, for example, R. Vekatesh, Ajay Kohli, and Gerald Zaltman, "Influence Strategies in Buying Centers," *Journal of Marketing* (October 1995), pp. 61–72; Gary L. Lilien and Anthony Wong, "An Exploratory Investigation of the Structure of the Buying Center in the Metal Working Industry," *Journal of Marketing Research* (February 1984), pp. 1–11; and Wesley J. Johnston and Thomas V. Bonoma, "The Buying Center: Structure and Interaction Patterns," *Journal of Marketing* (Summer 1981), pp. 143–56. See also, Christopher P. Puto, Wesley E. Patton III, and Ronald H. King, "Risk Handling Strategies in Industrial Vendor Selection Decisions," *Journal of Marketing* (Winter 1985), pp. 89–98.

27. "B2B E-Commerce Headed for Trillions," www.clickz.com (downloaded March 1, 2004).

28. This discussion is based on Jennifer Reinhold, "What We Learned in the New Economy," *Fast Company* (March 4, 2004), pp. 56ff; Mark Roberti, "General Electric's Spin Machine," *The Industry Standard* (January 22–29, 2001), pp. 74–83; "Grainger Lightens Its Digital Load," *Industrial Distribution* (March 2001), pp. 77–79; and www.boeing.com/procurement (downloaded February 6, 2004).

29. "B2B, Take 2," *Business Week Online* (November 25, 2003).

30. Mark Krauss, "EBay `Bids' on Small-Biz Firms to Sustain Growth," *Marketing News* (December 8, 2002), pp. 6, 7; "Ebay Realizes Success in Small-Biz Arena," *Marketing News* (May 1, 2004), p. 11; and www.ebaybusiness.com.

31. This discussion is based on Robert J. Dolan and Youngme Moon, "Pricing and Market Making on the Internet," *Journal of Interactive Marketing* (Spring 2000), pp. 56–73; and Ajit Kambil and Eric van Heck, *Marking Markets: How Firms Can Benefit from Online Auctions and Exchanges* (Boston: Harvard Business School Press, 2002.)

32. Sandy Jap, "An Exploratory Study of the Introduction of Online Reverse Auctions," *Journal of Marketing* (July 2003), pp. 96–107. Lands' End: This case is based on information available on the company Website (www.landsend.com) and the following sources: Robert Berner, "A Hard Bargain at Lands' End?" *Business Week* (May 28, 2001), p. 14; Rebecca Quick, "Getting the Right Fit—Hips and All—Can a Machine Measure You Better Than Your Tailor?" *The Wall Street Journal* (October 18, 2000), p. B1; Stephanie Miles, "Apparel E-tailers Spruce Up for Holidays," *The Wall Street Journal* (November 6, 2001), p. B6; Dana James, "Custom Goods Nice Means for Lands' End," *Marketing News* (August 14, 2000), p. 5.

Lands' End: This case is based on information available on the company website (www.landsend.com) and the following sources: Robert Berner, "A Hard Bargain at Lands' End?" *BusinessWeek,* May 28, 2001, p. 14; Rebecca Quick, "Getting the Right Fit—Hips and All—Can a Machine Measure You Better than Your Tailor?" *The Wall Street Journal,* October 18, 2000, p. B1; Stephanie Miles, "Apparel E-tailers Spruce Up for Holidays," *The Wall Street Journal,* November 6, 2001, p. B6; and Dana James, "Custom Goods Nice Means for Lands' End," *Marketing News,* August 14, 2000, p. 5.

CHAPTER 7

1. Lisa Bannon and Carlta Vitzthum, "One-Toy-Fits-All: How Industry Learned to Love the Global Kid," *The Wall Street Journal* (April 29, 2003), pp. A1, A4; "Mattel, Inc.," *Hoover's Online,* www.hoovers.com (downloaded March 25, 2004); and "Mattel Recharges Its Batteries," *NYSE Magazine,* www.nyse.com (downloaded July 3, 2003).

2. These estimates are based on data from *International Trade Statistics 2004* (Geneva: World Trade Organization). Global trade statistics reported in this chapter also came from this source, unless otherwise indicated.

3. Masaaki Kotabe and Kristiaan Helsen, *Global Marketing Management,* 3rd ed. (New York: Wiley, 2004), p. 440.

4. "Bartering Gains Currency in Hard-Hit Southeast Asia," *The Wall Street Journal* (April 6, 1998), p. A10; and Beatrice B. Lund, "Corporate Barter as a Marketing Strategy," *Marketing News* (March 3, 1997), p. 8.

5. Statistics in this section were derived from Statistics Canada, CANSIM 228-0003.

6. Michael E. Porter, *The Competitive Advantage of Nations* (New York: Free Press, 1990), pp. 577–615. For another view that emphasizes cultural differences, see David S. Landes, *The Wealth and Poverty of Nations* (New York: Norton, 1998).

7. Roger L. Martin and Michael E. Porter, "Canadian Competitiveness: Nine Years After the Crossroads."

8. Dennis R. Appleyard and Alfred J. Field, Jr., *International Economics,* 4th ed. (Burr Ridge, IL: McGraw-Hill/Irwin, 2001), chap. 15; "A Fruit Peace," *The Economist* (April 21, 2001), pp. 75–76; and Gary C. Hufbauer and Kimberly A. Elliott, *Measuring the Cost of Protection in the United States* (Washington, DC: Institute for International Economics, 1994).

9. This discussion is based on information provided by the World Trade Organization, www.wto.org (downloaded March 17, 2004).

10. "A Survey of EU Enlargement," *The Economist* (November 22, 2003), special section.

11. "Free Trade on Trial," *The Economist* (January 3, 2004), pp. 13–15.

12. www.juniper.net/company (downloaded March 15, 2004); and "Alliances in Consumer and Packaged Goods," www.corporate finance.mckinsey.com (downloaded Autumn 2003).

13. For an excellent overview of different types of global companies and marketing strategies, see Warren J. Keegan, *Global Marketing Management,* 7th ed. (Upper Saddle River, NJ: Prentice Hall, 2002), chap. 2.

14. Johnny K. Johansson and Ilkka A. Ronkainen, "The Brand Challenge," *Marketing Management* (March–April 2004), pp. 54–55.

15. Kevin Lane Keller, *Strategic Brand Management,* 2nd ed. (Upper Saddle River, NJ: Prentice Hall, 2003), p. 693.

16. "Golden Boys and Girls," *The Economist,* February 14, 2004, pp. 37–38; Elissa Moses, *The $100 Billion Allowance: Accessing the Global Teen Market* (New York: Wiley, 2000); and www.mtv.com/company (downloaded March 22, 2004).

17. For an extensive discussion on identifying global consumers, see Jean-Pierre Jeannet and H. David Hennessey, *Global Marketing Strategies,* 4th ed. (Boston: Houghton Mifflin, 1998).

18. "The Net's Second Superpower," *BusinessWeek* (March 15, 2004), pp. 54–56; "B2B E-Commerce Headed for Trillions," www.clickz.com (downloaded March 27, 2004); and "EU B2B Expected to Explode," www.clickz.com (downloaded March 27, 2004).

19. For comprehensive references on cross-cultural aspects of marketing, see Paul A. Herbig, *Handbook of Cross-Cultural Marketing* (New York: Halworth Press, 1998); Jean-Claude Usunier, *Marketing across Cultures,* 2nd ed. (London: Prentice Hall Europe, 1996); and Philip R. Cateora and John L. Graham, *International Marketing,* 12th ed. (Burr Ridge, IL: McGraw-Hill/Irwin, 2005). Unless otherwise indicated, examples found in this section appear in these excellent sources.

20. "Clash of Cultures," *BrandWeek* (May 4, 1998), p. 28. Also see R. L. Tung, *Business Negotiations with the Japanese* (Lexington, MA: Lexington Books, 1993).

21. These examples appear in Del I. Hawkins, Roger J. Best, and Kenneth A. Coney, *Consumer Behavior,* 9th ed. (Burr Ridge, IL: McGraw-Hill/Irwin, 2004), chap. 2.

22. "Greens Protest Coke's Use of Parthenon," *Dallas Morning News* (August 17, 1992), p. D4.

23. "Japanese Products are Popular in the U.S.," *Research Alert* (November 17, 2000), p. 8; and "Buying American," *American Demographics* (March 1998), pp. 32–38; and Sharon Younger, "Marketing Overseas? Keep it Canadian," *Strategy Magazine* (February 11, 2002), p. 23.

24. "Marketing by Language: Oracle Trims Teams, Sees Big Savings," *Advertising Age International* (July 2000), pp. 4, 38.

25. Terrence A. Shimp and Subhash Sharma, "Consumer Ethnocentrism, Construction and Validation of the CETSCALE," *Journal of Marketing Research* (August 1987), pp. 280–89.

26. Subhash Sharma, Terrence Shimp, and Jeongshin Shin, "Consumer Ethnocentrism: A Test of Antecedents and Moderators," *Journal of the Academy of Marketing Science* (Winter 1995), pp. 26–37; Joel Herche, "A Note on the Predictive Validity of the CETSCALE," *Journal of the Academy of Marketing Science* (Summer 1992), pp. 261–64; Richard G. Netemeyer, Srinivas Durvasula, and Donald R. Lichtenstein, "A Cross-National Assessment of the Reliability and Validity of the CETSCALE," *Journal of Marketing Research* (August 1991), pp. 320–27; and Jill Gabrielle Klein, Richard Ettenson, and Marlene D. Morris, "The Animosity Model of Foreign Product Purchase: An Empirical Test in the People's Republic of China," *Journal of Marketing* (January 1998), pp. 89–100.

27. "The Net's Second Superpower," *BusinessWeek.*

28. "Betting on a New Label: Made in Russia," *BusinessWeek* (April 12, 1999), p. 122; "Russia and Central-Eastern Europe: Worlds Apart," *BrandWeek* (May 4, 1998), pp. 30–31; and "We Will Bury You . . . with a Snickers Bar," *U.S. News & World Report* (January 26, 1998), pp. 50–51.

29. www.wto.com (downloaded February 15, 2004).

30. "Mattel Plans to Double Sales Abroad," *The Wall Street Journal* (February 11, 1998), pp. A3, A11.

31. Cateora and Graham, *International Marketing.*

32. For an extensive and recent examination of these market entry options, see, for example, Johnny K. Johansson, *Global Marketing: Foreign Entry, Local Marketing, and Global Management,* 3rd ed. (Burr Ridge, IL: McGraw Hill/Irwin, 2003); Keegan, *Global Marketing Management;* Kotabe and Helson, *Global Marketing Management;* and Cateora and Graham, *International Marketing.*

33. *McDonald's 2003 Annual Report.*

34. "A Survey of Business in China," *The Economist* (March 20, 2004), special section.

35. This discussion is based on Keller, *Strategic Brand Management,* pp. 709–10; "Machines for the Masses," *The Wall Street Journal* (December 9, 2003), pp. A19, A20; "The Color of Beauty," *Forbes* (November 22, 2000), pp. 170–76; "It's Goo, Goo, Goo, Goo Vibrations at the Gerber Lab," *The Wall Street Journal* (December 4, 1996), pp. A1, A6; Donald R. Graber, "How to Manage a Global Product Development Process," *Industrial Marketing Management* (November 1996), pp. 483–98; and Herbig, *Handbook of Cross-Cultural Marketing.*

36. Jagdish N. Sheth and Atul Parvatiyar, "The Antecedents and Consequences of Integrated Global Marketing," *International Marketing Review* 18, no. 1 (2001), pp. 16–29. Also see D. Szymanski, S. Bharadwaj, and R. Varadarajan, "Standardization versus Adaptation of International Marketing Strategy: An Empirical Investigation," *Journal of Marketing* (October 1993), pp. 1–17.

37. This discussion is based on John Fahy and Fuyuki Taguchi, "Reassessing the Japanese Distribution System," *Sloan Management Review* (Winter 1995), pp. 49–61; and Edward Tse, "The Right Way to Achieve Profitable Growth in the Chinese Consumer Market," *Strategy & Business* (Second Quarter 1998), pp. 10–21.

38. "Stores Told to Lift Prices in Germany," *The Wall Street Journal* (September 11, 2000), pp. A27, A30.

CNS Breathe Right Strips: This case was prepared by Mary L. Brown based on interviews with Kevin McKenna, vice president, International and Nick Naumann, Sr. Marketing Services Manager of CNS, Inc., September 2004.

CHAPTER 8

1. John Horn, "Studios Play Name Games," *Star Tribune* (August 10, 1997), p. F11; and "Flunking Chemistry," *Star Tribune* (April 11, 2003), p. E13.

2. *2000 US Economic Review*, Worldwide Market Research Department, Motion Picture Association of America, pp. 14, 16.

3. Bruce Orwall, "'Commander' Finds Wind in Its Sails," *The Wall Street Journal* (November 17, 2003), p. B10.

4. "Spider-Man 2," www.boxofficemojo.com (downloaded July 31, 2004).

5. Willow Bay, "Test Audiences Have Profound Effect on Movies," *CNN Newsstand & Entertainment Weekly* (September 28, 1998); see www.cnn.com/SHOWBIZ/Movies/9809/28/screen.test/.

6. Thomas R. King, "How Big Will Disney's 'Pocahontas' Be?" *The Wall Street Journal* (May 15, 1995), pp. B1, B8.

7. Helene Diamond, "Lights, Camera . . . Research!" *Marketing News* (September 11, 1989), pp. 10–11; and "Killer!" *Time* (November 16, 1987), pp. 72–79.

8. Joel Ryan, "Gigli 'Razzed'," att.eonline.com/News/Items (downloaded January 26, 2004).

9. Carl Diorio, "Tracking Projectings: B. O. Calculations an Inexact Science," *Variety* (May 24, 2001); see www.variety.com/index.asp?layout=story&articleid=VR1117799996.

10. For a lengthier, expanded 2004 definition, consult the American Marketing Association's website at www.marketingpower.com; for a researcher's comments on this and other definitions of marketing research, see Lawrence D. Gibson, "Quo Vadis, Marketing Research?" *Marketing Research* (Spring 2000), pp. 36–41.

11. Joseph Pereira, "Unknown Fruit Takes on Unfamiliar Markets," *The Wall Street Journal* (September 9, 1995), pp. B1, B5.

12. Lisa D'Innocenzo, "Focus Groups for a New Age," *Strategy Magazine* (August 23, 2004), p. 10.

13. "Focus on Consumers," *General Mills Midyear Report* (Minneapolis, MN: General Mills, January 8, 1998), pp. 2–3.

14. Michael J. McCarthy, "Stalking the Elusive Teenage Trendsetter," *The Wall Street Journal* (November 19, 1998), pp. B1, B10.

15. Roy Furchgott, "For Cool Hunters, Tomorrow's Trend is the Trophy," *The New York Times* (June 28, 1998), p. 10; and Lev Grossman, "The Quest for Cool," *Time* (September 8, 2003), pp. 48–54.

16. Joshua Grossnickle and Oliver Raskin, "What's Ahead on the Internet," *Marketing Research* (Summer 2001), pp. 9–13.

17. Patti Summerfield, "Will PPMs Mean Higher Rates, " *Strategy Magazine* (February 9, 2004), p. 2.

18. Mark Maremont, "New Toothbrush Is Big-Ticket Item," *The Wall Street Journal* (October 27, 1998), pp. B1, B6; Emily Nelson, "P&G Checks Out Real Life," *The Wall Street Journal* (May 17, 2001), pp. B1, B4.

19. Gerry Khermouch, "Consumers in the Mist," *Business Week* (February 26, 2001), pp. 92, 94.

20. Dina Elboghdady, "Naked Truth," *Portland Press* (March 5, 2002), pp. C1, C5.

21. www. Mria-arim.ca; and www.pmrs-aprm.com (downloaded, June 11, 2005).

22. Patrick E. Murphy and Gene R. Lacznick, *Marketing Ethics: Cases and Readings* (Upper Saddle River, NJ: Pearson Education, 2006).

23. www. Mria-arim.ca; and www.pmrs-aprm.com (downloaded, June 11, 2005).

Ford Consulting Group, Inc.: This Video Case was written by David Ford.

CHAPTER 9

1. Joseph Pereira and Stephanie Kang, "Phat News: Rappers Choose Reebok Shoes," *The Wall Street Journal* (November 14, 2003), pp. B1, B4.

2. Ibid., p. B4.

3. Stanley Holmes, "The New Nike," *BusinessWeek* (September 20, 2004), pp. 78–86; and Tim Gray, "The Bounce Is Back for Sneaker Manufacturers," *The New York Times* (May 23, 2004), p. BU8.

4. Material on sneakers is based on the SGMA Report 2002, "The U.S. Athletic Footwear Market Today," which is published annually by the Sporting Goods Manufacturers Association (www.sgma.com) based on a study by the NPD Group (www.npd.com), which polls 35 000 consumers weekly and collects data from over 3500 retailers to provide this information; and April Y. Pennington "Heeling Art," *Entrepreneur Magazine* (May 2002), www.entrepreneur.com.

5. Information obtained from press releases from www.reebok.com, www.nike.com, www.vans.com, www.footlocker-inc.com, and www.cmax.com, as well as Terry Lefton, "Mike Likes Spite for Nike's New Jordan Line," *Business Journal—Portland* (July 29, 2002), www. portland.bizjournals.com.

6. Jeffrey A. Trachtenberg, "Magic Numbers," *Star Tribune* (June 17, 2003), pp. E1, E3.

7. David Leohnardt, "Two-Tier Marketing," *BusinessWeek* (March 17, 1997), pp. 82–90.

8. "Special Report on Mass Customization: A Long March," *The Economist* (July 14, 2001), pp. 63–65.

9. Patti Summerfield, "The Death of Demographics," *Strategy Magazine* (October 20, 2003).

10. These examples were supplied by Millward Brown Golfarb, 2005.

11. The discussion of fast-food trends and market share is based on: *National Consumer Survey© Choices 3 Crosstabulation Report: Fast-Food Restaurants* (New York: Simmons Market Research Bureau, Inc., Spring 2001).

12. Del J. Hawkins, Roger J. Best, and Kenneth A. Coney, *Consumer Behavior*, 9th ed (Burr Ridge, IL: McGraw-Hill/Irwin, 2004).

13. The discussion of Apple's segmentation strategies through the years is based on information from its Web site, www.apple-history.com/history.html.

14. Dennis Sellers, "Business Journal: Digital Hub Plan Just Might Work," *MacCentral* (January 16, 2001), Mac Publishing, LLC.

15. "The iPod's Big Brother," *BusinessWeek* (September 13, 2004), p. 46.

16. Nicholas Zamiska, "How Milk Got a Major Boost by Food Panel," *The Wall Street Journal* (August 30, 2004), pp. B1, B5.

17. Betsey McKay, "Mooove Over, Milkman," *The Wall Street Journal* (June 9, 2003), pp. B1, B5.

18. Ibid.

19. Rebecca Winters, "Chocolate Milk," *Time* (April 30, 2001), p. 20.

20. Lisa McLaughlin, "This Moo's For You," *Time* (September 22, 2003), p. 77.

21. Patricia R. Olsen, "Adding Fizz to the Dairy Case," *The New York Times* (November 2, 2003), p. BU1.

22. Mark A. Moon, John T. Mentzer, Carlo D. Smith, and Michael S. Garver, "Seven Keys to Better Forecasting," *Business Horizons* (September–October 1998), pp. 44–52.

23. Interview with Bill McKee, manager of Corporate Communications/Public Relations, Xerox Corporation, and annual reports available at www2.xerox.com/go/xix/about_xerox/T_archive.jsp?view=annualreports.

24. Cybersurf Corp. Homepage. *Cybersurf Announces Sale of High Speed Cable over Shaw Network in Western Canada*. 18 May 2004. (Accessed 4 June 2004.) http://www.cybersurf.net

25. Industry Canada Web site. *Telecommunications Service in Canada: An Industry Overview*. 4 May 2004. (Accessed 4 June 2004.) http://strategis.ic.gc.ca/epic/internet/insmt-gst.nsf/ en/sf06090e.html

26. Industry Canada Website. Internet Usage Increasing in Canada. 9 January 2004. (Accessed 4 June 2004.) http://strategis.ic.gc.ca/epic/internet/inimr-ri.nsf/en/gr107229e.html

Case: Written by Sherry Finney of Cape Breton University.

CHAPTER 10

1. Personal interview with Dr. George Dierberger, 3M (April 2004).
2. Michael Arndt, "3M's Rising Star," *BusinessWeek* (April 12, 2004), pp. 62–74.
3. Press releases from Motorola, Nokia, Samsung, Apple, and PalmOne; "Portable Media Devices: Beyond Music," e-mail newsletter from Jupiter Research (March 10, 2004); "Gartner: Mobile Phone Sales Grow by 20 Percent," *InfoWorld* (March 10, 2004); "Consumers Win as Turf War Rages over TVs, Cameras," *USA Today* (January 8, 2004), pp. B1, B2; and "Telematics: Coming to a Car Near You," *Technology Review*, Web log (April 21, 2004), www.technologyreview.com.
4. Jyoti Thottam, "Plasma's Bright Future," *Time* (April 12, 2004), pp. 42–44.
5. Greg A. Stevens and James Burley, "3,000 Raw Ideas = 1 Commercial Success!" *Research-Technology Management* (May–June 1997), pp. 16–27.
6. R. G. Cooper and E. J. Kleinschmidt, "New Products—What Separates Winners from Losers?" *Journal of Product Innovation Management* (September 1987), pp. 169–84; Robert G. Cooper, *Winning at New Products,* 2nd ed. (Reading, MA: Addison-Wesley, 1993), pp. 49–66; and Thomas D. Kuczmarski, "Measuring Your Return on Innovation," *Marketing Management* (Spring 2000), pp. 25–32.
7. Julie Fortser, "The Lucky Charm of Steve Sanger," *BusinessWeek* (March 26, 2001), pp. 75–76.
8. John Gilbert, "To Sell Cars in Japan, U.S. Needs to Offer More Right-Drive Models," *Star Tribune* (May 27, 1995), p. M1.
9. See Productscan Online at www.productscan.com.
10. Amy Merrick, "As 3M Chief, McNerney Wastes No Time Starting Systems Favored by Ex-Boss Welch," *The Wall Street Journal* (June 5, 2001), pp. B1, B4; see General Electric's Web site (www.ge.com) for an in-depth explanation of Six Sigma that 3M and other Fortune 500 companies use to improve quality: "The Road to Customer Impact: What Is Six Sigma?"
11. Morgan L. Swink and Vincent A. Mabert, "Product Development Partnerships: Balancing Needs of OEMs and Suppliers," *Business Horizons* (May–June 2000), pp. 59–68.
12. C. K. Prahalad and Venkat Ramswamy, *The Future of Competition* (Boston: Harvard Business School Press, 2004); Steve Hamm, "Adding Customers to the Design Team," *BusinessWeek* (March 1, 2004), pp. 22–23.
13. Anthony W. Ulwick, "Turn Customer Input into Innovation" *Harvard Business Review* (January 2002), pp. 91–97.
14. Adam Aston and Gail Edmonson, "This Volvo Is Not a Guy Thing," *BusinessWeek* (March 15, 2004), pp. 84–86.
15. Bruce Nussbaum, "The Power of Design," *BusinessWeek* (May 17, 2004), pp. 86–94; the article gives many techniques for idea and concept generation, as do Appendixes A, B, and C in Merle Crawford and Anthony Di Benedetto, *New Products Management,* 7th ed. (Burr Ridge, IL: McGraw-Hill/Irwin, 2003).
16. Personal interview with David Windorski, 3M (April 2004).
17. Steve Hoeffler, "Measuring Preferences for Really New Products," *Journal of Marketing Research* (November 2003), pp. 406–20.
18. Interview with Susan Graham, Atkins Canada (November 9, 2004).
19. Gray Hammel, "Innovation's New Math," *Fortune* (July 9, 2001), pp. 130–31.
20. Thomas M. Burton, "By Learning from Failures, Lilly Keeps Drug Pipeline Full," *The Wall Street Journal* (April 21, 2004), pp. A1, A12.

21. Danny Hakim, "Change Coming for Car Safety," *Star Tribune* (December 4, 2003), pp. A1, A8; Jayne O'Donnell, "Automakers Plan to Make Trucks Less of a Threat," *USA Today* (November 28, 2003), p. B1; and Dee-Ann Durbin, "Safety Official Softens Stance on SUVs," *Star Tribune* (February 27, 2003), p. A11.
22. Ben Elgin, "Can Google Hit It out of the Park Again?" *BusinessWeek* (April 19, 2004), pp. 38–39.
23. Tom Molson and George Sproles, "Styling Strategy," *Business Horizons* (September–October 2000), pp. 45–52.
24. Yuhong Wu, Sridhar Balasubramanian, and Vijay Mahajan, "When Is a Preannounced New Product Likely to Be Delayed?" *Journal of Marketing* (April, 2004), pp. 101–13.
25. Ben Elgin, "Can HP's Printer Biz Keep Printing Money?" *BusinessWeek* (July 14, 2003), pp. 68–70.
26. Peter Burrows, "Architects of the Info Age," *BusinessWeek* (March 29, 2004), p. 22.

The 3M Griptile Grip Golf Glove video case was written by Michael J. Vessey based on interviews with Dr. George Dierberger, 3M personnel, 3M sources, and other published sources, including: "3M Introduces 3M Golf Glove With Griptile Grip," 3M Press Release, May 5, 2004; "Who We Are," National Golf Foundation. See www.ngf.org; "The Golf 20/20 Vision for the Future Industry Report for 2003, (published June 8, 2004). See www.golf2020.com; "Core Golfers Gain Ground in 2003." National Golf Foundation Press Release (May 21, 2004). See www.ngf.org; National Sporting Goods Association E-mail newsletter (received June 21, 2004). See www.nsga.org; 3M Golf Griptile Grip Business Plan; and Golf Datatech 2003 Retail Market Share Report. See www.golfdatatech.com.

CHAPTER 11

1. Information Supplied by Clearly Canadian Beverage Corporation (January 10, 2005).
2. For an extended discussion of the generalized product life-cycle curve, see David M. Gardner, "Product Life Cycle: A Critical Look at the Literature," in Michael Houston, ed., *Review of Marketing 1987* (Chicago: American Marketing Association, 1987), pp. 162–94; and Donald R. Lehmann and Russell S. Winer, *Product Management,* 4th ed. (Burr Ridge, IL: McGraw-Hall/Irwin, 2005), pp. 261–65.
3. "Gillette Unveils Advertising In Revolutionary New M3 Power Razor." (May 17, 2004), www.gillette.com (downloaded June 20, 2005).
4. Harper W. Boyd, Jr., Orville C. Walker, John Mullins, and Jean-Claude Larréché, *Marketing Management,* 4th ed. (Burr Ridge, IL: McGraw-Hill/Irwin, 2002), p. 444.
5. Portions of this discussion on the fax machine industry are based on "Brother Wins Gamble in Shifting to Faxes," *The Wall Street Journal* (June 24, 2004), p. B6; "When Your Time Has Come—and Gone," *EDN.com* (November 27, 2003); "Electronics: 2003 Market Share Report by Category," *Reed Business Information* (January 8, 2004); and "Atlas Electronics Corporation," in Roger A. Kerin and Robert A. Peterson, *Strategic Marketing Problems: Cases and Comments,* 8th ed. (Upper Saddle River, NJ: Prentice Hall, 1998), pp. 494–506.
6. "Population Explosion" www.clickz.com (downloaded April 24, 2004); and "There's No Replacement—Not Even E-Mail," *Purchasing Online* (downloaded June 15, 2001).
7. "Why Coke Indulges (the Few) Fans of Tab," *The Wall Street Journal* (April 13, 2001), pp. B1, B4.
8. "Gillette Creates a Little Buzz with its New Razor," *Boston.com* (downloaded January 16, 2004).
9. "How to Separate Trends from Fads," *BrandWeek* (October 23, 2000), pp. 30, 32.
10. "More Guns, More Noise: What's Next for Videogames," *The Wall Street Journal* (May 6, 2004), pp. D1, D5; "Worldwide Videogame

Hardware and Software Forecast and Analysis: 2003–2007," *IDC Research* (November 2003); and "Console Wars," *The Economist* (June 22, 2002), pp. 57–58.

11. Everett M. Rogers, *Diffusion of Innovations,* 4th ed. (New York: Free Press, 1995).

12. Jagdish N. Sheth, Banwasi Mitral, and Bruce Newman, *Consumer Behavior* (Fort Worth: Dryden Press, 1999).

13. "When Free Samples Become Saviors," *The Wall Street Journal* (August 14, 2001), pp. B1, B4, and www.marketingmag.ca (March 9, 1998).

14. For a historical perspective on the product/brand manager system, see George S. Low and Ronald A. Fullerton, "Brands, Brand Management, and the Brand Manager System: A Critical-Historical Evaluation," *Journal of Marketing Research* (May 1994), pp. 173–90.

15. "Wrinkle-Stain-Resistant Apparel Boost Sales," *DSN Retailing* (June 9, 2003), pp. 25–26; John Heinzl, "Heinz Squeezes out Purple Ketchup," *The Globe and Mail* (August 7, 2001), p. B8; and "Hurdles on the Road to Hog Heaven," *Business Week* (November 19, 2003), pp. 96–98.

16. "Molson Canada's New Brew First of its Kind to Hit Beer Shelves," www.molson.com/newsroom (downloaded June 6, 2005).

17. "Dried Plum Print Push Paces Prunes," *BrandWeek* (August 12, 2002), p. 6; and "PlayStation 2 Software Update," press release at www.sony.com (downloaded November 15, 2003).

18. www.newbalance.com (downloaded May 6, 2004).

19. "St. Joseph: From Babies to Baby Boomers," *Advertising Age* (July 9, 2001), pp. 1, 38.

20. "Food Marketers Latch on to Health," *Advertising Age* (February 23, 2004), pp. 4, 41; and Daniel Kadlec "The Low Carb Frenzy," *Time* (May 3, 2004), pp. 47–54.

21. "The Shrink Wrap," *Time* (June 2, 2003), p. 81; "Don't Raise the Price, Lower the Water Award," *BrandWeek* (January 8, 2001), p. 19; and "More For Less," *Consumer Reports* (August 2004), p. 63.

22. Matthew Benjamin, "A World of Fakes," *U.S. News & World Report* (July 14, 2003), pp. 46–47.

23. This discussion is based on Kevin Lane Keller, *Strategic Brand Management,* 2nd ed. (Upper Saddle River, NJ: Prentice Hall, 2003).

24. This discussion is based on Kevin Lane Keller, "Building Customer-Based Brand Equity" *Marketing Management* (July–August, 2001), pp. 15–19.

25. Susan Heinrich, "The Leafs Budding Brand," *National Post* (June 4, 2001), p. C4; and Frederick G. Crane and Jeffrey E. Sohl, "Imperatives for Venture Success: Entrepreneurs Speak," *The International Journal of Entrepreneurship and Innovation* (May 2004), pp. 99–106.

26. This discussion is based on John Deighton, "How Snapple Got Its Juice Back," *Harvard Business Review* (January 2002), pp. 47–53; and "Breakfast King Agrees to Sell Bagel Business," *The Wall Street Journal* (September 28, 1999), pp. B1, B6.

27. "Hummer Markets Shoes for Offroad Set," *Advertising Age* (January 12, 2004), pp. 3, 40; Bruce Orwell, "Disney's Magic Transformation?" *The Wall Street Journal* (October 4, 2000), pp. A1, A15; and Keller, *Strategic Brand Management.*

28. Rob Osler, "The Name Game: Tips on How to Get It Right," *Marketing News* (September 14, 1998), p. 50; and Keller, *Strategic Brand Management.* Also see Pamela W. Henderson and Joseph A. Cote, "Guidelines for Selecting or Modifying Logos," *Journal of Marketing* (April 1998), pp. 14–30; and Chiranjeev Kohli and Douglas W. LaBahn, "Creating Effective Brand Names: A Study of the Naming Process," *Journal of Advertising Research* (January–February 1997), pp. 67–75.

29. "When Brand Extension Becomes Brand Abuse," *BrandWeek* (October 26, 1998), pp. 20, 22.

30. For an in-depth discussion on co-branding, see Akshay R. Rao and Robert W. Ruekert, "Brand Alliances as Signals of Product Quality," *Sloan Management Review* (Fall 1994), pp. 87–97.

31. This discussion is based on David Aaker, *Brand Portfolio Strategy* (New York: Free Press, 2004); and "To Lure Older Girls, Mattel Brings in Hip-Hop Crowd," *The Wall Street Journal* (July 18, 2003), pp. A1, A6.

32. "Unilever Finally Pares Down to Core Brands," *Mergers & Acquisitions* (February 2004), pp. 6–9.

33. Matthew Boyle, "Brand Killers," *Fortune* (August 11, 2003), pp. 89–100.

34. "Elizabeth Arden Unveils Wal-Mart Only Brand," *Advertising Age* (February 9, 2004), p. 2; and www.Kodak.com/international (downloaded December 3, 2003).

35. www.pez.com (downloaded May 10, 2004); David Welch, *Collecting Pez* (Murphysboro, IL: Bubba Scrubba Publications, 1995); and "Pez Dispense with Idea It's Just for Kids," *BrandWeek* (September 26, 1996), p. 10.

36. "Just the Facts," *Research Alert* (January 2004), p. 2.

37. "L'eggs Hatches a New Hosiery Package," *BrandWeek* (January 1, 2001), p. 6.

38. "Packaging is the Capper," *Advertising Age* (May 5, 2003), p. 22.

39. Theresa Howard, "Frito-Lay's New Stax to Take a Stand," *USA Today* (August 14, 2003), p. 12B.

40. "Asian Brands Are Sprouting English Logos in Pursuit of Status, International Image," *The Wall Street Journal* (August 7, 2001), p. B7C.

41. Stuart L. Hart, "Beyond Greening: Strategies for a Sustainable World," *Harvard Business Review* (January–February 1997), pp. 66–77; and Ajay Menon and Anil Menon, "Enviropreneurial Marketing Strategy: The Emergence of Corporate Environmentalism as Market Strategy," *Journal of Marketing* (January 1997), pp. 51–67.

BMW: This case was written by Giana Eckhardt and Steven Hartley based on company interviews and the following sources: Claire Billings, "Continuously Building the BMW Brand for 25 Years," *Campaign,* September 24, 2004, p. 16; Larry Armstrong, "BMW's Brand-new 6-series Convertible is Powerful, Elegant, and Eye-catching," *BusinessWeek,* August 9, 2004, p. 73; "BMW Reaches Out To the Affluent Young Urbanites," *Campaign,* July 23, 2004, p. 18; Gail Edmondson, "BMW: Crashing the Compact Market," *BusinessWeek,* June 18, 2004, p. 36; Gail Edmondson, "The Web Smart 50," *BusinessWeek,* November 24, 2003, p. 94; Troy Dreier, "BMW and iPod: Two Exclusive Names That Now Go Well Together," *PC Magazine,* September 21, 2004, p. 176; "Thrill Ride: With Three New BMW Shorts, Fallon Pulls Off Another Creative Coup," *ADWEEK,* October 28, 2002; Scott Donaton, "Cannes Fest Can Recognize Mad + Vine is Not Just a Fad," *Advertising Age,* June 16, 2003, p. 16; and "The New BMW M5," News and Press Release from www.bmwusa.com.

CHAPTER 12

1. "One-of-a-kind Music and Dining Experiences Ready to 'Rock' the Live Music Capital of the World," *PR Newswire* (June 25, 2001); "Hard Rock Café Reveals Its Own Treasures in New Book," *PR Newswire* (June 18, 2001).

2. B. Joseph Pine and James H. Gilmore, *The Experience Economy* (Boston: Harvard Business School Press, 1999); and Lawrence A. Crosby and Sheree L. Johnson, "Manufacturing Experiences: Tapping Emotions Can Create Value for Your Consumers," *Marketing Management* (January-February 2004), p. 12.

3. John E. G. Bateson and Douglas Hoffman, *Managing Services Marketing,* 6th ed. (Fort Worth: Dryden, 2004).

4. Statistics Canada, "Services Indicators," (February 12, 2003); www.statcan.ca (downloaded February 4, 2004); and Hebert G. Grubel and Michael A. Walker, *Services Industry Growth* (Vancouver: The Fraser Institute, 1989).

5. www.cfa.ca (downloaded January 15, 2005).

6. Christopher Lovelock and Evert Gummesson, "Whither Services Marketing?" *Journal of Services Research* 7 (August 2004), pp. 20–41.

7. Christopher Lovelock and Jochen Wirtz, *Services Marketing, 5th ed.* (Upper Saddle River, NJ: Pearson, 2004).

8. Valarie A. Zeithhaml, 'How Consumer Evaluation Processes Differ Between Goods and Services," in James H. Donnelly and William R. Georges, eds., *Marketing of Services* (Chicago, IL; American Marketing Association, 1981).

9. Keith B. Murray, "A Test of Services Marketing Theory: Consumer Information Acquisition Activities," *Journal of Marketing* (January 1991), pp. 10–25; and F. G. Crane, *Professional Services Marketing: Strategy and Tactics* (New York: The Haworth Press, Inc., 1993).

10. Vicki Clift, "Everyone Needs Service Flow Charting," *Marketing News* (October 23, 1995), pp. 41, 43; Mary Jo Bitner, Bernard H. Booms, and Mary Stanfield Tetreault, "The Service Encounter: Diagnosing Favorable and Unfavorable Incidents," *Journal of Marketing* (January 1990), pp. 71–84; Eberhard Scheuing, "Conducting Customer Service Audits," *Journal of Consumer Marketing* (Summer 1989), pp. 35–41; and W. Earl Susser, R. Paul Olsen, and D. Daryl Wyckoff, *Management of Service Operations* (Boston: Allyn & Bacon, 1978).

11. John Ozment and Edward Morash, "The Augmented Service Offering for Perceived and Actual Service Quality," *Journal of the Academy of Marketing Science* (Fall 1994), pp. 352–63.

12. A. Parasuraman, Valarie A. Zeithaml, and Leonard L. Berry, "Reassessment of Expectations as a Comparison Standard in Measuring Service Quality: Implications for Further Research," *Journal of Marketing* (January 1994), pp. 111–24; and Leonard L. Berry, *On Great Service* (New York: Free Press, 1995).

13. Amy Ostrom and Dawn Iacobucci, "Consumer Trade-Offs and the Evaluation of Services," *Journal of Marketing* (January 1995), pp. 17–28; and J. Joseph Cronin, Jr., and Steven A. Taylor, "Measuring Service Quality: A Reexamination and Extension," *Journal of Marketing* (July 1992), pp. 55–68; Alain Genestre and Paul Herbig, "Service Quality: An Examination of Demographic Differences," *Journal of Customer Service in Marketing and Management*, vol. 3, no. 3 (1997), pp. 65–83; and Jack Dart, "Professional Service Quality: The Practice or the Professional?" *Journal of Customer Service in Marketing and Management*, vol. 3, no. 2 (1997), pp. 7–21.

14. Stephen S. Tax and Stephen W. Brown, "Recovering and Learning from Service Failure," *Sloan Management Review* (Fall 1998), pp. 75–88; Stephen S. Tax, Stephen W. Brown, and Murali Chandrashekaran, "Customer Evaluations of Service Complaint Experiences: Implications for Relationship Marketing," *Journal of Marketing* (April 1998), pp. 60–76; Stephen W. Brown, "Service Recovery Through IT," *Marketing Management* (Fall 1997), pp. 25–27; and Leonard L. Berry and A. Parasuraman, "Listening to the Customer—The Concept of a Service-Quality Information System," *Sloan Management Review* (Spring 1997), pp. 65–76.

15. Gordon Fullerton, and Shirley Taylor, "Mediating, Interactive, and Non-linear Effects in Service Quality and Satisfaction with Services Research," *Canadian Journal of Administrative Sciences* (June 2002).

16. Leonard L. Berry, "Relationship Marketing of Services—Growing Interest, Emerging Perspectives," *Journal of the Academy of Marketing Science* (Fall 1995), pp. 236–45; and Katherine N. Lemon, Tiffany Barnett White, and Russell S. Winer, "Dynamic Customer Relationship Management: Incorporating Future Considerations into the Service Retention Decision," *Journal of Marketing* (January 2002), pp. 1–14.

17. Christopher Lovelock and Jochen Wirtz, *Services Marketing, 5th ed.*; and Valarie A. Zeithaml and Mary Jo Bitner, *Services Marketing, 3rd ed.* (Burr Ridge, IL: 2003).

18. Sundar G. Bharedwaj, P. Rajan Varadarajan and John Fahy, "Sustainable Competitive Advantage in Services Industries: A Conceptual Model and Research Propositions," *Journal of Marketing* (October 1993), pp. 83–99.

19. F. G. Crane, "The Relative Effect of Price and Personal Referral Cues on Consumers' Perceptions of Dental Services," *Health Marketing Quarterly*, vol. 13, no. 4 (1996), pp. 91–105.

20. Christopher Lovelock, *Services Marketing.*

21. Robert E. Hite, Cynthia Fraser, and Joseph A. Bellizzi, "Professional Service Advertising: The Effects of Price Inclusion, Justification, and Level of Risk," *Journal of Advertising Research* 30 (August/September 1990), pp. 23–31; and F. G. Crane, *Professional Services Marketing: Strategy and Tactics.*

22. F. G. Crane, *Professional Services Marketing: Strategy and Tactics*; and Kathleen Mortimer "Services Advertising: The Agency Viewpoint," *Journal of Services Marketing*, No. 2 (2001), pp. 131–146.

23. Patriya Tansuhaj, Donna Randall, and Jim McCullough, "A Services Marketing Management Model: Integrating Internal and External Marketing Functions," *Journal of Services Marketing* (Winter 1988), pp. 31–38.

24. Christian Gronroos, "Internal Marketing Theory and Practice," in Tim Bloch, G. D. Upah, and V. A. Zeithaml, eds., *Services Marketing in a Changing Environment* (Chicago, IL: American Marketing Association, 1984); and Dennis J. Cahill, *Internal Marketing* (New York: The Haworth Press Inc., 1996).

25. Ibid.

26. Hong Lee and Robert Boissoneau, "Empowering People in Modern Organizations for Improved Customer Service," *Journal of Customer Service in Marketing and Management*, vol. 3, no. 2 (1997), pp. 55–69; and Scott W. Kelly, "Developing Customer Orientation among Service Employees," *Journal of the Academy of Marketing Science* (Winter 1992), pp. 27–36; Stephen W. Brown, "The Employee Experience," *Marketing Management* 12 (March-April 2003), pp. 12–13; Lawrence A. Crosby and Sheree L. Johnson, "Watch What I Do," *Marketing Management* 12 (November-December 2003), pp. 10–11; and Hong Lee and Robert Boissoneau, "Empowering People in Modern Organizations for Improved Customer Service," *Journal of Customer Service in Marketing and Management*, vol. 3, no. 2 (1997), pp. 55–69.

27. F.G. Crane, *Professional Services Marketing: Strategy and Tactics;* and Leonard L. Berry and Neeli Bendapudi, "Clueing in Customers," *Harvard Business Review* (February 2003), pp. 100–106.

28. Frederick H. deB. Harris and Peter Peacock, "Hold My Place, Please," *Marketing Management* (Fall 1995), pp. 34–46, and Lovelock, p. 17.

29. Christopher Lovelock, *Services Marketing*

30. Ramin Setoodeh, "Technology: Safer Surfing for Love," *Newsweek* (April 19, 2004), p. 66; and Ginny Parker, "Looking for Prince Charming? In Japan Check your Cell Phone," *Time* (June 4, 2001), p. 88.

31. Stephen L. Vargo and Robert F. Lusch, "Evolving to a New Dominant Logic for Marketing," *Journal of Marketing* 68 (January 2004), pp. 1–17; and Stephen J. Grove, Raymond P. Fisk, and Joby John, "The Future of Services Marketing: Forecasts from Ten Services Experts," *Journal of Services Marketing*, vol. 17, no. 2 (2003), pp. 107–121.

32. Pine and Gilmore, *The Experience Economy.*

33. Ibid.

NHL: This case was written by Frederick G. Crane. Source: National Hockey League.

CHAPTER 13

1. www.confederationbridge.com; and interview in CBSL (August 2004).

2. www.lamborghini.itg.net and www.kbb.com.

3. Adapted from Kent B. Monroe, Pricing: *Making Profitable Decisions*, 2nd ed. (New York: McGraw-Hill, 1990), chapter 4. See

also David J. Curry, "Measuring Price and Quality Competition," *Journal of Marketing* (Spring 1985), pp. 106–17.

4. For a thorough review of the price-quality-value relationship, see Valerie A. Ziethaml, "Consumer Perceptions of Price, Quality, and Value," *Journal of Marketing* (July 1998), pp. 2–22.

5. F.G. Crane, *Professional Services Marketing: Strategy and Tactics* (New York: The Howard Press, Inc, 1993).

6. F. G. Crane, "The Relative Effect of Price and Personal Referral Cues on Consumers' Perceptions of Dental Services,"*Health Marketing Quarterly*, vol 13, no. 4 (1996), pp. 91–105.

7. N. Craig Smith and John A. Quelch, *Ethics in Marketing* (Homewood, IL: Richard D. Irwin, 1993); and F. G. Crane, "What's Ethical and What's Not with Canadian MBA Students," *Working Paper*, 2004.

8. Ron Winslow, "How a Breakthrough Quickly Broke Down for Johnson & Johnson," *The Wall Street Journal* (September 18, 1998), pp. A1, A5.

9. Jeff Lobb, "The Right (Pepsi) Stuff," *Marketing* (July 8, 1996), p. 15.

10. "Price War Is Raging in Europe," *Business Week* (July 6, 1992), pp. 44–45.

11. Michael Garry, "Dollar Strength: Publishers Confront the New Economic Realities," *Folio: The Magazine for Magazine Management* (February 1989), pp. 88–93; Cara S. Trager, "Right Price Reflects a Magazine's Health Goals," *Advertising Age* (March 9, 1987), pp. 5–8ff; and Frank Bruni, "Price of Newsweek? It Depends," *Dallas Times Herald* (August 14, 1986), pp. S1, S20.

12. "Nintendo Gamecube Set at Mass Market Price of $199.95"; "Dedicated Gameplay System Launches November 5, 2001, with Six First-Party Titles Priced at $49.95," Nintendo of America, Inc., Press Release (May 21, 2001).

13. "Time Is Money," *Forbes* (September 18, 2000), pp. 178–85.

14. "Premium AA Alkaline Batteries," *Consumer Reports* (March 21, 2001), p. 54; Kemp Powers, "Assault and Batteries," *Forbes* (September 4, 2000), pp. 54, 56; "Razor Burn at Gillette," *Business Week* (June 18, 2001), p. 37.

15. "Why That Deal Is Only $9.99," *Business Week* (January 10, 2000), p. 36. For further reading on odd–even pricing, see Robert M. Schindler and Thomas M. Kilbarian, "Increased Consumer Sales Response Through Use of 99-Ending Prices," *Journal of Retailing* (Summer 1996), pp. 187–99; Mark Stiving and Russell S. Winer, "An Empirical Analysis of Price Endings with Scanner Data," *Journal of Consumer Research* (June 1997), pp. 57–67; and Robert M. Schindler, "Patterns of Rightmost Digits Used in Advertised Prices: Implications for Nine-Ending Effects," *Journal of Consumer Research* (September 1997), pp. 192–201.

16. Thomas T. Nagle and Reed K. Holden, *The Strategy and Tactics of Pricing*, 3rd ed. (Englewood Cliffs, NJ: Prentice Hall, 2002), pp. 243–49.

17. www.rogers.com.

18. Kent B. Monroe, *Pricing: Making Profitable Decisions*, 2nd ed. (New York: McGraw-Hill, 1990), pp. 326–27. For a recent discussion of this topic, see Ramarao Desiraju and Steven M. Shugan, "Strategic Service Pricing and Yield Management," *Journal of Marketing* (January 1999), pp. 44–56.

19. Robert J. Dolan and Hermann Simon, *Power Pricing: How Managing Price Transforms the Bottom Line* (New York: Free Press, 1996), p. 249.

20. Peter M. Noble and Thomas S. Gruca, "Industrial Pricing: Theory and Managerial Practice," *Marketing Science*, vol. 18, no. 3 (1999), pp. 435–54.

21. George E. Belch and Michael A. Belch, *Introduction to Advertising and Promotion*, 5th ed. (New York: Irwin/McGraw-Hill, 2001), p. 93.

22. www.strategis.ic.gc.ca.

23. Monroe, *Pricing*, p. 34.

24. F.G. Crane, "The Relative Effect of Price and Personal Referral Cues on Consumers' Perceptions of Dental Services," *Health Marketing Quarterly*, vol. 13, no. 4 (1996), pp. 91–100.

25. Charles Fishman, "Which Price is Right," *FastCompany* (March, 2003), p. 92. (http://www.fastcompany.com/magazine/68/pricing.html.).

26. For an extensive discussion on discounts, see Monroe, *Pricing*, chapters 14 and 15.

Washburn International: The case is based on information amd materials provided by the company.

CHAPTER 14

1. "Show Time!" *BusinessWeek*, February 2, 2004, pp. 56ff; www.ifoapplestore.com/stores, downloaded June 7, 2004; and Jonah Bloom, "Apple, Song, Hershey Ring Up More than Sales at Their Shops," *Advertising Age*, February 2, 2004, p. 16.

2. See Peter D. Bennett, ed. *Dictionary of Marketing Terms*, 3rd ed. (Chicago, American Marketing Association, 2000).

3. PepsiCo, Inc. Annual Report, 1997.

4. Donald V. Fites, "Make Your Dealers Your Partners," *Harvard Business Review* (March-April 1996), pp. 84–95.

5. Bert Rosenbloom, *Marketing Channels: A Management View*, 7th ed. (Cincinnati, OH: South-Western College Publishing, 2004).

6. www.the-cma.org

7. www.generalmills.com (downloaded November 15, 2004); www.nestle.com (downloaded November 15, 2004).

8. For an overview of vertical marketing systems, see Lou Pelton, David Stutton, and James R. Lumpkin, *Marketing Channels*, 2nd ed. (Chicago: Irwin, 2002), chapter 14.

9. Joshua Levine and Matthew Swibel, "Dr. No," *Forbes* (May 28, 2001), pp. 72–76.

10. "Gillette Tries to Nick Schick in Japan," *The Wall Street Journal* (February 4, 1991), pp. B3, B4.

11. Christine B. Bucklin, Pamela A. Thomas-Graham, and Elizabeth Webster, "Channel Conflict: When Is It Dangerous?" *The McKinsey Quarterly*, No. 3, (1997), pp. 36–43.

12. "Black Pearls Reacast for Spring," *Advertising Age* (November 13, 1995), p. 49.

13. F. Robert Dwyer and Julie Gassenheimer, "Relational Roles and Triangle Dramas: Effects on Power Play and Sentiments in Industrial Channels," *Marketing Letters*, Vol. 3 (1992), pp. 187–200.

14. "FTC Pinpoints Slotting Fees," *Advertising Age* (February 26, 2001), p. 52; "Ca-ching," *Forbes* (June 12, 2000), pp. 84–85; and Paul N. Bloom, Gregory T. Gundlach, and Joseph P. Cannon, "Slotting Allowances and Fees: Schools of Thought and Views of Practicing Managers," *Journal of Marketing* (April 2000), pp. 92–109.

15. This discussion is based on Robyn Meredith, "Harder than Hype," *Forbes*, April 16, 2001, pp. 188–94.

16. Major portions of this discussion are based on Sunil Chopra and Peter Meindl, *Supply Chain Management: Strategy, Planning, and Operations,* 2nd ed. (Upper Saddle River, NJ: Prentice Hall, 2004), chaps. 1–3; and Hau L. Lee, "The Triple-A Supply Chain," *Harvard Business Review* (October 2004), pp. 102–12.

17. This discussion is based on Kathryn Jones, "The Dell Way," *Business 2.0* (February 2003), pp. 61–66; Charles Fishman, "The Wal-Mart You Don't Know," *Fast Company* (December 2003), pp. 68–80; and Chopra and Meindl, *Supply Chain Management*.

18. Portions of this discussion are based on "A Perfect Market: A Survey of E-Commerce," *The Economist* (May 15, 2004), special section; Donald J. Bowersox, David J. Closs, and M. Bixby Copper, *Supply Chain Logistics Management* (Burr Ridge, IL: McGraw-Hill/Irwin, 2002), chap. 10; and Chopra and Meindl, *Supply Chain Management*.

19. Erik Schonfeld, "The Total Package," *eCompany* (June 2001), pp. 91–97; and Kurt Hoffman, "Snapple Found Handling Logistics In-House Left a Sour Taste," www.supplychainbrain.com (April 2002).

20. Douglas M. Lambert, James R. Stock, and Lisa Ellram, *Fundamentals of Logistics Management* (Burr Ridge, IL: McGraw-Hill/Irwin, 1998).

21. Eck and Mitchell, "Transformation at IBM"; and David Simchi-Levi, Philip Kaminsky, and Edith Simchi-Levi, *Managing the Supply Chain: The Definitive Guide for the Business Professional* (New York: McGraw-Hill 2004), p. 78.

22. Jeffrey Davis and Martha Baer, "Some Assembly Required," *Business 2.0* (February 12, 2001), pp. 78–87.

23. Marshall Fisher, "What Is the Right Supply Chain for Your Product?" *Harvard Business Review* (March–April 1997), pp. 105–17.

24. Harvey Meyer, "The Greening of Corporate America," *Journal of Business Strategy* (January–February 2000), pp. 38–43; and M. Fleischmann, J. van Nunen, and B. Grave, "Integrating Closed-Loop Supply Chains and Spare-Parts Management at IBM," *Interfaces* (November–December 2003), pp. 44–56.

Amazon.com: This case is based on material available on the company website, www.amazon.com, and the following sources: Robert D. Hof and Heather Green, "How Amazon Cleared That Hurdle," *BusinessWeek* (February 4, 2002), p. 60; Heather Green, "How Hard Should Amazon Swing?" *BusinessWeek* (January 14, 2002), p. 38: Robert D. Hof, "We've Never Said We Had To Do It All," *BusinessWeek* (October 15, 2001), p. 53; "Amazon.com Selects Mercator E-Business Integration Brokers as Key Technology for Supply Chain Integration," *Business Wire* (November 28, 2000); Bob Walter, "Amazon Leases Distribution Center from Sacramento, Calif., Development Firm," *Sacramento Bee* (July 19, 2001).

CHAPTER 15

1. Information supplied by Tim Horton's (May 2005); and Rebecca Harris, "Down-Home Smarts," *Marketing Magazine* (February 7, 2005).

2. Ibid.

3. www.retailcouncil.org (downloaded March 1, 2005).

4. Daniel Thomas, "Suppliers Will Meet RFID Deadline," *Computer Weekly* (May 11, 2004), p. 14; Laurie Sullivan and Darrell Dunn, "HP, Sun Ramp up RFID Services," *Information Week* (May 10, 2004), p. 16; Irene M. Nunii and Adam Aston, "Radio ID Tags So Cheap They'll Be Everywhere," *Business Week* (October 20, 2003), p. 147; and "Target's RFID Goal Is to Have All Vendors Tagging by 2007," *HFN* (March 22, 2004), p. 26.

5. "Franchise 500," *Entrepreneur* (January 2005).

6. Kristen Vinakmens, "Small But Mighty." *Strategy Magazine* (December 15, 2003), p. 1.

7. Carol Matlack and Adeline Bonnet, "What's Shackling the Big Chains," *Business Week* (May 17, 2004), p. 26.

8. Kwan Weng Kin, "Vending Machines in Japan Get Smart." *The Strait Times* (Singapore) (October 26, 2003); and Andy Reinhardt, "A Machine-to-Machine Internet of Things," *Business Week* (April 26, 2004), p. 102.

9. Vito Pilieci, "The IKEA Catalog: It's Bigger than the Bible," *Ottawa Citizen* (August 27, 2003), p. A1.

10. Carrie Johnson, "The New Face of Canadian E-commerce," www.forrester.com (downloaded October 26, 2004).

11. Ibid.

12. www.forrester.com (downloaded October 26, 2004).

13. CBS News, "Canada May Block Drug Exports" (January 6, 2005); and Justin Thompson, "Cross-Border Rx," *CBC NewsOnline* (August 12, 2004).

14. Kristen Vinakmens, "Digitizing the Experience," *Strategy Magazine* (December 1, 2003), p. 11.

15. "My Virtual Model Inc. Acquires EZsize," *PR Newswire* (June 21, 2001); Steve Casimiro, "Shop Till You Crash," *Fortune* (December 21, 1998), pp. 267–70; and De' Ann Weimer, "Can I Try (Click) That Blouse (Drag) in Blue?" *BusinessWeek* (November 9, 1998), p. 86.

16. www.the-cma.org

17. Nanette Byrnes, "The New Calling," *BusinessWeek* (September 18, 2000), pp. 137–48.

18. Bill Vlasic and Mary Beth Regan, "Amway II: The Kids Take Over," *Business Week* (February 1, 1998), pp. 60–70.

19. Mathew Schifrin, "Okay, Big Mouth," *Forbes* (October 9, 1995), pp. 47–48; Veronica Byrd and Wendy Zellner, "The Avon Lady of the Amazon," *BusinessWeek* (October 24, 1994), pp. 93–96; and Ann Marsh "Avon Is Calling on Eastern Europe," *Advertising Age* (June 20, 1994), p. 116.

20. The following discussion is adapted from William T. Gregor and Eileen M. Friars, *Money Merchandizing: Retail Revolution in Consumer Financial Services* (Cambridge, MA: Management Analysis Center, Inc., 1982).

21. Gail Tom, Michelle Dragics, and Christi Holdregger, "Using Visual Presentation to Assess Store Positioning: A Case Study of JCPenney," *Marketing Research* (September 1991), pp. 48–52; and Chris Daniels, "Memories of Wal-Mart," *Marketing Magazine* (June 13, 2005).

22. Francis J. Mulhern and Robert P. Leon, "Implicit Price Bundling of Retail Products: A Multiproduct Approach to Maximizing Store Profitability," *Journal of Marketing* (October 1991), pp. 63–76.

23. Amy Haggar, "Dixie: Cheap Is Out, Value Is In," *Strategy Magazine* (August 25, 2003), p. 4; and Leonard L. Berry, "Old Pillars of the New Retailing, *Harvard Business Review* (April 2001), pp. 131–37.

24. Neil Gross, "On beyond Shoplifting Prevention," *BusinessWeek* (October 2, 2000), p. 170; and "A Time to Steal," *Brandweek* (February 16, 1999), p. 24.

25. Rita Koselka, "The Schottenstein Factor," *Forbes* (September 28, 1992), p. 104, 106.

26. Ira P. Schneiderman, "Value Keeps Factory Outlets Viable," *Daily News Record* (July 20, 1998), p. 10; Stephanie Anderson Forest, "I Can Get It for You Retail," *Business Week* (September 18, 1995), pp. 84–88; and Adrienne Ward, "New Breed of Mall Knows: Everybody Loves a Bargain," *Advertising Age* (January 27, 1992), p. 55.

27. Anne Faircloth, "Value Retailers Go Dollar For Dollar," *Fortune* (July 6, 1998), pp. 164–66.

28. Pierre Martineau, "The Personality of the Retail Store," *Harvard Business Review* (January–February 1958), p. 47.

29. Julie Baker, Dhruv Grewal, and A. Parasuraman, "The Influence of Store Environment on Quality Inferences and Store Image," *Journal of the Academy of Marketing Science* (Fall 1994), pp. 328–39; Howard Barich and Philip Kotler, "A Framework for Marketing Image Management," *Sloan Management Review* (Winter 1991), pp. 94–104; Susan M. Keaveney and Kenneth A. Hunt, "Conceptualization and Operationalization of Retail Store Image: A Case of Rival Middle-Level Theories," *Journal of the Academy of Marketing Science* (Spring 1992), pp. 165–75; James C. Ward, Mary Jo Bitner, and John Barnes, "Measuring the Prototypicality and Meaning of Retail Environments," *Journal of Retailing* (Summer 1992), p. 194; and Dhruv Grewal, R. Krishnan, Julie Baker, and Norm Burin, "The Effect of Store Name, Brand Name and Price Discounts on Consumers' Evaluations and Purchase Intentions," *Journal of Retailing* (Fall 1998), pp. 331–52. For a review of the store image literature, see Mary R. Zimmer and Linda L. Golden, "Impressions of Retail Stores: A Content Analysis of Consumer Images," *Journal of Retailing* (Fall 1988), pp. 265–93.

30. Mary Jo Bitner, "Servicescapes: The Impact of Physical Surroundings on Customers and Employees," *Journal of Marketing* (April 1992), pp. 57–71.

31. Jans-Benedict Steenkamp and Michel Wedel, "Segmenting Retail Markets on Store Image Using a Consumer-Based Methodology," *Journal of Retailing* (Fall 1991), p. 300; and Philip Kotler, "Atmospherics as a Marketing Tool," *Journal of Retailing*, vol. 49 (Winter 1973–1974), p. 61.

32. Kristen Vinakmens, "How Would You Turn Around Sears," *Strategy Magazine* (October 20, 2003), p. 2.

33. Kusum L. Ailwadi and Bari Harlam, "An Empirical Analysis of the Determinants of Retail Margins: The Role of Store-Brand Share," *Journal of Marketing* (January 2004), pp. 147–65; Joseph Tarnowski, "And the Awards Went to . . ." *Progressive Grocer* (April 15, 2004); Betsy Spethmann, "Shelf Sets," *Promo* (May 1, 2004), p. 6; and "Study Shows Continued Support for Category Management," *CSNews Online* (March 17, 2004).

34. The wheel of retailing theory was originally proposed by Malcolm P. McNair, "Significant Trends and Development in the Postwar Period," in A. B. Smith, ed., *Competitive Distribution in a Free, High-Level Economy and Its Implications for the University* (Pittsburgh: University of Pittsburgh Press, 1958), pp. 1–25; see also Stephen Brown, "The Wheel of Retailing—Past and Future," *Journal of Retailing* (Summer 1990), pp. 143–49; and Malcolm P. McNair and Eleanor May, "The Next Revolution of the Retailing Wheel," *Harvard Business Review* (September–October 1978), pp. 81–91.

35. Kenneth Hein, "Upfront 2004—The Advertisers: Fast Food," Adweek.com, April 26, 2004; "McDonald's Tests In-Store McCafes," ddimagazine.com (downloaded November 14, 2003); and "New McDonald's Ad Pushes Health," restaurantbiz.com (downloaded May 12, 2004).

36. William R. Davidson, Albert D. Bates, and Stephen J. Bass, "Retail Life Cycle," *Harvard Business Review* (November–December 1976), pp. 89–96.

37. Jim Carter and Norman Sheehan, "From Competition to Cooperation: E-Tailing's Integration with Retailing," *Business Horizons* (March–April 2004), pp. 71-78.

38. Carrie Johnson, "Getting Multichannel Marketing Right," www.forrester.com (downloaded January 7, 2005).

39. Ellen McCarthy, "Biometric Payment Systems Show Both Promise and Peril," *Portland Press* (June 12, 2005), p. F1, F2.

Case: Courtesy of Vaughan Mills.

CHAPTER 16

1. Interview with Susanne Boyce; and Susanne Boyce, "Cooking with Gas," *Marketing Magazine* (May 10, 2004), www.marketingmag.ca (downloaded June 22, 2005).

2. Wilbur Schramm, "How Communication Works," in Wilbur Schramm, ed., *The Process and Effects of Mass Communication* (Urbana, IL: University of Illinois Press, 1955), pp. 3–26.

3. F. G. Crane and T. K. Clarke, *Consumer Behaviour in Canada: Theory and Practice*, 2nd ed. (Toronto: Dryden, 1994), pp. 287–98.

4. Cynthia L. Kemper, "Biting Wax Tadpole, Other Faux Pas," *The Denver Post* (August 3, 1997), p. G–04.

5. Rik Pieters and Michel Wedel, "Attention Capture and Transfer in Advertising: Brand Pictorial, and Text-Size Effects," *Journal of Marketing* (April 2004), pp. 36–50.

6. Kusum L Ailawadi, Scott A. Neslin, and Karen Gedenk, "Pursuing the Value-Conscious Consumer: Store Brands versus National Brand Promotions," *Journal of Marketing* (January 2001), pp. 71–89;

7. B. C. Cotton and Emerson M. Babb, "Consumer Response to Promotional Deals," *Journal of Marketing*, vol. 42 (July 1978), pp. 109–13.

8. Robert George Brown, "Sales Response to Promotions and Advertising," *Journal of Advertising Research*, vol. 14 (August 1974), pp. 33–40.

9. Adapted from *Economic Impact: U.S. Direct Marketing Today* (New York: Direct Marketing Association, 1998), p. 25.

10. Siva K. Balasubramanian and V. Kumar, "Analyzing Variations in Advertising and Promotional Expenditures: Key Correlates in Consumer, Industrial, and Service Markets," *Journal of Marketing* (April 1990), pp. 57–68.

11. Don E. Schultz, "Include SIMM in Modern Media Ad Plans," *Marketing News* (May 15, 2004), p. 6; Don E. Schultz, "TV Advertisers Defy Logic, Pay More for Less," *Marketing News* (June 9, 2003), p. 14; Catherine Arnold, "Tech Design," *Marketing News* (January 15, 2004), p. 4; Gail Edmondson and Michael Eidam, "The Mini Just Keeps Getting Mightier," *BusinessWeek* (April 5, 2004), p. 26; Don E. Schultz, "Consumer Marketing Changed by Advent of 29.8/7 Media Week," *Marketing News* (September 24, 2001), pp. 13, 15; Pamela Paul, "Getting Inside Gen Y," *American Demographics* (September 2001), pp. 43–49; Charles Pappas, "Ad Nauseam," *Advertising Age* (July 10, 2000), pp. 16–18; and Dan Lippe, "It's All in Creative Delivery," *Advertising Age* (June 25, 2001), pp. S8, S9.

12. Dunn Sunnoo and Lynn Y. S. Lin, "Sales Effects of Promotion and Advertising," *Journal of Advertising Research*, vol. 18 (October 1978), pp. 37–42.

13. John Palmer, "Animal Instincts," *PROMO* (May 2001), pp. 25–33.

14. F. G. Crane and T. K. Clarke, pp. 237–38, 346.

15. James M. Olver and Paul W. Farris, "Push and Pull: A One-Two Punch for Packages Products," *Sloan Management Review* (Fall 1989), pp. 53–61.

16. Ken Riddell, "Advertising Sees Share of Pie Dwindling," *Marketing* (January 7, 1994), p. 2.

17. David Ciekiewicz, "Wired World," *Marketing Magazine* (June 18, 2001); www.marketingmag.ca (downloaded, June 22, 2005).

18. Eve Lazarus, "Branching Out," *Marketing Magazine* (October 20, 2003); www.marketingmag.ca (downloaded, June 22, 2005).

19. Robert J. Lavidge and Gary A. Steiner, "A Model for Predictive Measurement of Advertising Effectiveness," *Journal of Marketing* (October 1961), p. 61.

20. Brian Wansink and Michael Ray, "Advertising Strategies to Increase Usage Frequency," *Journal of Marketing* (January 1996), pp. 31–46.

21. www.marketingmag.ca/media-digest/html (downloaded June 2005).

22. Don E. Schultz and Anders Gronstedt, "Making Marcom an Investment," *Marketing Management* (Fall 1997), pp. 41–49; and J. Enrique Bigne, "Advertising Budget Practices: A Review," *Journal of Current Issues and Research in Advertising* (Fall 1995), pp. 17–31.

23. John Philip Jones, "Ad Spending: Maintaining Market Share," *Harvard Business Review* (January–February 1990), pp. 38–42; and Charles H. Patti and Vincent Blanko, "Budgeting Practices of Big Advertisers," *Journal of Advertising Research*, vol. 21 (December 1981), pp. 23–30.

24. James A. Schroer, "Ad Spending: Growing Market Share," *Harvard Business Review* (January–February 1990), pp. 44–48.

25. Jeffrey A. Lowenhar and John L. Stanton, "Forecasting Competitive Advertising Expenditures," *Journal of Advertising Research*, vol. 16, no. 2 (April 1976), pp. 37–44.

26. Daniel Seligman, "How Much for Advertising?" *Fortune* (December 1956), p. 123.

27. James E. Lynch and Graham J. Hooley, "Increasing Sophistication in Advertising Budget Setting," *Journal of Advertising Research*, vol. 30 (February–March 1990), pp. 67–75.

28. Jimmy D. Barnes, Brenda J. Muscove, and Javad Rassouli, "An Objective and Task Media Selection Decision Model and Advertising Cost Formula to Determine International Advertising Budgets," *Journal of Advertising*, vol. 11, no. 4 (1982), pp. 68–75.

29. Don E. Schultz, "Olympics Get the Gold Medal in Integrating Marketing Event," *Marketing News* (April 27, 1998), pp. 5, 10.

30. Cornelia Pechman, Guangzhi Zhao, Marvin E. Goldberg, and Ellen Thomas Reibling, "What to Convey in Antismoking Advertisements for Adolescents: The Use of Protection Motivation Theory to Identify Effective Message Themes," *Journal of Marketing* (April 2003), pp. 1–18.

31. Jill Kipnis, "Picture This: New Line Breaks Ground with HD Promos," *Billboard* (May 29, 2004); David Finnigan, "The Biz," *BrandWeek* (October 14, 2002); "The Fellowship of the New Line," *Promo* (September 2001), p. 84; and "Sneak Preview of Trailer for New Line Cinema's 'The Lord of the Rings: The Fellowship of the Ring'" *PR Newswire* (September 21, 2001).

32. Kate Fitzgerald, "Beyond Advertising," *Advertising Age* (August 3, 1998), pp. 1, 14; Curtis P. Johnson, "Follow the Money: Sell CFO on Integrated Marketing's Merits," *Marketing News* (May 11, 1998).

33. "Measure for Measure," *Marketing Management* (January–February 2004), p. 7.

34. www.the-cma.org (downloaded on June 22, 2005).

35. Ibid.

36. Ibid.

37. "Household Internet Use Survey," Statistics Canada (Sept 2004), Ottawa.

38. Carrie A. Johnson, "Getting Multichannel Retailing Right, www.forrester.com (downloaded January 7, 2005).

39. "Consumers Worried about Online Privacy"; "Online Privacy and You," www.cyberdialogue.com (downloaded June 10, 2004); David Stark "Online Retailers Missing out on Sales," *Marketing Magazine* (October 7, 2002); www.marketingmag.ca (downloaded June 20, 2005); and Michael Weiss, "Online America," *American Demographics* (March 21, 2001), pp. 53–60.

UPS: This case was written by Steven Hartley based on taped interviews of company personnel and the following sources: Dean Foust, "Big Brown's New Bag," *BusinessWeek*, July 19, 2004, p. 54; David Rynecki, "Does This Package Make Sense?" *Fortune*, January 26, 2004, p. 132; "The UPS Store and Mail Boxes Etc. Expand to 5000 Worldwide Locations," *Business Wire*, September 13, 2004; Charles Haddad, "The Websmart 50," *BusinessWeek*, November 24, 2003, p. 92; and information contained on the UPS website (www.ups.com).

CHAPTER 17

1. Information supplied by AdFarm (May 2005).

2. David A. Aaker and Donald Norris, "Characteristics of TV Commercials Perceived as Informative," *Journal of Advertising Research*, vol. 22, no. 2 (April–May 1982), pp. 61–70.

3. Larry D. Compeau and Dhruv Grewal, "Comparative Price Advertising: An Integrative Review," *Journal of Public Policy & Marketing* (Fall 1998), pp. 257–73.

4. Jennifer Lawrence, "P&G Ads Get Competitive," *Advertising Age* (February 1, 1993), p. 14; Jerry Gotlieb and Dan Sorel, "The Influence of Type of Advertisement, Price, and Source Credibility on Perceived Quality," *Journal of the Academy of Marketing Science* (Summer 1992), pp. 253–60; and Cornelia Pechman and David Stewart, "The Effects of Comparative Advertising on Attention, Memory, and Purchase Intentions," *Journal of Consumer Research* (September 1990), pp. 180–92.

5. Bruce Buchanan and Doron Goldman, "Us vs. Them: The Minefield of Comparative Ads," *Harvard Business Review* (May–June 1989), pp. 38–50.

6. Lewis C. Winters, "Does It Pay to Advertise to Hostile Audiences with Corporate Advertising?" *Journal of Advertising Research* (June/July 1988), pp. 11–18; and Robert Selwitz, "The Selling of an Image," *Madison Avenue* (February 1985), pp. 61–69.

7. Mary Lou Quinlan, "Women: We've Come a Long Way, Maybe," *Advertising Age* (February 22, 1999), p. 46.

8. Jean Halliday, "Of Hummers and Zen," *Advertising Age* (August 6, 2001), p. 29.

9. "Claritin Springs into Allergy Season with New Consumer Programs," *PR Newswire* (February 20, 2001).

10. Ira Teinowitz, "Self-regulation Urged to Prevent Bias in Ad Buying," *Advertising Age* (January 18, 1999), p. 4.

11. Bob Donath, "Match Your Media Choice and Ad Copy Objective," *Marketing News* (June 8, 1998), p. 6.

12. Michael S. LaTour and Herbert J. Rotfeld, "There Are Threats and (Maybe) Fear-Caused Arousal: Theory and Confusions of Appeals to Fear and Fear Arousal Itself," *Journal of Advertising* (Fall 1997), pp. 45–59.

13. Bob Garfield, "Allstate Ads Bring Home Point about Mortgage Insurance," *Advertising Age* (September 11, 1989), p. 120; and Judann Dagnoli, "'Buy or Die' Mentality Toned Down in Ads," *Advertising Age* (May 7, 1990), p. S-12.

14. Cornelia Pechmann, Guangzhi Zhao, Marvin E. Goldberg, and Ellen Thomas Reibling, "What to Convey in Antismoking Advertisements for Adolescents: The Use of Protection Motivation Theory to Identify Effective Message Themes," *Journal of Marketing* (April, 2003).

15. "You Respond to Planned Parenthood Ad," *Marketing Magazine* (June 21, 2004).

16. Anthony Vagnoni, "Best Awards," *Advertising Age* (May 28, 2001), pp. S1–18; Dana L. Alden, Wayne D. Hoyer, and Chol Lee, "Identifying Global and Culture-Specific Dimensions of Humor in Advertising: A Multinational Analysis," *Journal of Marketing* (April 1993), pp. 64–75; and Johny K. Johansson, "The Sense of 'Nonsense': Japanese TV Advertising," *Journal of Advertising* (March 1994), pp. 17–26.

17. Michelle Halpern, "Love it, Loathe it," *Marketing Magazine* (October 4, 2004); and "Yellow Seeks a Pledge from Students," *Marketing Magazine* (August 5, 2004); and www.marketingmag.ca (downloaded June 5, 2005).

18. www.cmdc.ca (downloaded June 3, 2005).

19. Giles D'Souza and Ram C. Rao, "Can Repeating an Advertisement More Frequently than the Competition Affect Brand Preference in a Mature Market?" *Journal of Marketing* (April 1995), pp. 32–42.

20. Lowell L. Lunden, "Secrets for Powerful Advertising: Strategic Implications of Recency," *Canadian Advertising Research Foundation Newsletter* (December 2003), pp. 9–13.

21. William F. Arens, *Contemporary Advertising*, 9th ed (New York: McGraw-Hill/Irwin, 2004), pp. 268; R20; and William G. Nickels, James M. McHugh, and Susan M. McHugh, *Understanding Business*, 7th ed. (Burr Ridge, IL: McGraw-Hill, 2005, p. 493).

22. www.cmda.ca (downloaded June 3, 2005).

23. Ibid.

24. Surendra N. Singh, Denise Linville, and Ajay Sukhdial, "Enhancing the Efficacy of Split Thirty-Second Television Commercials: An Encoding Variability Application," *Journal of Advertising* (Fall 1995), pp. 13–23; Scott Ward, Terence A. Oliva, and David J. Reibstein, "Effectiveness of Brand-Related 15-Second Commercials," *Journal of Consumer Marketing*, no. 2 (1994). pp. 38–44; and Surendra N. Singh and Catherine Cole, "The Effects of Length, Content, and Repetition on Television Commercial Effectiveness," *Journal of Marketing Research* (February 1993), pp. 91–104.

25. www.cmdc.ca (downloaded June 3, 2005).

26. Michelle Halpern, "Ready for Satellite Radio," *Marketing Magazine* (December 13, 2004).

27. www.marketingmag.ca/media-digest/html (downloaded June 3, 2005).

28. Ibid.

29. www.cmdc.ca; and Chris Daniels, "Ready, Set, Go!" *Marketing Magazine* (January 10, 2005) www.marketingmag.ca (downloaded June 10, 2005).

30. www.iabcanada.com (downloaded June 10, 2005).

31. www.cmdc.ca (downloaded June 3, 2005).

32. The discussion of post-testing is based on William F. Arens, *Contemporary Advertising*, 9th ed. (Burr Ridge, IL: Richard D. Irwin, 2004).

33. www.adstandards.com (downloaded, June 10, 2005).

34. Lisa D' Innocenzo, "Selling to the Store," *Strategy Magazine* (February 9, 2004), p. 1.

35. *Couponing Trends* (Markham, ON: NCH Promotional Services, 2002).

36. Kapil Bawa and Robert W. Shoemaker, "Analyzing Incremental Sales from a Direct-Mail Coupon Promotion," *Journal of Marketing* (July 1998), pp. 66–78.

37. Roger A. Strang, "Sales Promotion—Fast Growth, Faulty Management," *Harvard Business Review*, vol. 54 (July–August 1976), pp. 115–24; and Ronald W. Ward and James E. Davis, "Coupon Redemption," *Journal of Advertising Research*, vol. 18 (August 1978), pp. 51–58. Similar results on favorable mail-distributed coupons were reported by Alvin Schwartz, "The Influence of Media Characteristics on Coupon Redemption," *Journal of Marketing*, vol. 30 (January 1966), pp. 41–46.

38. This discussion is drawn particularly from John A. Quelch, *Trade Promotions by Grocery Manufacturers: A Management Perspective* (Cambridge, MA: Marketing Science Institute, August 1982).

39. Scott Hue, "Free 'Plugs' Supply Ad Power," *Advertising Age* (January 29, 1990), p. 6.

40. "PETA Ads Target of Complaints to ASC," *Marketing Magazine* (February, 22, 2005); www.marketingmag.ca (downloaded June 10, 2005); and Martin O'Hanlon, "Meat Lovers Not Complete Lovers," *The Chronicle-Herald* (August 11, 1999), pp. A1, A2.

Case: Courtesy of Adfarm.

CHAPTER 18

1. "Xerox Turns a New Page," *CNNMoney.com* (March 16, 2004); "Anne Mulcahy Has Xerox by the Horns," *BusinessWeek Online* (May 29, 2003); and Kathleen Cholewka, "Xerox's Savior?" *Sales & Marketing Management* (April 2001), pp. 36–42.

2. Statistics Canada, *Canada Year Book*, (Ottawa, 2005).

3. "America's 25 Best Sales Forces," *Sales & Marketing Management* (July 2000), pp. 57–85.

4. Mark W. Johnston and Greg W. Marshall, *Relationship Selling and Sales Management* (Burr Ridge, IL: McGraw-Hill/Irwin, 2005).

5. "Increasing Face Time," *Sales & Marketing Management* (January 2004), p. 12; and Barton A. Weitz, Stephen B. Castleberry, and John F. Tanner, Jr., *Selling: Building Partnerships,* 5th ed. (Burr Ridge, IL: McGraw-Hill/Irwin, 2004), p. 10.

6. For representative research and commentary on team selling, see Keith A. Chrzanowski and Thomas W. Leigh, "Customer Relationship Strategy and Customer-Focused Teams," in Gerald J. Bauer et al., *Emerging Trends in Sales Thought and Practice* (Westport, CT: Quorum Books, 1998); and Mark A. Moon and Susan Forquer Gupta, "Examining the Formation of Selling Centers: A Conceptual Framework," *Journal of Personal Selling & Sales Management* (Spring 1997), pp. 31–41.

7. Steve Atlas and Elise Atlas, "Team Approach," *Selling Power* (May 2000), pp. 126–28; and Neil Rackman, Lawrence Friedman, and Richard Ruff, *Getting Partnering Right* (New York: McGraw-Hill, 1996), pp. 47–48.

8. Carol J. Loomis, "Have You Been Cold-Called?" *Fortune* (December 16, 1991), pp. 109–15.

9. Jim Edwards, "Dinner, Interrupted," *BrandWeek* (May 26, 2003), pp. 28–32.

10. Paul. A. Herbing, *Handbook of Cross-Cultural Marketing* (New York: Holworth Press, 1998).

11. "Japanese Business Etiquette," *Smart Business* (August 2000), p. 55.

12. This discussion is based on Weitz, Castleberry, and Tanner, *Selling,* chap. 6; F. Robert Dwyer and John F. Tanner, *Business Marketing,*

2nd ed. (Burr Ridge, IL: McGraw-Hill/Irwin, 2002), p. 400; and Jeff Golterman, "Strategic Account Management in the Age of the Never Satisfied Customer," *Velocity* 2 (2000), pp. 13–16.

13. For an extensive discussion of objections, see Charles M. Futrell, *Fundamentals of Selling* (Burr Ridge, IL: McGraw-Hill, 2002), chapter 12.

14. Philip R. Cateora and John L. Graham, *International Marketing*, 11th ed. (New York: Irwin/McGraw-Hill, 2002), pp. 128, 131; and Herbing, *Handbook of Cross-Cultural Marketing*, p. 60.

15. Theodore Levitt, *The Marketing Imagination* (New York: Free Press, 1983), p. 111.

16. Weitz, Castleberry, and Tanner. *Selling.*

17. *Management Briefing: Sales and Marketing* (New York: Conference Board, October 1996), pp. 3–4.

18. Ellen Neuborne, "Know Thy Enemy," *Sales & Marketing Management* (January 2003), pp. 29–33.

19. Alan J. Dubinsky, Marvin A. Jolson, Ronald E. Michaels, Masaaki Katobe, and Chae Un Lim, "Ethical Perceptions of Field Sales Personnel: An Empirical Assessment," *Journal of Personal Selling & Sales Management* (Fall 1992), pp. 9–21; and Alan J. Dubinsky, Marvin A. Jolson, Masaaki Katobe, and Chae Un Lim, "A Cross-National Investigation of Industrial Salespeople's Ethical Perceptions," *Journal of International Business Studies* (Fourth Quarter 1991), pp. 651–70.

20. See Gilbert A. Churchill, Jr., Neil M. Ford, Orville C. Walker, Jr., Mark W. Johnson, and John F. Tanner, Jr., *Sales Force Management*, 7th ed. (Burr Ridge, IL: Irwin/McGraw-Hill, 2003), pp. 101–4.

21. Churchill et al., *Sales Force Management*, pp. 110–13. Also see Arun Sharma, "Who Prefers Key Account Management Programs? An Investigation of Business Buying Behavior and Buying Firm Characteristics," *Journal of Personal Selling & Sales Management* (Fall 1997), pp. 37–30; Dan C. Weilbaker and William A. Weeks, "The Evolution of National Account Management: A Literature Perspective," *Journal of Personal Selling & Management* (Fall 1997), pp. 49–50; and Paul Dishman and Philip S. Nitse, "National Accounts Revisited," *Industrial Marketing Management* (January 1998), pp. 1–9.

22. Douglas J. Dalrymple, William L. Cron, and Thomas E. DeCarlo, *Sales Management,* 8th ed. (New York: John Wiley & Sons, 2004), chap. 4; and Churchill et al., *Sales Force Management,* chap. 5.

23. "Look Who's Calling," *Sales & Marketing Management* (May 1998), pp. 43–46.

24. This discussion is based on Dalrymple, Cron, and DeCarlo, *Sales Management.*

25. Julia Chang, "Born to Sell?" *Sales & Marketing Management* (July 2003), pp. 34–38.

26. Weitz, Castleberry, and Tanner, *Selling*, p. 21. For further reading see Daniel Goleman, "What Makes a Leader?" *Harvard Business Review* (November–December 1998), pp. 93–102; A. Fisher, "Success Secret: A High Emotional IQ," *Fortune* (October 26, 1998), pp. 293–98; and Daniel Goleman, *Working with Emotional Intelligence* (New York: Bantam, 1999).

27. Joanne Thomas Yaccato, "Through the Gender Lens," *Marketing Magazine* (June 30, 2003); and Lesley Young, "Strange Hybrids," *Marketing Magazine* (February 11, 2002); www.marketingmag.ca (downloaded, June 22, 2005).

28. Ibid.

29. See, for example, Nora Wood, "What Motivates Best?" *Sales & Marketing Management* (September 1998), pp. 71–78; Melanie Berger, "When Their Ship Comes In," *Sales & Marketing Management* (April 1997), pp. 60–65; William L. Cron, Alan J. Dubinsky, and Ronald E. Michaels, "The Influence of Career Stages on Components of Salesperson Motivation," *Journal of Marketing* (January 1988).

30. Rosann Spiro, William J. Stanton, and Gregory Rich, *Management of the Sales Force* (Burr Ridge, IL: McGraw-Hill/Irwin, 2003), chap. 9.

31. www.marykay.com/recognition (downloaded June 21, 2004).

32. "Number Crunching," *Sales & Marketing Management* (September 2000), pp. 79–88.

33. For further reading, see Goutam N. Challagolla and Tasadduq A. Shervani, "A Measurement Model of the Dimensions and Types of Output and Behavior Control: An Empirical Test in the Salesforce Context," *Journal of Business Research* (July 1997), pp. 159–72; and Gregory A. Rich, William H. Bommer, Scott B. McKenzie, Philip M. Podsakoff, and Jonathan L. Johnson, "Apples and Apples or Apples and Oranges? A Meta-Analysis of Objective and Subjective Measures of Salesperson Performance," *Journal of Personal Selling & Sales Management* (Fall 1999), pp. 41–52.

34. "Measuring Sales Effectiveness," *Sales & Marketing Management* (October 2000), p. 136; "Quota Busters," *Sales & Marketing Management* (January 2001), pp. 59–63.

35. "Corporate America's New Sales Force," *Fortune* (August 11, 2003), special advertising section.

36. Cravens, "The Changing Role of the Sales Force," *Marketing Management*.

37. www.toshiba.com/technology (downloaded May 15, 2004).

38. "Going Mobile, Part 2," *Sales & Marketing Management* (June 1994), p. 5.

39. "Supercharged Sell," *Inc. Tech* (November 1998), pp. 42–50.

40. "Intranets Grow Up," *Sales & Marketing Management* (December 2000), p. 105.

Reebok: This case was prepared by Giana Eckhardt.

CHAPTER 19

1. www.westjet.com (downloaded on June 27, 2005); interview with Sean Durfy, VP Marketing, WestJet (June 28, 2005); and Norma Ramage, "WestJet on the Fly," *Marketing Magazine* (June 20, 2005), www.marketingmag.ca (downloaded June 20, 2005).

2. Roger A. Kerin, P. Rajan Varadarajan, and Robert A. Peterson, "First-Mover Advantage: A Synthesis, Conceptual Framework, and Research Proposition," *Journal of Marketing* (October 1992), pp. 33–52; and Pankaj Ghemawat, "Sustainable Advantage," *Harvard Business Review* (September–October 1986), pp. 53–58.

3. Nitin Nohria, William Joyce, and Bruce Roberson, "What Really Works," *Harvard Business Review* (July, 2003), pp. 42–52; and "Who Gets Eaten and Who Gets to Eat," *The Economist* (July 12, 2003), pp. 61–63.

4. Chad Terhune and Betsey McKay, "Behind Coke's Travails: A Long Struggle Over Strategy," *The Wall Street Journal* (May 4, 2004), pp. A1, A6; and Betsy Morris, "The Real Story," *Fortune* (May 31, 2004), pp. 84–98.

5. Faith Arner, "No Excuse Not to Succeed," *BusinessWeek* (May 10, 2004), pp. 96–98.

6. Jack Gordon, "Wall Street Curls Its Lip at Costco's Ungreedy CEO," *Star Tribune* (December 19, 2003), p. A33; and John Helyar, Ann Harrington, and Sol Price, "The Only Company Wal-Mart Fears," *Fortune* (November 24, 2003), pp. 158–63.

7. Kathleen Kerwin and Paul Magnusson, "Can Anything Stop Toyota?" *BusinessWeek* (November 17, 2003), pp. 114–22.

8. Murali K. Mantrala, Prabhakant Sirha, and Andris A. Zoltners, "Impact of Resource Allocation Rules on Marketing Investment-Level Decisions and Profitability," *Journal of Marketing Research* (May 1992), pp. 162–75.

9. John Reinan, "Keeping the 'O' Rolling," *Star Tribune* (July 20, 2003), pp. D1, D8.

10. Vanitha Swaminathan, Richard J. Fox, and Srinivas K. Reddy, "The Impact of Brand Extension Introduction on Choice," *Journal of Marketing* (October 2001), pp. 1–15; Deborah Roedder-John, Barbara Loken, and Christopher Joiner, "The Negative Impact of Extensions: Can Flagship Products Be Diluted?" *Journal of Mar-

keting* (January 1998), pp. 19–32; and Akshay R. Rao, Lu Qu, and Robert W. Ruekert, "Signalling Unobservable Product Quality through a Brand Ally," *Journal of Marketing Research* (May 1999), pp. 258–68.

11. *2003 Annual Report* (Minneapolis: General Mills, Inc., 2003), p. 5; *2004 Midyear Report* (Minneapolis: General Mills, Inc., 2004), p. 3.

12. This discussion and Figure 19–3 are adapted from Stanley F. Stasch and Patricis Longtree, "Can Your Marketing Planning Procedures Be Improved?" *Journal of Marketing* (Summer 1980), p. 82; by permission of the American Marketing Association.

13. Adapted with permission of The Free Press, a Division of Macmillan, Inc., from *Competitive Advantage: Creating and Sustaining Superior Performance* by Michael E. Porter. Copyright 1985 by Michael E. Porter.

14. Patricia Sellers, "P&G: Teaching an Old Dog New Tricks," *Fortune* (May 31, 2004), pp. 167–80.

15. Sandy Shore, "Coors-Molson Would Create No. 5 Brewer", Portland Press (July 23, 2004), p. 1C, 8C.

16. Adopted from Philip Kotler, *Marketing Arrangement* (Upper Saddle River, NJ: Prentice Hall, 2003), p. 299.

17. Stratford Sherman, "How Intel Makes Spending Pay Off," *Fortune* (February 22, 1993), pp. 57–61.

18. Bjorn Lomborg, "Prioritizing the World's To-Do List," *Fortune* (May 17, 2004), p. 60; and Alfred Marcus, Donald A. Geffen, and Ken Sexton, "Business-Government Cooperation in Environmental Decision Making," *International Journal of Corporate Sustainability* 9, no. 4 (2002), pp. 345–55.

19. Charles H. Noble and Michael P. Mokwa, "Implementing Marketing Strategies: Developing and Testing a Managerial Theory," *Journal of Marketing* (October 1999), pp. 57–74.

20. Jeffrey A. Krames, *The Jack Welch Lexicon of Leadership* (New York: McGraw-Hill, 2002), pp. 54–56, 105–8, 187–88; Robert Slater, *Jack Welch and the GE Way* (New York: McGraw-Hill, 1999), pp. 59–68, 77–88, 279–86; Nicholas Stein, "The World's Most Admired Companies," *Fortune* (October 2, 2000), pp. 183–91; and Jim Rohwer, "GE Digs into Asia," *Fortune* (October 2, 2000), pp. 165–78.

21. Daniel Roth, "This Ain't No Pizza Party," *Fortune* (November 9, 1998), pp. 158–64.

22. Thomas J. Peters and Robert H. Waterman, Jr., *In Search of Excellence: Lessons from America's Best-Run Companies* (New York: Harper & Row, 1982).

23. Tom Peters, "Winners Do Hundreds of Percent over Norm," *Minneapolis Star Tribune* (January 8, 1985), p. 5B; and Ben Rich and Leo Janos, *Skunk Works* (Boston: Little Brown, 1994), pp. 51–53.

24. Peter Galuska, Ellen Neuborne, and Wendy Zeliner, "P&G's Hottest New Product: P&G," *BusinessWeek* (October 5, 1998), pp. 92–96.

25. Robert W. Ruekert and Orville W. Walker, Jr., "Marketing's Interaction with Other Functional Units: A Conceptual Framework and Empirical Evidence," *Journal of Consumer Marketing* (Spring 1987), pp. 1–19. Shikhar Sarin and Vijay Mahajan, "The Effect of Reward Structures on the Performance of Cross-Functional Product Development Teams," *Journal of Marketing* (April 2001), pp. 35–53; and Amy Edmondson, Richard Bohmer, and Gary Pisano, "Speeding Up Team Learning," *Harvard Business Review* (October 2001), pp. 125–32.

26. Nelson D. Schwartz, "Colgate Cleans Up," *Fortune* (April 16, 2001), pp. 179–80.

27. Leslie M. Moeller, Sharat K. Mathur, and Randall Rothenberg, "The Better Half: The Artful Science of ROI Marketing," *Strategy + Business* (Chicago: Booz Allen Hamilton, 2003).

28. James D. Lenskold, "Customer-Centric Marketing ROI," *Marketing Management* (February, 2004), pp. 26–31.

Case: Courtesy of WestJet.

CREDITS

CHAPTER 13

p. 328, Jean Heguy/First Light; p. 330, Courtesy Bugatti; p. 336, © M. Hruby; p. 342, © Terry McElroy; p. 343, Courtesy of Air Canada Vacations; p. 346, Courtesy of Hudson's Bay Company; p. 347, Dick Hemingway; p. 348, Sharon Hoogstraten; p. 349, Courtesy of The Toro Company.

APPENDIX B

p. 363, Courtesy The Caplow Company.

CHAPTER 14

p. 364, Jill Braaten/The McGraw-Hill Digital Library. © The McGraw-Hill Companies, p. 372, Courtesy CPW; p. 375, © M. Hruby (left); p. 375, Dick Hemingway (right); p. 376, Courtesy of Kensington Florist, Calgary, Alberta. http://www.kensingtonflorist.com; p. 377, Courtesy of Visa; p. 378, Courtesy of Dai-Ichi Kikaku Co. Ltd. and Warner-Lambert; p. 384, Courtesy Dell, Inc. (left); p. 384, Courtesy Wal-Mart Stores, Inc. (right); p. 387, Courtesy FedEx Corporation (left); p. 387, Courtesy Emery Worldwide (right); p. 389, Rapistan Demag Corporation; p. 390, Fritz Hoffman/Image Works (left); p. 390, Fritz Hoffman/Image Works (right).

CHAPTER 15

p. 396, Cleo Photography; p. 400, Reprinted by permission of Tandy Corporation; p. 402, Courtesy Marconi Commerce Systems; p. 403, Courtesy L.L. Bean 2004 Fly Fishing Catalog; p. 404, Courtesy of QVC Network; p. 406, Courtesy My Virtual Model, Inc.; p. 413, Courtesy Taco Bell.

CHAPTER 16

p. 420, Courtesy of CTV; p. 423, BMW of North America, LLC; p. 425, Courtesy Best Buy; p. 426, © M. Hruby; p. 428, Courtesy MINI USA; p. 429, Courtesy of Fence Magazine; p. 430, © M. Hruby (top); p. 430, Courtesy Gulfstream Aircraft, Inc. (bottom left); p. 430, Courtesy H.J. Heinz Company. Used with permission (bottom right); p. 436, © M. Hruby; p. 445, McGraw-Hill IMC 2nd Edition Educational Video.

CHAPTER 17

p. 446, Courtesy of Adfarm; p. 449, Used with permission of Verizon Wireless (top left); p. 449, Courtesy Aventis Pharmaceuticals, Inc. (top centre); p. 449, Courtesy FTD (top right); p. 449, Courtesy DDB Worldwide and The Dial Corporation (bottom); p. 452, Courtesy of Planned Parenthood of Toronto (top); p. 452, Courtesy of Quiznos Canada (bottom); p. 457, Courtesy of Transcontinental Media; p. 459, Courtesy Captivate Network; p. 462, Courtesy NOP World; p. 464, Courtesy Val-Pak Direct Marketing Systems; p. 466, Courtesy of Canadian Tire; p. 466, © Shooting Star.

CHAPTER 18

p. 476, Courtesy Xerox Corporation; p. 477, Courtesy Medtronic; p. 479, Mitch Kezar/Stone (Getty Images); p. 482, Einzig Photography; p. 483, CB Productions/Corbis; p. 485, Ken Ross/FPG International; p. 493, Courtesy Mary Kay; p. 495, Courtesy of Toshiba America Medical Systems & Interactive Media; p. 496, Jose Peleaz/The Stock Market; p. 500, Courtesy of Reebok International Ltd.

CHAPTER 19

p. 504, Courtesy of WestJet; p. 507, Courtesy Costco; p. 508, © M. Hruby; p. 512, Courtesy Wal-Mart Inc. (left); p. 512, Courtesy Volkswagen of America, Agency: Arnold Communications (right); p. 517, © M. Hruby; p. 518, © M. Hruby; p. 520, GE Lighting Group; p. 521, Courtesy Lockheed Martin Corp.; p. 522, Courtesy Saturn Corporation; p. 526, Courtesy Colgate-Palmolive Company.

NAME INDEX

COMPANY/PRODUCT INDEX

SUBJECT INDEX